A
Popular History
of
The Great War

THE RIVER CLYDE AT GALLIPOLI. From this British steam collier, converted into a troopship, a memorable landing was made by British troops on "V" beach at Gallipoli. April 25, 1915.

A POPULAR HISTORY
OF THE GREAT WAR

Edited by SIR J. A. HAMMERTON

Complete in six volumes with
about 1000 maps & illustrations

Volume II
EXTENSION OF THE STRUGGLE: 1915

London
THE FLEETWAY HOUSE

Printed in Great Britain by The Amalgamated Press Ltd., London.

PREFACE TO SECOND VOLUME

THE second volume of A POPULAR HISTORY OF THE GREAT WAR covers the events of the year 1915, and is fittingly entitled The Extension of the Struggle. When 1914 ended Turkey had just joined the Central Powers, but the opposing group still consisted only of those countries which, in July and August, 1914, had combined to resist Germany—Great Britain, France, Russia, Belgium, Serbia, Montenegro, and Japan. Early in 1915, however, this alliance was strengthened by the adherence of Italy, while later in the year the Central Powers secured the aid of Bulgaria.

The struggle was extended, not only by the arrival of fresh combatants, but by the creation of new battle areas. The declaration of war by Italy on Austria, although not until later on Germany, made the borderlands of these countries, Trentino and Gorizia, a theatre of war. The entrance of Bulgaria into the field gave the Allies an opportunity for attack in the Balkans where were countries very inclined to throw in their lot with the winning side. Just before the opening of the year Great Britain, anxious to safeguard the supply of oil from Persia and to find a suitable field for the activities of the Indian army, had decided upon a campaign in Mesopotamia, the land " between the rivers," and, landing a force at the head of the Persian Gulf, this campaign was prosecuted with varying fortunes throughout the year under review.

A more formidable blow at the Turkish empire, at least so it seemed at the time, was the attack on its European territory. The naval attempt to force a passage through the Dardanelles was followed by the efforts of the army to establish itself on the rocky heights of the Gallipoli peninsula, an enterprise which occupied some nine months of the year. Although it failed in its main object, this campaign was not without its influence on the general fortunes of the war, while the feats of heroism performed there have not been surpassed by those in any field or in any age.

The struggle was extended, too, in other ways. One was the introduction by the Germans of unrestricted submarine warfare. The British Isles were declared in a state of blockade, a challenge which called forth counter measures that were successful in dealing with a new and terrible peril to the life of the nation. In the second battle of Ypres gas was used for the first time in warfare, and the aid of the scientist was called upon to enable the British and French armies to face this formidable danger.

Though fighting in the air had commenced before 1915, during that year it was greatly extended, and in its opening month a Zeppelin with hostile intent appeared for the first time over British soil. The use of other forms of aircraft for raiding purposes extended the area of the fighting zones and brought into it millions who would normally have been far from the scene of hostilities. To aid the armies in the field each combatant increased enormously the strength of its air forces, and fighting in that element became a regular and necessary part of every naval and military movement.

In other directions there was extension of activity during the year. The demand for more and more munitions and the establishment of a department of state under Mr. Lloyd George to provide them drew many thousands of workers, if not into the actual battle zone, at least into the orbit of war work, and huge establishments, such as those at Gretna and Chilwell, were created. The need for men, which became urgent in 1915, and led to the Derby scheme, and then to conscription, was an extension which few civilians had thought possible in August, 1914.

LITERARY CONTENTS
OF VOLUME II

MAPS AND ILLUSTRATIONS
IN VOLUME II

Maps and Plans

List of Plates

LIST OF PLATES—(*Continued*)

A POPULAR HISTORY

OF

THE GREAT WAR

Volume II

CHAPTER 1

The War Against Turkey

THE entry of Turkey into the Great War on the side of the
Central Powers has already been noted (Vol. 1, ch. 25),
as has the beginning of the operations at the head of the
Persian Gulf. Continuing the narrative, this chapter gives a
detailed account of Turkey's army and navy and the reasons
impelling her to wage war on the Allied Forces in the various
areas. The clash between the rival combatants in the
Dardanelles and on the Gallipoli peninsula forms the subject of
subsequent chapters in this volume.

Ever since the so-called Party of Union and Progress (the Young
Turk party, as it was familiarly known) came into power, and
deposed sultan Abdul Hamid, the Ottoman Empire had travelled
downhill at a greater rate than had ever been attained hitherto.
Abdul Hamid, with all his wicked ways, his callous massacres
of Armenians and oppression of Macedonians, his outrageous
dishonesty and admitted shiftiness, was at least a ruler who had
known how to keep the Ottoman Empire intact, and by playing
skilfully upon the jealousies of the Great Powers had managed to
misgovern his disjointed empire without undue interference from
the outside world.

The new diplomacy of the Sublime Porte was no longer framed
by one master diplomat as hitherto, but by a caucus of less

astute men, each jealous of his neighbour, and desiring more his own personal advancement than that of the Ottoman Empire.

Once the Entente Powers had declared war upon Turkey the die for her was cast. None knew better than Enver Pasha, the leader of the Young Turks, the vital issues at stake. Success might bring a recrudescence of Turkish power, and a rehabilitation of her sovereignty over the Balkans and northern Africa; but defeat would mean the dissolution of the Ottoman Empire into its component parts of Greek, Armenian, Circassian, Syrian, and Arab. Enver was gambling for the highest possible stakes, but so far as he himself was concerned it was a gamble well worth the risk. In the blackest days of the Balkan wars he had rallied all the polyglot fragments of the patchwork empire around the Crescent by an appeal to Ottoman patriotism.

He invited Syrian, Jew, and Christian alike to forget their diverse creeds and to concentrate their energies on winning back from Bulgaria the fair lands of the Maritza valley. In part the appeal succeeded, and when the recapture of Adrianople came to flatter this first effort, Enver found that his personal prestige —which had been sadly in need of a stimulant—soared once more into the zenith. Prestige of this kind, however, is only fed on victory. To maintain his political ascendancy in Constantinople it was necessary for Enver to be able to boast of some new conquest biennially. He was plotting a victorious war against Greece when the German intrigues suddenly pitched him into the seething cauldron of the great European war.

In view of the fact that Enver completed his military studies in Germany, it is probable that there was a good deal of reality in the warmth with which he espoused the cause of the new Triple Alliance. He realized that the adversary from whom Turkey had most to fear, or most to gain in the event of final victory, was Britain. It was against Britain, therefore, that expediency and strategy combined to suggest that he should make his greatest effort. Since at first he was powerless to strike at Great Britain effectively either by land or by sea, he determined to strike at her morally, and he induced the sultan to proclaim a jehad or holy war against the British Empire.

Whether Enver was hypnotised by the political miscalculations of Germany (who throughout the war proved herself as incapable in diplomacy and appreciation of national character as she showed herself capable in military organisation), or whether he was merely risking a false lead in the hope that it would draw a trump, it is impossible to conjecture; but there can be no doubt in fomenting a holy war Enver placed the seal of finality upon the crumbling destinies of the Ottoman Empire.

Religious fanaticism is not a force which can be lightly invoked; when once aroused it is calculated to carry all before it, overstepping, as it does, all considerations of nationality, race, and language. Had the sultan, when proclaiming a jehad, been able to rally the faithful to his standard by calling a war on Christianity, the move might have proved a feature of great strength; but all that he could do was to proclaim that as the ally of two Christain empires he proposed to make war upon a group of Christian states, one of which—Britain—ruled over a vast Mahomedan empire in India, and had nursed ten million Moslems in Egypt into a state of prosperity and religious freedom which they had never enjoyed under Turkish rule. Not unnaturally the jehad was a fiasco. The Moslems of India and Egypt refused to be entrapped into pseudo-religious fanaticism against their benefactors. All the great Moslem institutions and societies throughout Egypt and the British Empire hastened to assure the British government of their unswerving loyalty to the Raj, and deplored the fact that the sultan, the chief of the Moslem faith, had dragged their religion into so sordid a political intrigue.

In the days of Abdul Hamid only the Moslem Turk was subject to military service, but the Young Turk party altered the conscription laws, making every Turkish subject liable to be called up, irrespective of creed or race. The war against the Balkan League showed the utter futility of this new regime, for it was found that only a small percentage of the Armenian and other Christian races answered the mobilisation summons, while the vast majority of these who actually joined the colours seized the first possible opportunity to desert or to go over to the enemy. Again, another cause which contributed even more powerfully to the collapse of the Turkish armies was their faulty mobilisation scheme. To give an example: the 23rd independent division, stationed at Janina, in Albania, had a war strength of some 15,000 men. In peace time it actually numbered about 6,000 all told, one-third of whom had less than one year's service. The reservists, stores, and equipment for this division were supposed to come from Smyrna, in Asia Minor, and as a matter of fact never reached their destination.

Ever since January, 1913, the Turks under German guidance had been making desperate efforts to put their house in order, to remodel and equip their army, and to replenish their military stores. Each of the active (nizam) divisions was allotted a mobilisation centre. At these centres the nizam units were brought up to war strength and fully equipped, and to each nizam division a redif (or reserve) division was affiliated.

It was part of Germany's commercial policy to discourage the Turks from creating a large arsenal capable of constructing guns or ammunition on a big scale, since the firm of Krupp wished to sell such warlike stores to Turkey. But the Germans had reason to regret their short-sighted policy, for as soon as war broke out it became impossible to ship further ordnance stores from Essen to Constantinople. There was a great shortage of guns and artillery material in the new Turkish army. The arrangements for providing the troops with clothing broke down entirely, and the men had to undertake a winter campaign in cotton garments.

The modernised Turkish army of 1914 was organized as follows: The army on a peace footing was to consist of 25 nizam (or regular) divisions, each consisting of 13 battalions of infantry, 24 guns, one squadron of cavalry, and various details, in all about 15,500 men.

Five of these divisions (i.e., two at Adrianople, one at Constantinople, one in Turkish Caucasia, and one in Arabia) were to be maintained at full strength. The remaining 20 divisions, however, while kept nominally at about half strength were, for one reason or another, allowed to fall to anywhere from one-third to one-quarter of the established strength. On mobilisation all these divisions were to be brought up to full strength by drafts of reservists who had recently left the colours, or by men supposed to be serving, but who were actually on permanent leave; and, moreover, the strength of each battalion was to be augmented from a nominal 1,000 to an actual 1,250. Thus it was contemplated that the 25 nizam divisions, each numbering about 19,000, would muster 475,000 men. It was, moreover, intended to add one redif (reserve) division to each nizam formation, each pair making an army corps; the men of the redif formations being either middle-aged reservists who had finished their service, or younger men who, by hook or by crook, had escaped the net of conscription. The army corps were to be grouped into five armies, each consisting of five nizam divisions, five redif divisions, a mixed cavalry division composed of regulars, reservists, and irregulars, and two regiments (40 guns) of artillery, both light and heavy. This organization was calculated to bring the effective field armies up to about 1,150,000, the remaining 50,000 men being accounted for in garrison artillery and gendarmerie. There is reason to believe, however, that the utmost Turkey could hope actually to arm and muster during the war would be only about 640,000 men.

ESTIMATED STRENGTH OF THE TURKISH ARMIES

			MEN.
The Army of Europe (Adrianople).	5 Nizam divisions, 2 Redif divisions, and 3,000 cavalry		140,000
The Reserve Army (Constantinople).	5 Nizam divisions (under strength)	70,000	
	3 Redif divisions (under strength) ..	35,000	
	Irregular cavalry	2,000	
			107,000
The Caucasian Army (with part of Smyrna Army).	8 Nizam divisions (under strength)	120,000	
	8 Redif divisions (under strength) ..	80,000	
	Mixed cavalry	5,000	
			205,000
Arabian Garrison ..	2 Nizam divisions (1 under strength)	30,000	
	2 Redif divisions (probably unarmed, and very doubtful if they would mobilise at all)	10,000	
			40,000
Smyrna Garrison ..	1 Nizam division (under strength and badly armed)..	12,000	
	3 or perhaps 4 Redif divisions (under strength and badly armed)	40,000	
	Cavalry and details	8,000	
			60,000
Available against Egypt.	4 Nizam divisions (under strength)	60,000	
	1 strong Redif division (for lines of communication)	20,000	
			80,000
	TOTAL AVAILABLE		632,000

The troops of the nizam and those of the five redif divisions raised in Anatolia would have been fine fighting material had time and money been spent on their training; but the days were now past when sheer courage alone sufficed to make a good soldier. Some 95 per cent. of the Turkish rank and file were illiterate and of low intelligence; their musketry was inferior, and their knowledge of entrenching most elementary. The vast majority of the officers had very little education, either military or otherwise. There were, however, some 1,500 officers in the

Turkish army who had either studied abroad or completed their military education under German instructors, and these for the most part were very intelligent and eminently capable. The chief characteristic of the Turk as a fighting man is his wonderful doggedness in defence, even when vastly outnumbered. His tactics, however, are clumsy and devoid of originality, and he is terribly slow in seizing an opportunity.

Taught by the bitter experience of the Balkan League war, Turkey had at last realized the value of sea power, and had determined to create a fleet which would at least secure her own home waters, and keep open the fairway through the Aegean Sea. During the campaign of 1912-13, the Greek fleet had kept the Turkish navy mewed up in the Sea of Marmora, an impotent onlooker, while Greek shipping furrowed the narrow seas and Greek warships effectively blockaded the Turkish coasts. Under the guidance of the British naval mission at Constantinople, Turkey had caused two Dreadnoughts to be laid down in British yards; these were being completed by the Armstrong and Vickers firms when war broke out between Great Britain and Germany, and the British authorities promptly took them over. They were: Sultan Mehmet Rechad V., 23,000 tons, ten 13.5 in. and sixteen 6 in. guns, designed for a speed of 21 knots; and the Sultan Osman, 27,500 tons, fourteen 12 in. and twenty 6 in. guns, designed for a speed of 22 knots. The former was renamed the Erin, the latter the Agincourt.

Thus the two principal units were not available; but by way of consolation the German vessels Goeben and Breslau, previously described, were henceforth to form part of the Turkish fleet, which consisted of the following obsolete units: the battleships Barbarosse and Torgud Reis, built in 1891 for the German navy, and sold by Germany to Turkey in 1910, of 10,000 tons, with six 11 in., and eight 4.1 in. guns each, and capable of steaming at most 17 knots. The Messudiyeh, built in 1874, and reconstructed in Genoa in 1903, was of 9,250 tons displacement, speed 16 knots, with two 9.4 in. guns as her main armament, and twelve 6 in. guns in her secondary battery. She was sunk in the Dardanelles by the submarine B11. The Muin-i-Zaffir, built in 1869 and refitted in 1907, was little better than a gunboat. Of 2,400 tons displacement, she could steam only 12 knots, and was armed with four 6 in. guns. The light cruisers Hamidieh and Medjidieh, of 3,500 tons, with only 22 knots, and each carrying two 6 in., and eight 4.7 in. guns. Fifteen obsolescent gunboats, four modern destroyers and older ones, together with 15 torpedo boats, completed the Turkish Navy. As a fighting force it was entirely a negligible quantity, since had it been possible to coax it into a fight in the open, one British armoured cruiser would have sufficed to sink the whole collection in a very short time.

Nothing could have been less sound than was the Turkish strategical situation. On all sides Turkey was isolated and surrounded by superior hostile elements. In the Black Sea she was face to face with a Russian squadron which made up in efficiency for what it lacked in paper strength. Outside the Dardanelles was concentrated a vastly superior Franco-British naval force. In European Turkey the Balkan situation was so unstable that Turkey had of necessity to keep a large army ready in order to cope with any recrudescence of a Balkan coalition against her.

Although Turkey had to keep at least 250,000 men under arms in the vicinity of Constantinople, in order to deal with the Balkan political situation and to safeguard the capital against a sea-borne expeditionary force, this army could not hope in any way to co-operate with those of Turkey's allies in Europe. In the Caucasian area she was called upon to put into the field an army capable not only of holding back any Russian invading force, but also of maintaining Turkish suzerainty over the Armenian Christian population, long since seething with revolt. In this one theatre of war alone Turkey had more than enough to occupy all her remaining resources, for Russia could put in the field the whole of her Caucasian army of 750,000 men.

Again, in the Arabian theatre of war was a huge sub-continent, all the important cities of which were at the mercy of a sea-borne army or of naval power; and here again, as in Armenia, there was a local population only too anxious to throw off the hated yoke of the Turkish tax-collector. The Arab has little in common with the Turk, under whose domination he has suffered for many centuries all the hardships of misgovernment and over-taxation. The one sentiment Turk and Arab share in common is the religion of Mahomet, but the fact should not be lost sight of that Mahomet himself was an Arab, and it was the Arabs who built up the great empire of which Constantinople was the centre. For many generations local rebellions had recurred, and sometimes succeeded in shaking off the Turkish yoke both in Africa, Asia Minor, and Arabia; and so it might be again.

Inspired by her German advisers, Turkey determined to forestall her troubles; and, applying the axiom that a vigorous offensive is the best defence, she prepared two armies of invasion. The one, based on Erzerum, was to cross the Caucasus and invade Russian territory; the other, based on Damascus, was to cross the Sinai Desert and invade Egypt. Both of these ambitious expeditions were foredoomed to failure, but the fact that they should ever have been undertaken at all is strong testimony to the wonderful driving power of the German officers attached to the Ottoman army.

The Egyptian campaign had these ostensible reasons: 1. A vigorous offensive by land was necessary to counter-balance the Allies' predominance of sea-power in Near Eastern waters. 2. To strike at the very spring of British trade, wealth, and power —the Suez Canal. 3. By extending the authority of the Turkish Raj over a Moslem Egypt, the holy war might be partially justified in practice.

The true reasons for the invasion of Egypt may be summarised as follows:

1. Every British soldier retained to garrison Egypt would mean one man less on the Allies' line in Belgium and France, and therefore would set free a Prussian soldier to march on Warsaw and to liberate Eastern Prussia from the heel of the invading Russian host.

2. The war was already sufficiently unpopular in Turkey, and if a revolution were to be avoided, then an early success for Turkish arms was essential. Although the prospects of success in Egypt were extremely meagre, there was at least a faint possibility of achieving some military feat of arms; while in the only other area of war available to Turkish armies—the Caucasus —there was no probability of success whatever, owing to the rigours of the climate in winter and the known superiority of the Russian armies both in organisation and numbers.

Having once decided upon the invasion of Egypt, it must be admitted that the Turco-German staff set about their task in a most businesslike manner. All Turkish officers suspected of political intrigue against the Young Turk party were drafted to the army of Syria, while those who were known to have Anglophile tendencies were drafted to the army of the Caucasus. It is impossible to obtain definitely detailed information regarding the troops told off to form the army of Egypt, but the following estimate is approximately correct:

The advanced guard was formed of a redif division from Arabia, consisting chiefly of Arab Bedouins, who had no military training whatever, and no organization save on paper. This was 8,000 to 10,000 strong. This collection of nomad irregulars was concentrated between Jerusalem and Akabah, and it is estimated that at least 50 per cent. of them deserted before the advance even began.

In the main body were four nizam divisions, drawn from Asia Minor, consisting of the best fighting material in the Turkish army, but considerably under strength. These divisions were numerically strengthened but morally weakened by attaching to each certain redif formations, raised in Syria and Palestine. This combined force, amounting to about 60,000 nizam (regulars) and 10,000 redifs, were concentrated at Smyrna and Damascus, and were moved forward, when completed, by successive half-divisions along the Hedjaz railway, through Jerusalem, and thence by steady marching toward the Sinai Peninsula, where, on the confines of the desert wastes, an immense camp was formed during the middle of December, 1914.

From then onwards the Turkish army came under the almost daily observation of the British reconnoitring aircraft. The movements of the Bedouin camelry and horsemen were watched also by patrols of the Egyptian and Bikanir camel corps. During December, 1914, and January, 1915, two minor skirmishes took place between the opposing desert riders, the advantage in each case being with the British. A general forward movement from its rest camp was begun at the end of December, striking out into the wilderness on the march that Moses had taken 40 years to accomplish, but which, with modern organisation, was completed in as many days.

Some features of the Turkish arrangements are worthy of being placed on record. The guns and limbers of the artillery were equipped with cast-iron wheels, some six inches wide on the tread, in order to distribute the weight of the guns on the sand of the desert. Some 2,000 draught animals, above and beyond the 6,000 baggage-camels employed in carrying food and ammunition, were utilised in dragging sand-sledges. A Turkish bridging train of 36 galvanised-iron pontoons, German army pattern, was intended for bridging the Suez Canal. These pontoons, somewhat resembled an iron punt, pointed at one end, 19 feet by 4 ft. 6 in., and could be used either as boats or as floating piers for the construction of bridges wherewith to span the canal. Each pontoon was furnished with wide rollers to act as wheels on uneven ground; but where the surface of the sand was smooth, the rollers were unshipped, and the pontoon with its iron bottom slid like a sledge across the desert behind its team of draught animals. The pontoons were also used for the transport of stores, and thus served the double purpose of cart and boat.

Fortune at first appeared to favour the Turkish venture. During the months of November, December, and January there had been plentiful rains—in fact, the best rainfall that had occurred for seven years—and the water-holes and wells of the desert were unusually well supplied with precious liquid, vegetable in taste, gritting to the teeth, café au lait in colour, which people in this part of the world call water.

The desert well may belong to either one or two varieties. The visible well, or water hole, is reminiscent of an English horse pond, and is the result of innumerable generations of industrious digging on the part of desert wayfarers and of long-forgotten convict gangs in the days of the Pharoahs. Usually with a steep bank at one end and steps reaching down to the waterside, the water level may be six to 16 feet below the level of the bank. At the other end, however, a shelving ramp runs down to the water so as to enable beasts of burden to drink. A large well will be sometimes as big as a tennis lawn, with four or five feet of water in it after heavy rains; but in summer time this same well will be reduced to the size of a dining-room table, in which are eight to ten inches of water exposed to the scorching rays of the sun. The other, the invisible variety of well, is nothing more nor less than the damp surface of an underground streamlet. In order to obtain water, it is necessary to dig down between two and 12 feet, when the supply will be fairly constant but very small in quantity. In the rainy season, however, these hidden streams will often run above ground for 24 hours or so after a downpour. The comparatively copious rainfalls at the end of 1914 and in January, 1915, greatly facilitated the task of the invading army, and solved their principal administrative problem—transport.

During the early spring there is a desert wind that blows at times for a period of two or three days at a stretch. It comes charged with all the intolerable heat and minute sand particles of the surrounding desert, and is called the khamsin (fifty), because from its first to its last visit is supposed to be a compass of 50 days. When this wind blows the atmosphere is superheated and is surcharged with sand. Even though there is no cloud in the sky, it is impossible even to guess the direction of the brilliant Egyptian sun, so thick is the sand fog. To face the gale, which often reaches a velocity of 50 miles an hour, is an impossibility unless eyes and mouth be firmly closed. On February 2, 1915, the first khamsin of the new year blew in from east by south, and that night the Turkish

forces coming from the north-east determined to test the defences of the Suez Canal, trusting, no doubt, to the darkness and noise of the sandstorm to hide their approach, and to the biting sand particles to serve as their allies.

The British force in Egypt, under General Sir John Maxwell, at this time consisted of a strong force of Indian troops, with a fine Lancashire territorial division. The latter were somewhat weedy and only partially trained when they first arrived, but had grown into as fine a body of well-disciplined, lusty manhood as could be wished. There was also a very strong contingent from Australia and New Zealand. Splendid though these men were in physique, they had not at this time been sufficiently trained to that iron discipline which is essential in modern warfare. They were, therefore, held in reserve in the garrisons of Cairo, Alexandria, Mansourah, Tanta, and Zagazig.

To complete the truly imperial nature of this composite force, the native Egyptian army also furnished a not inconsiderable quota of its effectives to the force either holding the canal or immediately in reserve. Thus, along the western bank of the canal, in trenches which had been carefully prepared and strengthened for months previously, was a British force of about 50,000 men, with another 40,000 men behind it as a reserve.

It was against this highly-trained army, perfectly equipped in every detail, completely entrenched and serenely confident, that Djemal Pasha, the Turkish commander, launched his attack at dawn on February 3, 1915. The issue was never in doubt for a moment, for even had the Turkish general obeyed the first rules of tactics and strategy instead of setting them at defiance, he could have hardly hoped to overcome the obstacle of the Suez Canal and take the British trenches with the weary army at his disposal. When on February 1 he arrived within striking distance of the canal, the obvious thing for him to do would have been to push forward reconnoitring columns to ascertain the strength of the British positions. He could hardly hope to take these by surprise, since British aeroplanes had watched his footsteps across the desert. If, on the other hand, he was determined to attack at all costs, he should have struck with all his available force. He did neither. He blundered up against the British defences with his advance division, a second division being some three miles in rear as a support. The rest of his army might just as well have never left Syria for all the assistance they afforded.

It seems extremely probable that the German staff officers urged Djemal to attack at once in the sandstorm without making a preliminary reconnaissance, trusting to their luck, and hoping for a laxity in British vigilance. It may well be that Djemal was over-persuaded to fall in with these views, but, not wishing to risk his whole army in such a hazardous adventure, he decided to compromise and attack with a part of his strength only. Like most military compromises the effort was foredoomed to failure. The battle itself, if battle it can be called, offers very few points of interest. The British force allowed the enemy to come on well within close range before they opened fire upon them with murderous precision. At one point, indeed, the Turks were actually allowed to bring two of their pontoons up to the canal bank and to launch them on the water before the defenders opened fire. The Turks fought pluckily, as is their wont, but they had no chance from the very first.

At Serapeum, where the main Turkish attack culminated in a disastrous retreat, a Turkish 6 in. gun opened a fairly effective fire upon the British position and some of the war vessels lying in Lake Timsah, off Ismailia. The Indian marine service vessel Hardinge was struck twice by shells; a gallant old pilot of the canal company, Captain Carew, was standing on the bridge piloting the ship when a 6 in. shell burst on the bridge, tearing off his leg and wounding him in no fewer than 19 places. He therefore called down to those who were still alive amongst the débris: " Bring me a chair, and I'll take her into port!" Though he could not do this, it is pleasant to know that he recovered from his terrible injuries.

A short while afterwards, however, one of the warships on Lake Timsah took an ample revenge on the Turkish gun, killing the crew and silencing the gun with a well-aimed salvo from its 12-pounder guns, while the old French battleship Requin shelled the enemy's positions with 10.8 in. guns. By six o'clock, as night was falling, the enemy's reserves were in full retreat, but it was not considered advisable to follow them up into the desert. However, after nightfall, sniping broke out from the eastern bank of the canal, and two British companies were sent across the canal next morning to round up the snipers. These were met by a quite unexpected fire from a deep trench which had been well screened from view. The two companies sat tight until reinforcements were brought up, when the trench was cleared with the bayonet. Some 250 of the original occupants were captured, all of whom were picked men.

It will never be known what losses the Turks actually incurred in the battle of the canal, for many hundreds of fugitive soldiers must have been lost in the subsequent retreat; but, in any case, their losses were not less than 4,000 officers and men killed, wounded, and prisoners, while the British casualties barely totalled 60. Perhaps the most bitter blow of all to the Turks was the loss of practically the whole of their bridging train, which was partly destroyed and partly captured, for they did not make any attempt to save it. The loss of these pontoons precluded the possibility of any further Turkish attack upon the canal for many a long week, even if the Turks had the stomach for more fighting.

Meanwhile, on the shores of the Persian Gulf, an Anglo-Indian force was engaged in strengthening its position. General Fry's measures included the despatch of a garrison to Ahwaz, a town well inside the Persian frontier on the Karun river, and important because the pipe line from the oilfields passes near it. On January 21, 1915, a brigade, supported by three gunboats on the river, was sent out from Mezera in order to ascertain the strength and disposition of the Turkish force gathering in the neighbourhood which, during the previous two or three days, had been harassing the British patrols and outposts. After a northward march of about six miles, the enemy's outposts were sighted on a range of sandhills, behind which was the Ratta canal. After an artillery duel, the British advanced, drove within six hundred yards of it, whence they were able to shell the Turkish dhows and camp. About noon, having fulfilled their mission, they received orders to retire, and returned unmolested to Mezera. Their total casualties were about 50, and the loss of the Turks was estimated at 400 or thereabouts. The report brought back to General Barrett was that the enemy had about 5,000 men and six guns.

In February and March the Tigris and the Euphrates usually overflow their banks and flood the surrounding country, and for the time being this put a stop to the fighting. In Persia, however, there was an engagement on March 3, in which the British forces lost heavily. Near Ahwaz a few Turkish regiments were gathering around them a body of discontented tribesmen from Persia and Arabia, and to discover the strength of this force, a British contingent was sent out from the town. At Ghadir the Turks and their allies were located, but unfortunately they were much stronger than had been believed possible, and in the face of an enemy force of 12,000 the British had no option but to retire without undue delay. This they did in good order and without serious loss.

The withdrawal was effected, but not without difficulty. The Turks made determined efforts to cut off the retreat, and several times hand-to-hand fighting took place. However, Ahwaz was reached at last, and as the enemy did not return to the attack, it was assumed that he had lost heavily. His casualties were estimated at 600 killed and many wounded. The losses of the Anglo-Indian force were nearly 200. The 7th Rajputs had four of their white officers killed and their colonel severely wounded.

On the same day (March 3) a body of British cavalry made a reconnaissance towards Nakaila, a place about 25 miles north-west of Basra. While returning to camp they were followed by 1,500 enemy horsemen; but these were skilfully drawn on to a position where infantry with machine guns and field artillery were concealed. These opened fire, and the Turks having suffered heavily fled back to Nakaila. Unfortunately, in this little affair four British officers were killed and two were wounded severely.

In anticipation of the end of the flood season, the authorities in India sent further reinforcements to Ahwaz and Kurna, and with these went Lieut.-General Sir J. E. Nixon, K.C.B., who on his arrival took over the command of the whole force, which in this theatre of war now amounted to between 30,000 and 40,000 men. The Turks also received considerable reinforcements, and on April 11 they advanced on three of the British positions. Kurna, Ahwaz, and Shaiba, one of the forts protecting Basra, were attacked; but one only was seriously assaulted. On the 11th, and also on the 12th, Kurna was bombarded at long range, but no infantry attack followed, and the only damage done was the destruction of part of the bridge across the Tigris. British guns, both those on shore and those in H.M.S. Odin, however, appear to have inflicted a good deal of loss upon parties of the enemy who were seen in boats. Similarly, at the same time, Ahwaz was bombarded; but here again no damage was done, and although large bodies of cavalry appeared on the horizon nearly all round the British position, they made no offensive movement.

On Shaiba the attack was more determined, but was equally ineffective. After a certain amount of artillery fire, the Turkish infantry, led by some German officers, advanced in extended order towards the south, south-west, and west of the British lines. For three hours in the morning they came steadily on, and then they began to dig themselves in. In the afternoon the attack from the south was renewed, but this made no further progress. During the night of the 12th the Turks kept up a desultory fire, and early on the following morning it was found that a party of them had occupied some rising ground about a mile to the north of the British position. These men were easily dislodged by an Anglo-Indian attack, and the enemy next approached from the west but was driven back with ease.

When the British ceased the pursuit they had taken 18 officers, 300 men, and two guns. Many of the prisoners were in a starving and hopeless condition, and some had marched the whole of the 500 miles from Bagdad. The prisoners reported that the attacking force was composed of about 10,000 regular infantry, 1,000 regular cavalry, and perhaps 12,000 irregular levies of Kurds and Arabs. They had assembled at Nakaila and were commanded by Suliman Askeri and Ali Bey. In addition to the direct attacks, armed parties of them were sailing about on the flood-water between Basra and Shaiba, with the object of interrupting the British communications. The time had now come for a British offensive, for although the Turkish attacks had been repulsed, the enemy was still entrenched near the town of Basra.

On April 14 there was an engagement which really deserves the title of a battle. The whole Anglo-Indian force moved out from its camp near Basra towards Zobeir, a few miles to the south. Very soon the Turks were driven from an advanced position about two and a half miles away from their main line. This was in the shape of a crescent with tamarisk woods behind it and on either flank. In the wood and in well-concealed trenches before it were some 15,000 Turkish soldiers, with six big guns. Towards them the Anglo-Indian troops advanced steadily for five hours, from 11.30 in the morning until 4.30 in the afternoon. The plain was absolutely bare, the heat and glare were terrific, and although the enemy could not be seen, a constant and accurate rifle fire came from the trenches. Nevertheless, the attackers struggled on, and about 4.30 the Dorsets and the 117th Mahrattas led the way into the trenches, a great charge made by the whole line driving out the defenders at the point of the bayonet.

In this battle the casualties were about 700, and the list contained the names of 17 British officers killed. The victory, however, was worth the heavy price paid for it, for the Turks were thoroughly routed; they fled in great disorder to Nakaila, and their leader, Suliman Askeri, was reported to have committed suicide. The report was probably true.

The action was followed by a vigorous pursuit. By river and by road the Turks sought safety in flight. Twelve boats full of fugitives were either taken or sunk, and the total Turkish losses were about 2,500, of whom over seven hundred were prisoners. The booty taken included large quantities of tents, equipment, stores, and ammunition, as well as several machine-guns. The neighbourhood of Basra was entirely cleared of Turks, who soon continued their retreat beyond Nakaila, which was occupied by British cavalry on the 17th, and it was ascertained that there were none nearer than Rattava, 50 miles from the city.

This victory near Shaiba was decisive, and the month of May was mainly occupied in clearing the country of the remnants of the Turkish forces. Only near Ahwaz and Kurna were the Turks at all troublesome. In the former locality they were found to be in some strength on the Kharkhed, and thither an advance was made against them. The march, however, was delayed by severe sand-storms and by a rapid rise of the river, and before their camp was reached, the Turks had fallen back to Amara, thus vacating Persian soil. The British column, therefore, which was led by General Gorringe, was occupied in punishing the tribes which had assisted the enemy. Of these one or two offered some resistance, but this was soon beaten down, and their strongholds, with some of their other property, were destroyed. Others asked for terms and surrendered a number of rifles.

The Turks near Kurna were dealt with on May 31, soldiers and sailors both taking part in the enterprise. Starting at 1.30 a.m., partly by wading and partly in boats, the British succeeded in turning the enemy's position, while his guns were soon silenced by artillery and naval gunfire. By noon the heights had been seized and the Turks were in flight, leaving behind them three guns and about 250 prisoners.

As the force from Ahwaz had done, the Turks from Kurna retreated to Amara, an important town on the Tigris about 60 miles from Kurna, which was the next object of British attention. A flotilla consisting of the Comet and some launches, carrying General Townshend and Sir Percy Cox, the chief British resident on the gulf, reached the place on June 3, which was at once surrendered by the Governor, the garrison of 1,000 men becoming prisoners of war. In and around Amara the British captured about 80 officers and 2,000 men, seven field and six naval guns, 12 large steel barges, four river steamers, and a quantity of rifles and ammunition. This ended a successful campaign. The Turkish forces in Mesopotamia had been defeated and partly destroyed, and the whole of the country between Amara and the sea was in British hands. The delta of the Shat-el-Arab was protected by the garrison firmly planted at Kurna and Mezera, on either side of the Tigris, and the mouths of the river were guarded by British warships.

About the same time as the Persian Gulf operations were taking place, a campaign was begun in Mesopotamia. In ancient times, it is said, a cock could hop from house to house from Basra, the city of Sindbad, past Babylon and Seleucia, to Bagdad. But since the Mongol, the Turk, and the nomads of Arabia swept over that one-time fertile country, the tract between the Tigris and the Euphrates has lapsed into desert sand and riverside jungle of cane-brake. Instead of a land of vines, orange groves, and rose gardens, Babylonia has become one of the most desolate wastes in Asia, and the reason why neither the Turk at Mosul nor the Briton at Koweit had succeeded in occupying the wilderness became apparent in the spring of 1915.

In April the commander of the Indian expeditionary force, Sir Arthur Barrett, fell so seriously ill that Sir John Eccles Nixon had to take over his command. In the following month many men of the British regiments began to go sick, and when the full heat of the summer smote the Indo-British force the sufferings of the whole force were extreme. Among the British were the 2nd West Kents, the 1st Oxfordshire Light Infantry, the 2nd Norfolks, 2nd Dorsets, 1st Hampshires, and some territorial battalions. Among the Indian troops were the 20th, 22nd, 24th, 66th, 67th, 76th, and 90th Punjabis, 120th Infantry, 104th Wellesly Rifles, 103rd and 117th Mahrattas, 110th Light Infantry, 7th and 11th Rajputs, and 1st and 2nd Battalions of the 7th Gurkhas. Among the mounted troops were the 7th Lancers, 16th, 26th, and 33rd Cavalry, and Royal Horse Artillery (S Battery), and others. The heat was not much worse than that of the Punjab, yet the Indian troops suffered almost as much as the British troops. This was due to the fact that the steaming marshlands of the great rivers not only gave a trying, humid quality to the tropical sunlight, but also the vast stretches of stagnant water, full of rotting refuse, formed the breeding places of an innumerable swarm of mosquitoes, biting flies, and like pests.

It was the insect-borne diseases of the immense river marshes that had for nearly three centuries stayed the march of both Turk and Briton. Only the Bedouin, immunised for thousands of years to the plague insects of the swamps, was able to drag out a wretched existence amid the ruins of the earliest civilization in the world. His children were infected with all the diseases of the region in infancy, but their inherited constitution had been so toughened that what killed stranger adults troubled them not at all. The flies produced dysentery and typhoid, while the mosquitoes injected the malaria germ; when this was kept down by means of quinine, strange new kinds of tropical fever were encountered, which filled the British base hospital with patients. Such was the effect of the heat that a fine body of troops, inured to hardships, were seldom able to do more than eight miles a day. Indeed it would have been absolutely impossible for the Indian Expeditionary Force to do more than hold on to Basra and guard the pipe-line of the oilfields in Persia but for the help given to the soldiers by the sailors.

The men of the Royal Indian Marine, the Royal Navy, and the Royal Naval Reserve transformed the campaign into the most adventurous example of amphibious warfare in history. Owing to their foresight and resource, the army was practically transformed into a naval force that operated upon rivers, across stretches of flood-water, and through reed-grown marshes haunted by the wild beasts of Babylonia. Every form of craft was employed, from the most primitive punt to the latest type of oil-driven vessel. There were three old sloops, which had been doomed by the Admiralty to destruction when the war broke out, but which were saved to do great work in the river battles.

There were some flat-bottomed Irrawaddy paddle steamers, in which Sir Harry Prendergast had conquered Burma, brought across the ocean in their old age to bombard the Turkish trenches at Kut-el-Amara. Motor boats, light-draught river motors—which had seen service off Belgium, the Dardanelles, and German East Africa—sailed round the garden of Eden by Temptation Square and Serpent's Corner. There was an aeroplane which had flown at Singapore, and had afterwards shed its wings and become a launch with an aerial propeller, moving down the river with a series of detonations like a badly-firing motor-bicycle, and spreading dread among the Bedouins. There were tugboats (mounting 4.7 in. guns), horse barges, and the Meso-potamian steamers belonging to the Lynch firm. But the foundation of the operations was the bellum—a native punt drawing less than a foot of water, which can carry ten armed men. A great flotilla of bellums often fought strange infantry battles, while the steam-driven and motor-propelled vessels scouted in advance and acted like a cavalry division.

For some weeks in the spring the whole brigade stationed at Kurna was engaged in learning the art of navigation in bellums. This type of boat has a length of about 35 feet and a beam of $2\frac{1}{2}$ feet; it is propelled in shallow water by poles, and in deep water by paddles. Two men are required to work it, and as it was likely they would both be shot down when the action opened, all the men in the flat-bottomed craft had to learn how to punt and paddle, so as to be able to look after themselves if their boatmen fell. It was also at this time that a considerable part of the British field artillery was put on the water, and, by great feats of carpentry and smith work, mounted on rafts, sailing-boats, tugs, and launches. Machine-guns were also mounted in large numbers, and at dawn on May 31 the extra-ordinary new Indo-British navy moved out to attack.

In front of the hundreds of river-boats were the three sloops Clio, Odin, and Espiègle, each with six 4 in. guns, and the Royal Indian Marine steamer Lawrence, with the rafts and boats containing field-guns. This remarkable squadron had to steam through something that was neither land nor water, but a tract of mud thinning into a liquid form, while retaining the appear-ance of land by reason of the reeds growing out of it. The progress of the boats was much impeded by the reeds, and the Turks, with their Kurdish levies and German officers, entrenched on the low hills to the north, had a magnificent target. But their 6 in. field-guns used only the old segment shells, sold by the British Government to the Ottoman Empire soon after the South African War. These shells made a noise, but did very little damage. What was more important, the Turks had no machine-guns, and their musketry fire was not good. After the steamer-squadron had bombarded the enemy trenches, the sailor-soldiers of the bellum brigade—2nd Norfolks, 110th Mahratta

MESOPOTAMIA. Map showing the country between the Tigris and Euphrates which was the battle ground of the 1914-18 campaign:

Light Infantry, and 120th Rajputana Infantry—beached their
boats among the reeds, squelched through the marsh and charged
with the bayonet up the high, dry ground. The entrenched
Turks, on the hill now known as Norfolk Hill, put up a good
fight, but they were rushed and shattered, and the Turks in the
other six positions fled in disorder up the Tigris to Amara.
Some of them were cut off in the marshes, but the main force
could not be pursued; for an ingenious German engineer, who had

been working on the river when war broke out, blocked the
stream by sinking a line of large barges, surrounded by mines.
It took two days to clear away the mines and the wrecks. On
the evening of June 1 the steamers worked through the
obstruction and puffed away in pursuit of the Turks.

It was expected that they would make another stand at
Amara, which lies 87 miles above Kurna. The Turks, however,
were too deeply alarmed by the amazing boating army and its
gun-rafts and machine-gunned bellums, exercising all the extraordinary advantages of sea-power in the heart of a desert,
hundreds of miles from the sea. Had they made a stand at
Amara the British could have sailed by, have landed well in
their rear, and have cut their line of communications. It was
necessary to counter the naval tactics by constructing a
miniature system of Dardanelles forts on both banks of the river
with some powerful long-range guns capable of sinking the
largest ship that could be brought up-stream. The Turkish
commander, Nuredin Pasha, therefore, kept his men on the
march until they reached Kut-el-Amara, near Bagdad, where
the great cross-desert canal, Shat-el-Hai, runs from the Tigris
to the Euphrates at Nasiriyeh. Here he built a formidable
system of fortifications.

With the advance to Amara, the original plan of the Persian
Gulf campaign was concluded. The Admiralty oil supply had
been secured, and the enemy had been swept far back from the
British sphere of influence. The port of Mesopotamia, Basra,
had been taken, and a complete end had been put to the river
commerce of Bagdad, Mosul, and other towns. So far as India
was concerned, the danger of any Turkish movement was
restricted to Kurdish raids across the mountains to the north.
These raids led into the northern provinces of Persia, which were
under Russian influence; and the Russian army in the Caucasus,
possessing quick and easy transport across the Caspian Sea,
was excellently situated to meet any menace. So when the
very hot weather came the Indian Expeditionary Force stood
fast on the ground it had won, and consolidated the newly-
conquered territory. There were 136 miles of river communications to be maintained between Amara and Basra; and though
the Turks had been pushed back, there were large numbers of
armed Arabs scattered about the country. Some of them were
friendly to Britain—but many of them had helped the Turks,

and, under the influence of their priests, these continued to snipe British advanced detachments and to raid British stores.

At Basra things settled down so quietly that the British engineers began to transform the city of Sindbad. Dykes were cut to control the flood-water, the creeks were bridged, and roads made through the pathless marshes. Then a large scheme of town-planning was put into execution, in preparation for the day when a British engineer would dam the Tigris and Euphrates, and, by a vast system of irrigation, transform Babylonia into one of the great wheat-fields of the world. A beginning was made in establishing law, order, and industry by purchasing considerable tracts of land from the local owners. Much to the surprise of these Arab merchants, their land was bought from them at a fair price, instead of being seized by force, according to the immemorial custom of all other conquerors. Customs were established, and trade encouraged in every way; and by the institution of settled and progressive government, the improvement of land and water communications and the public health system, the benefits of British occupation were brought home to the townspeople.

The result was that some of the Arab tribes began to work heartily for the new government, and did much to relieve its troops when the terrible heat was seriously telling on the white men. Not a shot was fired for months, and in spite of the fact that large quantities of firearms had been concealed by the Turks in the mosques, every Arab in the towns except the mullahs was friendly.

This garrison work, though unexciting, was a relief from the rigours endured by the troops engaged in nomad-hunting in the neighbouring desert lands amid constant sandstorms. At times the temperature rose to 130 degrees in the small tents, and on very sultry days the sandstorms came. A dense khaki-coloured cloud would rise on the horizon, and then roll towards the encampment. The men would rush about strengthening their tent-pegs and ropes, and collecting all the loose kit; but often no preparation was adequate to meet the storm. The tents would be blown down like packs of cards, and all had to hide their heads under tent-flaps, bedding, or boxes, as it was impossible to face the blasts of cutting sand. In violent tempests the sand made a black darkness which lasted for hours. When the storm passed, and the troops emerged, their eyes were bloodshot, their mouths and nostrils coated with sand and mud, and all their bodies were a mass of sand.

It was in difficult circumstances that the work of chasing down hostile Arab tribes and burning their camps had to be carried out. The actual conflicts with mounted bands of Bedouin guerillas were not much of a trial. As the Bedouins usually had no guns, they scattered among the dunes when offered battle, and reconnoitring aeroplanes were hard put to it to trace the lines along which they would next concentrate. The Indian cavalry, with a section of horse artillery concealed behind them, managed at first by feigning a flight and leading the unsuspecting Bedouins towards the guns, to ambush some of the more daring. But the Bedouin, being a born guerilla fighter, mounted on a fine desert horse, soon learned all the tricks of the cavalry, and had to be hunted down by converging columns of infantry. When the Indo-British troops took up the work, he retired deep into the sandy waste, where were springs known only to himself. There he tried to outfight his foe by his last and most terrible weapon of defence—thirst.

Many of the Indian troops came from the desert regions in North-West India, yet even they could not march in the strong sun of the Mesopotamian summer through ten miles of waterless sand. In fact, as we have seen, they could not walk five miles when their waterbottles were empty. The heat from the sun above and from the scorching sand beneath dried up the blood in the body, and produced a condition of hallucination which quickly merged into coma, ending rapidly in death.

Yet even in the heat of the summer the work of daunting and disarming the hostile tribes went on at a surprising speed. And as the armed vessels had a range of over a week's march down both the Tigris and the Euphrates, and the steamers were able to tow large flotillas of troop-filled bellums and barges to any point at which the hostile Arabs assembled, not only was the pacification of the occupied territory ensured, but far-distant raiding tribes could also be unexpectedly attacked. During this phase of the campaign the Turks had no flying machines, while the Indian Expeditionary Force had both aeroplanes and seaplanes which bombed remote entrenched camps. In this fashion the first phase of the campaign ended. A period of comparative inaction ensued, until in April the British and Indian troops were ready for a fresh advance.

Stretch of the Suez Canal looking north. The famous water way was the objective of Turkish offensives on February 2, and March 22, 1915. These attacks were defeated by the British forces guarding the canal. On the latter occasion the Turks advanced to El Kubri, near Suez, and on being attacked retreated towards Nakhl.

British blimp, or naval observation airship, being towed by warship against a strong headwind. The blimp was a non-rigid type used by the Admiralty for scouting purposes.

SUEZ CANAL AND THE EYES OF THE NAVY

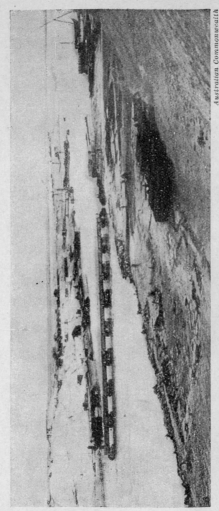

Australian Commonwealth

HEADQUARTERS OF AUSTRALIANS GUARDING SUEZ CANAL. Turkey's entry into the war on the side of Germany was the result of a scheme to divert the attention of the Allies to fresh frontiers and to weaken their forces in Europe. Defence of the Egyptian frontier and the Suez Canal necessitated the speedy dispatch of troops to the East. Among the contingents sent to this area were Australian troops, who built the floating bridge over the Canal shown in this photograph. Throughout 1915 Turkish attacks on the Canal were repulsed by British and other Empire forces.

Plate 2

Volume 11

COSSACK CAVALRY AMID THE SNOWY WASTES OF THE CAUCASUS. In January, 1915 the Turkish army operating against Russia in the Caucasus was decisively defeated at Sarikamish by the Russians under General Yudenitch. This area was the scene of severe fighting throughout the war The illustration shows Cossack cavalry patrolling in the snowbound mountainous country.

The main street of Kolomea, an important junction in
E. Galicia. Captured by the Russians in 1914, it was
re-taken by the Austrians in February, 1915.

General view of the town of Kovno, Lithuania, the scene of an Austrian victory
in August, 1915. The Russians put up an heroic defence of the fortress.

Novo Georgievsk, in Poland, was the scene of another
Russian defeat, in 1915, the town falling to the Germans
on August 19. The illustration shows the southern
gateway of the fortress.

NOTED LANDMARKS OF THE EASTERN CAMPAIGN

Plate 4   *Volume II*

CHAPTER 2

Russia in Wartime

Notwithstanding the reverses to which her giant army was subjected, Holy Russia never questioned the result of the war. France remained animated by a splendid chivalry, and Britain was determined at whatever cost to defend her empire. It was, however, not so much the spirit of nationality that bound the one hundred and sixty million people of Russia together, as a deep-seated abiding belief that their holy country could never be subject to an alien Power. One has to understand the religious sentiment which permeated the whole of Muscovy to appreciate how the Russians felt in regard to the conflict which was waged on her frontiers. She had her setbacks. Millions of her sons yielded their lives, but the end had to be—the Russian mind was incapable of thinking otherwise—a victory for Holy Russia.

It was this state of thought that made Russia in war time so incomprehensible to the foreigner. The people were moody and emotional, poetical rather than practical, and while bad news depressed them, good news never elated them. They took victories as a matter of course, because they knew they were to come. The Russians were in many ways the most charming people on the earth. They had the simplicity of children. Their hospitality was unbounded. A Russian would go out of his way, and spend much more than the condition of his purse justified, to give the visitor a good time. He knew perfectly well that men of other countries looked upon him as something of a savage, with a considerable tincture of wild Tartar blood in his veins. He was aware that, compared with other lands, he was backward; but he modestly reminded you that Russia, as a great people, had been in existence for not much more than one hundred years.

Yet with all its hindrances, the Russian empire had widened and extended until the dawn of the twentieth century found it the greatest cohesive nation on the earth. Indeed, it had grown so much, and drawn within its territory so many people of other races, that it may be said to have become fenced around with non-Russian speaking Russians. It was its size, its majesty, that filled the imaginative Russian with the conviction that it had a mighty destiny, not to be interfered with by the incursions of German soldiery. Much was heard about the numberless millions of men that Russia could put into the field. From the cold regions below Archangel, from the warm lands in the region of the Caucasus, from the prairies beyond the Volga, and from the illimitable stretches of Siberia the Russian was called to arms. He responded, not because he had a thirst to slay Germans, but because he felt it his duty to defend Holy Russia.

Frenchmen and Englishmen proceeded to war laughing and with gay songs upon their lips. Russian soldiers never did that. They went to their church and humbly prayed before their icons, the sacred pictures of their particular saints; they stood with bowed head while the picturesque and long-haired priests sprinkled holy water upon them, and then, singing hymns, they marched to their fate, never letting go of the faith that, whatever may befall them individually, Holy Russia must be triumphant. During the first year of the war the calm confidence of the people was most impressive. In Petrograd, in Moscow, the ancient capital, in all the great cities, life progressed much as it did in normal times. Business was conducted in the ordinary way. All the entertainments, the theatres, and the pleasure gardens were in full swing. It was only by witnessing hymn-singing battalions of soldiers marching through the streets, or coming across groups of pale-faced wounded fellows hobbling along, that one was reminded that a great war was in progress.

When the alarm was first sounded, the Russian authorities had a mighty difficulty to face. During the Russo-Japanese war the efficiency of the troops was much impaired by drunkenness. The principal beverage in the country was vodka, a fiery spirit mostly made from rye, the manufacture of which was a government monopoly, and the effect of which was direful. Germany calculated that the mobilization of the Russian army would be a slow and laborious process. The belief which prevailed in Berlin was, on the outbreak of hostilities, that first a swift blow should be levelled against France, and when France was in the dust, it would be time enough for the hordes of the kaiser to sweep round and deal with the soldiers of the tsar. But the Emperor William forgot the power of the Emperor

Nicholas. The Tsar of All the Russias was the Little White Father to his people. Whatever order he issued was not in the nature of a law, but was a religious ordinance which must be obeyed. Therefore, swiftly grasping the necessity for action, the Emperor Nicholas issued his famous ukase, proclaiming that the government manufacture of vodka should cease, so that the work of the army should not be retarded by the drunkenness of the soldiers.

It was generally accepted that the Russian was a drunkard— the worst drunkard, indeed, in Europe. This is quite a mistake. The European country where the least amount per head of the population was expended on alcohol was Norway. The country which came next was Russia. Per head of the population, the Russian, in normal times, spent 18s. a year on drink, while in England the amount spent each year per head of the population was estimated at 66s. The difference is that, whereas in England the money was disbursed chiefly on so innocuous a beverage as beer, practically all the money in Russia was spent on this fierce vodka spirit, which did tremendous harm physically, morally, and industrially to the subjects of the tsar.

Forbidding the state manufacture of vodka did two things. It lopped off a revenue of £67,000,000 a year which went into the Imperial exchequer, and it shut off the supply to the ordinary civilian. Freedom was given to the Zemstvos (local assemblies) and the municipalities to follow up the action of the tsar in what way they pleased. With few exceptions, all the authorities throughout the realm, from Archangel to Tiflis and from Moscow to Vladivostok, prohibited the sale and consumption of alcohol in any form. Not only was vodka removed, but the police put seals on cellars, and prevented the consumption of brandy, of wines, and of beer. Within a few days the whole of Russia, which had been a byword to the world, became teetotal. In a constitutionally governed country such a thing would have been impossible. It was only by the exercise of autocracy that such a revolution could be effected in the land of the tsar. Because the original command came from the Little White Father, the Russians accepted it without question. It is not to be assumed that even then men with money could not obtain wine and spirits by subterranean means. They could. But, speaking in a broad and general sense, it may be said that after the issue of the ukase ninety-nine per cent of the people of Russia never touched a drop of alcohol. Drunkards, of course, were distressed, and had recourse to methylated spirit and other beverages. But that means of ministering to the appetite was checked, because even methylated spirit could not be procured except through complicated formalities, which practically put it out of the reach of the former toper.

The essential fact to be realized is that, without demur, Russia fell in with the new condition of things. Temptation being removed, the artisans of the towns and the moujiks of the steppes, unable to dispose of their earnings as they did formerly, found themselves in possession of more money than ever they had before. They were able to spend it on better food, on giving better clothing to their children, in providing themselves with healthy amusements; and so, although in Russia the cost of living was materially increased in consequence of the war, the people were in every sense much better off than they were formerly. The soldiers responded to the call of their monarch with greater alacrity than they would have been able to do if they had fuddled their brains in the vodka taverns.

The speed with which Russia was able to mobilize was a marvel to the world. In the early weeks of the struggle, when the German armies were engaged in their first great attempt to sweep through the north of France and gain possession of Paris, it was the action of the Russian troops in the north-east, rushing into Prussia—until at one time there was a belief that nothing could restrain them from reaching Berlin—that caused the kaiser to slacken the pressure on the western front. He required German troops to contest the progress of the Russians in the north-east. Not only that, but the abstinence of the nation had a beneficial effect industrially. The Russian workman had never ranked high as an artisan; but the point is not to be missed that his efficiency was increased by at least fifteen—some people say twenty-five—per cent owing to his inability to reach the vodka bottle.

Another great change which the war produced in Russia was the development of public opinion. In old days public opinion, such as it is understood in England, was non-existent in the dominions of the tsar. The government was paternal, it was autocratic, it watched over and cared for the people. Those who were irritable under constant surveillance, who hungered for a condition of government different from that which existed, and who gave vent to their views by joining in revolutionary movements, were harshly—and no doubt in many cases cruelly—treated. One of the things upon which the German government calculated was that, with Russia at war, the various revolutionary parties would endeavour to upset the existing régime, produce internal trouble, and so make Russia an easy prey.

Now, for the first time within knowledge, the war was not waged by the Russian tsar or government, but by the Russian people. The war of 1903 between Russia and Japan was regarded by the majority of the Russian people as a dispute between the government and Japan. When Japan was able to overthrow Russia, the Russians themselves did not feel that their national dignity had been lowered. The blow had been struck at the government. The present war was from its outset different from that. Instead of the struggle on the frontiers providing the revolutionary party with a chance to push their propaganda into effect, it completely obliterated all political dissension throughout the whole of the tsar's realms, in precisely the same way as political differences were sunk throughout the British empire.

Doubtless many of the advanced thinkers looked forward to a change for what they considered to be the better in the administration of affairs when the war should be over. For the time being, however, the revolutionaries—the men who had been nurtured on western ideas, who resented autocracy as out of date, and desired their country to be administered on lines akin to those laid down in England—were just as true and as loyal to their emperor as were men who had spent their lives within the precincts of the court. Men who were exiled because of their opinions voluntarily returned to Russia, risking imprisonment, but eager to be of some service to their motherland.

Such loyalty, which in all probability the Russian government never contemplated, had its effect in another direction. The grip of autocratic administration was slackened. There was a revolution in progress in Russia, but it was all to the good. Men discussed what was happening in the world, and in Russia particularly, with a freedom which 20 months previously would have been impossible. Newspapers criticised ministers in a manner which, if attempted a little while back, would have landed the editors in the fortress of Peter and Paul, or have sent them on a long visit to Siberia. Public meetings were held, especially in Moscow. What was happening in the war was debated with as much freedom as in England itself, while at concerts, with the police standing by, songs were loudly applauded which would have meant the arrest of the singers, if not of the audience, but a couple of years before. Russia had some incompetent ministers. The public knew they were incompetent; they said so in conversation in the cafés; they said so at public meetings. Writers said so in newspaper articles. And the consequence was that a number of these inefficient highly placed personages was removed.

The war gave birth to healthy public opinion in Russia. During the first year of the war there was a remarkable development of public consciousness that action should be taken—violent, if necessary—to remove the black spots which disfigured the national escutcheon. It was common knowledge that in public as well as in commercial life Russia tolerated and practised what honourable men could not defend. Everyone was aware that little business was transacted without someone taking what he would have called a "commission," but which others would have described as a bribe. Of course, there were officials actuated by motives as worthy as those in any land, and whose hands were clean. But in the past every Russian shrugged his shoulders and was ready to admit that the accomplishment of services was slow, chiefly because there was someone who needed a little—and occasionally a very large—stimulus to do his duty. In what is called corruption, Russia was perhaps no worse than some other lands which consider themselves enlightened; but the practice of men receiving payment to do their duty was far too prevalent. In great government contracts there were officials who wanted their commission from the manufacturer before the documents were allowed to go forward to the minister to sign them. Right down to the humble policeman, badly paid, the same practice was usual. In most ordinary business transactions, the straightforward deal was generally held up by someone who wanted to know what his commission was to be before the negotiations advanced to completion.

That was the state of things before the war. It was the state of things at the beginning of the war. The public, however, soon became acquainted with the fact that even the supply of munitions and war material of all sorts, so necessary for the equipment of the army, was being retarded in delivery because of the pernicious practice of delay until the commission was arranged.

Then there swept through the nation a feeling of resentment, followed by a vociferous declaration that this sort of proceeding must cease. It would be idle to say that the frank indignation of the populace was the means of purifying public life. The point is that the Russians, who had been in the habit of acquiescing in or explaining that the receiving of a reward by an official was an old custom hard to remove, no longer defended it. It was vehemently denounced. There came forth a zealous belief that Russia was hampering herself by allowing such conditions to continue. There was clamour that certain prominent men, who were supposed to have exploited the necessities of their country to their own advantage, should be shot.

The government took manufacturers into counsel, and all government contracts had to pass through a committee, thus preventing the " go-between " from lining his own pockets. With regard to the old practice it has to be remembered that officials in Russia were not too well paid. The defence often put forward for the niggardly pittance that was handed to them was that they could easily find other means to secure recompense for their labours. The war not only stirred up the sentiment of the nation, but it moved men's minds to think of the future. One of the consequences of this was to create an ideal Russia in the popular imagination, where officials would be well paid for their labours, and where there would be purity in public life and fair dealing between men, so that the country, instead of being pointed at by other peoples, would be accepted as a model. Thus the conflict was not only one waged to overthrow the Germans. It was one between old habits and new ambitions, with the thought ever at the back of men's minds that not only would the unhappy days end by the repulsion of the invaders from Muscovite territory, but in the regeneration of Russia itself.

Another great change which was evolved during the first 12 months of the war was in Russia's attitude toward other nations. Easy-going and poetical, visionary and religious, more given to theorising than to working, the Russian people awakened to the fact that in modern matters, commerce particularly, she had slipped under the domination of other races. It was the break with Germany that caused her to appreciate how dependent she had allowed herself to be upon neighbouring countries, particularly Germany. It is to be remembered that a considerable section of Russian territory was comprised in what were known as the

Baltic provinces, where the people were not Slav, like the mass of the rest of the nation, but rather Teutonic in origin, with a part of the population speaking German as their usual tongue. These Baltic province Russians had always regarded themselves as superior to the ordinary Russians ; which, let it be admitted, they were in commerce and in manufacturing. For while the Slav is a dreamer, the Teuton is a practical man. With a German origin and bearing German names, it is not to be wondered at that many of these people had sympathy with the great progressive neighbouring country of Germany.

The Russians of the Baltic provinces showed business aptitude. Travelling into the interior, establishing commercial concerns, finding that the needs of the country in manufactured articles could not be supplied by the Russians, they let Germany make good the deficiency. For a generation Russia was subjected to a much more drastic invasion than that which took place during 1915. It was a commercial invasion, which percolated throughout the land until it may be said that, from a trading point of view, Russia was but a colony of Germany. More than half the manufactured goods which went into Russia from abroad came from Germany. A vast proportion of the principal shops in the great cities carried German names. Official life was permeated by German-speaking Russians. So even in government departments it was no unusual thing to find employees of the state conversing between themselves in the German language.

Beyond this, the war had not been in progress many weeks before the Russians became dimly aware—and ultimately glaringly aware—that subterranean endeavours were being made to swing public opinion in favour of Germany. Stories got about, no doubt ill-founded, that even in the highest circle Germanic influences were at work.

The war compelled Russia to examine her own condition. She was alarmed. She heard rumours that there was a peace party in Russia, and that it was chiefly composed of people of German origin. Her ears were filled with scornful references to France and to Great Britain, and she discovered that the instigators were men with German names. There was a shortage of manufactured goods. Every household was brought to a realization how great had been the German hold on Russia.

It required no agitation to rouse the Russian people to a decision that too long had she been subservient to another

Power which had been exploiting them. Accordingly there flamed into existence a movement which may be described as "Russia for the Russians." The questions were asked: Why should Russia purchase so much from Germany? Why could not Russia make more of the necessaries of life than she did? What was wrong with the skill of Russian working men that they did not produce a multitude of useful articles for themselves instead of paying Germany for them?

The asking of these questions led to a speedy decision. Russia must wake up, must shed her old-time torpor, must adapt herself to modern manufacturing conditions, must develop her own illimitable resources, must advance in industry without reliance upon other lands, and thus demonstrate to the world that she was not encompassed with a sort of semi-Oriental indolence, but was quick, alert, adaptive and capable of taking her place alongside any of the western nations. The war jogged the national liver, it stirred the latent national feeling, and caused Russia to take stock of her own potentialities and capabilities with the purpose of utilising them to the advantage of her own people.

What animated Russia most against the enemy was not so much the invasion of her territory as the bitterness engendered by the fear that Germany might impose her own commercial conditions upon Russia to the retardment of Russian industries. The firm determination to do more for herself and accept less from the foreigner was one of the direct results of the war.

Hatred towards the Germans developed to such an extent that the German tongue, although it had previously been the commercial language of the country, was prohibited. No one was allowed to speak German over the telephone; there were notices hung over the receivers threatening terrible punishments if such a thing were attempted. Hotels which had German names had quickly to change the description. In the big hotels of Petrograd, Moscow and elsewhere it was customary for notices to be hung up in three or four different languages for the instruction of visitors; but in every case German was obliterated. If anyone was heard speaking this language there was a hue and cry, and frequently the offender was maltreated at the hands of an infuriated mob. Many people could not differentiate between German and English, and there were quite a number of cases of both English men and English women being insulted because over-ardent and patriotic Muscovites imagined they were speaking

German. It is, indeed, difficult to realize the intensity of the hatred toward Germany which grew up and increased in volume during the war.

One notable explosion of public wrath occurred in Moscow. As already mentioned, most of the huge emporiums, though legitimately Russian, were conducted by men who, to their misfortune, bore German names. The folk of Moscow, always more vehement in their patriotism than the cosmopolitan population of Petrograd, frequently demonstrated against suspects of any kind being allowed to remain in the city, and conceived the idea that while the shops pretended to be Russian, they were in fact German.

With the breaking of a few windows a riot commenced. Shops were gutted ; goods were cast into the streets and appropriated or destroyed. Great clothing stores were reduced to ruins; valuable furniture was smashed to atoms; bookshops had their contents completely spoilt, and from the upper windows of music warehouses grand pianos were hurled into the thoroughfares, and there their demolition was completed. Under the new law the wine and spirit vaults were under lock and key and sealed; but the mob broke in and took possession of enormous quantities of liquor, and in one cellar where barrels of wine were broken open there was a flood four feet deep, and at least a dozen men, overcome by the fumes, were drowned. Russians with German names but whose families had been in the country for at least a century, men whose sons were actually fighting in the Russian army, were chased by the crowd, caught, and some of them subjected to the most cruel deaths. The police apparently did nothing to check the disorder, even when a number of the shops were set on fire. The best explanation is that they seem to have regarded it to be their duty not to interfere with a patriotic demonstration.

For two days the rioting continued. Many lives were sacrificed. It is right to say, however, that the governor-general of the city, who was on a sick-bed when he heard of the outrages, sent soldiers into the disturbed districts. A few volleys into the crowd, killing between thirty and forty people, brought a quick cessation of the trouble. There was a government inquiry, with the result that the chiefs of the police were removed from their offices. This particular case is recorded as evidence of how swiftly the fire of animus flamed against the obnoxious Teutons.

It was a little singular that while the passions of the people could scarcely be restrained against the Germans, comparatively little dislike was displayed towards the Austrians. When, for example, prisoners of war were marched through the streets, German soldiers were execrated, and responded with sullen, scornful looks, marching along black-browed and resentful, whereas a kindly sympathy was extended to the Austrian prisoners, who generally seemed merry and exchanged chaffing remarks with the spectators. Most of the Germans were transferred to Siberia; but the majority of the Austrians were drafted into farming districts, where their labour could be utilised in tilling the land.

At Moscow there was little on the surface to suggest that the country was at war. Business proceeded as usual. It was only by seeing long ambulance trains at the railway stations, by coming across long processions of wounded in the streets, by seeing the parade ground within the Kremlin constantly occupied by troops under drill, and the little groups of open-mouthed spectators before the guns which had been captured from the enemy that one was reminded of what was happening in the history of the world. A little investigation soon revealed that the nation was under the strain of war. There was a shortage of men's labour, so that in many occupations women had to be employed.

Then, owing to the check put upon the importation of manufactured articles, not only was there a scarcity, but prices considerably increased. Food rose to something approaching famine prices, and once or twice there was a distinct shortage of beef. This, however, was due not to lack of herds in Russia, but to the government commandeering so many head of cattle in order to provide beef for the soldiers, who, in their peasant occupations during peace time, could rarely afford such a luxury. Although the Russian army was short of many things, the commissariat department was efficient and the transport effective. No soldiers in this dreadful struggle were better fed or better clad than the troops of the tsar.

It was very much the same in St. Petersburg, the official capital of the country. Hotel prices were always high in Russia; but they were never so high as during war time. One of the reasons was that the proprietors, deprived of their profits because of the stoppage in the sale of wines, endeavoured to recoup themselves by increasing the prices of everything else. Russia, while possessing so enormous an army, had been rather unpractical in her preparations for the great inevitable bout between herself and Germany. In many respects she was caught unawares. Germany knew how ill-provisioned she was in munitions. Russia on her part had been slow in taking notice of what the long years of warlike preparation in Germany really meant. Many of the absolute essentials for war could not be provided in Russia to equip a fair proportion of her soldiery. She had to seek supplies from abroad. The German market was shut off, and France and Britain were much too busy preparing for their own requirements to offer much assistance to Russia, though they did help in many ways.

The result was that the representatives of big manufacturing concerns in neutral countries descended upon St. Petersburg in considerable numbers. They were mostly Swedes and Americans. One of the biggest hotels in the city was crowded with Americans who were seeking to secure contracts with the Russian government. Many of them did. The difficult point was the delivery. War goods could enter Russia without much hindrance by means of the back door. That is to say, they could be landed at Port Arthur or Vladivostok and brought into the country through Siberia. That, however, was a long and difficult route. The quickest ways were by Archangel and Odessa; but the gateway to Odessa through the Dardanelles could not be forced by the French and British Allies, and an entrance by way of the White Sea was hampered by the Arctic ice which encloses Archangel for several months of the year. It was this difficulty of getting absolutely necessary supplies from Allied and neutral countries that had much to do with the compulsory retirement of the Russian troops. They were brave enough; but bravery without munitions does not count for a great deal.

However, there was great confidence in the ability of the British and French warships and soldiers to knock a way through the Dardanelles, clear the passage of the Bosphorus, and thus provide an open route from the outer world to Odessa. As a preliminary to this the chiefs of the principal trading firms went to Odessa, furnished offices, and laid the train not only for supplying the soldiers with requisites from England and America, but also for providing the civilian population with goods of which the people were in need.

Russia was hard put to it to obtain supplies from abroad. During the dark days of winter the only means through which she could receive help from Britain and France was by way of Sweden. The population of Sweden was not particularly enthusiastic over the cause of the Allies. It could not be said that Sweden put facilities in the way of communication. Sweden had been laid under the intellectual spell of Germany, and, while the folk of this part of Scandinavia did not look with a fond eye upon the manner in which German goods were flooding the country, they had, according to their point of view, less to fear from Germany than from Russia; because the Swedes had long nursed a dread that if ever Russia had the power she would cut a way from Finland across the northern parts of Sweden and Norway and create for herself a port on the North Sea.

The Swedish attitude was not dictated by any resentment toward Britain, although the Swedish trading classes did not like ships being held up by the British Admiralty on the ground that the cargoes, while destined for Sweden, were really intended for Germany. It was perfectly natural that Sweden should not wish to incur the enmity of Germany. Therefore it can be easily understood that when she provided the only route between France, Great Britain, and Russia, her responsible authorities did not go out of their way to help in the conveyance of goods to the enemy of Germany.

The journey across the North Sea from Newcastle to Bergen, thence to Stockholm, then due north to the real "land of the midnight sun," and to the very edge of Lapland, round the top of the Gulf of Bothnia, and so across the Swedish frontier into Finland and down to Petrograd occupied eight days. There was only a single line to the north of Sweden. There was no railway communication with Finland. The Russians laid a temporary line on the frozen earth to a place opposite Karungi, on the Swedish side of the Tornea river; but when this fell into disuse owing to the spring thaw, it was necessary to convey all goods by vehicle a distance of some twenty miles along the frontier, and then ferry across the Tornea river to a point where the Finnish railway could be touched. Taking goods into Russia by this means in bulk was an impossibility.

The Swedes themselves made a very close examination to prevent the transit of contraband supplies. The only plan by which articles from France and England could be sent to Russia was through the parcels post. Millions of small packages travelled by that circuitous route. Trainloads upon trainloads of parcels took sections of small machinery into the country, where they could be put together. All this was very hampering and most expensive, and will convey to the mind of the reader to what a pass Russia was brought.

But with the coming of spring, although the Karungi route was still available, large articles, such as machinery, had to be taken into Russia by way of the White Sea and Archangel. As soon as the ice broke, fleets of merchant ships made their way to Russia's northern port, although many of them were impeded or prevented altogether by the enemy submarines which were on the watch at the mouth of the White Sea. The single line from Archangel to the south was in process of being doubled. It was over these metals that Russia got most of her supplies during the summer of 1915. Ordinary merchandise had practically to be ignored; the railway was requisitioned by the military authorities. Mountains of goods were stacked on the quaysides at Archangel, exposed to damage by the tempestuous weather.

Traders also suffered to a considerable extent. The Manufacturers' Association of Moscow, however, did what was best in the circumstances—sent representatives to Archangel, and by the utilisation of the waterways in that part of the world were able to forward much merchandise, though the delay was great. With the prospect of a famine in particular articles, several representatives of the principal Moscow firms made search throughout the empire, particularly in towns where trade had come to a standstill, and were able to purchase from the retailers many of their goods, and forward them to Moscow and to Petrograd.

The war, instead of reducing the populations of the great cities, increased them. The wealthier classes, who had been in the habit of travelling abroad, principally to German spas, remained at home. They did not even go to Yalta, the beautiful watering place in the Crimea; nor did many of them take up their abode on their country estates. They were anxious to keep in touch with what was happening in the great drama. They remained in the capital, or took up their residence in Moscow, Kieff, Jaroslav and other centres. There was a great inflow of refugees from Poland and from the south-western districts of the country.

For months Warsaw was a hustling military centre. Most of the troops chosen to fight the Germans in the north-eastern

theatre were sent that way, Endless processions of regiments marched through the streets, unarmed in many instances,
for the soldiers were to receive their rifles at the front;
which meant that they were to get their weapons from brother
soldiers who were wounded, or to have them passed on from men
who were dead. Hotels were packed with Russian officers.
Though the boom of the guns could be heard, and German
aeroplanes frequently flew over the city, life proceeded gaily
enough. There was little news of what was taking place at the
fighting line, except that the return of enormous convoys of
wounded men indicated that the resistance to the invaders had
been stubborn. Weeks before the actual evacuation there were
indications of what was going to happen. The treasury was
removed ; the wives of officials were provided with permits to
leave ; British residents were given the hint they had better go.

So matters proceeded until the last few days of the movement
when there was a rush of people making their escape before the
enemy entered the city. Never was railway traffic so congested.
Civilians had to be content with travelling under disagreeable
conditions in cattle trucks. The journey from Warsaw to
Moscow took over two days. Thus Moscow had a larger population than in normal times. It was the same down at Kieff, the
Holy City of Russia. Refugees from the region of Galicia all
made for this town. Thousands of them came without any possessions except the clothing in which they stood. It says much
for the warm-heartedness of the Russians that, although there
was little organization, kindness and hospitality to the unfortunate were abounding, and for fifty miles around there was scarcely
a house which did not shelter and care for some family which
had been obliged to fly before the invaders.

There were periods when the Russians were depressed. They
knew of the sacrifices which they were making, and there was
little opportunity for them to learn what their Allies were doing.
They became somewhat critical. They recalled how, when the
French and British were being pressed by the Germans on the
western front in the autumn of 1914, the Russians put up a
vigorous attack in the north-east in order to draw off some of
that pressure, and they asked the question why, when they were
being pressed in Poland and Galicia, the French and British
armies did not act vigorously in order to withdraw some of the
German pressure on the Russian front. They mourned that the

passage of the Dardanelles had not been forced. They grieved that the ammunition which they expected from their Allies, was prevented from being delivered. Still, though depressed, they were determined. Always at the back of their thoughts was the conviction that whatever might be the misfortunes which they might suffer they were but temporary, and that the foe must ultimately be repulsed.

No better proof of the spirit which animated the nation could be found than the way in which the whole of the civilian population recognized what was incumbent upon it. Slowly—for the Russian was incapable of doing things quickly—munition factories were organized, and the people set about producing war material for their troops. Frequently there was such a shortage that the soldiers were obliged to retire long distances before the superior equipment of the Germans. In time that trouble was surmounted. Within their capabilities, not so great as those of England, all the factories of Russia were engaged in turning out munitions of war.

It has been said, and rightly, that the people of Russia, the civilian population, did more than the government itself. The government attended to all military matters, the arming and the provisioning of the troops. Everything else was left to organizations and private individuals. For instance, the whole of the nursing and the wounded was left to the Red Cross Society and Russia's innumerable benevolent institutions. The Russian Red Cross Society had been active for many years, because within the scope of its operations was the improvement of the housing of the poorer classes as well as the care of the sick.

Practically all the ladies of the better classes engaged in hospital work. Each province, every Zemstvo, and every municipality had not only to look after the injured, but also to make provision for the dependents of the fighting men. Representatives of all the local authorities met, and schemes were drawn up whereby each district could do its share in caring for the maimed or sick. Some municipalities could accept a thousand men; others were only able to look after fifty men. Above this, all private individuals with houses of any size set apart either the whole dwelling or a certain number of rooms, and undertook at their own charge to minister to the wants of some poor fellows. The consequence of all this was that the wounded and the poor were looked after by municipal or private philanthropy.

You could not take a walk in any of the main streets of the big towns or drive through any of the villages without constantly seeing the Red Cross flag, indicating the existence of a hospital, great or small. Of course, some of these hospitals were much better equipped than others. But within their means all sections of the community gave freely. The dowager empress was at the head of the Red Cross Society, while the empress herself and her daughters made comforts for the wounded and gave the lead to other ladies by taking their share in hospital nursing.

The emperor himself ultimately took command of the Russian army, but long before then he had shown solicitude for his soldiers by travelling to the seat of war, and by visiting the Cossack soldiers who were fighting below the Caucasus. He went to arsenals and witnessed the manufacture of implements of war; he paid informal and quite unostentatious visits to hospitals, arriving often in a simple carriage, and attended by a single aide-de-camp, moving amongst the wounded, talking to them, and addressing the humblest private as "Brother."

CHAPTER 3

Battle of the Dogger Bank

FROM the beginning of January, 1915, reports were received of great activity in the German seaports, and it was thought that the comparative immunity with which the German squadrons had bombarded the English coast might tempt them to a similar or even more ambitious undertaking. At any time, it was felt, the Germans might decide to leave the defence of the Baltic to their minefields and come out to the North Sea in full force; and with several of his battleships out of the line for repair or on detached duty, Jellicoe had only 18 dreadnoughts against the 17 German ones, and Admiral Beatty but five battle cruisers against four German. This left too small a margin for accidents; and though ship for ship the British were far superior, the situation was not without its anxieties. On January 15 the German battle cruisers Seydlitz and Derfflinger were reported to have left the Jade, and such feverish preparations were going on at Kiel that it was felt that offensive action must be imminent. A British reconnaissance on the 19th discovered nothing, and only by two Zeppelin raids did Germany show any signs of enterprise.

All seemed quiet when intelligence arrived that a German sortie would take place on the 23rd, and on that Saturday afternoon the battle cruisers of the German High Seas Fleet with their attendant craft put out to sea. First the destroyer flotilla steamed out in fan formation beyond the minefields in the Bight of Heligoland. Then, as twilight was falling, a line of long, narrow shapes— the light cruisers—threaded its way l 'tween the mines to support the destroyers. While the last glimmer of daylight lasted the destroyers and light cruisers continued their work of hunting about for some sign of a British submarine; but none was visible. So as the early winter night drew on, the defences of Wilhelmshaven opened, and four grey battle cruisers, with the sharp bows of ocean racers, came out at full speed, under the guard of the destroyers. Their object was to scout round the Dogger bank, and there to destroy any British light forces they might meet—possibly, if no opposition had been met a more ambitious programme would have been carried out.

The four battle cruisers were the Seydlitz, which carried the flag of the admiral in command, Hipper, the Derfflinger, the Moltke, and the Blücher. Of Germany's remaining battle cruisers the Von der Tann was out of action, as she had been damaged after the raid on the Hartlepools and the air raid on Cuxhaven in 1914, and the Goeben was in Turkish waters. The Lützow was building.

The history of the Blücher is interesting. In 1906, when Lord Fisher was working out his plan for a fleet of all-big-gun ships, the German Admiralty heard a rumour of the creation of a British ship of the new type—the battle cruiser. With much trouble and expense the intelligence department obtained a forecast of the plan of the Invincible. On this plan the design of the Blücher was carefully modelled, being given the same displacement (about 15,500 tons) as the British ship would possess. She was armed with what was thought to be an over-powering armament for a cruiser—twelve 8.2 in. guns—and engines were made to give her a speed of a little over 26 knots. But all the information obtained at considerable cost by German spies was false. The first three battle cruisers of the

Invincible class (completed in 1908) were not cruisers in the old sense of the word, but racing battleships, with two knots more speed than the Blücher, a tonnage of 17,250 tons, and—the grand surprise—eight 12 in. guns apiece.

Admiral Hipper made full preparations for a running fight. He laid a new minefield north of Heligoland, and arranged for the Zeppelins on that island to come out and drop bombs, with the assistance of a squadron of seaplanes, laden with smaller shells. He also concentrated a large flotilla of submarines between the minefield and the Dogger Bank, with a view to torpedoing his possible pursuers, while his own ships were threading the mine area. All this, however, was only a precautionary measure. He seems to have hoped to have been able to start a different operation at some distance from the northern British coast, during which one or more of his fastest battle cruisers would be able to slip out on to the trade routes, while the British squadron was being hammered in an unexpected way. The minefield, submarines, Zeppelins, and aircraft were arranged to protect the weakened but successful squadron as it turned homeward after the accomplishment of the first part of the design.

Mr. Winston Churchill in " The World Crisis, 1915," has described how by intercepting wireless messages, and in other ways, the information about the German movement reached the Admiralty, and how arrangements were made to meet it. He had just gone into his room about noon on Saturday, the 23rd, when Sir Arthur Wilson entered unannounced. " First Lord," he said, " these fellows are coming out again." "When?" asked the first lord. " To-night. We have just got time to get Beatty there." A plan of campaign was decided upon, and telegrams were sent ordering the units to a rendezvous in the North Sea. The telegram sent to Sir John Jellicoe and the other commanders was as follows :

Four German battle cruisers, six light cruisers, and 22 destroyers will sail this evening to scout on Dogger Bank, probably returning to-morrow evening. All available battle cruisers, light cruisers, and destroyers from Rosyth should proceed to a rendezvous in 55° 13′ N., 3° 12′ E., arriving at 7.0 a.m. to-morrow. Commodore (T) is to proceed with all available destroyers and light cruisers from Harwich to join vice-admiral Lion at 7.0 a.m. at above rendezvous. If enemy is sighted by Commodore (T) while crossing their line of advance, they should be attacked. Wireless telegraphy is not to be used unless absolutely necessary. Telegram has been sent to commander-in-chief home fleet; vice-admiral Lion; vice-admiral third battle squadron; and commodore (T).

Four units are mentioned in the telegram, and from four bases they set out. Commander Tyrwhitt, described as T, or of torpedoes, left Harwich with four cruisers and two flotillas of destroyers, while in a dense fog Commodore Keyes, with the Firedrake, Lurcher, and four submarines made for Heligoland. Farther north Sir David Beatty steamed out of Rosyth with his squadron of battle cruisers—Lion, Tiger, Princess Royal, Indomitable, and New Zealand. Beatty himself was in the Lion, Sir Archibald Moore, his second in command, in the New Zealand. Four light cruisers, Nottingham, Birmingham, Lowestoft, and Southampton, came out of Cromarty Firth to join the battle cruisers. Finally, to support this force, Admiral Bradford led out his squadron of battleships and cruisers, and Sir John Jellicoe, with his Dreadnoughts, three squadrons of cruisers and other auxiliary craft, steamed out of Scapa Flow.

The vessels met as ordered at the rendezvous at seven on the Sunday morning, and soon afterwards the Aurora, leading one of the flotillas, sighted the leading German light cruisers near the Dogger Bank. At 20 minutes past seven she opened fire with her two 6 in. guns, on the Kolberg, and wirelessed her flagship that she was engaging the enemy. After a short exchange of salvos, an explosion was seen under the Kolberg's fore bridge, and she turned away. Sir David Beatty at once altered course towards the direction of the gun flashes, which were south-south-east, ordered all his battleships to increase speed, and commanded the light cruisers and destroyers to get in touch with the enemy.

The German vessels had been steering north-west, but now without waiting to see clearly what he had to meet, their admiral at once turned his ships about, and went full speed on a south-east course. Meanwhile the British light cruisers kept closely in touch with the hostile ships and wirelessed all their movements to Sir David Beatty, whose battle cruiser squadron was working up to full speed and was steering south-eastward to close with the enemy. The weather this time was extremely favourable from the British point of view. A north-east wind swept sea and sky clear of mist, and allowed a long vision over the grey-foam-flecked waste of waters. At 7.30 a.m. the German squadron was sighted from the flagship. It was seen on the port bow, about 14 miles away, steaming fast, and steering towards the south-east.

It was supposed that the last ships of the German line were preparing to drop contact mines in their wake, on the chance of blowing up some of the pursuing British vessels. But this simple trick was easily countered, for the first thing Sir David Beatty did, on receiving the report of the enemy's position, was to steer his ships outside the enemy's track, getting on their quarter. In other words, he so altered his course as to pursue them on a

line parallel to theirs, instead of following directly behind them. Thus the course of the fugitives and the line of the pursuers formed two parallel lines at least six or seven miles distant from each other.

The British squadron settled down to a long stern chase, all the battle cruisers working up their speed until they reached a speed of 27 knots. This was an easy speed for the new ships, Lion, Tiger, and Princess Royal, which were, indeed, able to add another couple of knots to it. But for the Indomitable, an older battle cruiser, it was an excess over her normal rate of movement. She would have tailed away out of the line, but for the tremendous exertions of her engineers and stokers. The New Zealand, completed in 1912, four years after the Indomitable, had also some difficulty in keeping up with the three leading ships. For while the Tiger could do over 30 knots, the Princess Royal 30 knots, and the Lion nearly 30 knots, the older New Zealand could only do a fraction over 25 knots at her best.

It was in the first place a battle between British engineers and stokers and German engineers and stokers. The Germans had 14 miles start, which the British engine-room men had to wipe out before the danger spot was reached. The speed of the newly completed Derfflinger was not known, but it was certainly less than that of the latest British battle cruisers. The speed of the Seydlitz, a 1913 ship, was about equal to that of the Princess Royal, a 1912 ship. The Moltke, completed in 1911, was just a little faster than the New Zealand, completed a few months later. The Blücher and Indomitable, with actual sea speeds of about 25 knots, were out of the running.

At about nine o'clock when within 20,000 yards of the rear German ship, the Lion fired ranging shots. The enemy at this time were steaming in single line ahead, with their six light cruisers tearing away in front of them, and a number of their destroyers on their starboard beam. Ten minutes later, at about 17,000 yards, the Lion got her first shell home on the Blücher. A terrific mass of high explosive and hardened steel, weighing more than half a ton, screamed through the air at a speed of more than a mile in two seconds, and crashed on the armour of the doomed Blücher. A blue light showed where steel struck on steel, and then came the smoky explosion of the lyddite tearing open the six-inch thickness of Krupp armour plate. The Lion's third salvo carried away the Blücher's after superstructure, disabled two turrets, and killed and injured 250 men. Eleven minutes afterwards shells from the Tiger also began to fall on the Blücher. Seeing this, the chief gunnery lieutenant of the Lion took another target, and, with the help of his fire-control officers, dropped the shells from his four bow guns on to the third ship in the German line, the Moltke, and struck her with salvo after salvo, from a distance of 18,000 yards. Now, three of the enemy's ships were concentrating on the Lion, and at 9.30 a shell took her on the water line and penetrated her bunkers.

The position at 35 minutes past nine in the morning was that the Blücher had dropped astern, and had come within the range of the four forward 12 in. guns of the New Zealand, after having been terribly bombarded in turn by the Princess Royal, the Tiger, and the Lion. They had set her on fire, and done a great deal of damage to her, even knocking one of her gun turrets out of its holdings, and hurling it with its guns and its crew into the sea.

The three leading British battle cruisers now passed the doomed rear ship of the enemy's line, and steaming ahead on their parallel course, attacked the more powerful and swifter German vessels. The British flagship, the Lion, had gained so much on the enemy that she could now straddle the German flagship, the Seydlitz, leading the enemy's line, this being to pitch a number of shells at her simultaneously, some of them perhaps falling short or going over, but some of them hitting. The first salvo from the Lion had terrible effect. It pierced the upper deck of the stern and the armour of the stern turret, where it exploded. The officers' quarters were destroyed, but, worse still, a charge in the reloading chamber ignited, spreading down to the ammunition chamber below, through a connecting passage, and thence up into the second turret, the crews of both being instantly killed, and the turrets put out of action. The Tiger also massed her guns on the Seydlitz, while the Princess Royal continued to batter the Moltke, the third ship in the German line.

Only the second German ship, the Derfflinger, escaped much damage. The reason for this was that she was, during the earlier part of the fight, hidden in smoke. Smoke was the great trouble that the British gunners had to contend against. When the action opened, the flotilla cruisers, the Arethusa, Aurora, and Undaunted, with their destroyers, were steaming ahead of the line. They immediately dropped back so as not to foul the range with their smoke. At a distance of about ten miles, when the Lion first got home on the Blücher, the target was extremely small. The principal German ships were from 600 to 650 feet long, and about 95 feet wide amidships. On the skyline they make a mark that could be covered by a large pin's point. Hold a lead pencil by the point, one and a half feet from the eye, and the small black centre of it will more than cover the target presented by the whole German battle cruiser squadron. Naturally, therefore, any drift of smoke between this remote target and the fire-control stations on the leading battle cruisers seriously interfered with the aim of the gunnery officers.

BATTLE OF THE DOGGER BANK

The British vessels were moving at something over 28 knots, the enemy's ships were driving along at nearly the same pace. Thus the calculations for throwing a shell at a pin's-point target ten to eight miles away were continually changing. The battle was really fought by mathematicians, armed with various kinds of range-timing and range-finding instruments. In most cases the man who actually aimed and fired the great guns never saw the guns he fired or sighted on the mark at which he aimed. Other men supplied him with visual information, and all he had to do was to make his rapid calculations, then give his guns the right elevation and deflection, and fire them by an electrical signal when his chronometer marked the fraction of a second to which he had calculated.

Getting a gun on the mark is now a fairly easy matter with modern telescopic sights and range finders. The trouble is to calculate the elevation at which the shot shall be pitched into the air, so that, at the end of its curve, it shall plump down right on the mark. A gun may be truly brought into line with the target, but if the elevation is not correct the shell will pitch harmlessly into the sea, either in front or behind the enemy's ship. At a distance of ten miles, a 13.5 in. shell would be about 20 seconds making its aerial voyage. During this time, a 29 or 30 knot target would have shifted an appreciable distance. So the shell has to be pitched at the spot a vessel will reach in about a third of a minute. To make more sure of hitting it, all the attacking guns are fired at once by the chief officer of the fire control, with the result that if his calculations are correct he straddles his target, and gets at least one terrible wrecking shell full on the mark.

Both the British and the German squadron began the action under the best conditions for good gunnery effects, for each of the principal opposing ships presented only her bow or stern at the target as a mark. This meant that each ship could be more easily hit by the opposing guns than if it had shown one of its long sides to the enemy. This is a curious paradox, well known to all fighting seamen, but scarcely understood by the general public. When a ship shows only its bow or stern, leaving merely the beam of 90 to 95 feet clear on the sky-line, it is a better mark then a ship broadside-on, showing its long grey side, 600 to 650 feet in length. The explanation lies in the old problem of raising the gun to its right elevation. When a ship is fighting bows-on or stern-on the entire length of its deck comes under fire. A shell pitched at its bow, but falling short, will strike amidships or aft. In the same way, a shell pitched at its stern, and falling over the mark, will strike amidships or forward. In short, when a ship fights broadside-on, there is only the narrow breadth of her deck as a target. When she fights a running action, showing her bow or stern, the entire length of her deck forms a receptacle for the enemy's shells.

For this reason a fighting admiral will not usually run away when he meets the foe, but will turn and engage in a sound, regular broadside action. In so doing he exposes his ships less to the enemy's fire than if he ran away. He puts spirit and courage into his men, and if he wins the victory it is an absolutely decisive one. To steam away, trying to escape at full speed, and expose the entire length of the ships' decks to the salvos of a confident enemy, exhilarated by the feeling of mastery, is to ride for a fall.

Rear-Admiral Hipper had four ships against five, and 32 big guns against 40, but these were of smaller calibre than the British. The odds in gun power were, we may admit, fully two to one against him. But this is only a paper calculation. It was for him by skilful manœuvring, to get certain massed fire effects which would give him the advantage. Nelson was always ready to fight against heavy odds, and yet, by his genius in handling his ships, to bring superior forces to bear on the enemy at the critical point. Only a few weeks before, Admiral Cradock, with only two large guns, had faced an enemy with eight times his gun power. He attempted the impossible, perhaps, but Admiral Hipper was offered a fighting chance that any British squadron would have gladly taken; but there is just a possible explanation of his apparent want of fighting energy. He may have been trying to lure Sir David Beatty into a trap.

The only manœuvre of importance that Admiral Hipper attempted was to send in his destroyers in the hope of saving his battle cruisers. This movement began at a quarter to ten, when Beatty's two leading ships were pounding the flaming Seydlitz, while the Princess Royal was hammering at the Derfflinger, and the New Zealand was crippling the Blücher. The British flotilla cruisers and destroyers had previously withdrawn from the front to the left of the line, to prevent their smoke from obscuring the chief targets, and the enemy's destroyer flotillas now swept away from their battle cruisers and charged across at the leading British ships. In answer to this movement the destroyer Meteor, backed by the M Division of destroyers, steamed out to meet the enemy's attack.

All through the critical period of the remaining part of the action the position of the Meteor was terrifying. She was clean in the line of fire, shells whistling over and all around her, with now and again an enemy's broadside aimed directly at her. Imagine a frail little vessel, steaming 35 knots, with four battle cruisers on either side belching forth flame and smoke continually, and the screech of the projectiles flying overhead seeming to tear the air into ribbons. Big shells, dropping perilously near, sent columns of water 100 feet above the sea, just a few yards away from her deck, and the descending spray drenched every man. All around was the noise of the great guns, the yellow explosions, the blue flashes, as the shells struck the armour-plate, with massive tongues of fire shooting up, and dense clouds of black or yellow smoke, which obliterated the whole ship from view when the shells burst upon her. She was hit twice without suffering any material damage, though most of the crew continually missed death by inches. It seemed as though they possessed a charmed life, until they tried to torpedo the Blücher, which had at last fallen out of the line, a raging furnace amidships, helpless, and been left to her fate. She had been battered by the 13.5 in. guns of Beatty's three leading ships. Then the New Zealand turned her 12 in. guns upon her; and lastly the stokers of the Indomitable brought up their vessel in time to do the final killing.

This was about 11.20. To hasten the job, the little Meteor circled round the doomed ship that was settling down, though still on an even keel. But even then she was not dead. For, firing her last round, she sent an 8.2 in. shell into the Meteor, which killed four men and wounded another. What next happened is not clear. On the one hand the Meteor, two minutes after the shell struck her, discharged her torpedo. On the other hand, the Arethusa had also approached the stricken enemy ship, with the same idea of finishing her off, and of releasing the Indomitable for more important work. The Arethusa discharged two torpedoes. As at this time the

Blücher was almost stationary, it is possible that other torpedoes got home, for the crew of the Arethusa admit that the doomed ship had a terrible list before they fired their first torpedo. At 11.45 Commodore Tyrwhitt signalled that she had struck her flag. The Arethusa, steaming up within 100 yards of the stricken ship found the German crew game to the last. They lined up to the taffrail, standing rigidly to attention, and in this attitude they would have met their death if a British sailor had not warned them. One of the officers of the Arethusa took up a megaphone and shouted to them to jump if they wanted to save their lives. They understood him, and after gallantly waving their caps and cheering, they all took to the water. The last torpedo had done its work, and the Blücher slowly turned over on her port side. For some minutes she floated bottom upwards, and at last sank slowly, leaving the survivors of her crew struggling in the water. Most of the Germans wore indiarubber airbags, fitting in front of their chests, and these floats kept up over 250 of them in time to be rescued.

More would have been saved; but while boats were picking up the survivors, a German seaplane came into view and, soaring above, began dropping bombs upon the men who were being given their lives. One bomb fell among the drowning men, and blew four of them to pieces as they were clinging to one of the hundreds of planks which the British sailors had thrown overboard to help them till the boats came along. In the distance the German airmen must have mistaken the Blücher, which had been battered out of all recognition, for a sinking British ship, thus giving rise to the report afterwards made by the German Admiralty, that a British battle cruiser had been seen to sink. In any case it was not chivalrous of the German airmen to bombard drowning seamen, and the fact that these seamen were their own countrymen, with whose rescue they interfered, was in a way a fitting punishment. The appearance of a Zeppelin and the prospect of a repetition of the outrage made it necessary for Commodore Tyrwhitt to recall his boats.

While the destruction of the Blücher was proceeding, the enemy's destroyer flotillas got between the opposing battle cruiser lines, and emitted vast columns of smoke to screen their beaten and flying remaining big ships. Then, under cover of the thick drifting curtain of smoke, the three German battle cruisers turned northward in order to increase their distance from the Lion and the Tiger. But the manœuvre was at once discerned by Sir David Beatty, and he ordered his squadron also to alter course, form a line bearing north-north-west, and drive on at utmost speed.

Thereupon the commander of the German destroyer flotillas attempted a brave but impossible thing. He sent his frail small boats full steam ahead at the two leading British battle cruisers, with the intention of closing for a torpedo attack. On a dark, cloudy night with a little mist, these mosquito tactics might produce an important result. It was for such work in the darkness that destroyers were specially suited. But to attempt it on a bright winter morning, in an air of extreme visibility, was not gallantry but utter desperation. The battle cruisers had each a broadside of eight 4 in. guns, directed by a special subsidiary system of fire-control for beating off destroyers and so when the Lion and the Tiger both opened fire on the enemy's mosquito craft the effect was so overwhelming that all the German destroyers withdrew from the tempest they had drawn down upon themselves, and resumed their original course alongside their own battle cruiser line.

Soon after they withdrew, about six minutes to eleven, when the Blücher was a fiery, shapeless wreck, a new source of danger to the British squadron was observed. Enemy submarines were reported to be steering under water towards the cruisers from the starboard bow. Whether or no German submarines were present is not definitely known, but the peril of this underwater attack was not great in the circumstances. The leading ships were then being driven along at a pace of 32 knots, and no submarine was quick enough in action to get a torpedo on a target going at this speed.

Everything was going excellently from the British point of view. From 9.20 o'clock to 11 o'clock the Lion had been hurling her terrible shells at the three German battle cruisers. From 9.45 o'clock the Tiger and the Princess Royal had also been hammering the Seydlitz, Moltke, and Derfflinger; and the New Zealand had also brought her 12 in. guns to bear on the rear enemy ships. For the last 75 minutes the Seydlitz and the Moltke had been repeatedly on fire, and the Derfflinger, which had first been obscured by the drifting smoke of her flagship, had also become a clear target. There were more than 1,000 men dead and wounded in the three ships, and some of their guns were out of action. An hour more and the three of them would have been at the bottom of the sea. But the luck which had enabled the raiders to escape from Sir John Jellicoe in person (on Dec. 16, 1914) again favoured them, but not to the same extent. The enemy's concentrated fire was especially directed upon the British flagship, which therefore suffered the most in Sir David Beatty's squadron; but for a time no vital damage was done. Between 10.30 and 11 a.m. she was constantly hit and more than one fire had broken out. At 11 o'clock she was shaken from stem to stern by a direct hit that drove in the waterline armour abreast of the boiler rooms and so damaged the feed tank that the port engine had to be stopped. The same shot put the dynamos out of action so that light and power failed, and the ship took a decided list to port. She could no longer continue the chase, and had to fall out of line under a guard of destroyers. Though Sir David Beatty at once transferred his flag to the Attack, it was some time before he could rejoin his squadron, which he did when he had shifted his flag to the Princess Royal at about 20 minutes past twelve.

With the withdrawal of the Lion, Rear-Admiral Sir Archibald Moore took over command in circumstances of peculiar difficulty. Obeying Admiral Beatty's last signal the squadron had just turned at right angles to the enemy's course to avoid the reported submarine attack. Thus the German ships were rapidly getting out of range. Admiral Moore had no information as to the submarine attack, and the last signal he had taken in from the Lion was the " alter course " signal. As the Lion's wireless was out of action and there were only two signal halliards usable, all that Admiral Beatty could do before she pulled out of line was to hoist two short flag signals, " Attack enemy's rear," and " Keep closer to the enemy." These, it is said, were hoisted before the compass signal " course N.E." was lowered, with the result that the rear-admiral understood that the compass signal governed the rest. The misunderstanding might have been cleared if the signal " Keep closer to the enemy " had been taken in; but the flags were blowing fore and aft and in the smoke and general confusion, not one of the battle cruisers received it. The Blücher, therefore was taken to be the objective and the three British battle cruisers continued on the new course; the other German battle cruisers rapidly getting out of range.

Thus the action was broken off and the British squadron withdrew. Of the three surviving German battle cruisers, one was seriously damaged, and the other two, according to German reports, were able to make good their injuries. Some damage was also done to the German destroyers, and one of their light cruisers of the town class, the Kolberg, was engaged by the light cruiser Aurora, and much battered. It was at first thought that she had been sunk, but the Berlin authorities denied this. In the Blücher alone the Germans lost 1,100 men; another 1,100 wounded were reported to have been treated in Hamburg, and the Seydlitz arrived at Wilhelmshaven with 250 wounded. The British loss in lives was very slight. Eleven men were wounded in the Lion. In the Tiger, the engineer-captain and nine men were killed, and three officers and five men wounded; and four men were killed and two wounded on the destroyer Meteor.

The condition of the Lion gave cause for anxiety. Her starboard engine began to give trouble, owing to priming and it gradually stopped. At thirty-eight minutes past three the Indomitable was ordered to take the Lion in tow. Submarines were reported to be in the vicinity and at any moment she might be attacked. Under difficult circumstances this task was accomplished in a seamanlike manner, and the injured ship was brought safely to the Forth on January 26. Though the Germans claimed a partial victory, it is worthy of note, however, that soon after the action Admiral von Ingenohl was superseded from the command of the German High Seas Fleet. This looked as though Rear-Admiral Hipper had played well the part assigned to him, but had failed to receive proper support from his chief. Somewhere about the same time Sir John Rushworth Jellicoe was promoted. These two changes of command and rank in regard to the contending leaders of the opposing fleets were fairly indicative of the results of the British and German naval operations at the end of the first six months of the war. The German commander had failed; the British commander had succeeded. Though complete success was not attained in the action of the Dogger Bank, in a large measure it established certain points.

AN ANXIOUS VIGIL

While the fight was proceeding the Admiralty was kept informed of its progress, and the tense moments there have been vividly described by Mr. Churchill in his book " The World Crisis." He describes first of all the happenings of the Saturday, the day before the battle.

The reader may imagine the tense feelings with which the long hours of the afternoon and evening were loaded. We shared our secret with none. That night I attended a dinner which the French ambassador was giving to Monsieur Millerand, then minister of war, and in London on a mission of consequence. One felt separated from the distinguished company who gathered there, by a film of isolated knowledge and overwhelming inward preoccupation. In December we had hardly credited our sources of information. All was uncertain. It had even seemed probable that nothing would occur. Now with that experience wrought into one's being, only one thought could reign—battle at dawn! Battle for the first time in history between mighty super-Dreadnought ships! And there was added a thrilling sense of a beast of prey moving stealthily forward hour by hour towards the trap.

And then he continues:

There can be few purely mental experiences more charged with cold excitement than to follow, almost from minute to minute, the phases of a great naval action from the silent rooms of the Admiralty. Out on blue water in the fighting ships amid the stunning detonations of the cannonade, fractions of the event unfold themselves to the corporeal eye. There is the sense of action at its highest; there is the wrath of battle; there is the intense, self-effacing, physical or mental toil. But in Whitehall only the clock ticks, and quiet men enter with quick steps laying slips of pencilled paper before other men, equally silent, who draw lines and scribble calculations, and point with the finger or make brief subdued comments. Telegram succeeds telegram at a few minutes' interval as they are picked up and decoded, often in the wrong sequence, frequently of dubious import; and out of these a picture, always flickering and changing rises in the mind, and imagination strikes out around it at every stage flashes of hope and fear.

CHAPTER 4

First Winter on the Western Front

THE months of January and February, 1915, which preceded the action at Neuve Chapelle were not productive of any very encouraging results so far as the British force was concerned. Indeed, although, in April, Italy acceded to the allied cause, the whole of the year 1915 was marked by actions mostly in favour of the enemy. On the Western front the small British expeditionary force was undergoing a drastic reconstruction. As a regular army it had ceased to exist, and the task of absorbing thousands of newly trained troops was in process. The problem of supplying these new armies with munitions had not yet been properly tackled. The supply of certain forms of artillery and of high explosive was still inadequate, and the appeals of commanders in the field failed to move to any effective degree the obstinate intransigeance of the War Office.

The British armies in early 1915 were in no condition to take part in any prolonged offensive action. The advantage was with the Germans, and the best that could be hoped for was to hold the ground already occupied and to achieve success in local actions. Indeed, it was at this time that the " raid " was first employed as a regular feature of trench warfare. This form of operation, which became anathema to every battalion commander, for it almost always meant the loss of officers and men whom he could least afford to spare, was intended mainly to gain ground, to " put the wind up " the enemy, and keep him tied to his positions. It was also used to secure prisoners for identification, and was supposed by the higher command to have a heartening effect on the attacking troops. This may have been so when the operation was completely successful, but when, as often happened, heavy casualties were incurred to very little purpose, it is difficult to believe that the effect on moral could ever have been encouraging. The raid became such a persistent feature of trench warfare that it is interesting to record that the first of these operations is believed to have

Cribb

The British battle cruiser Tiger was prominent in the Dogger Bank action, January 24, 1915. Completed in 1914, she carried eight 13·5 in. and twelve 6 in. guns. Her length was 670 ft., and displacement 28,500 tons.

Cribb

The battle cruiser Indomitable also took part in the battle of the Dogger Bank. Of the Invincible class, she was completed in 1908 and had a displacement of 17,250 tons. Indomitable was engaged in the battle of Jutland.

The German battle cruiser Moltke, completed in 1911, took a notable part in the naval warfare. She was one of the enemy ships that bombarded Scarborough, and was present at the big engagement of January 24, 1915, but escaped much damage, being hidden in smoke during the earlier part of the fight.

SHIPS OF THE DOGGER BANK BATTLE

BEATTY'S FLAGSHIP AT DOGGER BANK AND JUTLAND. Badly hit by German shells at the battle of the Dogger Bank on January 24, 1915, Sir David Beatty's flagship, Lion, was compelled to retire from the line, and was sent to Newcastle for repairs. She was one of the battle cruisers under Beatty's command at the battle of Jutland, in 1916, and again had a narrow escape, being badly damaged.

Plate 6

Volume 11

Cribb

BIG GUNS OF THE PRINCESS ROYAL. This photograph shows the 13·5 in. guns in the forward turret of the battle cruiser which established a world's record for speed of capital ships. It also shows the small 4 in. guns in casemates. The turrets of big warships are revolved by hydraulic power. This cruiser took part in the battle of Dogger Bank, January 24, 1915.

Daily Mail

THE SINKING OF THE GERMAN CRUISER BLÜCHER. One of the most remarkable pictures of the war, the above shows the German armoured cruiser Blücher heeling over before sinking in the battle of the Dogger Bank. Badly on fire, Blücher dropped out of the line and was sunk by two torpedoes fired by the British light cruiser Aurora. The photograph was taken from a British cruiser.

Plate 8

Volume II

been carried out on the night of February, 3-4, 1915, by Lieutenant F. C. Roberts, with 25 men of the 1st Worcestershires.

At this period other afterwards well-known features of life at the front began to make their appearance. Much of the instruction of the new officers and men in specialised branches of warfare now began to be carried out behind the lines. Courses for officers, non-commissioned officers, and men were instituted in machine gunnery, in signalling, in bombing, and later in gas protection. A few weeks only could be allowed to give a handy acquaintance with the use of new weapons, but men, stimulated by the thought of promotion and relieved for a short interval from the strain of the trenches, proved apt pupils. These schools of instruction were abundantly justified by results, and if (since there was not the time available) they could not turn out the magnificent marksmen of the regular army, it must be remembered that the rifleman, robbed of his target by entrenchment, was becoming of less importance. It was highly needful that he should become adept in the more effective machinery of trench warfare. It was a time of experiment in bombs, in mortars, in rifle grenades—though it must be made clear that at the beginning of 1915 these weapons were still in a very primitive stage of development and often highly dangerous to the user.

Two other innovations about this time will be recalled by men who were there. One was the introduction of the green envelopes in which private communications could be sent home free from regimental censorship—a privilege greatly appreciated by the men and by the company officers, to whom this censorship was always a disagreeable duty. It was about this period too that the British front began to take on an English nomenclature. Trenches and tracks and headquarters were christened with English names, many of which were to become famous through the ensuing years. The idea is credited to the fertile imagination of General Hunter-Weston, then commanding an infantry brigade. Once adopted it spread rapidly. Communication trenches were called after London thoroughfares (such as Clarges Street), a duckboard track was christened "Peter Pan," and for obvious reasons dangerous cross-roads near Ypres became the famous "Hell Fire Corner."

During January, 1915, considerable reinforcements continued to arrive. Two new regular divisions had been organized and

C2

despatched from England: the 27th composed of garrison troops, and another, the 28th, under Major-General E. S. Bulfin, composed of troops who had been serving in India and were not included in the 27th. In February there followed the Canadians, commanded by Lieut.-General Alderson, and in numbers rather greater than a normal division. They arrived to take over trenches under conditions which were far from easy. The winter was a hard one, and the line was under constant shell fire and the observation of snipers. The weather, in January, was at its worst, and the troops suffered badly from what afterwards became known as " trench feet." This very painful complaint was brought on by imperfect circulation, which could not be properly maintained under the conditions of trench life. It was never properly mastered, but as precautions (such as rations of dry socks) became possible its incidence was considerably lessened.

On January 1, 1915, the French commander-in-chief ordered a movement of advance in Alsace at the extreme southern end of the German front. Here the Chasseurs Alpins, working through the snow, sleet, and frozen slopes of the Vosges mountains, had a happy success. They placed most of their light guns in concealed positions on their front, so as to command the valley through which they were moving. On the lower ground they came out to attack, dragging a single battery with them. When the Germans, based on Mulhouse, counter-attacked with 6,000 men, the French made a feint retreat, abandoning their guns, and the Germans, elated by their supposed victory, swept down in full force to capture the battery. The result was that 2,000 of the enemy were killed, 2,000 surrendered, and most of the German guns were taken, the French losses amounting to scarcely more than 200 men. It was one of the most successful ambushes of the war.

Having broken the defending force, the French advanced and captured the approaches to Mulhouse. This was a test action, for it took the German commander four days to collect a force capable of making a counter-attack. This long delay showed that he had no powerful reserves, but had to detach men by companies all along his line, some coming from such a distance from the scene of conflict that it took them four days to arrive at their new position. General Falkenhayn, it was clear, had no large reserves on the western front.

It was then that Field-Marshal Hindenburg, in the East, was refused any more first-line troops. They were all needed badly in France and Flanders, and the kaiser came to Laon, the headquarters of Field-Marshal Heeringen, to hold a council of war. For the situation immediately in front of Laon, along the heights of the Aisne, threatened to become serious. From the natural fortress, formed by the seamed and broken plateau, most of the troops urgently needed north and south had been taken. The German commander relied upon his strong artillery power, sited on the most formidable line of heights in the western field of war, to beat back any attack. For both British and French troops had failed to carry the plateau in September, 1914, when they came to it from the Ourcq and the Marne. But in midwinter the new French army east of Soissons, which had replaced the British force when it was transferred to the Ypres sector, had been supplied with a new armament of heavy howitzers, designed to keep down the German fire.

For this reason the heights around Soissons had become more open to assault, and on January 8, 1915, ten thousand French infantrymen crossed the Aisne by pontoon bridges and attacked the hill, four hundred and thirty feet high, against which the British 3rd army corps had failed in September. Since that date the Germans had strengthened their barbed-wire defences, and had extended their trenches. But the lines were now held so feebly that, after a bombardment, the French carried the firing line, the support line, and the reserve line at ten separate points, and then broke the counter-attack at the point of the bayonet. For forty-eight hours the struggle went on, the French general feeding, munitioning, and reinforcing his troops by a series of pontoons thrown over the Aisne.

On the night of January 9 two more strong German counter attacks were repulsed, and then at dawn, after throwing the enemy back yet again, the French stormed two further lines of trenches, and captured also a copse on the plateau. A considerable body of Moroccan troops, cut off two days before from the attacking French division, had managed to hide between the opposing armies. The new French advance released them, and it was their unexpected attack on the enemy's flank that helped to decide the second battle. The next day was marked by an increasing violence in the German counter-attacks. General von Kluck was being reinforced. The French general commanding the Soissons army also brought up reinforcements. But on the night of January 11 a thaw set in, and the flood from the melting snow swelled the river Aisne into a fierce, broad torrent, and all the bridges except one at Venizel were swept away. Not only could the French commander send no reinforcements, but his troops fighting on the plateau were unable to retire.

In the darkness they got some of their guns over the Venizel bridge, while the Germans were making their grand counter-attack under cover of a very violent fire from all their guns. Two pieces of artillery had to be rendered useless and left in the hands of the enemy, but even after the French division sent most of its artillery back over the bridge, and could not hope for reinforcements, or even for a safe retreat, it fought on with great bravery for two days. On January 13 the French troops made a furious counter-attack against the hill, four hundred and thirty feet high, which they had lost, and the Moroccans advanced against the hill of Crouy. In spite of the steepness of the slopes and the bogs of mud in the hollows, and the massed fire of the enemy's guns, the French captured a trench and a considerable number of prisoners. Then, having checked the enemy, they retired on the night of January 13 apparently without serious molestation.

The German staff proclaimed that they had won a notable victory, which was compared with the battle of Gravelotte, but they undoubtedly exaggerated the losses they had inflicted on the French, who at least were left strong enough to counter-attack at the end of the battle and instal themselves in the curve of the Aisne covering Soissons. On the top of the plateau the French were still entrenched at the sugar factory of Troyon, won by Sir Douglas Haig's men in September; and by the river, going towards Soissons, they held on to a bridge-head at Venizel and Missy, where Sir Horace Smith-Dorrien's troops had fought.

General Joffre continued to exert an increasing pressure on the enemy's line from the North Sea to the Swiss frontier. He threatened to break through in one of three places. Neuve Chapelle, near Lille, Perthes, near Reims, and Eparges, between Metz and Verdun, formed the three points against which the Allies pressed. In between these foci of attack were several places of minor importance, from which railways and roads serving the German lines were imperilled. And far to the south the menace of a sweeping movement through Mulhouse to the

Rhine was maintained for several months. Then there were many places of small importance in themselves, where a scarcely perceptible swaying movement went on all through the winter. The ferry town of Berry-au-Bac, on the Aisne, became famous through frequent mention in the official communiqués, and the Four de Paris, in the Argonne, acquired a similar renown. Tracy au Val, below the western slopes of the heights of the Aisne, and Cuinchy, near La Bassée, on the British sector, were other little points of note in the history of this phase of the war.

The first serious attempt by the Germans to renew their offensive was made on January 25, 1915. Apparently one of the reasons it was made was that the birthday of the kaiser was approaching, and the Duke of Württemberg, on the Ypres front, and the Crown Prince Rupert of Bavaria, on the Lille front, wished to present their emperor with a birthday gift of some valuable strategical positions. But the operation was not planned in a large way. The French troops holding the trenches near Zonnebeke, eastward of Ypres, were assailed at dawn by a German brigade, the leading companies of which advanced to the attack without any preliminary bombardment of the allied position. The French batteries opened fire when the Germans were hung up in the wire entanglements. None of the storming parties reached the French trenches. Three hundred German troops were killed round the wire entanglements, and many more were caught by the allied artillery as they retired.

More serious was the attempt to penetrate through the allied line in front of Béthune, which town was a principal railway-head for the Allies' positions north of the Lys river. Béthune was as important as Ypres; for if it had been taken, the Germans would have been able to threaten the British communications with Boulogne and the French communications with Calais. Prince Rupert of Bavaria, therefore, thought that Béthune would be a handsome birthday present for his emperor on January 27. He began by attacking Neuve Chapelle at dawn on January 25. This was only a feint to induce Sir John French to concentrate in the wrong direction. The grand attack was launched against the French and British trenches on the south of the canal from La Bassée to Aire. At the same time another fierce assault was made on the British position north of the canal at Givenchy

The German guns round La Bassée massed their fire to clear a path for their infantry, but the British artillery answered by shelling the enemy's gun positions, and won the artillery duel. At eight o'clock in the morning the German infantry attacks were made against Givenchy and Cuinchy, by the canal, and against the Béthune road, south of the canal. In both places the Germans succeeded in capturing some of the allied trenches. At Givenchy they swept over the defenders' firing line and captured the village. But as they surged forward down the street they were met by bayonet charges, and in a fight at close quarters, lasting for four hours, were driven back. But the Germans were remarkably resolute. After being bayonetted out of the village they made five attacks on the north-east corner of the position, but finally were obliged to withdraw.

Meanwhile the German attack on the other side of the canal went on all day. As the Germans came along the main Béthune road they were caught by British machine-guns, but with fine determination the Bavarians held together, and took a part of the trenches in the brickfields near La Bassée. Then, at one o'clock in the afternoon, British troops made a counter-attack, with the help of a section of General Maud'huy's army, and drove the enemy back a considerable distance in furious hand-to-hand fighting. The recaptured trenches, however, were so strongly held by the Germans with machine-guns that the British had to make a fresh line close behind the one they had lost.

But the Germans paid dearly for one small and unimportant gain of ground they had achieved, and that was soon lost, for on the night of January 27 the British troops made a night attack up the Béthune road, and won back some of their trenches with little loss. This brought the Germans out again, south of the canal, on February 1. Advancing before dawn, they took a small trench by the canal, but as soon as the sun rose and aerial observation became possible the Germans were shelled out of their position. Then the infantry swept out in strong force, and not only drove the Germans from the trench they had captured but seized one of the German posts upon the canal embankment. Supports then came up, and, rushing through the firing line, pushed on to the second German post, driving out the garrison at the point of the bayonet.

They fought their way along the German trench southward, throwing hand-grenades in it until they had dislodged the foe from a considerable length of his line, and captured two of his machine-guns. The hero of this dashing and important little affair was Sergeant Michael O'Leary, of the Irish Guards. He was one of the leaders of the storming party which captured the German posts. Rushing ahead of his comrades, in the face of a sweeping rain of fire, he shot some of the Germans holding the first barricade and bayonetted the others. Then he went on alone towards the second barricade, sixty yards behind the first, and captured it single-handed after killing three more German soldiers and taking two others prisoner. The remarkably small losses of the attacking party were due to the skill and audacity of the heroic Irish Guardsman.

While the action at Cuinchy was proceeding the French on the right flank were being heavily engaged on the Béthune road. Here the Germans made three attacks. The first two were beaten back by the French artillery, but in the third attack the enemy reached the trenches of the Allies. The French, however, had only been holding their fire, so as to give the Germans no means of escaping. They opened upon them at point-blank range, brought down all the front line, caught the supports as they rose, and then shrapnelled the last line of reserves. Only three Germans got back to their own trenches.

The reason for all this activity round La Bassée, at a time when the boggy ground was unfavourable to any movement, was learned from the German prisoners. From the position on the canal the British machine-guns had brought to bear an enfilading fire on some of the German trenches. The machine-gun officers could not see what damage they were doing, but according to the prisoners the German losses had been heavy.

General Joffre, maintaining the threat of a general offensive movement on Perthes in the Champagne sector, at the same time made the feint of a decisive attack against the weakest part of the German lines at St. Mihiel, between Verdun and Toul. At the beginning of the new year the French troops round Perthes were four miles from a railway in the German lines, which fed the German front and helped to link the German army in Champagne with the German army in the Argonne. The loss of this cross-country railway would have been serious for Germany, and if an attack were made in overwhelming force, with cavalry and motor-artillery ready to make a sweeping movement through the gap, the result would have been decisive

So, in the second week of February, 1915, a French army of a quarter of a million men was collected near Perthes, in front of a section of German trenches not more than 12 miles long. The section extended from the village of Souain to Ville-sur-Tourbe in the Argonne. This part of the front rested mainly on a chalk soil, through which the rain drained rapidly, leaving the surface—a rolling waste with the rises topped by fir plantations—dry enough for military movements. The Germans brought up 80,000 more men. Some of them came from the La Bassée position, others were fresh troops originally intended for an offensive movement in the north. It was the knowledge that the Germans were bringing up reinforcements in order to attempt to resume the offensive that led General Joffre to concentrate in great force at Perthes.

He wished to impose his will upon the enemy commander and thus direct the movement of the German troops This he did by throwing large bodies of men against the hostile lines in Champagne. The German troops then massed just where he required them so to do. The battle lasted twenty days, from February 16 to March 7. The French won scarcely a mile of ground in depth, capturing a ridge overlooking the railway line feeding and connecting the German armies. At the rate at which they progressed it would have taken them a lifetime to push the enemy over the frontier. The achievement of the long battle was not, however, the capture of the ridge overlooking the railway, for the French artillery had already been able to bombard this hostile line of communication by indirect fire.

The sole object of the French commander, General Langle de Cary, was to press against the enemy and force him to concentrate round Perthes. This pressure was continued, until at least 220,000 German troops were massed against the 250,000 French troops who were attacking. Then an enormous number of French howitzers and guns, brought up behind the twelve-mile front, opened fire in an extraordinary way Over 100,000 shells, it was said, were dropped into the German lines, and though the Germans in turn brought up 64 field batteries, 22 batteries of heavy guns, and an additional regiment of field artillery, the vast volume of French shell fire could not be kept down. The German casualties were undoubtedly heavy, and though the French could claim no decisive victory the battle of Champagne played its part in the war of attrition.

CHAPTER 5

The Russian Front

ALTHOUGH early in January, 1915, there was a pause in the war of movement on the eastern front, as there had been on the western front, yet the whole character of the struggle there differed essentially from that in the west. In the east there was a great deal of debatable ground between the Russian defensive line of the Niemen and the Narew, passing south only a few miles west of Warsaw, and the German defensive line upon or within the Prussian frontier. Over that debatable ground the battle swung, now backward and now forward, though for a long time the position remained stationary from the front of Warsaw to the front of Cracow, where the enemy territory was no longer Prussian but Austrian. Similarly, where the Russian line swept eastwards through Galicia, the ground in front of it was debatable. In Russian Poland the invading German armies were for the moment safely held west of Warsaw.

At first their position was difficult. Their hastily dug trenches afforded scant protection against the hail of shells poured upon them from the carefully prepared Russian positions, and the fact that in the November retreat they had laid waste the country right up to the German frontier, destroying villages and farm houses, and tearing up the railways and the roads which they had themselves laid during their victorious advance, made the problem of supplies and transport one of great urgency. The first of these difficulties was soon overcome. Rapidly the Germans constructed a line of trenches and dug-outs comparable to those in France and Belgium.

The second difficulty could only be overcome in one way— by taking Warsaw, where Hindenburg's armies would find comfortable winter quarters and an excellent taking-off ground for an advance towards Petrograd when the long Russian winter was over. At the extreme north and extreme south of the Russian line there was no deadlock, and there were two reasons why Russia should strike with all her power on these two flanks. One was that the Grand Duke Nicholas had been asked to do all he could to prevent reinforcements being sent from the German armies operating in the east to strengthen those operating in the west.

The other was that Austria had begun to collect another army to avenge her defeat by Serbia, and it was imperative that the Serbian army should be given breathing space after its great effort in the autumn. The only means by which this double purpose could be achieved was by pressure upon the Germans in East Prussia, and upon the Austrians in Hungary. Accordingly on January 5, 1915, a Russian division equipped with mountain guns came down from Galicia and captured Czernovitz, and began to work its way through Bukovina. By January 13 nearly the whole of Bukovina was in the hands of the Russians, and they were advancing by the Kirlibaba pass over the Carpathian mountains, which rise to a considerable height by the Rumanian frontier. Here the Russians attacked the last Austrian fortress guarding the path to Transylvania.

At the same time the main Russian armies in Galicia, under the command of General Brusiloff, stormed certain of the Carpathian passes, 200 miles north-west of the Bukovina pass. Brusiloff had to give up for the time his easy method of fighting with the Galician railway system immediately behind his line, and send several of his army corps over the snow-buried summits. In spite of the difficulties of their enterprise, they hurled back the great Austrian army, with its first reinforcement of three German army corps. The Dukla pass and the Uzsok pass were captured, and an advance was made into Hungary along the river valley leading to the town of Ungvar. In conjunction with the advance towards the Kirlibaba pass, the Russian movement threatened to sweep over all the Hungarian plain to the east of Budapest. So no troops could be spared for another invasion of Serbia, and on January 23, 1915, the new Austro-German army assembled near the Danube was sent up to the Carpathians.

In East Prussia Russia was maintaining constant pressure upon the German defences with four army corps under General Sievier. Hindenburg's plan to meet this situation was simple. He intended to move against both extremes of the Russian line. The village of Prasnysch, north of Warsaw, and the railway junction of Stanislav, south-east of Lemberg, were the points he aimed at. He sent an army into East Prussia to advance in two columns past Prasnysch, force the passage of the Narew, cross the Bug river, and cut the trunk railway between Warsaw and Petrograd. About the same time he launched another army over the easternmost Carpathians into Bukovina, on the Rumanian frontier, to fight its way towards Stanislav. This new operation was conducted while the main battle in the Carpathians raged with increasing fury. If Hinden burg's plan were to succeed it was necessary to prevent any of the Russian armies of the centre being detached to reinforce the flanks. To achieve this object Hindenburg decided upon another frontal attack upon Warsaw.

On January 31, 1915, seven " divisions of death," composed of picked troops who did not expect to return from the attack, massed behind the troops holding the German line in front of Sochachev on the Bzura and Bolimoff on the Rawka. At the same time an unusual number of heavy and light batteries was concentrated on this section of the front, and the kaiser came to Hindenburg's headquarters at Kutno to watch the great offensive. Then on the last day in January, after the Russian lines had been bombarded heavily with high-explosive shells, many of them of 11 and 12 in. calibre, the attack was made.

The German infantry advanced in close formation and with strong supports, bridged the Bzura in three or four places, and moved on the eastern villages of Sucha, Borzimov, and Gumine, between Sochachev and Bolimoff. The Russians were forced back from the Bzura into the forest stretching to Warsaw. For a week the fight went on, with desperate tenacity and intensity. So long as the German divisions retained their cohesion, they went forward, but at the edge of the forest the Russian guns caught them in dense masses, and broke them up. Then the Siberian riflemen swept down and recaptured their trenches, and by the middle of the week they won back the important position of Volya Shidlovska, near Gumine. At night the Russian searchlights revealed the last of the Divisions of Death marching to the support of their comrades; but the columns were dispersed by field-guns and machine-guns, and by February 6 45,000, out of the original 84,000 bayonets composing the seven divisions, were put out of action. Thereupon the attack came to an end. It may have been intended for more than a demonstration. But though it failed as an attack, it certainly succeeded in holding all the Russian armies before Warsaw, and thus facilitated Hindenburg's main plan.

On the day it ended, the more important battle of East Prussia began. In three broad columns the great north-eastern German army, under General von Eichhorn and General von Bülow, advanced in the rear of Warsaw. The first column, containing an army corps of first-line troops railed from the French front, operated against Grodno. The second column advanced against the Russian fortress town of Osoviec and the important railway junction of Bielostok. The third column marched on Prasnysch, immediately north of Warsaw. At the beginning of the struggle the main battle raged round the forest town of Augustow, and extended to the line of the Niemen. One Russian army corps was threatened by an enveloping movement, and hurriedly retired on Kovno. It had formed the extreme right wing of the Russian force, and its hasty retreat exposed the neighbouring Russian army corps at Augustow to the fate from which it had itself narrowly escaped. This was the 20th army corps under General Bulgaroff.

The northern German column swerved southward and half encircled Bulgaroff's men in the wilderness of wood and water round Augustow. Then, as the Russians were fighting their way out, another German column crossed the frontier still more to the south, and engaged them on the other side, completely cutting their line of communications. There were six German army corps against the single Russian army corps. The Russians were entirely encircled, and compelled to fight incessantly on four fronts. In a different terrain they might have been annihilated in twenty-four hours, but the ground favoured them. It was a wilderness of lakes, swamps, and dense brushwood, above which rose the gaunt boughs of great forest trees. In this spot a force of Cossacks had annihilated a section of the former German army of invasion in the autumn of 1914.

Bulgaroff still retained many of the Russian woodsmen of the district who had guided the troops in the former victory. This gave him a notable advantage in the use of the difficult and intricate system of paths across the swamp lands. There were no dominating heights from which the enemy could bring to bear his overwhelming number of field-guns. The 20th army corps was clearly doomed, but this fact did not disturb the Russian commander. To General Bulgaroff had fallen the same task as that which the Russian commander of the two army corps at Kutno had carried out in the same circumstances of peril. He had to put up so fierce, stubborn, and long a resistance that the victorious enemy would be checked by the arrival of stronger Russian forces. He had to fight for time, to enable the Russian commander-in-chief to alter his dispositions, and bring up an army to defend the Warsaw-Petrograd railway.

This Bulgaroff accomplished. As late as February 24 battalions of the heroic 20th corps were cutting their way through the German ring and rejoining the main Russian forces. Detachments continued to fight their way out of the forest, after a struggle lasting three weeks. Most of the corps fought on until their ammunition was exhausted, and then surrendered. General Bulgaroff, by his long and splendidly handled defence, had saved the situation. By the time he was captured, the Russian line along the Niemen and Narew rivers had been so greatly strengthened that Hindenburg's last attempt to obtain a decision was verging upon disaster.

The disaster occurred at the village of Prasnysch. Here the third force of invasion, operating in two streams from Soldau and Willenberg, swept down towards Warsaw. By Saturday, February 20, a brigade of Russian troops holding Prasnysch was partly forced back. The Germans did not at first directly attack them, but swept in two strong lines southward on either side of the village, in an encircling movement. A third German force marched still more southward to capture a ridge on which part of the Russian brigade was retiring. But though Prasnysch was about to fall, the men on the ridge, overlooking an endless waste of snow, held out. One German column attacked them on the west, while another column tried to storm them from the east. Their food supplies began to run out, and the ammunition for their small number of field-guns got low.

But from their dominating position they held out against terrible odds from February 20 to 24. It was on the last date that Prasnysch fell, with half the brigade involved in its fall. But the ridge was still defended by about a thousand Russians, with their dead and wounded lying near them, and all the slopes around strewn with the bodies of their enemies. For one day and one night more they held out. Just twenty miles away were the two Russian army corps that had escaped defeat. These two Russian corps were extended along the river Narew, where they were greatly reinforced by the new army brought up to defend the frontier rivers.

Their general was using the remnant of the brigade on the Prasnysch ridge to lure the enemy onward. When the village of Prasnysch fell, he crossed the Narew and advanced up the Orzec, and thence in a swift night march on Thursday, February 25, he cut off the leading German army corps. The German commander tried to retrieve the position by swinging the whole of his force on the line of the Orzec. But the Russians were too strong for him. They captured half his first army corps and killed a great part of the other half. Then they turned upon the main German force, and fought it back from the Orzec river to the hills of Prasnysch, in an incessant battle of four days, and on March 1 their full victory was achieved.

Hindenburg had sacrificed in vain his seven divisions on the Bzura river. For the surprise he had thereby hoped to accomplish against the Warsaw line of communications had completely failed. His strongest column, with the first-line 21st army corps from the French frontier, had forced the passage of the Niemen beyond Suvalki, but could do no more than make a bridge-head, from which it was unable to advance against the distant railways. The second column of invaders was entirely held up in front of the fortress of Osoviec, the garrison of which fought with great skill as well as superb courage.

With the defeat of the Germans at Prasnysch, and their containment at Osoviec and the Niemen line, Hindenburg's first main attempt to create a diversion from the battle of the Carpathians came to an end, but Brusiloff's advance had been checked. Half his forces were entrenched around Przemysl, patiently waiting for it to fall by famine. This left him with about a quarter of a million men, and with them he had to meet and hold up the whole Austrian forces on the Carpathians, not less in number than his troops, reinforced by 400,000 fresh soldiers, many of them being first-rate German fighting men. The Germans advanced towards the end of January on the Uszok and Beskiden passes, and captured them. On this section of the front Brusiloff was compelled to fall back on the Galician slopes, where he could use his railways. He also withdrew from the Kirlibaba pass the single division operating there. It slowly retired, fighting in the upland forest against two army corps which were trying to reach General Brusiloff's railway communications at Stanislav. The Russian division had to fight for time, by ambushing the advance guards of Hungarian troops, and generally impeding the enemy's advance. This it did in a month's incessant fighting in the Bukovina, that only cost the Russians in dead, wounded, and prisoners 1,007 men.

Early in 1915 there was some heavy but inconclusive fighting in the Caucasus. The Turkish operations were dictated by the German headquarters staff, and the Turkish armies in the Caucasus were at first employed not so much to attain any definite objective as to engage the attention of as large a portion of the Russian army as possible. In the first week in January the Turks made an advance in considerable force in the region of Kars, but met with overwhelming disaster. The movements took place among mountains and passes covered with snow, across extremely steep ridges, at a height of 10,000 feet. The Turks, with three army corps estimated to be bodies numbering from 30,000 to 40,000 men, delivered a frontal attack from Sarikamisch and a flanking attack from Ardahan. The outcome of it was that two of the army corps were almost annihilated, and the third was enveloped. After hard fighting its position was found to be so hopeless that it surrendered almost en masse, the number of prisoners being so large as to cause serious embarrassment to the victors.

The fighting here was of an altogether exceptional character, very different from the trench warfare of the western front. The Russians often found themselves forcing their way knee-deep in snow up mountains to carry the Turkish positions. The Turkish invasion of the Caucasian regions, especially under winter conditions, was, from the Turkish point of view, an enormous blunder, forced upon them apparently by the exigencies of German strategy. The object of diverting Russian troops from other fronts did not succeed, as the Russians did their fighting in this area entirely with that army of observation which they could not in any case safely withdraw, but which they found it unnecessary to reinforce, so that it did not draw off a single soldier from the other areas of conflict. The result of these engagements was that the Russians were enabled to advance in the direction of Erzerum, though a sufficient Turkish army was there concentrated to hold them in check.

The Turks then turned the Caucasian front into an affair of siege warfare, and each side deeply entrenched on the mountain slopes and drew off many troops to participate in the more important operations in Europe.

As 1915 wore on it became increasingly clear that the Caucasian front would become more important. With British forces operating in the Persian Gulf and in Mesopotamia the help of Russia in striking an effective blow against Turkey's eastern frontier would have been invaluable. It was with this purpose in view that in September, 1915, the grand duke Nicholas was made viceroy of the Caucasus with supreme command of the Russian armies operating there. After conducting with success the retreat of the Russian armies from Galicia, Poland, and Lithuania, the grand duke had apparently retired under a cloud from the command on the Eastern Front, his disgrace being, it seemed to some critics, merely mitigated in consideration of his royal birth and undoubted personal merit, by his appointment to the command-in-chief in the Caucasus. But the truth of the matter was far different.

By the defeat of the Franco-British expedition to the Dardanelles large Turkish forces had been set free. It was obvious that in the spring of 1916 the Caucasian front would become important, and the Grand Duke's appointment to the command of the armies there was not merely an attempt to save his face. There can be little doubt that he was a fine soldier, that he had taken his profession seriously, and that he had qualities as a general equal to those of many who were pitted against him. But his task as commander-in-chief of the Russian armies in 1914 had been a supremely difficult one. This failure, in so far as he failed, was brought about by conditions over which he had no real control. His troops were of incomparable bravery; they outnumbered the enemy, and his own strategical conceptions were sound. But these were factors which could not overcome the great deficiency of the Russians in arms and munitions. What the Grand Duke might have done with armies as completely equipped as those of Germany or France is a problem which may be propounded but cannot be answered. The fact remains that the victories for which the Russians hoped and upon which the Allies counted at the beginning of the war were not achieved by the Grand Duke Nicholas. His removal in those circumstances from the supreme command of the Russian armies was inevitable, but it should not be allowed to cloud his military reputation.

CHAPTER 6

Battle of Neuve Chapelle

THE same considerations which led the French to adopt the offensive in the early days of 1915 governed the decision of Sir John French to make a carefully prepared attack on March 10 on the German positions around Neuve Chapelle. It was essential at this stage to hold every possible German division to the Western front, and so relieve pressure on the Russian armies. Unless the Germans were to be allowed an immediate success in the East, it was necessary that they should be so harassed in the West that they dare not deplete their trench garrison to any great degree. As early as January 3, Sir John French had written to the War Office in these terms:— " In view of numbers and German commitments in Russia, it seems of the utmost importance that we should strike at the earliest possible moment with all our available strength."

But apart from this strategic inducement to give battle, Sir John French cherished the hope that he would be able to make a break through. Had his plans not been affected by local breakdown of communications it is possible that he might have made a serious gap in the German lines. As it was, the action at Neuve Chapelle achieved its object in holding German troops to the Western front and certainly inflicted heavy losses upon them. In military history it stands as the first battle of the war which was deliberately planned for some time in advance and was preceded by adequate artillery preparation. Although the Germans expected an attack on this front, the exact time at which it would be delivered, the nature of the attacking force, and the number of guns to be employed in the preliminary bombardment were unknown to them. Thus valuable elements of surprise accrued to the advantage of the British generals.

The enemy's lines in front of the 1st army had been weakened, and the only force capable of reinforcing the menaced trench garrison was a body of Saxons and Bavarians, resting at Tourcoing after a turn in the trenches near Ypres. It was hoped that the 7th division and the 8th division, forming the

4th army corps, and the Indian army corps, composed of the Meerut division and Lahore division, would break through the German front and recapture Lille, while the 1st army corps advanced against La Bassée.

One of the reasons why this was not done was the difficult nature of the ground. Beyond the trenches, set in low-lying, flat, marshy country, was the village of Neuve Chapelle, also on the plain. But east of Neuve Chapelle, and near the villages of Aubers, Fromelles, Herlies, and Illies, there was a large, low, horse-shoe ridge, formed by the edge of an upland running towards Lille, Roubaix, and Tourcoing, three of the most important industrial towns of France, lying just below the easternmost slopes. On the upland were the principal batteries defending the captured centres of French industry, and themselves defended by the last earthworks of German infantry at Neuve Chapelle. The British advance in October, 1914, had been arrested at Illies on the ridge, when an attempt was made to turn the German position at La Bassée. The British troops now had to move across boggy ground, through barrier after barrier of wire entanglements, over streams, past hedges, fortified houses, ditches, orchards, and woods, with hostile artillery sending a plunging fire from the horse-shoe ridge on which their guns were placed.

Sir John French could muster 48,000 men for the most important offensive movement in the western field of war since the battle of the Marne. He had no more troops to spare, and thus could not make a more comprehensive effort. At home, new battalions of otherwise well-drilled soldiers of the new volunteer armies were still waiting for rifles and cartridges in order to begin their musketry training. The artillerymen necessary to support them in battle were either waiting for guns or for shells in order to acquire battle efficiency by actual practice. Neither in camp nor in munition factories had the work yet been carried out necessary to equip a large British Army.

In these circumstances, Sir John French improved upon the example of the commander of the French army round Perthes, and massed still more artillery than usual in support of his storming parties. Weeks of rigid economy in the use of shells resulted in there being sufficient available for an intensive preliminary bombardment, although, in fact, this could not last more than half an hour in the first instance.

In addition, Sir John French and his chief of staff, Sir William Robertson, with the general of the 1st army, Sir Douglas Haig, were planning to use the striking force of some of the Flying Corps in a then novel manner. Bombing pilots were ordered to impede the enemy's communications while his front was being attacked. In particular, the railway bridge at Menin, over which reinforcements from the Duke of Württemberg's army might be sent to the help of Prince Rupert of Bavaria's forces, was marked for bombardment. Also the Courtrai railway junction, by which German troops could come southward from neighbouring Belgian depots, was selected for attack.

In the course of the battle one airman, Captain G. I. Carmichael, flying at a height of only 120 feet above Menin bridge, dropped a bomb which destroyed a pier, and another aviator did some damage to Courtrai railway-station. Later, the railway junction at Don was bombarded, and part of a train destroyed there, by Captain G. F. Pretyman, and Douai junction was also badly damaged. The artillery also took part in this bombardment of the enemy's lines of communication. On March 10 the railway-station at Quesnoy, east of Armentières, was shelled just as German troops were entraining to reinforce the fighting line. Many casualties were caused by this long-range fire, directed by a British aerial observer.

The idea was to cut off the attacked German force at and around Neuve Chapelle from any considerable channel of reinforcements. In a more immediate manner, the British artillery was partly directed at a critical moment in the action to the same end. Altogether, the planning of the battle was distinguished by boldness and originality. All the practical lessons of the war were digested into a sound example of modern offensive tactics.

Only by a surprise attack could a position of such strength as the Germans occupied be carried. And the opening surprise was effective. At a quarter past seven on Wednesday morning, March 10, 1915, the British guns started ranging. Then, at half-past seven, began the concentrated bombardment. Pieces of every kind took part in it. The field guns fired low to smash paths through the wire entanglements. The howitzers sent a fire of high-explosive shells into the excavated earthworks in front of the village.

This preparatory barrage, the first of its kind to be employed before a British attack, was raised about eight o'clock, and the lines of attacking troops were able to advance towards their objective. The Indian troops advanced in a flanking movement from Richebourg St. Vaast and the Rue de Bois, against the south side of Neuve Chapelle; the British troops swept up in rushes against the main western German position in front of the village; for the weakness of the German lines at Neuve Chapelle was that they formed a salient, jutting into the British front. The salient was attacked on two sides, just as the enemy had continually assailed the salient at Ypres.

The design was to envelop, by attacks directed both west and south of the village, the enemy force that would be driven by artillery fire from the entrenchments into the houses. As a matter of fact, when the British and Indian troops met in Neuve Chapelle they captured or killed the Germans in the village, taking many prisoners. This result was largely due to the effective plan of attack arranged by Sir Douglas Haig. Against the German trenches on the north-west of the village there advanced the 23rd brigade and the 25th brigade, forming part of Sir Henry Rawlinson's corps. Then against the German entrenchments south of Neuve Chapelle went forward the Garhwal brigade of Sir James Willcocks's Indian army corps.

The right battalion of the Garhwal brigade met with misfortune immediately, taking a wrong direction and advancing against barbed-wire entanglements that had not been destroyed. The remainder of the Indian brigade and the 25th brigade were more fortunate, for the German wire entanglements in front of them had been reduced to four-inch lengths, and blown over with their supporting posts into the German trenches. This result had been achieved by very accurate fire from the field artillery. It was the first time in the war that the direct fire of field-guns had been scientifically used in this manner. Combined with a plunging, heavy howitzer fire on the entrenchments, it enabled the attack in favourable circumstances to be carried out at less cost than the defence.

Thus the success of the action depended mainly upon the accuracy of direct fire by the light field-guns, for where the gunners had not shot away the German wire entanglements the troops were held up by these obstacles. Such was the case with the 23rd brigade, that rushed forward on the left of the 25th brigade but was held up by an unbroken tangle of barbed-wire in front of the first German trench. The leading companies of the Middlesex and the Scottish Rifles (Cameronians) suffered heavily. It was believed at first that the Middlesex had captured their objective, for not a man came back to report otherwise. The men of this first wave were afterwards found lying dead in the formations in which they had advanced. The utmost the 23rd brigade could do was to lie down and scrape up cover under a murderous fire, and thus hold the enemy.

BATTLE OF
NEUVE CHAPELLE
English Miles

British front before the battle
Railways   Roads

Meanwhile the two more fortunate brigades, better served by their artillery, swept along unimpeded, taking prisoners and capturing trenches. The Lincolns and Berkshires led the British brigade, while the Second 39th Garhwalis were the foremost troops of the Indian brigade. With hand-grenade work and bayonets they cleared the first hostile line, assembled the prisoners, and then held the captured positions in preparation for the next step of the advance.

Behind the Lincolns and Berkshires were waiting the Royal Irish Rifles and the Rifle Brigade. It had been arranged that, on capturing the trenches, the leading troops should swerve to right and left, so as to let through the Irishmen and the Rifle

Brigade to capture the village. In the same way the Second 39th Garhwalis had to stay in the trenches they took, and let the First 39th Garhwalis rush out and capture the dense woodland of the Bois du Biez, behind Neuve Chapelle. But at this point there was a hitch in the execution of Sir Douglas Haig's plan. The trenches had been captured in a swift rush, much quicker than had been expected by the artillery. British guns were still forming an impassable curtain of fire in front of Neuve Chapelle, to prevent any German supports in the village reinforcing the firing-line. But the firing-line had been captured, and this gun fire prevented the men from making a surprise attack on the village. The field telephones had been cut by the enemy's fire, and there were no means available for swift communication between infantry and artillery. In spite of this interruption, the village of Neuve Chapelle and the roads leading north and south-west from its eastern end were captured in the morning; for at ten o'clock the Rifle Brigade charged into Neuve Chapelle, where they were met by the 3rd Gurkhas. The two regiments had been together in India, and when they met in the captured village, Briton and Indian hailed each other in a renewed friendship.

Neuve Chapelle was wholly in British hands by eleven o'clock on the morning of March 10, but on other parts of the attacking line matters had not proceeded so promisingly. Delays and confusion had occurred. Heavy losses had resulted from attacks on strongly fortified trenches and time wasted in bombarding a supposed strong point, which turned out to be quite undefended. It was, however, only a temporary set-back, and by 1.0 p.m. the 23rd and 25th brigades had reached their objectives. They were then ordered to consolidate, while the 24th brigade, behind, was ordered to prepare to advance.

It appears that at this juncture Sir Douglas Haig believed that there was a possibility of a break through by cavalry, and ordered a brigade to move forward and hold themselves in readiness. Unfortunately delay in communications, the impossibility of rapid co-ordination, and one or two minor obstacles which had not yet been removed, made a further immediate advance impossible. Five clear hours were given to the Germans in which to prepare new defensive positions, place their machine-guns, and ensure that they could bring cross fire to bear on further British advances north of Neuve Chapelle.

About 3.0 o'clock in the afternoon General Rawlinson ordered the 4th corps to advance in a direction towards the village of Aubers. The 7th and 8th divisions were supported by artillery bombardment, but this was not very effective. It had not been possible to register the supposed German strong points, and communication with forward observation officers had been cut off when telephone wires were blown to pieces by shell fire. Concentrations of troops were erratic, and while one brigade considered itself in a fit position to jump off, it was delayed by the lack of knowledge of the readiness of its right- or left-hand neighbour. Finally an advance was made of about 500 yards, into the gathering dusk, by the Sherwood Foresters and the Northants. The country was difficult; there were ditches to be waded, and in the disappearing light units got hopelessly mixed. It was necessary to halt them for sorting purposes when they were already under German fire.

Along the rest of the line this renewed advance made little progress. It was everywhere started too late in the afternoon and the forward movement of the Indian division was cancelled when the news arrived that German reinforcements were in the Bois du Bieze, but at the end of the day considerable progress could still be reported as the result of the earlier ,fighting. The advantages gained amounted to the capture of the German front line defences on a front of four thousand yards and, at its maximum, a depth of twelve hundred yards. The whole of the village of Neuve Chapelle had been occupied and some hundreds of prisoners taken. The general reserve had not been called upon. On the other hand subsidiary actions had not produced any very fruitful results.

Immediately the news of the loss of Neuve Chapelle reached the German command, orders were given for a counter-attack to recapture the village, but the troops on the spot were so shattered and depleted in numbers that they were unable to carry out the operation. Reinforcements were sent up and the Germans spent the night March 11-12 consolidating their new front line, throwing up breastworks, strengthening their strong points and arranging more machine-gun nests. It was intended that the reinforcing battalions should counter-attack at dawn, but their arrival was delayed and this plan had to be abandoned. Sir Douglas Haig, acting on the information brought him by air observers, which accurately reported movements of troops by road but failed to note any great concentration by rail, issued orders on the night of March 10 for the general attack to be continued in the morning. His operation orders detailed the following plan :

The objectives of the 4th corps were from Aubers to a farm called La Cliqueterie. The Indian corps was to take the Bois du Biez and advance until its right rested on the hamlet of Ligny le Grand. The 1st corps was to continue its attack on the trenches east of Givenchy. The 5th cavalry brigade was ordered to be ready to march at any time after 9.0 a.m. " From information received," it was added in the operation order, " it appears that the enemy before us is in no great strength." Orders were also given for an artillery bombardment to precede the advance of the infantry.

The new German front line, in the rear of their strong points of the day before, had not as yet been observed and the artillery landed their shells where they were least needed. Attempts made by the 21st brigade to advance after the preliminary bombardment were all in vain, so intense was the machine-gun and rifle fire which they had to meet. The German guns too, in position on the Aubers ridge, maintained a three hours' bombardment along the entire British line. Very little progress was made at any point, telephone communications were destroyed and orders failed to reach the battalions. On the 4th corps front the attack may be said at this point definitely to have failed.

Meanwhile the Indian divisions were in no better case and no effective advance was made towards capturing the Bois du Biez. The difficulty of identifying the new German dispositions led again to waste of artillery preparation and the Indians were kept mostly to their ground by well directed enemy fire. Towards the middle of the day the belief was gaining ground that the Germans were preparing to attack, and it was thought that possibly the best chance of further advance might lie in receiving and repulsing this attack. But it soon became apparent that the Germans had no such immediate intention, and in consequence it was decided in the afternoon to continue the assault. Communications, however, were so lamentably bad that orders failed to reach many of the companies and such attempts as were made were the sporadic efforts of those who did receive instructions. This is well reflected in the message of one battalion commander who reported to his brigadier: —

"I received a note from the Worcestershires: 'We have *got* to advance. Will you give the order?' I answered 'No, it's a mere waste of life, impossible to go more than 20 yards, much less 200 yards. The trenches have not been touched by the artillery. If artillery cannot touch them the only way is to advance from right flank. A frontal attack will not get near them.'"

The Worcestershires did in fact advance, but their front lines were shot down, and the Sherwood Foresters in the attempt to establish themselves in some partially wrecked farm buildings sustained very heavy casualties. Indeed, the day as a whole was one on which practically no British gain could be counted and on which losses in men steadily mounted up. At the end it became clear that no further advance would be possible until the new German line had been to some degree shattered by gun fire.

On the evening of March 12 the main reinforcements which had been expected by the Germans arrived in their positions. These consisted of no less than six battalions and their participation in the counter-attack was fixed to take place at 5.0 a.m. the next morning. The enemy force available for this action numbered 16,000 men. The artillery bombardment of the whole of the front of the British 4th and Indian corps was opened at 4.30 a.m. It fell beyond the front line, which escaped injury, but it caused considerable casualties amongst troops in reserve. Under cover of a morning mist the Germans advanced to the attack at 5.0 a.m. The mist covered the plain and the ridge, and checked the fire of the British artillery.

Airmen had to drop 200 or 300 yards above the enemy's position in order to reconnoitre for the guns. The enemy's shells continued to break the telephone wires between the leading brigades, and the artillery officers with them directed the fire of the guns from advanced observation posts. At 9.30 in the morning, for instance, over a hundred feet of wire was destroyed, and there was a long delay in getting it mended. At forty minutes past ten the Germans made their attempt to get back Neuve Chapelle. They came down in masses along the whole front round the village and to the north of it. The troops that tried to debouch from Biez Wood were held back by the British guns, which had ranged very accurately at this point. Elsewhere the Germans were broken by four bursts of rapid fire from the breastworks, and thrown back with heavy loss. The ease with which the Germans were repulsed was so remarkable that they only reached the trenches at one point north-east of the village. There they were driven out and pursued with the bayonet. As the afternoon wore on the Westphalians especially began to surrender. Many of the men were exhausted. They said they had had no food for days, that all their officers were killed, and whole battalions destroyed.

This condition of things induced Sir Douglas Haig to counter-attack in turn. At half-past two in the afternoon there was a period of artillery preparation. Every British gun was brought to bear on Aubers ridge, north of Neuve Chapelle. This was the battle in which the heaviest British losses occurred. The 2nd Scots Guards, the 1st Grenadier Guards, the K.O.S.B., the 2nd Gordons, and their 6th Territorial battalion were among the troops that tried to storm the ridge. For four hours the struggle went on. Near to Neuve Chapelle there was a fierce contest round Pietre Mill, where the 6th Gordons, under Lieutenant-Colonel Maclean, who was killed in the action, fought their way up to the houses, using grenades and bayonets. The Rifle Brigade made heroic attempts to reach the ridge. They rushed through the zone of shrapnel, and then faced the German machine-guns and rifles, and with heavy losses took a trench. More troops tried to advance towards Aubers, and reached the line by the Rifle Brigade, but could not get any farther.

At one time it looked as though Sir Henry Rawlinson, with the 4th army corps and its supports, would achieve one of the grand successes of the war. The cavalry, under General Gough, came from Estaires, with the North Midland division. At four o'clock on Friday afternoon the 5th cavalry brigade, under Sir Philip Chetwode, rode out for immediate action along the Rue Bacquerot, fronting the Aubers ridge. The cavalrymen were to charge through the gap made by the infantry, take the enemy's batteries on the high ground, and open the road for a general advance to Lille. But the infantry attack against the heights failed just when it seemed to be almost successful. It was impossible to win the ridge, and as Sir John French had no reserves to call upon, he ordered Sir Douglas Haig on the night of Friday, March 13, to suspend offensive operations and hold and consolidate the ground won by the 4th and Indian corps. The commander-in-chief wrote afterwards in his despatches:

Most of the objects for which the operations had been undertaken had been obtained, and there were reasons why I considered it inadvisable to continue the attack at that time.

It is important neither to underestimate nor to exaggerate the British achievement at Neuve Chapelle. The plan of attack was brilliantly conceived, and executed generally with remarkable skill and gallantry. The check in regard to the breaking of telephone communications and the failure to destroy part of the hostile wire entanglements were ordinary incidents of battle. Such accidents though they may be foreseen cannot be quickly remedied. The actual success of the first attack was so rapidly achieved as to be a surprise to the British staff. The attacking forces won more ground at Neuve Chapelle by artillery fire and infantry charges in a single hour than the French at Perthes had gained in a week.

But the success might have been far greater. In the considered opinion of Sir John French, the fault that prevented the grand extension of the offensive movement rested with Sir Henry Rawlinson, commanding the 4th army corps. He did not use his reserves at the critical moment. He was rather too cautious and prudent. He should have thrown his reserves forward into the fight on the morning of March 10. At eleven o'clock on that morning when the village had been won, the disorder in the British fighting line, caused apparently by tactical errors, might at once have been restored if strong reserves had then taken on the work of pushing back the enemy. For the Germans were still reeling from the surprise attack, and their line might have been completely pierced if the whole of the 4th army corps had been brought to bear quickly at the critical point.

A delay of four and a half hours in restarting the attack prevented progress being made before nightfall, and interrupted the work; for by the next morning the enemy had recovered from his surprise, and by making new entrenchments and bringing up reinforcements he was able to check the advance. The victory of Neuve Chapelle was won in three hours on the morning of March 10, and won with comparatively little loss. It was afterwards that the heaviest casualties occurred during the days of repeated attacks and German counter attacks. On the British side the casualties amounted to 583 officers and 12,309 other ranks. The German losses were slightly less and included 30 officers and 1,657 other ranks taken prisoner.

BATTLE OF NEUVE CHAPELLE

The work of the Royal Flying Corps at the battle of Neuve Chapelle was greatly hampered by bad weather and poor visibility. Pioneer photography work (for the science of air photography was still in its infancy) had, however, provided sufficient material for maps of the enemy trenches to be drawn and circulated in sufficient numbers to the attacking army. Air photographs, too, were used in framing orders for the artillery and directing the preliminary bombardment. "For the first time in history the British army went into action with a picture of the hidden intricacies of the enemy defences, and, after the first assault, bombing parties were able to make their way, without loss of time, to their separate objectives." Moreover, the probable line of advance of the enemy could be judged from the clearly defined position of their communication trenches.

The German reply to Neuve Chapelle, in which they sought to rival the suddenness of the British blow of March 10, fell upon the line at St. Eloi. This was situated at the junction of two main roads, running from Ypres to Armentières and Warneton. The British second army, under General Smith-Dorrien, was holding that portion of the line which encircled the village eastward, and included a large mound to the south-east of it. The Germans, on March 14, 1915, after mining the mound, launched a heavy bombardment on the British positions, followed by an infantry attack which occupied the village.

On the following day the British counter-attacked. The 82nd brigade left their positions in the darkness and at the point of the bayonet captured part of the enemy's trenches in the village. It was on this occasion that the Canadians first met the Germans in actual battle, and the Princess Patricia's Canadian Light Infantry, with the 4th Rifle Brigade, distinguished themselves in attacking the ruined mound, while elsewhere Irish and English troops made supporting attacks. Just before dawn, men of the 80th and 82nd brigades stormed the barricades erected in the village streets and recaptured all the lost trenches east and west of the village, and, except for the mound, all the lost ground was ultimately recovered. The battle then died down.

CHAPTER 7

The Attack on the Dardanelles

WITH the coming of 1915, the British war council was faced with a problem of some complexity. It seemed that on the western front a static condition had been reached in which neither the Allies nor the Central Powers could hope for an immediate and decisive victory. Russia was already beginning to show signs of disintegration and appealed for a diversion which would relieve her hard pressed and ill-supplied troops in the Caucasian area. The Baltic was closed to any attempt of this kind, and eyes naturally turned to the Near East and the tempting thought of an operation in the Dardanelles, which, if successful, would strike at the very heart of Turkey and do incalculable good to British prestige in the Near East and the Balkans, which had suffered somewhat by the escape of the Goeben and the Breslau.

If the Dardanelles could be forced, Turkey would be obliged to turn to defend her own country, and so the pressure on the Caucasus front would be relieved. If the Bosporus could be passed the Black Sea would be open for the supply of munitions to Russia, whose position in regard to war material would become critical in the spring of 1915. If successful, it would check the Turco-German intrigues in Persia, Afghanistan, and the Indian border. Also, an attack upon the waterway between the Mediterranean and the Black Sea would appeal to Italian sympathy, steady Bulgaria, and stimulate Rumania. Indeed, the mere fact that Britain and France were assailing in force the heart of Turkey would be sufficient to paralyse all German and Austrian designs in the Balkans.

The danger of a purely naval expedition up the Dardanelles was well known to the naval officers at the Admiralty. It had been placed on record in 1877 by Admiral Hornby, who in that year was directed to force a way to Constantinople. He warned the authorities at home that, while it was practicable for a squadron to run past the forts—which were far weaker in those days, and were not supplemented by mines and torpedoes—

the fleet would, none the less, be helpless in the Sea of Marmora. Its supply of coal, ammunition, and food would be cut off, because the enemy would be certain to mount guns on the cliffs, which for more than six miles overhang the northern shore of the Dardanelles at the point where the channel closes to little over half a mile. It is never more than two miles in width. " Guns thus placed," he said, " could not fail to stop transports and colliers," and the fleet would be exposed to terrible danger. He therefore urged the necessity of occupying the Gallipoli peninsula with British troops before entering the Sea of Marmora. When, by a stroke of singular daring aided by good luck, he passed the Dardanelles, the Turks offered no resistance, but he had no illusions as to his position. " There seems to be an idea," he wrote from the Sea of Marmora to the first lord of the admiralty, " that this fleet can keep the Dardanelles open. Nothing can be more visionary. Not all the fleets in the world can keep them open for unarmoured ships."

Still earlier, in the days of the sailing ship, Admiral Duckworth, who with a British squadron ran past the forts and anchored before Constantinople in 1807, pronounced the operation " the most dangerous and difficult ever undertaken." It was also fruitless, as the Turks refused to be terrified, and he had to beat a speedy retreat as the only alternative to finding himself without water and food. The evidence of history was certainly not encouraging.

In the naval operations off Zeebrugge, British ships had to some slight extent hindered the German advance along the coast; yet in spite of long-range naval guns, the German army had succeeded in bringing up heavy batteries, and though there were 12 in. guns in the British battleships, skilfully directed by observers in aircraft, the ships were at last compelled to withdraw. It is true that the British warships carried out their main work of assisting the Belgian army to hold its positions in the inundated polders north of Furnes, but they were unable to prevent the German artillerymen from fortifying the coast and establishing a dangerous submarine base at Zeebrugge. The work which the Germans did under continual bombardment by naval guns was a remarkable achievement pointing to the impotence of ships against land batteries in the conditions of modern warfare. By using part of the siege train from Antwerp, including several of the monster Krupp howitzers, the

Germans were able to fortify all the coast, and lay a new minefield round Zeebrugge.

The idea of forcing a passage through the Dardanelles was considered at a meeting of the war council in November, 1914, just after Turkey had entered the war. Nothing was done, however, beyond collecting a few transports until January 15, 1915, when the appeal for help came through from Russia. The matter was then discussed again. The proposal before the council was for an attack by the army and navy combined, but when Lord Kitchener stated that it would be impossible to find the necessary men, estimated at 150,000, for the land operations the idea of the naval attack was entertained, its chief advocate being the first lord of the admiralty, Mr. Churchill.

The Admiralty next decided to ask for the views of the man on the spot, Vice-Admiral S. H. Carden:

Do you think that it is a practicable operation to force the Dardanelles by the use of ships alone? It is assumed that older battleships would be employed, that they would be furnished with mine sweepers and that they would be preceded by colliers or other merchant vessels as sweepers and bumpers. The importance of the results would justify severe loss. Let me know what your views are.

His reply was, " I do not think that the Dardanelles can be rushed, but they might be forced by extended operations with a large number of ships." Three days later he was told that " high authorities here concur in your opinion," and was asked to send detailed particulars of the proposed operations. Meanwhile, Sir Henry Jackson, then chief of the staff, was asked to prepare a memorandum on similar lines.

On January 11 Vice-Admiral Carden sent his answer. Four operations, he said, were possible, and he estimated that it would take a month to carry them out. They were (a) The destruction of defences at the entrance of the Dardanelles. (b) Action inside the Straits so as to clear the defences up to and including Kephez Point battery No. 8. (c) Destruction of defences of the Narrows. (d) Sweeping of a clear channel through the minefield and advance through the Narrows, followed by the reduction of the forts farther up and advance into the Sea of Marmora.

Mr. Churchill said that this telegram made a great impression on every one who saw it, but the plan met with only a qualified approval from Sir Henry Jackson, whose idea evidently was to confine the attack to the outer forts, as an attempt by the fleet alone to get through the Dardanelles was not a feasible operation. Lord Fisher disliked the idea, not because he considered it impossible, but because he thought the ships could be employed to better advantage elsewhere. Nevertheless, on January 12 he initialed a minute which said:

> The forcing of the Dardanelles as proposed and the arrival of a squadron strong enough to defeat the Turkish fleet in the Sea of Marmora would be victory of first importance and change to our advantage the whole situation of the war in the East. It would appear possible to provide the force required by Admiral Carden without weakening the margin necessary in home waters as follows: (Mr. Churchill here mentions the forces and arrangements he considers necessary.)

With these views before it, the matter was discussed by the war council on January 13, when the following decision was reached. " The Admiralty should prepare for a naval expedition in February to bombard and take the Gallipoli peninsula with Constantinople as its objective." The matter was further discussed on January 28, after which Mr. Churchill pressed forward preparations for the naval attack.

At the outset it was hoped that some part of the Greek army would assist in the operations. A small French expeditionary force, composed of Senegalese troops and Zouaves, was actually collected in North Africa, under the command of General d'Amade. There may also have been some arrangement for detaching a small portion of the British forces in Egypt to help in attacking the gates of Constantinople and the Black Sea. But all this part of the scheme fell through when the king of Greece refused to follow the advice of his prime minister, M. Venizelos, who had promised the Allies to send one division (20,000 men) to the Dardanelles. The effect was that practically no military help against the Turkish 5th army, entrenched on the Gallipoli peninsula, could at the time be granted to the combined British and French squadrons which were preparing to attack the Dardanelles forts. Both the British and the French navies had a large number of powerfully-armed warships which were too slow to take part in the manœuvres of a general fleet action. There were battleships, such as those of the Canopus class, which could not be used in the North Sea with the swift super-

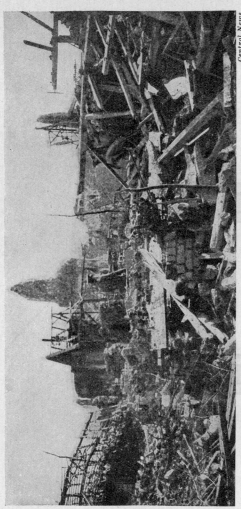

Central News

VILLAGE OF NEUVE CHAPELLE AFTER THE BATTLE. The "grand offensive" planned by the Allies in March, 1915 began with Sir John French's determined attack on Neuve Chapelle, a village north of La Bassée, which had been in German hands since 1914. The British bombardment began on March 10, and, although the casualties were heavy, Neuve Chapelle was captured the same day. The battle wore on, without further ground being gained, until March 12. This photograph conveys some idea of the effect of the British artillery fire.

"Queen Elizabeth"   "Lord Nelson" "Agamemnon" "Inflexible"   Destroyer

NAVAL ATTACK ON THE DARDANELLES. This sketch, made by a naval officer during operations in the Dardanelles in March, 1915, shows the British battleships, Queen Elizabeth, Lord Nelson, and Agamemnon and the battle cruiser Inflexible, opening up a long-range bombardment on the Narrows on the 18th. This attempt to force the Narrows ended in heavy losses for the Allies, the Inflexible suffering serious damage from collision with a mine.

Plate 10   Volume II

H.M.S. QUEEN ELIZABETH LEAVING MUDROS. The battleship Queen Elizabeth was flagship of Vice Admiral Carden, and then of Vice-Admiral de Robeck, at the Dardanelles, 1915. The surrender of Rear-Admiral von Reuter on behalf of the German fleet, to Sir David Beatty took place in the after-cabin of this ship. She was the first British warship to carry 15 in. guns, and to be driven entirely by oil fuel. She carried eight 15 in., twelve 6 in., and four 3 in. guns, and five submerged torpedo tubes.

Russell

Swaine

Meley

LEADERS OF THE GALLIPOLI LANDING.—Left, Sir Ian Hamilton commanded the British force on the Gallipoli peninsula in 1915. He led it in the terrible fighting until he was superseded in October. On minor points he was censured by the commission that inquired into the conduct of the operations. Centre, Sir William Birdwood led the Australian corps in Egypt and Gallipoli, his fine leadership in the latter campaign earning for him the title "Soul of Anzac." He succeeded Sir Ian Hamilton in command of the army in Gallipoli. Right, General Gouraud led the 1st Colonial Army of France in 1915, and in the Gallipoli operations, when in command of the French forces, was severely wounded.

Plate 12

Volume 11

Dreadnoughts, for it was clear that any great battle in the North Sea would be a running fight. Any slow British battleships present would tail off during such an engagement, and be left without the protection of destroyers—a prey to enemy submarines. Moreover, the Grand Fleet was so strong in both gun power and speed that even the newest battleship with 15 in. guns—the Queen Elizabeth—could safely be detached from it. There were also battle cruisers, like the Inflexible, which could safely be spared from Sir John Jellicoe's command.

Altogether, there was a surplus of British naval force, over and above the Grand Fleet and Mediterranean Fleet, and no immediate use for it could be found except in the Dardanelles. A considerable portion of this surplus was composed of old and slow types that were destined for the scrap-heap at the end of the war; but their guns in most cases were very powerful, and it seemed well worth while to use them against the land forts of the Dardanelles, even at the risk of serious injury in an attempt to force a passage.

One thing was evident. If the attack on the Dardanelles were pressed by land as well as sea, and any severe reverse were experienced by the Allied forces, withdrawal from the situation created thereby was politically impossible. Britain, France, and Russia were important Mahomedan Powers. They were fighting the Ottoman Caliphate, which had for centuries been recognized by Moslems as the directing force of their religious world. So long as the Powers of the Triple Entente conserved their military prestige, the Ottoman sultan, and the Young Turk war party using him as their marionette, were unable to influence seriously the Mahomedan subjects of the Christian nations; for the Ottomans themselves were leagued with Christian Germans, Austrians, and Hungarians. There was no sound pretext for a holy war. On the other hand, if the prestige of Britain and France were temporarily lowered in the Orient by a great Turkish victory in the Dardanelles, the consequences might be grave in India, Egypt, and Northern Africa. Thus, even in the political field, the advantages won in one quarter by a serious display of activity might be fully balanced by disadvantages elsewhere, unless the naval attack on the Dardanelles were backed by the landing of a very large Franco-British army.

Even in 1912, the Italians, then fighting the Turks, had decided against an attempt on the Dardanelles, though at that time the Turkish defences were weak, the forts were out-of-date, and the minefield at Dardanos was covered by batteries which mounted few guns of large calibre; in the Narrows, the forts of Kilid Bahr and Chanak were armed only with plunging fire batteries. So weak were the defences in 1912 that another minefield was laid in front of the Narrows to supplement the batteries. Nevertheless, the Italians were so daunted by the difficulties of that tortuous waterway that they would not risk their fleet in attempting to force the passage.

The Turks had begun to strengthen the defences of the Dardanelles some time before they opened hostilities against the Allies. They were greatly helped by a cargo of mines brought to Constantinople in the second week in August by the German steamer that accompanied the Goeben and the Breslau in their flight from Mediterranean waters. A considerable number of powerful guns and howitzers, some of 14 in. calibre, were obtained. Motor batteries, worked by German gunners, were largely used, and rails were laid on one shore at least for the employment of very heavy but mobile howitzers. On the Gallipoli peninsula four distinct lines of trenches were dug near Krithia, and carried from this point round all the important heights which dominate the line of advance towards the Narrows.

The works at Bulair, in the neck of the peninsula, which had proved a strong defence against the Bulgarian army in the Balkan war, were further strengthened. Some 40,000 troops were entrenched on the peninsula to prevent the forts on the European side of the Straits from being attacked in the rear by a landing-force. Another Turkish army corps was held ready to reinforce the Gallipoli garrison if need should require. The forts on the Asiatic shore were supported by well-entrenched troops, amounting to at least another army corps. Large reinforcements were available in the interior of Asia Minor and round Smyrna. It looked as though an army of 500,000 British and French troops would be needed to attack from the land the forts and Turkish armies on both sides of the Dardanelles. At the time it was quite impossible to spare this immense force from the Franco-Belgian front, so the fleet was ordered to try to carry the waterway by gun power alone.

Chief among the bombarding warships was the Queen Elizabeth, with her eight 15 in. guns, each throwing a shell weighing 1,720 lb. to a distance of 15 miles or more. She had also a secondary battery of twelve 6 in. guns, and a powerful anti-aircraft armament. She used only oil fuel, giving her a designed speed of 25 knots, was 650 feet long, and had a displacement of 27,500 tons. Her high-explosive shell, when it made a direct hit at a distance of 10 miles or so, produced the most tremendous destructive effect of any missile used by man; her shrapnel shell threw out 2,000 bullets on explosion. Black Bess, or Lizzie, as the pride of the British Navy was called by admiring seamen, was a potent influence on the political side of the action by the Allies. It might indeed be said that she did more harm to the Turks by the popular interest she excited in the Balkan states than by the actual blows she dealt to the Turkish forts.

When neutrals realized that the Grand Fleet in the North Sea was so strong that a new battleship with eight 15 in. guns could be spared for the Mediterranean, their confidence in the eventual victory of the Allies was restored. Among the other important ships was the early battle cruiser the Inflexible, with a nominal speed of 25 knots, and eight 12 in. guns, and the two last pre-Dreadnought battleships, the Lord Nelson and the Agamemnon, with a speed of about 18.5 knots, each armed with four 12 in. guns and ten 9.2 guns. Then there were several older battleships, armed with four 12 in. guns and twelve 6 in. weapons apiece. Such were the Irresistible, Duncan, Cornwallis, Vengeance, Ocean, Goliath, Albion, and Canopus. Of the same general type, but still older, were the battleships Majestic and Prince George. The Swiftsure and Triumph were newer ships, purchased from Chile in 1903. They mounted four 10 in. guns and fourteen 7.5 in. guns apiece. A number of cruisers, such as the Euryalus, Amethyst, Dublin, and Sapphire, with destroyer flotillas, mine trawlers, and a seaplane carrier, the Ark Royal, made up the British fleet.

The French navy, whose main forces were occupied in the Adriatic, detached a group of old battleships. These were the Suffren, with four 12 in. guns and ten 6.4 guns; the Bouvet, with two 12 in., two 10.8 in., and eight 5.5 in. guns; the Gaulois, with four 12 in. and ten 5.5 guns; and the Charlemagne, equally ancient, with four 12 in. and ten 5.5. guns. The top speed of the Suffren was only 16 knots, and that of the three older ships was less. The only representative of the Russian navy was the Askold, a 1903 cruiser, with twelve 6 in. guns

The British fleet was at first under Vice-Admiral S. H. Carden; but after the early operations he was replaced by Vice-Admiral John de Robeck. The French squadron was commanded by Rear-Admiral Guépratte, who carried out his part of the work very gallantly from his flagship the Suffren, while not concealing his opinion that the naval attack was useless without the simultaneous co-operation of a large allied military force. Vice-Admiral Peirse, with some of the ships of the East India squadron, conducted operations against Smyrna and neighbouring points with a view to distracting the enemy by the feint of a landing on the Asiatic coast.

The German emperor had sent one of his best naval men, Admiral Usedom, with a large number of gunnery officers and gunners, to direct the defences of the Dardanelles. General Liman von Sanders, with a multitude of German officers, controlled the Turkish land forces in Gallipoli, and everywhere the Ottoman troops were commanded by German officers. Deeply embedded between the hills were enormous position-guns, with ammunition chambers dug out of the earth, and filled with waggon-loads of explosives and vast quantities of shells. Close at hand were tents in which the officers had been living for months past. In the Sea of Marmora a great flotilla of boats maintained communication at night between the Gallipoli peninsula and the Asiatic shore, thus preventing any attempt at reduction by famine in the event of the Allies getting command of the Bulair lines at the neck of the peninsula.

For some months before the main attack opened there had been desultory firing at the entrance forts to the Dardanelles, and this had to some extent put the Turks on the alert. But the main attack was a surprise for the enemy, for they had then ceased to expect that so daring a thing as the forcing of the greatly strengthened defences of the Straits would be attempted. On February 14, 1915, the gunnery lieutenants of some of the battleships set out in a destroyer to have a good look at the forts they were to attack. Four miles off the land they came under fire, but none of the German shells struck the reconnoitring ship.

Admiral Carden's plan of operations, which was mentioned in page 79, may usefully be repeated here: 1. The bombardment and reduction of the defences at the entrance to the straits. 2. Minesweeping up to the Narrows and the reduction of the defences on the way. 3. Bombardment and reduction of the forts at the Narrows. 4. Sweeping the principal minefield (off Kephez). 5. Bombardment of the forts above the Narrows. 6. Passing into the Sea of Marmora. 7. Operations in the Sea of Marmora and the patrol of the Dardanelles.

The scheme of the bombardment was to be carried out in three phases : first a long-range bombardment (direct or indirect) out of range of the forts; next a bombardment with the secondary armament by direct fire; and finally an intensive concentration at decisive ranges of 3,000 to 4,000 yards. It was laid down that in the earlier stages if ships found themselves in danger of being hit they were to withdraw out of range.

At eight o'clock in the morning of Friday, February 19, the engagement began. The allied fleet of battleships and battle cruisers steamed to their positions, and at 9.45 the bugles sounded action stations. About ten minutes afterwards the fore turret of the Cornwallis opened fire on Orkanie Fort. Its 12 in. shell fell over the forts. The next fell short, but near. Then, by these bracketing shots, the range was obtained; the third shell got home, and a great cloud of stone and brickwork rose high in the air. Soon after, the fort at Helles was engaged by the Triumph, and the Suffren was taking Kum Kale by indirect fire over Cape Yeni Shehr. For an hour the leading ships worked hard at their guns, then, about noon, they drew back, and another squadron of big-gun vessels took their place. At each crash of the guns great clouds of grey smoke rose from the forts, and flames appeared from a Turkish camp on the hillside and from a large barracks in the town by the forts. The Germans and Turks attempted no reply, as the allied fleet kept beyond the range of their guns.

But the long-range bombardment had not put the hostile batteries out of action. An exciting time followed when at three o'clock in the afternoon the Vengeance, Cornwallis, and Triumph, with the Suffren, Gaulois, and Bouvet, closed in to try to finish off the first forts of the Dardanelles. Far out to sea the Inflexible and Agamemnon kept up a long-range covering bombardment with their 12 in. guns, while the ships that closed in used only their secondary armament. By nightfall the forts round Cape Helles had been very badly battered, and had ceased to reply, and on the other side of the Straits only one battery remained active. The German shells had pitched close to the

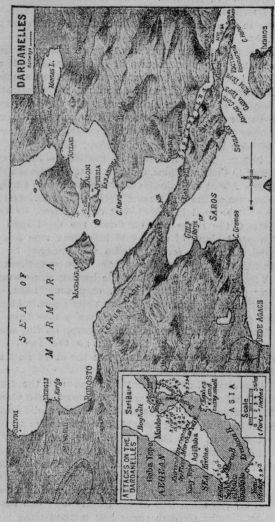

THE NAVAL ATTACK ON THE FORTS OF THE DARDANELLES

Relief map of the Dardanelles in relation to Thrace and Asia Minor. Inset, sketch of the S. extremity of the Gallipoli Peninsula; the figures show the number of guns and their calibre in the Turkish forts in 1915

A DARING DEED

French and British ships, and some had passed between the masts. But the enemy's shooting was not good; not a single hit was obtained on any unit of the fleet.

For a week afterwards the great battle between ships and forts was interrupted. There was a hurricane of wind, with short, high seas, that made aerial reconnaissance and steady naval gunnery impossible. By this time General Trotman had arrived with the Plymouth and Chatham divisions of Royal Marines, who were to be used, if and when required, as demolition parties. But the weather became quieter from February 25, and the attacking fleet steamed up again to see if anything were left of the forts. Naval airmen found that in the interval the enemy had prepared several new gun-positions, but no guns had been mounted in them. Two or three of the guns, overturned by the first bombardment, seem also to have been set up again. But the entrance forts, with their nineteen guns, ranging from 6 in. to 11 in., and their smaller armament of another eleven guns less than 6 in. calibre, were not able to withstand the terrific fire brought against them. The Germans seem to have left the old entrance forts unstrengthened, except for one new earthwork and a mobile howitzer battery working behind Kum Kale.

Day after day the operation continued. The next phase of the operation was the reduction of the forts between the entrance and the narrows known as the Dardanos group and the Messoudieh group. Preceded and followed by minesweepers, the Albion, the Triumph, and the old Majestic steamed up on February 26 harassed by concealed batteries, but getting admirable results. On this day marine demolition parties were landed on both sides of the entrance to complete the work of the ships. In spite of heavy resistance in places, they blew up guns or destroyed breech pieces. It was then than Lieut.-Commander Robinson observed that Fort Orkanie was silent. He went forward single-handed with a demolition charge, and, finding the fort deserted, blew up one gun and returned to bring up his party and complete the destruction of the remaining guns. For this act of heroism he was awarded the Victoria Cross. The landing parties were withdrawn with very slight loss. Again the weather intervened. On February 27 a strong gale interfered with the landing of the demolition parties, but in the afternoon the mortars at Sedd el Bahr were blown up, the last two standing in the open, by Lieut. Sandford, the officer in charge.

THE ATTACK ON THE DARDANELLES

By Monday, March 1, both entrance forts and their magazines were destroyed, and under the shelter of the battleships the minesweepers began their work. At eleven o'clock in the morning the Triumph, Ocean, and Albion entered the Straits and bombarded Eren Keui and Dardanos Fort, some ten miles up the Dardanelles, towards the Narrows. Under cross fire the ships were constantly hit, though not seriously damaged, and after a rather fruitless day they retired; but in the meantime Lieut. Sandford and his demolition party had landed at Kum Kale, and had found that seven of its nine guns were untouched. These he promptly demolished and returned without accident.

Even at this early stage the view was expressed by a leading officer that there was little hope of dealing effectively with the widely scattered and cleverly hidden guns from the sea. Sir Julian Corbett, in the Official History of the War: Naval Operations, states that: " It was . . . becoming evident that . . . the choice lay between abandoning the attempt to break through, or using troops at once to clear the shores."

In the night the minesweepers, with daring and skill, swept within a mile and a half of Kephez Point, with land batteries and field-guns firing at them furiously as they worked along. A squadron of allied destroyers answered the hostile guns and succeeded in keeping down their fire. The next day Fort Dardanos, on the Asiatic side, and Fort Saundere, on the Gallipoli side, were bombarded by the Canopus, Swiftsure, and Cornwallis. Every available field-gun and howitzer on Achi Baba, or Tree Hill, and on the southern slopes of Pasha Dagh pitched high-explosive shells against the three British battleships. And Fort Suandere worked all its guns with the utmost speed. Each ship was struck, but their armour held good, and only one man was wounded. At 4.50 p.m. the forts ceased to fire, being apparently damaged, and after continuing the bombardment for another forty minutes the battleships withdrew.

On Wednesday, March 3, the French squadron steamed into the Gulf of Xeres, and bombarded the forts on the Bulair line, blowing up several ammunition depots. On Thursday British battleships were able to advance about four miles into the Straits, which brought them to within two miles of the danger zone. Ten miles ahead of them was Chanak, with Kilid Bahr opposite, where the channel narrowed to a breadth of less than two miles. Here it was that forts, field-batteries, and mobile howitzers were thickly clustered on both sides of the waters leading to Nagara Point. On this day, too, landing-parties were put ashore at both Kum Kale and Sedd el Bahr, but in both cases a stiff resistance was met with, and they were withdrawn, with a loss of 20 officers and men killed, 25 wounded, and 3 missing. It was a regrettable setback.

In addition to their numerous guns of position, their field howitzers, shore torpedoes, and electric mines fixed on the bed of the channel, the Germans and Turks had a formidable weapon of defence in the strong current flowing from the Black Sea to the Mediterranean. In the month of March the rivers of the Black Sea were in flood, and the consequence was that there was a great volume of water flowing through the Narrows. A modern torpedo, the Leon, was admirably suited to the circumstances. It consisted of a powerful floating mine which could be set in torpedo fashion to drift in a current, bobbing up and down, and with a good knowledge of the direction of the current it could be employed with deadly effect against any target in narrow waters.

The only protection used against this torpedo was an old-fashioned torpedo net round each battleship. But by reason of its curious movement the Leon mine was likely to pass under the net and explode on the ship's hull. Moreover, if a battle-ship went into action with her torpedo-nets out, her speed was much reduced; and the old slow vessels, constituting the main part of the attacking fleet, wanted to get every knot possible out of their engines. It was by moving in curves in Erenkeni Bay, within the basin of the Dardanelles, that they managed to disconcert the aim of the German and Turkish gunners and escape from the shells. But no satisfactory means of protection could be devised against the formidable Leon torpedoes.

On March 5 the main business of destroying the modern-gunned and newly-strengthened defences of the Narrows was taken in hand. The Queen Elizabeth opened fire from a position near Gaba Tepe, throwing her huge shells over the Gallipoli peninsula and across the Narrows on to the Kilid Bahr forts of the European coast. The next day, March 6, the Queen Elizabeth again took up the bombardment, but owing to the Albion's difficulty in spotting for her inside the Strait she could not make effective practice. Moreover, coming under fire from concealed howitzers, the Queen Elizabeth had twice to shift her position, at last moving to a range of more than 20,000 yards from her target.

A modern aeroplane, carrying an officer with range-finding instruments and an instrument for wireless telegraphy, would have made the bombardment of the Narrows practicable. Airmen, darting about the sky, could alone direct the elevation and traverse of the great battleship's guns. The gunnery officers of the Queen Elizabeth could see nothing except the sandstone cliffs of the Gallipoli peninsula and the scrub-covered heights of the Pasha Dagh beyond. Even if observation balloons had been used, at a distance of thirteen miles from the low-placed and masked forts and earthworks, no exact work of position-finding and spotting would have been possible. The three seaplanes at the Admiral's disposal were able to give little help: one crashed into the sea, the pilot of the second was wounded, and the third went up too late to be of great use.

In the absence of satisfactory air reconnaissance officers in the fire-control stations of battleships circling within the Straits were able to watch certain of the bombarded forts and signal the results of the fire to the Queen Elizabeth. But this was not practicable in the attack on the most difficult defences of the Narrows, and whenever there was a fog, or even a mist, the work of the fleet was seriously interrupted. The conditions of this extraordinary naval action were the same as those governing the action of land artillery in Flanders and France. Everything depended upon clear vision for observation of fire. When the scene of action was veiled with haze, the guns could only be trained by means of measurements on the map, and as the effect of their fire was then incapable of being known, they were just as likely to be wasting costly ammunition and uselessly wearing away the tubing of the great naval guns, as to be damaging to the enemy and his defences.

Little progress therefore was made in the bombardment during hazy weather, and there were also continual delays owing to storms. The tail-end of winter was indeed the worst of all seasons for naval operations in and round the Dardanelles. As it was a mild winter, the flooding of the Black Sea set up an especially strong current in the Straits in February and March, and the general moisture of the air at the opening of spring led to the hostile forts and field-batteries being blanketed by mist for a week or more at a time. The upshot was that, soon after every hostile bombardment, the Germans were able to repair much of the damage done. Only the old forts at the entrance were quite destroyed, and even at Helles and Kum Kale motor-batteries and new gun-sites were prepared close to the landing places, thus making the destruction of the old entrance forts an affair of small permanent importance.

The most notable achievement of the Allied fleet in the first week of March was the effect produced upon the Italian mind. The Giornale D'Italia, a newspaper closely connected with the Government of Signor Salandra and Baron Sonnino, urged the necessity for an Anglo-Italian agreement with a view to the intervention of Italy on the side of the Triple Entente. Other powerful organs of Italian opinion advocated the same policy, and the Government began to act in a most vigorous way with a view to the denunciation of the treaty with Austria and Germany. In Bulgaria and Rumania there was a similar strong current of public opinion in favour of intervention on the side of the Allies, the Bulgarians especially being excited by the prospect of renewing their struggle with their old enemies the Turks. In Constantinople was a widespread feeling of alarm.

All this, however, was due more to the prestige of the British navy than to the actual amount of progress made in forcing the Dardanelles. On March 8 the Queen Elizabeth entered the Straits and attacked the forts in the Narrows by direct fire. The visibility was bad, however, and the results of the fire disappointing. According to Turkish accounts no damage of military importance was effected, and there were no casualties. At 3.30 p.m. Admiral Carden withdrew his ships.

Strong efforts were now made to clear the Kephes minefield. Trawlers and picket-boats, escorted by one or more destroyers, carried out sweeping attempts on the nights of March 9 and 10, but with small success. They were picked out by the enemy's searchlights, and came under very heavy fire. On March 14 a grave mishap to the British cruiser Amethyst revealed the signal dangers of the whole enterprise. While inside the Dardanelles, covering the mine-sweepers, she was suddenly fired upon by a concealed Turkish battery and suffered terrible loss in a few minutes. As a result of a dozen hits by the Turkish guns one-fifth of her crew were put out of action.

The defenders of the Straits displayed an admirable patience and restraint in handling their big guns, allowing small targets, such as destroyers and light cruisers sent to draw their fire, to steam up without being attacked. Only the German motor-batteries, as a rule, fired on these small vessels. The allied naval commander naturally wanted to discover the positions of all the enemy's guns; and, like a chess-player sacrificing pawns with a design to get a strong line of attack on his opponent's more important pieces, Admiral de Robeck threw out his destroyers and a light cruiser or two and watched for the flashes from the great guns along the waterway. But the Germans were not to be drawn in this fashion. They suffered terribly at times from the long-range fire of the allied battle-ships, and if Turkish officers had been controlling the forts and earthworks the position of all the guns might more quickly have been revealed. The Teutonic discipline, endurance, energy, and ingenuity with which the defence of the Dardanelles was conducted deserved high praise.

The Germans had their full reward when the first great attempt was made to approach the Narrows. This took place on Thursday, March 18, a day of good weather and clear air, when the entire scene of operations was spread out in a bright picture at the feet of the observers on the island mountain of Tenedos. Above the low-lying hills on the Asiatic shore the view extended down to the wide first basin of the Dardanelles, with the shattered forts of Sedd el Bahr by Cape Helles, and the stretch of low land at the village of Krithia, rising up to Tree Hill. Beyond Tree Hill was the valley of Suandere, from which mounted the great rocky clump of the Pasha Dagh.

At the foot of the Pasha Dagh were the white walls of the village of Kilid Bahr, and it was here that the chief defences of the Straits were. They consisted of ten forts, lying opposite to the forts on the Asiatic side of Chanak. Immediately north and south of the main forts were five other batteries at the base of Pasha Dagh. On the Chanak side there were also three additional forts. Then, farther to the north, in the rocky bend of the Narrows by Nagara, there were two forts on the Gallipoli cliffs and three forts on the Asiatic promontory. As already explained, the Germans also had guns on the hill-sides, some of them running on rails in and out of excavated caves, while others were moved by motor-vehicles, or hauled along on a light railway track. Below the Narrows there was a fort at Kephez Point, and another fort opposite it on the Gallipoli cliff. Still more southward there was another fort by the ravine of Suandere. This was thought to have been silenced, as for some days it had made no reply to the fire of our ships, and the forts almost opposite it at Dardanos and White Cliffs seemed to have been put out of action. But, as a matter of fact, Suandere and Kephez forts, guarding the first narrow strait, were not much damaged by the preliminary long-range bombardment. The German gunners there were only reserving their fire for the great struggle.

At a quarter to eleven o'clock on Thursday morning the Agamemnon, followed by the Triumph and Prince George, entered the basin and began to shell these two forts. Then from the entrance to the Dardanelles the warships Queen Elizabeth, Inflexible, and Lord Nelson shelled the forts at Kilid Bahr and Chanak. Every gun and howitzer on both sides of the Straits returned the fire, when at about twenty-two minutes past twelve Admiral Guépratte led his squadron up the Dardanelles and engaged the forts at close range. All the ten battleships engaged were hit, but they silenced every gun at Dardanos and Suandere, and put Fort J at Kilid Bahr and Fort U at Chanak out of action. A German war correspondent at Chanak said that the town looked like being reduced to a rubbish heap. Gigantic walls, that had stood all the storms of four and a half centuries and seemed to have been built for eternity, heaved under the earthquake shock of the great shells and went up in hurtling lumps of earth and stone. Ship after ship steamed into the bay, fired her guns, and then swerved round in an ellipse, followed by other vessels, each in turn coming into the firing line. Shells flew in all directions towards Dardanos and the howitzer batteries by Suandere and on the forts on both sides of the Narrows.

At Chanak there was a tremendous fire caused by the great shells of the Queen Elizabeth. The camp, barracks, and buildings used by the Germans were a heap of rubbish, and though according to the German statement only one gun was destroyed, most of the others were overthrown and buried in the earth, or otherwise temporarily disabled. The same condition of things seemed to obtain right round Kilid Bahr when the action ceased at nightfall. Most of the batteries were upset or covered with earth or thrown out of position by great holes made beneath them. Had it been entirely a contest of gun against gun, the battleships would have dominated the Narrows sufficiently to allow landing-parties of the Royal Naval Division to complete the work of destroying the enemy's main defences. The forts on the Gallipoli side especially suffered badly from the long-range fire which the Queen Elizabeth poured into them from her position under Kum Kale. One of her shells produced a tremendous outburst of flames, rising like a volcanic eruption above the hills, and followed by a great canopy of smoke. She also exploded a powder magazine at Chanak.

Among the allied ships some little damage was done by the enemy's shells. The battle-cruiser Inflexible was badly hit, and her forward control position shattered by a heavy shell, and the old Gaulois was also badly damaged. All this, however, was less injury to the fleet than had been reckoned in the most hopeful estimate of the cost of the grand attack at close quarters. But just when things were going well the first disaster occurred. At 25 minutes past one all the forts ceased firing, and six more old battleships steamed inside the Straits to relieve the Suffren, Gaulois, Charlemagne, and Bouvet, with the Triumph and Prince George. But as the Bouvet was returning in the basin, north of Erenkeni village, she struck a mine. There was a column of vapour followed by a spout of dense black smoke which suggested her magazine was struck, and in less than three minutes the old battleship sank with most of her crew, 600 officers and men. There was only a patch of bubbling water when the Charlemagne steamed up to try to rescue the drowning sailors.

This disaster was the first of a series which was to have a dire effect upon the operations, and to bring about an entire change of policy in the Dardanelles theatre of war. At about nine minutes past four in the afternoon, as the Irresistible was steaming along in the firing-line, she also was mined, and began to list heavily. Happily, she remained afloat, and in spite of the massed fire which the Turkish guns poured upon her and upon all vessels that stood by to rescue her crew, destroyers managed to save most of the officers and men. But scarcely had this been done when, at five minutes past six, the Ocean also struck a mine. Again, with great skill and gallantry, practically the whole of the crew was safely removed under a hot fire. The work of rescue was done in a way that excited the admiration of the French sailors.

Soon after four o'clock the Inflexible, which somewhat earlier on the same day had been badly damaged by gunfire, also struck a mine which killed every man in the foremost submerged flat. Though down by the head and listing badly, her devoted crew were able to save her, and she was able to get back to Tenedos. The loss of life on the British ships was slight, having regard to the large scope and importance of the operations, and the loss of three old battleships was not a heavy price to pay for an attack upon all the principal fortresses of the Dardanelles. Though the Secretary of the Admiralty remarked at the time, " The power of the fleet to dominate the fortresses by superiority of fire seems to be established," this appears to have been a surprisingly sanguine interpretation of the results achieved.

Unfortunately it was not a question only of the comparative strength in gun fire of the ships and the forts. There were the mines to be reckoned with. By these hidden instruments of defence the Turks undoubtedly transformed the artillery duel on March 18 into an important victory over the bombarding fleet. The admiral in command of the allied naval forces was unable to resume the attack upon the forts until means had been devised for protecting the ships against mines. The check was an affair of a more serious nature than the British Government were inclined to admit at the time.

As Mr. Churchill says in his book, The World Crisis, 1915, " the operation of sweeping the area from which the ships were to bombard . . . was the indispensable preliminary to any naval attack upon the forts. This was not achieved because the sweepers were inadequate . . . and this fact led directly to the losses in the attack of March 18, and indirectly to the abandonment of the whole naval enterprise." It appears that on the night of March 8 a small Turkish ship had laid a line of moored mines in Erenkeni Bay, in waters occupied by the British ships during the bombardment of March 5 and 6. These mines had not been detected by the sweepers, and on them the Bouvet and the three British vessels had come to grief. Some of these were, in fact, encountered by sweepers on March 16, but the line of moored mines was not suspected.

THE ATTACK ON THE DARDANELLES

The Turk, after being badly defeated by Bulgarians, Serbians, and Greeks in the recent Balkan War, had come to Gallipoli and Chanak oppressed by the legend of the invincible British and with a romantic sympathy for the gallantry and daring of the French. Without the help of the German he would certainly have crumpled up and broken out in riot in Constantinople when the allied fleet assailed him with 12 in. and 15 in. shells. But the upshot of his victory in the Dardanelles was that the Turk fully recovered his self-confidence and became, as his father had done at Plevna, one of the most formidable fighting men of the world.

Equally important was the result of their victory upon the minds of the German commanders and officers who had conducted the principal work of defending the Dardanelles. They had been almost ready to accept defeat when the bombardment was proceeding vigorously. But when night fell on March 18 they became inspired to more severe efforts by a success with which they were themselves surprised. For example, the German officer in charge of the battery at Chanak had most of his guns damaged when he ceased fire at half-past six on Thurday evening. But by working all night at high pressure he repaired the battery, and on Friday morning all the guns except one were again ready for battle. By the end of March even Kum Kale Fort, at the entrance to the Straits, was again active, a motor-battery having been placed in operation there by the Germans. Then across the water at Sedd el Bahr field-guns were placed in earthworks to command the bay. Every night for five weeks, from March 18 to April 25, the work of strengthening all the Gallipoli peninsula and the Asiatic shore went on under the direction of the German officers. British airmen could see long camel transport trains coming from the interior of Asia Minor towards the coast, and troops were concentrated from north and south to form a large army.

For some time the general opinion held that the allied fleet, which was reinforced by three more battleships—the French Henri IV. and the British Queen and Implacable—would again attempt to force the Dardanelles without waiting for a landing army. But stormy weather set in, and though the Black Sea fleet of the Russian navy tried to disconcert the enemy on March 29 by bombarding the outside forts and batteries of the Bosporus, the attack on the Dardanelles was not resumed.

The fact was that the allied admirals had decided at a council of war that nothing more could be done without the help of a large army. The difficulties of the situation continued to increase. After the intervention policy of the Greek prime minister, M. Venizelos, was defeated by King Constantine, everything went wrong, and it was the withdrawal of the offer of Greek aid that led to the disastrous use of naval forces alone. For the Allies lost their arranged bases at Salonica and Mitylene, and though with the tacit consent of M. Venizelos the fleet continued to use as a base the Greek island of Lemnos, this very slight measure of assistance was also withdrawn by the new Greek premier, M. Gounaris.

The failure of the attempt to conquer the Gallipoli peninsula was attributed by many to mismanagement and incompetence, and there arose a pertinacious demand for an enquiry. In consequence a royal commission, with the earl of Cromer as chairman, was appointed to deal with " the origin and inception of the attack," and its report was issued on March 8, 1917. In this certain criticisms were passed on Lord Kitchener and Lord Fisher, and the commissioners expressed the view that greater care should have been taken by the prime minister and the first lord of the admiralty to see that the views of their naval advisers were properly put before the war council.

The actual words of the Report are :

We think that there was an obligation first on the first lord, secondly on the prime minister, and thirdly on the other members of the War Council to see that the views of the naval advisers were clearly put before the council; we also think that the naval advisers should have expressed their views to the Council, whether asked or not, if they considered that the project which the council was about to adopt was impracticable from a naval point of view.

The final conclusions of the commissioners, however, is not wholly condemnatory. They say:

We think that although the main object was not attained certain important political advantages, upon the nature of which we have already dealt, were secured by the Dardanelles expedition. Whether these advantages were worth the loss of life and treasure involved is, and must always remain, a matter of opinion.

As more than any other individual the first lord of the admiralty, Mr. Winston Churchill, was responsible for persistently prosecuting the idea of an attack on the Dardanelles we may fittingly quote the opinion of the commissioners about his actions in this matter.

He ought, instead of urging Lord Fisher, as he seems to have done at the private meeting after luncheon on January 28, to give a silent, but manifestly very reluctant, assent to the undertaking, not merely to have invited Lord Fisher and Sir Arthur Wilson to express their views freely to the council, but further to have insisted on their doing so, in order that the ministerial members might be placed in full possession of all the arguments for and against the enterprise. We have not the least doubt that, in speaking at the council, Mr. Churchill thought that he was correctly representing the collective views of the Admiralty experts. But, without in any way wishing to impugn his good faith, it seems clear that he was carried away by his sanguine temperament and his firm belief in the success of the undertaking which he advocated. Although none of his expert advisers absolutely expressed dissent, all the evidence laid before us leads us to the conclusion that Mr. Churchill had obtained their support to a less extent than he himself imagined.

Mr. Churchill's defence of his actions will be found in Vol. II. of The World Crisis, 1915; there he says:

I have asked myself in these later years, what would have happened if I had taken Lord Fisher's advice and refused point blank to take any action at the Dardanelles unless or until the War Office produced on their responsibility an adequate army to storm the Gallipoli peninsula? Should we by holding out in this way have secured a sufficient army and a good plan? Should we have had all the advantages of the Dardanelles policy without the mistakes and misfortunes for which we had to pay so dearly? The Dardanelles commissioners, studying the story from an entirely different angle, obviously felt that if there had been no naval plan in the field, there would later on have been a really well-conceived and well-concerted amphibious attack. No one can probe this imaginary situation very far, and it is impossible to pronounce.

But I think myself that nothing less than the ocular demonstration and practical proof of the strategic meaning of the Dardanelles, and the effects of attacking it on every Balkan and Mediterranean power, would have lighted up men's minds sufficiently to make a large abstraction of troops from the main theatre a possibility. I do not believe that anything less than those tremendous hopes, reinforced as they were by dire necessity, would have enabled Lord Kitchener to wrest an army from France and Flanders. In cold blood, it could never have been done. General headquarters, and the French general staff would have succeeded in shattering any plan put forward so long as it was a mere theoretical proposal for a large diversion of force to the southern theatre. At one moment they would have told us that, owing to the Russian failure, great masses of Germans were returning to the West to deliver an overwhelming offensive; at another, that they could not spare a round of ammunition and were in desperate straits for the want of it; at a third, that they had a wonderful plan for a great offensive which would shatter the German line and drive them out of a large portion of France. All these arguments were in fact used, and their effect was, as will be seen, to cripple the Dardanelles operations even after they had actually begun. How much more would they have overwhelmed any paper plan for an eastern campaign? There would have been no Dardanelles with its hopes, its glories, its losses, and its ultimate heartbreaking failure.

But who shall say what would have happened instead? A few weeks' more delay in the entry of Italy into the war, and the continuance of the great Russian defeats in Galicia, would have rendered that entry improbable in the extreme. A few more months acceleration of the Bulgarian declaration of war against us, and the whole of the Balkans, except Serbia, might have been rallied to the Teutonic standards. The flower of the Turkish army, which was largely destroyed on the Gallipoli peninsula, would certainly have fought us or our Allies somewhere else. The destruction of the Russian army of the Caucasus could not have been long averted. I do not believe that by adopting the negative attitude we should ever have got our good and well-conceived amphibious operation. We should have got no operation at all. We should have done nothing, and have been confronted with diplomatic and military reactions wholly unfavourable throughout the southern and eastern theatre. Searching my heart, I cannot regret the effort. It was good to go as far as we did. Not to persevere—that was the crime.

CHAPTER 8

The Landing on Gallipoli

BEFORE the failure of the naval attack on the forts of the Dardanelles the original idea of a combined naval and military effort had again been brought forward, and on February 16, 1915, while preparations for the bombardment of the 19th were being made by the fleet, the Cabinet decided " to mass a considerable force in the Mediterannean to be used as occasion might require." At the same time the Admiralty was instructed " to build special transports and lighters suitable for the conveyance and landing of a force of 50,000 men at any point that might be required."

Early in March it was decided to send Sir Ian Hamilton to command the troops that were being collected, although the scope of the proposed military operations had not yet been decided. Sir Ian was instructed to confer with Vice-Admiral Carden and his successor, Admiral de Robeck, who took command of the fleet about this time, and these officers soon reached the conclusion that a joint operation against Gallipoli was desirable. The War Council accepted this opinion, although Mr. Churchill, the first lord of the Admiralty, expressed " regret and anxiety " at the abandonment of the naval operations after the failure of March 18. At this time, therefore, the Government's policy was not that the attack should be abandoned, but that it should be made both by the navy and by military forces who would be employed on a large scale.

Although in origin the expedition was a joint operation by Great Britain and France, yet practically the whole of the forces employed were supplied by Great Britain, only a small contingent coming from France, as General Joffre refused to spare any troops from the Western Front. The French contingent consisted of a body of troops drawn from the Armée Coloniale and the Foreign Legion which had been sent to Egypt to be used in occupying the Gallipoli peninsula if the naval effort to force the Straits were successful. They were under the command of General d'Amade.

Sir Ian Hamilton had under his command a force of about 120,000 men, the nucleus of which was the 29th Division under the command of Major-General A. Hunter-Weston. It consisted of the 86th infantry brigade comprising the 1st Lancashire Fusiliers, the 2nd Royal Fusiliers, the 1st Royal Munster Fusiliers, and the 1st Royal Dublin Fusiliers; the 87th infantry brigade consisting of the 1st King's Own Scottish Borderers, the 2nd South Wales Borderers, the 1st Border Regiment, and the 1st Royal Inniskilling Fusiliers; the 88th infantry brigade in which were the 4th Worcesters, the 1st Essex, the 2nd Hampshires, the 5th Royal Scots, and a territorial battalion, a squadron of the Surrey Yeomanry, and two batteries. The Naval Division comprised a brigade of royal marines and two naval brigades. To these forces was added the British army in Egypt consisting of 16 battalions of Australian, and four of New Zealand infantry commanded by Sir William Birdwood, and the East Lancashire Territorial Division comprising the Manchester brigade, in which were the 5th, 6th, 7th, and 8th Manchesters, the East Lancashire brigade consisting of the 4th and 5th East Lancashires and the 9th and 10th Manchesters, and the Lancashire Fusilier brigade comprising the 5th, 6th, 7th, and 8th Lancashire Fusiliers. There was also a body of Indian troops.

On his arrival in the East on March 17 Sir Ian Hamilton had selected Mudros as the base of his operations, and there in the middle of April the expedition began to assemble. One of the difficulties that confronted Sir Ian was the fact that secrecy was impossible. The Turks and their German commander-in-chief, General Liman von Sanders, were well aware that a landing was intended, and they were thoroughly prepared to meet it. Nor could there be much doubt as to the point which would be chosen for the attack; there was no practicable alternative to the southern extremity of the peninsula. After reconnaissances Sir Ian Hamilton had selected as landing places the beach at the north-east corner of Morto Bay, designated beach S; the beaches on each side of Cape Helles, that on the east being called beach V and that on the west beach W; the beach above Tekke Burnu known as beach X, and the beach due west of Krithia called beach Y. The landings at V, W, and X were to be the main operations, the landings at S and Y being intended only to protect the flanks and harass the Turks.

THE LANDING ON GALLIPOLI

In addition to the landings at the southern extremity Sir Ian Hamilton decided also to effect a landing at Gaba Tepe, in the Gulf of Saros north of the main Turkish position, which was to be carried by the co-operation of the two forces. The task at Gaba Tepe was assigned to the Australian and New Zealand troops. About 150 ships were necessary to transport the troops from their Egyptian base, and by April 21 they were all assembled in the Bay of Mudros, on the island of Lemnos. The spectacle in the bay was imposing. The ships varied in size from the Queen Elizabeth to the fishing smacks of the islanders. Famous liners, which had carried the British flag in every sea, were collected into a great fleet of transports, and they were protected by an imposing fleet of warships. For three days they waited in Mudros Bay for the period of settled calm weather which was necessary for the landing.

Sir Ian Hamilton's army had to land in face of an enemy who had had full warning for two months that a landing in force would be attempted. He had to put on shore food, water, guns, horses, ammunition, and a thousand articles necessary to keep an army in the field, and to make arrangements to remove a large number of sick and wounded. All these operations were dependent on the state of the capricious spring weather, and a rough sea would leave one part of the army ashore while its main force and its supplies were held off the coast.

On Friday morning, April 23, the stormy weather subsided, and at five o'clock in the afternoon the first transport steamed out of Mudros Bay, followed by other huge liners, all their decks yellow with khaki battalions. The bands of the fleet played them out, and the crews of the warships cheered them on to victory. The Australasian division of liners, with its assistant battleships, steamed towards Gaba Tepe, which was made about one o'clock a.m. on Sunday, April 25. It was a beautiful, calm night, with the sea lit by a brilliant crescent moon; the soldiers rested in preparation for their tremendous exertion, and were afterwards served with a last hot meal. At 20 minutes past one the boats were lowered, and the troops fell in on deck and embarked in the boats, in complete silence and with great rapidity, without a hitch or accident of any kind.

The steam pinnaces towed the boats towards the shore, the battleships also steaming towards the land. By 10 minutes past four the three battleships arrived 250 yards from the coast, which was just discernible in the starry darkness, the moon having sunk. The boats, which had been towed behind the warships, now went ahead, in snakelines of 12, each boat being crowded with troops so that the gunwale was almost flush with the water. The operation was timed so as to allow the boats to reach the beach in darkness before daybreak, so that the Turks would not be able to see the targets before the Australasians reached the land. Every eye was fixed on the grim, sombre sweep of cliff and hill just in front, which was so dark and silent that it seemed as if the enemy had been completely surprised.

But at 10 minutes to five, as the leading boats approached the beach, an alarm light on the hill flashed for 10 minutes. It was soon followed by a burst of rifle fire from the beach, where the Turks were entrenched. Soon a British cheer rang out and the rifle firing diminished as the dawn broke in a haze at half-past five. As some of the steam pinnaces returned men learnt what had happened. When the Australians were about 200 yards from shore the enemy opened fire with rifles and machine-guns. Happily, most of the bullets went high, yet many men were hit in the crowded boats. In grim silence the others rowed with all their might till they reached the five-foot watermark. Then, without waiting for orders, the troops leaped into the sea and waded to the beach, and there, forming up roughly, they charged at the line of flame marking the first Turkish trench. The men of the landing party had been warned not to fill their magazine rifles until daybreak, as a hot rifle fire from them would have given the enemy's batteries the target they were vainly searching for in the darkness. The Australians, therefore, used only their bayonets.

In about a minute they had taken the trench on the beach, captured a Maxim gun, and killed or dispersed all the defenders. Facing the small victorious force was a steep cliff. It was covered with thick undergrowth, and about halfway up it was another trench, from which the enemy directed a terrible fire on the beach and on the boats. Three boatloads of men were wiped out before they could land, and the troops of the first landing-party dropped in large numbers from bullets poured on them from three sides. The Australians flung down their packs and climbed up the cliff, lifting themselves up from foothold to foothold by clutching at the shrubs. In less than a quarter of an hour most of the Turks holding the cliff trench were killed by the bayonet or put to flight. The Australians cut through the wire entanglements just before daybreak and made a complete surprise attack.

When the sun rose, and the outlines of the yellow coast and the green hills beyond became clear, it was seen that a fortunate mistake had been made. Instead of landing at Gaba Tepe, just north of the rocks, the boats had turned in the darkness towards Sari Bair, a great clump of sandstone rock rising from nine hundred and fifty to nine hundred and seventy-one feet. This luckily proved to be a better landing place than that actually planned, as it afforded some cover for the invaders. But the boats bringing them ashore were continually under fire as they passed to and from the transports, and during the early part of the day it was impossible to check the enemy's fire. It was here that British midshipmen, some of them boys of 16 fresh from Dartmouth, where they had only received a few months' training, conducted themselves with an heroic coolness recalling the best traditions of the midshipmen of Nelson's days.

By the time the sun had fully risen the Australians had gained the first ridge of Sari Bair, and by a quarter-past nine the first landing battle was won; for the covering force of Australians held such a firm footing on the crest that the intense fire of the enemy died away, and though sniping went on throughout the day the disembarkation of the remainder of the force proceeded without interruption save from shrapnel shells. The position of the victorious battalions was, however, very difficult. The proper thing for them to have done was to have entrenched on the conquered ridge and waited for the main force to disembark. But the ground was so broken and scrubby that it was hard to find a good entrenching line. When the troops thought they had cleared a space they were still subjected to a continual and punishing fire from the snipers.

Then as the light became good the German gunners on the heights brought their artillery into action. There were first two guns at Gaba Tepe, which enfiladed the landing beach with shrapnel. But one British cruiser moved in close to the shore and battered the sandstone rocks with high-explosive shell so that the enemy guns there were silenced. In the meantime the Australians on the crest, smitten on both flanks and worried all along their front, began to move out in search of their foes. The fact was their landing at Sari Bair had been a surprise for the German commander. A weak force had held the beach, and only scattered snipers occupied the mountain, trying to hold back the Australians until the Turkish divisions, sent towards the wrong places round Suvla Bay in the north and Gaba Tepe in the south, collected in the afternoon at Sari Bair.

The Australians worked northward and eastward in a series of fierce bayonet rushes. Then, encouraged by the slightness of the opposition they met, they went ahead in a burst of charges down the ravines and up the ridges. This bayonet work went on all the morning, the Australians still advancing by the fury and rapidity of their onset. Their leading troops worked down the Khelia Valley, and by tremendous efforts they crossed the last and third ridge and got within a few hundred yards of Maidos, the key to the Narrows. In front of them, across the water, was Nagara Point. Had it been possible to make this attack in force and bring up guns and entrench on the ground won in the extraordinary impetuous charge, the road to Constantinople would have been conquered in a few hours.

But the Australian covering force had gained more ground than it could hold. There were only 2,000 or 3,000, without food or guns, and lacking even machine guns. Most of their work had been done with the bayonet, and in the afternoon the German commander brought his main force against them and almost outflanked them. But at the critical moment the New Zealanders came to the help of the Australians, and after retiring from the third ridge back to their early position on the first ridge, the troops dug themselves in. Then the Indian troops disembarked, and after the second rush of the Australasians, the combined and strengthened force of Australians, New Zealanders, and Indians again advanced to the third ridge, after repulsing some furious counter-attacks by the Turks.

As twilight fell the enemy brought up more reinforcements, and his counter-attacks were supported by a heavy bombardment of the Australian position from hostile batteries which the naval guns could not reach. So dangerous did the pressure on the lines become that Sir William Birdwood drew the troops back to the first ridge during the night, and his staff devoted all their energies to strengthening the position and getting some field-guns ashore to deal with the enemy's artillery. The Australians had suffered heavily in their first retreat from the point near Maidos.

When Monday morning dawned, however, the landing battle at Sari Bair was won, in spite of the fact that another Turkish army corps was moving up on the north-east for the grand assault which was to drive the invaders into the sea. The German artillerymen had brought all their guns into play and had moved up more batteries for the final bombardment. During the whole of Sunday night the hostile gunners had maintained a rain of shrapnel over the landing beach, with a view to hindering disembarking operations. The battleships had tried to support the troops by a heavy fire from their secondary armament, but as the enemy's gun-positions at this time were not known the ships could not do much to keep down the enemy's fire.

But on Monday morning the position was reversed. The Turks could clearly be seen moving in large numbers along the heights, and the position of their supporting batteries could be spotted by the flashes. Moreover, every time they had fired in the darkness of Sunday night naval fire-control officers had been spotting the flashes and comparing notes and measurements. The Queen Elizabeth and seven other warships steamed up to take part in the battle. The seven older ships moved close inshore, each of their chief gunnery lieutenants having a marked map of this section of the enemy's territory. The Queen Elizabeth stood farther out to sea, so as to get a howitzer effect with her guns by pitching the shells as high as possible into the dales, where airmen reported the enemy were gathering for shelter preparatory to the advance. Then, as the Turkish infantry moved forward to the attack, they were met with a terrific bombardment. Every kind of shell carried by the warships was thrown at them, from the 15 in. shrapnel of the Queen Elizabeth to the little shell of the 12-pounders.

On land the advancing Turks were met by rifle and machine-gun fire. For two hours the Turks pressed their attack, while the naval guns inflicted terrible losses on them. On Monday afternoon the Turkish attack was definitely repulsed, the position at Sari Bair was secure, and the trenches were deepened so that the men could not be shaken by shrapnel fire.

On Tuesday morning, April 27, a fresh Turkish division was brought up to Sari Bair and launched against the British trenches after a heavy bombardment by the German batteries. But the result was the same as on Monday. The Turks came on time after time, and were shot down in multitudes, and by three o'clock in the afternoon all the spirit of the twelve thousand fresh hostile infantrymen was broken. The Australasians again advanced with the bayonet and won more ground, enabling them to strengthen their defences.

All the German leader could do was to maintain a curtain of shrapnel over the beach and the neighbouring waters, in order to impede the disembarking operations. But the hail of bullets made little impression on the work of the pinnaces, boats, lighters, and tugs, and the seamen who manned them; for though the shrapnel bullets churned up the water with the spectacular effect of a hailstorm, the material damage inflicted by the intense bombardment was slight. Nothing could budge the Overseas troops, and by building roads, making concrete works, dragging guns up the cliff, constructing bombproof shelters, they fortified their position between Sari Bair and Gaba Tepe so that they were able to reduce the garrison and send a force to help the British troops at Sedd el Bahr, at the end of the peninsula.

Simultaneously with the Australian landing the main body of Sir Ian Hamilton's army was carrying out its attempt upon the southern extremity of the peninsula. On the Asiatic shore of the entrance to the Dardanelles was Kum Kale, from which Turkish batteries had command of all six landing beaches. It was a vital necessity to master the fire of the enemy on the Asiatic shore, in order to enable the 29th Division to land and establish itself. So, by arrangement with Sir Ian Hamilton, the French Colonial Division, under General d'Amade, steamed in its transports to Kum Kale, protected by three French battleships and other craft.

The French general selected as his landing ground the most historic battlefield in the world—the far-famed windy plain of Troy, stretching below the hill on which Troy stood, to the mouth of the river Meander, or Simois. The landing was made west of the river by the mouth of the Meander, where the French transports poured the marines and Senegalese troops into small boats early on Sunday morning, April 25, when the landing conflicts were raging on the other side of the Strait. The boats were towed by trawlers and torpedo craft to the mouth of the river at half-past nine in the morning, under a fire of shells and bullets from the ruined citadel of Kum Kale. Some distant German batteries at In Tepe were also trained on the French marines and coloured troops. But after fierce hand-to-hand fighting the French gained sufficient mastery of the position to avert the danger that Turkish artillery operating from this point would seriously hamper the British landing. The following day the French force was able to re-embark and join the British force on beach S.

The 29th Division was meanwhile making its memorable landing on the southern extremity of the Gallipoli peninsula. In his despatch describing the landing Sir Ian Hamilton wrote:—

The transports conveying the covering force arrived off Tenedos on the morning of the 24th, and during the afternoon the troops were transferred to the warships and fleet-sweepers in which they were to approach the shore. About midnight these ships, each towing a number of cutters and other small boats, silently slipped their cables, and escorted by the 3rd Squadron of the Fleet, steamed slowly towards their final rendezvous at Cape Helles. The rendezvous was reached just before dawn on the 25th. The morning was absolutely still; there was no sign of life on the shore; a thin veil of mist hung motionless over the promontory; the surface of the sea was as smooth as glass. The four battleships and four cruisers which formed the 3rd Squadron at once took up the positions that had been allotted to them, and at 5 a.m., it being then light enough to fire, a violent bombardment of the enemy's defences was begun. Meanwhile the troops were being rapidly transferred to the small boats in which they were to be towed ashore. Not a move on the part of the enemy; except for shells thrown from the Asiatic side of the Straits, the guns of the fleet remained unanswered.

But though the enemy were silent they were far from being unprepared. The task of the Australians had been rendered easier by the fact that their landing had to a certain extent taken the Turks by surprise. But the 29th Division could make no surprise attack. The cliffs at Cape Tekeh, Cape Helles, Sedd el Bahr, and De Totts Battery, at the eastern point of Morto Bay, rose from 50 to 100 feet. Above the cliffs was an open plateau, rising in places not far from the sea's edge to 138 feet, 141 feet, and 256 feet. Two miles inland the hills began sloping up to the dominating ridge of Acha Baba, or Tree Hill, 730 feet above sea level. Then, hill over hill, the ground ran to the rocky, broken clump of Pasha Dagh, at the Narrows. The Germans had everywhere the finest possible field for direct gun fire, innumerable ravines and hollows, in which to shelter their howitzers, and mile-long slopes like the glacis of a mighty fortress, down which their entrenched infantry could shoot with

their machine-guns helping them, and preparing for their charges.

The plan of attack was different from that at Sari Bair. No surprise in the darkness was possible, as the beaches were defended by underwater wire entanglements and by the main forces of the 5th Turkish Army entrenched on the high ground and flanking all the beaches. The defending troops were supported by light field-guns and 6 in. howitzer batteries in formidable numbers, working with marked ranges, and completely swept the whole field of fire. It was hoped that a terrific bombardment of the enemy's positions by every gun in the battleships, including the Queen Elizabeth, would master the enemy's fire. But as the ships, apparently, used shrapnel shell chiefly, against which the German engineers had skilfully made deep trenches, the extraordinary volume and fury of our naval bombardment did not in most cases have an effect commensurate with the tremendous effort made. What was needed was high-explosive shell in immense quantities. Only high-explosive shell could smash up the enemy's earthworks. But as is well known, shell of this kind was sadly lacking. At the Dardanelles, where the enemy was magnificently entrenched for a long siege warfare, the lack of high-explosive shell seems to have been the principal factor of failure in the military operations.

The only real success in the preliminary bombardment was obtained round Beach X, north of Cape Tekeh. It was due to the bold tactics of the captain of the Implacable. At dawn the covering

ship, the Swiftsure, started a fierce fire against the cliffs—using, of course, shrapnel. But at eight minutes to six the Implacable, also employing shrapnel for her 12 in. and 6 in. guns, closed for action. Instead, however, of remaining in deep water, the captain navigated his ship within five hundred yards of the shore, till there were only six fathoms of water to float the battleship that displaced 15,000 tons. With her four 12 in. and her twelve 6 in. guns she smote the cliffs at point-blank range, so that the shrapnel smashed into the enemy's trenches and machine-gun chambers in the sandstone with a shattering effect. Not a Turk was able to show his head above the bluff of shrub-grown rock, and the British troops were towed into the beach and there they landed without any opposition, climbed up the cliff and entrenched. When they advanced inland they were badly worried by a Turkish battery at the village of Krithia. But again the gunnery lieutenants of the Implacable came to their aid, and when the position of the battery was signalled to the battleship the guns were knocked out of action. Had the other naval bombardments been as rapidly successful as the affair on Beach X, remarkable progress might have been made.

The landing on Beach Y, northward nearer Krithia, also went well. The disembarkation at this point was a greater surprise to the enemy than the operations round the end of the peninsula. Only three light cruisers, the Dublin, Amethyst, and Sapphire, helped with their guns—the Dublin having eight 6 in., and the two older warships twelve 4 in. pieces each. But the light draught of these unarmoured cruisers enabled them to get close to the shore, and with their small guns they bombarded the high cliff so that a covering force of two battalions and one company landed with scarcely any resistance from the Turks and obtained a firm footing on the heights.

Far more difficult was the disembarkation on the next beach southward, known as Beach W. It consisted of a bay with a wide stretch of sand running like the mouth of a funnel into an inland valley, dominated on one side by the hills extending to Cape Tekeh, and commanded on the other side by the cliffs ending in Cape Helles. The natural defensive strength of the position was extraordinary, for the covering force had to land on a shelterless stretch of sand, with the enemy holding in front of them a crescent of broken, rising ground, pouring down a flanking fire on both sides and a frontal fire from the centre. The German engineers had much improved the natural advantages of the ground. There were wire entanglements in profusion, and a great system of shrapnel-proof trenches.

In vain did the battleships bombard the Turkish defences with all their armament for three-quarters of an hour. The guns were not able to destroy even the lines of barbed-wire on the foreshore. The boats that made for the beach were confronted by a hedge of undamaged wire entanglements, and the crowded troops were exposed to a murderous cross-fire from pom-poms, machine-guns, and entrenched riflemen. In the centre of the bay every man who waded ashore and heroically dashed forward to cut the wire was shot down. Meanwhile another beach party, consisting of engineers and Royal Naval Division men, made for the shelter of Cape Tekeh in the second line of tow-boats. Here another landing party had got into difficulties, and after rowing through a heavy fire the men climbed the cliff, holding on to the extreme edge of it with desperate courage.

Hearing the shouts of these men the party in the second tows came to their assistance, scrambling up the cliff, rifles in hand. The two parties then advanced and captured a Turkish trench in a furious bayonet charge, and thus checked the enfilading fire which was still being poured on the foreshore. About the same time the cliffs on the other side of the bay were carried, and both landing parties on the horns of the crescent displayed such marksmanship that the Turks were afraid to leave their trenches and charge them. At ten o'clock another regiment was landed. The reinforced covering column then worked up the valley and cleared the enemy from their central position. Only then was it possible to cut the barbed-wire entanglements, remove the wounded from the beach, and begin disembarking ammunition and stores. For the British troops then held the crests commanding the terrible death-trap of Beach W. The men there were in somewhat the same position as the Australians and New Zealanders between Sari Bair and Gaba Tepe. Snipers and distant hostile batteries rained rifle and shrapnel bullets over the disembarking operations; but the holes in the cliffs from which the German machine-guns had been firing were in the possession of the invaders.

All round the southern part of the coast, however, the troops were not able to advance. They were most successful when they merely entrenched on the cliffs they had won and covered the principal work of disembarkation. At Beach Y the men tried to work inland, and thus clear all the southern plateau from the opposing Turks. But they were outflanked and punished

THE LANDING ON GALLIPOLI

so heavily that all the force at Beach Y re-embarked on Monday morning. This was the only landing failure the British had in the peninsula.

The troops at the next landing-place, Beach X, also moved forward on Sunday morning, according to the co-ordinated plan of attack arranged by Sir Ian Hamilton. They were checked, after fighting their way inland for a thousand yards. At this point the landing force on their right at Beach W had been timed to meet them. But, as has been shown, Beach W had proved to be a death-trap, and the men there had enough to do to win a footing. The consequence was that the right flank of the troops advancing from Beach X was exposed, and the men retired towards the cliff, where a desperate battle went on all Sunday night. It ended, however, in a British victory, and on Monday morning the troops north of Cape Tekeh again advanced.

On the other side of the end of the peninsula, at Beach S, by Morto Bay and De Totts battery, the landing was effected with few losses and a fine dash. For though the enemy had a trench along the shore, the British battleship at this point was more successful than the ships that fired at the wire entanglements on Beach W. The Turkish position was battered by the naval guns, and then carried at the point of the bayonet by a landing party of seven hundred men.

The enemy howitzers then swept the lost beach with shrapnel, but the British troops were in a fairly safe position in the circumstances, as they were swarming up the cliff and also working round the shoulder of a hill on the left. They reached the old battery on the top by ten o'clock in the morning, and in the afternoon they had made a line of trenches on the plateau, from which they were able to hold the 2,000 Turks in front of them. They formed the right wing of the force that was trying to get astride of the peninsula, occupying the position it was intended that the French troops should work from when the demonstration against Kum Kale was completed. On Tuesday morning the French force took over the trenches by De Totts battery, leaving the landing force free to strengthen the British line on the left.

Between De Totts battery and Beach W was the worst of all the landing places. This was Beach V, lying under the old castle of Sedd el Bahr, and extending towards the high cliff that rose

CHARGE BY THE NAVAL DIVISION AT GALLIPOLI. The Royal Naval Division was a body of volunteers raised by the Admiralty. A detachment was sent to Antwerp in October, 1914. Part of the force fought in Gallipoli in 1915, and was among the troops that assaulted the fortified hill of Achi Baba on June 3, 1915.

Imperial War Museum

A QUIET MOMENT AT ANZAC COVE. The term "Anzac," popularly applied to troops from Australia and New Zealand, was adopted for official use by the War Office in 1916. It is derived from the initial letters of the words Australian (and) New Zealand Army Corps. This cove north of Gaba Tepe, Gallipoli, was christened "Anzac" by the troops who landed in April, 1915—the first occasion on which the use of the name is recorded.

Plate 14

Volume II

sharply from the foreshore round Cape Helles. The beach was only a few hundred yards wide, and the strong current of the Dardanelles swept round it with great power, making any landing by row-boats almost impossible. The lie of the ground was similar to that of Beach W, with a smaller sandy foreshore, fronted by a broken valley and enfiladed from the heights on either hand. On the left, at Sedd el Bahr, was the modern entrance fort to the Dardanelles. Its two great guns had been put out of action by the fleet, but the bomb-proof chambers were intact, and the German engineers had constructed a system of trenches and barbed-wire entanglements extending round the valley and connecting with the solid masses of masonry of the ruined castle. The ruins still afforded excellent cover for sharpshooters and machine-gun parties, and the broken walls of the village of Sedd el Bahr had also been skilfully worked into the enemy's new system of earthwork defences.

Behind the village was a hill 141 feet high, afterwards famous as Doughty-Wylie's Hill. On this commanding position the enemy had constructed a maze of trenches and barbed-wire hedges from which the beach was dominated at point-blank range. As in the case of Beach W, the foreshore and valley were also trenched and set with barbed-wire. Farther inland were heavy howitzer batteries, further strengthening a position which even in the ordinary way would have been one of the most formidable that any troops had ever been called upon to take. But instead of coming overland against the stronghold and entrenching against the enemy's fire and working forward by saps, the British troops had to attack without any cover from the sea, advancing in little boats against an adverse current.

Only the ingenuity of Admiral de Robeck and his Staff made the landing attack practicable. They took a large collier, the River Clyde, cut great doors in her steel sides, and filled her with 2,000 troops. Her bridge was turned into a fort by means of steel plates, and casemates were built in her bows and lower bridge, from which twelve machine-guns were worked by the Naval Division. A string of lighters, towed by a steam-hopper, moved by the side of the River Clyde, the lighters being intended to form a sort of pontoon bridge from the ship to the shore.

It was proposed that the collier should be run ashore on Sedd el Bahr beach, as high up as possible. But the current swung her out of her course, and she went too far eastward close to a reef of rocks. The water above the reef was too deep for the men to wade through, but the steam-hopper also beached herself alongside, forming a gangway. Under a tornado of fire from the enemy, a lighter was also got into position, and the most difficult of all the landings began. While the River Clyde was grounding, a covering party in eight tows also reached the shore. But fifty yards from the water's edge was a barbed wire obstruction spanning the beach. It was undamaged by the naval guns, and the enemy waited till the covering party was held up on the wire, and then played on them with three machine-guns. All the men would have perished but for the fact that there was near the sea a sandbank about five feet high. Under the lee of this shelter the survivors dug themselves in. All the while the River Clyde was rattling under the tempest of machine gun fire, and shrapnel. One of the gangways was destroyed as soon as it was let down, and though the machine guns from the bridge and casemates answered the enemy's fire, they could not beat it down.

It was death to venture outside. But at the word of command, part of the Fusilier brigade, under General Napier, dashed out and tried to reach the foreshore. The short-range fire of the Turkish machine guns swept them off the planks as they ran, mowed them down in the barges, knocked them over in the water, and took a ghastly toll of those who reached the beach and rushed for cover to the sandbank. Of those who fell into the water during the race down the gangway and across the barges, many were drowned. Wounded and weighed down by their packs and full cartridge belts, many an heroic Fusilier perished in quite shallow water. Yet there was no hanging back. General Napier was himself among the killed.

There were the Dublin Fusilers, who had three companies wiped out; the Lancashires, who went with the first tows and suffered terribly, and the Munsters, some of whose platoons also reached the sandbank. The Lancashires got caught in an underwater entanglement, and were there swept by machine-guns. The survivors struggled out of the water into a minefield, and those who extricated themselves from this new peril were again enfiladed by machine guns. Only fifteen men were left alive in the platoon that reached the beach. But with amazing bravery they held on gamely, and tried to rush a Turkish trench. It was an impossible feat. The Turks poured a shower of bullets at them and then charged with the bayonet. Somebody in the Majestic was watching the Lancashires. Two shells from the battleship's guns struck the trench as the Turks were rising to the charge, and the survivors of the fifteen Fusiliers thereby accomplished the apparently impossible. For, rushing on the staggered enemy, they shot or bayoneted those that did not flee, and captured the trench.

Miracles of courage were performed by the men under the sandbank, who went out and brought to shelter their wounded comrades struggling in the water. Some of the rescuers also got the wounded men into the boats and away to the ships. Often the rescuers were killed and the wounded men shot a second time. The grandest figure in the scene of horror and heroism was a seaman from the River Clyde. Calmly smoking a pipe, he went about the beach amid a hurricane of bullets, getting the wounded into safety, and working all the time with an amazing unconcernedness. Meanwhile a party of the Fusiliers, who had landed in tow-boats, scaled the cliff to the village of Sedd el Bahr and carried on a close-range rifle fight with the Turkish infantry in the streets and ruined buildings. But they were too few in number and too much exposed in position to force their way into the town. They had at last to give up the unequal combat and scramble down the cliff to the shelter on the beach.

By the afternoon there were about two hundred men under the sandbank. Digging holes in the sand, they crawled under cover, and there they had to remain until nightfall. It had been seen that any further attempt at a landing would mean the entire destruction of the Fusilier Brigade and the 2nd Battalion of the Hampshires working with them. So the River Clyde remained all day by the beach with nearly 2,000 men inside her. Meanwhile the situation had been greatly improved by the success of the landing on Beach W, under Cape Helles. A battalion of infantry there began to climb up the steep slopes of the crest. So quickly did they move that the sailors watching them from the battleship could hardly realize that the troops were meeting fierce resistance and losing heavily at every step. But there was no stopping to count the cost. The troops swarmed out on the crest of Cape Helles and entrenched there, and in the afternoon a couple of guns were landed. It was hoped that the men holding Cape Helles would be able to work round towards Sedd el Bahr and facilitate the operations of the Fusilier Brigade by clearing the high ground round the sandbank.

But the German engineers had foreseen everything. They had reckoned on losing Cape Helles, while holding up our landing-party at Sedd el Bahr. Round the plateau eastward of Cape Helles lighthouse was a barrier. It consisted of meshes of wire, the barbs only an inch apart, supported on iron posts. This barrier was ten yards in depth. It ran from Cape Helles to Sedd el Bahr Fort. Behind it was a series of trenches, zig-zagging in a rough circle, forming a redoubt held by a strong body of German infantrymen, who were able to fire in any direction in order to prevent any troops which might force a landing at Cape Helles from giving any help to the landing-party in difficulties at Sedd el Bahr. It was precisely this situation which had arisen, all of which goes to show what science and foresight the Germans employed in fortifying the Gallipoli peninsula.

Yet, supported by the fire of the warships, the troops at Cape Helles worked up to the very edge of the barbed-wire by the end of Sunday afternoon. Then they began to cut a path through it while enduring a furious fire from the redoubt. And when some of our infantry tried to dash through in daylight the Turkish fire was too hot for an advance on so small a front as that possible through the wire barrier. Not till night fell were the men able to work forward and get some command over the Turks holding up the landing on Sedd el Bahr beach.

In the darkness of Sunday night the two thousand troops in the River Clyde at last managed to get ashore without a single further casualty. The operation was conducted with such silent skill that the enemy did not perceive until it was too late that anything was happening. Then they opened a raging rifle fire on the ship, and maintained it until close upon dawn. But the ship was empty, and while it was serving as a decoy target the troops, having got ashore with all the ammunition, food, and water they needed, began to push up under the shelter of the cliffs below the castle.

At eleven o'clock at night the Turks became seriously alarmed, and swept the entire beach with a violent fusillade. But the British troops were lying down under cover and suffered little loss. Again they went forward in the darkness, and worked their way into part of the ruined castle and the shattered fort. The centre also advanced, and won a firm hold on the shore; and when day broke on Monday, April 26, an attempt was made to close round the enemy from the castle cliff on one side and the central beach. The attack, however, was held up by machine-guns from one of the towers of the castle, and the men had again to take cover until the Cornwallis battered the towers down with her guns. Then, by hard fighting through the ruined village behind the castle, the British troops worked out in the open country, only to be again held up by the principal work of defence of the German engineers—Doughty-Wylie Hill.

This green mound, which stands about 140 feet above sea level, had been converted into a system of earthworks and wire entanglements, from which the machine-gun and rifle fire swept the beach in front, Cape Helles on their right and Sedd el Bahr on their left. The condition of the weary troops, who had been fighting all night and morning and losing heavily, was very serious. The loss in officers during the landing had been disastrous, and though all the men who had got through unwounded were desperately eager to close with the enemy, there was in many cases nobody left to lead them.

It was in these circumstances that Colonel Doughty-Wylie came ashore and began to talk to the men. He was a staff officer, and he had no business to be where he was. But the situation was critical, and it was because he knew the men had lost their officers that he assumed command. Carrying only a small cane, he walked about in the tempest of fire, talked to the men, cheered and rallied them, and formed them up for the charge. At his orders they fixed their bayonets, and, leading them with his cane, he took them up the fortress hill, and fell dead in front of them. The Fusiliers passed over his body, cut through the barbed-wire, bayoneted the Turks, and captured the height. And in honour of the man who led them they called it Colonel Doughty-Wylie's Hill.

The Dublin Fusiliers, with the Munsters on their left and the Hants on their right, made the great charge. Major Grimshaw, of the Dublin Fusiliers, was as heroic as Colonel Doughty-Wylie, and fell like him on the field of battle. A younger hero of the Dublins was Lieutenant Bastard. He led his men against the fort, only to have them all thrown back by a sweeping fire

from a machine-gun. While the men took cover Lieutenant
Bastard ran forward to the opening through which the machine-
gun was playing, thrust in his revolver, and emptied all its
chambers. He must have killed or wounded some of the
gunners, for the fire was at once reduced. The young lieutenant
escaped at the time by a miracle, but afterwards, while passing
a loophole in the fort, he got a bullet through his cheek.

The speed and dash with which the Irishmen took the fortified
hill were, according to the soldiers themselves, the grand feature
of the most remarkable landing battle in military history. But
the fact was that every regiment of the 29th Division distinguished itself by its dauntless courage and invincible tenacity.
In addition to the first battalions of the Dublin, Munster,
Lancashire, and Inniskilling Fusiliers, and the second battalion
of the Royal Fusiliers, the landing battles at the Southern end
of the Gallipoli peninsula were fought by the 1st Essex Regiment,
the 2nd Hants, and 1st Scottish Borderers, 2nd South Wales
Borderers, 1st Border Regiment, 4th Worcesters, and 5th
Territorial Battalion of the Royal Scots. Magnificent work was
also done by the Chatham, Deal, Portsmouth, and Plymouth
Marine Light Infantry, and the Drake, Hood, Nelson, Howe,
and Anson Battalions of the Naval Division.

It was at noon on Monday, April 26, that the Turks fled
from their last defences on the hill, enabling Beach V to be
cleared. This prepared the way for a further advance inland,
enabling the line to be stretched right across the southern end
of the peninsula. When General Liman von Sanders came down
in great force on April 28 to make the grand attack which
was to push the British back into the sea, they had constructed
a system of trenches from the Aegean coast to the Dardanelles.

In a sustained effort on the night of Wednesday, April 28,
the Turks pressed forward in close-order formation on the
thinly-held British line, intending, after the manner of the
Germans, to smash their way through by sheer weight of
numbers. But they were everywhere repulsed. Long lines of
their dead lying in front of the British trenches marked the
high-water mark of their onslaughts. They also attacked the
French in dense masses on the same night, but they were routed
by a fierce counter-attack at the point of the bayonet. Again
on the following Saturday the Turks concentrated against the
French front, while making only a spasmodic effort against

the British lines. Some of the Senegalese troops on Saturday gave way after their officers had fallen. But the Zouaves went forward in a bayonet charge and recaptured the ground.

The first stage of the great battle ended in the middle of May with the Turks entrenched across the slopes of Achi Baba, and the allied troops holding the ground south of Krithia village. The campaign had become a matter of trench warfare, and the winning of the peninsula was a question of how many men Sir Ian Hamilton could afford to lose in order to capture each trench and each hundred yards of ground. Nothing could be done without large reinforcements and an enormous supply of ammunition.

After the losses of the landing battles, Sir Ian Hamilton must have had less than 35,000 bayonets immediately at hand for the desperate work of attacking the Turkish position. The Turco-German commanders concentrated all their principal armies on the defence of the Dardanelles. The campaign against Egypt was discontinued, and the attack on Russia across the Caucasus was reduced to an unimportant defensive battle. Even the comparatively small Indo-British army advancing along the Euphrates up towards Bagdad was only opposed by a single weak Turkish army corps. All the main military resources of one of the greatest warrior races in the world were organized by capable German officers and set in a series of almost impregnable mountain defences, in order to safeguard the channel forts, which prevented the allied fleet from forcing the Dardanelles.

There were never less than 150,000 Turkish soldiers, with thousands of German engineers and artillerymen, holding the entrenched heights between Achi Baba and Sari Bair. To replace their losses new Turkish armies poured down the mainland track to Gallipoli, or were carried across the Sea of Marmora in transports. It is not surprising that the British advance was slow and the casualties terribly heavy. The enemy was deeply entrenched on one of the finest lines of natural fortifications in the world, with guns and howitzers commanding every site occupied by the British troops. He could bring most of his provisions and supplies up by road at night, with little or no interference from the fire of the British ships, and a huge flotilla of small sailing vessels, plying across the Sea of Marmora, greatly assisted in the provisioning of the defending army.

There was scarcely any water in that part of the mountainous peninsula occupied by the attacking troops. Even their machine-guns at times became unworkable through want of water in the jackets to keep the barrels cool. Everything necessary for existence had also to be brought to the bombarded beaches, and thence carried laboriously by hand through narrow communication trenches to the men in the firing-line. As summer came on, the white troops were almost prostrated by the tropical heat, and plagued by a monstrous number of flies. It became at last a feat of great ingenuity to swallow food without eating live flies also. The Australian and New Zealand Army Corps left off all their clothes, except for one garment around their loins, and their bare bodies were baked to a Red Indian colour.

In any other age than this, the Dardanelles expedition would have collapsed in the summer through an outbreak of deadly pestilence. For flies and vermin, those great disease carriers, filled the trenches, the flies feeding on the corpses left between the lines. Happily, since the South African War, there had been great advances in the science of preventive medicine, and for both enteric and cholera there were vaccine treatments, which greatly reduced the mortality from these two dreadful pestilences. The reversion of the Anzacs to a state of nudity was an excellent protection against the chief vermin-borne diseases, and it was combined with a system of disinfecting the clothes of all the troops which also removed at intervals the agents of pestilence. The water was filtered and boiled, and the troops supplied with an abundance of good food. In fact, the Army Service Corps rather overdid the food supply; for in the heat of the tropical summer, when the soldiers wanted light food, they were still supplied with tins of bully beef. There were times when they rolled the beef tins into the sea in order to avoid eating the meat, but the indefatigable and unchangeable director of food supplies in the Dardanelles went on throwing ton upon ton of bully beef at the troops.

At the end of April, 1915, the allied troops in the southern end of the Peninsular had forced their way forward for some five hundred yards from their landing-places. By this time both sides showed signs of exhaustion, but Sir Ian Hamilton judged that the troops who could first summon up spirit to make another attack would win some hundreds of yards of ground. And as his own force was crowded together under gun fire in a very narrow space, he determined to be the first to strike out. He therefore brought the 2nd Australian and New Zealand infantry brigades down from the Sari Bair region, and rearranged the 29th Division into four brigades, composed of the 87th and 88th Brigades, the Lancashire territorial brigade, and the 29th Indian infantry brigade. Then with the remnant of his forces he formed a new composite division, which he used as a general reserve, after reinforcing the French division with the 2nd Naval Brigade.

The 29th Division went into action at 11 a.m. on May 6, when it moved out leftward, on the south-east side of Krithia. Half an hour afterwards the French force on the right also advanced along the lower slopes of the river ridge of the Kereves Dere. The combined operation, however, made little progress. The British troops were held up outside a pine wood, which the enemy had transformed into a machine-gun redoubt; and the French also were checked by a terrible fire from a strong field-work after reaching the crest of the ridge. The following morning the Lancashire territorials charged gallantly up the slope towards Krithia. They were caught by the German machine-guns; but as they retired, another territorial force, the Queen's Edinburgh Rifles, took the pine wood.

In addition to dislodging the machine-gun parties, they brought down Turkish snipers working from wooden platforms on the trees, and thus cleared the way for the general advance. But just as all seemed to be going well, and the Inniskilling Fusiliers came up to maintain the hold on the pine wood, the Turks, by a gallant charge, won back this clump of trees in the centre. Nevertheless, the Inniskillings went on and captured three enemy trenches, till in the afternoon the advance was again held up by an enfilading fire from hostile machine-guns hidden on a ridge between the gully running towards Krithia and the sea. The operation looked like ending in a stalemate; but neither Sir A. Hunter-Weston nor Sir Ian Hamilton would submit to the check. The commander threw in all his reserves, and ordered a general advance; and despite their heavy losses, the men rose with a will, and in a bayonet charge recaptured the pine wood and advanced nearly all their line some 300 yards.

The troops were almost worn out, but Sir Ian Hamilton kept most of them working when darkness fell at the task of consolidating their new position. His airmen had told him that the enemy were receiving reinforcements, and he was resolved to make one more push before the new hostile forces got into position. At half-past ten the next morning (May 7) he flung out the New Zealand Brigade, and won another two hundred yards in front of the pine trees. Then at half-past four in the afternoon he threw the 2nd Australian Brigade into his front, and sent his whole line forward against Krithia. The Senegalese sharpshooters were broken by the storm of heavy shells from the ridge by Kereves Dere. But the black troops were rallied by their officers, and sent forward in another rush, supported by a small column of French soldiers. Their figures were seen outlined against the sky on the crest of their ridge just as darkness fell and veiled all the battlefield.

When morning came, Sir Ian Hamilton found that the French had captured the machine-gun redoubt on the ridge, and had entrenched in front of Zimmerman Farm. The 87th Brigade had taken another 200 yards of ground; while the Australian Brigade, though swept by shrapnel, machine-gun and rifle fire, extended the front for another 400 yards.

The gain of ground in the three days' battle was only six hundred yards on the right, and four hundred yards on the left-centre. It does not look much on the map, but in practice it meant a great deal, for it gave the allied troops just living room on the tip of the peninsula, enabling them to scatter sufficiently in bivouacs in a network of narrow ditches, to avoid annihilation from the high-placed enemy batteries. Sir Ian Hamilton confessed that it was only on May 10, 1915, that he felt that his footing below Achi Baba was fairly secure.

General Liman von Sanders showed an instant appreciation of the advantages won by the attacking troops. He made a furious attempt in the night to drive the allied line back; but after a desperate hand-to-hand conflict, the French and British retained the whole of their newly-won position. For the first time for eighteen days and nights the half-shattered but indomitable 29th Division was able to have an ordinary sleep. It was a sleep disturbed by shells, as the men were only drawn back to the dug-outs near the beach, while the newly-arrived 42nd Division took their places in the firing-trench. But even a dug-out with howitzer shell interludes was a place of peace and repose after the events of the preceding three weeks.

By this time the weary attacking troops had exhausted all opportunities of surprise and initiative. The enemy was well aware of their numbers and dispositions, and as the British were in possession of the Turks' first line of defence, no more battles in the open were possible. All further advances had to be conducted by the method of siege warfare, in which the ground was very gradually won by local efforts, after slow, methodical preparation. Sir Ian Hamilton prepared this change of tactics by arranging all his artillery under a central fire control, so that all the heavy pieces and most of the light pieces could be switched together by telephone for an intensive bombardment of a short section of the hostile front. The guns of the fleet were similarly placed under a central control by means of wireless stations, and the machine-guns were set in carefully chosen redoubts to strengthen the system of trenches.

Meanwhile the officer commanding the 6th Gurkhas had begun on his own initiative the new method of advancing by local efforts. Between Krithia and the open sea there was a deep river bed, known on the map as the Saghir Dere, and known in the camp as Gully Ravine, and crowned seaward by a steep bluff. Below the bluff was Y Beach, where some of the troops had fought their first landing battle. Since then the enemy had transformed the bluff into a powerful fortress, from which a number of machine-guns had continually broken up the left wing of the British attacks. To assail the fortified cliff across the gully was madness, but the Gurkhas worked their way along the shore, and then started in the darkness to crawl up the steep height on their hands and knees. They reached the top, but failed to surprise the enemy, who beat them back with a sweeping fire.

The Gurkhas, however, had shown how the bluff could be captured, and the next day Major-General H. V. Fox, commanding the 29th Indian infantry brigade, devised plans for a concerted attack. This was carried out in the evening of May 12, when the Manchester Brigade made a feint on the right of the enemy's position. The guns of the Dublin and Talbot opened fire seaward on the Turkish trenches, while the guns and howitzers of one of the British divisions kept up a heavy shell fire from the land. Evening deepened into night, and the great bluff flamed with bursting shell that kept the Turks below their parapets. Then again in the darkness a double company of

Gurkhas crept along the shore, and scaling the cliff, carried the position with a rush. They were followed by their machine-gun section, and another double company of their battalion, and when dawn broke the conquered position had been connected with the main line, advancing the British left flank by nearly five hundred yards.

Nothing of much importance was done for another fortnight. During this time the hardest work fell on the sappers, who tried to work up within rushing distance of the enemy's second line by means of winding saps from which the troops could debouch. On May 25 the Royal Naval Division and the 42nd Division were able to entrench a hundred yards nearer the Turks, and four days afterwards the entire British line was helped onward by means of engineers' work. At the same time the French force also progressed and captured a machine-gun redoubt on the ridge going down to the Kereves Ravine. But all this slow movement of approach against the hostile mountain fortress was suddenly complicated by a series of naval disasters. Some German submarines worked down to the Dardanelles in the third week in May, and all British naval dispositions and transport work were abruptly checked.

The Goliath, an old battleship but a useful one, had already been sunk by a Turkish destroyer. This disaster was followed by the torpedoing of the Triumph on May 26 and of the Majestic on May 27. The position then became serious. The large steamers which had been supplying the troops with food and ammunition could no longer be safely used, and it seemed at first as if the Germans and Austrians had only to send half a dozen more submarines to the Dardanelles in order to maroon the troops on the Gallipoli peninsula. It was a situation to test to the uttermost the ability of the British sailor; but by fine ingenuity and inventiveness he saved the army which he had put ashore with such remarkable skill. All the transports were sent into Mudros Bay, where there was only a narrow channel to guard. Men, stores, guns, and horses were henceforth conveyed across forty miles of water from Mudros to the peninsula in mine-sweepers and other small, shallow vessels, which did not lie deep enough in the water for a torpedo to strike them at the ordinary depth. Then the large warships, whose guns were very useful, and sometimes of vital value in the military operations, were sheltered near the shore by means

of submarine defences, while destroyers and patrol boats tracked
the hostile under-water craft and assailed them in various ways.

During the first phase of the submarine menace, when it was
doubtful if disaster was not impending, Sir Ian Hamilton planned
another attack on the Turkish position. He was ably seconded
by General Hunter-Weston. The French expeditionary force
now commanded by General Gouraud brought up two divisions
to act round Kereves Dere. Almost every night the Turks
assailed the allied line, hoping, no doubt, to find that the
attacking troops were weakening under the submarine menace.
But the British positions remained intact, and Sir Ian Hamilton
on June 3, 1915, made his first deliberate assault on the Achi
Baba fortifications. For his line of battle he deployed the
29th Division on his left, the 42nd (East Lancashire) Division
in his centre, with the Naval Division linking on with the French.

General Sir A. Hunter-Weston, who was directing the British
troops on a front of four thousand yards, had about 17,000 men
in the firing-line, with 7,000 men in reserve. The action began
on the morning of June 4 with a preliminary bombardment
which lasted for more than three hours, after which the British
troops moved out on a feint attack to draw the fire of the
enemy's artillery and machine-guns. The device was successful,
and amid a heavy fire the British artillery renewed its bombardment with increasing intensity, being able to mark more
exactly the hostile targets. Precisely at noon the range of the
guns was lengthened, and the entire British line charged.
Both the French divisions moved forward at the same time.

The Lancashire territorials and the new recruits of the Anson,
Howe, and Hood battalions of the Naval Division did extremely
well. They captured the first Turkish line in front of them in
from five to 15 minutes, and then burst through the second
Turkish line in another spurt. In less than half an hour the
men of the East Lancashire Division and the Naval Division had
penetrated a third of a mile in the enemy's front, and were
consolidating the conquered ground. The 29th Division was less
fortunate, as its left wing was held up by a wire entanglement,
so placed as to have escaped damage from the British shells.
It was an Indian brigade that was checked in this manner, and
though a company of the 6th Gurkhas battered their way into
the Turkish works, they had to be withdrawn with the rest of
the brigade in order to avoid being cut off.

While a fresh attack was being organized, the French corps on the British right got also into difficulties. The 1st French Division carried the opposing enemy trench, while the 2nd Division stormed in a magnificent fashion the strong Turkish redoubt on the Kereves Ridge, known as the Haricot. But the French left wing, acting on the right flank of the Naval Division, was unable to gain any ground, and this led to a disaster. In the afternoon the Turks, pouring out through the series of communication trenches, delivered a massed counter-attack on the Haricot redoubt, while their guns prepared the way for them with a storm of shrapnel and high-explosive shell. The French lost the redoubt and fell back, and in so doing completely uncovered the right flank of the Naval Division. The men of the 2nd Naval Brigade were enfiladed and forced to retire with heavy losses from the position they had captured, and the Collingwood battalion, which had gone forward in support, was almost completely destroyed.

It looked as though the Turks were about to roll up the whole of the attacking line, for when the Naval Brigade was compelled to retreat across the open, sloping fields under a terrible fire, the exposed flank of the Manchester Brigade was in turn caught by Turkish and German machine-guns, and swept by volleys of rifle fire, and then hammered by hostile bombing-parties. But the Manchester men—nearly all of them territorials—fought with great courage to hold what they had won.

The fighting around Krithia in the afternoon of June 4, 1915, was a matter upon which every territorial can look back with deep pride. The Manchester Brigade equalled the finest exploits of the old regular army. They answered the attack on their flank by throwing back their right wing. Their position was one of extreme peril, for they were surrounded on two sides, and the Turks were making a sustained and furious effort to drive across the salient and cut off the brigade. So the British commander-in-chief formed up the Naval Division, and asked General Gouraud to co-operate in making an attack that should advance the right of the British line, and connect and protect the flank of the Manchester men. But the French corps was itself still in great difficulties. Twice the attack was postponed at the request of General Gouraud, and at half-past six in the evening he reported that the pressure of the Turkish masses against him was so heavy that he could not advance.

Nothing remained but to withdraw the Manchester men from the second Turkish line which they were holding to the first Turkish line. The net result of the day's operations was an advance on a depth of 200 to 400 yards, along a front of nearly three miles. It was less than had been hoped for, but it was still a very considerable gain. Not only was there a substantial and very useful extension of ground, but the Turks were so severely punished that, though flushed with the victory of regaining their second line, they had not enough spirit left to attempt a counter-attack to recover their firing-trenches and forward machine-gun redoubts. Four hundred prisoners were taken, including five German officers, who were the remnant of a machine-gun party from the Goeben. Most of the captures were made by the Lancashire territorials, whose divisional commander was Major-General W. Douglas.

General Gouraud was not the kind of man to rest under the loss of the Haricot redoubt. This maze of trenches and communicating saps, with its machine-gun emplacements, commanded the top of the ravine of Kereves Dere, and threw a deadly enfilading fire along the allied front. It had to be captured. Therefore at dawn on June 21 the French commander launched both of his divisions against the Kereves ridge. The 1st Division, forming the right wing, stormed through a Turkish advanced trench, only to be counter-attacked and driven out; for the German engineers had arranged a fan-work of saps by which the Turks could advance safely through shell fire and continually reinforce the fighting-line. Meanwhile the 2nd Division had driven through Two Turkish lines and re-captured the Haricot fort. When their comrades on the right retired, the Turks took the victors of the Haricot position on their flank, and got them in a position similar to that in which the Manchester Brigade had been caught.

But the French would not give up their conquest, and while they were hanging on desperately, Gouraud sent up his 1st Division in assault after assault. Just as the sky was shading over at evening, some of the latest recruits of the French Army, striplings of the new drafts, fought their way up the ridge with the impassioned courage of youth, and in ten minutes captured six hundred yards of the enemy's trenches. There were Zouaves and men of the Foreign Legion in the two victorious battalions, but these veterans were the first to praise the lads of the 1915 class. All the night the Turks counter-attacked, and their violent efforts to return into the Haricot redoubt did not cease till June 23, by which time some seven thousand of them lay dead or wounded in front of the French firing line. The French losses were heavy, amounting to two thousand five hundred men, but they had gained a very important position, and had annihilated the best part of a Turkish division.

After this blow against the Turkish left on the ridge over-looking the Strait, it was the turn of Hunter-Weston to hammer at the enemy's right on the cliff overlooking the open sea. The Turks had all along held with great tenacity to the coast, where their position was one of extraordinary strength, owing to the deep ravine running between Krithia and the sea. Near the shore the Turks had a formidable system of five lines, prolonged inland by two trenches. The ravine, the famous Gully Ravine, stretching inland in the neighbourhood of Gurkha Bluff and twisting in a north-eastern trend between overhanging hills, was two hundred feet high in places, and covered with thick green undergrowth. There was good water in the ravine, which in-creased its value. Therefore the Turks held to it with all their might. General Hunter-Weston drew up a scheme of attack, the feature of which was a peculiar pivoting movement, and he put it into action on the morning of June 28. His design was to hold the enemy at a spot about a mile from the coast, and, on this pivoting point, swing his left flank upwards and through the Turkish positions.

The movement began by the Border regiment rushing a redoubt known as the Boomerang, when the wire entanglements had been smashed by a brief, intense burst of gun fire. A few minutes afterwards the 87th Brigade stormed three lines of Turkish trenches, while the Royal Scots advanced and took the two trenches in front of them. Then, as this first British wave spread out and flattened over the conquered ground, the 86th Brigade, led by the 2nd Royal Welsh Fusiliers, pushed through the three lines captured by their comrades and bayoneted the Turks out of their last two lines of trenches. It took scarcely more than half an hour for the two brigades of the indomitable 29th Division to carry all the five Turkish lines, and their swift hammer-stroke was consummated by the success of the Indian Brigade, which secured a spur running into the sea from the rearmost Turkish trench. The gully, with its solid hedge of barbed-wire was not attacked until the high ground on either side was won. Then the barbed fence was left uninjured, to hold back the Turks in the ravine, who were hurled down and trapped by their own defences. Altogether the enemy was driven back along the coast for a thousand yards, enabling the British left flank to establish itself firmly high up the coast, and prevent any enfilading fire against its centre.

The importance of the advance was seen by the way in which Ali Riza Pasha, the commander at Achi Baba, and his superior, Liman von Sanders, regarded it. For many nights and days they launched the Turkish infantry from Achi Baba in heavy counter-attacks, until the best part of another Turkish division was vainly destroyed. In front of Krithia and Achi Baba the laborious Turk constructed by the end of June the finest modern fortress in existence. It was a network of trenches and earthwork forts, all protected by barbed-wire, and linked by saps and communication trenches. No infantry could storm the position, because all the works and all the approaches, including the embarkation beaches, were swept by a cross-fire of artillery from the commanding heights of Achi Baba and from mobile batteries working near In Tepe, on the Asiatic shore, close to the buried ruins of Troy.

Sir Ian Hamilton had not sufficient men or sufficient heavy howitzers and high-explosive shell to tear through the lines around Achi Baba. Still less did he possess, in the region dominated by the higher peak of Sari Bair, the means of forcing his way across the five miles of broken rock and dense shrub to the forts guarding the Narrows. His position for the time was one of stalemate, but it was one in which stalemate meant defeat.

Sir Ian Hamilton asked for a larger force, and the Dardanelles Committee in Downing Street managed to arrange for the despatch of modest reinforcements, which would arrive at Mudros base by about the middle of August. In the meantime the British commander had to keep the enemy in check, and so daunt him by constant attacks as to reduce him to a defensive attitude. After the advance by the French on Kereves Dere on June 21 the enemy had counter-attacked in a desperate fashion day and night for a week, winning only a transient footing between two of the lost trenches. The Turks, who recaptured the lines by a violent night assault, were surrounded at daybreak and either slain or taken prisoners. All the hostile efforts to recover the ground slackened completely by June 30, and at this sign of weakening Gouraud struck out again.

At early morn on June 30 the French left wing charged under cover of massed gun fire and stormed a subterranean fortress at the head of Kereves Dere, known as the Quadrilateral. It consisted of seven deeply-cut lines, connected by shrapnel proof communications and defended by machine-guns. Some platoons of the Colonial infantry swept over their objective in the vehemence of their movement, and drove some hundreds of yards beyond it. They were encircled, but they fought their way back to the Quadrilateral with but slight loss. In the afternoon came the inevitable Turkish counter-attack against their lost redoubt, but despite the large mass of troops employed by the enemy commander, he won back no ground, and his forces were so severely punished that the customary nocturnal counter-attack was not delivered.

In the meantime the Australians and New Zealanders, now known as the Anzacs, had been fiercely attacked in the position, now called Anzac cove, which they held. The Australasians were perched upon the cliff below Sari Bair, where their immediate purpose was to hold up as large an enemy force as possible, thus lessening the pressure on the 8th army corps and the French army corps along the Krithia front. They also kept open the gateway to the vitals of the Turkish positions along the Strait, but the British commander designed this rather as a demonstration than a serious line of attack. As Sir Ian Hamilton remarked in his despatch, the Australians and New Zealanders were not able to fulfil the part allotted to them and play second fiddle to their comrades round Krithia. Their dare-devil spirit would not let them rest on the defensive, and from the moment they landed they protected themselves by attacking and continuing to attack. Their position round Anzac cove was a rough semicircle, with a radius of about 1,100 yards. The farthest point was Quinn's Post, consisting of ledges on the brink of a precipice, falling for two hundred feet almost plumb to the valley below. The Turkish line was only a few feet away, and, by a surprise attack, an enemy brigade captured some of the fire trenches on the ledge on May 10. But the Australians sold the ground dearly.

At Anzac there was no room to live. The position was far worse than at Krithia, where the two attacking army corps had a large plateau on which to bivouac and shelter. The men of Anzac had only a footing on a single scrubby ridge by the edge of the sea, and their entire position was open to close-range shell fire from the amphitheatre of sombre heights immediately around them. In point of range the Turkish rifles could reach every spot in Anzac; it was only the lee side of Maclagan's Ridge and of the neighbouring lower fall of cliff by the water's edge that saved the men from direct fire. The enemy's howitzer batteries could pitch their shells everywhere, and the Turkish and German guns, operating on the mountains, had an easy plunging fire on nearly all the trenches. As many as 1,400 shells an hour fell at times on Anzac, the calibre of the projectiles ranging from 11 in. high-explosive to 3 in. field shrapnel.

Gun fire, however, could not dislodge the Australasians, so on May 18 General Liman von Sanders came to Sari Bair and used 30,000 troops in an attempt to close the gateway to the Narrows. After a heavy bombardment, lasting twenty hours, the German commander-in-chief launched, before dawn on May 19, a great infantry attack against the left flank and centre of Anzac. Six waves of Turkish infantry were broken by the New Zealanders and Australians by sunrise, and the men on the right flank at Quinn's Post and Courtney's Post, both south-west of the main masses of Sari Bair, also repulsed furious attacks on the right flank. Then at five o'clock in the morning, when the air cleared, a large additional number of enemy guns, of 12 in. and 9.2 calibre, intensified the cannonade, and after four and a half hours of fighting the Turkish infantry on the British right flank began to press hard against Courtney's and Quinn's Posts. This vehement attack, however, was so severely handled by the Australians on the British right that the column swung away and tried to advance towards the left. But again it was caught by machine-gun fire and gusts of shrapnel, and the Turks at last drew back beyond Quinn's Post at eleven o'clock in the morning, and gave way in their crowded trenches under the searching artillery fire.

The Australasians had only 100 killed and 500 wounded, while, plainly visible in front of their trenches, were thousands of dead Turks. Fighting went on around Quinn's Post for five weeks, but in the meanwhile Enver Pasha, the leader of the Young Turks, who had become all-powerful in Turkey, had decided that a great effort must be made to drive the invaders from Gallipoli. This was to be done by direct attack with an overwhelming force and after careful artillery preparation. On June 29 with thirty fresh battalions and a great mass of artillery, he began his attack upon the Anzac position. Every gun or howitzer was worked as quickly as possible for an hour and a half, and all the Turkish trenches were tipped with darts of flame from the rifles of the infantry, and with the steadier blazes of the machine-guns.

Only twelve hours before, during General Hunter-Weston's drive along Gully Ravine, near Krithia, the enemy batteries on Achi Baba had seemed to be short of ammunition; but it was patent that, at Sari Bair at least, Enver Pasha had hurried from Constantinople with large fresh supplies and charges, in addition to his reinforcement of thirty more battalions of new troops. Yet the unexpected bombardment at Anzac did not produce on the well-constructed and deep trenches and dug-outs the effect intended. For each heavy column of Turks was shattered before it reached the Anzac trenches. First the troops under Major-General Sir A. J. Godley knocked a great column to pieces simply by musketry and machine-gun fire. All the British guns were laid on their targets, but they did not come into operation until the grand Turkish attack was launched on a wide, deep front. The conflict scarcely lasted an hour, and by half-past two in the morning of June 30 none of Enver's men remained in the open ground between the trenches. Out at sea the British destroyers had caught them with an enfilading fire; heavy howitzers had torn great holes in the columns, while field-guns swept the charging multitudes with direct fire.

The Turk displayed remarkable bravery of a characteristically apathetic kind. He came on with fixed bayonet, apparently quite indifferent to death. On the other hand, little or no organized use was made of this personal attitude of courage of the enemy private. There was no science in the leadership of the company officers. Before each attack the battalions were massed under cover of some rising ground or shrub; but when the mass emerged for the bayonet charge against the British position, it seemed more a mediæval swarm of fighting men than a modern military machine. No regular formation was apparent, and no telling manœuvre under fire produced any surprise effect. Leaving the invincible men of Anzac to Essad

Pasha, Enver went to the south of the peninsula with ten thousand new levies from Asia, and a great banner was hoisted on Achi Baba to announce his arrival. The local general was still opposed to any attempt to recover the lost ground, and wanted merely to strengthen the trenches and await the next Franco-British advance.

But Enver Pasha was determined to carry out his own plan, and he delivered his attack from Achi Baba on the night of July 4, 1915. There was the customary artillery preparation by the batteries on the European and Asiatic shores of the Dardanelles. Fire was opened on the first lines of the British and French troops, and curtained off the support trenches with a rain of shrapnel. The men of Anzac were also kept occupied by a furious bombardment, in which a ship of the Barbarossa class stationed in the Narrows assisted. The battle began about three o'clock in the morning of July 5. The inexperienced Turkish levies were allowed to approach the British and French trenches, and were shot down almost at point-blank range. Very few of them were able to retire. The principal attack was made at the point where the British Naval Division connected with the French.

Some 50 Turks gained a footing in one trench, only to be destroyed. The 29th Division wiped out their enemies by musketry and machine-gun fire, and along Gully Ravine, where the Turks massed in great force, they were broken by naval guns and infantry volleys. By noon the battle ended. Not a single allied position had been seriously menaced, but the Turks' casualties were heavy. The British losses were also great, being due to a few Turkish high-explosive shells bursting exactly in the trenches. In the evening a large squadron of allied seaplanes circled over Krithia, in spite of the strong wind, and darted over the Strait to the town of Chanak, on the Asiatic shore. There the Germans had built their aerodrome, and the structure was bombed and set on fire as an answer to a bombing sally made by the German airmen early in the morning.

By this time British submarines, having crept safely through the mine-fields in the Narrows, and established themselves firmly in the Sea of Marmora, began to exert an important effect upon the course of operations; for they seriously restricted the transport of troops from the Asiatic coast, and took to shelling the convoys and columns winding down along the road near the shore. Then on Monday, July 12, Sir Ian Hamilton, pursuing his design to daunt the enemy, delivered another furious assault on the lines round Achi Baba. He used a new instrument of attack, consisting of an armoured motor car, with iron hooks attached to short chains. The plan was for a number of these cars to dart towards the wire entanglements of the Turks and fling the great hooks over the obstacle, and then drive back at full speed, while using the guns against the troops defending the trenches. It was calculated that large gaps could thus be made more quickly than the entanglements could be broken with shrapnel by field guns.

The attack began in the usual way with a terrific bombardment, but, instead of throwing the shells all along the hostile front, the central fire control massed the fire on the enemy's centre, where a territorial brigade flung out and, smashing through two of the enemy's lines, just reached the third Turkish position. Then the advanced troops were forced back, and as they failed to establish a connection with the French on their right, there was severe hand-to-hand fighting on the exposed flank. Meanwhile the French also stormed two strongly-fortified lines near Kereves Dere, and the combined attack drove back the Turks on Achi Baba to a depth of some four hundred yards.

Naturally the Turkish commander concentrated for an attempt to win back the lost ground. As, however, his reserves came up the communicating trenches with their supplies of hand-bombs, the 29th Division rushed into action at an unexpected point. On the left of the British front, just by the Achi Baba gully, the Turks had built a powerful rectangular redoubt, perched on the edge of the ravine, down which machine-guns were concealed. At four o'clock in the afternoon, when trench warfare was raging furiously on the centre and the right wing, all the available guns were suddenly turned on the Achi Baba nullah earthworks. Hundreds of high-explosive shells burst in trenches and saps, throwing up masses of earth, sand-bags, and wooden beams. The Turks scurried down the communicating trenches, but the gunners lengthened their range and reached the enemy's reserve positions, while a battleship pitched 12 in. shells on the Turkish observation station on Achi Baba.

As the smoke was lifting from the battered nullah redoubt, a British brigade charged forward, and the enemy's batteries, which had been waiting for this movement, tried to counter it

by smashing up the redoubt with shrapnel and explosive shell.
The ground about the ravine steamed like an active volcano,
but the British troops leapt through the tornado of death and,
capturing the position, found what shelter they could in the
twice-battered trenches. There was a considerable number of
Turks taking shelter in dug-outs amid the earthworks, and so
bravely did they stand their ground, with steel and hand
grenades, that it looked for a moment as if they would keep
the position. But the Scotsmen who had made the charge
continued their work with the bayonet, and after an underground
fight of an hour and a half, all the works were captured.

The artillery contributed greatly to this success. Throughout
the furious combat it maintained so thick a curtain of shrapnel
that the Turkish reserves could not get into the fight. In this
manner another four hundred yards of ground were won. In
the night the Turks sought to retrieve their defeat. The Turkish
brigadier-generals varied their efforts to counter-attack. Some
launched their infantry in bayonet charges, all of which were
beaten back; others sent their men creeping up through the
low scrub and the saps with girdles of bombs. These bombing
parties were the most formidable of the assailants, and at the
point where the British right wing had advanced too far and
got out of touch with the French left, a section of the trenches
was recaptured by the Turkish bomb throwers. But some French
gunners swung up their " 75's," and, using melinite shell, cleared
a path for one of the naval brigades, which hacked its way
into the midst of the bomb throwers and slew them.

In order further to occupy the enemy the French general
suddenly thrust out his extreme right wing, and made the
important gain of all the ground right down to the mouth of the
River Kereves Dere, where it runs into the sea. These and
other small local successes, however, together with the increasing
activity of British submarines, did not have any important effect
upon the general position. The enemy's main works of defence,
which protected the forts along the Dardanelles, were as strong
as they had been three months before.

CHAPTER 9

Second Battle of Ypres (I)

THE early days of April, 1915, were occupied by the British in taking over from the French a further five miles of front between the Ypres-Menin road and the Ypres-Poelcapelle road. This increased the length of line held by Sir John French to thirty miles. The new trenches were, in many cases, in a very poor condition, and everything possible was done by way of revetment to strengthen them. In some places the nature of the ground made anything but very shallow trenches impracticable, for if dug deep they became little else than running dikes, and in such a case it was necessary to erect breastworks which would at least be bullet proof. Everywhere, too, an effort was made to protect the front line with adequate barbed wire entanglements. An interval of comparative quiet was utilised in the same manner by the Germans, who had far better material resources for this kind of work.

About the middle of the month warnings began to reach the allied commands that, before their next attack, the Germans intended to use asphyxiating gas to be projected along the ground against the defending troops. A prisoner, captured by the French, gave a circumstantial account of having seen cylinders of gas in position in the trenches. He gave the date of the attack as April 15, and professed himself well acquainted with the German plans and dispositions. Indeed it seemed to the French general Putz that he knew far too much for a private soldier, and had probably been sent over deliberately to mislead with a cock-and-bull story. He was, in fact, right in his details, for an attack by gas had been intended for April 15 and was only postponed because the wind was unfavourable.

But this prisoner's treachery was not the only source of warning. From Belgian agents came the news that respirators for the German troops were being made in great quantities in Ghent. But one sign alone, it has been pointed out, should have been sufficient to warn the allied leaders of the gravity of the threat. Recently the German Press had published accusations that poison gases had been used by their enemies, thus paving the way for a necessary " reprisal." Not for the last time did they use this ingenious method of finding justification for some new " frightfulness." At least they could make use of the fact that this method of warfare was the invention of an English chemist, and had been offered for use in the Russo-Japanese war.

But however they sought to justify the use of a method of warfare condemned by international agreement, they certainly achieved a remarkable degree of surprise when they first let loose their gas clouds. Whether the French and English commanders can be held entirely blameless in neglecting rumours and reports, passing them on " for what they were worth," and making no provision for protection against gas is open to question. When as afterwards happened thousands of home-made respirators began to reach the front, troops who had suffered in the first attacks must have wondered why some such simple provision could not have been made for them in the first instance. It is said that the allied commands could not believe that the Germans would so transgress the rules of war as to use gas, but this can be no excuse for a lethargy which condemned thousands to injury and death.

For a time the looked-for attack did not develop, aerial reconnaissance detected no new activity which might be expected to precede a coming battle, and in the meantime the assault on Hill 60 diverted the attention of the higher command from rumours which, in any case, they discredited.

The famous Hill 60 is a low, artificial eminence, raised by the earth dug from a railway cutting, two and a half miles south of Ypres, and between the villages of Zillebeke and Hollebeke. It had come into the possession of the Germans in December, 1914, and was of tactical importance, as the fire from it enfiladed the British position in the Ypres salient, and the summit gave the Germans good observation of the British movements. During April six mines were run under it by Northumbrian and Monmouthshire troops, each containing a ton of explosives, though owing to the wetness of the ground mining operations here were of peculiar difficulty. The date fixed for their explosion was April 17.

The explosions took place at 7.0 p.m. They were immediately followed by an artillery barrage, and the storming parties of the Royal West Kent, the K.O.S.B., with a machine-gun section of the Queen Victoria's Rifles, were consolidating their capture within a quarter of an hour. The German artillery was immediately turned on them, and all through the night of April 17-18 German bombing parties attacked, working forward amidst the numerous shell craters which covered the slopes of the hill. At dawn there was a more resolute advance by the Germans, and they actually reached the crest, on part of which they established themselves. In the evening of the 18th the British infantry once more assaulted this German lodgment and cleared it out after a desperate struggle in which the British losses were over 1,500. Next day the Germans redoubled their bombardment, with serious effect.

The summit was small and only a few men could be stationed on it without dangerous overcrowding. All April 19, 20, and 21, the crest was held, though the casualties multiplied fearfully. By the night of April 21, when the Germans temporarily ceased their attacks and relaxed the vehemence of their fire, the British losses on the hill exceeded 100 officers and 3,000 men.

Anticipating events which were to follow elsewhere, it may be added that Hill 60 remained in British hands without challenge until May 1, when the Germans attempted to overwhelm its small garrison with chlorine gas, discharged from cylinders, and did actually kill or put temporarily out of action most of the garrison, but they were not able to establish themselves in the British works owing to the fumes.

On May 5 they repeated this gas attack and rendered the sole British trench on the summit untenable, seizing it when the fumes were dissipated. Thus, the crest once more passed into their possession, though the British could not be dislodged from the western slope, to which they clung resolutely. As may be imagined the assault on Hill 60 gave many opportunities for deeds of gallantry and, in all, four V.C.'s were awarded for conspicuous heroism during the fighting on April 20-21. One of these was earned by 2nd Lieutenant G. H. Woolley, of the 9th London regiment (Queen Victoria's Rifles), who was the first Territorial officer to receive the decoration.

In the meantime the entire salient of Ypres had become the scene of a long and desperate battle. The British delay in resuming the offensive after Neuve Chapelle was an undisguised revelation of weakness, and the German Staff decided therefore to attack. Reinforcements were sent through Belgium. In the matter of men, however, the odds were not against the British 2nd army. Falkenhayn, who directed the operations, was not relying on infantry power. In this respect he had had a severe lesson at Ypres in the autumn, and he profited by it. He had resources of artillery which still gave him overwhelming superiority in gun fire. He brought up the great Krupp naval guns, and the howitzers which had been used along the Belgian coast in repelling Admiral Hood's battleships and monitors.

This new siege train was placed in position against Ypres, and provisioned with an extraordinary amount of shells. But even this was not enough to ensure absolute success. So a new weapon of destruction was brought to the front. All along the German lines round Ypres—northward, southward, and eastward—gas-cylinders, it appears, were placed as early as March 30. Each steel cylinder was about fifty-three inches long, and was filled with chlorine. The cylinders were stored in bomb-proof casemates, in the proportion of one to every six and a half feet of the front. The officers directing the gas operations then waited until the wind was in an easterly or north-easterly direction. They had a long time to wait as the south-westerly spring breezes were blowing.

They patiently whiled away the time by putting their troops through the respirator drill. For more than three weeks the Germans vainly waited for a steady, favouring wind. It never came, and on Thursday, April 22, they resolved to profit by a south-easterly wind blowing towards the French part of the front, north of Ypres. Here a French Colonial division of Zouaves and Turcos held the line stretching from Dixmude to Langemarck. Behind them was the Yser canal, and in front of them a tract of wooded country held by part of the Duke of Württemberg's army. At Langemarck the allied line was continued by the men of the Canadian division under General Alderson. Behind the Canadians was the village of St. Julien, and on their right was Zonnebeke and the Roulers road, from which the line swerved round south-west to Hill 60. The German general calculated that, if the French Colonial division was broken north of Ypres, the line of the Canadians could be turned and then Ypres could be captured in a sudden, driving, overwhelming sweep.

The morning of April 22 broke fine, and nothing remarkable occurred during the early part of the day except an unusually heavy bombardment of the Ypres neighbourhood. This was intensified about 5.0 p.m., and it was at this hour that the gas-cylinders were opened. The gas had been pumped in under great pressure, so that when the cylinders were opened it spurted out with great force, and did not float upon the wind until it was some distance from the German trenches. There, losing its impetus, it gathered into a low-lying cloud of greenish colour, which turned yellow as it streamed upwards. The ghastly fog-bank drifted slowly down the wind, remaining thick on the ground owing to the density of the gases, and pouring into the French trenches and surprising all the troops there.

First their eyes began to smart under the influence of the poisonous vapour, then the deadly chlorine acted on the membrane of their throats, and so thickened it that they began to choke. Last, and worst of all, the chlorine entered the delicate fabric of the lungs and ate it away with a torturing, burning effect, leaving the helpless victims outstretched in the trenches, fighting in vain for air, and perishing in agonies. It is recorded that those who stayed in their position suffered less than those who ran away—for the action of running accelerated the effect of the poison. Those who stood on their fire-step or even mounted their parapets felt the least effect. Those who suffered most cruelly were the wounded who fell to the ground and could not be removed.

There was no defence against the gas. The unprepared Frenchmen and Algerians either died, or fell back towards the Yser canal, half blind, and suffering greatly. Then behind the gas-cloud came the German troops. Their advanced outposts wore gas-proof helmets, while the main force of infantry was provided with respirator masks. They brought up machine-guns and occupied the low ridges north of Ypres, and forced a passage across the canal by Steenstraete and Het Sas villages, and constructed fortified bridge-heads on the western bank. Thirty guns were captured, including four 4.7 British guns which had been lent by the Canadian division to strengthen the lines held by their French comrades.

The position of the Canadian division was then one of extreme peril. They were holding a line of about 5,000 yards, with two brigades in the trenches and the third in reserve. The 3rd brigade had joined on with the French line at Poelcapelle. The 2nd brigade continued the British line down towards

Zonnebeke. Brigadier-General Turner, of the 3rd brigade, ordered up his 3rd battalion as soon as the attack started, and Canadian artillery was sent to support the French. Nearly all the Zouaves and French territorials, who held positions on the left, were in flight; but next door to the Canadians a battalion of Tirailleurs, who had suffered less from the gas, stood their ground. But a very considerable gap, from Steenstraat on the left to Poelcapelle towards the centre of the salient, had been made, and through this the Germans began to advance.

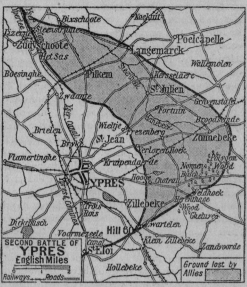

Amidst the confusion it was at first thought that the Canadians had been driven back, but four hours afterwards, at 8.25 p.m., Brigadier-General Turner reported that his line still held. It was, however, becoming obvious at G.H.Q. that a very serious situation had arisen, and reserves were hurried up to the threatened flank; but so extensive was the gap that the new flank could, in any case, be little more than an outpost line. Later reports showed how grave the danger was, for the gap, which at first had been thought to be 3,000 yards in length, was in reality 8,000 yards and the way was clear to Ypres. Fortunately for the British, the Germans showed no inclination to push on farther that evening. They dug themselves in and allowed a further respite to the British to bring up reinforcements. Their shell fire, however, did not cease, and attacks on the line held by the British 27th and 28th divisions, though they were repulsed, tied possible reinforcements to that sector.

The Canadians held their ground and at midnight launched the counter-attack which was one of the most dashing features of the action. In front of the Canadian Scottish of the 3rd brigade and the 10th battalion of the 3rd brigade was a wood, known as Kitchener's Wood, containing the four lost guns that had been lent to the French. The trees could be seen in the light of the misty moon about five hundred yards away. The wood was occupied by 7,000 German troops, who had built forts defended by machine-gun parties with sand-bags. No enemy was visible as Colonel Leckie led the Canadian Scottish forward and Colonel Russell Boyle led out his 10th battalion. But when the leading companies were in the hollow, about two hundred yards from the mass of trees, the line of hostile machine-guns squirted upon them a continuous sheet of bullets.

Yet the four charging lines never wavered. When one man fell another took his place. The survivors of the two battalions burst over the low ridge and through the hedge where the Germans were entrenched, and then entered the shadowy wood. Here it was wild hand-to-hand fighting in clumps and batches amid the brushwood, the Canadians having only their rifles against the machine-gun forts forming the German support line. Their casualties were very severe, the two battalions being reduced to ten officers and 400 men, and with so light a force they could not possibly hold such an advanced position without support. This was not forthcoming, and, the French offering no assistance, it was decided to withdraw from this advanced position to one south-east of the wood. It had been " a true counter-attack," and had been carried out " with rapidity, decision, and courage." As a feat of arms it redounded greatly to the credit of the Canadian forces.

The general position by the morning of April 23 was far from reassuring, but some kind of outpost line had been established throughout the length of the gap. Ten battalions were in position, although far from being in continuous touch. Nor were they properly entrenched or protected by barbed wire.

It appeared afterwards that the tactics which were being employed by the Germans were directed towards securing a limited objective and that there was no intention of pushing the attack at once to its possible conclusion. This method of capturing a desired line, holding and consolidating it until the attacking force is ready to make another well-prepared leap forward, is one that became very familiar as the war progressed. Sir Douglas Haig employed it on the Somme and throughout the 3rd battle of Ypres; but in 1915 it represented a new form of tactics and explained the action of the Germans on the night of April 22 in digging in and attempting no further advance.

On the morning of April 23, therefore, there were no signs of any great reinforcement of the German line and British counter-operations which had been started the evening before were continued. On this morning the first very primitive protections were suggested against a repetition of gas attacks. Troops were advised to dip their handkerchiefs in water, or, if they could obtain them, use respirators made of lint and tape dipped in a solution of bicarbonate of soda; but to units in the most exposed positions neither lint nor tape nor bicarbonate could have been available. Shortly afterwards also an appeal was made to willing workers at home to set about making respirators of gauze and cotton, which was naturally responded to most eagerly. But the bulk of the defending troops were still without any adequate protection and having seen the terrible effects of the gas attack of the day before it is remarkable, to say the least, that they should have stood so steadfastly in the face of a recurring menace.

On April 22 a detachment of four English battalions—the 4th Rifle Brigade, the 2nd K.S.L.I., the 2nd Buffs, and the 3rd Middlesex—which were in reserve billets had been detailed to the assistance of the Canadians. This force with a divisional engineer company (2nd Wessex) reached St. Jean on the morning of April 23 and was placed under the command of the senior officer, Colonel Geddes of the Buffs. Hence it was known as the Geddes detachment.

Colonel Geddes received orders on the morning of the 23rd to join up with the Canadians at Kitchener's Wood, a mile southeast of St. Julien and extending his force left to get in touch with the French, and so proceed to clear up any German forces which might have established themselves in this gap. Colonel Geddes had only a small staff to keep touch with his scattered force, and it was impossible for him to complete his arrangements and make a start with the attack until daylight. This proceeded gradually, not without considerable German opposition. The Canadians advanced simultaneously and three battalions of Zouaves on the left were also thrown into the fight.

It resulted in a fairly continuous line being formed from the former Canadian left flank to a point 1,200 yards from the Yser canal. To north and south of this new left flank French territorials still held a line which was for the greater part of its length on the north bank of the canal, but had been forced back over the south bank between Het Sas and Lizerne by the German gas attack of the day before.

To call this section of the front a " line " is too flattering a description. It was nowhere properly entrenched, the battalions holding it were depleted, many of them to half their strength, and there were gaps which urgently required filling up. Seventeen and a half British battalions were facing 42 German battalions which were supported by artillery with a superiority of five to one. The position was extremely serious.

For the time being the Germans remained stationary, contenting themselves with shelling heavily all along the line; but aerial reconnaissance revealed the fact that they were massed against the Canadian flank and that they were vastly strengthening their positions. Further British attacks seemed impossible without reinforcements, which were not immediately available, and yet the longer an attack was delayed the more strongly entrenched the Germans would become and the more difficult it would be to take their positions.

Reinforcements were in fact being sent up as quickly as possible by both the French and the English. Colonel Geddes' detachment was increased to seven battalions. The infantry of the 50th (Northumbrian) division was allotted to General Sir Horace Smith-Dorrien, cavalry was ordered up in support, and units of the Indian division were ordered to be in readiness.

But the movements involved took time and time was the most important factor. Orders were issued at 2.40 p.m. for a general attack to be made from the line (between Kitchener's Wood and the Yser) in the direction of Pilkem supported by a French attack along the canal. But a delay in the arrival of the 13th brigade caused a postponement of the hour of attack until 4.15 p.m.

When the assaulting battalions were finally launched it was under circumstances which precluded any possibility of a successful issue. They advanced over the open, in full view of the Germans; they had had no opportunity of properly reconnoitring the ground; they had no adequate artillery support. It

Chanak is the chief town of the sanjak of Bigha, Asia Minor. It stands on the Dardanelles, at its narrowest part, opposite Kilid-Bahr (seen below). It was unsuccessfully attacked by the Allied Fleet in March, 1915.

The illustration shows Kilid-Bahr, on the European shore of the Narrows, looking towards Gallipoli. It faces Chanak (shown above). It was here that Turkish forts, field batteries and mobile howitzers were thickly clustered on both sides of the water.

TARGETS OF THE ALLIED FLEETS IN THE DARDANELLES

ANZACS AT GULLY BEACH. During the Gallipoli operations many ingenious and interesting names were given to the various camps and bases. The illustration shows a typical piece of scenery on the peninsula. Gully Beach is situated on the west coast, about two miles north of Cape Helles. Krithia, which was the scene of severe fighting, lies two miles to the north-east, whilst Achi Baba lies a few miles farther on.

Plate 16

Volume II

was not clear what progress the French were making, though it was afterwards learnt that they had made none at all. The British line did advance towards their objective but at great cost, particularly in the loss of officers, for the attacking troops were raked with rifle and machine-gun fire and were heavily bombarded. The action undertaken according to a promise made by Sir John French to General Foch gained very little. The tragic irony of the situation as the official historian points out is that " actually no ground was gained that could not have been secured, probably without any casualties, by a simple advance after dark, to which the openness of the country lent itself." As a result of the attack it could be said that the British line was nowhere driven in though preparations were made for a withdrawal from the apex of the salient by Poelcapelle held by the Canadians and a company of the Buffs, which had become untenable owing to enfilading fire on both sides. This was carried out during the night.

The actions which occupied the six days between April 24-30 bear the official title of the battle of St. Julien. During the morning of the 24th a German attack was definitely expected. Opinions differed as to where this might fall, but a general order to be vigilant was issued by General Smith-Dorrien. The first blow, in fact, fell on the extreme left of the allies' line where the Belgians had lost touch with the French through the capture the day before of the village of Lizerne. The attack which took place at 3.0 a.m. was an attempt to turn the Belgian flank. It was repulsed, and the Belgians were able to get in touch with the French and prevent any further German advance over the Yser canal. A French counter-attack failed to make any progress.

During the same early hours of the morning a strong attack was developing against that jutting point of the Canadian line which was opposite the village of Poelcapelle. This was preceded by an intense bombardment and by the release of a wave of gas. Twenty-four German battalions then advanced in an attempt to encircle the eight British battalions which were holding the salient. Despite the fact, however, that they had only the flimsiest protection against gas, such as moistened handkerchiefs and bandoliers, the Canadians succeeded in holding the enemy. Only on a half-company front did the Germans succeed in gaining a foothold, and this after every officer of the battalion (the 15th Canadians) had been killed or made prisoner. The 8th battalion of the Canadians also behaved magnificently. Many of them were suffocated by the gas fumes; but they managed to defeat a heavy German bombing attack and even recapture some of the lost ground.

Brigadier-General Turner had little artillery support and no reinforcements except tired troops who had been sent out for a rest which they had earned but not enjoyed. These were his 10th and 16th battalions, which had suffered such heavy losses the day before. They were brought into action again but not in time to be a support in the immediate emergency. Salvation, by an accident of war, came from the enemy who, startled by the ferocity of the resistance which they met, and possibly deterred by a fear of penetrating into the gas-affected area, paused, leaving the pursuit of the attack to troops on the north-western side of the salient. Fortunately for the Canadians there was artillery in position to defeat this, supporting a concentrated rifle fire from the trenches. The Germans advanced in close formation and suffered very heavy losses.

But they were persistent in their attempts to break this line, and about 9.0 a.m. with fresh troops to take the place of those who had fallen they forced the decision to retire. This retirement was disastrous in two ways. Those who succeeded in making the retreat were so heavily shelled that they lost half their numbers, and a company of the Buffs and two platoons of the Canadian 15th battalion were left standing without having received the order to retire. They fought until their last cartridge was expended and the survivors, most of whom were wounded, were forced to surrender.

The retirement left a gap of 1,500 yards defended only by cross fire. The news of the break through quickly reached Canadian headquarters and General Alderson ordered up what reinforcements he could command. Sir Herbert Plumer (5th Corps) also was informed of the hazardous position and took steps to send help as soon as it could be summoned.

Between the hours of nine and eleven there appears to have been a cessation of the attack while the enemy were repairing their losses and reorganizing their line for further offensive action. This took place at 11.0 a.m. preceded by heavy gun-fire and was directed against the second Canadian position. A decision was made by battalion commanders on the spot to withdraw to a position between Fortuin and St. Julien (see map p. 157), and this retirement of the right half of the 3rd Canadian brigade took place shortly after 11.0 a.m. under a shattering artillery fire and a close pursuit by the infantry. What small reply the British guns could make was at least effective in preventing the Canadian force from being annihilated, though they suffered the most severe losses. Two York and Durham battalions were sent up to assist the retiring Canadians to dig in in front of St. Julien, but they arrived too late to be of any practical use. Again time was given by the Germans, who waited for further artillery support before continuing the attack.

This supporting gun-fire soon began and about mid-day a furious bombardment fell on the positions about St. Julien. Three-quarters of an hour afterwards the Germans occupied the trenches in front of this village. The Canadians drew back to a line on the Gravenstafel-Wieltje road (see map p. 157).

During this day the battle fluctuated but at the end the advantage lay with the Germans. The necessity for even stronger counter-attacks became evident. Foch promised assistance in the shape of very heavy reinforcements, but it was taking time to bring these up. Meantime every possible effort was made to press the enemy.

With the retirement of the Canadian left the Canadian centre held. The brigadier-general extended his line and flung his left flank southward and fought on until Sunday afternoon, April 25. By this time his field fortifications had been wiped out by the high-explosive shells of the enemy's heavy artillery. But the men held on until they were relieved on Sunday by British troops. Sir John French had given orders that the line near St. Julien should be immediately restored. These orders were passed down through General Plumer, who ordered General Alderson to make the strongest possible attack. He placed at his disposal the 10th and 15th infantry brigades and six battalions, and General Alderson gave the command of the attack to Brigadier-General Hull.

The idea was that the attack should begin at 3.30 a.m., and instructions were that it should proceed northwards as far as possible. Again there had been no opportunity for reconnaissance, and General Hull was asked to throw his forces into a battle ground the natural features of which were obscure.

Also he was not at all sure that he could keep touch with the fifteen battalions which he commanded. In fact this turned out to be impossible, for he was understaffed and telephonic communication had not been established. There was not sufficient time to summon any conference of battalion commanders. As the units moved up to their battle positions on a pitch-dark night they were heavily shelled, and they were delayed by the fact that they had to defile through two narrow gaps in the defensive wire of the British support or, as it was called, the G.H.Q. line. It became obvious that there was not the smallest hope of making the attack at the appointed hour of 3.30 a.m. The French had not progressed, and elsewhere on the British front serious gaps were being reported. The situation was more confused and dangerous than it had been on the morning before.

On Sunday, April 25, at about the same time that Sir Ian Hamilton's divisions were making the landing at Gallipoli, matters looked gloomy enough for the British troops in the west. General Hull had perforce postponed his attack until 5.30 a.m., and news of this postponement did not reach the batteries which fired uselessly between 2.45 and 3.15 a.m., and then closed down. When the attack started he had no artillery support that was of any value to him. Moreover, the difficulty of communicating with the battalions allotted to his command resulted in orders miscarrying and when the attack was launched it was made by five battalions only and not the fifteen that had been originally intended should share in the operation.

As they advanced they came at once under the fire of snipers and machine-guns. With a precision worthy of the autumn manœuvres, the attacking lines spread out into open formation and advanced over a quarter of a mile. By this time they had reached the outskirts of the village of St. Julien. Here, caught in the open by the most devastating machine-gun fire, they were checked and could make no further progress. The losses on this hopeless adventure were very heavy, the 10th brigade losing 73 officers and 2,346 other ranks. The Germans made no attempt to exploit their success, and the best that could be said of an expensive failure was that it had, at least, prevented the enemy from making further trouble in this sector.

A FRUITLESS ATTACK

Meanwhile, however, a strong enemy attack developed against the 85th brigade holding a position between Gravenstafel and Broodseinde. This was preceded by a heavy bombardment of shrapnel, high-explosive, and gas shell. The German infantry charge which followed was repulsed except at one point where a lodgment was made on a front of sixty yards held by an exhausted battalion of the East Surreys. The enemy also obtained minor successes at other points, and the Canadians were obliged to retire a short distance thus leaving the flank of the 85th brigade exposed. The line was very thinly held but the enemy, unaware of the precarious state of the troops opposing them, attempted no further advance that evening.

An attempt was made during the night of April 25 to reorganize the line and redistribute the commands. This was only partially successful owing to the difficulty of assembling the scattered units in the darkness. There appears also at this time to have been some difference of opinion between the British and French commands which made united action impossible. Sir John French took the view that as it was the French who had in the first place retreated it was their responsibility to repair the line. General Putz was not prepared to accept such an enlarged view of his task. The French were willing to enter into the attack later in the day (April 26) and in the meantime the Indian division was brought up on General Smith-Dorrien's front to be in readiness to renew the attack in the afternoon.

This attack was timed for 2.0 p.m. with an artillery preparation to begin at 1.20 p.m. Assistance from the French was relied upon and other units of the British 5th corps were ordered to co-operate. The advance, which began to time, started under every disadvantage. It was made in full view of the enemy whose artillery was able to direct its shells with deadly accuracy. Indeed, it is remarkable that despite the fact that whole platoons of infantry were wiped out to a man, the attack did proceed to within a hundred yards of the enemy's trenches. At this point it was hopelessly checked. The French advance was dissipated by clouds of gas which also badly affected the Indian troops. The Northumberland brigade which attempted an advance at the same time suffered even more severely.

To the right of Gravenstafel the Germans had attempted to dislodge a battalion of the Hampshires first by a surprise attack which failed and secondly by an intensive bombardment levelled on the trenches with deadly accuracy. But by the end of the day neither side had done anything materially to alter the position and there were to be more days of fighting before the lines became stabilised.

On the morning of April 27 both French and English generals ordered renewed offensives with the object of regaining any ground that had been lost. Sir John French continued to act against his better judgment, which was to withdraw from the Salient, shorten his line and thus spare his troops and improve his communications. But co-operation had been promised to the French and in consequence it was necessary to conform with their movements. Accordingly two brigades of the Lahore division moved forward between St. Jean and La Brique about 12.30 p.m. They immediately came under very heavy artillery fire and underwent a perfectly useless slaughter, for the French never moved from their trenches. During the day the Indian division made further efforts to advance, but at nightfall, summarising the day's events, Sir John French merely recorded the fact that they were where they were and had suffered very heavy casualties.

Thus ended the action which was known as the battle of St. Julien. The night was quiet, and except for a further vain attempt to recover a lost trench at Broodseinde, was uneventful. It was employed in reorganizing the units of the 5th corps and in contemplating the arrangements for shortening the salient. An important piece of wiring enclosed an unoccupied area discovered by the engineers, thus effecting a gain of ground without loss. But retirement was in the air, and Sir H. Smith-Dorrien, in a long communiqué to the chief of General Staff, expressed himself " doubtful if it is worth losing any more men to regain French ground unless the French themselves do something really big." Despite the fact that he was soon to be engaged in retiring his troops, Sir John French replied through his C.G.S.: " Chief does not regard situation nearly so unfavourably as your letter represents. . . . He wishes you to act vigorously with the full means available in co-operating with and assisting the French attack."

CHAPTER 10

Second Battle of Ypres (II)

A T half-past four on the afternoon of April 27 while
fighting was still in progress, Sir Horace Smith-Dorrien,
at 2nd army headquarters, received the following
telegram :—

Chief directs you to hand over to General Plumer the command of all troops engaged in the present operations about
Ypres. You should lend General Plumer your brigadier-
general, general staff, and such other officers of your staff as
he may require. General Plumer should send all reports direct
to G.H.Q. from which he will receive his orders.

This meant the virtual dismissal of Sir Horace Smith-Dorrien
from the command of the 2nd army, though his actual removal
to England did not take place until May 6. The message was
followed the same evening by more explicit instructions to Sir
Herbert Plumer.

With reference to the failure of the French attack to-day,
and to the Chief's instructions given you by Brig.-General
Maurice, the Chief wishes you to consolidate the line you now
hold so as to render it more secure against further attack.
You are also requested to prepare a line east of Ypres joining
up with the line now held north and south of that place ready
for occupation, if and when it becomes advisable to withdraw
from the present salient. . . . It should be such as to avoid
withdrawal from Hill 60.

Following these orders a reorganization of units in the line
took place. The battalions that had been placed under the
command of Colonel Geddes were returned to their brigades; the
divisions again assumed their regimental establishment. General
Plumer alone was in an anomalous position for he was still
G.O.C. the 5th corps, and also in command of a miscellaneous
body of troops known as "Plumer's Force." Fortunately the
night was very little disturbed by enemy action (except for continuous shelling) and the reorganization of the line was proceeded
with without much molestation.

Throughout these days of comparatively futile battles Sir John
French seems always to have entertained the idea that the most
sensible course would have been to withdraw his line to one
more capable of defence which was removed from the dangers
which accompany the attempt to hold a sharp salient. But the
French, and particularly General Foch, were convinced that

they could re-take the lost ground and were violently opposed to any withdrawal. In this argument the British commander-in-chief appears to have been worsted, a matter for no surprise when it is realized with what force the French general advanced his opinions. The two commanders had had an interview at Cassel on the afternoon of April 28.

Some hours later General Foch sent an unequivocal message to Sir John French. He acknowledged the difficulties with which the British were contending, that they were tired, that they had suffered heavily, and that it was far from easy to keep them properly supplied. He also agreed with Sir John French that the operations in the salient had now become subsidiary to the offensive which was being planned for a point farther south, and that it would be injudicious to employ more troops or resources than were actually available on the spot; but he had " the honour to observe " that the new British positions were badly chosen. They were at the foot of the ridges and would be more difficult to hold than those on the crest.

The enemy, Foch pointed out, " master of the abandoned crest," would be able to attack again under favourable conditions; he would be able to bring his artillery nearer to Ypres from the east, and thus shell from a new direction that junction of communication. He further pointed out that the British line of supply, Ypres, Vlamertinghe, Poperinghe was commanded by the German guns, and nothing less than the recapture of the Langemarck region could remove this menace. He argued that if a retirement was made to the line Fortuin—Hill 60 it would be " a confession of impotence " and would " simply invite a very strong German effort." He saw in such a retirement the possibility of being driven farther back on Ypres and the canal to positions less and less strong, of being forced to fight yet another " battle of Ypres " with the Germans in the moral ascendancy. Further, he regarded retirement in the Ypres salient as the worst possible preparation for the attack which it was hoped to make farther south.

Summing up, General Foch urged that the proposed retirement should not only *not* be ordered but should be definitely forbidden, and in conclusion he had " the honour to request the Field-Marshal not to consider any further the retirement from the line on account of the serious consequences which would ensue, but to be good enough to keep to his present intention and to support the French offensive to retake the Langemarck region at all costs beginning at noon on the 29th."

Sir John French, pledged as he was to the spirit if not the letter of co-operation, was yet obliged to reply that unless the French could make good their losses the British must carry out their proposed retirement—and a line was chosen for the new position along the forward slope of the Frezenberg ridge. This would mean that the retirement would be on a base at least five miles long and at some points of a distance in length of 2½ miles. Meanwhile the French made an ineffectual attempt with three battalions to retake their former trenches round Steenstraat, with the help of British and Belgian artillery; but the remainder of the French on the left did not move, and so a brigade of the Indian division which had been ordered to support them also remained in their trenches.

On the next day (April 29) General Putz again announced his intention to attack, but General Foch cancelled the order on the ground that the artillery were too newly arrived to have registered their targets. A postponement of twenty-four hours was suggested, and Sir John French agreed to delay his retirement for that period. The situation at this time appears to have been more than ever confused; with the French promising to regain their ground if the British would stay where they were and offer assistance, and on the other hand the British generals straining to begin their retirement but consenting to delay it until the French attack was made. For a number of reasons Generals Foch and Putz could not fulfil their promise and for the next two days the two armies were for all practical purposes inactive.

Sir John French grew tired of waiting and on the afternoon of May 1 General Plumer received the order to begin his retirement that night. It was to be effected by stages and by the morning of May 2 the first of these had been completed without interference. So quiet was the enemy during the forenoon that it was hoped that the further stages of the retirement would be also without incident. Shortly after noon, however, the enemy's fire flared up along the front and the line on the north of the salient, held by troops of the 27th division, was heavily bombarded, first by high-explosive and later with gas shells. This bombardment was followed at 4.30 p.m. by the release of a gas cloud along three miles of front.

At some parts of the line the gas was very much denser than at others and local withdrawals were necessary; but so quickly were reinforcements brought up that there were troops everywhere in position to meet the assault when the gas clouds cleared away. Some units (for all were still inadequately protected) suffered heavy losses particularly a battalion of the Lancashire Fusiliers who had 18 officers and 431 other ranks incapacitated. But thanks to the brilliant charge of the reinforcing troops through the gas cloud, and the readiness of artillery support to help in destroying the assaulting columns, the attack was completely repulsed. The night was quiet, and General Plumer was able to continue his retirement.

There was yet one day to go, and during this the Germans made a further heavy attack on the British lines near Gravenstafel. The troops who were attacked suffered heavy casualties; but despite the fact that they were without proper artillery support (for batteries had been moved back during the retirement of the night before) they were able to hold their line. There were still sufficient men of the regular army left in the shattered battalions to establish a superiority of rapid fire against the enemy, upon whom they inflicted very severe punishment.

There followed during the night the withdrawal of all the remaining units to the agreed line. This was carried out without casualty with the enemy in complete ignorance of the movement. Indeed on the following morning the evacuated trenches were heavily shelled. Sir John French had at last secured his object and rescued his force from a position in which it was exposed to enemy fire from three sides. Undoubtedly this move should have been made before, and had it been, many casualties would have been saved. The blame for the delay must rest on both the French and British staffs who failed to advise proper co-ordination.

From Hill 60 the new line formed a rough semi-circle by Hooge, through Frezenberg until it joined up with the French right again, at a point known as Turco Farm. Divisional headquarters were withdrawn to positions behind Ypres. There followed a period marked only by small attacks and heavy shelling of British trenches. Work was carried out to strengthen these and consolidate the line generally. The French, on the left, continued to make minor assaults with the idea of preventing the withdrawal of German troops to the south. The fall of Hill 60, on May 5, has already been recorded (see chapter 9) and the next set battle, which was one of the fiercest of the whole operations, did not open until May 8. It lasted six days, and is officially known as the battle of Frezenberg ridge.

The new line was in no condition to withstand continuous bombardment and to this it was now subjected day after day. The trenches were shallow, at places no more than three feet deep. It was impossible to dig further without their becoming waterlogged and with such flimsy protection the British infantry were called upon to endure the heaviest shelling they had yet experienced, and according to General Plumer's order of May 8 to hold the line with all possible tenacity. There were few reinforcements available, for the 1st army was about to be engaged in the battle of Aubers ridge further south.

The bombardment of the morning of May 8 fell most heavily on the front held by the 83rd brigade, but it was very intense along the whole front. Considering that practically every trench was destroyed and support lines were equally inundated by shell fire it is extraordinary that the line held. The 3rd Monmouthshire, the 2nd King's Own, the 1st Suffolks, and the 2nd Cheshires of the 83rd brigade holding the front of the Frezenberg ridge made a particularly heroic resistance, and only when the defending troops were wiped out to a man did the enemy succeed in obtaining any foothold. The 80th and 83rd brigades on the right were also subjected to very heavy shell fire, but succeeded in resisting the German advance.

To the north of the 83rd brigade, between Frezenberg and Mouse Trap farm, the 84th brigade was most violently bombarded and attacked. It was gradually overwhelmed and the remnants of battalions fell back. A very serious gap of about two miles was left, and though some kind of flank had been formed to protect this the necessity for a counter-attack became obvious. This was entrusted to the 83rd brigade under General Boyle. Though prosecuted with the utmost energy it could not dislodge the Germans. At least it succeeded in nailing them to their ground, though at immense cost, and prepared the way for a further counter-attack by the 10th brigade that evening. This was eventually successful and forced the Germans to abandon their positions which they had captured. At the end of the day they could claim very little advantage, though if their aim had been purely to reduce the numbers against them their success had been terrible indeed. The British losses on May 8 were particularly heavy amongst officers, both senior and junior, at a time when they could least be spared and were needed to lead and to inspire the new drafts of inexperienced troops which were arriving.

From the German point of view the present attacks were not regarded in the light of main assaults. At no time during this phase of the battle did they reinforce their offensive troops in any notable way. Their plan, it appears, was to rely on their immense superiority in artillery, backed up by their command of the air, to break down the resistance of the defending troops. When and where this object was achieved they looked to their trench garrison to follow up the advantage.

During the next three days, although the battles of Arbois and Aubers ridge had directed their attention to the south, the Germans did not desist from their attempts to break in towards Ypres. They seemed most anxious to make this break on the front of the 27th division between Hooge on the Menin road and the extremity of Sanctuary Wood in front of Zillebeke. They achieved a small local success on May 9, but failed to penetrate the divisional front in any broad sense. Next day they tried again, obliterating front line trenches and destroying their garrison, but were held back at first by strong opposition from the support line, which managed to resist repeated enemy attacks supported by further bombardment and clouds of gas. On May 11 the Germans, though part of their assaulting troops, owing to a sudden change of wind, were caught in their own gas clouds, did succeed, mostly by bombardment, in forcing a partial retirement to a prepared line. On the 12th they contented themselves with shelling the 27th divisional front and attempted no further advance. To give the tired infantry of the 28th and 27th divisions a necessary rest sectors of the trenches were taken over by men of the cavalry divisions under General de Lisle.

But theirs was to be no mere trench duty for on the next day the front between Hooge and the Ypres-St. Julien road, a sector of which they held, was one of the most heavily shelled and one of the earliest attacked. The Germans were successful in taking part of the front line, but were held up from making any further advance by the well-directed fire of cavalrymen in the support line. On other parts of the battle-field the day was marked by attacks and counter-attacks during which the famous Mouse Trap farm was taken and won back again. By the evening, and at the end of the battle of Frezenberg the Germans, after six days' fighting, had shelled the British off the forward slope of Frezenberg ridge and could count a net gain in ground of a thousand yards between Hooge and Mouse Trap farm. Casualties on both sides had been very heavy. The Germans say that lack of men and ammunition were reasons for calling a halt at this stage.

There remained one most important action before the 2nd battle of Ypres may be said definitely to have closed. This is known as the battle of Bellewaarde ridge and was fought on May 24-25. Bellewaarde lake and Bellewaarde wood were immediately beside Hooge on the Ypres-Menin road. The bombardment which preceded the attack fell on the whole 5th corps front from Hill 60 to Turco farm (see map p. 157). (Turco farm was at a point south of Pilkem, a little to the right of the Ypres-Pilkem road. The largest wave of gas which the Germans had yet released was directed towards nearly the whole of this front, not far short of five miles in length. As the wind was in a favourable direction for them the defending troops were awake to their danger and were able to repulse the first attacks with rifle and machine-gun fire. Mouse Trap farm, for what it was worth, again fell to the enemy. As the attack proceeded the Germans began to gain advantages. On the 83rd brigade front they were able to overwhelm a section of the front line; between Hooge and Bellewaarde they penetrated the line held by the cavalry division. On the 4th division front, on the left of the line the Germans began to exploit their success at Mouse Trap farm by bombing and capturing the front line trench. The centre of the British line held fast.

During the afternoon and evening counter-attacks were made by troops of the 84th and 85th brigades. Though carried out with great determination they achieved little, and in the evening (on May 24) it was decided to withdraw and form a new connected front. This involved giving up ground in front of Mouse Trap farm of about a thousand yards in depth, which it was decided it was impossible to hold. The day of May 25 passed without much incident.

At this point it may be said that the second battle of Ypres had come to an end. It had been waged with little intermission for nearly five weeks and had been fought to a standstill. Both sides were exhausted, and both had suffered enormous casualties. At Hill 60 and during the battles of Ypres the British losses were 2,150 officers and 57,125 other ranks. The German losses were given as 860 officers and 34,073 other ranks, but it must be remembered that the Germans did not include in their casualty lists those who were only slightly wounded. Even so, it is only reasonable to suppose that their losses were much lighter than the British, who suffered throughout from the enemy's superior artillery fire, from gas attacks and from the constant necessity of making counterattacks without proper artillery support.

The Germans complained that they were getting short of ammunition, but they, who were so much better supplied to begin with, could not at any time have suffered the serious deficiencies of the British. Long before the battle ended guns had to be discarded, worn out by over-use. Many were employed long after they should have been withdrawn, which accounted for much inaccurate ranging. But not only in heavier guns was the British lack of material so disastrously apparent; there was a deficiency in all lighter forms of weapons, in machine-guns, in trench-mortars, in hand grenades, and even in rifles. Ammunition, too, was quite inadequate to serve the needs either of defence or attack. Sir John French made repeated representations to the Government at home, but many months were to pass before these bore fruit.

As far as the air services were concerned the Germans could also command far more aeroplanes and trained pilots and observers. During " 2nd Ypres " the Royal Flying Corps did much excellent work, despite continuous interruption from bad visibility, but throughout the battle they were outnumbered by the enemy. It is interesting to record that the first Victoria Cross won by an airman was awarded in this battle. The honour fell, unhappily posthumously, to 2/Lt. W. B. Rhodes-Moorhouse, who bombed Courtrai from a low altitude and though mortally wounded flew his machine back to the aerodrome in Merville. He died of wounds next day. Throughout the battle the Royal Flying Corps carried out their dangerous duties with dash and intelligence. When it died down they proceeded to the systematic photography of the new positions.

After an interval of years the impartial student may well wonder whether any military advantage was gained by the Germans, with whom lay at least the superficial victory. Their use of gas weighed morally against them in neutral countries, and inflamed still further the hatred of their enemies. They could boast their victories at home and so encourage their own spirits, but at most they had flattened out a salient and were but a short step further towards their objective—a break in the allied line followed by a flanking movement towards the Channel ports. And what could the British boast for their 60,000 casualties? At least that they had held that line in the face of the most severe onslaughts. They could say also that they had no other course but to accept the challenge made to them and fight the battle to a finish.

Undoubtedly the losses would have been less had Sir John French had the full strength of his opinon and had he not repeatedly delayed his retirement. For during these days of hesitancy the British line was most severely attacked and the necessary counter-attacks resulted in whole battalions being wiped out. Indeed, it has been questioned whether those counter-attacks were always as necessary as they seemed to the higher commands. They were made under every possible disadvantage— lack of artillery support, lack of communications, lack of any preliminary reconnaissance by the leaders concerned. But pledged by daily promises to the French to hold his line it is difficult to see how they could have been honourably avoided.

Those to whom nothing but praise can attach were the troops in the field, many of whom at this time were untried men called upon to fight under conditions of great hardship. They seldom had adequate trench protection, they were often left in the open without rations or supplies, and they were in that discouraging position of receiving shell-fire to which their own guns could not answer. When Sir John French addressed the survivors of his army he congratulated them on having performed " the most difficult, arduous and terrific task of withstanding a stupendous bombardment of heavy artillery, probably the fiercest artillery fire ever directed against troops."

The eye-witness account of a battle recorded by the private soldier has illuminating flashes which serve to enlighten the official record. This account of the 2nd battle of Ypres may well conclude with extracts from a contemporary document, the impressions of a private of Queen Victoria's Rifles who took part in the action.

We are soon busy firing. Dawn (21st) gradually appears, and the enemy begins bombarding with hand-grenades. One by one I see my pals fall. Mr. Woolley (the first Territorial V.C.) takes command after Major Lees and Mr. Summerhayes have been killed. What a roar and tumult! Maxim guns are hammering away, shrapnel bursting above us, and blinding flashes follow the explosion of hand-grenades. My rifle becomes too hot to hold, and I throw it aside for another. A bomb explodes a few yards away on my left among the Bedfords. What happens to them I don't know. I feel no longer a human being. Simply mechanically I continue firing. Mr. Woolley appears at the mouth of the communication trench and encourages us by saying reinforcements are coming up. A blinding flash, and something hits me full in the face —a feeling as though someone has smacked the bristle side of a stiff brush in my face. My hand goes up—no, there is no blood. Only fine particles of earth have reached me.

The Devons begin to arrive, and as they come up, we make our way to the rear—crawling on hands and knees along the low, badly-damaged communication trench into the original fire trench, and from there to the communication trench leading on to the railway cutting. Passing the Northumberland Fusiliers on our way, we reach another communication trench, leading from the railway to the support dug-outs, which are in what was once a wood. But few trees are left— mostly short stumps, for the tops have been blown off. Here we are gathered into some sort of order, and go across a couple of fields to some more dug-outs.

About midday (April 22) we receive orders to be ready to move. We work our way back across the fields, keeping well under cover of hedges till we reach Zillebeke, turning off from there to the left and once more regaining the railway. A few minutes' halt, and we proceed along the embankment to the Lille road into Ypres. A mile the other side of Ypres a halt is made, and the battalion is formed up once more. Food is eaten. Presently we again fall in, and General Smith-Dorrien makes a speech congratulating the regiment on the part it had played, after which we proceed to a new hut encampment about a mile farther back, arriving there about 4 p.m. Most of the fellows, being very fatigued, dropped down in their places in the huts to sleep; the more energetic went in search of water for washing, others to surrounding farms for coffee and eggs; I was among the last.

A SOLDIER'S ACCOUNT

Presently French transports come hurrying from the direction of the firing-line. No notice was taken at first, but the stream seems never ending. All manner of rumours fly around. I return to the camp. Everywhere troops are asking questions, yet all is marvellously orderly. Soon comes the order to "stand to." We are paraded, magazines are charged, and all ready to march off. Official news comes that the enemy has broken through the first line of the French, but the Canadians are holding the second line. We are marched across a couple of fields, and begin digging a trench. We are on this for a couple of hours or so, and then return to our huts, being told to be ready to move at a moment's notice. Two hours' sleep is snatched, and we are on the move again, and go along the railway track in the direction of Vlamertinghe. We bivouac in a field. Our field kitchens supply hot tea, and rations are issued.

Dawn breaks (Friday, April 23rd), and we take cover from aeroplane sight, lining the hedges. About 10 a.m. the brigade starts on the move. Our battalion brings up the rear. We pass Vlamertinghe and proceed towards Elvertinghe. No one knows where we are bound for, yet we are all under the impression we are going to a permanent encampment for a rest. We reach a farm and rest in a field.

Another meal is made, and about 4 p.m. the brigade is on the move again. We pass a village, and after about a three-mile march we reach the Yser Canal and cross a pontoon bridge. Our battalion is spread out in extended order on the bridge. The attack is successful, and we are told certain trenches are taken. We remain on the embankment all night, and about mid-day the following day, (Saturday, April 24), orders arrive to be ready to move. We tramp across fields, recently ploughed and sown, passing the village of St. Jean on our right. Everywhere troops are on the move. An enemy aeroplane has seen what is happening, and soon shells begin to drop—not a few here and there, but a perfect hailstorm of metal. Troops are moving up everywhere. Order is kept marvellously considering. We stumble along as quickly as we can. I don't know who is leading us, or where we are making for. The air is thick with smoke, and breathing becomes difficult. Presently we reach a partly-built rampart, and are told to spread ourselves out as much as possible, and dig ourselves in behind it. Operations are soon begun. Higher up a shell has burst among our men; another bursts within a few yards of the spot where I am working. I have just time to fall flat—surely that can't have missed me?—yes, I am quite all right, though Chalmers has got a nasty piece in his thigh. We are only digging a few minutes when orders come to advance towards a farm building. Making our way in our own time we reach a pile of mangel-wurzels—I stay behind this for a breather. Half-right from this, about two hundred yards away, is a trench, and it is there we are to make for. Having recovered my breath, I make a dash. The enemy have evidently spotted us, and a machine-gun is soon busy. Gad, I never heard so many bullets whistle past me before! I reach a sort of " don't care " mood, and I plod across to the trench as best I can, for I am absolutely whacked. I reach it in safety, and flop down on some straw in the bottom, thoroughly exhausted.

The trench is held by Canadians, but they are very few, and my company links up with them. Apparently this was originally a support trench, but owing to the enemy having been successful in taking some trenches of ours in front of a wood, this position is now a front-line one. We arrive just after the Germans had made an attack on some other trenches, and had been repulsed, and as they retreat across an open space, between a farm building and the wood, we are able to pepper them well from our position. The range was eight hundred yards, but I think we accounted for a few—anyhow, not many reached the wood. This is the first occasion on which I have had a real target—and didn't I enjoy it, too!

As darkness came, we began to get busy improving the trench. There was a plentiful supply of good turf to be dug behind the trench, and very soon we began to make ourselves a fairly safe shelter. Rain, however, began to fall, and this did not cheer our spirits. Dawn arrives (Sunday, April 25). About 7 a.m. heavy rifle fire opens from the wood, which is half-left from our position, and presently we observe the cause —a kilted regiment is advancing to attack. The bark of a dog sounds above the rifle fire, and, sure to behold, there is the figure of a big black dog running ahead of the Scotties. What a fine sight—yet what a terrible sight!—for an enormous lot of the poor chaps are falling. The distance is far too much to cover (about eight hundred yards), and in broad daylight, too. Very soon the attack is given up, and those who are left make their way back. Things quieten down a bit. I snatch an hour or two's well-needed sleep.

About 2 p.m. the enemy start shelling some farm buildings about fifteen yards on the rear of our trench, but about one hundred yards from the spot where I am. They are sending over some very heavy stuff. My pals must be having a pretty hot time up that end. The farm buildings are used as a head-quarters by the Canadians. The range is soon found, and smoke issuing from the buildings shows us a fire has occurred. Soon ammunition begins to crackle off, and this goes on for some hours. A lot of stores, etc., must have been lost. The bombardment lasts about three-quarters of an hour, during which time I count ninety shells that have been sent over. Dusk comes on, and being anxious to fill my bottle, I volunteer to get some water from the pump at the farm. I take another fellow with me, and we pick our way through the ruin to the pump, and begin filling the bottles. There are a lot of other fellows (Canadians) also on the same search; others are in search of whatever they can find in the way of spare rations, etc.

Suddenly another shell comes over, bursting beyond the buildings. Fellows scuttle away like rats; my pal and I make hasty tracks for our trench again. Having reached it in safety I sit down and laugh, for it is really most amusing to see everyone suddenly dart away in all directions, dropping the tins of jam which they had been confiscating. The rest of the night passes peacefully, and we are able to continue the work of fortifying our trench.

The grey dawn (April 26) begins to appear, and with it a heavy mist. About 4 a.m. our adjutant appears, and tells us to hurry and get ready to be relieved. It is most essential to get away before the mist rises, for it is now almost broad daylight. We file out and are led across fields, reaching the village of St. Jean, through which we pass. What havoc and devastation has been done! A few days ago people were living here, and now, roofless houses, shattered walls, shell-holes dotting the cobbled road. Furniture is lying in the streets, the smouldering remains of a motor-ambulance stand on the side of the road; dead men and horses are lying everywhere, and not always whole bodies, alas! We leave the road, and go across country once more; at last, striking the canal, we move along the banks. This embankment is now a mass of dug-outs, for it has been heavily shelled since we were last there. All had seemed so undisturbed before, and I plucked cowslips which grew among the grass. We rest a few minutes when we have crossed the pontoon bridge, and then continue our march back to the farm near Elverdinghe. We are all played out by this time, and many have had to fall out on the way. Now for a wash and a shave for I have had neither for the seven days. A pond close by, though not very clean is very welcome, and after a good scrub down I feel a new man. The rest of the day is spent in lounging about and feeding. There is plenty to eat, for beyond our own parcels, those of our killed and wounded pals are split up amongst us, and these are not inconsiderable in number. We remain at this farm resting till Thursday, April 29, getting three full nights' sleep. On this day we receive orders to parade at 6 p.m. for the trenches again. We are going to reinforce another regiment.

CHAPTER 11

The Fight for Przemysl

IN January, 1915, the Carpathians again became the chief scene of activity on the Eastern front. From Tarnov the Russian line ran south-east to the Rumanian frontier. Along the range of the Carpathians Brusiloff's army held the Duka Pass and the Lupkowa Pass, but farther east it only touched the northern foothills. In the extreme south-east Russia had occupied practically the whole of the Bukovina. Early in 1915, General von Linsingen, commanding the southern army of the Central Powers, attempted a movement against Brusiloff in the Carpathians. But operations on the snow-clad mountains were extremely difficult, and it soon became clear that neither the relief of Przemysl nor any other major success could be expected in the immediate future. The German attempt on the left flank had failed by the Niemen and Narew; the Austrian attempt on the right flank in the Bukovina had also been checked. All along the central river front—along the Bzura, Pilica, Nida, Vistula, and Dunajec—the Austro-German forces were for the time completely exhausted by their enormous losses, and on both sides of this section of the fighting-line a condition of stationary trench warfare obtained.

This left the Russian commander free to choose his own point of attack and concentrate all available troops there. There was, however, one very important factor that interfered with his free choice of the scene of his offensive movement. He had fewer guns and howitzers of the heavy class than the enemy possessed. What was worse, his store of large, high-explosive shells was almost exhausted, and even his field-artillery had to be exceedingly economical in the use of ammunition. In these circumstances he could not take the proper line of attack and drive in on Cracow and the industrial district of Galicia.

The extraordinary change in the conditions of modern warfare told most heavily against Russia, for the Russians were almost entirely an agricultural people. General Sukhomlinoff, the Russian chief of staff, displayed great energy in mobilising all available factories in the Empire. But, unfortunately, the only industrial region of much importance in Russia was that extending from Lodz to the frontier of Silesia, and it was in the possession of the enemy. Most of the Russian seaports were closed by ice, and though some ammunition was obtained through Port Arthur it was not sufficient for the needs of the Russian armies. The result was that they had to rely on the bayonet and shrapnel-proof trenches. Millions of Russian peasants were ready to take the field, but were held back by lack of rifles and artillery.

In these circumstances the grand duke selected as his region of attack the wooded sandstone heights of the eastern Carpathians, for here, at a mean altitude rising from 3,250 feet near the sources of the tributaries of the Dunajec to 5,000 feet south of the sources of the San, the wooded and snow-clad mountains gave back to the Russian infantryman his natural advantage over his opponent. For one thing the climate suited him. He was accustomed to bear a greater rigour of cold than any other European. The Austrians of the plains were killed or crippled in thousands by the severity of the winter mountain weather. The Bavarians showed more powers of endurance, but they suffered from frost-bite, while the Russian troops lost few men from this cause.

The only men in the Austrian armies who could fight in the snow on the Carpathian heights with the resisting powers of the Russian troops were the Tyrolean sharpshooters. Good men they were, and greatly enduring, but there were too few of them. The Russians had only to work round the Ondava valley, from which the Dukla Pass ran; then, on a front of twenty miles or so, they would get astride the branching lines of communication, which were feeding the Austro-German front of one hundred and fifty miles in Galicia and the Carpathian rampart. In other words, by advancing southward from the Dukla Pass the Russians could turn the enemy's front and attack him in the rear, after cutting off all his supplies.

This was the reason why General Brusiloff held on only to the Dukla region, and slowly pushed forward there against a desperately stubborn resistance. On all the rest of the front he was content to hold back the Austrians and Germans. He occupied at Dukla the decisive position, and by continually pressing forward he compelled the hostile commanders to mass against him for the defence of the Austrian communications. So hard pressed were the Austrians that three Bavarian army corps, under the command of General von Linsingen, were sent to the Carpathians to assist them. The Bavarians held the Lupkow, Uzsok, and Tuchla Passes, but they were not strong enough for their task. More German aid had to be sent, until the German forces under Linsingen amounted to half a million men. These operations by General Brusiloff had the desired effect not only of preventing the transfer to the Western front of German troops which had been lent to Austria, but actually made it necessary that they should be reinforced. Brusiloff could not undertake a bigger offensive until he was reinforced and had received fresh supplies of rifles and ammunition.

In the meantime the siege of Przemysl was vigorously pressed. The great Austrian fortress on the San river had been remodelled and strengthened by a famous Swiss engineer after the affair of Agadir in 1911. When the new fortifications of Przemysl were completed in 1913 the experts of the German staff examined the fortress very carefully, and congratulated the Austrian staff upon the strength of the new works. In the considered judgment of the German authorities, Przemysl had been transformed into a stronghold superior to Thorn, and at least equal to Metz. That was as much as to say that it was the finest modern fortress in Central Europe. It consisted of nine main works, arranged in a circle around the town.

In these main works were guns of enormous size, mounted in armoured towers, operated by electricity, and automatically disappearing after the gun had discharged its shot. Each of these works was placed on one of the foothills of the Carpathians, at an altitude of 1,000 to 1,350 feet above sea-level. The distance between the main works ran from 2,000 yards to 10,000 yards, there being marshes and other natural obstacles in the wider spaces to help in the defence. In the gaps between the main works there were nine smaller forts, with armour-plated cupolas, quick-firing guns, armoured machine-guns, and motor-batteries. Further, in the course of the siege, a considerable number of temporary works was erected all along the twenty-five-mile ring. There was also a girdle of closed trenches, wire entanglements, and land mines. The railway running from the Russian frontier to Lemberg and Cracow was bent round so as to pass through Przemysl.

So as long as the fortress held out, an invading army fed from Kieff would lack the use of the main railway when operating in Eastern Galicia. This is what occurred when the armies of Generals Brusiloff and Dmitrieff advanced in September, 1914, from Lemberg towards Cracow. Their railway communications were cut by Przemysl, and all through the autumn, winter, and early spring General Dmitrieff in particular had to rely entirely upon the small railway bending up and down by Rava Russka.

The Russian forces in and near the Dukla Pass were also hindered by the control over the Galician railway system exercised by the enemy at Przemysl. The Russians could not maintain their offensive movement over the Dukla Pass against Hungary by a long, strong, persistent culminating effort until the trunk railway was in their hands. In other words, the Russians could not feed and munition an overwhelmingly numerous army in the battle of the Carpathians until they had captured Przemysl. But as the munitions were not yet available the fall of Przemysl was not a necessity in the Russian plan.

There had been an occasion when its swift capture would have been of considerable benefit to the Russian forces. This was in September, 1914, when General Dmitrieff, advancing with amazing speed from Lemberg, hoped to take Cracow by surprise and capture it. Przemysl stood in his way. He massed his artillery against two of the forts, shattered them in a fierce, swift hurricane of shell, and then launched an army corps at the gap. But the main works of defence held good, and the leading Russian brigades were felled in thousands with such rapidity that the attempt to take Przemysl by storm came abruptly to an end. Then in the middle of October, 1914, Hindenburg's advance against Warsaw and Ivangorod compelled the Russian commander-in-chief to alter his entire front; for the Germans and Austrians were superior in number to the Russians and were able to choose their points of attack and to force the Russians to concentrate in answer to their movements. The troops investing Przemysl had to be drawn off to strengthen the fighting front.

But when Hindenburg was thrown back, and his right wing, composed of Austrian and Hungarian troops under General Dankl, was severely handled and almost broken on the Upper Vistula and the Lower San, the situation in Przemysl became serious. General Kusmanek, the commander of the fortress, did not at first know whether the strength of his position had been augmented or decreased. His proper garrison numbered about eighty thousand troops. But after the blow delivered by General Dmitrieff against the Austro-German force, seventy thousand more fugitives—German, Austrian, and Hungarian soldiers—retired into the fortress to avoid capture.

Thus on November 12, 1914, when the second siege began, Kusmanek had double the number of troops that had originally been assigned to the defence of the stronghold. In itself this was a matter of congratulation, for the ring of forts measured twenty-five miles round. The proper garrison for a system of trenches of this extent, reckoning on the estimate of two men to a yard, was eighty-eight thousand men. That left no reserve of the original garrison to fill the gaps caused by casualties and sickness, and to provide for the sorties in great strength which would be required when the Russian front was pressed by the grand relieving army of Austrians and Germans. Thus, from a purely military point of view, General Kusmanek could look with satisfaction on the enormous increase of his forces.

Unhappily for him, the economic situation was not so favourable. The store of food in Przemysl had been measured only by the requirements of the original garrison. After the fall of Lemberg streams of civilian fugitives besides the soldiers had passed into the city. By the middle of November, 1914, the year's food supplies had so diminished that even the original garrison would not have been able to live on the stores for more than eight months. The enormous addition of seventy thousand more soldiers reduced the period for which the fortress could hold out, without further supplies, to five months.

General Kusmanek reckoned on being able to use the larger part of the fugitive troops in strong and vehement sorties before they brought his stock of provisions down to danger point. His superfluous troops were so numerous that it seemed possible they might battle their way through the investing force near the road to the Lupkow Pass, at a time when the main Russian southern army near Lupkow was straining every nerve to meet the attacks of the relieving army from Hungary. If only the troops making the sortie could break through the line of invest-ment they would take Brusiloff's men in the rear at the moment when the relieving forces were pressing on the Russian front. The result of this would be something more important than the relief of Przemysl. The Russian forces round the Dukla Pass would be cut off, together with a considerable portion of Dmitrieff's army fronting Cracow, in Western Galicia. All the land between Cracow and Przemysl would be cleared of Russians, and there would be an admirable opportunity, after the Russian front was broken, of turning and encircling the entire Russian forces in Galicia. In short, what was contemplated, as the result of an overwhelming sortie from Przemysl, was the complete destruction of the southern Russian army.

Brusiloff had no siege artillery, and even his available force of field-guns was not large. No idea of a duel with the great pieces of ordnance at Przemysl could be entertained. The Russian commander could profit only by the enormous number of troops in the fortress and revert to the old-fashioned method of reduction by famine. Only five divisions of Russian troops of the third class, old reservists more than forty years of age, were detached for the siege operations. They were placed under the command of General Selivanov, a veteran of seventy years, who had served in all the Russian wars since the Turkish war of 1877. His forces at first were much inferior to the Przemysl garrison, there being about 100,000 Russians to 170,000 Germans, Austrians, and Hungarians. General Selivanov's field-guns were largely the outworn artillery of the southern army, the tubes having lost their exact rifling by constant use since the beginning of the previous August. When new field-artillery arrived for the army in Galicia General Brusiloff, instead of sending the old guns back to Kieff to be re-rifled, gave them to General Selivanov.

The Russian general kept his batteries well out of range of the great new guns of Przemysl, and entrenched on a wide circle of hills at a long distance from the girdle of forts. His sole object was to stop anybody from getting in or out of the beleaguered fortress-city. He made no attack, but simply waited until General Kusmanek attempted a sortie. Then, as the enemy troops advanced beyond the shelter of their great guns of position, they were shot down close to the wire entanglements in front of the Russian trenches. But in the middle of January Kusmanek began to grow seriously alarmed at the rapid diminution of his food supplies. More of the garrison was sacrificed in vain attempts at a successful sortie, while the Russian sappers began to drive their trenches closer to the ring of forts. The decisive struggle took place in the middle of February, when the southern Russian army was swinging round from its position on the Dukla Pass and winning ground towards Lupkow. Instead of the relieving army in the Carpathians helping the garrison of Przemysl, the garrison troops had to fling themselves out in fierce night attacks, less with a view to breaking through than with the design to compel Selivanov to ask for more reinforcements.

Selivanov had a difficult task. As his line ran in a much larger circle than the ring of forts he was investing, he needed many more troops to hold his positions than did the enemy. As the power of making attacks really rested with the beleaguered Austrians, they could mass at night and break forth for an advance in any direction they chose. The Russian commander could not concentrate in advance against them, but had to leave the defence of the assailed section of trenches in the hands of the ordinary number of men there. The only consequence of the repeated attempts to break through the investing line, conducted by the valiant Hungarian General Tamassy, was that General Selivanov was compelled to use the proper number of men in garrisoning his trenches—two to a yard—which, on a circular front of fifty miles required an army of 176,000 troops. These were infantrymen, and the total Russian besieging forces towards the end of the siege amounted to 200,000 men.

Even this was not very much more than the number of foes against whom they were operating. And these foes had an overwhelming superiority in heavy artillery. But with undaunted courage the Russians sapped forward, building their trenches by special devices, perfected since the outbreak of hostilities, which gave some protection to the troops against even the heaviest projectiles. The outer forts and field fortifications soon fell into the hands of the Russians, who mined and counter-mined, completing each part of their mole-like work by a night attack with bayonets and hand-grenades. But though they were able to push their trenches so near as to bring in view the churches and roofs of Przemysl, they remained incapable of capturing one of the main forts. The Austrians asserted that from November 12, 1914, to March 1, 1915, only three shells fell in the city. Having only short-range artillery, all that the Russian commander could do with it was to cover every path and road by which the enemy could make sorties. He relied almost entirely on shrapnel, which he employed against the hostile troops as they came into the open. Every night the Russian searchlights on the distant hills swept all the country, seeking for signs of a sortie, and telegraphing to the gunners the range and direction of any advancing body of hostile troops. In the second week of March the situation of the defenders became desperate. For some time they had been subsisting on short rations, but these had given out suddenly; for it was found that a large store of tinned meat on which the garrison had been depending was unfit for food.

General Kusmanek informed the Austro-German armies along the Carpathians of the situation by wireless messages, with the result that everything possible was done to relieve the falling fortress. The battles upon the crest and slopes of the mountains raged with terrific fury. Large German reinforcements arrived for General von Linsingen, and every man that Austria-Hungary could at once put into the field was railed up through the Latorcza valley to strengthen General Böhm Ermolli.

In a magnificent spirit of heroism the Germans, Austrians, and Hungarians fought their way through the snow, ascending and descending the frozen rampart of rock, and deploying around the upper vast reaches of the San River. Holding again the Lupkow Pass, the Austrians swept out toward Baligrod, and at the same time advanced from the Uzsok Pass northward. By a tremendous effort and an enormous sacrifice of men the Teutons and Hungarians almost touched the railway thirty miles south of Przemysl. Unfortunately for them, General Brusiloff, knowing the position of affairs in Przemysl, had foreseen all the attacks of the relieving armies. Indeed, one of the chief reasons why only a few shells fell in the beleaguered city during the siege of five months was that the Austrian movements had been long foreseen. The Russians had saved their ammunition to shatter the supreme attack by the relieving armies.

General Brusiloff was offered a powerful park of heavy siege-guns in January, 1915, but he said he could do without it, if it could be used with effect elsewhere. The park was, in fact, employed along the opposite flank of the great Russian battle-front, and the siege of Przemysl went on with extraordinary quietness except for the sorties of the famishing garrison. When, however, in March, 1915, the offensive movement of the German and Austrian relieving armies culminated in an attack upon

Brusiloff's Carpathian front, there was no need to prolong any further the agony of the beleaguered fortress town. By then the siege had served its main purpose, and had dragged the forces of Austria-Hungary beyond the limit of their strength. To complete his grand design Brusiloff needed at once the 200,000 men detained around Przemysl. So General Selivanov was ordered to close in upon the doomed city and carry it, if need be, by storm.

On March 14 the veteran general opened the attack, for which all the means had been available since the previous January. The operations were started in the north by the village of Malkovice, along the railway line from Jaroslav. Heavy howitzers were brought up by the railway, and the bombardment of the strong main fort dominating the highway to the north was begun. At the same time the smaller works on this northern section were assailed, and the hostile batteries were so well mastered that on March 16 the Russian infantry carried the heights and entrenched themselves within rifle-shot of the forts. The Austrians tried to recover some of the ground by using an armoured train along the railway. The train came along at night with a large body of troops in the hinder carriages, but the Russian searchlight men spotted it and directed the guns on it, and the armoured train was swiftly and completely wrecked by shell fire.

The Russians advanced in open formation, by crawling in short rushes, and drove the defenders from the miles of trenches along the high-road and railway. The ground was covered with snow, making it easy for searchlights on both sides to light up advancing or retreating troops, who then came under a tempest of shrapnel. Fortunately for the Russians there was a birch wood, with a stretch of thick, short undergrowth, along the line the Russians were taking, and it served them as cover from observation till they were close on the railway. The great forts tried to retrieve the defeat on the northern section by a continual bombardment of the closing-in lines of Russian trenches. Twenty thousand rounds of big-gun ammunition were fired daily on March 15 and March 16. But the Russians were too deeply entrenched to be shattered by even this terrific fire. They continued to advance from the south as well as from the north, occupying the village of Krasiczyn south-westward. It was against the southern Russian trenches that most of the great shells were flung on March 17, preparatory to the final sortie of the garrison.   General Kusmanek served out the last rations, and issued a proclamation to the troops :

Soldiers, half a year has passed while we children of almost all the nationalities of our beloved country have incessantly stood shoulder to shoulder against the enemy. Thanks to God's help and your bravery, I have succeeded, despite the enemy's attacks, despite cold and privations, in defending the fortress against the enemy. You have already done much to win the acknowledgments of the Commander-in-Chief, the gratitude of the country, and even the respect of the enemy.

Yonder in our beloved country, thousands and thousands of hearts are beating for us. Millions are waiting with held breath for news of us.

Heroes, I am about to make my last demand of you. The honour of our Army and country requires it. I am going to lead you out, a steel wedge, to break through the iron ring of the foe, and then, with unflagging efforts, move farther and farther till we rejoin our Army, which, at the price of stubborn battles, has already approached quite near to us. We are on the eve of a big fight, for the enemy will not willingly allow the booty to slip through his fingers. But, remember, gallant defenders of Przemysl, each one of you must be possessed by the single idea, " Forward, ever forward !" All that stands in our way must be crushed.

Soldiers, we have distributed our last stores, and the honour of our country, and of every one of us, forbids that after such a hard-fought, glorious, and victorious struggle we should fall into the power of the enemy like a helpless crowd. Hero-soldiers, we must break through, and we shall !

This appeal appears to have been made to all the infantry and cavalry forces of the garrison. But such was the feeling of utter dispiritment, due perhaps partly to want of sufficient food, that only 20,000 men answered it.   These were mainly Hungarians, comprising the 23rd Honved division, part of the 23rd Landwehr brigade, and the 4th regiment of Hussars. Led by the brave Hungarian General Tamassy, this fighting remnant of the garrison marched out beyond the forts at five o'clock on Friday morning, March 19. They advanced in an easterly direction in a determined manner, but were unable after nine hours' fighting to reach the Russian trenches. Eight thousand of them were killed, and nearly four thousand were taken prisoners. At the same time as the Przemysl garrison made its last vain essay to break through, a furious battle was opened by the relieving armies. The attack raged especially west and east of Gorlice. The Austro-Hungarians used 12 in. howitzer fire, under cover of which twenty battalions flung themselves against the Russian trenches, but they were held up on the wire entanglements, and there shot down by machine-guns and magazine rifles. Another attack was delivered by a Honved brigade against the height held by the Russians near Ciezkovice. Only a Russian battalion held the position at first, and their line was taken, but they counter-attacked, with two battalions hurrying to their aid, and beat the enemy back by noon.

An hour afterwards the 30th Honved division swept out in a great charge. Despite their heavy losses, the Hungarians got through the wire entanglements and took the height. But the Russians were reinforced, and drove them back. Three times the position was lost and won, but at four o'clock in the afternoon the remnant of Russians made a fourth counter-attack. Such was the fierceness of battle on both sides that neither asked nor gave quarter; and after slaughtering all their foes the Russians recovered their trenches. The swaying battle-line extended from Gorlice in western Galicia, across the Carpathians, to Svidnik in Hungary, then back over the Carpathians near the Lupkow Pass, to Baligrod and Lutoviska; thence over the Dniester and along the Stry River. In no place did the relieving armies break through. All their vigorous and costly attacks were intended solely to withdraw attention from Przemysl, and to provide favourable conditions for the final sortie of the garrison.

After the Hungarian division was repulsed, no course was left to General Kusmanek but to prepare for surrender. Meanwhile the Russians pressed the attack relentlessly on Friday night and Saturday against the east and north front. But across the sound of the guns there suddenly came a series of thunderous explosions. The Austrians were blowing up the great forts, motor-batteries, magazines, bridges, and everything likely to be useful to the victors. One of the smaller forts with quick-firing guns was captured by the Russians in time to save it from entire destruction. But all the main works of defence were so thoroughly dynamited that Przemysl lost all its importance as a place of strength. The famous 12 in. Skoda howitzers were blown into fragments; every soldier was ordered to destroy his rifle. Then, as the Russian shells began to fall on the aeroplane sheds, four Austrian airmen made their last flight from the fortress in the two last machines left intact. The scene below them was indescribably terrible. From the exploding ammunition stores smoke and flame shot up in clouds, the military buildings and warehouses were on fire, and the flying machines were in danger of being overturned by the force of the explosions. Then on Monday morning, March 22, 1915, General Kusmanek, who had opened negotiations for surrender on March 20, gave up the fortress.

The fall of Przemysl, which gave the Russians control over the trunk railway of Galicia, and thus strengthened their hold on the recovered duchy, was an event of high importance; for the Austrians then lost about one quarter of the territory of the Dual Monarchy, with a population of eight million. As Galicia had contributed to the Austro-Hungarian army about one-fifth of its recruits, the effect of the loss was increased. Moreover, Galicia was a province of enormous natural wealth. It was the only centre of oil production in the Teutonic Empire; its coal reserves were vast, and its great salt-mines almost within reach of Dmitrieff's army were of great importance. The fall of the fortress released General Selivanov's army, together with a large portion of that of General Dmitrieff, which had assisted in the final assault. By the fall of Przemysl the main-line railway communication with Kieff through Lemberg became available for the supply of munitions to the Russian army. The garrison which surrendered to the Russians numbered about 120,000 officers and men. Nearly a thousand guns were taken, but fewer than two hundred were fit for use.

The day after the fall of Przemysl the Russians began to advance over the Carpathians towards Hungary. Half the 200,000 troops released by the success of the siege operations were sent southward towards the Dukla and Lupkow passes. There they strengthened the front of the Russian southern army, and the reinforced troops began steadily to push both the Austrians and the Germans over the crests of the mountains. In the neighbourhood of the Dukla the three road passes of Polyanka, the Dukla, and the Jaliska were won by the Russians, and they descended the Hungarian slopes towards Bartfeld, Svidnik, and the valley of the Laborcz river. Then in the higher and more densely-wooded heights between the Lupkow and the Uzsok passes they conquered, in the first week of April, 1915, the towering forested ridge of the Polonina mountains and approached Rostok Pass. From this point they progressed by fierce and incessant forest fighting through the deep snow to the Smolink Hills, situated beyond the main Carpathian ridge, on the Hungarian decline. The Lupkow Pass was captured and an advance was made from the Hungarian side against the Uzsok Pass. This threatened to cut off the German force defending the pass, and when this was done there would be a gap of seventy miles in the Carpathian defences— quite a large enough door for Brusiloff to flood the Hungarian plain with a large force of troops. Such was the position in the last week in April, 1915.

At this time the Central Powers decided to make a determined attempt to retrieve the situation in this theatre of war. The former minister for war, General Falkenhayn, who had succeeded Moltke as chief of staff, took over the enormous task of directing operations on both the eastern and western fronts, and General Mackensen was appointed to lead the main German forces in Galicia. General Linsingen, commanding the German troops on the Munkacs-Stry line, was further reinforced and given larger powers of command. The Austrian Archduke Friedrich, nominally in chief command over the Austro-Hungarian forces, was placed under the control of Mackensen; the Archduke Ferdinand, commanding the army along the Dunajec, was also subordinated to Mackensen, and similarly all the other Austrian and Hungarian commands were strictly subjected to German leadership.

All through the winter and early spring the German artillerymen in France and Flanders had been ordered to observe a strict economy in the use of high-explosive shells. This was the explanation of the momentary allied ascendancy in artillery power, remarked by both the French and British commanders at the close of 1914. Germany was quite as formidable in heavy armament as she had been, and it was calculated that in the manufacture of munitions she was still seventy-five per cent. more efficient than Britain and France combined. In all German and Austrian armament factories the work had been kept going day and night by three eight-hour shifts in the early months of the war. But after the defeat at Ypres the supply of munitions was increased, by engrossing every power-lathe formerly used for ordinary work, and setting the armament mechanics

FRENCH CAMP AT SEDD-EL-BAHR. In the Gallipoli operations the French forces co-operating with the British were commanded at first by General d'Amade. The village of Sedd-el-Bahr was one of the landing places of the Allies, and was used as a base for men and stores. Sedd-el-Bahr stands on the north side of the entrance to the Dardanelles, and being of great strategic importance was formerly strongly fortified by the Turks.

EARLY GAS ATTACK AT "PLUGSTREET" WOOD. Chlorine gas—the first poison gas used in the Great War—was stored under pressure in cylinders in the trenches and discharged as a cloud against the enemy, the wind carrying the cloud along. Later, phosgene was employed in the same way, and was also used as a shell charge. Chlorosulphuric acid was used to some extent in smoke pots, and was sometimes mistaken for a defensive smoke screen. Gas-cloud discharges largely depended for their efficiency on wind direction and other meteorological conditions. Plugstreet Wood was the popular name for the wood in Belgium correctly called Ploegsteert, prominent in the German gas attack in April 1915.

Plate 18

Volume 11

Cribb

BRITISH "E" CLASS SUBMARINE. There was a rapid increase in tonnage of under-sea craft up to the end of 1914. The first British submarines were of the type ordered by Lord Fisher in 1901. The latest pre-war "E" class, of which the above is one, were of 750 tons. These submarines did excellent work early in the war. The E11 torpedoed the Stambul off Constantinople on May 25, 1915, and sank other enemy craft, including a transport.

THE TORPEDOED LUSITANIA ABOUT TO SINK. The Lusitania, one of the world's largest liners (tonnage 31,500) was torpedoed and sunk by a German submarine off the Old Head of Kinsale on May 7, 1915. She had on board nearly 2,000 persons, of whom 1,195 lost their lives, being either drowned or killed.

Plate 20

Volume 11

and labourers on a general twelve-hour shift, the men working in weekly turns of twelve hours' day work and twelve hours' night work.

The fierce winter battle on the Bzura, Pilica, and Nieder rivers, and the operations of the German army of half a million men north of Warsaw along the Bobr, Narew, and Niemen rivers, necessitated the use of a vast number of high-explosive shells. In all their battles against the Russians the Germans used their superior artillery power in a wasteful manner. This waste was partly balanced by the economy observed upon the western front, and with the extreme speeding up of all the gun-making work and munition factories, General Falkenhayn had his new war machine ready for operations by the middle of April, 1915. Krupp and Skoda and other gunmakers had provided him with two thousand new heavy pieces of ordnance, and three millions of large, heavy, high-explosive shells. There were also 2,000 new or fairly unworn pieces of field-artillery, and for these also there were truckloads of high-explosive shell ready. At the same time the manufacture of machine-guns had gone on at high speed, enabling the ordinary fire-power of the infantry to be enormously increased.

It was Falkenhayn's original intention to use this new war-machine to break the Franco-British front, but with Hindenburg's complete failure in the eastern theatre of war, Falkenhayn's scheme for a decisive spring campaign in the west had to be postponed. So successful was the southern Russian army under General Brusiloff that by the middle of April it was in a position to advance into the Hungarian plain and cut the communications of all the German and Austrian troops on the Carpathian front. By his extraordinary success, combined with the general lack of munitions of war in Russia, General Brusiloff drew on his men the blow intended originally for the French and British troops.

The part of the Russian line chosen by Falkenhayn for his attack lay between Tarnov and Gorlice and faced towards Cracow. It was held only by a small entrenched army of 160,000 men, under the Bulgarian commander, General Dmitrieff. By selecting for attack two places on this short front, the existence of all the Russian armies in Galicia and Hungary could be menaced. The Austro-German means of communication round Cracow were excellent. There were two lines of railways running from Cracow to Dmitrieff's positions at Tarnov, near the Dunajec river, and at Gorlice, on the Ropa stream. Then, midway between Cracow and Tarnov, the two railways were connected by a cross-country line, enabling troops to be manœuvred in trains from south to north or north to south. In the south, on the Lower Dunajec, was the railway junction of Neu Sandez, from which another railway ran into northern Hungary. There were thus three railways, by means of which the heavy howitzers and high-explosive shells could be transported for action against the narrow lateral Russian front in Western Galicia.

Towards the end of April General Dmitrieff observed the concentration of enemy forces against his line. He was far from suspecting that the greatest military machine known in history was being brought against his comparatively small forces. He asked for reinforcements, and General Ivanoff, on the Nida front north of him, and General Brusiloff, on the Carpathian front south of him, sent what men and guns they could spare. But when the blow fell on the night of April 28, 1915, the force of it was beyond anything that man had experienced.

About seven hundred guns were employed by General Dmitrieff to defend his lines along the Dunajec and the Biala rivers until the fall of Przemysl enabled him to increase his artillery. When reinforced, he had about 250,000 troops between the Lower Vistula and the Carpathian heights, but a good many of them lacked their artillery corps, as there was still a serious shortage of munitions. The front was far too short for the deployment of Mackensen's forces. Both the guns and the troops were arranged in a step formation, or echelon system. Yet the echelons were so close together that there was a practically solid line of front from the point where the Dunajec flowed into the Vistula to the point where the Biala valley merged into the Carpathian heights.

The Archduke Ferdinand advanced on the night of April 30 against the Dunajec front. Mackensen attacked south of Tarnov, between that town and Gorlice. His front extended only about twenty-five miles, from Tuchov to Gorlice. He had at least half a million men, including all the remnants of the Prussian Guard and the best Bavarian and Saxon troops from the French and Flemish front. His crack troops numbered 150,000, and the rest of his men were mainly drawn from the

First German Reserve. He had 1,500 heavy guns, including most of the available 17 in. howitzers. Opposed to him were two army corps of General Dmitrieff's army, reduced by the wastage of war to 60,000 men. There was thus somewhat less than one Russian to every yard of front, and as there were three lines of Russian trenches, the trench garrisons amounted to about one man to four yards. Mackensen began the attack with what the Germans called a hurricane fire. For four hours every gun and howitzer was worked as fast as human hands could work it, and 700,000 high-explosive shells were pitched into the Russian trenches—more than ten shells to each Russian soldier.

The quantity of projectiles used by Mackensen's forces on this narrow front in four hours was double the amount formerly regarded as necessary for a six months' siege of a great and well-provisioned fortress. There was no escape from the 17 in. Skoda shells. Each shell weighed 2,800 pounds; in its flight it rose nearly five miles in the air, and it penetrated twenty feet into soft ground before it exploded. Every living thing within one hundred and fifty yards of the explosion was killed, and many persons farther off were also slain. The main damage was not done by the metal fragments, but by the enormous pressure of the exploding gas. The gas got into the body cavities, and in its further process of expansion tore the flesh apart. Men who happened to be close by entirely disappeared; not the slightest remains of their clothes or of their flesh could be found. Scores of men at a distance who escaped metal fragments, stones, and showers of earth, were killed, lacerated, or blinded by the pressure of gas. The gas also broke in the partitions and bomb-proof roofs of shelters, and as the force of the explosion travelled everywhere along the air, no winding of the trenches was a defence against the terrible pressure.

At Ciezkovice on May 1 the Russians managed for a time to hold their ground even under the hurricane of shells. They remained silent and motionless until the German infantry advanced to occupy the wrecked trenches; then they opened fire at six hundred paces and repulsed them. But farther south, at Gorlice, there was no battle. The famous naphtha town was battered into a heap of ruins, only one wall with a tower standing in the midst of unimaginable devastation. The immense oil-tanks were set on fire at the first attack, and for days the flames shot up into the clouds, making the place look in the distance like a gigantic torch. The Russians who survived the first inferno of shell fire beat back the advancing infantry and retired in the night north-eastward to Biecz. Then, on the fourteen-mile front from Tuchov-Biecz, Mackensen, by means of long-range fire from his heavy artillery and a bombardment at shorter range by his field guns, delivered another attack on May 2. But between Tuchov and Biecz there are three streams and the Branka Mountain, with a peak 1,600 feet high. The peak dominates a considerable stretch of the lower course of the Biala. General Dmitrieff made full use of this advantage in the lie of the land, and though he had only light field-artillery firing shrapnel he held the enemy up for another three days.

It was not until May 5 that Mackensen's enormously gunned army succeeded in blowing a path through the Russians' three lines of defences east of the Biala. Thus General Dmitrieff, by a magnificent six days' resistance on his southern front and flank, gave the southern Russian army, operating in Hungary from the Zboro, Dukla, and Lupkow passes, full time to withdraw in good order away from the mountains and back to the San. Only the 48th Russian division, under General Korniloff, was cut off by the enemy while retiring from the Dukla pass on May 6. Korniloff's troops were surrounded on all sides, but their commander skilfully massed them in the direction of the San Valley, and by a violent attacking movement through the densely wooded foothills the division shot and bayoneted its way out of the German ring of flame and steel and rejoined its parent corps on Friday, May 7.

What, however, the Russian commander could not do was to extemporise an artillery power equal to that of the enemy. A thousand heavy guns of position are not made in a day or a month, and three million high-explosive shells from 6 in. to 17 in. in diameter cannot be manufactured on the spur of the moment. The port of Archangel was closed to ordinary traffic in May to enable the British and French Governments to pour into Russia every gun and shell, rifle and cartridge, that could be spared. The operations of the British armies were to some extent delayed by the necessity to help Russia. At the same time the Siberian railway was working at high pressure, connecting the Galician battlefield with the armament factories of Japan and America. With all this outside help Russia could not, in a few weeks, get anything like the artillery power of her enemies; but she did equip a fresh army and get some hundreds of howitzers of a lighter model, which were the most useful of all in battles of manœuvres on the open field.

The Grand Phalanx which Falkenhayn had built up was the hugest battering-ram ever constructed, but naturally it could only act in battering-ram fashion. Placed in position, with a solid, definite obstacle to work against, it could quickly smash that obstacle into fragments. But when the obstacle withdrew at a speed of twenty miles a day, the battering-ram could not at once pursue it and immediately get to work again. Mackensen's extraordinary number of heavy artillery, and his store of thousands of high-explosive shells, some weighing more than a ton each, could only be moved along a railway. The Russians thoroughly destroyed all railway lines as they retreated, and badly damaged every metalled roadway. The consequence was that the battering-ram could only move forward when the Germans and Austrians had rebuilt the railway. The speed varied from three miles to five miles a day at the most. Something like four miles a day was therefore the average rate of progress of Mackensen's army and its enormous siege train.

The German commander-in-chief had sacrificed mobility to power. Basing his plan entirely on the conditions of the trench warfare system obtaining throughout the western front, and extending over the larger section of the eastern front, he had constructed a war-machine that could break through any trench system and shatter any fortress, but which could not pursue an enemy. As a matter of fact, both the Germans and the Austrians were too eager to pursue. On each occasion when the Russian lines withdrew from the zone of heavy shell fire the attacking infantry advanced in an attempt to transform the retreat into a rout. The Russians waited for them with light field-guns, machine-guns, and infantry concealed in woods and ditches from the eyes of reconnoitring airmen. Thus time after time they struck a damaging counter-blow.

But on May 9 Mackensen's army was further reinforced from Cracow. It crossed the Wislok at Krosno, and the troops deployed in dense lines along the high range of hills running from Stryschov on the Wislok to Brozov on the tributary stream of the Stobnica. It was only a sixteen-mile front, ending about thirty miles west of Przemysl. Covered only by their light field-artillery, the German troops, with the battered Prussian Guards still at their head, manœuvred in a brave and impetuous manner under the most brilliant of German commanders, and making a frontal attack against the Russian centre, broke it by pressure of massed numbers. It was a well-fought, well-managed victory in the old, orthodox Prussian manner. Mackensen sacrificed his men in tens of thousands at the decisive point until they had advanced so close that neither the Russian bayonet nor the Russian shrapnel could master its final charge. Mackensen broke clean through the Russian front.

No orderly retirement was possible. The Russian general gave way in his centre, making no attempt to retrieve the position there, but sent all his reserve troops in a march southward. By means of their magnificent marching powers the Russians rounded the enemy's flank, and in a series of furious charges worked round still farther and menaced his rear. First a German division gave way, then an army corps, enabling the Russians in front also to advance southward to take part in the surprise turning movement. Mackensen was losing on his right flank double what he was winning on his advanced centre. In fact, his whole line was in danger, the Russians having got a hook round it. He had to draw back his victorious troops and send them to his rear, and check the Russian flanking movement. The Russian commander was not able to press his advantage, through lack of a decisive number of men, but he completely stopped Mackensen's advance and was able to retreat to the San River in a tranquil manner. One of the reasons why the Russian counter-stroke was not fully driven home at Krosno was that a large part of the new reinforcements was operating in the Bukovina.

Here, on the same day as Mackensen in Galicia received his first severe check, a battle was raging on a forty-mile front from Obertyn to Czernovitz. A large Austrian army was trying to work up to the Dniester, and then, in co-operation with the German army moving towards Stry, envelop Lemberg from the east, and cut the Russian communications with Kieff. In conjunction with the severe pressure that the armies of the Archduke Ferdinand and Mackensen were exercising on the east, and the army of Linsingen and the army of Böhm Ermolli were exercising from the south, the enemy's flanking movement in the Bukovina was a very serious matter. But General

Brusiloff had good railway communications with Russia at Tarnopol, north of the Dniester. That is to say, he could get reinforcements and munitions quickly, and his local commander-in-chief agreed that the Bukovina front was the best suited for a counter-blow.

Therefore, on May 9 the Russians offered battle round Czernovitz, and advanced in impetuous attack for two days, throwing the enemy back with heavy losses. Some 5,000 prisoners were taken and six guns, and the advanced enemy forces holding the bridge-head on the Dniester at the railway town of Zalestchiki were routed. At the same time a strong attack was made upon the hostile forces working up from the Carpathian Mountains. More than 5,000 bodies were found in front of the Russians on the mountain slopes of the Javornik range. In five days 20,000 prisoners were taken between the Dniester and the Pruth rivers, and the Russians captured the town of Nadvorna, and cut the railway between Bukovina and Austria. This for the time being put an end to the Austrian attempt at a flanking movement from the Bukovina.

The Austrians still lacked driving power. All the chief work in the struggle for Galicia was done by German troops under Mackensen or Linsingen. Linsingen's fighting army was the chief force in the south. More than half a million men were employed by him, with a large amount of light field-artillery, including many 6 in. howitzers. Some 12 in. pieces of ordnance were also brought up over the mountain range as the railway was rebuilt. But the difficulties of communication were so great that the heavy artillery power of this second great German army remained very much inferior to that of Mackensen's force. The result was that Linsingen, having to meet Brusiloff on fairly equal terms, was continually defeated in his advance against Lemberg. Indeed, Linsingen was only able to advance when Brusiloff resolved to shorten his line with a view to assisting the 3rd Russian army.

As General Ivanoff viewed the situation, the entire success of Falkenhayn's scheme depended on the progress made by Linsingen. Mackensen and his mighty Phalanx, crawling forward at a speed of four miles a day, had failed to break the Russian front and encircle the southern Russian army. The movement of the Phalanx was therefore no longer a menace, but merely a new development of the war of attrition. The vast and cumbrous moving siege train could be left to exhaust itself in continual frontal attacks, with the Russians giving way very slowly as they wore down the enemy. If necessary, this kind of Russian retreat could be carried on for months, at the rate of four miles a day, without Mackensen getting farther into Russian territory than the Austrians had done in August, 1914, before they were completely overthrown and routed.

But the position of Linsingen's army was different. It was making a flank attack against the Russians at the same time as the Phalanx was making a frontal attack. If the flank attack succeeded, the consequence would be an overwhelming disaster to all the Russian forces in Galicia. So the Grand Duke Nicholas devoted special attention to the struggle between Linsingen and Brusiloff. Brusiloff completely retired from the Carpathian front in the middle of May, and took his stand in the valley of the Dniester from Drohobycz.

The Russian position on the Dniester was very strong. In the western reaches above Sambor and Drohobycz there was a twenty-mile stretch of wide river-swamps, fed by the melting snows of the Carpathians, and forming for the time an impassable defence. Then, in the more eastward reaches, there were open cultivated spaces with intervals of dense woodland along the northern bank. The Russian general strongly entrenched along the open spaces, and placed most of his guns there. In the forests he left only advance-guards with machine-guns to defend the crossings. On nearing the river, Linsingen made a general reconnaissance in force on a front of forty miles. He was beaten back at all the towns and open spaces, but won a bridge-head at last near Zuravno, where the northern bank of the river was thickly wooded. Here the army of Count Bothmer, which constituted the main striking force of Linsingen's command, crossed the Dniester on the night of June 6, after having lost some ten thousand men two days before in a fruitless attempt on the Russian bridge-head near the junction of the Stry and Dniester.

Having at last got across the Dniester by Zuravno, Count Bothmer advanced through the forest for two days, winning a stretch of ground on the northern bank some fourteen miles long and ten miles broad. But around this wooded tract the Russians closed in on the night of June 8, and then in a long, violent hand-to-hand struggle the Germans were pushed back over and into the river. It was a soldiers' battle with the bayonet, similar to that which had occurred in the forests near Ivangorod in October, 1914. All the Russians' stores of ammunition were running low, cartridges as well as shells; but by getting the enemy into a deep forest, where none of his guns was of much use, General Brusiloff, in spite of the heavy material odds against him, won on June 9 an important victory on the flank position along the Dniester.

Meanwhile, General Mackensen, with the large force called the grand phalanx and its supporting armies, continued to make good progress in the direction of Przemysl. In frontal attack after frontal attack Mackensen battered his way forward, losing many men, and yet increasing his infantry forces as his siege train crawled along; for the German Staff, directed by General Falkenhayn, fed the Phalanx with every available soldier in the two Central Empires. Mackensen's great siege train slowly moved along the railway, from Gorlice to Jaslo, and thence northward to Rzeszoff towards Jaroslav. He attacked Jaroslav on Friday, May 14, meeting only a single Russian division, entrenched for a rearguard action on the hills west of the town. For two days the division held back the Germans, while the main Russian forces crossed the river and entrenched along the eastern bank.

Then, on Monday, May 17, the real battle began. The Prussian guard corps, with the 10th army corps and the 41st reserve corps and a composite corps, advanced across the fords of the San, between Jaroslav and the town of Sieniawa. Their forward movement was heralded by a tempest of heavy shells from the German batteries. But such was the skill of the Russian general in choosing his ground and directing the counter-attack that Mackensen only won from one to three miles' depth of ground east of the river. Then, entrenching some of his reserve troops along the foothold won along the east bank of the San, the German commander put the larger part of his siege train on the railway, and travelled back to Sanok in the south, and thence towards Przemysl.

For the Russian general staff the solely vital problem was to keep the Russian lines intact for as long and wearing a fighting retreat as the German staff cared to impose upon the Russian armies. But in the last anxious days of May it seemed to some of Russia's western allies as if the obstinate attempt at a long defence of the perilous salient at Przemysl might give Mackensen the opportunity for the grand stroke of breaking through the Russian forces. It was almost with a feeling of relief that military circles in Britain and France heard that the enemy had recaptured Przemysl on June 3. The delay in retiring was then revealed. The Russians had filled the city full of military stores. To prevent these stores from falling into the hands of the Austrians and Germans, a small, heroic rearguard manned the entrenchments while the war material was being rapidly removed by the double-track railway to Lemberg and the broad highway running due east. What the Austrians recovered was nothing but the empty shell of what had been their mightiest stronghold.

CHAPTER 12

Politics and Munitions

PROBABLY before the end of 1914 the majority of the British people realized that the struggle to which the country was committed was different in degree from anything that had gone before, but it was not until later that it was realized that it was different also in kind. Britain's previous wars had been fought by a small professional navy and army, usually far from the country's shores, and with weapons manufactured in a single arsenal. The general public had only learned of the battles and other incidents, in which many of them took only a languid interest, after an interval of time. The classic instance, an oft-quoted one, of this detachment is found in the novels of Jane Austen. Writing in the midst of the struggle against Napoleon, she describes the social life of her own class, which included sailors and soldiers, without any reference to the war raging in Europe. It is impossible to imagine anyone writing of life in England in any rank or class during the Great War without showing almost on every page how it permeated every fibre of the nation's being and entered into every one of its manifold activities.

The inventions of science were responsible for the marked difference between the two epochs. In 1914 the word relativity had not been coined, but the principle it expresses was operating. The invention of the telegraph, both wire and wireless, made it possible for the reporting of the event in a distant land to be practically identical with its occurrence. The development of aircraft, and other forms of locomotion had so reduced distance that 600 miles had become nearer to one than 60 miles was a century before, while gunnery ranges had been lengthened in much the same proportion. The result of these changes was to place the population at home on the edge, as it were, of the battle area, while the demands of the forces for arms and ammunition made it necessary to set large numbers of civilians, both men and women, at work on producing and transporting them. The war had become not merely a battle of the nations, as was Leipzig in 1814, but a veritable war of the nations.

It was one of Napoleon's maxims that victory goes to the big battalions, but the experience of the Great War has been that it goes rather to the big batteries. The need of all the armies was for an enormous supply of guns and ammunition, especially perhaps of machine-guns and high-explosive shells; an amount far greater than anyone had previously thought possible was required, and the Germans were the first to realize this new and pregnant fact. They were first in the field with an overwhelming supply of munitions, as they had been, in August, 1914, with an overwhelming supply of men.

Great Britain was in a less fortunate position. The shortage was at first one of munitions generally, but as the struggle went on it became one of high-explosive shells which, because of their greater utility in modern warfare, were rapidly supplanting shrapnel. As early as October the French were using these high-explosive shells almost entirely, but the British continued to employ shrapnel.

Sir John French made constant appeals to the War Office for more munitions, and Mr. Lloyd George, in his War Memoirs, quotes a request sent by the commander-in-chief on December 31, 1914. Sir John said:

> The present supply of artillery ammunition has been found to be so inadequate as to make offensive operations, even on a small scale, quite out of the question. Recent experience has shown that the ammunition available suffices for scarcely one hour's bombardment of a small portion of the enemy's line, and that even this operation leaves no ammunition to repel

a counter-attack or to give the assaulting columns sufficient support. Owing to the nature of the operations in which we are, and shall continue to be, engaged, the supply of artillery ammunition is the governing factor.

The shortage became more evident in the early weeks of 1915, and on February 9 it was announced that the president of the board of trade had appointed Sir George Askwith, Sir Francis Hopwood, and Sir George Gibb to inquire into and report upon the best steps to secure that all the available productive power of the employees engaged in the engineering and shipbuilding establishments of the country should be utilised in the emergency. About this time, reasons for the shortage of munitions were being discussed. The failure to produce more was ascribed to the prevalence of strikes and the temptations of drink.

In a speech delivered at Bangor on February 28, Mr. Lloyd George referred to both of these reasons, and Lord Kitchener did the same on March 15, in the House of Lords. Mr. Lloyd George said that " For one reason or another we are not getting all the assistance we have a right to expect from our works," and added: " I say here solemnly that it is intolerable that the life of Britain should be imperilled for the matter of a farthing an hour." He spoke equally strongly about the lure of the drink, as he called it: " Drink is doing us more damage in the war than all the German submarines put together." Lord Kitchener mentioned the restrictions imposed by the trade unions as another reason for the inadequate output of munitions.

On March 9 Mr. George introduced into Parliament a bill called the Defence of the Realm Amendment (No. 2) Bill, which gave the Government power to take over the control of all works capable of being used for the production of munitions of war. This meant that at any time a manufacturer might be told that his works were required and he must turn out—a drastic, but in the circumstances a necessary proceeding. In his speech, Mr. Lloyd George said: " It is vitally important that we should increase the output, and every facility for the output of munitions of war," and he remarked that he was arranging for a central committee to take charge of the scheme and was looking out for " a good, strong business man with some go in him, who will be able to push the thing through." Six days later Lord Kitchener referred to the same subject. He mentioned the excellent response of the armament trades to the nation's need and the loyalty of a great majority of the employees, but added:

> Notwithstanding these efforts to meet our requirements, we have unfortunately found that the output is not only not equal to our necessities, but does not fulfil our expectations, for a very large number of our orders have not been completed by the dates on which they were promised.

It was on this occasion that he said that " the supply of war material at the present moment and for the next two or three months is causing me very serious anxiety."

On March 17 Mr. Lloyd George met the representatives of the trade unions and suggested to them that during the war all their rules and regulations restricting output should be suspended and that labour disputes should be arranged without any stoppage of work. The result was that a memorandum containing certain recommendations to workmen was signed by Mr. Lloyd George and Mr. Walter Runciman on behalf of the Government, and by Mr. Arthur Henderson and Mr. William Mosses on behalf of the workmen. Its chief points were as follows:

> During the war period there shall in no case be any stoppage of work upon munitions and equipments of war. All differences on wages or conditions of employment shall be the subject of conferences between the parties. In all cases of failure to reach a settlement of disputes by the parties directly concerned or their representatives, or under existing agreements, the matter in dispute shall be dealt with under any one of three alternatives as may be mutually agreed, or, in default of agreement, settled by the Board of Trade. An advisory committee representative of the workers engaged in production for government requirements shall be appointed by the Government. During the war period, the relaxation of the present trade practices is imperative. Any departure from the practice ruling shall only be for the period of the war. The relaxation of existing demarcation restrictions or admission of semi-skilled or female labour shall not affect adversely the rates customarily paid for the job.

On March 29 the Shipbuilding Employers' Federation sent a deputation to Mr. Lloyd George to advocate the closing of public houses and clubs in areas where munitions of war were produced. They brought forward evidence that much of the increased wages earned by the workmen was spent in drink, and pointed out the obvious fact that this drinking was detrimental to good and regular work and had already caused serious delays. Mr. Lloyd George's reply should be given in detail:

Having gone into this matter a great deal more closely during the last few weeks, I must say that I have a growing conviction, based on accumulating evidence, that nothing but root and branch methods will be of the slightest avail in dealing with this evil. I believe that to be the general feeling. The feeling is that if we are to settle with German militarism we must first of all settle with drink. We are fighting Germany, Austria, and drink; and as far as I can see the greatest of these three deadly foes is drink. Success in the war is now purely a question of munitions; I say that not on my own authority, but on the authority of our great general, Sir John French. He has made it quite clear what his conviction is on the subject. I think I can venture to say that that is also the conviction of the secretary of state for war, and it is the conviction of all those who know anything about the military problem—that in order to enable us to win all we require is an increase, and an enormous increase, in the shells, rifles, and all the other munitions and equipment which are necessary to carry through a great war. You have proved to us to-day quite clearly that the excessive drinking in the works connected with these operations is interfering seriously with that output. I can only promise you this at the present moment, that the words you have addressed to my colleagues and myself will be taken into the most careful consideration by my colleagues when we come to our final decision on this question.

Meanwhile, the British failure to pierce the German lines at the battle of Neuve Chapelle in March had brought about a crisis. On March 13 French telegraphed to Lord Kitchener "cessation of the forward movement is necessitated to-day by the fatigue of the troops, and, above all, by the want of ammunition," and five days later he wrote:

I desire to state, with all the weight of my authority as commander-in-chief of the British army in France, that the object of his majesty's Government cannot be attained unless the supply of artillery ammunition can be increased sufficiently to enable the Army to engage in sustained offensive operations, and I further desire to impress on them the very serious nature of the effort that it is necessary to make to achieve this end.

In his despatch of April 5 the field-marshal again mentioned this matter.

> An almost unlimited supply of ammunition is necessary, and a most liberal discretionary power as to its use must be given to the artillery commanders. I am confident that this is the only means by which great results can be obtained with a minimum of loss.

Under the stimulus of Mr. Lloyd George's energy more vigorous steps were now taken, and in April he found his " good, strong business man " in Mr. G. M. Booth, of Liverpool, who became secretary of a new departmental committee of the War Office. Of this Lord Kitchener was chairman, and its business was " to give assistance in expediting and, if possible, accelerating the supply of munitions of war." In addition a larger committee was appointed to work with this War Office one. This was called the munitions of war committee, and its duties were " to ensure the promptest and most efficient application of all the available productive resources of the country to the manufacture and supply of munitions of war for the army and navy." Its chairman was Mr. Lloyd George, and among its members was Mr. Balfour.

Everything seemed going well when a bomb fell from a very unexpected quarter. The trade unionists of Newcastle-on-Tyne welcomed the new departure, which included the establishment of local committees for increasing the output of munitions, promised to " deliver the goods," and " do their bit," and ended by inviting the prime minister to address them. Mr. Asquith accepted the invitation, and on April 20 spoke at Newcastle. He said:

> I saw a statement the other day that the operations of war, not only of our army but of our Allies, were being crippled, or, at any rate, hampered, by our failure to provide the necessary ammunition. There is not a word of truth in that statement.

He declared that it was neither true nor fair to suggest that there had been anything in the nature of general slackness in the armaments industry on the part of either employers or employed, and throughout took an entirely opposite line from that followed by Mr. Lloyd George, and, to a less extent, by Kitchener. The speech aroused a general sense of perplexity, which was the reverse of reassuring. It should be said, however, that the prime minister laid great stress upon the need for a large and rapid increase in the output of munitions, this being " one of the first necessities of the state."

On the following day Mr. Lloyd George spoke on the question in the House of Commons. He gave some account of the work done in providing more munitions, being on the whole optimistic, but he said nothing by way of modifying his earlier warnings. He stated that the output of munitions had grown from 20, an arbitrary figure taken to represent the output in the month of September, to 90 for October and November, 156 for December, 186 for January, 256 for February, and 388 for March. In other words, the factories in March had turned out more than 19 times the amount they produced in September. He added that the production of high explosives had been placed on a footing which relieved us of all anxiety and enabled us to supply our Allies.

On the liquor question Mr. Lloyd George met with a rebuff. In order to deal with " the lure of the drink," he brought in on April 29 a bill giving the Government power, during the period of the war, to control or close all public-houses in areas where munitions were produced or transport was carried on, or troops were quartered, if they thought such action was desirable. Moreover, he proposed to double the tax on spirits and to put a heavy tax on beer and wine. There was a good deal of opposition to the new duties, and they were abandoned, for many, reassured by Mr. Asquith's speech, considered that such drastic remedies were hardly called for. However, as a substitute, the sale of spirits under three years of age was entirely prohibited. This, it was hoped, would put an end to the drinking of raw and fiery spirits. Shorn of its taxation proposals, the bill became law, and the Government appointed a central control board to deal with the drink problem in the munitions, transport, and camp areas. This set to work, its chairman being Lord D'Abernon, better known as Sir Edgar Vincent, and in a short time it had issued regulations closing public houses earlier in the day in certain industrial areas, notably those around Glasgow and Newcastle, and in general making it more difficult for workmen to procure drink.

On Sunday, May 9, the British troops made an attack upon the Aubers Ridge which resulted in heavy losses, revealed piecemeal in the long lists of casualties published in the papers.

On May 14 The Times printed a telegram from its correspondent in Northern France, who said that the attack failed because of " the want of an unlimited supply of high explosive." The British troops were unable to level the German parapets to the ground after the French practice, and, consequently, they came up against unbroken wire and undestroyed parapets. Five days later, The Times, in a leading article, said: " Men died in heaps upon the Aubers Ridge ten days ago because the field guns were short, and gravely short, of high-explosive shells." A yell of anger broke from that section of the press which had consistently opposed all measures for the defence of the country, whether on sea or on land; but the statements in The Times were true, and Mr. Asquith had evidently been misinformed when he spoke on April 20.

The shortage of shells was not the only difficulty that confronted Mr. Asquith's ministry. Like most other British governments during the previous 200 years it was a party ministry appointed in time of peace to direct the affairs of the nation at peace, and its members were not therefore necessarily fitted to direct the operations of war, especially of such a war as the one that early in 1915 was attaining such vast proportions and creating such novel and perplexing problems.

For some time it had been rumoured that Mr. Winston Churchill, the first lord of the admiralty, and Lord Fisher, who had become first sea lord on October 31, 1914, were not working very harmoniously together, and with two such masterful personalities this is not perhaps surprising. Although remaining in office, Lord Fisher disliked the attempt to force the passage of the Dardanelles, a scheme very dear to Mr. Churchill. There were other reasons for grave disquiet in the minds of those who were responsible for the conduct of affairs, and one of them, Mr. Churchill himself, has vividly described the situation at this time.

The War Council of May 14 was sulphurous. We were in presence of the fact that Sir Ian Hamilton's army had been definitely brought to a standstill on the Gallipoli peninsula, was suspended there in circumstances of peril, was difficult to reinforce, and still more difficult to withdraw. The fleet had relapsed into passivity. Lord Fisher had insisted on the withdrawal of the Queen Elizabeth; German submarines were about to enter the Aegean, where our enormous concentrations of shipping necessary to support the Dardanelles operations lay in a very unprotected state. At the same time the failure of the British attacks in France on the Aubers Ridge was unmistakable. Sir John French's army had lost nearly 20,000 men without substantial results. The general headquarters naturally demanded increased supplies of men and ammunition. The shell crisis had reached its explosion point—the shortage had been disclosed in The Times that morning—and behind it marched a political crisis of the first order. The weakness and failure of Russia were becoming every month more evident. Intense anxiety and extreme bad temper, all suppressed under formal demeanour, characterised the discussion.

He then tells how Lord Kitchener and himself in turn put their views before the council, how he wrote to the prime minister and how he arranged for the co-operation between the fleets of Great Britain and Italy, which country had just entered the war. The next morning he received the following note from Lord Fisher:—

May 15, 1915.

First Lord,

After further anxious reflection I have come to the re-gretted conclusion I am unable to remain any longer as your colleague. It is undesirable in the public interests to go into details—Jowett said, " never explain "—but I find it increasingly difficult to adjust myself to the increasing daily requirements of the Dardanelles to meet your views—as you truly said yesterday I am in the position of continually vetoing your proposals. This is not fair to you besides being extremely distasteful to me. I am off to Scotland at once so as to avoid all questionings.

Yours truly,

FISHER.

In these circumstances Mr. Asquith decided to ask the leaders of the other political parties to unite with him in forming a coalition government to carry on the war. He did this, as he was entitled to do, without consulting his colleagues as a whole, although he may have talked the matter over with one or two more intimate friends among them, and to clear the way he asked them to place their resignations in his hands. They did so, and the Liberal Government, which had been in office since December 1905, came to an end. Mr. Asquith then wrote to Mr. Bonar Law, the Unionist leader in the House of Commons, asking him and those associated with him, " to join forces with us in a combined administration," and telling him that he intended also to ask the leaders of the Irish and Labour parties to participate. The prime minister gave his reasons for taking this step in the following words:

> After long and careful consideration, I have definitely come to the conclusion that the conduct of the war to a successful and decisive issue cannot be effectively carried on except by a cabinet which represents all parties of the state.

Their common action, he added, "should be exclusively directed to the issues of the war." Mr. Bonar Law accepted the invitation in the following sentences: "The considerations to which you refer have for some time been present to the mind of Lord Lansdowne and myself. We have now communicated your views and your invitation to our colleagues, and we shall be glad to co-operate with you in your endeavour to form a national government."

In the following words Mr. Asquith stated the position to the House of Commons:

> I think it right, at the earliest possible moment, to say two or three words to the House in regard to the matters which have been the subject of public report and rumour. I cannot say more at the moment than that steps are in contemplation which involve the reconstruction of the Government on a broader personal and political basis. Nothing is yet definitely arranged, but to avoid any possible misapprehension, and as the House is about to adjourn, I wish here and now to make clear to everybody three things. The first is that any change which takes place will not affect the offices of the head of the Government, or of the secretary of state for foreign affairs. They will continue to be held as they are now. The second is that there is absolutely no change of any kind in contemplation in the policy of the country with regard to the continued prosecution of the war with every possible energy, and by means of every available resource. The third and last point, one of great importance to my hon. friends behind me, and I have no doubt also to hon. gentlemen who sit behind the leader of the opposition, is this: Any reconstruction that will be made will be for the purposes of the war alone, and is not to be taken in any quarter as any reason for indicating anything in the nature of surrender or compromise on the part of any person or body of persons of their several political purposes and ideals.

For a week the newspapers and the public were busy guessing at the names of the members of the new Government. One or two were certain, and several others practically so. Mr. Asquith, Lord Kitchener, and Sir Edward Grey would stay at their posts, and room would be found for Mr. Bonar Law, Mr. Balfour, Mr. Austen Chamberlain, and possibly Lords Lansdowne and Curzon. Mr. Lloyd George would remain a member of the cabinet, and Mr. Arthur Henderson, the leader of the Labour Party, would join it, but there was more uncertainty about the position of Mr. Winston Churchill and the attitude of Mr. John Redmond.

On May 26 the newspapers contained the names of the members of the new Cabinet. There were one or two surprises, but on the whole the forecasts had been tolerably accurate. The late cabinet had consisted of 20 members—19 Liberals and Lord Kitchener—but the new one contained 22. Twelve of these were members of the retiring cabinet—Mr. Asquith, Sir Edward Grey, Lord Kitchener, Lord Crewe, Mr. Lloyd George, Mr. McKenna, Mr. Harcourt, Mr. Birrell, Sir John Simon, Mr. Runciman, Mr. McKinnon Wood, and Mr. Winston Churchill. The eight who retired were Viscount Haldane, Lords Beauchamp, Lucas, and Emmott, Mr. Herbert Samuel, Mr. Hobhouse, Mr. J. A. Pease, and Mr. Montagu. Of these, two—Mr. Samuel and Mr. Montagu—received positions in the new Government, but outside the Cabinet. Mr. Samuel returned to his former position of postmaster general, and Mr. Montagu became financial secretary to the Treasury. Of the 10 newcomers eight were Unionists, one was a Liberal, and one the leader of the Labour Party. The Unionists were Lord Lansdowne, Mr. Bonar Law, Lord Curzon, Mr. Balfour, Mr. Austen Chamberlain, Mr. Walter Long, Lord Selborne, and Sir Edward Carson. The Liberal was Sir Stanley Buckmaster, afterwards Lord Buckmaster, who succeeded Lord Haldane as lord chancellor.

There was a good deal of shuffling of positions to find suitable places for these men. Mr. Asquith, Sir Edward Grey, Lord Kitchener, Mr. Runciman, president of the board of trade, Mr. Birrell, chief secretary for Ireland, and Mr. McKinnon Wood, secretary for Scotland, remained at their posts, but all the others were moved. Mr. Balfour took Mr. Churchill's place as first lord of the admiralty, but this did not surprise people so much as the appointment of Mr. McKenna to succeed Mr. Lloyd George as chancellor of the exchequer. Mr. Churchill became chancellor of the duchy of Lancaster, and Mr. Lloyd George minister of munitions.

Important positions were reserved for Mr. Bonar Law and Mr. Austen Chamberlain, who became secretary for the Colonies and secretary for India respectively. Mr. Walter Long was made president of the local government board, Lord Selborne president of the board of agriculture, while Lord Curzon succeeded Lord Crewe in the sinecure office of lord privy seal. Sir John Simon became home secretary in place of Mr. McKenna, and Sir Edward Carson took the former's place as attorney general. Lord Crewe became lord president of the council instead of secretary for India, and Mr. Harcourt first commissioner of works, a position he had formerly filled, instead of colonial secretary. Lord Lansdowne entered the cabinet without any particular office, a member " without portfolio," as he was styled. In the 18th and earlier part of the 19th centuries it was not unusual to have members of this kind in the cabinet, but since then the custom had been dropped. Curiously enough, the last minister previously to hold a position of this kind in Great Britain was Lord Lansdowne's grandfather, in 1855. Mr. Arthur Henderson, Labour's representative in the new cabinet, became president of the board of education.

Little need be said about the appointments to offices outside the cabinet. They were divided fairly evenly between Liberals and Unionists, with two representatives of Labour—Mr. William Brace, the under-secretary for home affairs, and Mr. G. H. Roberts, a junior lord of the treasury. Of the other appointments, perhaps the most interesting were those of Lord Robert Cecil to be under-secretary for foreign affairs, and of Mr. F. E. Smith (afterwards Lord Birkenhead) to be solicitor general. Mr. John Redmond declined Mr. Asquith's invitation, and consequently the Irish Nationalists were unrepresented in the coalition government. The party, at a meeting held in Dublin on May 25, supported Mr. Redmond in his refusal, but decided to give to the new government the support they had accorded to the old one.

The change was for the better, but in certain important respects the new cabinet was as unsatisfactory as the old one had been. It was all to the good that the leaders of the Unionist and the Labour parties should take a share of the responsibility of the war; but two main objections to the old cabinet had not been removed by the advent of the new one.

As before, the Cabinet was too big and too civilian. Its membership, originally far too large, had actually been increased, and a body of this size cannot, in the very nature of things, conduct a war efficiently. Decisions cannot be taken promptly when 22 persons have to weigh and discuss the pros and cons, and much valuable time is lost in talking. Again, with the solitary exception of Lord Kitchener, the cabinet was still exclusively civilian, and several of these civilians were, by training and inclination, the last men in the world to take prompt action on any question whatsoever. They were essentially men of inaction.

Resulting from the crisis and the reconstruction of the Government was the creation of the ministry of munitions, a department founded to look after the supply of arms and ammunition. Mr. Lloyd George became the first minister, and while the bill establishing the department was passing through Parliament he visited Manchester and Liverpool, where he spoke on the need for increasing the output. The bill, criticised on the ground that it gave excessive power to the minister, became law on June 9, and Mr. Lloyd George threw his tremendous energies into getting his department to work on the enormous task entrusted to it. He took with him a number of civil servants, but for many responsible positions he called upon prominent business men, who were soon installed in buildings in Whitehall. Among them were Sir Eric Geddes and Sir Arthur Duckham.

In his War Memoirs Mr. Lloyd George has thus described the department:

> The Ministry of Munitions was from first to last a business man organisation. Its most distinctive feature was the appointment I made to the chief executive posts of successful business men, to whom I gave authority and personal support that enabled them to break through much of the routine and aloofness which characterised the normal administration of Government contracts.

The Act gave the ministry authority to take what land or buildings it required, to engage what labour it wished, and to make conditions governing labour for the period of the war. The board of trade was constituted referee in all disputes between employers and employed; lock-outs and strikes were forbidden, employers being liable to a fine of £5 a day for every worker locked out, and employees to the same fine for striking. The profits of controlled establishments, that is, establishments having to do with manufacture for the ministry of munitions, were limited to not more than 20 per cent. over the average amount of net profits for two years before the war. This was later supplemented by a scheme of costing, by which prices were greatly reduced. At first employees were not allowed to leave one establishment for another without permission, but later leaving certificates were made necessary. Munition workers were given a badge.

A campaign was begun to enlist labour for war factories. Piece work was established and workers were encouraged to earn as much as they could. Women of every class volunteered for the hard, dangerous, and physically exhausting work of the machine shops, explosive factories, and steel works. While there was undoubtedly some waste and overlapping in the work of the ministry, these were, when all the circumstances of the hasty creation of a vast enterprise were numbered, insignificant compared with the results accomplished.

Production was divided between the great munition firms, assisted by thousands of small manufacturers all over the country and the government factories. In some cases private firms, in addition to managing their own works, managed national factories for the government. To facilitate the transport of munitions to France a port was built at Richborough, in Kent. A train ferry across the Channel and a barge service were opened. Railway trucks were run directly on the train ferries, taken across to France without unloading, run on the rails there and carried straight to their destination.

The work of the ministry covered much more than production. Lord Moulton became, under the ministry, director general of explosives, and a vast chemical research department was created. New propellants were evolved and vast plants were erected for the production of nitric, sulphuric, and picric acids and ammonium nitrate. National industries not at first apparently directly connected with the war, like soap making and dye production, had to be directed in order that they should yield the maximum amount of necessary chemicals, such as glycerine, for war service. When poison gas was introduced by the Germans the chemists had not only to provide protection for their own men against the German gas, but to supply the army with still more effective gases in reply, which they did. They produced the best gas mask and the most deadly gases known.

The largest of the munition works erected by the Government was at Gretna on the Scottish border. There 16,000 workers were employed, and for them not only houses but refreshment rooms, clubs, and other buildings were provided. Near Woolwich, at Well Hall, a new town was built to house the extra employees at the arsenal, and at Chilwell, near Nottingham, arose a vast factory where over 56 per cent. of the shells required by the British army were filled.

The vast organization at Chilwell owed a great deal to Lord Chetwynd, whose services were vividly described and thoroughly appreciated by Mr. Lloyd George in his War Memoirs:

To help us with the problem of shell filling I had the good fortune to secure the services of Lord Chetwynd, who was recommended to me as the best man to help us in our difficulty. He had practical experience in dealing with explosives, and had a tremendous store of resource and ingenuity, but I was warned that he was very sensitive to any attempt to control him by a bridle of red tape. We told him he was wanted to build and run a factory that would fill 1,000 tons of high explosive shells a week. He stipulated for and got a very free hand, without control by the departmental managers of the Ministry, and a contract valid till after the cessation of hostilities.

Thus equipped, he went straight ahead in glorious independence. He found a site at Chilwell, near Nottingham, and designed and built his own factory there. While it was being erected, he went over to France in October, 1915, as one of the deputation I sent to study the French methods of shell filling, and satisfied himself that the French practice of filling with powdered explosive, by pressing it in through the nose of the shell, could be adapted for amatol. This was important, for to make our supplies of T.N.T. go as far as possible, it was desirable to use it with 80 per cent. of ammonium nitrate, which involved filling dry, as such mixture could not be poured. At Woolwich they had designed a process for filling with this " 80/20 " amatol, by compressing the powder into cakes and insetting these in the shell. But that meant either having a detachable bottom for the shell or a detachable tapered end, and both these devices proved in practice not only an additional complication and delay, but unsatisfactory and a cause of premature explosion.

Lord Chetwynd went back to Chilwell and determined to fill 80/20 powder by pressing through the nose. He hastily designed and ran up a small experimental plant to show it could be done, and when there was a talk of abandoning the 80/20 amatol on account of the unsatisfactory results achieved by the Woolwich shells, he challenged a test of those filled by him by pressing through the nose—a test from which they emerged triumphantly.

Lord Chetwynd designed his own plant and processes, aiming always at speed, simplicity, and the fullest use of machinery on mass-production lines. He passed his raw material through machines originally used for coal-crushing, stone-pulverising, sugar-drying, paint-making, sugar-sifting. The T.N.T. he ground between the porcelain rollers of a flour-mill; a bread-making plant did the mixing. He bought up a derelict works that had been producing lace-making machinery, and used it to manufacture the appliances he designed for filling shells. People objected that it must be highly dangerous to treat high explosives so unceremoniously. Lord Chetwynd's retort was to move to a house at the end of his press houses. If anyone is to be blown up, I'll be the first! he remarked; and his action greatly encouraged his workers.

Chilwell was a controlled establishment and in all the ministry of munitions was responsible for about 5,000 of these works wherein materials of war were turned out and in which about 3,000,000 persons were employed. Over these controlled establishments the ministry had very extensive powers. Their profits were limited, and their rates of wages could not be altered without its consent. More important was the provision that ordered the removal of all rules, practices and customs which tended to restrict production or employment.

The work of making munitions done in these establishments included the manufacture or repair of arms and ammunition, ships, vehicles and aircraft, and any other article intended for use in war and of any metals, machines, or tools required for such manufacture; the construction, alteration or repair of buildings for naval or military purposes or for munitions work, and of houses for the accommodation of persons engaged therein; the construction and alteration of docks and harbours; and the supply of light, heat, water, or power.

CHAPTER 13

Conquest of South-West Africa

By the end of the 19th century Africa, like the rest of the world, had been explored and divided up between the great European powers, and in this division Germany secured a share—or, rather, several shares. One of these was a big stretch of land on the west coast, north of the Orange River, which divides it from the Cape Province. In April, 1884, the German Government announced that Herr Lüderitz, a Bremen merchant who had taken possession of certain points on this coast, was under the Kaiser's protection. From that time, the territory became known as German South-West Africa. The northern part, however, was sometimes called by its older name of Damaraland, and the southern part Namaqualand.

The colony contained 320,000 square miles, and was therefore just about the size of Germany and Italy together. On the west the country has a sea coast of about eight hundred miles; on the north it is bordered by the Portuguese colony of Angola; and on the east by Bechuanaland, a British protectorate. Its southern frontier, the shortest of all, is the Cape Province. In 1914 it had a population of about 100,000 natives, mainly Bushmen and Hottentots, and about 15,000 German settlers. A large part of the colony was mere desert, but much of it was suitable for farming, and in this the Germans made their homes and introduced their cattle. South-West Africa is fairly rich in minerals, especially diamonds. In 1906 extensive diamond mines were discovered near Lüderitz Bay, and subsequently proved very rich. Copper is also found in the country, but little gold has as yet been discovered.

On the coast there were two ports—Swakopmund about the centre, and Lüderitz Bay, called also by its older Portuguese name of Angra Pequena, in the south. Near Swakopmund the British had a little settlement called Walvis Bay. The capital of the colony was Windhoek, a town in the interior about two hundred miles from Swakopmund. On this possession the Germans spent a considerable amount of money, chiefly in building railways and in developing their two ports. The main lines of railway formed three sides of a square of which the sea coast was the fourth. Starting from Swakopmund, a line ran east to Windhoek, and then turned south, and made for Keetmanshoop, completing the round by reaching the coast again at Lüderitz Bay. In addition to these main lines there were two others. One ran south from Seeheim to Warmbad, a place only a few miles from the British frontier, and the other served the extreme north of the colony.

It is at first difficult to see what induced the Germans to build the southward line. The country it served was largely arid desert and certainly never justified railway development to the exclusion of other centres. The explanation is that it was of political rather than commercial importance, giving a railhead conveniently close to British territory. The political history of the German occupation of the country lends colour to this view, and there can be no doubt but that Germany was counting upon a Boer rising in the Union of South Africa, in the event of the outbreak of war, which would effectually prevent any attempt by Union forces to invade the German colony, and might well create a situation in which the Germans themselves could do the invading.

With regard to the northward line it is clear that its primary importance was commercial since it served the valuable copper mines round Grootfontein. But here again it cannot be doubted that the Germans had for long been casting covetous eyes at the largely unexplored and more undeveloped territory that is now Southern Rhodesia. Like Cecil Rhodes, German colonists were dreaming of an " Empire to the northward." It is conceivable that the clash of interests which was rapidly developing in that area of the dark continent, together with the undoubted machinations of German agents amongst the Boers of the Union territory, might have precipitated in Africa that conflict which became inevitable, after the outbreak of the war in Europe.

The colony was by far the most suitable of all Germany's African possessions for development by white men. The heat is intense at some seasons, but except in the swamps to the north, is always dry, and malaria is rare. The greatest difficulties are presented not by the climate, but by the natural features of the country. Along the coast extends a broad strip of low lying desert, almost waterless and practically useless for commercial purposes. Inland the country rises to a series of plateaux 2,000 to 6,000 feet above sea level. On these higher plains cattle rearing is profitable, and the climate very favourable to Europeans. But the great barrier to rapid development is everywhere lack of water. Only the Orange river on the southern boundary, and the Cunene river in the north are running streams all the year round. Innumerable river beds and water courses dissect the country, but except at certain seasons in the year these river beds are always dry. Elsewhere what water there is is found below the ground, and only at great depth.

In spite of this drawback German development had been steady. Immigration of whites other than Germans was steadily discouraged, although a number of Boers had settled in the country before the outbreak of war. As in most cases, Germany ruled her colony with an iron hand. The administration although efficient, was autocratic and harsh. Whites and natives alike suffered from the severe discipline. But German ambition was not to be denied and the very expensive administration was encouraged in its unpopular methods. The inevitable result happened, and in 1904, the Hereros, the warlike but industrious race of natives who inhabited the country, revolted.

The struggle was long, violent, and bitter, and only after nearly 20,000 German troops had been despatched to the country was the rising finally quelled. The Germans acted with ruthless cruelty. They had waged war with all the power of modern science against a people who were legitimately fighting for their liberty. Against such power human bravery alone was useless. The revolt was quelled, and the Germans almost exterminated the Hereros, who were estimated to number about 85,000 in 1900 and numbered less than 25,000 in 1911. Neither age nor sex was spared, and the pitiful remnants were herded into reserves and kept in a condition of semi-slavery. In spite of this the economic progress of the country was rapid; but it is an interesting fact that fully half the capital investments were British. Minerals were the chief source of wealth as has been said, diamonds and copper being the main exports, but animal products and some agricultural raw materials were also produced.

As early as 1895 Germany had given an indication of her policy in South Africa. The Kaiser's notorious telegram to President Kruger after the Jameson Raid was the beginning of the cultivation of friendly relations with the Boer republics.

During the South African war, Germany had given them every evidence of sympathy, but at that time she was unprepared to precipitate the crisis, and the Kaiser even refused to see Kruger when he visited Germany. The effect of this duplicity upon the Boers was considerable, and although energetic steps were taken by German agents to repair the damage done, the progress made in that direction in the intervening years was small. Dr. Seitz, the German governor, was himself sceptical of the position. He said he had ample evidence of the " mistrust of the Boers of the German race and the German character," and although his agents kept in touch with Boer politicians it was clear to him that little could be hoped for from Boer sympathy. Nevertheless, on the outbreak of war he issued a manifesto in which he declared that Germany made war " not on the Boer people as such but on the English and their adherents." The effect of German intrigue and the disaffection of the Boers has already been dealt with in an earlier chapter. The only measure of success achieved by German diplomacy in South Africa was to postpone the conquest of their colony for three or four months.

German preparations for war were, as usual, rather better advanced than the British. Von Franke, the German commander, had a nucleus of trained troops numbering 2,500. To this he was able to add a considerable number of men recruited from amongst the German colonists. The majority were old soldiers, who had served against the Hereros and had settled in the colony instead of returning to Germany. But he was unable to mobilise any African force, nor dare he try, in view of the unquenchable hostility with which the natives were filled. Throughout he had to rely upon his small white army. Exact figures are uncertain, but it probably numbered under 9,000.

A compact and well-equipped little force, it represented a formidable enemy when operating in its own country. Of material supplies the Germans had plenty, and they were also well provided with rifles, machine and field guns. Their one aeroplane was of great service in the early days; but it broke down and thereafter the Union planes had, for what it was worth, command of the air. The most useful of the German units was a small camel corps, which was handled with great efficiency, and caused considerable trouble to the Union forces. Several hundred Boer malcontents fought on the German side, but the enemy's most valuable ally was the nature of the country.

Protected along its eastern and western faces by a belt of arid and almost impassable desert, it was everywhere waterless, and generally presented great difficulties to transport. The British were faced with the constant problem of finding water and food, both of which were scarce, and as there was a complete lack of other supplies they were dependent upon their transport, which had to cover long distances across difficult country. It was almost impossible to quit the well-defined tracks, and the Germans were therefore able to concentrate at threatened points.

Thus on the west of the country the only practicable points of entry into the country were along the lines of the railways from Swakopmund and Lüderitz Bay. In the south, the Orange River could be crossed in two places, the more important of which was just south of Warmbad, while on the east any advance was impossible except through a narrow belt of country along the Malopo river bed. Dr. Seitz and his associates realized quite well that they would get no help whatever from Europe, but they had high hopes that a successful rebellion of the Boers in British South Africa would be of material assistance to them. Accordingly, early in August, 1914, their two ports—Swakopmund and Lüderitz Bay—were abandoned and all works of naval importance were destroyed; and their garrisons, with their stores, retired to Windhoek.

The question of South-West Africa did not escape the attention of the Imperial Government, and soon after the outbreak of the war there was some correspondence on the subject between the colonial secretary, Mr. Lewis Harcourt, and General Botha. Mr. Harcourt said that the authorities in London attached a good deal of importance to the conquest of this German colony, and asked the South African people to undertake the work, and so to perform a great and urgent Imperial service. Botha's reply, which partly precipitated the rebellion, was an unequivocal promise of support. Towards the cost of the campaign the British government gave a loan of £7,000,000.

Owing to the rebellion, it was some months before Botha was able to give his mind and the resources of his country to this task, but he never lost sight of it, and as soon as the back of the Boer revolt had been broken, preparations were made for an invasion of German South-West Africa. As early as September 18, 1914, Lüderitz Bay had been seized by the navy;

a little later the valuable diamond mines passed into British possession, and on Christmas Day a body of South African troops reoccupied Walvis Bay, which had been temporarily in the possession of the Germans. On December 31 the Union Government announced that they proposed to commandeer men for the coming campaign, and not to depend wholly on volunteers; for, as their communiqué said:

> In view of the danger of invasion, it will be necessary to employ much larger forces than at first intended, in order to destroy the enemy and rebel forces, so that they may never again menace the peace of South Africa.

Further proof of the ubiquity of the navy was given on January 14, 1915, when Swakopmund was occupied. It was found absolutely deserted, but undamaged. The Germans, however, had sown the place with mines, and before these had been discovered and removed two troopers of the Imperial Light Horse had been blown to bits. The two German ports were now in Botha's hands, but there were other entrances into South-West Africa, and these, too, had to be secured. The Orange is crossed at two main drifts—Schuit Drift and Raman's Drift—and the latter of these had been seized by the South Africans during the rebellion, when there was a good deal of fighting along the line of the river. Early in January, 1915, an attack was made on Schuit Drift. This was seized, and the Germans driven across the river.

At the beginning of February the four principal gates into the German colony were held by the Union forces, the climatic conditions were becoming more favourable, the rebels had been crushed, and Botha could press forward with his plan of invasion. This was well conceived, well planned, and well executed, and as it was furthermore justified by its complete success it deserves to be studied by all those interested in military operations. It cannot, of course, be compared with the gigantic movements in Europe, but within its own limited sphere it was a triumph of forethought and preparation.

The plan proposed was an enveloping advance on Windhoek from the coast and from the south, the railways to be taken on the way. For this purpose the Union forces were divided into two armies, called the northern and the southern. The former, which was commanded by Botha himself, was to assemble at

Swakopmund, and to march along the railway line to the German capital. The southern army, under General Smuts, was entrusted with a more complicated task. For the first part of this it was divided into three columns. One under Sir Duncan Mackenzie was to advance inland from Lüderitz Bay, while another, under Colonel van Deventer, was to move across the Orange and along the railway leading from Warmbad. The third column, under Colonel Berrange, was to start from Kimberley, and after crossing the Kalahari Desert, was to clear the enemy from the south-eastern section of the colony. In the neighbourhood of Keetmanshoop the three were to unite, and Smuts was to lead them northwards to join Botha.

While this circle of steel was being drawn around the Germans they made one effort to break through. At Kakamas, on the Orange, a British garrison stationed there to protect Schuit Drift was suddenly and violently attacked by about six hundred Germans on February 5. At eight o'clock in the morning big guns and Maxims opened fire upon the station, but the defenders were ready, and in a short time the assailants were beaten off. They lost nine men killed, twenty-two wounded, and fifteen taken prisoners, while on the Union side the casualties were one killed and two wounded. On hearing of the engagement, Colonel van Deventer marched out from Upington to cut off the enemy's retreat, but the Germans retired too quickly, and escaped envelopment.

Since its occupation by the British, Swakopmund had been a very busy place. Men and stores were landed there in considerable quantities, and a railway line, protected by blockhouses and sea walls, was built along the few miles of coast which separate the port from Walvis Bay. Early in February General Botha left Cape Town to take over the direction of operations, and on his way he called at Lüderitz Bay, near where Sir Duncan Mackenzie's men had been encamped for some time past, engaged in making preparations for their campaign.

On the following day, February 12, Botha reached Swakopmund, and on the 22nd his army moved out, a heavy fall of rain having made its task easier. On the 23rd Nonidas and Goanikontes, two stations on the line to Windhoek, were occupied without serious fighting, although some resistance had been expected, as the Germans were in strength at the former place, and with their outposts and patrols there had been several

Humphrey Joel

DESTROYER THROWING OUT SMOKE SCREEN. The British navy adopted many ingenious devices during the war. That of the smoke-screen to conceal a ship's movements from the enemy, as illustrated above, proved very successful.

Plate 21

Abraham & Sons

NAVAL INVENTION AND DEVELOPMENT. The illustration shows a British mystery ship of the merchant type used to fight submarines, having concealed guns and wireless. An early attempt at dazzle painting or camouflage is seen on the side of the ship and the funnel. This term was used in the war for all such schemes of concealment, which were particularly valuable in the case of ships at sea. Dummy funnels and false decks were also among the devices adopted to deceive the enemy, and as the war proceeded even more elaborate mystery ships were evolved by the British naval authorities.

Plate 22   *Volume II*

Imperial War Museum

A striking illustration showing the explosion of a depth charge in the wake of a destroyer attacking a U-boat.

Sport & General

Naval tactics were greatly changed by the invention of floating mines, with which German destroyers sowed the seas, thus rendering all vessels liable to sudden destruction. This photograph shows a floating mine washed ashore.

DEPTH CHARGE AND FLOATING MINE

British monitor Mersey, which helped to destroy the German light cruiser Königsberg, in the Rufiji river, German E. Africa, July 11, 1915.

The British battleship Majestic which was torpedoed by the U23 off Cape Helles, Gallipoli, on May 27, 1915.

The monitor Severn also helped to destroy the Königsberg. Previously, along with a sister ship the Mersey, the Severn was employed in bombarding German positions on the Belgian coast.

A BATTLESHIP AND TWO MONITORS

Plate 24   *Volume 11*

skirmishes. Nearly a month was then spent in preparing an advanced base, and in finding out something about the strength and disposition of the enemy.

On March 19 Botha was ready for another advance. In accordance with his orders, two brigades of mounted men left Husab, he himself accompanying the first, which was commanded by Colonel Brits. Its object was to attack Riet, an important place south of the railway, which commands the high road to Windhoek, where the enemy was known to be in strength; and to complete its work, the Bloemhof commando was ordered to move round its flank, to seize the dominating height of Schwarze Kopje, and to cut off the Germans retreat.

At daybreak on the 20th the brigade came in front of the German position, which was a very strong one. Its right rested on the Swakop and its left on the foothills of the Langer Heinrichberg, while its guns, skilfully placed, commanded both the main road and the river. A frontal attack was necessary, but the South Africans advanced without flinching, their progress being splendidly assisted by the guns of the Transvaal horse artillery. At length they reached the German lines, and after a sharp engagement the enemy was driven out in disorder. Unfortunately the Bloemhof commando failed to reach its allotted place, and so the retreat was unhindered. During the engagement a party of snipers under Captain Lemmer did good work in preventing the Germans from destroying the water-holes.

Meanwhile, the second mounted brigade was carrying out its part of the programme, which was to seize an important section of the line running to Windhoek. For this purpose it was divided into two columns. One under Colonel Celliers cut the line between Jakalswater and Sphinx, and seized a train full of supplies; and then, having thus hampered the movement of any reinforcements from the direction of Windhoek, attacked Jakalswater itself. There, however, the German position was strong, and the assault on it failed; but it served the secondary purpose of preventing the enemy from sending assistance to other parts of the field. Forty-three prisoners were taken by the Germans. The second division of this brigade, led by Colonel Alberts, marched against Pforte, another station on the line, where the Germans had taken up a position. An encircling movement was carried out successfully, and the position was surrounded. One battery was disabled by shell fire, and the other was rushed.

For the next five or six weeks after these operations Botha was busy clearing the railway system of the enemy. Two main lines ran from Swakopmund, the northern to Grootfontein, Tsumeb, and the north of the colony, and the southern to Windhoek. The main line of advance for the Union force was along the second of these; but to prevent any attack on its flank it was necessary also to hold the other. For fifty miles this was secured, and to guard it the Kimberley regiment, under Colonel Skinner, was stationed at Trekkopje, then the railhead of the Union advance.

On April 26 some seven hundred Germans with twelve guns attacked this encampment, and a hard fight, lasting about four hours, took place. The object of the enemy was, while shelling the defended lines heavily, to get round the two ends of the trenches and enfilade them. But the plan miscarried, although the Germans got within about one hundred and fifty yards of their objective. Some armoured cars belonging to the Naval Air Service forced them into a position whence guns and rifles could reach them easily and they retired, leaving twenty-five killed and wounded behind them. The Union force had three officers and eight men killed and about forty wounded.

While Botha had been making this satisfactory progress in the north, the southern army had not been idle. The column commanded by Sir Duncan Mackenzie cleared out the Germans and took some stores from one or two places in the neighbourhood of Lüderitz Bay, and then without difficulty seized a substantial stretch of the railway line. On February 22 the advanced guard was at Garub, a station 70 miles inland, which was occupied without opposition, and from there some scouts pushed out and fought a skirmish with a force of mounted Germans who were covering the retirement of a troop train. The attack was rashly executed and the Union scouts were driven off, fortunately with small loss.

Having reached Garub, Mackenzie had the worst part of his march behind him. He had crossed the desert which fringes the sea coast, and was approaching the hills and the fertile land beyond. At Garub there was a plentiful supply of water, and henceforward his anxieties on this score, although not removed, were considerably lightened. While here, the British camp was attacked by a hostile aeroplane, which dropped shells and hand-grenades.

GERMAN STATIONS OCCUPIED

Fifteen miles beyond Garub is the important station of Aus, the principal resting-place for the caravans journeying from north to south, and in searching the mountainous country between the two places the Union forces had a stiff task. There was much sand, and food and water were scarce. The difficulties were not lightened by the action of the Germans who had filled up the bore-holes and poisoned some of the wells. Towards the end of March the Germans blew up the railway and prepared to evacuate Aus. The position was naturally strong, and the Germans had added considerably to its defences. Mines had been laid, trenches dug, and the passes through the hills fortified, but everything was abandoned without a struggle.

This was partly due, no doubt, to the strength and skill of the advancing force. On the night of March 30 a body of mounted infantry marched silently out, and in the morning was in possession of two of the important passes giving access to Aus. Once there they threatened the flank and the retreat of the Germans, and the whole position at once was weakened. The success of the British in the north was sufficiently alarming, and withdrawal became a necessity.

On the following day the British entered the place. Several mines were exploded, but without any serious casualties. One of the mines was composed of thirty pom-pom shells and a hundred sticks of blasting gelatine. The buildings in the town were found undamaged, but they had been stripped of everything useful, and the bridges and culverts had been destroyed. In a short time, however, these and also the railway line had been repaired, and a further move was possible.

The success of the southern column under Colonel van Deventer was equally striking. Safely across the Orange at Schuit Drift, Van Deventer soon came into touch with the Germans. Sweeping over a wide district in the south-east of the colony he occupied a group of stations, including Ukamas, Nabas, Jerusalem, Velloor, and Heirachabis, and before the end of March had seized two or three German camps, containing a large quantity of supplies, horses, and live-stock. One of these was at Platbeen, about fifty miles north of Ukamas, and another was at Geitsaub. At both there were skirmishes, and at the cost of one man killed and two wounded his force made twenty-eight prisoners and killed six of the enemy. On March 30 Van Deventer reached the railway at Warmbad, its terminus, 25 miles from the frontier, and occupied it without opposition. From there he pushed along the line so rapidly that two days later his men entered Kanus, a station sixty-five miles to the north.

He established his headquarters at Kalkfontein, a station twenty-five miles north of Warmbad, and here on April 11 he was joined by General Smuts. The task immediately before them was that of driving the Germans from the slopes of the Karras Mountains. The plan adopted was to advance in three columns. Van Deventer himself marched near the railway and to the west of the mountains, while a second detachment moved to the east of them; somewhat in the rear and acting as a reserve was a third column, which took the road through the hills. The manœuvre was completely successful. Threatened on all sides, the enemy withdrew without putting up the semblance of a fight, and the region passed entirely into the hands of the South Africans. On April 18 a mounted brigade, under Colonel Villiers occupied Seeheim, the place where the line from Warmbad joins the railway from Lüderitz Bay. According to one account, the Germans hurriedly evacuated this junction because they mistook a party of scouts for the main body of the enemy. Their departure was so rapid that they did not destroy the bridge across the Great Fish river.

By this time Van Deventer's column was in touch with Colonel Berrange's force, which, it will be remembered, had set out from Kimberley. British Bechuanaland had been crossed without hindrance, the only difficulties encountered arising from the nature of the country, and in March the enemy was first sighted near the border. At Hasuur, fifteen miles north-west of Rietfontein, on April 1, Berrange captured an entrenched position with slight loss, and from then he fought his way steadily westward to the neighbourhood of Keetmanshoop.

Keetmanshoop was now surrounded, and its occupation, either peaceably or otherwise, was only a question of days. This town, the business capital of German Namaqualand, was the eastern terminus of the railway line, nearly two hundred miles from the coast. On April 19 the Germans quietly vacated it, having first rendered the telegraph and telephone wires useless, and on the 20th it was occupied by the British. A day or two later General Smuts travelled along the railway from Keetmanshoop to Aus, thus showing how completely the line was in the hands of the Union forces.

Before Smuts could concentrate his whole force it was necessary for Sir Duncan Mackenzie's column, which had reached Aus, to join the others. This junction was effected during May. From Aus there was no need for Sir Duncan to keep to the railway line, for it was already cleared of the enemy; and so, with his mounted men, he struck out to the north-east. The towns of Bethany and Berseba were occupied without hindrance, and the railway line was reached on April 24 at Aritetis, a station seventy miles north of Keetmanshoop. Once on the railway line Mackenzie began to act in conjunction with Van Deventer against the enemy retreating from Seeheim and Keetmanshoop. On the 22nd part of Van Deventer's pursuing force had come up with the Germans at Kabus, 20 miles to the north, where an indecisive engagement had taken place. The Germans, about 600 strong, beat off the attack and continued their retreat, although they left most of their wounded in their pursuers' hands. The Union force lost 22 men taken prisoners.

Mackenzie now joined in the chase. He learned that the Germans who had fought at Kabus were taking train at Gibeon, a station forty miles to the north of Keetmanshoop, and at once he decided upon his method of attack. His whole force having approached within two miles of Gibeon, a small party was despatched to destroy the railway to the north of that place, and one brigade, the 9th, was sent forward to engage the enemy. The 9th brigade was unequal to the task before it, and having suffered severe loss and left seventy prisoners in the hands of the enemy, it fell back upon the main body. This skirmish took place during the night of April 27, and on the following morning Mackenzie attacked the Germans with his whole force.

The battle of Gibeon was soon over. The Germans, outmanœuvred, outnumbered, and outfought, were driven from the field and pursued for about twenty miles, only the rocky and difficult nature of the ground preventing the destruction of the whole force. As it was, the seventy prisoners captured the previous day were rescued, and seven officers and two hundred men were captured, as well as both of the Germans' field-guns and several Maxims. In addition, the cutting of the railway line delivered into the hands of the victors a train, a number of transport wagons, and a quantity of livestock. The British losses were three officers and 20 men killed, and eight officers and 47 men wounded.

The success of Mackenzie's march, first across the coastal desert, and then over the one hundred and twenty miles of arid country which lie between Bethany and Gibeon, was due very largely to the exertions of his quartermaster-general, Sir George Farrar, and it was, therefore, a great loss to the Union forces when Sir George was killed in a railway accident near Gibeon on May 18. It was the end of a full and adventurous career. He had been sentenced to death for his share in the Jameson Raid, had fought against the Boers in the war of 1899-1902, and until the last was the controlling spirit of a great mining organization.

Meanwhile Botha was faring well in the north. After the fighting around Jakalswater on March 20 the northern army halted for a while in order to organize its supplies, and it was not until May 1 that Kubas, a place thirty miles nearer Windhoek, was occupied by Colonel Brits. It was hastily evacuated by the Germans, and around it miles of entrenchments were found, and over 100 contact mines were discovered and removed. Botha despatched General Myburgh and a small force, and ordered him to sweep round to the south and envelop Karibib. He struck at Otyimbingue, which is only 60 miles from the capital, and a skirmish there resulted in the capture of twenty-eight prisoners. On May 5, as the result of this operation, the important railway junction of Karibib was reached and occupied, whence a march of 20 miles took the army to Johann Albrechtshöhe, and a further ten to Wilhelmstal.

Windhoek was now almost in sight, as the van of the army under General Myburgh was rapidly approaching it, and on May 10 General Botha, who was then at Karibib, was informed by telephone that the place was prepared to surrender. With a small escort he set out at once in his motor car, and on reaching the capital on the following day he was met by the burgomaster, with whom the terms of capitulation were arranged. On the 12th a detachment of the Union forces under Myburgh formally entered the town, and at noon there was an interesting and historic ceremony. Escorted by a long and imposing array of mounted burghers, Botha took up his station before the courthouse, from the steps of which a proclamation was read in English, Dutch, and German. This placed certain districts of South-West Africa under martial law, promised protection to those who obeyed its provisions, and expressed regret at the intention of the Germans to continue a hopeless struggle. The Union Jack was then hoisted, and the troops presented arms. In an address to his men Botha thanked them for their services in carrying out an enterprise " of the utmost importance to the Empire and the Union, as it means practically the complete possession of German South-West Africa."

Before the arrival of the British the German troops had withdrawn to Grootfontein, which, it was stated, was now their capital. However, some 3,000 Europeans, mostly women and children, remained in Windhoek, and with them were 12,000 natives, who thus passed under British rule. The valuable highpower wireless station, situated about a mile from the town, was found intact, and with its capture Germany had lost all those she possessed outside Europe. A quantity of rolling-stock also fell into the hands of the British. The government of the capital was entrusted to Colonel Mentz.

Something still remained to be done before the German field force was destroyed, but the major operations were over. These had been carried out with a maximum of skill and a minimum of loss. To Botha himself the very highest praise is due, but neither the ability of his subordinates, nor the endurance of his men should be overlooked. Their chief enemy, indeed, was not the Germans, but the desert, waterless and arid. Water was always scarce, often very scarce, as may be inferred from this quotation from a divisional order: " It has been observed that water is being used for washing purposes. This practice must cease immediately." The dust storms and heat were very trying. As one soldier said: " Every day we have awful dust storms lasting for hours, and the shade temperature always over 100 degrees." Sometimes tents were blown to ribbons, and the sand came along at times like sleet.

As a result of the violence of these storms about 200 Cape boys were employed day and night shovelling the sand off 40 miles of railway line, and although they made a clear passage for the train in the morning, when it returned in the evening there was sometimes as much as four feet of sand over the rails. A further hardship, which happily was only experienced once or twice, was due to lack of provisions. Now and again, especially in the final rapid advance, the troops got too far in front of the transport wagons, and after the capture of Windhoek they were for some days on half and then quarter rations.

But the difficulties attributable to nature were increased by the action of the Germans. In filling up the bore-holes with sand the Germans were quite within their rights; but in poisoning the wells they violated one of the best known and respected conventions of warfare.

We have already stated that near Aus Sir Duncan Mackenzie found the wells of drinking water had been poisoned, the only extenuating circumstance being that warning notices had been affixed to them. At Swakopmund, in January, the British on seizing the town discovered that six wells had been poisoned by means of arsenical cattle dip. On his arrival Botha took up the matter, and on February 23 he wrote to Lieutenant-Colonel Francke, the German commander, drawing his attention to the fact that such an act was contrary to Article No. 23 (a) of The Hague Convention, and informing him that, if the practice was persisted in, he would hold the officers concerned responsible and he would be reluctantly compelled to employ such measures of reprisal as might seem advisable. In reply, Francke defended the action of his men, who had orders " not to allow any water supplies to fall into the hands of the enemy in a form which allows such supplies to be used either by man or beast." He added that to prevent injury to the health of the enemy, instructions had been given to mark with warning notices the wells which had been so treated. Botha answered that this reply was unsatisfactory, and repeated his former threat.

However, all his difficulties were at length overcome, and these cannot be summarised better than in the words of Mr. Asquith. Speaking at the Guildhall on May 19, a week after the capture of Windhoek, the prime minister said :

> Their undertaking has been no slight one. A force of about 30,000 men, rather over half of whom are mounted men, with guns, horses, medical stores, mules, and transports, have been conveyed oversea five hundred and seven hundred miles, in addition to the large land force which has been operating on the German-Union frontier. All supplies, every pound of provisions for the men, much of the water for their consumption, every ton of forage for horses and mules, have had to be brought from Cape Town. All the railway material for rapid construction had also to be brought from Cape Town, and all these men, horses, guns, supplies, and materials had to be landed at two ports, Lüderitz and Walvis, at which appliances for disembarkation for such operations had not been constructed.

The campaign had been so successful that there was no need for General Smuts to keep his whole force in the field, and in May a portion of it was sent back and disbanded. In thanking these men for their services, Smuts mentioned that the country had been subdued in much shorter time than had been anticipated, and that the casualties had been comparatively few.

The position of the Germans had become hopeless. With the fall of Windhoek, the whole of the country south of the capital had been lost to them, and they had been driven into the difficult country to the north, where they were cut off from their supplies and surrounded by bitterly hostile natives. Their losses in killed and wounded, like those of the South Africans, had been comparatively light, but they had lost a considerable number as prisoners. Although Francke had a fighting force that was still well equipped, it was hopelessly outnumbered and its reduction was simply a question of time.

April and May, 1915, were the months that marked the high tide of the German successes in Russia. Most Germans and many of their enemies were convinced that those successes were the prelude to a speedy termination of the war. Dr. Seitz, the governor of German South-West Africa, certainly was of that opinion, and in order to gain time he commenced negotiating with General Botha for terms of surrender. A conference was arranged and was held at Giftkuppe on May 21, but the discussion proved abortive, Botha demanding only unconditional surrender. Dr. Seitz returned to his countrymen and prepared to continue his resistance.

With the demobilisation of the larger part of General Smuts' army, the task of finishing the campaign devolved upon General Botha. He began operations without delay. One column marched along the railway towards Grootfontein, while others swept the country to the south-east of it. A few days after the occupation of the capital, Colonel Mentz came up with a party of Germans at Seeis thirty-seven miles to the east, and there, without loss to himself, he took 152 prisoners, and several wagons full of provisions, guns, and ammunition. About the same time General Manie Botha had a skirmish with the enemy about fifteen miles from Wilhelmstal, and a mounted brigade had one somewhat farther to the east. Meanwhile, on the railway line General Botha occupied the station of Omaruru, about 80 miles from Windhoek, where he took some prisoners, and a day or two later he was in possession of Kalkfeld, 40 miles farther north. This place had been entrenched and prepared for resistance, but as a result of flanking movements the Germans were compelled to abandon it. Still the Germans declined to give battle, and Botha's mobile column swept victoriously on. On June 26 Otjiwarongo, a station on the railway, and Okandyande, a town eight miles to the south, were occupied, while wide encircling movements gave possession of the whole of the district around Waterberg. At Okandyande two hundred and fifty interned civilians were liberated.

Fifty miles, or thereabouts, beyond Otjiwarongo the railway line forks, one branch going to Grootfontein and the other to Tsumeb. Near the junction stands Otavi, near which place are extensive deposits of copper, and as soon as the Union forces were securely planted at Okaputu and Omarasa, two intermediate stations, they made a dash for it. At 6.30 on the evening of June 30 General Manie Botha, with the 5th brigade, left Okaputu, and at dawn on the following morning his scouts came into touch with the enemy. Later in the day a general action developed near Osib, and although the nature of the ground gave certain advantages to the defenders, and the attacking force had covered forty-two miles in sixteen hours, yet Manie Botha's skill and promptitude and his men's courage and endurance prevailed, and before nightfall Otavi was occupied. At Otavifontein—to give the town its full name—there is a good supply of water, and so arid is the neighbourhood that the possession of this town practically means the possession of the surrounding country.

From Omarasa, five miles south of Okaputu, another mounted brigade—the 6th—led by General Lukin, had set out at the same time as the 5th, and between the two came General Botha with the headquarters staff. Unlike Manie Botha, Lukin did not have to fight, but the excellent condition of his men was proved by the fact that they covered the forty-eight miles to Otavi in twenty hours without appreciable pause. The casualties among the Union forces in this operation were four killed and seven wounded. They took 27 German prisoners and a machine-gun. A single day's rest was all that Manie Botha's men needed after their strenuous march and their running fight through a country covered with bush, and while they were taking this a regiment of mounted rifles was sent to seize the pass through the hills at Eisenberg. This having been done, the main body was soon on the move again towards Grootfontein.

This fight near Otavi was the last real stand made by the Germans. Brave as they unquestionably were, their position was hopeless. Supplies were failing, for Botha's generalship had deprived them of one advantage after another. They had been driven into the wildest and most inhospitable parts of the country; they were losing, one after the other, the places where food could be stored and water found; and, moreover, they were in a district as has been said, where the natives—with good reason, if half the stories told are true—were fiercely hostile to them. Above all, Botha's columns were closing round them. They could either fight heroically but senselessly to the last, or they could surrender. They chose the latter alternative, and during the first days of July were making preparations for it.

Away to the west of the line of Tsumeb two columns were sweeping through the country. At Asis General Myburgh had left the railway, and at Chaub, sixteen miles south of Tsumeb, he had met a body of Germans. What followed can scarcely be called a fight, for with only one man killed Myburg took 86 prisoners, and on July 8 marched right into Tsumeb, where 500 or 600 more surrendered. He also captured some field-guns, and released a number of South Africans who had been captured by the Germans. Colonel Brits was moving in a still bigger arc. On June 30 he left Otyisasu, five miles west of Otjiwarongo, and passing through Otyo and Okakeua, he reached the German port of Namutoni. There he took 150 German prisoners, seized their supplies and, like Myburgh, liberated a number of prisoners. It was then officially stated that all the Union prisoners in German hands had been released.

By this time Dr. Seitz was again in communication with General Botha about a surrender. Botha presented his terms in the form of an ultimatum, and while they were being considered his men stood to arms ready, if need be, for a final battle. This, however, was not to be. On the stroke of time the terms were accepted, and at two o'clock on the morning of July 9, at a spot described as Kilometre 500 on the railway between Otavi and Khorab, the conditions of the capitulation were agreed to and signed by Botha, Seitz, and Colonel Francke. All the Germans surrendered unconditionally. It is a tribute to civilization that in that distant part of the world Botha was able to ring up Myburgh on the telephone, and to inform him of the surrender. The terms of surrender provided that the officers should be released upon parole, and that the men should be interned in the country. The two paragraphs dealing with this question may be quoted in full:

> The active troops of the said forces of the said Protectorate surrendered shall in the case of officers retain their arms and may give their parole, being allowed to live each under that parole at such places as he may select. If for any reason the Government of the Union of South Africa is unable to meet the wish of any officer as regards his choice of abode, the officer concerned will choose some place in respect of which no difficulty exists.
>
> In the case of other ranks of the active troops of the said forces of the said Protectorate, such other ranks shall be interned under proper guard in such place in the Protectorate as the Union Government may decide upon. Each non-commissioned officer and man of the other ranks last referred to shall be allowed to retain his rifle, but no ammunition. One officer shall be permitted to be interned with the other ranks of the artillery, one with the other ranks of the remainder of the active troops, and one with the other ranks of the police.

These conditions referred only to the regular troops and to the police. Reservists were allowed, upon surrendering their arms and signing a form of parole, to return to their homes and their civil occupations. Civil officials were allowed to retain their homes, but not, of course, their positions. Government property and all warlike stores became the property of the Union.

The work of attending to the details of the surrender was entrusted to Brigadier-General H. T. Lukin, and a revised estimate of the number of prisoners gave it as 204 officers and 3,293 of other ranks (of these rather less than half were regulars); 37 field-guns and 22 machine-guns were given up at this time. The formal surrender took place at Otavi, where the prisoners began to arrive on July 11. Several of them were wearing a cross, not of iron, but of black cloth edged with white cord, this being apparently the nearest approach they could get to the decoration so dear to the Kaiser's heart. They stated that their provisions were almost at an end. Two brigades, one mounted and one infantry, remained with General Lukin to look after the prisoners, but as regards the others, arrangements were made for their return to the Union, where the victorious conclusion of the campaign was hailed generally with great enthusiasm. The whole operation had been carried out with singularly little loss. Under 2,000 casualties were sustained by the Union forces both in the rebellion and in the campaign in South-West Africa, and of these less than 500 were killed.

The Germans suffered even less, and although no accurate figures are available it is fairly clear that not many more than 150 were killed and 200 wounded. But nearly 6,000 prisoners were taken, which accounts for two-thirds of the German force. A considerable number without doubt returned to their homes during the final stages of the campaign.

At a cost of some 2,000 casualties—less than many a single day's loss suffered by British armies in Flanders—General Botha had captured a territory over 300,000 square miles in extent, and had brought 15,000 whites and 100,000 natives under the rule of the British Empire. It was an undeveloped land, but a rich one, and under British rule was capable of great development. Before the surrender the damage done to the 1,400 mil^s of railway had been made good, and a regular service of trains was running. Moreover, the line from Upington in Cape Colony was, in June, extended to Kalkfontein, thus linking up the Union system with the German one.

And what shall we say more? Just this, that General Botha and his men deserved the praise showered upon them by the King and his subjects all over the world. On July 13, in moving that the thanks of the House of Commons be given to General Botha and Smuts and the forces under their command, Mr. Asquith said :

I ask the House at this, the earliest opportunity, to testify to the admiration and gratitude of the whole Empire, first to the illustrious General, who is also Prime Minister of the Union, and who has rendered such inestimable service to the Empire, which he entered by adoption, and of which he has become one of the most honoured and cherished sons, and to his dauntless and much enduring troops, whether of Burgher or British birth, who fought like brethren, side by side, in the cause which is equally dear to all of us—the broadening of the bounds of human liberty.

CHAPTER 14

Submarine Warfare

E VER since the introduction of the submarine it had been realized that a new and untried factor had been introduced into modern warfare, and the year 1915 was to show the extensive uses, lawful and unlawful, to which it could be put. The German submarine vessels had the prefix U (*unterseeboot*) followed by a number, for example, U 28, or were named U A, U B, U C, followed by a number. The later U-boats were a great improvement on the earlier, in size, cruising radius, and service qualities, being more of the cruiser type; *e.g.*, U 139 was 303 ft. in length, 29½ ft. in beam, and had a surface displacement of 1,950 tons, as compared with the 450 tons of U 13-20, and 650 tons of U 21-32. At this time the largest was the U 142 type. These were 320 ft. in length, with a surface displacement of 2,160 tons. They carried a crew of 83, and their radius of operation was far beyond the limits of the North Sea. The English Channel having been closed by nets, booms, and patrol vessels, they went north round Scotland, and were soon in evidence in other theatres of war.

The genesis of submarine warfare waged upon peaceful trading ships, can be traced to two main sources, and the principal of these was undoubtedly the failure of those schemes which Germany had prepared for the embarrassment and destruction of British oversea trade. From the opening of hostilities down to the inglorious exit of the Kronprinz Wilhelm, over a period of nearly nine months, German commerce destroyers had succeeded in capturing or destroying only 54 British merchantmen out of a total of over 20,000.

Another point which weighed heavily with the enemy was the dwindling success of his submarines when used for their legitimate purpose of attacking warships. In the first five months of the war enemy submarines destroyed eight British warships in home waters, their total tonnage being 67,700. In the second five months the record fell to two ships of 6,333 tons, and only one of these, the old destroyer Recruit, of 385 tons, was a regular warship. The result was that the submarines were diverted from the hunt for battleships and cruisers and concentrated upon the merchantmen using British ports. On February 4, 1915, Germany made a definite declaration of policy:

> Just as Britain has designated the area between Scotland and Norway as an area of war, so Germany now declares all the waters surrounding Great Britain and Ireland, including the entire English Channel, as an area of war. For this purpose, beginning from February 18, 1915, it will endeavour to destroy every enemy merchant ship that is found in this area of war, without its always being possible to avert the peril that this threatens to persons and cargoes. Neutrals are therefore warned against further entrusting crews and passengers and wares to such ships. Their attention is also called to the fact that it is advisable for their ships to avoid entering this area, for even though the German naval forces have instructions to avoid violence to neutral ships in so far as they are recognisable, in view of the misuse of neutral flags ordered by the British Government and the contingencies of naval warfare, their becoming victims of an attack directed against enemy ships cannot always be averted.

Thus did Germany declare war upon merchant ships of whatever nationality that might be found by their submarines in the waters surrounding the British Isles. The organized submarine blockade was not due to start until February 18, but it really began at the end of January, although numerous merchantmen had been sunk before then. On the 31st of that month half a dozen British merchantmen were attacked. Some were torpedoed in the neighbourhood of Liverpool and some in the Channel, and among the latter was the steamship Tokomaru, which was bringing from New Zealand 97,000 carcases of mutton. No warning was given in this instance, but the crew were saved by French torpedo boats.

A submarine in the Irish Sea, the U 21, made a practice of giving the crews time to leave before sending the ships to the bottom. But the vessels in the Channel were either commanded by men of a different stamp or they were acting under a different set of orders. The latter seems the more probable explanation, in view of an official statement issued by the German Admiralty at this time, which ran: " England is about to ship to France a large number of troops and a great quantity of war material. We shall act against these transports with all the military means at our disposal."

In the afternoon of February 1 an attempt was made to sink the British hospital ship Asturias. This vessel, carrying a staff of doctors and nurses, was making for Havre to embark wounded British soldiers and bring them across to England. In accordance with the Hague conventions, to which Germany had subscribed, she was painted white, with a broad band of green running from stem to stern, and huge red crosses painted in prominent positions on her sides. It was broad daylight when, at about five o'clock in the afternoon, the conning tower of a German submarine was sighted at a distance of about five hundred yards, and immediately afterwards the track of a torpedo was seen making directly towards the ship. The master immediately altered his course, and rang down to the engine-room for full speed, the torpedo missed its aim.

There was great confidence in Germany in the moral effect of the submarine blockade. It was firmly believed that, with this menace facing them, British shipowners would refuse to risk their ships at sea, and that officers and men would decline to place their lives in jeopardy. On February 10 the steamer Laertes, bound for Amsterdam, was intercepted in the North Sea by a German submarine, and peremptorily ordered to stop. Instead of doing so, the Laertes clapped on extra speed and proceeded to steer an erratic course, hoisting the Dutch flag; but a torpedo was fired, dodged by the Laertes; and then the submarine opened fire. She kept on her way at full speed, and soon saw the submarine drop astern and give up the chase.

The inauguration of the blockade was accompanied by no diminution of British shipping or in the volume of traffic dealt with at British ports, though ships were torpedoed and crews were wantonly murdered. On February 19 the Cardiff steamer Cambank was attacked without warning off Anglesey. On the same day the campaign against neutral shipping was opened by the torpedoing off Folkestone of the Belridge, a Norwegian ship carrying oil from New Orleans to Amsterdam. Fortunately, the vessel did not sink, and was towed into the Thames.

On March 27 the steamship Aguila was intercepted in the Irish Sea by the U 28 and ordered to stop. Instead of doing so, the vessel put on her best speed in an endeavour to escape; but the submarine proved the faster, and when at last the Aguila was overhauled and came to a standstill the Germans gave the passengers and crew only four minutes to take to the boats. Almost before it was possible to begin to get the boats out the submarine opened fire on them. On the same day the steamer Falaba, outward bound from Liverpool, and carrying nearly 200 passengers—men, women, and children—was stopped at the mouth of the St. George's Channel by the U 36. The submarine gave them only ten minutes to get into the boats and away, and then drove a torpedo into the ship. Many were killed by the explosion. Boats were shattered and their occupants thrown into the water, while the liner rapidly took a heavy list that precipitated the others into the sea. The result was that 123 lives were destroyed.

On April 18 a German submarine torpedoed the trawler Vanilla. Refugee ships, hospital ships, and passenger ships were also torpedoed. One ship, the Harpalyce, engaged in bringing relief from the United States for the stricken and impoverished people of Belgium carried a safe conduct issued by the German minister at The Hague, intended to save her from all interference at the hands of German warships.

Yet on April 10 this ship was torpedoed in the North Sea by a German submarine and sent to the bottom. Many were the occasions when a threatened British ship refused to be cowed, and the feat of the Laertes was repeated under even more difficult circumstances by Captain John Green, of the steamer Vosges, on March 27.

Equally plucky was the behaviour of the steam-tug Homer. On April 8 this little vessel was towing the French sailing ship General de Sonis up the Channel, when, off the Isle of Wight, a German submarine appeared and called upon them to surrender. Captain Gibson, of the Homer, paid no attention, but, awaiting his opportunity, slipped the tow rope and drove straight for the submarine under a shower of bullets from the enemy's machine-guns. The Homer missed the submarine's stern by no more than a yard and then steered for the Owers Lightship, pursued by the enemy, who fired a torpedo that missed its mark. The tug got safely into port with seven shot holes in her and the General de Sonis arrived later under sail.

The first merchantman which actually sank a submarine was the Thordis, a vessel of less than 800 tons, commanded by Captain J. W. Bell. The incident occurred on February 28, when the ship was off Beachy Head. The look-out sighted a submarine, and Captain Bell immediately ordered all hands on deck in case of emergency. In a few minutes the track of a torpedo was seen making towards the vessel; but the weapon passed clear. For some unknown reason the submarine drifted towards the Thordis, and the latter was steered so as to bring her bows on to the vessel. A heavy wave came and lifted the steamer on its crest, and when she descended there was a tremendous crash as she fell on to the hull of the submarine. Large quantities of oil appeared on the surface, and the submarine was not seen again.

In view of the fact that the German declarations had laid special stress on the assumption that large numbers of men and quantities of material were about to be shipped from England to France, their failure to attack the British transports with any success was most remarkable. In the first ten months of the war only one vessel was even hit. This was the horse-transport Wayfarer, torpedoed 100 miles off the Scilly Isles on April 11. She was towed into Queenstown. Only five lives were lost, and all the 763 horses were got ashore safely.

It was not until March 1 that the British Government announced any special retaliatory measures against the submarine blockade. Hitherto, although the enemy's shipping had been wiped off the seas, commerce was still carried on with German ports by neutrals, provided that they were not carrying contraband. On March 1 Mr. Asquith reviewed the policy and behaviour of German submarines and added:

Germany is adopting these methods against peaceful shipping and non-combatant crews with the avowed object of preventing commodities of all kinds, including food for the civil population, from reaching or leaving the British Isles or Northern France. Her opponents are therefore driven to frame retaliatory measures in order, in their turn, to prevent commodities of any kind from reaching or leaving the German Empire. These measures will, however, be enforced by the British and French Governments without risk to neutral ships or to neutral or non-combatant lives, and with strict observance of the dictates of humanity. The British and French Governments will therefore hold themselves free to detain and take into port ships carrying goods of presumed enemy destination, ownership, or origin.

In short, the British Government declared a blockade of German ports—a measure which, in the opinion of many, should have been taken earlier in the war.

A U-BOAT SUNK

The first enemy submarine to be accounted for after the institution of the submarine blockade was the U 8, which was sighted off Dover on March 5 by a flotilla of British destroyers. When the U 8 rose again she was promptly attacked by the destroyers Ghurka and Maori, so that she quickly sank, the whole of her crew being taken prisoners.

Another enemy submarine, the U 12, was destroyed on March 10 off the Firth of Forth. The first intimation of her whereabouts was given by two trawlers, and a hunt was immediately organized. The submarine discharged two torpedoes at the destroyer Attack, and as she came to the surface to see the result, was discovered by the destroyer Ariel (Lieut.-Commander J. V. Creagh), which proceeded to charge full speed at the vessel. The submarine dived, but she was too slow in sinking. The Ariel, keeping dead on her course, sped over the spot where the submarine had disappeared, and as she did so she struck the periscope and bent it completely over in such a way as to blind the submarine. She came to the surface again, and the Ariel and other destroyers immediately opened fire on her, maintaining it until the crew came out of the hatches with their hands raised in token of surrender. Eighteen of the crew of 28 were drowned.

The next success was recorded by the Admiralty on March 26 in the following brief statement: "The Admiralty have good reason to believe that the German submarine U 29 has been sunk with all hands." As the Grand Fleet was returning to Scapa, an alarm of submarines was given, and the track of a torpedo was seen to pass just astern of the Neptune. At the same time the Dreadnought caught sight of a periscope and steered directly for it, handled with such precision that she struck the U-boat before she could dive. As the great bulk of the Dreadnought passed over her, a conning-tower reared out of the water for just long enough to allow the figures 29 to be clearly seen.

Submarines joined with a will in these attacks on neutrals. The Dutch steamer Medea was sunk in the Channel by the U 28 on March 25 after she had been stopped and her papers examined. At about the same time the Italian steamer Luigi Paradi was sunk, to be followed early in April by the Swedish vessel Folke. A Dutch steamer Katwyk, carrying grain from Baltimore for Rotterdam consigned to the Dutch Government was torpedoed and sent to the bottom, the crew fortunately being able to save themselves. Norwegian, Danish, Greek, and American vessels were treated in the same way. On May 1 the United States steamer Gulflight, carrying a cargo of oil, was torpedoed off the Scilly Isles; but did not sink.

Driven to desperation by her impotence to affect the position seriously, Germany planned a grand coup. She advertised her intentions extensively in America. On May 1, 1915, the giant Cunard liner Lusitania was due to leave New York for England, and the same morning the following announcement, issued from the Imperial German Embassy, Washington, appeared in a number of American newspapers:

> Travellers intending to embark for an Atlantic voyage are reminded that a state of war exists between Germany and her Allies and Great Britain and her Allies; that the zone of war includes the waters adjacent to the British Isles; that, in accordance with the formal notice given by the Imperial German Government, vessels flying the flag of Great Britain or any of her Allies are liable to destruction in those waters; and that travellers sailing in the war zone in ships of Great Britain or her Allies do so at their own risk.

To emphasise the warning, most of the prominent Americans who had booked a passage by the Lusitania received a telegram on the morning of the vessel's departure in these terms: " Have it on definite authority Lusitania is to be torpedoed. You had better cancel passage immediately." Hardly anyone was deterred by these warnings. It was felt that the Lusitania's speed would protect her in case of attack, although considerable submarine activity had recently been reported off the west coast of Ireland.

The Lusitania crossed the Atlantic at a speed of 21 knots—considerably below the rate she was capable of. As she came into the British waters the vessel reduced speed to about 18 knots, so that she might arrive off the Mersey at such a time as to be able to proceed straight in without waiting for the tide. Actually four wireless warnings of the presence of submarines were despatched from Valencia on May 6 and May 7. Nevertheless, at a speed of 18 knots she steamed along the south coast of Ireland on a lovely spring day, only a few miles off the coast, not even taking the trouble to steer a zigzag course.

It was well past midday of May 7, and many of the passengers were down below at lunch. The look-outs had been doubled, and Captain Turner was pacing the bridge anxious, no doubt, but confident. Suddenly from the other end of the bridge there came the cry, " There's a torpedo!" Captain Turner rushed across, but it was too late to do anything to save the ship. Almost as soon as he had seen the track of the weapon, the torpedo struck the Lusitania on the starboard side between the third and fourth funnels. A second struck her aft a few minutes later.

Instantly the great ship began to heel, but never at any time was there the slightest disorder among the passengers or crew. The vessel was so huge that many on board did not for a moment imagine that the dull boom they heard was the explosion of a torpedo against her hull, and those who did know what had happened were confident that a vessel of such a size would not succumb. Every available boat was ordered to be launched at once. Lifebelts were served out, and as the ship listed more and more, confidence gave way to despair. The boats on the port side could not be lowered—they simply dropped against the side of the ship; and many of those on the starboard side had to be attended to by the passengers themselves. The tragedy was over, so far as the ship was concerned, in 18 minutes. She was struck just before 2.15 p.m. She gave a final lurch and disappeared just after 2.30.

There was no ship in the vicinity at the time, but fortunately there were watchers ashore who in the far distance had seen the disaster, and with all possible dispatch a swarm of vessels was sent out from Queenstown. But this was locking the stable door after the horse had been stolen, and the rescuers arrived only to save those who had been fortunate enough to get into the boats, or to find some other sure means of keeping afloat. There had been nearly 2,000 people on board the Lusitania, and of this large company 1,195 were drowned. The sinking of the Lusitania was hailed in Germany as a master-stroke. Time was to prove how great a mistake political and psychological had been made. The effect on the conduct of the war was to intensify the anti-submarine campaign, and to antagonise the United States of America.

Though the Grand Fleet had improvised means of defence against submarine attack for its capital ships, the Franco-British armada, operating off Gallipoli, and the supply ships and transports of the unhappy Dardanelles expedition were in much danger. In home waters oversea food supplies and ocean-borne commerce were seriously imperilled, and the general position was one of great anxiety.

In the last vain attempt to disguise from Americans, Scandinavians, and Dutchmen the true nature of their aims, the Germans held that the campaign of submarine piracy, which formally opened in February, 1915, was merely an answer to the plan for starving out the Central Empires by a naval blockade. When Germany opened her submarine campaign against non-combatants in cargo and passenger steamers, she was being fed by the Americans with fat and cotton for making smokeless powder, and large food supplies were reaching her from the Balkans and through neutral ports.

The Liberal Government, which had tried to force the Declaration of London upon the navy, did not, when hostilities opened, extend its list of contraband to the raw material of such things as dynamite, nitro-glycerine, and gun and rifle ammunition. Even when the Coalition Government was formed, no member of it had sufficient first-hand scientific knowledge to enable him to know what was properly contraband. Lard, oil, and similar substances used in the manufacture of nitro-glycerine were overlooked in drawing up the list of contraband. Meanwhile, British freights continued to rise. Between 200 and 300 British steamers were sold to neutrals, partly with a view to avoiding the submarine menace, and at the same time British shipbuilding declined seriously.

It was calculated that on some important lines the homeward and outward freight, after deducting extra expenses, amounted to 39 times as much as the pre-war profit. The special tax of 50 per cent. later raised to 80 per cent., on excess profits still allowed the shipowner to tax the import and export trade enormously. It was estimated that in the first 19 months of the war the indirect cost to the British people of the rise of freights was £400,000,000. The net profits in the shipping industry were reckoned at £250,000,000 for 1915, as compared with £20,000,000 for 1913.

In addition to the results of the German submarine campaign in home waters and the Mediterranean, there were many fires and explosions in vessels bound from North and South America to Europe. During the year 321 British vessels and 212 foreign vessels were directly sunk by German agency, but there were other heavy losses through incendiary fires, which accounted for much of the grand total annual loss of 726 vessels of 500 tons gross register and upwards, of the value of nearly thirty million pounds. Putting the matter briefly, the losses of British and neutral shipping in 1915 exceeded 1,800,000 tons, while the heaviest loss in any year before the war was 500,000 tons. The British public after first watching with keen anxiety the successes of the enemy, concluded that we had practically won on all points when the underwater raiding flotillas were destroyed, captured, or hunted away. Germany made a great sacrifice of her trained submarine crews and submarine vessels, but her losses in this respect were more than repaid by the heavily-increased economic pressure exerted upon our nation by her campaign against the mercantile marine.

The difference between the freights at the end of 1914 and those at the end of 1915 cannot, of course, be accepted as the measure of the enemy's success. The British Government had taken for war service about half the available tonnage, and by grave lack of initiative and foresight neglected to buy a large number of foreign vessels in the early weeks of the war, when neutral shipowners were timid and ready to sell cheaply. Instead, it was the British who lost some hundreds of vessels, after hostilities opened, by sale to neutrals.

The Dardanelles adventure—by reason of the huge fleets of merchant steamers, trawlers, and other trading vessels it distracted from commercial work—was a factor of high import-ance in checking the supply of iron ore, wheat, and other food and materials. Then the extension of the operations in the Persian Gulf to Bagdad diminished the number of steamers engaged in Oriental trade. The Government attempted in November, 1915, to concentrate its resources by forbidding British ships to trade between only neutral ports to the neglect of the carrying requirements of itself and Allies.

Towards the winter of 1915, when the Dardanelles adventure was about to close and release a considerable amount of shipping, the Salonika adventure, in which still larger armies needed transport and seaborne supplies, made a still larger deficiency in the commercial carrying power of the mercantile marine. But it might fairly be maintained that Britain could have borne the burden of the Dardanelles, Bagdad, and Salonika expeditions without being seriously inconvenienced by them if the blow struck by the U-boats had not turned the muddle into complete economic disorder.

From the purely military point of view, however, the German was not so successful. In the period under review he developed his submarine campaign by a series of very rapid and striking successes, which caused the allies much perturbation. But the fighting British seaman, by reason of his extraordinary versatility and intelligence, rose quickly to the occasion, and in a long, bitter struggle, conducted in absolute silence, defeated the Germans. Never had the silent navy so well deserved its epithet. Sir John Jellicoe had at last 3,000 vessels under his orders; and Admiral de Robeck could also number his large and small craft by the thousand. The Admiralty did not announce its successes though these occurred every week. The German marine office seldom knew at any time what was its own strength in underwater craft.

The boats went out, and stayed often with means of supply lasting for weeks, but very many of them did not come back. It was not known where, when, or how they had been destroyed. The deadly silence told on the nerves far more than any triumphant announcement would have done. It is credibly reported that the trained and well-disciplined sailors of Germany were at last wrought up into such a state of dread that they could not be got to volunteer for submarine work. The small crews needed were offered work on Zeppelins, which they regarded as much less risky, and after being removed for this supposed purpose from their comrades, they were dragooned into service in the U-boats.

About the time when the Goliath was torpedoed by a Turkish destroyer in the Dardanelles, and went down with 500 British sailors there came to the combined French and British fleets off Gallipoli a rumour which caused intense anxiety. German submarines of the most powerful type, it was said, were coming from the North Sea into the Mediterranean. As a matter of fact, Lord Fisher had been expecting for months the appearance of enemy underwater craft round the Dardanelles. One of the reasons why he may have disapproved of the expedition was that he foresaw serious difficulties, arising from the fact that Austrian submarines could escape the blockade of the Adriatic, and the latest type of German U-boat could voyage from Emden to Constantinople. However, when the Cabinet decided on the great adventure, Lord Fisher prepared to help in the days of trial. At home great new naval machines of war were being made in haste to counter the submarine menace to our Mediterranean forces. But meanwhile a single German U-boat—U 51, under Lieutenant von Hersing—showed what serious injury could be done to an unprotected fleet. Hersing seems to have worked around Scotland to the Bay of Biscay, where by arrangement he was met by a neutral ship, that supplied him with oil. With extreme boldness he tried to pass Gibraltar without submerging, but was spotted by a French destroyer, and forced by gun fire to dive.

He obtained another supply of oil, either from a secret base at Sollum, on the Egyptian coast, or at one of the numerous secret bases off the islands and mainland of Greece. His periscope was first clearly seen by the British fleet at 1.30 p.m. on May 22, 1915, near Rabbit Island. All the battleships, cruisers, and transports were at anchor, presenting a series of easy targets, but the Prince George fired two rounds that made the submarine dive, while the destroyers dashed out and screened the helpless fleet in dense columns of black smoke. Had Hersing been ready to venture the lives of himself and his men, he might have got in a blow at some of the modern capital ships, but he was hunted away by the destroyers, while all the ships started a series of evolutions at full speed, heading to all points of the compass, then rounding on their wake in the hope of ramming the enemy, and then spurting off in another direction.

When the alarm had subsided the ships returned to their anchorage, with the tireless destroyers forming a guard round them; but it was recognized that the protection of the destroyers was inadequate, and in the night all the valuable new battleships and battle cruisers departed for home waters, and the work of making Mudros Bay a submarine-proof harbour was hurriedly carried on. The task of supplying the armies at the Dardanelles was seriously interrupted, as no unarmed steamer had a fighting chance against the German U-boats. But the Swiftsure remained at her old anchorage, off Cape Helles, with some old battleships, while the Canopus, Vengeance, and Albion patrolled the coast round the Anzac positions.

At eight o'clock on the morning of May 25 Hersing sighted the Swiftsure off Cape Helles, and ran within three hundred yards of her, but being met by rapid fire disappeared without firing. The Majestic and Agamemnon were quite close to the Swiftsure, and it has never been explained why the German did not release a torpedo. Two and a half hours afterwards he tried a shot at the Vengeance, but missed, and then came up again, and caught the Triumph as she was steaming slowly near the Anzac position. The battleship had her nets down at the time, but they were utterly useless. Two terrible missiles either cut through them or went beneath them. The great ship listed, and in about eight minutes rolled over and turned upside down. Then after floating for half an hour bottom upwards she disappeared in a great cloud of steam. Fortunately, not many lives were lost, as a trawler and destroyer were quite close to the stricken vessel, and at once went to its aid.

Worse was to follow than the destruction of the Triumph. The submarine that sank her was perceived, and pursued until nightfall by the British destroyers, but Hersing escaped in the darkness, and two days afterwards again approached the Anzac position. Here the old battleship, Majestic, built in 1895 and armed with four 12 in. and twelve 6 in. guns, was acting as a huge heavy battery in support of the Australasian Expeditionary Force. Something like 12 destroyers were ranged about the battleship, to protect her against hostile underwater craft. But the German submarine officer, whose skill cannot but be praised, got under her guard and his torpedo sank her in a few minutes. Had it not been for the presence of the destroyers, the loss of life would have been very heavy. Some of the destroyers emitted a black cloud of smoke to veil the scene from the Turkish gunners on Sari Bair, and others steamed in for rescue work, with the happy result that most of the crew—about 760 officers and men—were saved.

But the blow, by reason of the skill and daring with which it had been delivered, entirely upset Admiral de Robeck's plan of naval co-operation with the Mediterranean Expeditionary Force. It was quite clear that the British and French admirals had no defence against the German submarines operating around the Gallipoli peninsula. One U-boat, with a good officer and 30 men, practically drove off the battleships, battle cruisers and armoured cruisers collected by Britain and France against the Ottoman Empire.

For the next two months things went well in the Dardanelles for the Germans and their allies. Hersing took his submarine through the Straits to Constantinople and tried to fight the British craft. But in July the latest creation of the British designers, a raft almost flush with the waves floated into the Mediterranean. In the bows was a 9.2 in. gun, in the stern a long 6 in. piece. The newcomer was followed by a smaller monster, armed with only two 6 in. guns.

Then came Lord Fisher's contribution to the naval art of attacking land fortifications. It was a huge torpedo proof monitor, carrying only two 14 in. guns, and some anti-aircraft armament. The sides bulged some ten feet, and then slanted under, forming a platform just washed by the waves. This bulge made the vessel steer badly, and reduced her speed to a wobbling crawl. But despite her slowness, her awkwardness and her other defects, she was a good antidote to the submarine. The 14 in. guns were not of British make, and they showed it. But despite their serious faults they were able to pitch in the enemy's trenches a shell weighing three-quarters of a ton at a range of 15 miles. Four vessels of the 14 in. gun type came into action off Gallipoli, and, with a large number of other monitors of various shapes and sizes, they set to work to convince Turk and Teuton that the island race had not lost command of the seas. Then some ancient vessels of the British Fleet turned up in strange disguise. They were old cruisers, decorated with a ten-foot waist-belt which hung from their sides by wire ropes and steel stanchions. But with the new anti-torpedo protection they did some good work, and the Dardanelles operations proceeded for some months with remarkable security so far as the surface vessels were concerned.

It was not only the British navy that suffered losses from submarine action. The French navy which was charged with the duty of containing the Austrian fleet was exposed to similar risks. At the beginning of the war Austria had seven submarines in service, and seven in various stages of construction, but it was not until the war had been in progress nearly five months that their underwater craft made any attempt on the French fleet.

On December 21 a German submarine, U 12, commanded by Lieutenant Egon Lerch, reached the southern end of the Adriatic, and there, after lying in wait for some time, she succeeded in stalking the French Dreadnought Jean Bart. She fired two torpedoes, one of which missed its mark by 100 yards, but the other struck the 23,000-ton battleship in the bows and tore a huge rent in her side. Fortunately, however, her bulkheads and watertight doors stood out against the strain, and she was able to make her way into port, some hundreds of miles distant, under her own steam and without further mishap.

Three days after this, the French submarine Curie, a small but modern vessel of 390 tons, carrying seven torpedo-tubes, made a plucky attempt to enter the harbour at Pola with the object of attacking the Austrian ships within. She safely passed the outer defences, and was creeping slowly along towards the inner harbour, when she was suddenly fouled by a heavy steel net rigged across the entrance. In extricating herself from this obstruction the submarine rose to the surface, and the Austrians, having been warned by the movements of the buoys supporting the net, immediately opened a heavy fire, which rapidly smashed in the sides of the submarine and sent her to the bottom. All the crew were picked up, with the exception of the commander, who chose to go down with his ship.

The second Austrian submarine attack on the French fleet was more successful than the first. On the night of April 26-27 the armoured cruiser Léon Gambetta, flying the flag of Rear-Admiral Sénès, was steaming slowly across the mouth of the Adriatic, en route to Malta. Without any warning of impending attack, a terrific explosion occurred amidships, in the neighbourhood of the engine room. A few minutes later when the ship was already heeling dangerously, a second torpedo struck her, and she began to settle down rapidly. One or two boats full of men got away, and one or two were swamped as the 12,000-ton ship disappeared beneath the waves.

All the officers of the doomed ship gathered on the bridge, and not one of them was saved. The noise of the explosions was fortunately heard at the lighthouse on Cape Santa Maria di Leuca, and a flotilla of Italian torpedo craft was immediately sent out to search for survivors. It was a most gallant action on the part of the Italians, for their boats might easily have been mistaken for French vessels, and fired upon or torpedoed by the Austrians. They searched the sea for hours, but were only able to pick up 137 survivors out of a crew of some 720.

The Léon Gambetta was a serviceable armoured cruiser of 12,000 tons, completed in 1905, and armed with four 7.6 in. and sixteen 6.5 guns. Her successful assailant was the U 5, a submarine of 269 tons submerged displacement, carrying two torpedo tubes.

There seems to have been only one German U-boat besides Hersing's operating off the Dardanelles at the close of May, 1915, but quite a large flotilla of hostile underwater craft at last collected in the Mediterranean. Many of the vessels appear to have been built or assembled in the Austrian ports along the Adriatic coast; others continued to make the long voyage from Germany. The U officers changed their flags according to circumstances, showing the Austrian ensign when torpedoing Italian vessels, and flying the Crescent when there was danger of provoking the United States. Even the Bulgarian flag seemed to have been used by the German submarine officers who controlled, by reason of their superior skill, nearly all the boats used against the allies. But skilful though the Germans were they did not take full advantage of the opportunities offered by the battleships and transports presenting targets such as were dreamed of by submarine commanders. In fact they did no more damage than the British submarines in the Baltic and the sea of Marmora had wrought under more difficult conditions.

The enemy's submarine campaign in the Mediterranean opened in September, 1915. By this time the British warships were boomed or waist-belted against torpedo attack, and the U-boats sought and found easier victims in the allied troopships. As a beginning the Southland was torpedoed on September 2, but was not sunk. On September 14, 1915, however, occurred the first loss of a British transport in the war, when the great troopship Royal Edward was torpedoed in the Aegean Sea with the loss of 1,000 lives, most of the drowned soldiers being drafts for the 29th division. Five days after the Royal Edward was destroyed, a German submarine, operating south of Greece, caught another British transport, the Ramazan, and sank her by gun fire, causing the loss of 300 men. Another transport, the Marquette, carrying Indian troops, was torpedoed in the Aegean on October 26, when 100 lives were lost. On November 5 two submarines attacked an armed boarding steamer, the Tara, and sank her after 35 of her men were killed. The troopship Mercian was shelled by a U-boat on November 10, and 103 men were killed or injured, but the vessel was not sunk.

A French steamer, the Indien, was also torpedoed and sunk by a U-boat in the Aegean Sea on September 8, 1915. In the same waters the Provincia was destroyed on October 3, and a French transport, the Calvados, was torpedoed and sunk off Algiers on November 4, 1915. Altogether the toll taken by enemy underwater craft in the Mediterranean in six months in legitimate attack on warships and vessels employed for warlike purposes was considerable but not decisive. The naval losses at the Dardanelles, in addition to those already mentioned, included a mine sweeper, the Hythe, sunk in collision on October 28, and the destroyer Louis, which was stranded and wrecked the following month. Four submarines were lost in circumstances that will be described later, and the same number of underwater craft were also lost by the French either in the Strait or the Sea of Marmora.

The outstanding fact in the Mediterranean in the autumn of 1915 was that the British and French fleets did not succeed in defeating the activities of the German and Austrian submarines, although some were sunk, and some of their shore bases discovered. The U 12, of Austria, was torpedoed on August 10 by an Italian submarine, and the U 13 was sunk by a French destroyer, the Bison, on August 13. But the British, the French, and the Italians could not clear the sea and make it fairly safe for passenger liners and cargo steamers. For some time, indeed, a reign of terror prevailed over the great inland water. French, Italian, Japanese, and British passenger liners were torpedoed without notice.

The Italian passenger liner Ancona, proceeding from Naples to New York, stopped at Messina for more passengers and cargo. The passengers were mainly Greeks and Italians with large families, going to the United States to settle there, the majority being women and children. At one o'clock in the afternoon of Monday, November 8, 1915, as the liner was steaming between Sardinia and Tunis, a submarine appeared at a great distance and fired a shot across the bow. It was not a blank shot, but a live shell, and without observing any of the formalities accompanying the right of search, the submarine, while gaining rapidly on the steamer, continued to shell the Ancona when she had stopped. Not only was the wireless apparatus struck, but the sides and crowded decks of the ship were swept with shrapnel; even the lifeboats in which passengers sought for shelter were destroyed. Many of the non-combatants were killed outright by the exploding shells. A wild panic broke out when the shelling began. The liner was quickly torpedoed and sank in seven minutes, more than 200 men, women, and children being lost. The submarine flew the Austrian flag, and was afterwards acknowledged by the Vienna authorities to be one of their vessels; but some Italian naval officers maintained that it was a German U-boat. On the same day and near the same spot, a French transport, La France, bringing invalided soldiers back from Mudros, was sunk by a submarine.

Another French passenger steamer, Ville de Ciotat, was torpedoed. She was passing Crete on Christmas Eve, bound from Japan for Marseilles, with 135 passengers and 181 officers and men. It was ten o'clock in the morning, and a minute after passing near a Greek steamer, a terrific explosion shook the ship, and a submarine flying the Austrian flag appeared on the surface a short distance away. The crew worked steadily and coolly, and lowered five lifeboats and two rafts before the vessel sank. Seventy-nine lives were lost, including the women and children in one boat which capsized. About the same time one of the newest liners of the Nippon-Yusen fleet, the Yasaka Maru, was torpedoed without warning on her way to the Suez Canal. Happily, the ship did not sink for 49 minutes, and owing to the admirable skill and calmness of the Japanese officers and men, all the passengers and crew were saved. This was the second Japanese steamer torpedoed in the Mediterranean.

On December 30, 1915, the P. and O. liner Persia was attacked and sunk in five minutes. The loss of life in the Persia was very heavy. There were 350 persons on board, and only 180 were saved. Eleven of the survivors, including Lord Montagu of Beaulieu, were picked up after being thirty-two hours without either water or food. Soon afterwards another Japanese steamer—the Kenkoku Maru—was torpedoed. There was also an attack on an American tank steamer—the Petrolite—on December 5, 1915, which had an important sequel. The Petrolite was shelled in the Mediterranean by a submarine flying the Austrian flag, and the shelling continued, as in the Ancona case, after the steamer had stopped. The submarine then came alongside, and the commander offered to buy supplies. The captain of the Petrolite refused to sell, and the Austrian officer thereupon seized one American sailor and held him as hostage, while some of the submarine crew boarded the steamer and forcibly took supplies.

Here may be concluded our survey of the first phase of the enemy's submarine campaign in the Mediterranean area. It was in this area that the hostile underwater craft achieved their most remarkable successes, which included the sinking of two battleships and two troopships on the British side, as well as the destruction of several important French and Italian warships. The French cruiser Léon Gambetta was torpedoed in the Ionian Sea by a hostile submarine on April 26, 1915; the French submarine Mariotte was sunk on July 26, 1915, in the Sea of Marmora; one French armed merchantman—the Indien—was torpedoed in the Aegean Sea on September 8, 1915; and the French troopship Calvados was sunk off Algiers in the first week of November, 1915. Italy lost a fine cruiser—the Amalfi—which was torpedoed in the Adriatic on July 7, 1915; and eleven days afterwards a smaller cruiser—the Giuseppe Garibaldi—was also torpedoed in the Adriatic. Italy also lost a destroyer, a submarine, and a torpedo boat; and the Austrian submarines sank one of her transports during the expedition to Albania.

But having regard to the long period of warfare covered by this survey, and the large area of operations in Mediterranean waters, crowded in places with allied warships, troopships, and supply steamers, the damage wrought by the flotillas of enemy submarines in ten of the most critical months of warfare was much less than might have been feared; for in the Mediterranean circumstances favoured the attacking underwater boats.

The water-gate of the Strait of Gibraltar was in one place only about nine miles wide, and from the great British fortress rock there were only eleven and a half nautical miles of sea stretching to the Moorish coast. But it was impracticable to employ nets to stop or capture the submerged raiders coming from German ports; for the water was remarkably deep—some 950 feet—with a powerful current running in from the Atlantic, beneath which swept a strong counter-current flowing outward from the East Mediterranean. Just beyond the Strait, the midland sea deepened to 3,000 feet, and went down in a large tract to more than 6,000 feet. Except in the shallowing waters of bays, the use of nets against enemy submarines was, therefore, impracticable. The German naval experts helping the Turks could not even net the very narrow Dardanelles against our underwater craft. Natural conditions generally favoured the attacking submarines.

British battleship Triumph, sunk by a German submarine
on May 26, 1915.

Hospital ship used on the Tigris in Mesopotamia campaign.

Cribo

Another " E " class submarine, employed early in the war.

BRITISH SHIPS OF DIVERS SORTS

H.M.S. Formidable, torpedoed by enemy submarine in the
English Channel, January 1, 1915.

German cruiser Bremen, sunk by British submarine in the
Baltic, December 17, 1915.

British liner Falaba which was torpedoed in St. George's
Channel by a German submarine, March 28, 1915.

BRITISH AND GERMAN SUBMARINE ACTIVITY

Plate 26   *Volume 11*

Russell

FIRST MINISTER OF MUNITIONS. Previously pacifist in outlook,
Lloyd George threw all his immense vitality into the struggle to defeat
Germany. As Minister responsible for the organization of munition
factories, he served the country with unabated energy. When the
ministry of munitions was established on June 9, 1915, he became its
first minister, started an office at No. 6, Whitehall Gardens, with two
tables and a single chair, and gathered round him able business men
who served in an unpaid capacity. In addition to its chief work of
speeding up the output of munitions, the ministry had also a department
for suggesting and examining new inventions.

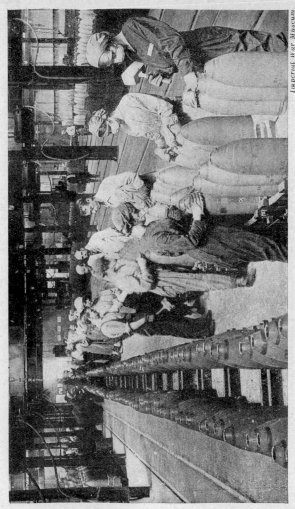

Imperial War Museum

HEROIC WOMEN MUNITION MAKERS. It was not long before the combatants in the Great War came to realize that the old conception of war as being the exclusive business of professional or conscript armies was outworn ; and the still older conditions returned in which war affected every citizen. All civilian activities were viewed in their relation to war needs ; this photograph shows male and female workers, the girls being masked for protection against fumes, filling shells in the famous British munition factory at Chilwell, near Nottingham.

Plate 28

Volume II

The enemy had bases on the strip of Anglo-Italian coast-line in Africa, dominated by the warriors of the Senussi tribes, and more bases along the Asiatic shores of Turkey, as well as numerous secret depôts on Greek islands. The task thrown upon the destroyers, light cruisers, and seaplanes was enormous, and though helped in their work of ferreting out the enemy by the French naval forces, the burden of incessant labour was such as often tested the men to the full stretch of their powers of endurance. The British policy of silence was founded on good tactics and on sound psychology in regard to the Teutonic temperament. The Germans and Austrians seldom knew where and how their underwater boats had been snared.

But it is worthy of remark that when the Salonika expedition was on the way, and the withdrawal from the Dardanelles undertaken, the military power of the U-boats was reduced, for the time at least, to a negligible factor. Armies numbering a quarter of a million men, with their vast war machinery and material, were transported over the midland sea without disaster, despite the German and Austrian underwater craft. While the Teutons were killing non-combatants in unarmed liners, such as the Ancona, Ville de Ciotat, and Persia, they were shunning, more from fear than from ignorance, their proper work of impeding the Salonika, Albania, and Dardanelles operations. In fine, for practical purposes, they were beaten.

There was, however, one extraordinary note of humour in the history of Teutonic submarine work in the Mediterranean. On December 7, 1915, the Austro-Hungarian ministry of foreign affairs sent an appeal to Sir Edward Grey, through the American embassy in London. Certain Austro-Hungarian subjects—chiefly women and children—were being repatriated from India in the British steamer Golconda, and an Austrian petition was forwarded to the British Government, pleading that the Golconda should be specially protected from the German and Austrian submarine attacks, and adding:

> The imperial and royal government will hold the British Government responsible for the lives and well-being of these passengers, the majority of whom are better-class people.

Sir Edward Grey's reply deserves to be quoted verbatim:

> With regard to that portion of the petition which asks that special precautions may be taken to prevent danger to the lives

I 2

of the Golconda passengers by submarine attack, I feel bound to express my astonishment that the Austro-Hungarian Government, itself one of the authors of the danger, should have thought it seemly to endorse this request.

Not content, however, with doing this, the Austro-Hungarian Government further states that it will hold his Majesty's Government responsible for the lives and well-being of those passengers, "the majority of whom are better-class people." I am at a loss to know why "better-class people" should be thought more entitled to protection from submarine attack than any other non-combatants; but, however that may be, the only danger of the character indicated which threatens any of the passengers in the Golconda is one for which the Austro-Hungarian and German Governments are alone responsible. It is they, and they only, who have instituted and carry on a novel and inhuman form of warfare which disregards all the hitherto accepted principles of international law, and necessarily endangers the lives of non-combatants. By asking for special precautions to protect one of their own subjects on board a British merchant vessel, the Austro-Hungarian Government recognises what is the inevitable consequence of their submarine policy, and admits that the outrages by which the Lusitania, the Persia, and numbers of other ships have been sunk without warning were not the result of the casual brutalities of the officers of enemy submarines, but part of the settled and premeditated policy of the Governments whom they serve.

It is needless to add that his Majesty's Government does not propose to take any precautions on behalf of Austro-Hungarian subjects which it does not take on behalf of its own, and that if they suffer any injury from submarine attack on the part of his Majesty's enemies the responsibility must rest solely with those who have made such attacks part of their ordinary methods of warfare. The proper and sufficient protection from this danger is that Austria-Hungary and Germany should observe ordinary rules of humanity in their methods of warfare.

While in the secondary field of operations, the Mediterranean, German underwater craft continued to cause much anxiety, the anti-submarine campaign in British waters was continued intensively. As generally happens, after the sickness was found the antidote: defence improved as offence intensified. Small patrol ships, improved indicator nets and net buoys, the microphone submarine detector, improved technique in submarine hunting all combined to harass the U-boat commanders. Fishermen proved to be admirably suited to this kind of work.

THE BARALONG

Among the watchers of the seas there were some, like the crew of the Baralong, who crowned many months of alert but uneventful activity with a great coup. Disguised as a tramp, she wandered apparently aimlessly in the area of the greatest submarine activity, and when the British liner Arabic had been reported sunk without warning off the Irish coast she steamed towards the scene of the disaster. She came upon a sufficiently dramatic scene. The Nicosian, with a cargo of army mules, had been torpedoed and was being shelled by a German submarine.

The men in the Baralong were angry because they had seen the submarine shelling the cattle ship while the British crew was getting into the lifeboat. As the patrol steamer came round the bows of the Nicosian the submarine again fired, but the shot went wide over the Baralong. The Baralong then opened musketry fire. The Germans at once left their guns, and rushed for the conning tower.

The Baralong then fired both her port and her stern guns. The first shot hit the U-boat below the water line, the second struck the conning tower and split it in half. The submarine was one of Germany's latest and largest, being about 300 feet long, with a displacement of about 1,000 tons. She had guns, mounted fore and aft, which were of slightly larger calibre than the two guns of the Baralong. But the action lasted only a few minutes, the submarine gunners only firing the one wild shot. There were no British casualties. The shattered submarine sank, and the crew jumped overboard. The Baralong's commander called the Nicosian's boats alongside and began to clear them. Then it was seen that a number of the submarine's crew had swum to the Nicosian and were climbing aboard.

Thus far, the facts as stated were admitted on both sides. But in regard to the final scene the German government published a curious version of the affair, set out in alleged affidavits by some of the American cattlemen. The sum of the allegations was that the crew of the Baralong murdered the men of the German submarine as they were struggling in the water. In a series of notes sent to the American ambassadors in London and Berlin, the German government demanded that the British government should try the officers and crew of the Baralong for murder. Sir Edward Grey replied by offering to submit the case to the arbitration of a board of American naval officers if Germany would, at the same time, submit to the investigation of three atrocities committed within forty-eight hours of the Baralong incident. These atrocities were: (1) The torpedoing of the Arabic without notice, whereby 47 non-combatants were drowned; (2) the attack made by a German destroyer on the helpless crew of the British submarine E 13, stranded in Danish waters; (3) the firing of a German submarine on the unresisting crew of the steamer Ruel, after the men had taken to their boats.

The facts, according to Sir Julian Corbett's account, are as follows: Fearing that the survivors of the submarine might scuttle or set on fire the Nicosian with her valuable cargo of mules and fodder, Lt.-Commander Herbert, of the Baralong, ordered a party of marines to board the Nicosian, warning the men to be on their guard against surprise and to be careful to get in the first shot. It appears that the Germans were found in the engine room and that the marines, believing that they were the same people who had sunk the Arabic that morning, shot them all in hot blood.

About this time the First Lord of the Admiralty (Mr. A. J. Balfour) wrote a famous letter concerning the U-boat campaign, the concluding paragraphs of which may be quoted:

It is true that by this method of warfare many inoffensive persons, women and children, as well as men, neutrals as well as belligerents, have been robbed and killed. But it is not only the innocent who have suffered. The criminals also have paid heavy toll. Some have been rescued and are prisoners of war. But from the very nature of submarines it must often happen that they drag their crews with them to destruction, and those who send them forth on their un-honoured mission wait for their return in vain.

Herein lies the explanation of the amazing change which has come over the diplomatic attitude of Germany towards the United States. Men ask themselves why the sinking of the Lusitania, with the loss of over 1,100 men, women, and children, was welcomed throughout Germany with a shout of triumph, while the sinking of the Arabic was accepted in melancholy silence.

Is it because in the intervening months the United States have become stronger or Germany weaker? Is it because the attitude of the President has varied? Is it because the arguments of the Secretary of State have become more persuasive? Is it because German opinion has at last revolted against lawless cruelty?

No. The reason is to be found elsewhere. It is to be found in the fact that the authors of the submarine policy have had time to measure its effects, and that deeds which were merely crimes in May, in September are seen to be blunders.

How many U-boats, with the finest-trained crews in Germany, were lost by Grand Admiral von Tirpitz and Herr Ballin remains a matter of speculation. As the work of destruction often took place far under the water, it was not always possible to say what the actual result had been. Sometimes bubbles and oil appeared on the surface, and these were fairly good evidence of a killing; sometimes a submarine with its suffocated crew was found in the nets. Among those known to have been destroyed in 1915 were: U 8 sunk by British destroyers, March 4, 1915; U 29 rammed and sunk, with all hands, by the Dreadnought, March 25, 1915, Lieut.-Comr. Weddigen, who torpedoed the Cressy, Aboukir, and Hogue in the U 19, going down with her; U 27 sunk by gunfire, Aug., 1915; U 41, sunk by auxiliary patrol ship, Sept. 24, 1915; U 14, sunk by a decoy trawler, off Aberdeen, June 5, 1915; U 40, torpedoed and sunk in the same month by a British submarine; U 27, sunk by the Baralong.

Around the British Isles a new type of submarine minelayer made its appearance which, working along traffic routes, did considerable damage. Dangerous to neutrals as well as belligerents, the practice was a flagrant defiance of the customs of war, and it was only because neutral nations were prospering so exceedingly by supplying belligerents with foodstuffs and ammunition that no more than diplomatic protests were made.

The enterprise of the British submarines in the Dardanelles showed a fearlessness that was beyond all praise. Handicapped by the strong current, the narrow channel and the innumerable obstructions they yet persisted in running the gauntlet. We have already related the opening incident of the submarine campaign against the Turks, in which Lieutenant N. D. Holbrook dived under five rows of mines in the Dardanelles and torpedoed the Turkish battleship Messudiyeh. The extraordinary difficulties which he overcame in contending with the strong current in the narrow strait, and in keeping his boat on a true course, were illustrated by the disasters which befell Lieutenant-Commander T. S. Brodie in submarine E 15. His boat was swung out of her course by the Dardanelles current, and stranded at Kephez Point on April 17, 1915. Brodie was killed; most of his crew were captured; and it was feared that the fine modern submarine would fall almost undamaged into the hands of the enemy. But Lieutenant C. G. MacArthur in a small, old-fashioned boat, B 6, made two very enterprising reconnaissances off Kephez Point on the same day; and though shelled by the Turkish batteries and very seriously endangered, saved his ship and brought back valuable information. Thereupon Commander Eric Robinson, with the picket-boats of the Triumph and Majestic, made a night expedition to Kephez Point on April 18, and torpedoed E 15 to prevent her from falling in a serviceable condition into the hands of the Turks. The enemy forts swept the picket-boats with a heavy fire, and the Majestic's boat was holed and sunk.

Altogether four British submarines, including E 15, were lost in the Dardanelles. AE 2, the submarine of the Royal Australian Navy, was sunk by Turkish warships in April, 1915, when trying to enter the Sea of Marmora. The E 7, missing since September 4, 1915, was caught in the nets. E 20 was sunk in the same waters on November 5, 1915, four officers being taken prisoners. One of these disasters was connected with the loss of the small French submarine Mariotte, which was sunk by a more modern and more powerful German submarine in the Sea of Marmora on July 26, 1915. A note of the place fixed for the rendezvous of British and French underwater craft in the Marmora Sea was discovered by the Germans in the wrecked Mariotte; and when E 20 arrived at the rendezvous, expecting to meet a friend, she was blown to pieces by U 14, who kept the appointment. A still smaller French submarine, of only 386 tons, the Turquoise, was also captured in the Sea of Marmora on October 30, 1915, while early in May the Joule, a 550-ton boat was mined in the Dardanelles, and in January the Saphir, of 390 tons, was lost while attempting to equal the feat of Lieutenant Holbrook.

But all these losses were outbalanced by the achievements of the British submarines in the Sea of Marmora. Lieutenant-Commander E. C. Boyle, in command of submarine E 14, won the V.C. by an eventful voyage through the Dardanelles on April 27, 1915. After making his way through the enemy mine-field, he had great trouble to escape the currents that had wrecked the E 15, and after overcoming the currents he was in danger from hostile patrol boats and shore batteries. But he remained in the narrow waters of the Strait, where he sank a Turkish gun-boat before entering his easier field of activity, the Marmora Sea. In this wider and more tranquil stretch of waters he opened operations on April 29 by sinking a Turkish transport. Four days afterwards he destroyed another Turkish gunboat. On May 10 he attacked two large transports escorted by destroyers. His torpedo got home on the larger of the two, and with a terrific explosion she sank quickly. An entire infantry brigade and several batteries of artillery—in all about 6,000 Turkish soldiers—were drowned. On May 13 he forced a steamer to run aground, and on May 18 he returned safely through the Strait. It was Commander Boyle's work in extending Lieu-tenant Holbrook's warlike explorations of the Strait that com-pletely opened the Sea of Marmora to the allied underwater craft. By the end of September, 1915, the E boats, ranging from Constantinople to Mudros base, had so interrupted and disorgan-ised the seaborne supplies of the Turkish army on the Gallipoli peninsula that if Germany, Austria, and Bulgaria had not opened the land route through Serbia to Constantinople the Mediterranean Expeditionary Force might have won the Dar-danelles gamble through the exhaustion of the enemy.

The British submarine campaign in the Marmora Sea was conducted in as chivalrous a manner as possible, yet its military results, and its effect upon the civilian population in Constan-tinople, were very striking. Especially when torpedoes exploded about the arsenal of the capital, the Turkish people were ready to give up the struggle, and a strong peace party was formed headed by the heir of the throne, who was afterwards assas-sinated. The Germans tried to net the Strait against the British submarines, and brought their best submarine officer, Hersing, to Constantinople to devise more defensive measures, and six or more German submarines operated round the Ottoman capital. But no defence was found against the astonishingly daring underwater attacks. In one action, a British submarine rose by the Turkish coast and fought against a squadron of Ottoman cavalry. The men on deck, handling the gun, and sniping with rifles, were swept by the enemy's fire, but they stuck to their strange work, and routed the hostile horsemen.

Still more remarkable was the feat of Lieutenant G. D'Oyly Hughes, serving in submarine E 11. On August 21, 1915, he swam alone from the submarine to the shore near the Ismid railway line. He took with him on his long swim some explosive, and with this he blew up the brickwork support of the Turkish railway. There was an armed guard scarcely 150 yards from the spot, in the enemy's line of communication, which he attacked. The gallant lieutenant fought a running fight with them for about a mile, and then dived back into the sea, and swam for another mile in his clothes, being at last picked up utterly exhausted by his comrades in E 11. In June, 1915, Lieutenant-Commander Nasmith sank a large Turkish transport, a vessel containing a large quantity of ammunition, and then chased a supply ship filled with stores, and torpedoed her alongside Rodosto pier. A small store-ship was next met and forced to run ashore, and as a crowning exploit the British submarine officer penetrated into the harbour of Constantinople and torpedoed a transport lying alongside the arsenal. The Goeben, Breslau, and other warships were, however, protected by heavily laden boats moored alongside them to form a rampart, and they could not be reached.

On August 5, Lt.-Commander Nasmith, in his second passage of the Straits, submerged to 110 feet and charged the net, which broke. An hour later he had torpedoed a transport; at dawn next morning he was attacked by an aeroplane, but was able a few hours later to sink a gunboat. On the 7th he was in action with troops ashore. On August 8, 1915, he sighted and sank the last Turkish battleship, the Hairredin Barbarossa, a 10,000-ton ship, carrying six 11 in, and eight 4.1 guns, built in 1891 for the German navy.

Lieutenant-Commander Cochrane, in E 7, swept the Sea of Marmora of much enemy shipping before his boat was sunk in September, 1915. Also he turned his gun on the Turkish railway line near Kava Burnu, and, after blocking the line by bombarding it from the sea, shelled a troop-train and blew up three ammunition wagons attached to it.

Lieutenant-Commander K. M. Bruce, with Lieutenant W. B. Pirie, likewise made a prolonged cruise in the Sea of Marmora, during the course of which they did much damage to enemy shipping, and outfought by gun fire a Turkish destroyer and a gunboat, put both to flight, and returned to their base, after extricating their submarine from a very difficult position. Their work of destroying Turkish shipping was continued in November, 1915, by Lieutenant-Commander David de Beauvoir Stocks.

Down to October, 1915, it was reckoned that there had been sunk in the Dardanelles and the Marmora Sea, mainly by British submarines, one battleship, one destroyer, five gunboats, 11 transports, 44 steamers, and 148 sailing vessels. And as E-boats continued to operate in November and December, 1915, in the waters around Constantinople, the total damage done to Turkish shipping sadly impeded the transport of war material and troops from the European to the Asiatic shore during the winter campaigns in Mesopotamia, the Caucasus, and Persia. Thus the strength of the new arm in underwater warfare told on the fortunes of land wars in places far distant from the scene of the operations of the E-boats.

While telling heavily against the Turkish military and naval power in the southern waters of the Dardanelles and the Marmora Sea, British submarines bore equally heavily upon the industrial military and naval power of Germany in the northern waters of the Baltic. In the spring and summer of 1915 the Germans were able to bring strong naval forces to the Courland coast to help the advance of the army under General Below. On March 23, for example, seven German battleships and 28 torpedo craft cruised off Courland, shelling towns, villages, and roads used by Russian troops, and Libau was captured on May 9. Early in June German surface warships, with submarines and reconnoitring aircraft, began to appear off the Gulf of Riga, and the Russian transport Yenissei was torpedoed and sunk on June 6. On the other hand, three German vessels were likewise sunk, and soon afterwards an attempt to storm Windau from the sea was defeated by Russian torpedo boats, which sank a German mine sweeper. Then on July 2 a mine layer, the Albatros, was driven ashore on Gothland during an action between Russian and German battle squadrons.

It was in this action that the British submarine flotilla won its first striking success. Commander Max Horton had penetrated, in E 9, far into the Baltic, and on July 2, 1915, he torpedoed the enemy battleship Pommern—the first German capital ship damaged by the British. She was a vessel of the Deutschland class, ten years old, with four 11 in. guns and fourteen 6.7 guns, six torpedo-tubes, and 9¾ in. armour amidships.

Then, on July 30, when Below was pressing forward in Courland and in need of reinforcements, one of his large transports, full of troops, was torpedoed by another British submarine, under Commander Noel F. Laurence. The same gallant officer played a decisive part in the naval action in the Gulf of Riga that lasted from August 18 to 21, 1915. We have already described, from the Russian point of view, the principal events of this naval attack on Riga. A German fleet, consisting of nine battleships, twelve cruisers, and strong destroyer flotillas, tried to force the passage of Moon Sound and the northern entrance to the gulf. Fog interrupted the execution of the enemy's plan to capture Riga from the sea, and the old Russian battleship Slava and the gunboat Sivoutch fought splendidly and destroyed several small craft.

But the blow that staggered and daunted the German admiral was delivered by Commander Laurence outside the gulf. The enemy's battle-cruiser squadron, including the Seydlitz and Moltke, was acting as a supporting force to the ships engaged near Riga, and the British submarine succeeded in stealing quite close. Commander Laurence released a torpedo at the Seydlitz, and narrowly missed her; then he fired at the Moltke, and struck her in the bow, crushing in one of the torpedo chambers. Four hundred tons of water entered the hull, but as 1,500 tons was needed to overcome the buoyancy of the watertight bulkhead system, the battle-cruiser was able to get safely to Hamburg. Nevertheless, Commander Laurence's blow at one of the finest of the enemy's ships had an effect more decisive than Lieutenant-Commander von Hersing's attack on the Triumph and Majestic in the Dardanelles earlier in the year. The German admiral, reported to have been Admiral von Ingenohl, feared to risk any more of his capital ships against British submarines, and broke off the naval operations against Riga and the right wing of the Russian armies.

On the same day as the Moltke was torpedoed there occurred the first disaster to the British submarine flotilla operating in the Baltic. E 13, under Lieutenant-Commander Layton, was passing in darkness through the Sound, but he grounded in the early morning on the Danish island of Saltholm, near Copenhagen, in the southern mouth of the Sound. At 5 a.m. a Danish torpedo boat appeared by the island, and the officer gave the commander of E 13 twenty-four hours in which to try to get the boat refloated. At the same time a German destroyer arrived on the scene, and stayed close to the E-boat until two more Danish torpedo craft came up. The enemy vessel then withdrew, but at nine o'clock in the morning two German destroyers steamed in from the south, and at a distance of 300 yards one of them fired a torpedo, which hit the bottom of the sea close to the stranded British boat and exploded. At the same time the enemy destroyer opened fire with all her guns and machine-guns. The helpless British crew was taken unawares by this illegal attack. The E-boat was in Danish territority, with three Danish torpedo craft anchored close to her, and in her stranded condition she could not fight. Her men were cut down by shrapnel and machine-gun bullets while struggling in the water, and fifteen of them were killed before one of the Danish torpedo boats steamed between the submarine and the German destroyer and made the Germans cease fire and withdraw.

Another submarine was lost, also by stranding, on January 6, 1916, on the Haags Bank, off the Dutch island of Texel. The crew of 33 men and officers were happily rescued by a Dutch cruiser. The rescue occurred outside Dutch territorial waters, but the three British officers and 30 men were interned, which was a loss of a finely-trained crew. Yet another boat was stranded and lost a few days later.

These strandings, however, were the only British submarine disasters in northern waters reported since D 3 was mined off Yarmouth in November, 1914. As against them, there was in the Baltic operations a long, magnificent record of successes. After the murderous attack on Lieutenant-Commander Layton and the crew of E 13, the Germans laid a new mine-field in the Sound between Denmark and Sweden, and later they so increased the extent of this field that only the narrow, shallow strip of Danish and Swedish territorial waters was left open. Moreover, the Swedish government put out the lights on their coast in order to make the passage through the Sound on the Swedish side impossible during the night. Even so, E-boats continued to penetrate, by mystic ways, into the Baltic.

On October 13, 1915, a remarkable naval action was witnessed off the Danish island of Moen, by the east coast of Zealand. A German cruiser and three German torpedo boats were fighting a single British submarine. The Germans manœuvred in circles at high speed in order to avoid being torpedoed, but a loud explosion was heard and one of the torpedo boats vanished.

The cruiser and remaining torpedo craft then fled, and the grey form of E 19 emerged and remained visible for some time. The next day there was another action between E 19 and a German torpedo boat off the island of Faroe, in which the enemy vessel was sunk. A greater British success was achieved off Libau on October 23, when the German armoured cruiser Prinz Adalbert, laid down in 1900, and armed with four 8.2 in., ten 5.9 in., and twelve 3.4 in. guns, was torpedoed. Two torpedoes struck home, causing the ship to sink so quickly that most of her company was lost.

How valuable was the work of British submarines in the Baltic may be gauged by a General Instruction issued by Prince Henry of Prussia to German submarine commanders of the Gulf of Finland patrol. It read: " I consider the destruction of a Russian submarine will be a great success, but I regard the destruction of a British submarine as being at least as valuable as that of a Russian armoured cruiser."

Lieutenant-Commander F. N. Cromie was among the British submarine commanders who won distinction in the Baltic as winter approached. He began his passage through the Sound during a severe bout of influenza, and directed operations from his bed. On November 7 he tried a spot in open waters where the train ferry between Germany and Sweden passed, but his plan was spoilt by two German destroyers and a cruiser, who stopped him in an exciting chase after the ferry. He dived when they left him, reckoning they would soon return to renew their search after him. So it befell. The cruiser was the Undine, convoying the German steam ferry Prussia from Trelleborg to Sassintz. When she returned for battle, with her two attendant destroyers, Lieutenant Cromie torpedoed her and set her on fire. Then, as a glimpse through the periscope showed him she was not sinking, he dived beneath her stern, and gave her another torpedo on the opposite side.

The Undine was a small cruiser of 2,175 tons, thirteen years old, armed with ten 4.1 guns, ten one-pounders, and two torpedo-tubes, with two-inch deck armour. A more improved vessel of a similar class was the Bremen, a 1903 ship of 3,250 tons, with the same armament and armour, but larger in size. The Bremen, with other light cruisers of the town class, was sent out with destroyer flotillas, swarms of trawlers, and Zeppelin airships, in a determined effort to hunt down the

E-boats in the Baltic, as the Grand Fleet had hunted down the U-boats round the British Isles. But the E-boats fought with daring and skill. They sank the Bremen on December 17, 1915, and another German torpedo boat.

Meanwhile, the fighting underwater flotilla in the Baltic was ruining German trade with Sweden, and completing the blockade cordon round the Central Empires. Had the Foreign Office allowed, a formal blockade of Germany could have been proclaimed by October, 1915, for the E-boats, without resorting to furtive mine-laying, and with mighty German naval forces actively opposing them, broke down both enemy seaborne trade and enemy troop transport in the northern midland sea. The cargo steamers stopped and sunk were very numerous, and the import of fine Swedish iron ore, vitally needed for military purposes, was impeded.

The insurance rates on German and Swedish shipping were considerably increased, and some underwriters even refused to cover the German risks against British submarines. All German ships taking the Baltic north and south route had to keep within territorial waters. This augmented the difficulties of navigation, owing to the irregular coastline of Sweden and the long fringe of islands. Moreover, an enormous number of mines got adrift in the Baltic, and added to the danger of shipping. The German mine-fields in the Sound were ineffective, the mines continually breaking loose; even in the Great Belt the mines could not be made to keep their anchorage. The intense activity of the British submarines, amid all the deadly confusion, produced a feeling of panic in German Baltic ports. So great were the losses to German shipping that information concerning most of the lost steamers was suppressed in the enemy's newspapers. As the Danish government organ, the Politiken, observed:

The tables are now turned on Germany in waters where the Germans have hitherto been unchallenged masters. This form of British warfare is no doubt exceedingly inconvenient to Germany, though the rigour of it is much mitigated, no neutral ships being molested; but Britain nevertheless hits harder than her opponent, because the effective isolation of Germany is being brought about. The submarine war against British commerce was a mere pinprick, as British supplies were in no way impeded, but the loss of a similar amount of tonnage would lame Germany.

CHAPTER 15

Aubers Ridge, Festubert and Hooge

W HILE the second battle of Ypres was still engaging all the resistance of the British 2nd army, Sir John French had promised his co-operation to General Joffre in a grand attack to be made farther south. The two first actions in which the British 1st army became involved are known as the battles of Aubers Ridge and Festubert. Neither brought much success to British arms.

The first advance was attempted on the morning of May 9. The fighting extended from the village of Bois Grenier to that of Festubert, the principal attack being delivered against the German position at Rouges Bancs, near Fromelles and the Aubers ridge, where British troops had been held up in the battle of Neuve Chapelle. At the same time that the 1st army, under Sir Douglas Haig, swung up against the low plateau in front of Lille, a large French force, under the direction of General Foch, made a fierce onslaught upon the German lines between La Bassée and Arras. The combined Franco-British offensive movement was undertaken partly with a view to relieving the pressure upon Ypres, and partly with a view to reconquering Lille and its rich coal-mining regions and breaking the German front. It was also designed to help the Russian armies retreating in Galicia.

Both the British and the French artillery tried to smash in the German trenches by an overpowering bombardment. But while the French gunners were fairly successful by reason of their enormous supply of high-explosive shells, which they used for weeks in a continuous bombardment, the British guns and howitzers, employing mainly shrapnel, made no practicable breach in the enemy's fortified lines. Yet this bombardment, which started about half-past five on Sunday morning, was on a larger scale than at Neuve Chapelle.

It was, moreover, a surprise bombardment. The French had adopted the principle of prolonged shelling over many days to reduce their enemy's defences before sending forward their infantry. To this object they sacrificed the element of surprise, for the Germans were kept always on the alert for the attack to which they knew that the bombardment must be a preliminary. The British generals had no adequate supply of shells to employ in this manner and had to content themselves with a few hours' shelling before sending troops forward.

During the quiet period which preceded the battle the Germans had greatly strengthened their defences. They had specially manufactured barbed cables of much heavier gauge than usual which could not be severed with ordinary cutters, and which resisted shrapnel fire. To make these cable entanglements more difficult of reduction by artillery, the Germans had thrown up banks, looking like trench parapets, behind which extended the entanglement area protecting the real trench. All that advancing troops could do when faced by an unbroken and uncuttable barbed cable defence of this kind, was to cast their overcoats upon the barbed edge, and then try to clamber over it while the German machine-guns were playing upon them. As well as this strong wiring the Germans had been working hard to render their machine-gun posts impregnable and to give their troops in the line protection from gun fire by means of dug-outs and strong parapets.

There was a varying space, often less than two hundred yards wide, between the British and the German trenches. In many places the sand-bag barricades, built man-high on the marshy lowland soil, were close enough for the opposing troops to hear each other talking, so very narrow was the long strip of No Man's Land running between the khaki-coloured sandbags on the British side and the piebald, black-and-white sandbags of the Germans.

In front of the British line was a horse-shoe ridge, forming the chief obstacle between it and the plains which led to Lille. At Rouges Bancs the ridge sweeps away in a north-easterly direction, and by the hamlet there lies a small wood, similar to that which had proved a stumbling-block at Neuve Chapelle. But the wood was quietly captured by Indian troops, the Pathans and Gurkhas, before the bombardment opened, and the way seemed clear for a great infantry advance. To meet the onslaught the Germans brought up men whom they had been concentrating in Lille. From their unbroken fortified lines they brought to bear such an extraordinary number of machine-guns that nothing but some hundreds of thousands of high-explosive shell could have blown a clear path for the British infantry.

In the famous triangle west of La Bassée, where the 1st army corps and Indian divisions tried to advance, the German commander used an admirable stratagem. He left his first two lines empty of men and material during the bombardment, and waited in great strength for the British infantry advance in his concreted and armour-plated third line.

At the same time he transformed the famous brickfield by La Bassée into a machine-gun fortress, from which a sweeping deadly fire was poured on the attacking troops. Heavy losses were incurred in this section when, after nearly carrying the enemy's position, British troops had to retreat back to their own trenches, the Bedfords and the Highlanders having especially distinguished themselves by the fury of their charge. Had reinforcements been at hand at this point at the critical moment, a victory might have been won; as it was, things remained after the battle in about the same condition as before. The 1st army was repulsed both south round La Bassée and north below Bois Grenier.

Nowhere along the line could the British claim much success. In the first attacks of the morning the German trenches were entered in places, but so fierce was the machine gun fire which met the reinforcing troops that no permanent foothold was gained. British casualties were very heavy even during the first two hours' fighting. The position was one of deadlock, and at 8.0 a.m. Sir Douglas Haig decided to make a further attempt to destroy the enemy's wire and to repeat the attack. He had information that the French on his right were progressing well and he was not aware of the full extent of the failure of the first attacks of his own divisions.

Owing to difficulties of reorganization this new attack on the part of the 1st and Indian divisions could not be made until 4.0 p.m., and by 5.0 p.m. it was decided to abandon the assault as a failure. It had been held up everywhere by German machine gun fire. The attack of the 4th corps, which held a line from Neuve Chapelle northwards to Bois Grenier, though it at first achieved minor successes, finally met with the same costly and discouraging repulse. British losses in a single day were over 10,000 officers and men. The failure was very largely due to the unexpected strength of the enemy's trench defences, and the lack of heavy calibre shells which alone could have reduced them. The Germans also seem to have been very well aware that the attack was coming and were awaiting it with the greatest composure.

While breaking off the action at Aubers ridge Sir John French still sought the opportunity for offensive action elsewhere. The French commander-in-chief continued to impress upon him the importance of driving the enemy from French soil, which, if it were not done quickly, he said, would mean the loss of the war. He appears to have been impatient of the situation at Ypres, forgetting, perhaps, that he had promised the British commander that he would throw his reinforcements into the salient to recapture the ground lost by the French. The British failure at Aubers ridge had, in fact, released German troops to withstand the French attack which proceeded farther south—and Sir John French agreed to relieve a French division and at the same time to attack once more in the neighbourhood of Festubert.

The point selected for an attack was a salient which formed a bulge between Neuve Chapelle and La Bassée. Viewed from the British trenches, the German position seemed to be a stretch of bare, flat fields, dotted with ruined cottages, farm buildings, and orchards. In reality it was a network of pitfalls. Hidden in the coarse, high grass were ditches, filled with mud and slimy water, and in some places the ground was hardly more than a morass. The German batteries, placed on the high ground westward, had all the ranges marked, and by means of telescopic sights could sweep every yard of the ground. But if the attacking troops could get quickly into the German trenches, from seventy to three hundred yards distant, the hostile batteries would for the time lose most of their advantages.

The front selected for the first attack ran from the neighbourhood of Festubert on the right to Richebourg l'Avoué on the left, and many very awkward obstacles had to be overcome before the first German trenches were reached. The attack was planned for May 12, and the 7th division was moved south to support it. The weather on the chosen day was misty and dull, interfering with the aerial observers. Sir Douglas Haig had determined, too, that success could only be obtained by demolishing the enemy's front line defences, and this had not been satisfactorily accomplished. So the operation was post-poned to May 15, the Canadian division being in the meantime also moved south to support the proposed advance of the 1st British army corps. There was no moon on the night of Saturday, May 15, and the sky was sombre, but not pitch dark. The position in front of the British line was held by the 7th Westphalian army corps.

The Indian corps began the attack, leaving their trenches at half-past eleven at night, advancing from Richebourg l'Avoué in a south-westerly direction. The enemy, however, was ready for an attack. The moment the attacking troops left the trenches the sky was lighted up with innumerable flares, shed-ding a clear white light over a very large area. Through this the German machine-guns and automatic rifles fired with terrible effect. Many of the Indians were shot as they clambered over their own parapets, and their advance was checked. Their comrades, the British troops of the 2nd division, were more fortunate. By a magnificent rush they broke into the enemy's first line and cleared the Germans out with bayonet and hand-grenade and got into their second line in some of the most furious fighting in the war; for the British troops attacked with great determination. The Indian troops, after their failure on the left, threw their flank back to connect with the original line. But the centre and the right of the line bombed and bayoneted their way through the German barricades, and completely cleared out the Germans in hand-to-hand fighting; and then joining hands stormed the German second line, penetrating six hundred yards through the hostile salient along a front of eight hundred yards.

All this was only a preliminary step in the plan of operations. About three o'clock on Sunday morning, when the German commander was massing men for a counter-attack to recover his two lines of lost trenches, the 7th division went into action and broke into another side of the German wedge at Festubert. The German entrenchments north of Festubert were of a most formidable character. Hundreds of thousands of high-explosive shells would have been needed to level them to the ground, and even then the bank-protected barbed cable entanglements might still have held up troops in daylight, and enabled the German machine-guns to destroy them. But in the darkness the British troops, moving forward in a swift wave, twelve hundred yards long, got over the entanglements by covering them with over-coats or blankets, and drove the Germans out of the front trench with hand-grenades and bayonet. They took the second German line in the same manner, and also the third line; and then rushed one supporting point a f t e r another until they had broken twelve hundred yards behind the German front in the direction of the Rue de Marais, running towards the village of Lorgies, just at the foot of the first ridge of the Lille plateau.

Many of the German prisoners were captured as they were sitting in their bomb-proof shelters. One German non-commissioned officer said that the attack by the 7th division had only come a quarter of an hour before it was expected. As it was, the newly-won positions formed on Sunday morning, May 16, a couple of formidable wedges driven into the German lines, with a distance of only a thousand yards between them. But small though the intervening space was, it was very strongly held and fortified. It included two lines of breast-works constructed so as to give a field of fire in both directions, and there was a series of redoubts, consisting of strongly-fortified farm buildings, all linked together by shrapnel-proof trenches. The hostile breastworks were armed with machine guns which were protected by steel shields, and these could only be destroyed by high-explosive shell.

Having no shells of this sort available, the attacking troops tried to advance towards Festubert by bombing their way with hand grenades. Another 40 yards was gained in this manner, but this success was followed by a check. At half-past ten on Monday morning another determined effort was made to cut off the Germans in the space between the two wedges by pressing across their communications northwards from La Quinque Rue. The operation could not be carried out, as by this time the Germans had been strongly reinforced, and their machine-guns, automatic rifles, and heavy batteries swept away the assaulting line.

Small bombing parties continued to work along the German trenches in spite of the terrific fire, making progress at various points during Sunday afternoon, and capturing two hundred prisoners. At the same time the British artillery had a field for shrapnel work all along the rear of the enemy's lines, where German troops were collecting to reinforce their front. When night fell on Sunday the British position was not unencouraging. In the night the German counter-attack, directed against the advanced position north of Festubert, where the British troops had penetrated the entire series of hostile entrenchments, and had built a rough barricade of sand-bags behind the German lines, succeeded in regaining lost ground.

At daybreak on Monday morning, May 17, Sir Douglas Haig closed in with all his force. Every available gun and howitzer was brought to bear on the two lines of breastworks and on the fortified posts and farm buildings. The Germans were already surrounded on three sides, and the British artillery got a smashing cross-fire effect, resembling that which the Germans had obtained on the salient at Ypres.

Round Festubert the British infantry closed with the enemy. The 7th division pushed on towards the Rue d'Ouvert, and the 2nd division more slowly forced its way towards the Rue de Marais and Violaines. The hand-grenade parties worked forward with furious skill under the cover of their artillery, and the two British wedges lengthened out and joined together before noon, cutting off all the Germans in between, closing on them with the bayonet. and taking some three hundred prisoners. The two assaulting divisions then joined hands and turned eastward, and worked all the afternoon against the machine-gun posts and network of entrenchments, and clusters of fortified buildings between La Quinque Rue and Rue de Bois. A fierce conflict raged especially round Cour de l'Avoué Farm, where the enemy had a series of very strong works. Among the German troops holding this position was a battalion of Saxons who had been hurried down from the north that morning and flung in to reinforce the hard-pressed garrison.

In spite of machine-guns and bullet-proof defences British troops worked round the farm, while the engineers looked after the telephonic communications with their distinct batteries. This was the most important task in the whole of the operations; for, as at Neuve Chapelle, the wire was continually getting broken just when the infantry needed the guns to knock out enemy machine-gun posts. The engineers had to work out in the open in the shell-swept zone of fire, patching up the wires in order to keep the telephones in working order. Splendidly did they work round the fortress-farm on Monday afternoon, with the result that at the critical moment the infantry held their hand while the British batteries poured a crushing fire into all the farm buildings.

There were then about 700 Saxons holding the position. They had already been badly handled by the bombing parties, and when attacked from the rear, they gave up the fight and came out to surrender. Then occurred an incident which is still a matter for dispute. There is no doubt that these retreating Germans were caught in the act of surrender by the fire of their own machine guns and artillery. They were killed almost to a man and it was believed at the time that this was a deliberate act on the part of the German command to discourage surrender under any provocation. Later consideration of the circumstances, however, makes it appear more probable that the German gunners genuinely mistook their comrades for their enemy, a not unknown blunder in the confusion of battle.

While these events were occurring on the British northern wing on Monday, May 17, good progress was at last being made in the south along the German trenches below Festubert. The hand-grenade and the bayonet continued to prove the best weapons of the British infantryman. The fighting south of Festubert was marked by many isolated and hand-to-hand combats. The German trenches were narrow, being so constructed to minimise the effect of shrapnel fire. But a narrow trench is an inferior protection against hand-grenades or a bayonet attack, and by using these weapons British infantry made certain creditable advances. By midday on Monday the 1st army had captured altogether two miles of the enemy's front. During the night of May 16 the Germans began to withdraw their line between South Breastwork and Ferme du Bois to a line three-quarters of a mile in rear. This movement escaped the notice of British aviators and patrols, and when an advance was made about 9.0 a.m. on May 17 little opposition was met with. By 10.0 a.m. possession was gained of the whole of that region known as the Quadrilateral.

Sir Douglas Haig while ordering a strong line to be consolidated instructed his brigadiers on the spot to take every opportunity of making local advances—but the waterlogged nature of the ground, enfilade fire from the new German positions, and the advancing darkness made further progress that evening impossible. Unfortunately the attacking troops suffered also from the misdirected fire of their own artillery. The country was particularly difficult, being riddled with dikes obscured to the distant view by patches of long grass. A very gallant assault was made by a party of Camerons, who secured a temporary foothold in the South Breastwork of the German line. Continuous rain added greatly to the difficulties of the troops.

Further attacks ordered for the morning of May 18 were postponed until the afternoon and where they were made were everywhere repulsed. The Guards brigade under Lord Cavan suffered particularly heavily from machine-gun fire from the new German trench, the exact position of which had not yet been identified and which had so far been left untouched by British bombardment. On the night of the 18th the 7th and 2nd divisions were relieved by the Canadian division, and the 51st (Highland) division under General Alderson. This body of troops known as "Alderson's Force" succeeded in making one or two minor advances. On May 23 the Canadian and the 47th divisions were ordered to attack against Chapelle St. Roch and Rue d'Ouvert. The 47th, a London division experiencing its first great battle, assaulted with the greatest gallantry. The 1/23 and 1/24 London battalions captured the German front and support trenches making an average advance of four hundred yards on a frontage of a thousand yards. The Canadian attack was not so successful, but despite heavy counter-attacks and intense enemy fire the ground captured was held.

This action was the last which took place during the battle of Festubert. General Joffre required support for his attack on Vimy ridge, and on the 25th the British 2nd division were ordered to march south to relieve the French 58th division. At the same time Sir John French suspended further offensive operations in the Festubert sector giving orders to Sir D. Haig to hold the line upon which his army was entrenched.

The lesson of the battle of Festubert was undoubtedly that had infantry attacks been supported by adequate artillery action a very considerable success might have been achieved. As it was, the British infantry had no reason to be dissatisfied with the advances which had been made in actions which were intended mainly to divert the attention of the enemy from the French attacking armies. They were still ill-supplied with essential munitions of assault and of trench warfare, but the British commanders could at least congratulate themselves on the fact that the drafts of civilian soldiers and hastily trained subaltern officers who were rapidly taking the place of the hardened regular troops, were their equal in steadfastness and initiative. Altogether during the battle of Festubert British casualties amounted to 710 officers and 15,938 other ranks.

During the months that intervened between Festubert and the battle of Loos in September the British troops were engaged in one or two actions which gained battle honours, but for the most part they were locked in their trenches, suffering that daily toll of casualties which is an inevitable feature of trench warfare. Readjustment was made in the positions held by the British expeditionary force, most important of which was that which left Sir John French in command of the defences of the whole of the Ypres salient. During this period, too, there was a welcome addition to the B.E.F. in the arrival of one or two newly-formed divisions from England. The requests of the French for further offensive action to support their attack had now to be treated with considerable reserve, for lack of ammunition made an attack on a large scale impossible. All that Sir John French could sanction were minor offensive actions requiring the minimum of artillery preparation.

As a beginning Sir Douglas Haig recommended an attack north of Givenchy towards the high ground near Violaines. This was to await the moment of General Foch's renewed attack and was to be launched against the line Chapelle-St. Roch—Rue d'Ouvert. Lack of heavy ammunition precluded any action more important than an assault, and this was made on the morning of June 15. It had been carefully prepared, with a slow bombardment to destroy trenches and barbed-wire and the explosion of a mine. The attack was made by two brigades, and though it achieved no element of surprise it succeeded in penetrating the German trenches at several points. But it failed to capture strong points or to make any breach in the support line. In bombing fights the German fire prevented supplies being sent forward to the attacking British troops. After a stubborn attempt to hold the positions gained they were forced gradually to retire. Two attempts to re-occupy the ground were not successful. As the French had been held up, orders were given to the 1st British army to hold their ground and not attempt any further advance.

The second important engagement of this period was the action of Bellewaarde carried out on the 2nd army front on June 16. This was intended to assist the 1st army operation at Givenchy and was also very carefully planned. As will be remembered during the 2nd battle of Ypres the Germans seized and held the Bellewaarde ridge and the objective of this attack was to re-capture that important point of observation. The assault was made by the 9th and 7th brigades of the 3rd division. After a bombardment lasting two hours the first line of attacking troops advanced and captured the German front line without great difficulty. Unfortunately the second wave was followed too precipitately by the third, and the advancing troops were caught in their own artillery barrage which had not yet lifted. Inextricable confusion resulted, though certain units succeeded in reaching the second and even the third line of German trenches.

After continuous fighting with bombs and bayonet, the attacking troops were obliged to fall back on the first line they had captured, although they had in the meanwhile resisted a heavy German counter-attack. A supporting attack by the 42nd brigade was held up by German shell fire. Altogether this action of Bellewaarde resulted in the capture of the German front line for a distance of about half a mile, but the Germans retained possession of the ridge with its advantage for observation. The British losses were exceptionally heavy. The final actions of this period took place round the village of Hooge. Hooge had fallen to the Germans during the 2nd battle of Ypres, and at this time (June 1915) an effort was made to recapture the village.

On June 16, after a violent bombardment, the 3rd division of Allenby's corps attacked near Hooge château, the outbuildings of which the British had captured by a skilful local operation on June 3. The object was to straighten out a German salient in the British front; after a severe struggle, the British secured the desired trenches and even pushed far beyond, taking 200 prisoners. The points, which were too far in advance of the new British line to be held, were evacuated during the day, but the original objective was gained and held.

Farther to the north troops of the 6th corps, on July 6, suddenly seized a considerable section of the advanced German position and beat off German counter-attacks with heavy loss. In all these local combats the British lost heavily from the continuous German artillery bombardment, as in the moist ground about Hooge it was almost impossible to construct satisfactory defences, and every trench was plainly visible. On July 7 the Germans attempted to retake their lost position, but ultimately were beaten back.

HOOGE & HILL 60
Scale of One Mile
British Front April 1915

Between July 22 and 26, the British, by skilful mining operations, in which they showed a g r e a t superiority over the Germans, made further gains of ground in the dismal terrain along the Menin road and near Hooge château, but the British trenches were continually bombarded by the German artillery, to which the supply of projectiles in the British artillery was insufficient to make an adequate reply. The Germans employed gas shells largely, against which the British gas-masks were a very inadequate protection, and the sufferings of the British troops along the whole salient front were cruel, the men of the 6th and 14th divisions bearing the brunt of these serious attacks.

On July 30 the Germans for the first time used against the British troops in this section of the front another weapon forbidden by the laws of war—flame-throwers, which had been previously tried against the French troops on other parts of the front. Early in the morning a mine was exploded under the British trenches near Hooge, and immediately afterwards jets of flame streamed from the German positions, only 20 yards away, into the British line, killing in the most horrible manner the men of the companies holding it. At the same time trench mortars poured bombs on the British front. Under cover of the sheet of flame and bombs, the German infantry assaulted and seized the advanced British line, after which they forced their way into certain of the support-trenches, making a total advance of some hundreds of yards. There they consolidated their position. In the afternoon four British battalions attempted a counter-attack, but were repulsed with heavy loss, leaving 50 officers out of 90 on the field. On the following night the Germans renewed their attack with liquid fire and a deluge of shells, behind which their infantry advanced, but without achieving serious progress.

Extensive preparations were made by the British to recover the ground lost, which was of tactical importance, and the whole 6th division was brought up ready to attack. On the night of Aug. 8 the British artillery opened a heavy fire on the German position, and at 3.15 on the following morning the troops of this division delivered an assault. It was immediately successful; 500 Germans were killed and 100 taken prisoners—but to hold the captured line was difficult in face of the enfilading fire which the Germans were able to concentrate upon it from Hill 60, whence they commanded its rearward communications. In the end most of the ground won with such courage was retained, though it was necessary to withdraw detachments which had pushed so far forward. The British loss in this action exceeded 2,000.

Thus ended the minor actions of 1915, in which no appreciable ground was gained. Undoubtedly they were of help to the French, through whose insistence they were mainly initiated. If they had any other value it lay in the experience which they gave to the British commanders and to regimental officers in the field of the exigencies of a new type of warfare. As a result of this, far more care was taken to secure the telephone communications between the front line assaulting troops and brigade headquarters—and in the later actions lines were laid in triplicate with the result that this communication was never entirely destroyed by shell fire.

CHAPTER 16

From the Vosges to Artois

DURING the spring of 1915 General Joffre sought to divert
the enemy's attention and keep him always vigilant
by minor attacks on widely separated parts of the front.
His favourite scene was the high pine-wooded ridge of the
Vosges between Münster and Thann, with a more southernly
point of advance towards Altkirch. In this long stretch of
difficult mountain country fighting went on continuously. Many
years before the war a school of French military writers had
worked out a plan for countering the German advance into
France by a movement on the right wing, beginning in Alsace
and continuing through Lorraine. Such a movement had been
attempted in the first month of the war, but had been severely
checked by the great battle in Lorraine which the French called
the battle of Morhange and the Germans the battle of Metz.
The French there lost very heavily and were thrown back by
the army of Metz and the Bavarian troops.

After Foch had saved the situation, when commanding
only a division, and had then, with an army corps, played the
chief part in helping General de Castelnau to check the Bavarians
on the hills round Nancy, the French invasion of Alsace-Lorraine
had been resumed. The army based on Belfort, composed
mainly of mountain troops from the French Vosges and the
Pyrenees, held the Col de la Schlucht in the High Vosges, near
Münster, and the country north of Thann as far as the last high
green ramparts of rock near Hartmannsweilerkopf and the hills
between Belfort and Mulhouse.

The mountain of Hartmannsweilerkopf, rising nearly 4,000
feet above sea level, north of the town of Thann, had been
occupied by the French, and then lost through the troops being
cut off on the icy slopes. But it was recovered and fortified in
the early spring after a series of fierce conflicts. The last battle
for the summit took place on April 27, after it had been occupied
for a single day by the Prussian Guard, who made use of gas
in the attack.

The famous lower height rises at the end of a valley which

overlooks the plain of Alsace and the Rhine, with the Black Forest directly in front of it. It was an observation station of dominating power, and as the French army had placed its heavy artillery on the next and higher peak of Molkerain, the guns could be directed by means of telephone from the observation mountain at any target in the Rhine valley. Such was the reason for the incessant conflict for the possession of the summit of Hartmannsweilerkopf, the principal battles occurring on January 19, March 26, April 26, and April 27, 1915. After the last victory the French batteries commanded the railway from Colmar to Mulhouse, and were ready to advance when General Joffre gave the order. In the meantime, in order to keep the Germans in Alsace from growing venturesome, another line of attack against Colmar was slowly cleared by continual fighting along the valley of the Fecht, where the village of Metzeral was captured by a storming attack on June 22, 1915. The French troops had then before them scarcely four leagues of the wooded, difficult river valley to conquer, in order to come to the plain of Alsace at Turkheim, where in ancient days the famous French commander Turenne had won Alsace by a great victory.

The German commander employed every possible means of checking the advance along the Fecht to Metzeral. The broken ground, as a Swiss observer remarked, had been divided into small fields, by hedges of barbed-wire and mazes of concrete and armoured trenches, with machine-gun redoubts—all strengthened by a large number of field-guns and siege-pieces, working in the rear of the marked ranges. Hosts of men laboured at the fortifications from dawn to dusk; the forests were also fortified, barbed-wire being stretched from tree to tree, and wolf-pits dug. In some places preparations were made for setting the pine-woods on fire by means of petrol and incendiary bombs.

But the French artillery scored many advantages. The light 3 in. gun, firing 20 rounds a minute, proved a handy weapon in mountain warfare. It blew away the wire entanglements, destroyed the trenches and machine-gun redoubts; and then, while the heavy artillery in the French rear shut Metzeral off westward by a curtain of shrapnel, the mountain troops charged down northward on Metzeral, while their comrades advanced on the other side by the hamlet of Altenhof. The German trenches on the slopes were carried and the enemy retired into the village houses, which had been strongly fortified.

But the French general did not waste his infantry in attempting to carry the village by storm. The light French guns were again brought into action close to the battle-line; and when night fell Metzeral smoked in the darkness like a gigantic torch. The French guns had set the village on fire, and as the survivors of the garrison troops fled, the guns caught them again. Then lengthening their range the French gunners caught also the German reinforcements vainly hurrying up to enable a counter-attack to be organized. The Germans drew back leaving the burning village in the hands of the French army.

The attack along the Fecht was directed from Gerardmer over the neck in the mountains known as the Col de la Schlucht. But it could not proceed at most much farther than Münster until another movement more to the north got under way. This second movement was based on the town of St. Dié. A few miles to the north of St. Dié is a line of hills with some scattered hamlets known as the Ban de Sapt. On this line the Bavarians had entrenched after their victory at Morhange in August, 1914. The French commander-in-chief, therefore, had first to clear the Ban de Sapt before resuming the sweeping movement through Lorraine in conjunction with the movement through Alsace. From this fortified position on French territory the enemy was able to threaten a flanking attack against any French force working up into Lorraine. The French army based on Nancy was operating still more northward close to the frontier and about five miles from the German town of Château Salins.

Meanwhile the Ban de Sapt, connecting with the high rampart of the Vosges, in front of Strassburg, remained a menace. But towards the end of April the French sappers began to win the mastery over the enemy. The first affair of importance took place at the village of La Fonteneile on the summit of a height 1,900 feet above sea level. Here the French troops had, by months of work, constructed a strong system of entrenchments protected by advanced posts. The Germans laid siege to the height, and at the end of March their saps were driven to within twenty yards of the French advanced posts. During the siege the German infantry made several attempts to carry the position by storm, but were repulsed.

The youngest French recruit could guess what the next stroke would be. The German sappers had sunk shafts, and begun to drive a mine under the summit. The French counter-mined and blew up one mine, then had a fierce struggle with hand-grenades and melinite bombs in one of their advanced works. The struggle was of a curious and terrible kind. The ground was swept by machine-gun and artillery fire on either side and no man could cross it and live. So the fighting took place underground in a maze of deep, narrow trenches and tunnels. After the struggle had gone on for three days, the French engineers brought it suddenly to a conclusion. They buried some hundredweights of high-explosive in their front trench, and constructed new traverses by which the garrison troops could retire. When the conflict was at its fiercest the French gave way and fled, and the victorious Germans crowded into the captured position crying: " Surrender, Frenchmen!"

The French maintained a strong resistance, to give the enemy a full opportunity of increasing the number of his attacking troops. Then the great mine of cheddite (a powerful high-explosive) was exploded, and when the fumes had lifted, the French went back to their position and put it in order, while their guns kept the enemy off by a barrage of shrapnel. Every German had been killed. Soon afterwards the French at last began to advance. It was their first movement of advance in this region since the August battle on the Grande Couronné de Nancy. They went forward slowly, as they had in turn to fight against a powerful system of defence works.

While the Ban de Sapt was thus being cleared for a further advance over the Vosges towards Strassburg by the army based on Epinal, the army based on Toul and Nancy performed a double work. By hard forest fighting in the woods around the Grande Couronné de Nancy and in villages such as Reillon, near the French edge of the frontier going towards Saarburg, it prepared the way for the old and much-studied plan of a grand advance through Lorraine. But at the same time the army of Toul co-operated with the army of Verdun in dealing with the situation created by the partially successful advance of the German forces from Metz. At the battle of the Marne, the army of Metz had made in September, 1914, a strong assault against forts running along the Meuse, and connecting Verdun with Toul. The object was to drive a wedge between Verdun and Toul from the east, while the army of the German crown prince drove another wedge eastward from the Forest of the Argonne. When the two wedges met, Verdun would be completely encircled, and it was hoped would quickly be captured. This design remained half completed for many months. The army of Metz carried out its part of the work, and all through the winter, spring, and summer maintained at St. Mihiel, on the Heights of the Meuse, the wedge it had driven into the French system of frontier defences.

But the army of the crown prince, which had suffered heavy losses in the forest fighting in the Argonne, was powerless to tighten and complete the German loop round Verdun. A decisive victory might have been obtained by breaking through the French fortified line at Verdun and Toul, and, completing the encirclement of Verdun, the crown prince would have struck an even heavier blow than the western German wing was attempting to deal in the neighbourhood of Calais. The breaking of the eastern line of fortresses would, at any time in the campaign, have brought the Germans round the eastern flank of the Franco-British armies, and compelled those armies to withdraw in furious haste south of Paris. The continual storming attacks along the road to Calais were of lesser importance in the large strategical problem of the war when compared with the plan of operations which the Crown Prince could not carry out.

This plan of operations had been designed by Moltke and the German staff long before the outbreak of hostilities, and the results of its breakdown were very disastrous when General Sarrail, with the Verdun army, and General Gouraud, with a single army corps of mountain troops, threw back the Crown Prince's forces, while General de Langle de Cary's army was hammering eastward at the German positions in the Argonne Forest during the advance from the Marne.

When the retreating Germans in the middle of September, 1914, made a firm stand along the Aisne and the Suippes rivers all that remained of the main German plan of attack was the wedge driven through the Heights of the Meuse by the army of Metz. For ten months or more the French commander-in-chief allowed the wedge driven from Metz to remain in the most dangerous part of his line. Even when the French and British forces at last outnumbered the Germans by nearly nine to five, the broad hostile spear-point at St. Mihiel was only slightly reduced in breadth by a little pressure against both its edges.

Between Metz and Verdun extends a clay plateau, seamed with water-courses, forming ponds and lakes of considerable size.

There are also many patches of woodland amid the moist and fertile farm-lands of the Woevre, as the flattish upland between the Meuse and the Moselle is called. Westward, above the sunken course of the Meuse, is a line of hills, mostly bare, known as the Heights of the Meuse. On these hills was constructed the chain of smaller isolated fortresses which connected Verdun with Toul. Then, running in a north-easterly direction along the highway from Commercy, through Pont à Mousson, were more hills, the most important of which, in the circumstances of the war, was the wooded height known as the Bois le Prêtre. The German wedge rested chiefly on the lower marshy ground between the Heights of the Meuse and the hills connecting with the Bois le Prêtre.

The heights occupied by the French forces rose on an average from three hundred to three hundred and fifty feet above the plain of the Woevre. The distance between the high position held by the Verdun army at Bois Haut near Les Eparges and the high position held by the Toul army at the Bois le Prêtre, on the opposite side of the wedge, was only about twenty miles. With the new powerful heavy siege-guns from the Creusot foundries, both French armies at Bois Haut and Bois le Prêtre could command every acre of the German salient running down to the Meuse at St. Mihiel.

Howitzer fire could be directed by aeroplane observers in the modern way against the railway line by which the Germans brought up artillery, ammunition, and general supplies from Metz. The railway ran from Metz to Thiaucourt, a town about five miles north-east of the Bois le Prêtre. But beyond Thiaucourt the line swerved away from the Heights of the Meuse and ran through the French trenches. It was therefore useful to the enemy only as far as Thiaucourt; but from this point they rapidly built a light railway along the old Roman road running to St. Mihiel. The distance of the new German railway, with all its windings, was less than twenty-five miles, and as the materials were stored in advance at Metz, the work was carried out quickly. By means of the new railway connexion a large number of very heavy howitzers was brought up to the heights around St. Mihiel, and the entire plain of the Woevre was transformed with remarkable speed into a fortress of earthworks, wire entanglements, machine-gun redoubts, and artillery pits, garrisoned by the larger part of the army of Metz. The Woevre

A MUSHROOM CITY IMPROVISED IN WAR TIME. During the Great War, several square miles of Gretna Green, which had formerly held only a couple of farmhouses, suddenly became a city of 20,000 munition factory workers, and their families, under the control of the Ministry of Munitions. In addition to huts for their accommodation, clubs, refreshment rooms and other buildings were erected for their benefit. The total value of the cordite produced here was £16,690,246.

Interior of a gunshop in the munition works of Krupps, the great German firm at Essen, where during the war 20,000 shells were turned out daily.

Austria's chief arsenal before and during the war was the Skoda Works at Pilsen, which town passed to Czecho-Slovakia by the peace treaty. The works were afterwards used for the making of machinery.

Large well-lighted shed in French munition works at Creusot, where high-explosive shells were made. Here was designed and produced the famous 75 mm. field-gun.

THREE GREAT EUROPEAN MUNITION WORKS

Plate 30

Volume II

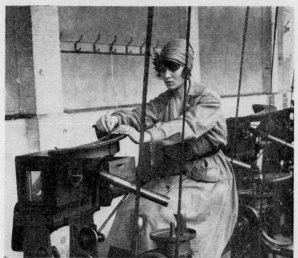

A woman operating a cartridge machine in a munition factory. Over 750,000 women were employed by the Ministry of Munitions.

Imperial War Museum

Training mules for the army. One of the open-air occupations for women providing an alternative to industrial life

WOMEN'S WORK IN THE GREAT WAR

ENEMY TRIUMPH IN PROUD PRZEMYSL. Przemysl, the Galician fortress, surrendered to the Russians in March, 1915 but they were unable to hold it long, for a successful Austro-German campaign in Galicia enabled Mackensen to advance on Przemysl in May and to recapture it in June. The Austro-German troops are here seen entering the town

Plate 32

Volume 11

thus became a grand extension of the entrenched camp of Metz. It was both the barbican of the Lorraine fortress and the gate by which half a million or more German soldiers could be sent forward to hew their way towards Central France.

The French commander made no attempt whatever to alter the situation. Under his orders the Verdun army on the north and the Toul army on the south of the wedge merely kept the enemy occupied by continual but local struggles for the hills above the plain. The fighting in the Bois le Prêtre went on for many months; and there was also a steady pressure through the Forest of Apremont, and its continuation northward—the Wood of Ailly—the latter being about a mile and a half from the fort of the Roman Camp, which defended St. Mihiel. Between Apremont and the Bois le Prêtre was a line of hills, some of which were four hundred and fifty feet above the plateau. These hills were held by the Germans. The French put little or no pressure against them, for it was unscientific and expensive to attempt to advance all along the line, when there were two key-positions from which the vast and formidable fortress system of the Germans could be commanded.

Both sides knew what these two keys were. The first was the Bois le Prêtre with a lower wooded hill in front of it—the Forest des Venchères, immediately overlooking Thiaucourt. The second key, and the more important, was the hill of Les Eparges, lying immediately in front of Bois Haut, and overlooking the hamlet of Combres. For all practical purpose Les Eparges was the winning position in the long wrestle for the Woevre between the army of Verdun and the army of Metz. The two fortress towns were really besieging each other, and each attacking the hostile works at the point where they met in the Woevre. The two cities were only thirty miles apart, and as their ring of main forts extended far into the intervening country they could have bombarded each other with 12 in. guns had it been worth while to waste expensive ammunition. Instead of doing so, they extended their field fortifications until there was only a hundred yards or less between the advanced trenches.

The Germans had earlier taken the village of Chauvoncourt on the further bank of the Meuse. This constituted the famous gateway through which a grand German attack might at any time be launched against the rear of the entire Franco-British-Belgian front. The gateway, however, was blocked from the outside, for the time being, by the French army in the Forest of the Argonne; for the high, wooded ridges of the famous forest, which for centuries have been one of France's great barriers against invaders, dominated completely the German positions around St. Mihiel. Holding the enemy at this point, the French commander began in the early spring of 1915 to master the Woevre by a movement in a more important direction.

While the battle of Champagne (see chap. 22) was at its height the French Staff gave an order for the Verdun army to attack the hill of Les Éparges. The first assault was made on February 17 by means of a mine explosion, after which the first German line was captured without a struggle. The enemy, however, counter-attacked, and there followed a terrible hand-to-hand struggle, lasting about seventy hours, in which the attacking French regiment was at last pressed into a part of the captured trenches and swept by heavy fire from the German guns. The position was untenable, and it seemed nothing remained but to retire or die fighting. But the Frenchmen found another and better solution to the problem. In their last desperate charge, in which they left the first German trench and tore farther up the hill, they completely shattered the 8th Bavarian regiment in front of them, and extended their footing on the height so that they were able to break down all the enemy's succeeding counter-attacks.

The German general commanding the Woevre operations did not feel satisfied that his key-position was safe with the French holding his first line. He brought up engineers, who worked on shifts, day and night for a month, strengthening the fortifications. They drove a tunnel from the village of Combres through the mountain of clay to the German defences near the summit. In the tunnel they built a light railway line, by which supplies and reinforcements could be hauled up by steam-power quickly, without interference from the French batteries. To provide against a heavy shell bombardment of the defence works, the troops were sheltered in large, underground chambers, eighteen feet below the surface. A large number of machine-guns in Metz was brought up, with many mine-throwers of large calibre, and the artillery was strengthened by sixteen additional batteries of heavy howitzers placed in concealed sites in the neighbouring plain. Aerial torpedoes were also forwarded by the new railway, and the garrison of 4,000 infantrymen and 5,000 engineers was given the support of an entire division of infantry. Orders were issued by the staff that Les Eparges must be held at any cost.

Meanwhile the army of Verdun made no further movement of importance until during the attack at Neuve Chapelle the German commander-in-chief reduced the garrison of his trenches at every possible point. In particular, a considerable number of men were moved from the army of Metz. This was the opportunity for which General Sarrail had been waiting; and on March 19 three French battalions charged up Les Eparges ridge and broke the 4th Bavarian regiment. The main work was done by the great new mobile Creusot howitzers which were moved by means of a light railway all round the entrenched camp of Verdun.

They were massed against the ridge, and their shells penetrated into the 18 feet-deep caverns, and by their blast put out all the lamps, while the falling earth closed the passages. Most of the men in the shelters were captured by the charging French infantry. The new first line of German trenches was occupied without a struggle by reason of the effectiveness of the French siege artillery. But from their second line the German troops violently counter-attacked, and in a fiercer struggle than that of February, they fought day and night until March 21, by which time the French troops had advanced 380 yards along the ridge, which had a total length of about 1,580 yards, and a height of about 1,135 feet above sea level.

On March 27 a single battalion of Chasseurs charged from the conquered trenches towards the summit, and though the colonel and all the company commanders were wounded, the desired result was obtained, and a new point of vantage rushed for the final attack on the summit. In the earlier fighting the Germans had tried to hold their front trenches by means of a few machine guns, the main body of troops retiring into the underground shelters when the bombardment began, and returning by tunnels to the open when the infantry attack was expected. After the success of the Chasseurs, the front German trenches had to be held continually in force to guard against another surprise assault by infantry, using only bomb and bayonet, and unheralded by heavy artillery fire. It will be remembered that Sir John French at Festubert, at a later date, omitted the preliminary bombardment, with a view to taking the Germans by surprise when they were trying to defend their front trenches in too economical a manner. No doubt the French staff had communicated to Sir John French full details of the Les Eparges surprise attack.

By this time at Les Eparges the attacking and defending forces were so closely approached that the Germans began to lose heart. The supporting division replaced the two shattered Bavarian regiments, and in the rainy evening of April 5 when the clay soil was a slide of mud in which men sank up to their thighs, the decisive attack was made. Two French regiments advanced through the curtain of rain towards the western side of the summit. A single aerial torpedo launched by the Germans caused enormous loss to one of the assaulting lines, but in the twilight most of the French troops escaped the fire of the defenders and entered the German trenches.

Night fell on a furious hand-to-hand struggle, that went on ceaselessly all through the darkness; but when dawn broke a large, fresh body of enemy troops fell upon the French battalions and compelled them to retire. Yet again, as soon as night fell, the French infantry charged forward into the trench on the east of the summit, and also climbed up some way on the west. In unceasing torrents of rain they fought all the night, and when dawn again broke they had won another five hundred yards. Once more the German commander sent up fresh forces through the tunnel; but fresh French forces also arrived, and the Frenchmen, wet through, muddied all over, and often dropping their mud-clogged rifles and using their bayonets as knives—knives being handier than fixed bayonets in a narrow trench—stabbed and bombed their way forward. All the enemy's counter-attacks were repulsed, and at five o'clock in the morning of April 7 the struggle suddenly ended.

The German commander, in an endeavour to carry out his plan of holding Les Eparges at any cost, sent out his last supports by the tunnel from Combres village; but as the troops debouched from the other side of the tunnel, the French howitzers caught them with shrapnel fire. Every man was swept away before he could reach the trenches held by the French infantry. In rear of these, meanwhile, an army corps from the Woevre was being rapidly collected with a view to pushing it up the hill. Large bodies of troops massed in Combres village; but it was now daylight, and French aerial observation officers, in communication with heavy French batteries concealed in the village of St. Remy, a mile and a half south-east of Combres, directed the howitzers against the gathering masses at the foot of Les Eparges. The larger part of the enemy's reinforcements was broken up by the French guns before it could form for attack. Those that escaped the French artillery were beaten back by the infantry, and so heavy were the enemy's losses that all the rest of the day and all the following day he attempted no further counter-attack.

All the while the rain continued, making the movement of French reinforcements through the muddy clay very difficult. It was not until the morning of April 8 that three fresh battalions arrived on the ridge. They at once went into action, and in an hour's bayonet fighting they captured the summit.

The enemy held only a little triangle of ground at the eastern extremity of the ridge, but the key to the position was in the hands of the French, and all counter-attacks were swept away by shell fire and machine-gun fire, without bayonet or bomb work. The French general conducting the operations then relieved his troops, and sent out sappers to put the trenches in order, and to reconstruct and enlarge the system of communicating earthworks. The fresh regiments brought to Les Eparges advanced in the rain in the afternoon of April 9 to complete the victory. It had been arranged that the French artillery should drop a heavy barrage on the defences still left in the enemy's hands.

But at the critical moment a blanket of mist fell upon the height, and this made aerial control of the guns impossible. In these conditions the French infantry had to carry out the work at more expense. They went forward in a charge in the evening, followed by hand-to-hand fighting in the darkness. Rain and fog made searchlights, star-shells, and other modern means of illuminating the battlefield practically useless; and at ten o'clock at night Les Eparges was completely won. Two counter-attacks were beaten off with ease on the nights of April 11 and 12, the French artillery being used in such a way as to make every attempted attack on the ridge on the part of the Germans only a laborious form of suicide.

While the attack upon Les Eparges was being conducted by the army of Verdun, the army of Toul profited by the severe strain which its comrades in the north were imposing upon the common foe. For many months part of the Toul forces had been fighting from the south against St. Mihiel and Thiaucourt. By the Heights of the Meuse they had withstood all the winter the shock of the enemy in the Forest of Apremont. Their lines in places were only two miles from the forts defending St. Mihiel, and the commander of Metz exerted all his strength to end the battle in this region which had begun in September, 1914. The largest siege-guns in Metz were brought down by the light railway, with millions of hand-grenades, hundreds of thousands of bombs, and thousands of aerial torpedoes.

The French were at first at a disadvantage, owing to their lack of heavy field-artillery, but the Creusot and other gun factories had, by now, improved their output of heavy howitzers. The result was that the army of Toul, which was still the most important army in France, as it guarded the flank of all the Franco-British-Belgian line, was put on a level of equipment with the enemy. By the spring of 1915 the positions along the eastern frontier fortresses were reversed. Instead of the Germans trying to invest or break the great French entrenched camps, the French began to press strongly against the German fortification protecting Lorraine. The army of Toul shelled, bombed, and mined its way through the Forest of Apremont.

Towards the end of March the French trenches had been driven through the Forest of Apremont towards the bare height crowning Ailly Wood. The advance was conducted by sapping until the French engineers issued from the north-west of the Forest of Apremont and dug their way along a ravine leading to a steep height in Ailly Wood known as the " fortress." Here the Germans had constructed a very strong system of armoured earthworks, forming the outer defence to St. Mihiel, less than two miles northward. Against this fortress the army of Toul massed their machinery of slaughter in the first days of April.

By this time they also possessed aerial torpedoes. These consisted of large, cigar-shaped tubes of metal, filled with high-explosive and steadied in their flight by a propeller. The aerial torpedoes were ejected from a kind of mortar, by means of a small charge of powder, and when they were thrown into the air the propeller and rudder kept them on the mark. The French used many of these new missiles, and the three German lines on the hill were destroyed, together with the accessory defences. All the garrison perished, many being thrown up into the air, with trees and sand-bags, when the land torpedoes struck home. At the same time the French gunners, acting as observers at a distance of only three hundred and sixty feet from the German lines, directed the new heavy siege ordnance against the enemy's machine-gun redoubts. Then, after some hours, the labours of the French engineers were completed. They had driven three mines into the hill, and at noon on April 5 the mines were exploded ; and before the fumes were blown away the French infantry advanced in three waves against the shattered fortress.

The troops were ordered not to enter the German trenches, for any purpose, but merely to clear them out. They used the ordinary hand-grenades, and also little boxes of high-explosive which they called colanders, thrown in the manner of the classic discobolus. Avoiding the German trenches, which had probably been mined by the enemy in case he lost them, the French infantry swept round and took their foes in the rear of the hill by means of two flank movements, which completely swept the ground, and then united behind the fort.

The entire German force on the hill was either blown up by torpedoes or heavy shells, or killed in the infantry-rush by bomb or bayonet. Only on the right of the hill were two French companies held up by machine-guns, after capturing three lines of trenches. In the evening the enemy tried to obliterate his lost positions by massed fire of his heavy guns, but the French artillery had been concentrated round Ailly Wood in superior force, and, directed by observers in aeroplanes, it poured so tremendous a fire on the German batteries that these were silenced. At six o'clock in the April evening the German infantry attempted a counter-attack. But it broke and retreated, being caught by shrapnel from both the light French field guns and the Creusot heavy howitzers.

On April 6, after the hill fort was captured, the French launched an attack on the left of the enemy's position. But as the German commander strongly reinforced his front, the French troops were obliged to retire through the deep cuttings, and the work was resumed by the heavy French howitzers and the aerial torpedo section. Once more they blew up three lines of hostile trenches, leaving to their infantry only the work of occupying the lines. The enemy then had no fresh force to continue the action, and two days elapsed before he could collect sufficient troops to make a counter-attack. Then all the German artillery in the region of St. Mihiel massed its fire on Ailly Wood, and under cover of this barrage the re-formed German infantry made eight distinct, massed attempts to recover the position by storm. But the French engineers had not wasted time in the two days' interval allowed them. Not a single piece of trench was lost; and, as the Germans came up in close formation to within sixty feet of the armoured trench, and then retired through a wide zone of French shrapnel fire, they suffered very heavy casualties.

During the struggle the thunder of the German artillery was continuous, and the entire hill disappeared in the fumes of the exploding shells and asphyxiating gases. According to the report of the French staff, every tree in the wood was destroyed, and every yard of ground was ploughed up by shells from the German siege-guns. Many of the trenches were wiped out by direct hits, and on this occasion the French telephone wires were cut for two hours. Yet the German counter-attacks were repulsed. The battle was concluded on April 10 by the advance of two French battalions, which captured the trenches from which the Germans had been issuing for their attack. The enemy then ceased to counter-attack, and the French engineers strongly fortified the new position in Ailly Wood.

Throughout these actions and those that followed, General Joffre was impressed always by the necessity of withholding enemy troops from the eastern front. He was encouraged also by the thought that the pre-occupation of the Germans in the east might give him his opportunity to break through, and drive them from their entrenched positions in the west. At this time he had decided on that series of attacks, north of Arras, which are known as the second battle of Artois. He was obliged from lack of men and munitions at this time to abandon a more ambitious plan of attack, which would have included offensives from Reims and Nancy.

He undoubtedly hoped from the meditated assault in Artois to pierce the enemy's line. His imediate objective was the Vimy Ridge, overlooking the plain of Douai from which, if successful, he could continue his advance towards Cambrai. The general attack was under the command of General Foch, whose group of armies consisted of the 10th (General D'Urbal) and the 8th (General Maud'huy).

Though still not so well supplied with heavy artillery and shells as the Germans, the French were in fact far better off in this respect than the small British expeditionary force. In the battle upon which they were now to engage, every means of destruction was necessary to demolish the immensely strong defences of the Germans, and it was fortunate for the French that they had those means available. The battle was preceded for six days by the heaviest bombardment so far employed in the war. It has been described as the first real bombardment, by which is meant that it was the first to approximate to the bombardment of the later stages of the war, when guns stood wheel to wheel, and for weeks poured shells of every calibre into the enemy's defensive lines.

The main attack which was fixed to start on May 9 was designed to reach Lens, the centre of the French coalfield, by penetrating the works which defended it. These were of great strength, with deep trenches, underground galleries, concrete and steel machine-gun posts, and were protected by extremely elaborate systems of mines and barbed wire. The most conspicuous point in the defences was the high hill of Notre Dame de Lorette, rising to a height of 500 ft., with, to the south of it, the fortified villages of Ablain, Carency, and Souchez, the cellars of which had been connected. The works were so designed as to be independent of one another and to flank each other, so that the fall of one or two would not involve the evacuation of the whole position. With this group of fortresses the Germans under Prince Rupert held the direct road from Arras to Bethune, and threatened the roads to Aire and St. Pol. It formed a most dangerous salient in the Allied front, threatening both Bethune and Arras.

All this system of works, with its underground passages, armoured forts, and light artillery pits, was covered by the fire of hundreds of siege-howitzers, heavy field artillery, and naval guns, sited on and behind the second line of hills to the east running through Vimy, below which, still farther eastward, extended the plain of the great French coalfields.

In a bird's-eye view, such as the French airmen enjoyed in their continual voyages of reconnaissance, the German line formed a wedge of hills, the point of the wedge being Ablain. General Foch used three main striking forces against the point of the wedge. The first force struck out at the hill of Notre Dame de Lorette, the second force struck at Ablain, and the third force at Carency. At the same time an advance was made from the north against Lens, the scene of conflict being the village of Loos, and another advance was made southward against the town, the battlefield being La Targette and Neuville St. Vaast. In addition to all these movements a severe and persistent pressure was maintained along the entire front of the armies commanded by the crown prince of Bavaria from Armentières to Arras. Prince Rupert was never allowed to weaken one part of his front to strengthen another part. He had to leave his men in the positions in which they found themselves, until reinforcements arrived.

At each point of attack the battle opened at the same hour and in the same manner. On the morning of May 9 some 1,200 French guns poured a hurricane of high-explosive shell into the German trenches. The artillery fire was especially concentrated on the Lorette spur; for as this rose some two hundred feet above most of the other hills, it was the main key to the general position. The Germans here had six lines of trenches, strengthened by concrete, and barred by two or three zones of barbed-wire. At every hundred yards the trenches were flanked by machine-gun redoubts. One of these redoubts, north-east of the chapel of Notre Dame de Lorette, was surrounded by a wolf-pit, lightly covered with turf, with bayonets stuck at the bottom, to catch those who fell in. The bombardment levelled many of the German trenches and inflicted severe loss, but did not seriously affect the maze of underground works, or the fortified cellars. Many of the machine-gun posts, which needed a direct hit to demolish them, remained intact.

The redoubts were connected by underground telephone wires, with batteries of field-guns, some of which at Ablain swept the hill on the south, while others at Souchez were able to get a flanking shrapnel fire on any hostile force advancing up the eastern slopes. There was also concentration of heavy German artillery north-east of the hill, at Angres and Lievin, which would cover every part of the height by means of direct or indirect fire.

A division of Baden troops garrisoned the Lorette height, and the divisional general was promised reinforcements in two days. The French commander waited until the attack on the

Aubers ridge by the British 1st army occupied the entire attention of the Prince of Bavaria. Then at ten o'clock in the morning the French gunners lengthened their range, and under cover of their fire the first French line clambered over their parapets and charged. The French field-guns had done their work well. All the enemy's wire entanglements were destroyed.

Moreover, the heavier shells had broken down all the trenches, and the three German lines were captured in a single movement of advance by the first French line. The men bombed their way into the remaining machine-gun redoubts with great gallantry and spirit, and before noon had advanced two miles. A barrage behind them prevented those of the Germans who remained unwounded from retreating, and also fresh German troops from coming up. Three thousand unwounded prisoners and ten guns were taken. La Targette was stormed and a house-to-house fight started in Neuville St. Vaast and Carency. But then, under a terrible flanking fire from the German machine-guns, and under the bombardment of the German artillery, the advance was held.

The French troops spent the night in rebuilding the German lines they had captured, while the sky was lighted by a continuous bombardment of the position by the enemy's distant heavy batteries. In the morning of May 10 the first French line was about to leap out again and try to capture the crowning entrenchments round the chapel, when an order came from General Foch to stand and prepare for a counter-attack, which had been seen by an aviator to be in preparation round the sugar factory at Souchez.

As the attacking column advanced, the heavy German guns deluged the hill with high-explosive shell, which would have swept away the French infantry had it been exposed. But owing to this timely warning it was the Germans that were caught in the open by the French guns. As they withdrew under shrapnel fire the French infantrymen made their charge and captured another line of trenches. The German counter-attack had been completely checked, but on the other hand no further progress could be made against the flat hill top at the chapel. The fortress there was so well supported by the German guns at Angres that each assaulting line was swept back. It was seen that more ground would have to cleared round the dominating height before the decisive assault could

be made. In the night the advanced line of troops was reinforced, and the next day the enemy was driven back from
the southern buttresses. Then in a fierce night attack, in which

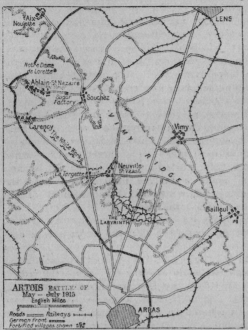

the French ad-
vanced by rushes
from one shell-hole
to another, the
spur commanding
Ablain was won.
On May 11 the
large church of
Notre Dame de
Lorette was taken
with knife, pistol,
and bomb, after
some of the most
desperate fighting
of the war. But
on the high ground
the Germans still
had strong posi-
tions which held
out resolutely and
had to be assaulted
one by one.

Not until the
fortress of Lorette
was in the hands

of the French was the capture of the village of Ablain possible;
for Ablain was a low-lying, double row of peasants' and working
people's houses, extending more than a mile, in the valley
road running from Souchez towards Servin. The straggling
village was dominated by the height of Lorette on the north
and by Carency Hill on the south. To add to the difficulty
of the attacking army, all the slopes on either side were
covered with fruit trees or forest trees, and under this screen
of foliage the enemy was able to manœuvre troops, machine-
guns, and light artillery, and the reinforcements sent up from
Souchez. The German engineers had left nothing to chance,
but had driven long, narrow, deep communication trenches to
Souchez and Givenchy en Gohelle, down which troops could

pass to the firing-line at Ablain and the neighbouring points without being exposed to shrapnel fire. From the fan-shaped sloping position at Ablain the Germans commanded the main road from Arras to Bethune.

The position was therefore one of great importance and, as it was the extreme point of the German wedge, it was fortified with an extraordinary amount of labour. Every house was connected by underground passages, and linked by means of deep communication saps with the wooded spurs north and south. All the winter the attacking army at this point had rested in the low-lying westward plain, where the trenches were very watery. But in March, 1915, when the Germans were weakened by the need for reinforcements in Champagne and at Neuve Chapelle, the French infantry of the line had, by a surprise attack, won some of the drier ground together with some of the foremost houses of the village. And there they remained quietly for two months, while the distant German howitzers conducted a regular bombardment against them. Their sappers, however, dug out deep shelters for them, and after beating back several counter-attacks, they lived on fairly peaceably, in spite of the interest which the German artillery-men took in them.

But on the morning of May 9 their gunners at last gave them the help they needed. Every house in the long village was destroyed by high-explosive shell, some 20,000 rounds being used for this purpose. At the same time the enemy's wire entanglements were shattered by the new weapon of trench warfare, the little quick-firing cannon, made on the revolver principle. Its small, powerful shells swept away the barbed-wire obstacles, and while the heavier guns were still playing on the eastern end of the village, the French infantry left their trenches and took a considerable number of the houses. They did not, however, advance very far, as they would have been enfiladed both from Lorette Hill and from Carency Hill, while the German siege-guns at Vimy, directly in front of them, would have battered them to pieces. Ablain did not fall until it could be encircled by the conquerors of Carency and Lorette. As a matter of fact, the village was won on May 12. Using incendiary shells, the gunners set on fire every ruined cottage in which the Germans were sheltering, and left the infantry to collect the spoil and prisoners and occupy the conquered ground.

Ablain was only an episode between the grand event of Lorette and the grand event of Carency. The capture of Carency was a very arduous affair. The village lay in a hollow, which was dominated by a wooded hill. The houses formed five groups, one in the centre, and the other four admirably placed for defence on the north, west, south, and east. Each group of walled buildings had been transformed by the enemy's sappers into a modern fortress. The shattered brickwork merely served as bullet-proof shelters for machine-guns. A single man watched with a periscope for a movement by the French troops. The garrison of machine-gun men, grenade-throwers, and sharp-shooters lived far underground at a depth no howitzer shell could penetrate. Tunnels and deep, narrow saps enabled the garrison to be relieved for a furlough, and to be kept well supplied with food and ammunition.

On the hill above them were light field-guns, tubes for firing aerial torpedoes, and hundreds of machine-guns. Other guns were hidden in the surrounding orchards, and also many useful field-howitzers, all the batteries being connected with observation stations on the hill-top. Then in front of this formidable and almost invisible system of fortifications were four lines of trenches, strongly garrisoned by troops, who moved in and out through tunnels.

The French were in as sorry a position before Carency as they had been before Ablain. They were in the Artois plain, and the water from the hills drained into their trenches where they often stood waist deep in the mud. They had tried to win a footing on the high ground on December 18, 1914, but as they advanced against the village from the north and west, they were stopped by machine-gun fire, and though they charged again on December 27 they were again mowed down and forced to retire. For some months afterwards the fighting was conducted by means of mine shafts and mining saps; but in spite of the underground struggles which occurred, no damage whatever was done to the enemy's position. On the contrary, this position was continually strengthened.

When Carency was attacked on the morning of May 9 the preliminary bombardment was conducted for a space of three hours. The new trench cannon broke down the wire entanglements and the parapets of the German entrenchments, while the heavy howitzer shells crashed into the fortified houses and into the underground caverns. Then, when the lines of Chasseurs swept out with fixed bayonets, the lighter French guns maintained a line of fire close in front of them; the trenches were carried and the village entered by one violent movement—in one bound, as the French themselves said. The attack was made mainly from the south and the east, across a ravine near the road running from Carency to Souchez.

At only one point on the right, where the enemy was sheltered from gun-fire in a hollow, was there any resistance. This spot in the fortification was, however, almost encircled the following day by another French advance across the Souchez road. The hostile island was then conquered, and in a series of house-to-house attacks the Chasseurs and the young French troops fought their way into the village. The struggle went on underground through the passages connecting the houses and in the shelter caverns where the garrison used to rest. The French suffered badly while trying to advance above ground against the loop-holed buildings from which machine-guns were trained on them. It was impossible to carry the village by storm, even when the French field batteries were brought up close to it.

The place was a warren; the defenders went underground when the French artillery opened fire, and by means of sub-terranean telephone wires they brought their heavy batteries to bear on anything they could not reach with their own machine-guns. The French infantry had to ferret them out with hand-bomb and knife, with little help from their own artillery. While this mole warfare was going on, the Saxon, Baden, and Bavarian troops holding Carency were able to communicate in almost absolute security with Souchez and Ablain by means of deep, narrow communication trenches. But on Tuesday, May 11, the French regiments entrenched on the Souchez road fought their way into Carency Wood, east of the village, and after a stubborn fight, in which they held off counter-attack after counter-attack launched from the direction of Souchez, they captured the main communication trenches.

The Germans in Carency then had only the route to Ablain open to them. General Foch tried to enclose this by a sudden double attack eastward and westward. But the French troops attacking from the east, over the position that they had con-quered in Carency Wood, were surprised by a large and formid-able fortification. On a wooded hill there was a great quarry hidden amid the trees, which had been excavated out of the chalk hill to a depth of two hundred and sixty feet, and strengthened by casemates and bomb-proof caverns. Another regiment was sent up to reinforce the attacking troops, and the battle for the quarry opened with a surprise success on the part of the French. Two hundred and fifty German troops came out into the open on the wooded hill, with the intention of making a stand behind the wire entanglements which they had laid between the trees. But instead of charging, the French colonel sent a message along his field telephone, and the light French guns, in a sharp, intense, massed fire, completely wiped out the hostile troops who had ventured above ground.

Then the attack on the quarry opened, and went on for 76 hours of incessant fighting. The French lost heavily in covering the open ground leading to the subterranean fortress, but the western wave of attack slowly mounted the hill on one side, preceded by a bombardment of high-explosive shell from the distant French batteries. At the same time the eastern line of attack swept into the forest, and at half-past five on Thursday, May 13, a line of waving handkerchiefs rose about 30 yards away from the advanced French trench.

As the prisoners were being collected a series of fires broke out in the valley northward. It was Ablain burning. Heralded by the fire of their guns, the victorious French troops swept down the northern slopes of the hill, and using the communication saps made by the Germans, they swung against the eastern end of Ablain, and after a grim hand-to-hand struggle that lasted all night they crowned the victory of Carency and Lorette by capturing the position at Ablain and another 1,000 prisoners.

On May 15 the French 10th army continued its attack against the Labyrinth, Neuville St. Vaast, and Souchez. After a two hours' bombardment three successive assaults were launched, but none of them succeeded in making any appreciable progress. A few houses were occupied in Neuville and short sections of trenches in the Labyrinth were captured. At this stage a temporary deadlock was reached and General Foch decided to break off the battle for eight or ten days to allow his troops rest and to accumulate a sufficient supply of munitions for a further intensive bombardment. In fact no further move was made until June 7, when an attack was made with the object of securing Neuville and the Labyrinth.

A CURIOUS VILLAGE

Neuville was a curious village. The Germans lived some thirty-three feet below the street. The cellars of the houses were strengthened by a topping of cement three feet thick, and underneath the strengthened cellars was a subterranean town, the caverns being connected by large, main tunnel thoroughfares with narrower side galleries. The garrison troops circulated like moles during the battle, coming up in the most unexpected places. There was one tunnel in particular that ran under the French lines, and in the rear of the attacking troops a hidden German officer studied the French preparations through a periscope, and telephoned fire directions to German batteries miles away eastward at Thelus and Vimy. There were indeed German guns and howitzers on three sides of Neuville, and they maintained a furious fire on the French soldiers. But in the long battle of Neuville neither the German nor the French guns were predominant; for it was a battle of cave-men, going on often at a depth to which no shell could penetrate. The final assault on Neuville lasted three days and the village became wholly in possession of the French on June 10.

On the same day nearly all the Labyrinth fell into French hands. It was a maze of blockhouses, shelters, saps, caverned chambers, and armoured concrete defences and tunnels, on which the German engineers had spent much skill and energy. It was built around two sunken country lanes, from which spread, for a mile and a half on either side, works of every kind, amply furnished with machine guns and bomb throwers.

Meanwhile the French sappers drove a parallel, in the ancient way, towards the Eulenburg Passage, one of the principal lines of the Labyrinth. A field of scarlet poppies stretched between the parallel and Eulenburg Passage, and on June 16 the French infantry charged through the poppies suddenly and leaped into the enemy's line. There followed a struggle in Eulenburg Passage lasting three days, which sealed the victory of the French. As a result of these operations the German had been thrown off the line of occupied heights; the biggest underground defences yet constructed had been captured; and the moral of his defending troops had been severely shaken when the operations came to a close on June 19.

CHAPTER 17

Italy Joins in the Conflict

WHEN the Great War broke out Italy was an unknown quantity in the European situation. Bound to Germany and Austria by the Triple Alliance, it seemed to many that she must inevitably fall into line beside them. Yet there was a complexity of forces within her which to the last moment seemed as though they might sway her in either direction or disintegrate her people in civil war.

In 1865, when Bismarck was working out his scheme for establishing Prussian instead of Austrian supremacy in Germany, he procured for Prussia the alliance of Italy, whose reward was to be Venetia. At the conclusion of the war of 1866 Austria ceded Venetia, and the boundary of the Italian kingdom was defined. Austria still retained the Alpine region known as the Trentino (so called from the city of Trent) geographically a part of Italy, and having an Italian population. She retained also Trieste and Istria, on the Adriatic. Thus, Italian nationalist sentiment held that there was still a portion of Italy unredeemed; this was Italia Irredenta.

When once the German Empire was thoroughly established and organized, there was no collision of interests between Germany and Austria; so, in 1882, Bismarck secretly formed the Triple Alliance between the three Powers of Central Europe— Germany, Austria, and Italy—the inducement to Italy being security against any revival of Austrian aggression, security against France, and economic advantages to be obtained from the friendship of Germany. Italy could hardly ever feel that, in a political sense, she had gained substantially by the alliance; in fact, the empires took very little account of her interests unless their own were directly furthered thereby; and there was never any love lost between Italy and Austria. Nevertheless, the alliance was renewed in 1912.

In 1913 Austria approached Italy on the subject of an aggressive war on Serbia, ostensibly to be undertaken as a necessary measure of self-defence for Austria—the scheme, in fact, which matured in the summer of 1914. Italy definitely declined to be a party to any such scheme, of which she disapproved in plain terms, as inevitably involving a European conflagration. When Austria issued her ultimatum to Serbia, Italy was not consulted. It was therefore clear that no conceivable obligation could rest upon her to support the Teutonic allies when the inevitable result followed. There began a long campaign of intrigue in Italy, supported with lavish bribery by German agents, and only ended when, all things being at last ready, the Salandra cabinet was able to demand of the country and the king a free hand to take such action as Italian interests required.

Perhaps in no country affected by the war was the drama of intrigue played with such a wonderful setting and, it may be added, to so rapt an audience. When the conflagration started, the head of the Italian Government was Signor Salandra, a man of whose personal characteristics so little was known that even his friends believed him mainly a party politician. He became premier, as most people had supposed, as a stop-gap when the great Italian dictator, Signor Giolitti, laid down the reins of power in 1914. Salandra's was a Conservative government. As such it could not actually command a majority, but, on condition of its becoming a war government, it received the support in the country of the " Radical-Interventionists," who believed in the necessity of Italy's intervention on the side of the Allies. Signor Salandra's cabinet had become a national one.

But there were difficulties, and the principal of these difficulties was the man who was called the Italian dictator, Signor Giolitti. His position had long been unique. At once the ablest politician in Italy, and one of the most skilful wire-pullers, he had for years dictated Italian policy just as he had filled Italian posts, prefectures, governorships and commands with devoted adherents. It is perhaps doubtful whether Signor Giolitti had any international policy which could give a clear lead in the circumstances which prevailed in Europe after August, 1914. He was not, as has sometimes been assumed, an enemy of Great Britain; on the contrary, his ideal for Italy was a naval agreement with Britain as the strongest sea Power, and at the same time a close military attachment to Germany as the most important land force.

The first business of Signor Salandra's cabinet was at once to restore the breaches in Italy's defensive armaments. The host of German spies very soon reported to the German War Office that the Italian preparations appeared to be of a thoroughly practical character, and their reports were presently backed by communications from Germany's diplomatic representatives at the Italian Court and at the Vatican.

We have said that Austria had omitted to consult Italy before presenting her German-made ultimatum to Serbia. In consequence there could be no doubt that Italy was at least relieved of all responsibilities under the Triple Alliance, and almost immediately she declared her neutrality. There was considerable indignation in Berlin where, a few days earlier, demonstrators before the Italian Embassy had acclaimed the Italian ally. Actually, the Italian declaration of neutrality had done the Allies one invaluable service—it had released for the struggle against the invading Germans a number of French troops which must otherwise have been kept on the Italian frontier.

In the breathing space given by the declaration of neutrality, the Salandra cabinet was busy calling up various classes of the reserves (many men being called by letters delivered by hand instead of through the post), piling up ammunition, and preparing down to the last detail the equipment necessary for the difficult mountain warfare; and German agents were busy all over the country in mobilising every kind of force against the Interventionists, as the war party was called.

The German campaign did not reach its maximum tension until the arrival in Rome of the German Imperial agent-general, Prince von Bülow. It was now pressed, not only with energy, but with a huge expenditure of money in all directions, and simultaneously Prince von Bülow himself began to open overtures with Baron Sonnino in order to discover what territorial concessions the existing Italian Government considered necessary.

It is easy to understand that, even though Prince von Bülow was in reality the agent-general for the Central Empires, certain diplomatic limitations had to be retained. Italy had no open cause of quarrel with her ally Germany, except in so far as she was bound to disapprove of the more brutal features of the German invasion of Belgium and northern France. Yet the Italian Government was not in the least in the dark as to the true authorship of the Serbian ultimatum or of the European War; nor could it disguise from itself the fact that circumstances being as they were, Germany could and did, to a certain extent,

AN ANTI-GERMAN CAMPAIGN

dictate Austrian policy during the war. It followed that while
Prince von Bülow was not charged with any mandate to make
concession on behalf of Austria, he was actually the person with
whom the Italian Government had to negotiate.

The primary object of the Italian Government was to gain
time until the military preparations were completed. The
objects of Prince von Bülow were two: First, if possible, to
make the Italian Government define the terms, territorial and
otherwise, which it considered the minimum acceptable; and
secondly, by dribbling out concessions, bit by bit, to convey
the impression that every reasonable demand was being granted,
and that Italy could gain, without firing a shot, at least as much
as she could hope to gain by successful war. The Giolittians also
were preparing for a coup. They knew, of course, that with
infinite patience the Salandra cabinet was making good the
deficiencies in arms and ammunition which the Giolitti cabinet
had left.

Meanwhile the Garibaldians—that is the remnant of those who
had fought for Italian freedom with the national hero in 1865
and those who formed their adherents now—were conducting a
vigorous campaign throughout Italy for the freedom of the
Italian districts still under Austrian rule; and, lastly, there was
a strong but much less obvious movement in northern Italy
which had for its object the democratisation of public control,
the prevention of another Giolitti tyranny, the diminution
particularly of Jesuit influence, and the introduction of demo-
cratic institutions such as they saw in England. They were
prepared to go to any length to prevent the Prussianising of
Italy as a result of the war. Their main objective was to combat
Germany through a war with Austria.

For many weeks Baron Sonnino held his hand. He refused
to be drawn by Prince von Bülow, and continued to insist that
since Austria had broken the terms of the Triple Alliance it was
for her to state what reparation she was prepared to make.
Austria desired that the cession of the Trentino and rectifi-
cation of the frontier at other points should be conceded after
the war as a reward for Italian neutrality. Italy demanded that
all territorial concessions should come into force immediately as
reparation for the Austrian breach of agreement. Italy demanded
that the Italian districts of Istria should be surrendered absolutely; Austria offered only to make Trieste a " free city "

under Austrian suzerainty. Italy demanded not only that concessions should be immediate, but also that Germany, as the obviously predominant partner, should give guarantees for the effective maintenance of the concessions after the war.

Mention must be made of one feature of the intrigue carried on by Germany in Rome—namely, the so-called Vatican Plot. Among the coadjutors of Prince von Bülow in Rome was a certain Herr Erzberger, the leader in the German Reichstag of the powerful Catholic Centre party. He was sent to Rome to encourage the resistance of the Roman Catholic Church to an Italian war with Austria.

So far as Germany was concerned the Church of Rome was most influential in the south and west, and here also were the strongholds of the political Centre party whose fortunes were bound up with Catholic influence. It was neither unnatural nor unintelligible that Roman Catholic Germany and Austria should endeavour to range on their side the influence of Italian Catholics and also through the Pontificate to appeal to Catholics in neutral countries. The grave factor in the situation was that Herr Erzberger personally and through his emissaries endeavoured to set on foot a secret agitation against the war—that is against the King's advisers—through the medium of the Roman Catholic clergy. Traps were laid for the Pontiff himself. He was induced to grant an audience to a German-American journalist who subsequently used the conversation for the purpose of affecting the sympathies of Roman Catholics in the United States and in other neutral countries. The Italian populace now began to show a restlessness under these contending forces. Companies of young men of the Interventionist persuasions were formed, and as a counterblast similar bands of neutralists paraded the cities.

Naturally there was no doubt felt that while a small proportion of the Neutralist leaders were genuinely convinced that Italy ought not to go to war, the violent Neutralist demonstrations, on the contrary, were both inspired and assisted by German intriguers, whose main desire was to make it appear that feeling against the war was so strong that something resembling civil war must result if the Government finally rejected the Austrian proposals. These demonstrations led to constant clashes between the factions and the Carabinieri were at times hard put to it to prevent open riot.

Further, the Garibaldi movement, too, had produced a crisis to which we must now turn our attention. Early in the war the Garibaldians had sent a special corps of Garibaldi volunteers who fought with the French troops in Alsace. The corps suffered severely in one of the German assaults, and one of the members of the Garibaldi family fell at the head of the volunteers. The news of this engagement had a wide-spread effect in Italy, and undoubtedly helped largely to popularise a movement for celebrating the fifty-fifth anniversary of the sailing of the one thousand Garibaldian volunteers for Marsala in 1860.

This anniversary fell on May 5, 1915, and it was decided to hold a great meeting on the scene of Garibaldi's embarkation with his thousand volunteers just below Genoa. A memorial statue was prepared, and was to be unveiled, while a great patriotic demonstration was to be addressed by Gabriele D'Annunzio, the Italian poet, who had come to be recognized as the spokesman of the Irredentist and Interventionist movement. There is no doubt that as the arrangements for the great demonstration took shape, the leaders of the movement believed that it might carry the Italian Government " off its feet," and that it would provide king and cabinet with a fitting opportunity for declaring their policy. Both the premier, Signor Salandra, and the foreign secretary, Baron Sonnino, announced their intention of being present, and finally it was announced that the King himself would witness the unveiling of the statue. An immense concourse of people from all parts of Italy was expected.

But two days before the ceremony the whole official programme was suddenly cancelled. It was announced in the morning that owing to the gravity of the international situation, neither the premier nor Baron Sonnino could leave Rome, and finally, towards noon, it was further officially announced that the King would not be present. At the beginning of May Italy finally made it clear that the concessions she demanded were no longer to be regarded as consideration for a maintenance of the alliance, but as the alternative to Italy's joining the Allies. The Triple Alliance was denounced by Italy on May 4—that is, the day before the Garibaldian ceremony.

Three factors had thus combined to prepare Italian public opinion for intervention. There was the desire to " realize national aspirations "—there is no better expression for the Irredentist and Garibaldian movement—and there was the growing sense of the hopelessness of any decent civilized life after the war unless Germany were crushed—a factor which Germany certainly underestimated—and, finally, there was the increasing exasperation as the plots of German and " Germanising " agents in Italy became clearer. The appalling stories of brutality to Italians within Austria's borders helped to fan the flame of Irredentist zeal, the sinking of the Lusitania and the use of poisonous gases broke the back of pro-German opposition.

After May 4 there was not really any question as to what the Salandra cabinet would and must do. There was only a question whether it could carry its measures into effect without an appeal to the country. There is, perhaps, little doubt now that Salandra's ministry would have precipitated events in the first week of May had not the Russian retirement begun in the north, and had not the Italian minister for war become cognisant of a shortage of munitions on the part of the Allies. These facts may have necessitated some revision of plans.

On May 10 German and Austrian consulates throughout Italy began to advise their nationals to quit Italy, and an hour or two after the issue of the warnings by express letter the consulates were besieged by people asking for passports. The exodus continued for about ten days, when the majority of Germans and Austrians who could get away had taken refuge in Switzerland.

May 11 saw demonstrations throughout the country no longer of a " Garibaldian " character, but of violent indignation at the sinking of the Lusitania, and the Union Jack began to appear combined in one flag with the French, Russian, and Italian colours. On the evening of the 14th occurred a treacherous attack with revolvers upon the Interventionists issuing from the Porta Venezia, and on the same day Giolitti, who had gone to Rome to take the measure of the situation, struck his blow.

Gathering all the weight of his authority, all the influence of his years of dictatorship, he forced his supporters to a declaration that they would not support the Salandra government in its existing form. This meant that when Signor Salandra should ask the Chamber of Deputies for a ratification of the measures already taken, and for the various votes necessary to give the Government a free hand for the prosecution of the war, he would —if Giolitti could make good his threats—be defeated. Signor Salandra and Baron Sonnino had expounded to him the situation as it had developed, but he professed himself dissatisfied and refused to advise the King to continue to support the Salandra ministry. Signor Salandra had no alternative. On May 14 he and his whole ministry resigned. Constitutionally the King was bound to attempt a compromise. Giolitti himself would not, or, as is more probable, dared not attempt to form a ministry. Alternatives were tried without success, and meantime Italy came nigh to civil war.

Printing presses worked all through the night of the 14th and the day of the 15th to turn out millions of little white cards bearing the inscription, " Death to Giolitti!" and huge red-white-and-green posters bearing the yet more significant warning " war or republic!" In Rome a furious mob stormed the Parliament house and threw up barricades in the streets; and in Milan, Turin, and Genoa men prepared for fighting in the streets.

It is impossible in short space to hope to give any impression of the fury of the crowds which throughout Italy demanded the return of the Salandra ministry. But there is no doubt that any alternative statesman who might have attempted in other circumstances to try to form a Cabinet must have recognized the warning that his first task would be to quell a civil war. And very wisely one and all refused to face a situation which called now for the one ministry that the people would tolerate. The die was cast. Italy declared war on May 23, 1915.

All Austria's principal mountain fortresses could easily have been forced at the end of the first week in May, if the war had opened in accordance with the plans of General Cadorna, King Victor Emmanuel, and his ministers; for both Austria and Germany had been taken unawares by the denunciation of the Triple Alliance. The mountain forts were held by only a few thousand troops, Austria's forces being employed against the Russians in the great Galician offensive, or massed along the Serbian front. But during the three weeks which Signor Giolitti won for his old friends, the mobilisation against Italy was carried out at high speed. The cemented trenches, the gun emplacements, the armour-plated casemates and strategic roads had long been ready; but the men to use them were mainly provided between May 4 and May 23. Every man who could be spared from Hungary and the southern Austrian provinces was railed to the Italian front, until, by May 23, more than 300,000 men had been got into position. They were mostly Tyrolese and Hungarian territorial troops, supported by first-line regiments in positions of importance. Against them General Cadorna brought up 700,000 first-line soldiers.

The fact that they had somewhat more than two men to the enemy's one was not of much importance. What counted was guns, and especially heavy siege-guns. The Austrians had their heavy artillery placed on every dominating height, fed by railways, defended by machine-gun redoubts on the mountain sides, with light quick-firers sheltered in caves or galleries hewed from the rock. The Italian guns were on railway lines in the plain, or being hauled up distant valley roads by ox teams. The Italians had to set about building mountain fortresses, from which their guns could work; and before they could build these fortresses they had first to conquer the mountains. The Italian position was similar to that of the Franco-British position in Gallipoli; but on the Austrian mountain line the peaks were higher and steeper; the front was enormously larger, giving the enemy room for grand manœuvres; and on the fortresses on the mountain heights millions of pounds had been spent, and the labour of ten years crowned by the recent work of thousands of engineers, with full and exact knowledge of all the recent developments in artillery fire and modern earthwork fortifications.

Had General Cadorna only retained his opportunity for surprise, he would have launched by night some hundreds of thousands of men, with Maxims and 3 in. mountain guns, to attack the Austrian forces in the rear before they were fully garrisoned. But after the long delay imposed by Signor Giolitti, the Italian commander, at midnight on May 23, only sent out battalions of Alpine troops to seize any ridges not held in strength by the Austrians near their main position. There was no surprise whatever about this movement, for the Austrian batteries had begun to fire on Italian redoubts five hours before hostilities were declared to be opened. The Austrian chief of staff, General von Höfer, was amply prepared for every manœuvre by his opponent. He, however, made the mistake of despising the men brought up against him.

Thus it befell that the Archduke Eugene, with General von Höfer as his chief of staff, and Dankl as army commander in the Tirol, made the mistake of holding the first line on the Austrian frontier with a ridiculously small number of troops. The Alpini and the Bersaglieri, with some battalions of the line and some gendarmes, crossed the frontier soon after midnight at all the strategical points, and by a hundred swift, fierce little skirmishes, began to reverse the positions of Austria and Italy. Among the points occupied at a singularly small loss of life to the victors were the Montozzo Pass, 8,585 feet high, and the Tonale Pass, 6,180 feet high, leading into the western Tirol, and Ponte Caffaro, running into south-western Trentino; the ridge of Monte Baldo, extending northward for fifteen miles towards Arco and Rovereto in the southern Trentino; some of the heights giving westward towards Trent; all the valleys in the labyrinth of the Dolomite Alps, and footholds on the Alps of Carinthia.

It was nearly all done by bayonet fighting, after splendid mountaineering feats. The cyclist sharpshooters advanced in a straightforward manner up the mountain paths till they were greeted with musketry fire. They then sought more carefully for cover, pushing forward from rock and tree with their wings extending up the mountain sides, and there engaging any enemy skirmishers. Meanwhile the Alpine troops were climbing the mountain, by ways only known to themselves, over trackless screes and rocky falls, over glaciers and snowdrifts, and then descended the opposite slopes at some distance behind the enemy vanguards, skirmishing near the entrance to the path.

By the evening of May 25, all the passes of the Dolomite Alps were won, and good breaches were made at Tonale Pass along the north-west and in the Carnic and Julian Alps along the north-east front. The gun trains began to move more rapidly towards the holes made in the great mountain rampart, and tens of thousands of Italian engineers went up by train and motor-vehicles, and started building trenches and making gun emplacements. Simultaneously the main Italian infantry force, consisting of the 3rd army, moved with great speed across the Friuli plain through Udine, Palmanova, and St. Georgio, where two railway lines ran into the Isonzo valley and the Torre valley.

Here the covering troops had moved forward over the frontier at midnight on May 24, and in a single day they captured nearly all the towns and villages between the frontier and the Isonzo river, from Caporetto, nestling in the north below the precipices of Monte Nero, to the hamlet of Belvedere southward on the Gulf of Trieste. In this region the Italians had a strong fortress town, Palmanova, lying about fourteen miles west of the great Austrian fortress town of Gorizia, to guard against any irruption into the Venetian plain. But General von Höfer had abandoned

the direct attack through Gorizia, and had made a mo
scheme of campaign. All he did was to place a stro
on the mountain of Korada between the Isonzo river
Judrio. The mountain dominated the middle cours
Isonzo, and was transformed into a fortress with a ne
deep trenches protected by wide wire entanglements
reckoned that by the time the Italians brought the
artillery into play on the trenches and began to cut
wire with their field-guns, supports could easily be
forward across the Isonzo. The bayonets of Italy,
carried the position. This and other early frontier s
ended in successes of high strategical importance for th
troops, and the perturbed Austrians and Hungarians co
find no better reply than to drop bombs on Venice an
battleship or two to bombard the open town of Ancona

The skirmishing along the mountain frontier conti
the end of May, by which time, the forces attac
Trentino southward had crossed the Lessini mountains
Verona, and, penetrating nearly ten miles into Austrian
had taken the town of Ala and brought forward he
against the Rovereto forts. Further advances were a
in southern Trentino towards the towns at the head
Garda and along the Sugana valley towards Trent.
actions, however, formed only a holding movement.

It will be seen on the map (page 317) that the Austria
system spread like the five fingers of a hand southward
Trentino. These five railway lines were never des
ordinary traffic; they were intended to transport and
large Austro-Hungarian army, to leap on Verona an
rich, busy cities of Lombardy, thus beheading Italy b
off her chief centres of industry. Then, according
scheme, the Italians were to be allowed to approach t
line on the way to Trieste. But when they had be
volved in this operation and the two railway lines run
Venice were choked with their supplies, another larg
Hungarian army was to advance through the pass
Carnic Alps and through the Julian Alps from the c
camp of Tarvis, and by a quick southward swoop ta
flank the Italian forces on the Isonzo line.

All this was well-known to General Cadorna. It w
the reason for his drives at all the mountain passes

at all the strategical points, and by a hundred swift, fierce little skirmishes, began to reverse the positions of Austria and Italy. Among the points occupied at a singularly small loss of life to the victors were the Montozzo Pass, 8,585 feet high, and the Tonale Pass, 6,180 feet high, leading into the western Tirol, and Ponte Caffaro, running into south-western Trentino; the ridge of Monte Baldo, extending northward for fifteen miles towards Arco and Rovereto in the southern Trentino; some of the heights giving westward towards Trent; all the valleys in the labyrinth of the Dolomite Alps, and footholds on the Alps of Carinthia.

It was nearly all done by bayonet fighting, after splendid mountaineering feats. The cyclist sharpshooters advanced in a straightforward manner up the mountain paths till they were greeted with musketry fire. They then sought more carefully for cover, pushing forward from rock and tree with their wings extending up the mountain sides, and there engaging any enemy skirmishers. Meanwhile the Alpine troops were climbing the mountain, by ways only known to themselves, over trackless screes and rocky falls, over glaciers and snowdrifts, and then descended the opposite slopes at some distance behind the enemy vanguards, skirmishing near the entrance to the path.

By the evening of May 25, all the passes of the Dolomite Alps were won, and good breaches were made at Tonale Pass along the north-west and in the Carnic and Julian Alps along the north-east front. The gun trains began to move more rapidly towards the holes made in the great mountain rampart, and tens of thousands of Italian engineers went up by train and motor-vehicles, and started building trenches and making gun emplacements. Simultaneously the main Italian infantry force, consisting of the 3rd army, moved with great speed across the Friuli plain through Udine, Palmanova, and St. Georgio, where two railway lines ran into the Isonzo valley and the Torre valley.

Here the covering troops had moved forward over the frontier at midnight on May 24, and in a single day they captured nearly all the towns and villages between the frontier and the Isonzo river, from Caporetto, nestling in the north below the precipices of Monte Nero, to the hamlet of Belvedere southward on the Gulf of Trieste. In this region the Italians had a strong fortress town, Palmanova, lying about fourteen miles west of the great Austrian fortress town of Gorizia, to guard against any irruption into the Venetian plain. But General von Höfer had abandoned the direct attack through Gorizia, and had made a more subtle scheme of campaign. All he did was to place a strong force on the mountain of Korada between the Isonzo river and the Judrio. The mountain dominated the middle course of the Isonzo, and was transformed into a fortress with a network of deep trenches protected by wide wire entanglements. It was reckoned that by the time the Italians brought their heavy artillery into play on the trenches and began to cut up the wire with their field-guns, supports could easily be moved forward across the Isonzo. The bayonets of Italy, however, carried the position. This and other early frontier skirmishes ended in successes of high strategical importance for the Italian troops, and the perturbed Austrians and Hungarians could then find no better reply than to drop bombs on Venice and send a battleship or two to bombard the open town of Ancona.

The skirmishing along the mountain frontier continued till the end of May, by which time, the forces attacking the Trentino southward had crossed the Lessini mountains north of Verona, and, penetrating nearly ten miles into Austrian territory, had taken the town of Ala and brought forward heavy guns against the Rovereto forts. Further advances were also made in southern Trentino towards the towns at the head of Lake Garda and along the Sugana valley towards Trent. All these actions, however, formed only a holding movement.

It will be seen on the map (page 317) that the Austrian railway system spread like the five fingers of a hand southward down the Trentino. These five railway lines were never designed for ordinary traffic; they were intended to transport and supply a large Austro-Hungarian army, to leap on Verona and all the rich, busy cities of Lombardy, thus beheading Italy by cutting off her chief centres of industry. Then, according to this scheme, the Italians were to be allowed to approach the Isonzo line on the way to Trieste. But when they had become involved in this operation and the two railway lines running from Venice were choked with their supplies, another large Austro-Hungarian army was to advance through the passes of the Carnic Alps and through the Julian Alps from the entrenched camp of Tarvis, and by a quick southward swoop take in the flank the Italian forces on the Isonzo line.

All this was well-known to General Cadorna. It was indeed the reason for his drives at all the mountain passes, for each

CAMPAIGNS IN
TRENTINO
English Miles
0   5   10
Railways

pass was a Thermopylæ where a battalion with a couple of
quick-firing guns and half a dozen Maxims could hold back an
army corps for days. The Italian commander-in-chief, having
conquered practically all the enemy's first line along a front of
three hundred miles, waited to see in what sector the Austrian
pressure would be most strongly felt.

The answering thrust came at Monte Croce pass, in the Carnic
Alps, on May 29. It was a foggy day, and under cover of the
mist the enemy massed a strong force by the railway from
Villach and brought them to Mauthen, from which they made
five stubborn attempts to regain the pass. The Alpini and

Bersaglieri swept away each wave of assault by musketry and machine-gun fire at almost point-blank range; then, leaping up after the last attack, they drove the enemy down the valley at the point of the bayonet.

This was only the beginning of the battle of Monte Croce. Each side had large forces within call, and fed the troops up the valleys as the fighting-lines wasted. So the struggle continued day and night, while the Italian commander pushed over the neighbouring passes and strengthened himself for the great counter-attack. The height known as Freikofel, commanding the Plöcken plateau, near Monte Croce pass, was stormed on June 8 and the pass of Valentina and the pass of Oregione, 7,590 feet high, overlooking the wooded Gail valley, were taken.

The last pass was won by the Alpini who climbed over the white mass of Paralba and fought their way down to the high saddle. The Austrians brought up another army corps, and on the night of June 14 made a great attempt to break through the rampart of Italian valour and turn the Carnic Alps, according to design, into the gateway for a flank attack on the main Italian army. Oregione's saddle, the snowfields of Paralba, and all the peaks and wild ravines extending to Monte Croce and Freikofel were dappled with groups of fighting men, some shooting from rocky cover, others trying to get home with a bayonet charge delivered at close quarters from some fold in the limestone. On Paralba, some 8,840 feet high, the Austrian troops were on Italian territory; but they were soon caught on the flank and threatened towards the rear, and scattered towards the Steinwand, a mountain towering above the Gail valley.

In this area of war the Austrians had the advantage of possessing a railway running through the Drave valley, and approaching closer to the frontier rampart than the Italian railway system did. They could therefore bring up fresh troops with more speed. In the Gail valley they had a wide, long region in which they could mass without being seen; they had a good road to the mountains from Mauthen, while the Italians had only rough valley tracks. Nevertheless, the Italians kept the gateway to Venice firmly closed, while they attacked the enemy force on both flanks. These flanks consisted of the Tarvis system of fortresses on the right, lying round the Predil pass, and the Cortina d'Ampezzo pass on the left, running towards the Austrian railway at Toblach.

The beautiful village of Cortina, lying 4,000 feet high amid the most superb scenery in Europe, was captured by the army on the Cadore section of the front on May 30. Most of the fighting took place on the great northern mountain height, crowned by the glaciers and snow-fields of Tofana, and around the Cinque Torri, a line of apparently inaccessible peaks. By June 9 Falzarego pass was won, and in the closing battle, in which the enemy lost a gun, a footing was obtained on a very important strategical position, three miles beyond the pass, on the Sasso d'Istria, close to the point at which the Dolomite road bends southward through its ravine and goes in two tunnels under the mountains.

It was this great and rapid success that disturbed the Austrian commander, and made him anxious about the western defences of the Tirol; for at Falzarego and Sasso d'Istria the Italian troops were approaching the rear of the Col di Lana, and its neighbouring mountain masses on which the fortresses defending Cordevole valley were constructed. By a double flanking movement along the Cordevole river and the Dolomite road, the Cadore army had begun to extend in a pincer-like formation around one of the main Austrian systems of defence. General Dankl had to pour more troops and light artillery on to the Cadore front; for the Italian thrust up the Cordevole valley was the most dangerous threat to southern Austria.

At the end of the valley, across another range of mountains, was the wrist of the Austrian hand-like railway system that fed both the Trentino forces and the forces in the southern Tirol. If the wrist were cut by the army of Cadore all the lands between Switzerland and the Carnic Alps would be lost. The southern Tirol and the Trentino form a great mountain wedge thrust into the Italian plain : but General Cadorna rightly decided that a thrust at the eastern base of the salient towards the only trunk line feeding the army of General Dankl would make the enemy so alarmed about his own safety that he would not think of erupting into the plain. The Austrians had only to advance some twenty miles across their Trentino frontier to reach Verona; Brescia was still nearer, with all the fertile, busy plain of Lombardy extending around. The conquest of Verona was largely a matter of heavy siege-guns, but it was General Cadorna who chiefly determined where most of these great hostile weapons should be used. Many of them were placed with great labour on the Cadore front, because the Italian pressure there was very severe. Many of them were also sited behind the Carnic and Julian Alps, especially in the corner near Predil pass; then the Isonzo front, between Tolmino and the Adriatic, needed more heavy guns for its defence. In the end none remained for any movement into Italy.

This was very important, because for a considerable time the Italian artilleryman fought at a disadvantage. To say that his guns and mortars were unequal to those of his opponent is to understate the case; the Austrians' heavy gun—the big Skoda— was the finest in the world. It had done much of the work of fortress smashing in Belgium and Russia, and the fact that the Austrians were in a position to lend heavy artillery to their allies for use on the western front is an indication of the wealth of big-gun power in Austria. And after ten months of war, when the great howitzers were being employed by the thousand in Galicia and along the Danube, the Skoda works could still produce an armament superior to that of Italy. Besides the 12 in. Skoda, with its extraordinary handiness, due to its consisting of two separate parts easily hauled along, and its magnificent force and precision, there were great and still increasing numbers of the new 6 in. Skoda, a gun designed at first, in the summer of 1914, for mountain warfare in the Carpathlans.

To meet this offensive the Italians had to create at top speed a new armament. They took as their field-gun the French 75 mm. quick-firer, newly improved by its inventor, Colonel Déport, and they built 6 in. and 12 in. howitzers for attacking the Austrian forts. But an army of a million men needs 4,000 guns, and the twenty-five Italian army corps required also several siege trains of great power. This ordnance could not be turned out in a year, even with help from other countries, and Italy, without coalfields, was not a steel-making nation.

So in spite of all the speeding up of production, the Italian armies entered on the war at a disadvantage. Their great peril was that an enormous quantity of heavy Austrian artillery might be released in the eastern theatre of war, by a decision against the Russians, and brought up against them.

For political reasons, too, General Cadorna could not afford to sacrifice his men in offensive movements costing 50,000 men a day, even with a view to reaching Trieste. Much less could

EARL KITCHENER AT THE FRONT. From 1914 onwards the secretary for war, took the greatest interest in the military operations in France, and paid repeated visits to the Allied G.H.Q. Here he is seen watching the effect of French shell fire.

BRITISH AT ARTOIS. The illustration shows a determined attack by British troops on a German trench in the prolonged fighting in May–July, 1915, to which the name battle of Artois is sometimes given. In the main it was a French offensive, but valuable assistance was given to their ally by the British under Sir John French.

Plate 34   *Volume II*

he contemplate doing it in order to attain some key position
in the mountain ramparts. His problem was to conserve his
forces for a possible, and sometimes probable, defensive campaign against mighty Teutonic forces, and meanwhile win
victories and keep his casualty lists low, while fighting heavy
howitzers with light mountain guns and 3 in. quick-firers.

It was a very difficult programme to carry out, but the
Italian commander at least equalled the achievement of General
Joffre and Sir John French under the similar conditions of a
parallel battle. The forces opposed to him were smaller than
those entrenched against the French and British troops. The
Austrians, Hungarians, and Bavarians on the Italian front seem
to have numbered 300,000, at first, increasing towards the autumn
to 700,000. But on a line of three hundred miles, walled in everywhere by great mountains, entrenched hill camps, and fortressed
plateaux, like the Carso, the actual fighting density of the
enemy troops was not much less at last than that of the Germans
on the Franco-Flemish front; in fact, the points of incessant
conflict in Italy may in the end have been more crowded.

Yet all the first striking successes by Cadorna, between the
last week in May, 1915, and the third week in August, 1915,
were accomplished with a total casualty list of less than 30,000.
The Austro-Hungarian losses in the same period on the same
front were 18,000 dead, 54,000 wounded, and 18,000 prisoners.
This is a very striking result, especially having regard to the
fact that the Italian troops were continually attacking fortified
mountain positions at a time when only part of their new
artillery was available. General Cadorna told his men that they
won their successes because they fought in a more scientific
manner than their foes. And this was no inspiriting flattery.

All the long series of small but highly important frontier
victories were won by light Italian troops, composed mostly of
Alpini, cavalry, cyclists, the Bersaglieri, and batteries of horse
artillery. On the Venetian plain, by the Lower Isonzo, a few
thousand men in two days conquered with little loss all the
territory which Prince von Bülow had offered the Italian nation
as the grudged price of her permanent neutrality.

After these troops had swiftly won the first round in the
Austro-Italian struggle, there was an apparent relaxation of
effort while the infantry of the line waited for their heavy siege
artillery to come into action. This was mainly a matter of

engineering, especially on the Isonzo front, where the river was in high summer flood owing to the melting of the snow on the mountain-tops. Bridging skill of an unusual kind was needed to get the new siege-guns across the floods, at the places where small bodies of the advanced troops were furiously holding bridge-heads on the enemy's side of the swollen waters. Along the Isonzo the retreating Austrians had broken down the high embankment used to carry off the snow-water, and had thereby inundated the plain in the manner of the Belgian Yser defences.

The gallant Italian sappers, working under a plunging fire from the enemy's batteries had rapidly thrown some light pontoon bridges over the flood. Along these frail temporary structures the first Italian contingents crossed in the darkness, took the first line of Austrian trenches near the waterside, and broke up the light artillery positions close to the river. But this was the utmost that could be done to prepare the way for the attack on the enemy's last systems of hill and mountain fortifications, and it was accomplished by the first week in June, 1915.

But though the enemy's main positions could not be assailed until the infantry of the line advanced with heavy guns, those troops on the Lower Isonzo made a happy stroke in a south-westerly direction in June. By the edge of the sea, just below a dominating height on the Carso tableland, was the seaport of Monfalcone, once belonging to Venice, but stolen from her by the Austrians in the Napoleonic era. Monfalcone had become the third most important port in Austria-Hungary, and at its yards, Cantiere Navale, warships were still being built for the Dual Monarchy. Monfalcone was only sixteen miles from Trieste, though the road and railway tracks by the sea were impracticable for an advance in force.

Monfalcone itself had been bombarded by the Italian fleet on May 30, when a chemical factory, in which asphyxiating gases were being made, was destroyed. The bombardment was continued by light cruiser squadrons on June 7. Then the Castle of Duino, the magnificent residence of the Hohenlohe family, standing on the edge of the sea, nearer Trieste, and defended by three batteries of artillery, was shattered and set on fire, in order apparently to prepare for operations against Monfalcone from the south-western side in the Gulf of Panzano. The design was to threaten an advance on Trieste by the sea-road leading down through the famous pleasure palace of Miramar. The destruction of Prince Hohenlohe's castle was calculated to make the Archduke Eugene anxious about the probable line of Italian advance. Some of his troops were therefore collected hastily, but in strong force, above Duino, in preparation against an Italian landing; but not an Italian landed. It was all a feint.

The attack on Monfalcone was launched from the opposite quarter, in a straightforward direction across the Isonzo, on June 8. Only the light troops—Bersaglieri, cyclists' corps, and grenadiers—were employed, but they broke the enemy's river-line at a point where it was considered impregnable. Then, as the over-confident enemy had prepared no line of retirement between the river and the plateau, Monfalcone was won in a rapid running fight through the villages around the Isonzo delta. Close to the hamlet of Aquileia the passage of the Isonzo was forced by a smashing bayonet attack, and the Italian troops, headed by motor-cyclists with machine-guns, cycling scouts, and aeroplane observers, flowed in two arms around every position at which the Austrians tried to make a stand. By this continual threat of an encircling movement they forced the Austrians into Monfalcone. The enemy then set fire to some of the slopes which the Italians were attacking. But while the pine-wood near Monfalcone flared to the skies, the quick-manœuvring Italians, headed by a battalion of grenadiers broke into the open town and occupied it, after storming the Rocca promontory.

Since the seaport reposed at the foot of the Carso plateau, with two large clumps of limestone, rising a thousand feet above the streets on the northern side, the enemy's heavy artillery on the heights had the power of turning the town into a shambles: but the Bersaglieri, grenadiers, and sharpshooters were not disposed to see the famous city they had captured ruined by 6 in. high-explosive shell. Moreover there were some warships lying in the shipyards in various stages of construction, and the Italians wanted to complete and gun these ships, and employ them. So the conquest of Monfalcone was completed by the brigade of light troops climbing up the limestone cliffs and hauling their 3 in. guns after them. With these they induced the enemy to drag his howitzers farther away from the seashore; and the town was won.

All went well during the week following the capture of Monfalcone. General Cadorna had the keen joy of recapturing the

Isonzo town of Gradisca, which his father had won from the same foe forty-nine years before. The capture of Gradisca on June 9 completed the Italian control of the Lower Isonzo, and the general attack on all the fortresses guarding Trieste was then prepared. Of these fortresses four were of supreme importance. On the south was the Carso tableland, immediately defending Trieste. Between this tableland and the foothills of the Julian Alps was the river-valley of the Vipacco, barring which was the fortress system of the cathedral city of Gorizia. Then north of Gorizia was a fortified system of heights round the Isonzo town of Tolmino, and above Tolmino was the vast entrenched camp of Tarvis, that extended to Malborghetto and other Alps of Carinthia. It was useless to mass an army against any one of these fortress systems. Had an attempt been made to win Trieste across the Carso tableland, the advancing forces would have been cut on the northern flank from the Gorizia area. It was also useless to attack merely the Carso and Gorizia. A well-defended advance towards Trieste could only be undertaken by using another large force in thrusting at Tolmino and the Tarvis fortresses, by which ran the road to Vienna.

In the centre of this long fortress-line was the railway town of Plava, lying on the eastern bank of the Isonzo, beneath the wooded heights of Ternovane forest. Plava, with its tunnels and entrenched heights, moated by the flooded river, formed the point of the middle Austrian salient. In short, it was a key position, and the general Italian offensive began by a night attack on Plava, from Mount Korada on the other side of the river. The Italian sappers, with great coolness and skill, built a pontoon bridge in the darkness; and the infantry crossed the water on June 17, and by a violent bayonet attack carried the town and the surrounding heights. Only by the most stubborn valour did the Italian troops overcome the tremendous difficulties of the position, and win a further foothold on the thickly-wooded heights. The Austrians returned with strong reinforcements, but the Italian general, having breached the enemy's second line in this place, poured strong forces into the gap, and a great battle took place on the edge of the forested highland. The local conditions were in favour of the Austrian army, for its forces could be massed amid the screen of trees where no Italian airmen could spy them. On the other hand, the Italian heavy artillery across the river on Mount Korada was able to send a plunging fire on the lower tableland, and with this help the dashing Italian troops drove the enemy back.

At the same time, the Hill of Podgora, directly covering Gorizia, and forming the barbican of the defence system of the city, was assailed, and a strong reconnoitring force advanced towards Mount Fortin. Then, with five hundred guns massed against the defences of Gorizia, the first great Italian offensive move was made. Cadorna wanted to discover exactly the enemy's new lines of defence and the new position of his heavy mobile artillery.

The Italian infantry of the line charged here with superb intrepidity, and penetrated both the northern and the southern entrenchments. These extended over a front of more than ten miles from San Gabriele Mount, below Plava, to San Michele Mount on the Carso tableland. The trenches were built in the latest German style, with concrete more than a yard in thickness and armour plate cover, so that not only was shrapnel futile, but even ordinary sized high-explosive shell did little or no damage. Bayonet and rifle also were of no avail in an assault; the lines had to be won and retained by hand-bombs and short knives. The Italian attack would have been a complete check, if the enemy had been content with having repulsed the four army corps operating under the duke of Aosta, between Gorizia and the sea; but the comparative ease with which the assault had been beaten back led the Archduke Eugene to take the offensive in turn. Therefore, as soon as the Italian attacking forces slackened, the main Austrian army advanced in full force across the Carso plateau.

Thus began the first great open field battle between the Italians and the Austrians. It opened on June 22, and it was not ended by July 6. The Austrian position had been found impregnable by the forces of the Italian commander, for the 500 guns which the Italian general employed were quite inadequate. The ground was unassailable. The Carso is a tableland of broken rock rising in places to a thousand feet, and almost uninhabited in peace time. It is dotted with trees, seamed with deep, narrow, winding gullies, with a few larger ravines, that resemble the picturesque limestone valleys of the Peak district in Derbyshire. Owing to the action of rain on the limestone the plateau is pitted with funnel-shaped holes, which form natural machine-gun redoubts. But General Boroevics lost all the natural advantages of this immense natural fortress when he sent his divisions charging across the open ground against the lines to which the Italians were clinging; for though the Italians only held on to the rim of the tableland with a flooded river a third of a mile broad beneath them, yet their well-built sand-bag trenches gave them excellent cover against the enemy's artillery. There seem to have been at first only a few 12 in. Austrian howitzers, the greater number of these heavy pieces having been diverted to the Carnic Alps line and the Tirol and Trentino salients. Though the 6 in. pieces were numerous, the heavier Italian guns across the river could search out the batteries, and every conceivable form of attack by infantry was repulsed.

By the second week in July, however, none of the conquered ground was wrested from the Italian army; and as soon as the enemy relaxed his efforts, the Italians began to work up the fortified hills overlooking Gorizia by means of sharp, dashing attacks with bayonet and bomb. In the cultivated ground the siege method of sapping forward could be practised; but on the bare rock dynamite was needed to excavate a trench, and the charging soldiers had to carry sand-bags to make temporary cover from machine-gun fire. This extraordinary kind of trench-making was indeed the general feature of warfare along the three hundred miles of mountain front, for though the rocky masses changed from limestone to granite, gneiss, and other kinds of hard stone, the depth of loose earth was usually small, and sand-bags had to serve as a defence until the engineering corps blasted channels and galleries up and down the slopes.

The first phase of the battle for Gorizia ended in the repulse of the Austrian counter-attack in the middle of July. General Cadorna then delivered a fiercer assault, based on the knowledge he had obtained by his first reconnaissance in force. For three days and nights—July 18, 19, and 20—the troops of the Italian 2nd and 3rd armies leaped forward all along the zone of the Isonzo, and broke through the wire entanglements and the armoured trenches, taking 3,500 prisoners.

The next morning General Cadorna stayed the forward movement of the Duke of Aosta, and bringing reinforcements, ordered every man to help the engineers in strengthening and extending the trenches; for the commander, either through his aerial observers or his secret agents, had obtained knowledge that the enemy was about to make a supreme effort. July 21 passed quietly; then, on July 22, a mightier concentration of heavy Austrian artillery opened a hurricane fire on the Italian lines. A large number of German gunners had been sent to the Carso and the railways from Trieste and Laibach were used to their utmost capacity in bringing up shells.

The main infantry attack was delivered towards Gradisca, where the Italians had built their chief bridges across the Isonzo. The design, of course, was to cut the Italian line of communications, interrupt their supplies of ammunition, and destroy or capture their forces on the tableland. Under cover of the bombardment the Austrian infantry advanced in close formation, after massing behind the neighbouring hills. The first line of Italian troops could not kill the close-packed lines of the foe quickly enough, and it seemed as though the position would be lost.

But the Italian gunnery officers, watching the operation from their observing-posts, had the situation well in hand, and at the critical moment a storm of shrapnel from 500 guns and howitzers fell on the large target in front of the first Italian line, and made such holes in it that the garrison of the fire-trench beat back the remnant of the attacking masses with little difficulty; and soon after they had stopped the great charge, they received, owing to the excellence of the Italian staff work, a strong reinforcement. The troops then charged the shattered ranks of the enemy, captured the lines from which they had delivered the assault, and took 2,000 prisoners.

The next day the Austrians launched another strong attack on the Italian positions near the sea-edge of the Carso tableland. This was an attempt to recover Monfalcone, but it failed completely, though the rough ground did not permit the Italians to make another fierce pursuit. Finally two Austrian divisions, which advanced from the heights of San Michele and San Martino to storm Sagrado, were so smashed up that, on July 25, the Italian troops were able to carry some of the entrenched slopes of San Martino, and to storm the hill of Sei Busi. Monte Sei Busi, with its seven caverns, was the scene of one of the most violent contests on the whole front, for in a single day it was won, and lost, and won again.

The crest of San Michele dominated a large part of the table-land, and the main tide of battle surged around and over it for many days. At last the Italian infantry, on July 27, bombed and bayoneted their way to the summit, along which they then tried to establish themselves, but under the torrent of high-explosive and asphyxiating shell the crest and the exposed slopes beneath it could not be garrisoned. All the fighting was an affair of artillery, with thousands of machine-guns serving as secondary armament. In the defence, especially, the infantry was a force only of the third order, and the commanding Austrian, Archduke Eugene, employed on the Isonzo front some hundreds of thousands of Slav and Italian troops, natives of the ancient Venetian territories which Italy was fighting to recover.

Like the grand drive of the Franco-British forces at Massiges and Loos, the Italian offensive on the Gorizia failed to break the enemy's resistance. Fighting went on night and day, with violent offensives and counter-attacks. By the middle of November, 1915, the situation on the Carso tableland resembled that in Champagne. The enemy had been driven back to his last line, and had been compelled to bring up half a million more troops. Having, however, won time to recover from the blow which he had received, General Boroevics constructed another system of lines behind the Doberdo plateau. To all appearance the Italian army, like the Franco-British forces on the western front, was in a position of stalemate. But the Italian soldier, like the French and British soldier, did not believe that this state of things was permanent. He had clearly shown such a marked personal ascendancy over his foe that he confidently waited for more guns, more shells, and a large store of stupefying gas, so that he could balance the enemy's extraordinary machinery of warfare, and then engage in a decisive hand-to-hand struggle in the fortress from which the road branched to Trieste and Vienna.

During this pause, the wildly picturesque work of Alpine warfare went on in the Julian, Carnic, Dolomite, Trentino, and Tirolean mountains. In the Julian Alps the fighting mountaineers of Italy had a startling stroke of luck in the first phase of the struggle. From an order issued by the Austrian commander, General Rohr, it appears that two of his companies were set to guard a formidable rampart of rock between Tolmino and Monte Nero. The position was one which five hundred men, with Maxims and quick-firers, could easily have held against an army corps. But the strength of the cliff of rock was so apparent that the Austrian troops took their duties very lightly. Leaving a few men at the post of observation, both companies used to sleep at night. The Alpini clambered over the mountain in the darkness, killed the watchmen silently with the knife, and then dropped in the rear of the two sleeping companies and captured them, so making a breach in the approaches to the entrenched camp of Tarvis.

The Italian siege-guns were able to use the peak of Monte Nero, which is a mountain in the form of a stump 7,370 feet high, as a fire-control station from which the 12 in. shells of their howitzers were pitched into the Tolmino forts, and the southern section of the Tarvis forts such as Flitsch, or Plezzo in Italian, a picturesque village only a few miles south of the famous pass of Predil, and connecting with it by an easy highway. Plezzo valley, where the Austrians had a mobile battery, was surrounded by a series of brilliant infantry actions in the mountains. At the western end of the great ring of fortified heights, barring the Predil pass and the highway and railway running into the heart of Austria, was Malborghetto. The Malborghetto forts formed a mountain salient in Italian territory, and the chief works, such as Fort Hensel—a great white oblong of armoured concrete—could be plainly seen from the Italian mountains. The Italians quickly brought their heaviest howitzers against the Malborghetto system, and reduced Fort Hensel and other permanent works to the same condition as that to which the Skoda guns had reduced the Liège forts.

This work of destruction, however, went on very slowly; for the high Alps, over which the shells had to be sent, were usually either veiled in mist or curtained by falling rain. Rare were the days when the air was clear and the observation officers could watch every shot and telephone the gunners what allowance they had to make for the winds above the mountains. When the forts were destroyed the work of the Italian artillery became more difficult. The enemy brought up batteries of new 12 in. guns, which were hidden on what is properly known as an Alp, that is a stretch of pasture-land, well below the summit, and covered with snow in winter, but used for pasturing cattle in the short summer. The guns were placed in tufted pits and their muzzles concealed from reconnoitring airmen, while dummy wooden guns were partly displayed at a safe distance in order to draw the enemy's fire. The heavy artillery on both sides could easily pitch a huge shell over the highest peak.

Close above the Tonale pass gleams one of the greatest glacier systems in Europe. The vast crown of ice extends from Alp to Alp for more than twenty miles. The broadest part is that which stretches for some six miles to Monte Adamello, 11,640 feet high. There are several easy paths over or by the glaciers, and the Alpini had seized and fortified these, but as they were watching the Austrian valleys eastward, while the infantry of the line hauled up big guns to dominate western Trentino, a force of the Tirolean mountaineers, in mid-July, 1915, came over the glaciers by a new track, and penetrated a few miles into Italian territory. At the well-known Garibaldi Hut, belonging to the Italian Alpine Club, there was a fight just beneath the Adamello, and the Tirolese were thrown back. They retained some peaks from which the Garibaldi Hut was afterwards shelled, but the intended threat of an invasive movement towards Lombardy was reduced to the shadow of a little Alpine skirmish.

Just north of the ice-capped Alps of the Adamello group was the upper part of the lovely Giudicaria valley, that runs by the fruitful lands of Lake Garda. The Italian troops seized here one of the northern passes by a surprise attack and worked forward towards the forts defending Riva and Arco. All the country south of the Ledro valley was gradually won by fierce artillery actions amid the mountains and densely wooded slopes, the duels between the Austrian forts and the mobile Italian batteries being followed by infantry attacks. A striking victory, which had decisive consequence, was the attack on Pregasina, by the edge of Lake Garda, which was undertaken in bad weather in the second week in October, 1915.

A similar movement of advance went on at the same time along the eastern lands of Lake Garda and down the Lagarina valley. As October closed, forces on either side of the lake were pressing on Riva and battering its fortified heights and bombarding the defences of Rovereto, which barred the road to Trent. Brezzecca, taken on October 22, 1915, was a place sacred to the memory of Garibaldi's exploits in 1866, and the joy of wresting this storied paradise from the ancient oppressors was felt by every Italian soldier. In some places the largest siege-guns were pulled to the tops of mountains by human force. The Austrians, it is said, tried to do the same thing; but after getting a 12 in. Skoda gun half-way up a mountain they had to let it down again. Probably not since the Pyramids were built have human hands successfully tugged at such gigantic weights as the hardy peasantry of Italy, Sardinia, and Sicily lifted at need a mile above sea level. The small guns were raised two miles above the sea by means of hand ropes, and by the same primitive method large stores of shells and provisions were hoisted above the clouds into the region of everlasting snow. Fuel was hauled up, and tools and dynamite for making caves in which to live in Eskimo fashion, when the valleys far below were still sweltering in heat. This work went on in the Dolomite maze, north-west of the Lake Garda region. There, on the western front of the Trentino and the Tirol, the Italian forces were thrusting against a series of vital points, along the Trent, Bozen, and Innsbruck railway line.

Trent was approached from the south by way of Riva, but the main advance was made along the Sugana valley. The Italians had advanced very rapidly down this famous valley, till in a few weeks they were east of Roncogno, and barely twelve miles from Trent. But the forts of Cantangel and the mobile siege-guns brought up by rail checked the advance, and the Austrian gunners distinguished themselves by an act of cruelty. They shelled the alarmed Italian population of the village beyond Roncogno.

The Bozen section of railway was menaced by the more northerly thrust along the Cordevole valley and the connecting swoop from the Cortina region, the first striking incidents of which we have already described. When General Dankl was strongly reinforced from the Serbian and Russian fronts, the Austrians made a very gallant and adventurous attempt to out-flank the advanced Italian position. A considerable force of Tirolean mountaineers climbed over the enormous masses of Mount Tofana, and on a great line of bastion crags, rising two miles above sea-level, there was a long, fierce struggle between large detachments of Alpine troops. It was a more important affair than the battle on the Adamello glaciers, and for some months the conflict went on at this extraordinary altitude. But the Italian Alpini proved themselves the better fighters, and by their powers of endurance, as well as by their skill in shooting, they cleared the larger part of the Tofana range, threw the enemy back towards Bruneck, and built a line of blockhouses.

In these little forts men had somehow to live in winter, when even on the lower passes there was a depth of ten to twelve yards of snow. It was also in this region of mountain warfare, where the Italians were curving round their enemy by the new Dolomite road, that a most remarkable example of engineering warfare was seen. A grandson of Garibaldi was colonel of a regiment which was trying to connect from the south with the forces advancing along the Dolomite road. One of the chief obstacles between the two tips of the Italian crescent was the rocky mass of the Col di Lana. This mountain, only 8,000 feet high, commanded a superb view, and for this reason it was an object of desire to the fire-control officers of the contending armies. In their first dash the Italians had reached the western slopes; but the Austrian engineers redeemed the faults of their commander on the Dolomite front by making the Col di Lana a perfect work of military art. A system of trenches and galleries began on the eastern slopes and wound in a spiral up the height, so that the Italians at the western foot were completely mastered. If they tried to charge up the steep, an avalanche of rock would fall on them. This avalanching method of re-pelling an Alpine attack had been elaborated by both sides. Masses of rock were drilled, filled with sticks of dynamite and other explosives, with an electric detonator which an observation officer could fire when he thought the enemy were clustered sufficiently thickly on the lower slopes.

The hand-bomb and the heavy high-explosive shell were use-less against the Austrian Col di Lana works, which had been excavated deeply in the solid rock. Colonel Garibaldi met this marvellous system of defence by engaging corps of skilled engineers, who had helped to drill and blast the great railway tunnels on the Swiss frontier. Under his direction, they tun-nelled right through the mountain into the Austrian galleries low down on the reverse slope where a hostile battery was working. When the fumes of the last blast of dynamite cleared away, a strong force of bombers leaped from the jagged hole at the end of the tunnel, cleared all the neighbouring galleries, and then, constantly fed by supports, smashed their way up and down the mountain.

CHAPTER 18

Russian Retreat from Galicia

A FTER the fall of Przemsyl, in June, 1915, the strength of
the German attacking forces became clearly apparent
to the Russians. At first the Russian general staff
thought that Mackensen's success was due to the fact that
Dmitrieff had been over-confident and had omitted to prepare
adequate positions on which to retire if he failed to hold
his line. This belief cost Dmitrieff his command, but the
threat to the whole of the Russian forces in Galicia was due
to something far more serious than the failure of one general.
The Central Powers had massed along the Galician front,
under the command of General Mackensen, every man and
gun they could spare from the west, and the Russians had
not sufficient armaments to withstand so furious an onslaught.
In the existing circumstances they had put up a remarkably
fine stand, but their armies in Poland and in East Galicia
had been compelled to fall back in conformity with Dmitrieff's
retreat, and there was no possibility of a big counter-attack.

The position of the combined German and Austrian forces
early in June was as follows: the army of the Archduke
Joseph Ferdinand was held along the lower San; Mackensen's
army was advancing east of Jaroslav along the railway towards
Rava Russka. Böhm Ermolli's army—mainly Austro-Hungarian
—was fighting on the road to Lemberg, at the town of Mosciska.
An army under Count Bothmer was working near the Dniester
marshes. Beyond these marshes in the south a group of armies
under Linsingen—mainly German in composition—had forced
the passage of the Dniester at Zuravno, and was trying to
advance on Lemberg and take on the flank General Ivanoff's
main forces. Then in the Bukovina the army of General
Pflanzer was fighting on the Pruth river and trying to connect
with Linsingen's right wing and take part in a flanking movement, which aimed at enveloping the southern Russian army.

The problem facing General Ivanoff was not an easy one.
Considerable reinforcements had been sent to the Russian

armies in Galicia from the north, and the Central Powers had also to reckon with what had always been a feature of Russian strategy—the sudden abandonment of large stretches of territory. An attempt by the Austro-German forces to recover Lemberg by a direct march from the south was held up by Brusiloff, who still held the Dniester and had been considerably reinforced. His resistance to the enemy advance would only have been effective if Mackensen's advance had been checked. But constantly reinforced and fully supplied with high explosives, Mackensen continued to advance, the failure of the Russians to make adequate preparations for a possible retreat having made his task far easier than it might have been. Mackensen's army was the spear-head of the Austro-German thrust, and the armies operating on his flanks had to wait until he had turned the Russian position before they could advance.

This Mackensen did in the battle of the Lubaczovka. The Lubaczovka is a tributary of the San, flowing down from the range of hills between Rava Russka and Lemberg. It is crossed near Jaroslav by a highway that runs in a north-easterly direction into the Lublin province of Russia; it is also crossed by a railway running to Rava Russka and the Russian frontier. Mackensen sent his heavy artillery along both the high road and the railway, and General Ivanoff concentrated against him along the river front and offered battle.

The struggle lasted more than a week. Mackensen, having at least half a million men arranged in échelon formation, brought them up group after group and flung them against the Russian river front. Each assault was prepared by the fire of thousands of guns, that hurled asphyxiating bombs as well as high-explosive shell and shrapnel on the Russian trenches. The Russian troops showed extraordinary endurance, but they were gradually worn down by the succession of fresh forces brought against them. They had no rest day or night for more than a week, while Mackensen's units had each some days of respite from fighting after they had delivered their attack and been withdrawn into reserve. Sheer physical exhaustion at last incapacitated the Russian infantry. On June 13 Mackensen was reinforced by fresh troops. They broke through the Russian lines west of the town of Lubaczov and began a rapid advance in a northerly direction. The Russian infantry was entirely exhausted. It had been fighting for ninety-six hours without relief, and the men had not enough strength left to march.

But at this moment General Polodchenko rode out with three regiments of cavalry—the Don Cossacks, the Kinburn dragoons, and the Chernigov hussars. These cavalrymen charged the unbroken lines of victorious German infantry, sabred them and put them to flight, and then galloped deep into the German rear, shook the enemy reserves and captured five machine-guns. The losses of the dragoons, hussars, and Cossacks only amounted to two hundred killed and wounded, but the force of their unexpected blow was such that it entirely checked the advance of the German army; for Mackensen made no further attack that day on the exhausted Russian infantry, and the Russian commander was able to withdraw with his front unbroken towards the hills near Rava Russka.

While the Russian commander had been contesting Mackensen's advance between Jaroslav and Rava Russka, the armies on his right and left had more than held their own, but as Mackensen drove onwards they had to be weakened in order to strengthen the Rava Russka front. Both had to give ground. This weakening of the Russian position was to some extent counterbalanced by a judicious choice of ground for the next battle. Between Przemysl and Lemberg was the famous lake line of Grodek, formed by a river running from north to south and flowing into the marshes of the Dniester. On a miniature scale the ground resembled that of the Masurian Lakes, and as the weather was very rainy the watery stretches and green swamps over which only four tracks ran, two of these being railway lines, needed but few men for their defence.

About ten miles north of Grodek the approaches to Lemberg were protected by entrenched hills extending to Rava Russka. It was the firm stretch of fairly level ground round the town of Janov, north of the lake system and south of the hill country, which formed the weak point in the new Russian position. This stretch of open country had been seamed with trenches and hedged with wire entanglements, and the troops brought from other parts of the front were massed there. Janov was also connected by railway with the depot at Rovno, and armoured trains with quick-firing guns were prepared for action.

But though the new Russian lines were marked by many unusual features of natural strength, General Ivanoff no longer thought of attempting to make any decisive stand against Mackensen's march. He did not intend to risk his armies in a battle for Lemberg. Lemberg was a city of both military and political importance. From the military point of view it was highly valuable as a great railway centre, from which a web of railway lines radiated in all directions. From a political point of view the loss of the capital of Galicia would be a severe blow to the prestige of Russia, would check the action of the Rumanians, and strengthen the German intrigues in Bulgaria and Greece. Lemberg certainly was worth fighting for, and if Ivanoff had had the guns he would have fought for it. But after the trial of strength with Mackensen on the San and at Lubaczov the Russian commander resolved that every apparent stand he made should be only a rearguard action on an important scale.

Though his army continued to fight with great fierceness, fighting was only the smaller part of the work of the troops. Their most laborious task was that of making new field fortifications, step by step, every few miles beyond their front, from the Bug to the Dniester. At every three to five miles the ground was broken by battle lines which showed where each wave of the slowly-advancing flood of invasion was temporarily checked. General Ivanoff, by means of his extraordinary series of defensive operations, reduced to a war of attrition the campaign intended to break him. At every three or five miles of his retreat he engaged the enemy forces and fought them until Mackensen brought his siege artillery into action. It was indeed at these times that the Russians got the opportunity of more than balancing their losses from gun fire, by a succession of swift, punishing counter-strokes. In the battle for Lemberg General Ivanoff only stayed long enough on his line of lakes and hills to take toll of the enemy's forces.

There was especially a furious battle near Komarno, where an advance of Böhm Ermolli's army was beaten back by the Russian artillery about June 18, and for the next three days there was a fierce struggle between the Austrian troops and the Russian forces holding the lakes. The Austrian attacks were broken in spite of the terrific bombardment that heralded every infantry advance. The Austrians were repulsed on the river, the Russian infantry there being unexpectedly assisted by an excellent supply of both light and heavy shells that were sent by rail down from Kieff.

It was Mackensen who again came to the help of the Austrians. He had made a great turning movement in the region of Zolkiev, some seventeen miles north of Lemberg. He first attacked the Russian positions in the open country round Janov, and forced the Russians there across the hills and across the Rava Russka railway to Zolkiev. At the same time his left wing, which had been resting on the former battlefield of Lubaczov, tried to swing farther northward in a wheeling movement round and above Rava Russka. This wing movement was defeated in a series of terrible contests that ended in the Germans being flung back towards Lubaczov. But Mackensen's centre was so strong that it was impossible to arrest its advance except by a pitched battle. This General Ivanoff was determined to avoid. So he slowly gave ground on the hill line between Rava Russka and Lemberg, and withdrawing his troops from the city he allowed the Austrian army, operating from the south under Böhm Ermolli, to recapture the capital of Galicia.

Sufficient resistance, however, was maintained against all the enemy forces to enable the city to be completely cleared of all war material. The stores were sent by railway into Russia or conveyed by long strings of carts behind the retreating armies. The main body of the troops about Lemberg withdrew towards the river line of the Bug, while strong rearguards held up the enemy in the regions of Rava Russka, Zolkiev, and Bobrka. Böhm Ermolli, emboldened by the ease with which he had taken Lemberg, tried to follow up the retreating Russians along the railway lines. But the Russians violently counter-attacked his forces in the region south-east of Lemberg, and there broke another of his divisions which was trying to connect with the German armies on the Dniester.

On the same date Mackensen's army was also attacked between Zolkiev and Rava Russka. Around Rava Russka the Russians brought an armoured train into action in an unexpected manner and broke a German division with the help of its quick-firing guns, making two thousand Germans prisoner and capturing a number of their machine-guns. This series of rearguard actions checked the enemy's advance and enabled the southern Russian army, which had been holding the Dniester line, to avoid being outflanked.

After the fall of Lemberg most of the weight of the enemy's attacks fell upon the forces under General Brusiloff. All through the war Brusiloff had never been defeated. It was he who had done most of the work in capturing Lemberg in September, 1914, and it was his troops that had stormed the rampart of the Carpathians and invaded the Hungarian plain. Even when he had been compelled to retire from the mountain line to the Dniester front, he had trapped Linsingen's army and had put at least half of its effectives out of action. His last great victory at Zuravno had been achieved just after the loss of Przemysl by Ivanoff's troops at the beginning of June. All the next week he fought back the armies of Bothmer, Linsingen, and Pflanzer along the Dniester, from Zuravno to Nizniov, and along the Pruth river through Bukovina to the Russian frontier.

There was a string of battles along a front of 150 miles, following the intricate course of the Dniester and its southern tributary streams. In many places the main river flowed in a large volume of water between high bluffs, making long, winding turns, with only a narrow neck of high land between the eastern and western channels. The Russian troops entrenched with artillery across the neck of each bend. The enemy threw his forces over the river in the unoccupied part of the loop, with the result that this force broke against the Russian position, and was thrown back in disorder to the bank of the river.

There were battles in forests, battles on the edge of the marshland, battles on the river cliffs, and at the towns where the railway lines from Hungary crossed the stream. All the battles ended in the same way—few of the enemy troops that crossed the river returned to their main armies, for Brusiloff had behind him the Tarnopol system of railways, and he was able quickly to manœuvre his troops and his artillery and reply to every move of the enemy. By the middle of June the German army under Linsingen was exhausted, in spite of the fact that it had received a continual stream of reinforcements by the Stry railway, and the assistance of several divisions of Bothmer's forces. The task of forcing the Dniester was then given to Pflanzer's army, which had been operating in the Bukovina. It advanced from the town of Kolomea over the hills to the hilly bend of the Dniester at Nizniov, where a railway line crossed the river. On the night of June 13 the Tirolese rifles were annihilated by a Russian cavalry charge across the railway bridge. The next day Pflanzer brought up his heavy artillery and made an infantry attack under an arch of shell fire, and after a struggle of three days he captured Nizniov. Then in a violent effort he pushed the Russians back from the river and captured some of the villages.

It was along the Zlota Lipa that Brusiloff had won his first important victory in the first Galician campaign in August, 1914. It was also along the Zlota Lipa that General Ivanoff had ordered the southern Russian army to make its final definite stand when the main Russian forces in Galicia had retired northward to the line of the Bug river. It was unfortunate for Pflanzer that he had used all the main strength of his army in capturing a position which, he imagined, Brusiloff needed, for the southern Russian army had not put out its strength in defending the bridge-head. It had acted against the Austrians under Pflanzer as it had acted against the Germans under Linsingen. It had allowed the enemy to capture the position with extraordinary loss of life, while firing from cover at the charging masses of infantry and pouring shrapnel at them and then giving ground before the pressure became severe on its own front. Meanwhile, fresh field fortifications were being constructed across the river for the decisive stand of the Russian army, and trainloads of shells were being brought from Tarnopol for the principal battle.

General Brusiloff always contrived to make his decisive attacks when the enemy troops faced him with their backs to the river, and with only a few pontoon bridges behind them when they retreated. It was a simple device which he had repeatedly practised throughout the Dniester combats. He placed a few heavy howitzers of long range in a position to command the pontoon bridges of the enemy, and then waited for them to cross the river before delivering his counter-stroke. Pflanzer crossed the Dniester at Nizniov in great force on June 19, but his troops were hemmed in between the deep windings of the river, and there bombarded furiously and swept by machine-gun and rifle fire for four days and nights. A remnant of some three thousand Austrians surrendered on June 22. On the same day Linsingen's army, which had also thrown large forces across the Dniester, higher up the stream near Zuravno, again met with a check. The German troops were driven back to the river and forced into the water, where some managed to swim to the islands in the middle of the stream. Those who remained on the northern bank were captured. This double blow at Linsingen and Pflanzer had an important effect upon the end of the Galician campaign. When Mackensen began a turning movement north of Lemberg he confidently expected that Böhm Ermolli's troops would shake the retiring forces directly in front of them and throw them into confusion. Then it was designed that Bothmer's army should drive in from the south-east, while Linsingen and Pflanzer were engaging Brusiloff's army and driving it back from the Dniester front. As planned, the operations promised to achieve Mackensen's and Falkenhayn's long-considered plan for enveloping and destroying the southern Russian army. But owing to the strength of this army and to the genius of its commander, it shattered the forces brought against it, and became the pivot on which all the other Russian forces swung in their long movement of retirement.

The deep-sunken waters of the Zlota Lipa, running up to the range of hills east of Lemberg, close to the sources of the Bug river, were chosen as the final line of the Russian retreat in Galicia. The line left the Tarnopol railway and the Brody railway in Russian hands, giving rapid means of transit to Odessa and Kieff. But instead of withdrawing with all speed to this river line, General Brusiloff continued to harry the German and Austrian forces in front of him. Having thrown Linsingen over the Dniester he swung away from the scene of his victory at Zuravno and joined in the attack on the central Austrian army at Bobrka, south-east of Lemberg.

Here the battle raged until June 27, when, after the enemy had been repulsed, a rearguard held the position until the main southern Russian forces were entrenched on the Grila Lipa, a river a hard day's march eastward. It ran into the Dniester, and at its confluence was the town of Halicz, scene of one of the famous battles in the first Galician campaign. During the retreat on Halicz, Linsingen made a final attempt to snatch a decisive victory, and sought with all his remaining troops and a large reinforcement from Germany to break across the Dniester and take the Russian army on the flank. He launched division after division across the river. The men came on in close-packed columns, but the columns were wiped out with shrapnel and machine-gun fire by the Russian rearguard. The fiercest drives failed at a hundred paces from the defending trenches, and in their counter-attacks the Russians took large numbers of prisoners. Böhm Ermolli's army and Bothmer's army co-operated with Linsingen's forces in trying for a week to break through the rearguard of the southern Russian army, but by the night of July 3 Brusiloff had effected a strong and orderly retirement from the Gnila Lipa to the Zlota Lipa, where a system of field fortifications enabled his army to hold out with ease for many months.

A victory by the extreme left wing of the southern Russian army helped to strengthen the general position. In the middle of June the Cossack forces operating in Bukovina retired to the frontier as a precautionary measure. But when General Ivanoff's troops were secure, and there was no danger of the Russian line breaking, the Cossacks advanced from the region of Chotin and delivered a succession of fierce actions south of the Dniester, and their driving force carried them in the last week of June within 15 miles of Czernovitz. All Pflanzer's troops in this region were badly shaken. More than a month elapsed before they were able to attack again the Dniester line. The attack occurred about July 18 on a river-town just to the north of Bukovina, but it failed completely.

In the main field of struggle, from the Stry to the Zlota Lipa, Brusiloff's army had conducted a fighting retreat for six weeks. In the course of this retreat it had taken 53,000 prisoners and had practically destroyed Linsingen's army. Having regard to the damage done to the enemy, it was one of the most extraordinary retreats in history. The explanation was that Brusiloff's forces were full of fight, and capable of standing their ground against the three hostile armies operating on their front. When they were obliged to retire, through the weakness of another part of the Russian line, they went back by forced marches to carefully chosen positions of great natural strength. At each of these positions they made a stand for several days, compelling the hostile infantry to advance across the open ground and attack them, while they themselves remained under cover, with excellent artillery at their back.

In all, some two hundred miles of ground were lost from May 1 to July 3 between the Dunajec and Gnila Lipa. The Russians continued to hold the country twenty-five miles east of Lemberg. Their lines ran from the Rumanian frontier along the Dniester as far as Nizniov. Thence they extended northward to Sokal, and continued along the marshy banks of the Bug towards Cholm, Lublin, and Brest Litovsk. General Ivanoff threw only a weak force along the river swamps, for the ground there was so bad that the enemy could not make any progress over it. General Ivanoff's chief forces withdrew from Rava Russka along a new Russian railway running to Cholm, built in the autumn of 1914. This new railway was of inestimable value to the Russian commander; for, after the battle north of Lemberg, Mackensen swung his army up northward towards Cholm, instead of endeavouring to complete the entire conquest of Galicia.

This retirement of the western wing of General Ivanoff's army had a marked effect upon the armies of General Alexeieff, which were defending Warsaw and Ivangorod in the great bend of the Vistula. Alexeieff and Ivanoff had the broad, swift waters of the Vistula between them, and they had to keep strong forces in line across the river, to prevent the enemy on either bank from breaking through. No overlapping was possible. As Ivanoff's force retired under pressure from Mackensen, Alexeieff's force had also to withdraw, to prevent the troops of the Archduke from crossing the river and getting on his rear.

Thus the decisive influence of Mackensen's movement began to extend in an enormous manner. From a position only a few miles north of the boundary of Eastern Galicia, it was able to shake the Russian line near Warsaw and, in particular, to compel the retreat of the Russian army on the Pilica, nearly two hundred miles east of the point at which he was striking. Such was the beginning of the third battle for Warsaw, which was to prove more successful than all the furious direct rushes that Hindenburg had made upon the capital of Poland. Mackensen's plan of attack was well made and carried out in a strong manner. But it had the defect of needing so enormous a train of heavy artillery that its movement of advance was extremely slow. It had taken him exactly two months to advance from Gorlice across Western Galicia to Tomaszov, the distance between the two towns in a straight line being under 120 miles.

CHAPTER 19

The Landing at Suvla Bay

B Y the end of July, 1915, it became clear that the original plan for taking the Gallipoli peninsula had failed. In the south the British front stretching across the peninsula in front of Krithia was faced by Turkish fortified positions which it was impossible to take by frontal assault. At Anzac Cove the ground which the Australians and New Zealanders had so dearly won was faced by a semicircle of Turkish trenches and batteries which provided a scarcely less formidable obstacle to any considerable advance. At this moment German diplomacy had succeeded in bringing about an agreement between Turkey and Bulgaria by which Bulgaria was to mobilize against Serbia. This fact made the British Government anxious to strike an effective blow against Turkey. The position in Gallipoli could only be changed by bringing about a war of manœuvre, and to this end Sir Ian Hamilton's new plan was directed.

To achieve it another landing with fresh forces was necessary, and the point chosen for this was Suvla Bay. Lying only a few miles north of Anzac Cove it was an advantageous point for the purpose, being protected by its natural formation, not only against the prevailing winds, but from the possibility of submarine attacks. Sir Ian's plan was that while the new force was thrown ashore at Suvla Bay the Anzac troops should make a move forward towards Sari Bair, and if the new army could advance to the Anafarta Hills the uplands commanding the whole width of the peninsula would be taken and the Turkish communications with Achi Baba and its defending lines could be cut. It was hoped that the landing at Suvla Bay would take the Turks completely by surprise, but the task lying before the Australasian army corps was extremely difficult. The main mass of rock and scrub at Sari Bair was higher than Achi Baba, and the seamed and broken mountain land was bounded on either side by other difficult summits, running down to plateaux which immediately overlooked the low cliff and ridge where the Australasian army corps was entrenched.

THE LANDING AT SUVLA BAY

But in his first despatch, Sir Ian Hamilton had commented
with admiration on the dare-devil spirit of the Anzacs, and
he now resolved that they should be his grand striking force.
The task he set them was one to appal any ordinary body of
troops. They had to storm and hold Sari Bair. They had
to take a position fortified by the best military engineers in
the modern world, and held in strong numbers by a race of
fighting men who had proved themselves magnificent in defence.

No operation of war could be more difficult than the attack
on Sari Bair; for the numerous and well-handled machine-guns
of the defending army, sweeping every slope with a stream of
five hundred bullets a minute, constituted a factor of resistance
of enormous value. The machine-guns, as employed under
the new tactical system by German officers, were more formidable weapons of wholesale slaughter than the quick-firing
field-guns, which projected a curtain of shrapnel to stop any
infantry charge. All this must be remembered when comparing
a modern offensive movement against fortressed heights with
the famous attacks on fortified positions made in the days when
cannon only fired slowly round shot or case over short ranges.

In about a hundred years of incomparable scientific inventiveness, the mechanical instruments of battle had been
developed to an inhuman power of general destructiveness. In
favourable circumstances a division of 20,000 men might be
defeated by ten men with two machine-guns. Personal bravery,
especially in an attacking force, seemed almost to be reduced
to insignificance by the enormously increased importance of the
mechanical means of destruction, in the production of which
the Germans were for the time supreme.

Everything that science could do for the Turks the Germans
had done. They had hedged the mountain slopes with barbed-
wire cables of remarkable thickness; they had converted the
heights into warrens, to shelter the Turks from both musketry
and shrapnel fire; they had provided them with more machine-
guns than the attacking force possessed, and had placed a large
number of guns and howitzers at the points commanding every
uphill field approach. Four months had been spent in fortifying
the heights, and any original local weakness in the dispositions
had been revealed in twelve weeks' incessant conflict, and
thoroughly remedied and again tested. Yet such was the confidence of Sir Ian Hamilton in the men of New Zealand and

Australia that, having set them the task of capturing Sari Bair, he took it for granted that they would succeed.

On their success he based the second part of his plan. He first reinforced the Anzacs with the Indian troops and two divisions from the new army. Then he arranged for troopships, containing the Greek Legion and supporting warships, to make a feint of landing at Karachali, on the Turkish mainland, threatening both the railway to Sofia and the Bulair lines.

This demonstration was designed to check for a day or two the movement of Turkish reinforcements into the Gallipoli peninsula, and to lead the enemy to concentrate on Bulair, while the real blow fell in Suvla Bay, only about twelve miles north of the Anzac position. The main body of the new army was to storm the Anafarta Ridge, lying close to the heights which the Anzacs were about to attack in the Sari Bair region. The aim of the operation, as planned by Sir Ian Hamilton, was to compel the Turks to concentrate against the New Zealanders, Australians, Indians, and British supports in a furious battle on the mountain slopes, and then to take the enemy on the flank with the advancing British army from Suvla Bay. It was expected that, if only the Anzacs could storm and hold Sari Bair, the hostile pressure upon them would suddenly be relaxed by the new army driving down on the Turkish flank. While this decisive manœuvre was proceeding, the British army corps and the French army corps in front of Achi Baba were ordered to make a violent assault upon the Turkish lines, in order to prevent the Turks at Sari Bair obtaining reinforcements from Achi Baba.

Lieutenant-General Sir F. W. Stopford was in command of the force to be landed at Suvla Bay. It was made up of two divisions of the new army, the 11th, under Major-General Hammersley, and the 10th, under Major-General Sir Bryan Mahon, and the 53rd and 54th Territorial Divisions. It sailed from Kephalos Bay on August 6, and so successful was the surprise movement that the troops were landed with only the slightest opposition. While General Stopford was landing at Suvla the pre-arranged attack against the Turkish lines was begun by the allied troops before Krithia and Kereves Dere. Though this action was only a holding movement, the fighting was of a terrible character, as the advance had to be made against an enemy in superior numbers who was receiving large reinforcements during the struggle. The brunt of the ordeal fell upon the Territorials of the East Lancashire Division, and they once more proved themselves extraordinarily brave.

This attack greatly facilitated the main operations in the Sari Bair region. The Sari Bair operations were also opened by a great movement on the right, which was skilfully devised to draw down the enemy forces and clear the path for the chief attack on the left. The point selected at Anzac for the holding movement was Lone Pine Plateau—an upland some four hundred feet above the level of the sea, extending south-eastwardly from the main mass of Sari Bair towards the promontory of Gaba Tepe, passing Courtney's Post, Quinn's Post, and Bloody Angle. On Lone Pine Plateau the Turks were dug in with all the science their German directors could command. The deep, narrow trenches in the broken highland of sand and scrub were roofed with great logs against shrapnel, machine-gun fire, and hand-bombs, the upper heavy timber work forming a road, with holes out of which the defending troops could leap for a charge. A row of loopholes in the parapets gave the machine-gun parties and riflemen a large field of fire, while leaving them under cover and safe from everything except a well-placed high-explosive shell.

An Australian division was given the task of capturing this upland, and the dismounted troopers of the 3rd Australian Light Horse made the attack. They went forward in three lines against Lone Pine at dawn on August 7. The first line was destroyed by the enemy's fire midway between the trenches. Exactly two minutes after the first regiment, the 8th, cleared the parapet, the second line went forward in turn without hesitation. It fell. For a minute the flag which the Light Horse had carried fluttered in a corner on the Turkish mountain fortress. A few men had got home. Then the flag vanished, and with it one of the bravest bodies of fighting men the world has seen. Then, ten minutes after the second line disappeared, the third line went over the breastworks, as steady, quick, and straight as the others, but it was stopped by order before reaching the fire zone. The movement was all over in a quarter of an hour. In the darkness of night one or two maimed figures crawled back over the British trenches. Meanwhile, the 1st Light Horse, attacking from Quinn's Post, had its first advancing line shattered by machine-gun fire, and, after taking a hill along with the Welch Fusiliers, had to retire with heavy losses. But the following day the infantry followed the dismounted cavalry, and, after a combat of extraordinary violence, Lone Pine was won. The Turkish general threw down reinforcements from the mountain and hurried out his reserves from the Maidos region. Night and day the furious counter-attacks went on, with every Turkish gun and howitzer within range turned on Lone Pine Plateau. But the Australian division could not be moved. What they had won they held, and their victorious thrust forward was an operation of the highest value.

While this attack was proceeding, something was happening on the left flank of Anzac which should have assured victory in Gallipoli. A large force of New Zealanders and Indians, with an Australian division in support, set out on a night march about half-past nine in the evening of August 6. Preparations had long been going on for this movement. Huge stores of ammunition and supplies had been secretly conveyed at night through the bush along the coast by Fisherman's Hut and towards the ravine of Asma Dere. The country was so rough, broken, and difficult that the Turkish commander did not foresee that an advance might be made against him from that side. He and his staff knew the ground intimately and regarded it as hopeless for European troops. At Lone Pine they expected an attack, but at Asma Dere they placed only patrol parties, instead of wasting a large force on connected entrenchments.

All this had long since been discovered by the Anzac scouts, and the plan of attack had been based on the knowledge thus obtained and on the peculiar gift of the Australasian and Indian troops for finding their way in darkness through unknown country. The expedition worked northward along the coast for a mile and a half, and then turned inland towards a height three miles away. By dawn the column of some six thousand men, under Sir A. J. Godley, had arrived within five hundred yards of the hill. The river course of Asma Dere had been occupied, and out at sea were British monitors, which since the losses of the fleet through submarine attacks had been substituted for battleships. They were linked by wireless with the troops inland, and ready to direct their 6 in. guns on any indicated point of the mountain heights.

It was one of the finest surprise movements in modern warfare. The design was to storm the crescent of peaks that blocked all direct advances from Anzac. Instead of attempting the absolutely impossible feat of climbing up the fortified slopes by a frontal attack from the cliffs around the landing beaches, the column had stolen along the coast northward and then swerved inland and opened a furious flank assault on the tremendous mountain position. The Australian division on the other flank was making sorties from Quinn's Post, Russell Top, and Pope's Post, and fighting desperately on Lone Pine Plateau, with the result that the attention of the enemy was distracted from the vital spot in the Gallipoli system of defence.

By daybreak on August 7 the Australian force forming the left of the secret advance force was based on Asma Dere, near Suvla Bay, where the new British army had landed. Its task was to move up Aghyl Dere towards Koja Chemen. On the right the New Zealand Infantry Brigade, with some other British and Indian troops commanded by Brigadier-General F. E. Johnston, was to advance on Rhododendron Ridge with Chunuk Bair as its final objective. The New Zealanders clambered up Rhododendron Ridge and, charging over the crest, won the south-western slope of the main peak of Sari Bair.

At the same time the Indian brigade drove upward and extended their ground beyond the farm and on the height that was known as Hill Q. The exertion needed in these upward drives was enormous. The ground was so steep and rough that it would have been hard work to climb it without opposition and without a burden. But the troops had to carry kit, rifles, food, and ammunition; they fought in a great heat, and had to go without water, and from every bush and hollow above their heads poured musketry fire or machine-gun torrents of bullets. Hostile batteries searched the clambering lines of attackers with shrapnel, and sudden counter-charges by resolute and hard-fighting Turkish troops forced the New Zealanders and Indians to bunch together in order to meet mass with mass.

The brigade fought for three days and three nights without ceasing, and conquered the south-west half of the main knoll of Chunuk Bair. They won the crest dominating the Narrows, and the roads leading to Bulair and Constantinople; but they withdrew their main line twenty-five yards from the summit, and did not retain their look-out posts to watch the enemy on the opposite slopes below. The fact was that the brigade was exhausted from fatigue, and in dire need of water and food. So hot had the fighting been that they had not had opportunity to dig trenches, but had merely scraped a few inches of earth out of the ground when groping for cover from the enemy's fire.

On the third night of the battle, two battalions of the new army—the 6th Loyal North Lancashires and the 5th Wiltshires—relieved Brigadier-General Johnston's brigade on Chunuk Bair. It was then, according to the point of view of the New Zealanders and their British companions, that the great mistake was made. The North Lancashires arrived in good time, but the 5th Wiltshires, being delayed by the intricate country, did not come up until four o'clock in the morning. The Lancashire men began to strengthen their trenches, while the belated Wiltshires were ordered by their officers to lie down in the mere scrapings. But none of the superior officers of these two bodies of fresh, untried troops grasped fully the

needs of the situation. Both battalions should have dug for their lives with every ounce of energy, got well under shelter, and, if possible, erected some defence against bombs rolled down the slope. Digging was all they were required to do, for the shattered Turks attempted no attack, and the relieving battalions were as fresh as possible in the circumstances, and would be in turn relieved by the rested veteran brigade. In fact, they had been sent for to dig rather than to fight. Apparently they were not instructed with sufficient emphasis by the retiring brigade, composed of veterans who thought that no soldier needed to be told to dig any more than he needed to be told to breathe.

An hour and a half after the Wiltshires arrived, the enemy batteries swept the slope with a storm of shrapnel, and a large Turkish column of fifteen battalions concentrated on the opposite slope and, storming over the crest in a huge mass, broke the North Lancashires and the Wiltshires, and then outflanked another British column. Swept by shrapnel and overborne by numbers, the small force withdrew farther down the slope of Chunuk Bair, and the victorious Turks then charged over the crest into the great gully south of Rhododendron Ridge. The gully led between the advanced lines of the Anzac forces and their base on the beach. Had the daring attack succeeded, there would have been a great British disaster. But Sir W. R. Birdwood, with Sir A. J. Godley and General Baldwin, and other able leaders, were equal to the sudden, dismaying situation. Part of the Anzac line on Rhododendron Ridge broke under the desperate valour of the Turk. Every man tried to stop the gap—colonels and generals fought by the side of privates in the ferocious hand-to-hand combats in the scrub.

The great counter-stroke was delivered by naval guns and land artillery. The Turks came on in four lines, the men in each line being set shoulder to shoulder with their fellows. So dense was the formation that the movement was clearly visible from all the British monitors, as well as from the neighbouring land batteries. Every gunner threw up on the mountain slope whatever shell was handiest to him—shrapnel, high explosive, or common shell—and a zone of death was formed in front of the position.

But the Turks were so impelled by the momentum of their flying charge down the steep mountain that they could not stop or turn back. They tumbled into the fume and flame and upwhirled earth, and in the explosions some of their bodies could be seen rising as a shell burst and then tumbling into the ravine. There were also ten machine-guns in the Anzac line, and the remnants of choking, half-dazed Turks that got through the zone of artillery fire were caught in a rain of bullets. For half an hour machine-guns were worked for rapid fire, and scarcely a Turk returned to the hills. About 12,000 of them were annihilated in about 30 minutes.

Throughout the rest of the day the enemy continued to attack, but hour by hour his force slackened, and at nightfall the battle ceased, with the Australian, New Zealand, Maori, Gurkha, Sikh, and British soldiers holding firmly to the spurs of Rhododendron Ridge with the farm there, and the Asma Dere position, extending to Damakjelik Bair.

While this set-back had done something to check the development of Sir Ian Hamilton's plan, the new landing at Suvla Bay had not been successful. The force under Sir F. W. Stopford consisted of the 11th Division, under Major-General Hammersley; the 10th division, called the Irish division, under Sir Bryan Mahon; and the 53rd division, composed of Territorial troops, without artillery, under General Lindley. The 54th division, also consisting of Territorial troops, without artillery, was brought into action as well.

On August 6 the 11th division landed around Suvla Bay, taking the Turks completely by surprise, but the generalship was in certain respects bad. On Hill 10 there was confusion among the men, and near the Karakol Dagh, where the 11th Manchesters had advanced with great pluck, there was no leader who could take hold of the two advancing brigades, and launch them in an attack. During the period of hesitation the Turks tried to drive the invading force back, but again the 11th Manchesters took them on with the bayonet, and, with the 9th Lancashire Fusiliers, broke them and drove them in disorder over Hill 10. The Turks retreated towards the Anafarta Ridges, followed by the 34th and 32nd Brigades, who were joined by some of Sir Bryan Mahon's men—the 6th Inniskillings, the 6th Dublin Fusiliers, and the 6th Irish Fusiliers. With more troops of his 10th division, Sir Bryan delivered a spirited attack to support the Manchester men of the 11th division, and conquered nearly all the ground as far as the Anafarta Hills. The 6th Munster Fusiliers especially distinguished themselves.

A swift and decisive victory seemed possible. The Turks had only four thousand men in the field, and they were not well-trained regular soldiers, but local levies and gendarmerie. The British had an army corps, less a brigade, landed, and twelve thousand more riflemen coming up as a reserve, with another twelve thousand behind them. So the odds against the Turks in infantry alone at the beginning were nearly 24,000 against 4,000. The attacking army had, moreover, a squadron of warships with long-range guns to strengthen the army corps artillery. But there was an extraordinary amount of mismanagement by some of the generals. Another disastrous fact was the failure of the water supply, and in his despatch Sir Ian Hamilton emphasized this point. He wrote:

> The weather was very hot and the troops suffered much from want of water. Except at the southernmost extremity of the Kiretch Tepe Sirt ridge there was no water in that part of the field, and although it existed in some abundance

throughout the area over which the 11th Division was operating, the Corps Commander reports that there was no time to develop its resources. Partly this seems to have been owing to the enemy's fire; partly to a want of that *nous* which stands by as second nature to the old campaigner, partly it was inevitable. Anyway, for as long as such a state of things lasted, the troops became dependent on the lighters and upon the water brought to the beaches in tins, pakhals, etc.

Undoubtedly the distribution of this water to the advancing troops was a matter of great difficulty, and one which required not only well-worked-out schemes from Corps and Divisional staffs, but also energy and experience on the part of those who had to put them into practice. As it turned out, and judging merely by results, I regret to say that the measures actually taken in regard to the distribution proved to be inadequate, and that suffering and disorganization ensued. The disembarkation of artillery horses was therefore at once, and rightly, postponed by the Corps Commanders, in order that mules might be landed to carry up water. . . .

The want of water had told on the new troops. The distribution from the beaches had not worked smoothly. In some cases the hose had been pierced by individuals wishing to fill their own bottles; in others lighters had grounded so far from the beach that men swam out to fill batches of water-bottles. All this had added to the disorganization inevitable after a night landing, followed by fights here and there with an enemy scattered over a country to us unknown.

Things were indeed so bad at Suvla at dawn on August 8 that Sir Ian Hamilton sent one of his Staff officers to observe and report. The Staff officer telegraphed that no Turkish gun was in action, that Turkish rifle fire was small, and that the enemy was very weak, but that the British troops were missing golden opportunities, owing to the inaction of their commanders. In these circumstances Sir Ian Hamilton surrendered his control of the Anzac and Achi Baba battles, and sailed for Suvla Bay, arriving there at five o'clock in the afternoon of August 8. All the day had been wasted, while the Anzac men and their comrades of the 13th division had taken the height known as Table Top and the ground beyond, where they should have connected with the Suvla Bay army. Even the patrols of the 11th division had not carried out orders to push forward in force and occupy positions waiting for them on the Anafarta Hills. A priceless 12 hours had been lost, and airmen reported that the Turkish army was on the march to Suvla.

FIGHTING IN THE ARTOIS WOODS. British troops storming up a slope to take a woodland position held by the enemy. This illustration is typical of the severe fighting in this battle. Both Allies and Germans lost heavily, and the gain of ground by the Allies was hardly worth the losses incurred. Throughout the battle the heroism of the British and French troops was most marked.

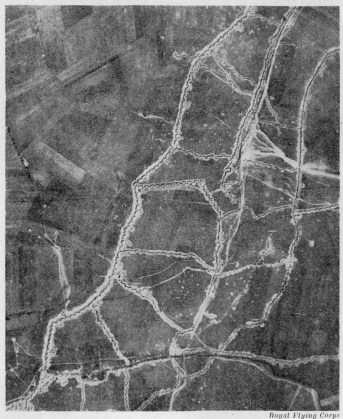

LAY-OUT OF THE MULTIPLE TRENCH SYSTEM. As the war proceeded on the West front it was found that a single trench system was very liable to penetration, so in 1915 the multiple system appeared, the main trenches being linked by communication trenches. Note, also, in this air view of a typical section, how the fire recesses have given place to traverses to restrict the effective range of shell bursts.

After examining the position, Sir Ian Hamilton urged that the 11th division at the eleventh hour should make an attack upon the hills. By this time the troops were well rested, watered, and fed. But the commander of the division did not like the idea of an advance by night, and General Stopford did not care to overrule his subordinate. Major-General Hammersley declared that the division was much too scattered for a night attack. Sir Ian Hamilton found, however, that one brigade—the 32nd—was fairly well concentrated and ready to move. Sir Ian Hamilton therefore overruled his generals, and ordered that the single brigade at least should try to make good the heights before the enemy occupied them. He gave his orders about 6 p.m. on August 8, but the four battalions did not begin their advance until 4 a.m. on August 9. One company of the East Yorks pioneer battalion topped one of the Anafarta Hills, but the rest of the battalion and the 22nd brigade were attacked on their flanks, and forced back. The hill that had been thus reached by a single brigade on the morning of August 9 commanded the whole battlefield.

It is quite probable that if the troops had been pushed up on August 8, when all difficulties about water had been overcome, the Turkish army marching on Suvla would have been thrown back, a connexion with the Anzac army would have been established on the high hills, and all the enemy positions in the Dardanelles dominated. As it was, the 11th division, under Major-General Hammersley, made its long-delayed attack on the Anafarta Ridges when the Turks had brought their guns back and had been strongly reinforced. The 32nd brigade was pushed off the slopes of the hill, and though Sir Ian Hamilton brought up his general reserve, the Territorial division, and gave it to General Stopford, no advance could be made. Many of the Territorial battalions fought with great gallantry, the Herefordshire men being remarkable for the impetuosity of their attack. On August 10 the division was launched against the Anafarta Ridge, but failed to take it. Then, on August 12, the infantry of the 54th division, which was just landed, was sent against the northern Anafarta position, but they only took one position.

On August 15 General Stopford was retired from his command, being replaced by Major-General De Lisle. By this time the 10th division, the 11th division, the 53rd, and the 54th division, originally consisting of 44,000 infantry, were reduced to fewer than 30,000 rifles. The Australasian and British forces at Anzac were reduced to 25,000, the British forces under Achi Baba numbered only 23,000 rifles, while the French corps consisted of 17,000 men. Sir Ian Hamilton estimated the Turkish forces in the Suvla Bay and Anzac region at 75,000 men. But the enemy had all the advantages of ground, sufficient ammunition, and drafts to refill all ranks depleted in action. On the other hand, the British divisions alone were 45,000 under their establishment, some of the finest battalions being so shattered that they had to be withdrawn from the fighting line. Sir Ian Hamilton, however, felt confident that if all his battalions were made up to strength and his munition depôts were refilled, he could still take the Narrows in the autumn of 1915, and clear a passage for the Fleet to Constantinople. But neither the men nor the ammunition Sir Ian needed could be spared for the Dardanelles operations.

When Sir Ian Hamilton found that he could not depend upon receiving drafts to fill out his wasted forces, he was disinclined to attempt another attack on a large scale; for he was likely to lose so many men in attacking the Turks, now strongly entrenched around Suvla Bay, that his weakened lines might be broken by a counter-attack. He therefore restricted himself to action on a small front, and selected the Anafarta Valley as his line of advance. The famous 29th division was transported from the southern Krithia area to Suvla Bay, and connected with the 11th division. These two divisions were set the task of winning the Anafarta Ridge, while the gunless Territorial army corps, composed of the 53rd and 54th divisions, held the enemy on the north. The attack was planned by General De Lisle, and launched on August 21.

But two mischances in the work of part of the 11th division led to another British defeat. The 34th brigade rushed the Turkish trenches near Hill 100, practically without loss; but the 32nd brigade, which should have connected with the victorious battalion and taken the south-west corner of the hill, was misdirected. The brigade lost its path in a light sea mist, and arrived at the north-east instead of the south-west corner of the spur. With magnificent courage and disregard of death, the men of the 32nd brigade still tried to carry the Turkish position, but could not succeed in rectifying the mistake of the Staff officers. Then the 33rd brigade, sent up in haste to capture the Turkish positions at all costs, fell into precisely the same error, and instead of reaching the vital south-west corner, wasted its effort in a north-easterly and south-easterly direction. Meanwhile, the 29th division, which set out half an hour after the 11th division, stormed Scimitar Hill, and despite the fact that one brigade was checked by a great forest fire across its front, the division pressed on up the Anafarta Valley until it was checked by the failure of the two brigades of the 11th division to take the south-west spur of Hill 100.

One brigade of the 29th division tried to carry out the work of the 11th division, but as it moved eastward across the spur of Hill 100 it was swept by a cross-fire of shell and musketry from the unattainable height and from another ridge. The leading troops were brushed off the top of the spur by storms of shrapnel and bullets, and the brigade had to fall back to a ledge near Scimitar Hill. It was then that the English Yeomanry division came into action in a magnificent manner. Under a steady and accurate fire from the Turkish batteries, it advanced in open formation across a plain for a mile and a half, moving like men marching on parade, while the Turkish shells made curtains of shrapnel bullets in its path.

Crossing the plain they formed up beside the 29th division, and as darkness fell, the troopers of Bucks, Berks, and Dorset pushed up the valley between Scimitar Hill and Hill 100. They took a knoll near the centre of this horse-shoe of heights, but the combined charge by the Yeomanry brigade and the 29th division could not carry the amphitheatre of Turkish trenches on the top of Hill 100. The 29th division lost nearly 5,000 men, and the yeomen also suffered very heavily. The poor staff work, which had allowed two brigades of the 11th division to work forward in a wrong direction, had brought about a general disaster which no skill or courage could retrieve.

Towards the end of the month of August, however, Major-General Cox, with a fine Anzac force, captured a very important height known as Hill 60, which overlooked one of the Anafarta valleys. During the vain attack of the Suvla Bay army on Hill 100, General Cox with 2,000 New Zealanders, 2,000 Irishmen, and a battalion of the South Wales Borderers, reinforced by the 18th Australian battalion, had carried one of the northern foothills of the Sari Bair clump, enabling trenches to be strongly made connecting the Suvla Bay army with the Anzac army. Then on August 27, General Cox again thrust out towards the Turkish lines around Anafarta. He used only detachments from the 4th and 5th Australian brigades, the New Zealand Mounted Rifles, and the 5th Connaught Rangers.

Owing to lack of shells the preliminary bombardment was ineffective. As soon as the Anzac troops swarmed out into the open they were met by a terribly hot fire of enemy field-guns, rifles, and machine-guns. The Australians on the right were held up by a battery of machine-guns, but in the centre the New Zealanders stubbornly fought upwards, and, after four and a half hours of fighting, took nearly nine-tenths of the summit. Then, on the left, a single company of the 5th Connaught Rangers stormed the northern communication trenches of the Turks. All the battalion then entered upon a ferocious bomb fight along the other Turkish trenches. The men drew many of the enemy's supports, and were promised the help of fresh troops by midnight. But before the fresh force arrived, the hostile commander launched some of his general reserve against the Connaught men, and drove them from the trenches as the 9th Australian Light Horse were coming up. The Australians made a plucky attempt to retake the lost communication trench, but were repulsed.

This left the New Zealand Mounted Rifles isolated on the top of the hill. Their holding was reduced to a hundred and fifty yards of trench, and all night and all the next day they were bombed, shrapnelled, blasted with heavy high-explosive shell, and attacked by dense masses of bayonets. But nothing that the Turk could do could shake them, and early in the afternoon of August 29, while the top of the hill was still in their possession, the Turkish communication trenches on the left were carried and held by the 10th Light Horse. Thus was won an important height, from which the attacking artillery officers gained an outlook over the Anafarta Sagir Valley, while the lateral communications between Anzac and Suvla Bay were thus made much safer.

Of the new troops, the Londoners who fought with the Australasians at Sari Bair won the praise of these veterans of Gallipoli ; and the Irish division that captured Chocolate Hill and Dublin Hill was composed of men of great valour; while the Yeomanry division, though defeated, was glorious even in disaster. On the other hand, there were some new troops that flinched when suddenly thrown into the furnace of battle; and the genius for leadership, which might have repaired the passing hesitation of untried fresh recruits, was not clearly visible throughout the first and decisive phase of the operations.

The explanation of the failure seems to be that, as the ground was very rough and difficult, the men had to advance in very open order, becoming separated from each other, and losing touch with their officers. It needed troops highly trained in skirmishing and very self-reliant, with each man eager to push on of his own accord towards the objective, without stopping for orders or waiting to see if his comrades were following him. But these requirements were not fulfilled by the unblooded, unhardened new battalions.

Despite the failure to reach the Narrows across the Anafarta Ridges and the vast rampart of Sari Bair, Sir Ian Hamilton reported that the troops remained confident that, with more help from their country, they would achieve victory. But in September the flow of munitions and drafts fell away, and sickness began to work still more terribly among the survivors of many arduous conflicts. Then, on October 11, the decision to withdraw was reached by the British Cabinet. Lord Kitchener cabled to Sir Ian Hamilton, asking for an estimate of the losses likely to be involved in an evacuation of the peninsula. Sir Ian Hamilton replied in such terms as showed that in his judgment an evacuation was unthinkable. The Government therefore decided to obtain a fresh, unbiased opinon, and on October 16, Sir Ian Hamilton was recalled to London, and Sir Charles Monro was appointed commander-in-chief of the armies on the Gallipoli peninsula. Such was the anxiety of the Government in regard to the evacuation that, in the middle of November, Lord Kitchener sailed for Mudros, and proceeded to study the position on the peninsula.

After Lord Kitchener's review of the position the evacuation was officially decided upon. Sir Charles Monro was convinced that evacuation was inevitable, and in a later despatch he gave the following reasons for his opinion :

> The positions occupied by our troops presented a military situation unique in history. The mere fringe of the coast line had been secured. The beaches and piers upon which they depended for all requirements in personnel and material were

exposed to registered and observed artillery fire. Our entrenchments were dominated almost throughout by the Turks. The possible artillery positions were insufficient and defective. The force, in short, held a line possessing every possible military defect. The position was without depth, the communications were insecure and dependent on the weather. No means existed for the concealment and deployment of fresh troops destined for the offensive; whilst the Turks enjoyed full powers of observation, abundant artillery positions, and they had been given the time to supply the natural advantages which the position presented by all the devices at the disposal of the field engineer. Another material factor came prominently before me. The troops on the peninsula had suffered much from various causes:

(a) It was not in the first place possible to withdraw them from the shell-swept area as is done when necessary in France, for every corner on the peninsula is exposed to hostile fire.

(b) They were much enervated from the diseases which are endemic in that part of Europe in the summer.

(c) In consequence of the losses which they had suffered in earlier battles there was a very grave dearth of officers competent to take command of men.

(d) In order to maintain the numbers needed to hold the front the Territorial Divisions had been augmented by the attachment of Yeomanry and Mounted Brigades. Makeshifts of this nature very obviously did not tend to create efficiency.

Other arguments, irrefutable in their conclusions, convinced me that a complete evacuation was the only course to pursue.

(a) It was obvious that the Turks could hold us in front with a small force and prosecute their designs on Bagdad or Egypt, or both.

(b) An advance from the positions we held could not be regarded as a military operation to expect.

(c) Even had we been able to make an advance in the peninsula, our position would not have been ameliorated to any marked degree, and an advance on Constantinople was quite out of the question.

(d) Since we could not hope to achieve any purpose by remaining in the peninsula, the appalling cost to the nation involved in consequence of embarking on an Overseas Expedition with no base available for the rapid transit of stores, supplies and personnel made it urgent that we should divert the troops locked up in the peninsula to a more useful theatre of war.

It had been expected that the autumn weather would do more to overthrow the Allies than even the Turks could do with their new guns. The Gallipoli peninsula and the neighbouring islands which were being used as bases were subjected to a series of terrible storms in the autumn and winter. British destroyers, which had been on duty off the coast since the opening of hostilities, showed by their logs that sudden and very heavy gales were to be expected; and it was thought that the storms would make it impossible for ships to ply to Anzac and Helles, so that the troops would be cut off from all supplies and unable to withdraw. To guard against this breakwaters were extemporised at Suvla, Helles, and Kephalos Bay. A number of old ships were filled with sand and sunk so that they extended in solid lines from the landing-places, and formed large harbours of fairly calm water. The French engineers at Helles did the same, and even sank a very old battleship to strengthen their system of sheltering piers. But a northern hurricane at the beginning of November undid some of this work, and damaged the lines of wrecks by rolling upon them with terrific fury from an unexpected direction. The breakwaters had been built against south-westerly gales, so that the northerly hurricane cleared the harbourages and made it necessary to reconstruct the rows of sunken steamers.

The memorable Gallipoli storm was that which began on November 26, 1915. In the night a violent thunderstorm broke over the peninsula, bringing down a cloudburst torrent of rain. The flood streamed downward for about twelve hours, in a volume of water so heavy that by the end of the first hour the trenches in some places were three feet deep in water, which cascaded down the saps, turned the dug-outs into drowning-pits, burst a dam of earthworks at Suvla, and then rushed down in all directions. Some of the trenches were full to the parapets, and men had to swim to avoid being drowned. But though the Turks were on higher ground, they suffered more than did the British. In certain parts of their line they had to stand on their parapets, where they were shot down by machine-guns. In other places, they had to crawl out into the open ground, and there also they were shot down.

Then, in the night of November 27, a still more terrible ordeal was imposed upon the opposing armies. A northern wind of Arctic severity swept over the hills of the peninsula. Many of the men of Anzac saw snow for the first time in their lives; and after the snow had fallen upon the soaking wet clothes of all the troops, a hard frost set in and froze the greatcoats of the men, so that these garments could be stood upright by themselves. There were men who had been up to their necks in water for a day, and had gone without food for thirty-six hours, as their ration parties had been lost; then their clothes had frozen upon them like boards. Soldiers were caught and frozen as they lay sleeping in utter exhaustion in the mud of the trenches, in a climate which scarcely a month before had been warm with the waning glow of a tropical summer.

The plight of the Turks was even worse. When it thawed on December 1, their bodies came floating down flooded gullies, where British soldiers had died of thirst in August. The Turks had no blankets or waterproof sheets; some of them were killed while they ran about looking for fuel; and large numbers gave themselves up in the hope of getting near a fire. As a matter of fact, there were then no fires in the British trenches; both officers and men were lucky who had cold bully beef and biscuit to eat. For the previous torrent had washed away the furniture of many dug-outs.

The extraordinary weather entirely upset the enemy's new plan of operations. The roads for the heavy howitzers were washed away in many parts, and the great vehicles, with their bullock-teams, were first bogged in the mud and then frozen there. Road-building in heavy autumn rain was bad enough, but when the ground alternately froze and thawed at the end of November, while the men failed in thousands from both sickness and frost-bite, the German engineers directing the job must have been reduced to a mood of black despair. In fact, they did not get their heavy guns into position until there was nobody on the peninsula remaining as a target for 12 in. shells. Even the shell supply was so delayed by bad communication and by naval bombardments that the Turks could not, even by the first week in January, 1916, maintain that intensity of gun fire which was required to level the British trenches and inspire their infantry with sufficient confidence to attack.

CHAPTER 20

The Fall of Warsaw and After

A FTER the fall of Lemberg German hopes of obtaining a final decision in the Eastern theatre of war during the summer of 1915 ran high. The Russians were now occupying the great defensive line passing from Novo Georgievsk, by Ivangorod, Lublin, and Cholm, to the river Bug, Lutsk, and Rovno; the northward line from Warsaw and Novo Georgievsk, the line of the Narew and the Niemen, being as yet intact. These two lines form roughly two sides of a triangle, with Novo Georgievsk and Warsaw as its apex. While they were held, Warsaw was secure; and Warsaw meant the bridges over the Vistula, the gateway necessary to a further advance into Russia. Novo Georgievsk, Ivangorod, and Brest Litowsk, east of Warsaw, formed also an angle covering Warsaw.

The German plan was to attack the Russian line both north and south of Warsaw, and taking the main Russian army on both flanks bring about a greater Sedan. With this purpose Hindenburg collected in the north a force of about a million men and divided it into three armies placed between Kovno and Mlava. The forces around Kovno were under the command of Eichhorn, who had been fighting in the Niemen river region for many months. Connecting with his southern wing were two great armies near Prasnysch, under Generals Scholtz and Gallwitz, who were further reinforced by an army under General Beseler, the conqueror of Antwerp, who was provided with a siege train of many 11, 12, 17, and 20 in. howitzers. He was to shatter and storm the great Russian entrenched camp of Novo Georgievsk on the Vistula river, while the armies of Gallwitz and Scholtz burst through the Russian lines on the Narew and Bobr rivers, and got in the rear of the Russian army defending Warsaw. In the south two great masses were concentrated, with Lublin and Cholm as their objectives.

The way in which the Russians had carried out the evacuation of Przemysl and Lemberg forbade the enemy to hope that he could break through the Russian line if it preferred retreating to imperilling its integrity. But it might be compelled to retire beyond the railway running from Cholm by Lublin to Ivangorod. If the Germans could get astride that railway Ivangorod would be cut off from the supplies and support on that side, and the maintenance of the line covering Warsaw would consequently be jeopardised. The German army, under Mackensen's command, was directed against Cholm; the Austrian army, under the Archduke Joseph Ferdinand, against Lublin. The object in view would be attained if either succeeded in its effort. In order that the encircling movement should succeed it was necessary to allow time for the armies under Mackensen and the Archduke to progress towards Cholm and Lublin, and the central Austro-German forces, operating in the great bend of the Vistula in the direction of Warsaw and Ivangorod, had also to be allowed time to fight their way closer to the central Russian armies.

The general position, therefore, remained for some weeks very deceptive in appearance. Nothing occurred to show that Warsaw was in immediate danger. Hindenburg remained quietly at his base in the East Prussian railway town of Allenstein, and forbade his corps and army commanders to exercise any marked pressure on the Russian forces entrenched around Prasnysch. Then his neighbour, Prince Leopold of Bavaria, commanding the Austro-German forces on the Rawka river in front of Warsaw, remained also very quiet, after a vain attempt to throw the Russian army back. On the right of the Bavarian prince was the remnant of the first-line Austro-Hungarian army, which General Dankl had led across the Russian frontier in August, 1914. Dankl had gone to the Italian front, and his twice-shattered army had been strengthened by fresh troops, stiffened with a large German element, and placed under the command of Woyrsch.

Woyrsch operated between the Pilica river and the Upper Vistula, but he was firmly held in front of Radom by the troops of General Alexeieff. He made progress only when Alexeieff had to swing down along the stream, in order to maintain connection with Ivanoff's forces between the Vistula and the Bug. Ivanoff was still opposed by the Austrian army under the Archduke Joseph Ferdinand and by that under Mackensen. And, as in the Galician campaign, it was the slowly-moving force of Mackensen which controlled the situation. On July 1 Mackensen occupied the Polish town of Zamosc, through which a firm road ran northward to the railway station of Cholm. The Archduke Joseph Ferdinand occupied the Polish town of Krasnik, through which a highway ran to the railway station of Lublin. Between the army of the archduke and the army of Mackensen there ran the river Wieprz, with marshland on either side of it soaked with the extraordinary rainfall of the previous month. The position is worth examining on a map. It will there be seen that Krasnik is barely twenty-five miles south of Lublin, and that Zamosc is about the same distance from the railway running to Cholm. As the Cholm and Lublin railway connected Ivangorod and Warsaw with the great Russian depot city of Kiev all the Russian armies in Poland were menaced by the forces at Krasnik and Zamosc.

Moltke's feat in shepherding the French army into the trap of Sedan was a small affair compared with that which Hindenburg was devising, in collaboration with Falkenhayn. They had taken a plan formed by General von der Goltz, and worked it out in terms of big gun transport. All that scientific calculation and prevision could do had been done, but the advent of reconnoitring aeroplanes made great strokes of surprise, that needed long preparation, somewhat difficult to conceal. The Grand Duke Nicholas learned enough to make him suspicious, and he sought for some means of delaying the immense movement of envelopment. He selected the weakest link in the chain that was being tightened around him. This weak link was the Austrian army at Krasnik, under the Archduke Joseph Ferdinand. Its artillery was more powerful than the Russian, but the Austrian guns were far from their railway base in Galicia, and the Russian army, with the railway behind it at Lublin, was able to get a quicker supply of shells.

The Lublin army was the Russian 3rd army, formerly commanded by Radko Dmitrieff. Its original four army corps had been half shattered on the Dunajec, but into its cadres was poured new material composed of the best fighting men available in Russia. The Russian 8th army had retired alongside the 3rd, and had also been severely handled. It also was reorganized from the best fighting material in Russia, for the design was that it should hold up Mackensen's forces at Cholm, while the 3rd army struck at the Archduke.

The battle began on July 2. With about a third of a million men, the archduke deployed on a front of ten miles at Krasnik, and tried to break the Russians in a series of fierce night attacks.

But his men were held up on the Wysnica, a tributary of the Vistula which runs through Krasnik. The battle continued for some days, with extreme fury, along the river and a brook flowing into it. After some heavy losses the Austrians managed on July 4, to push the Russians back and occupy the town of Bychava.

But the battle was only beginning. The Austrians had been merely attacking a rearguard, and after they had expended much of their strength in advancing over the river, the main Russian force came into action. It drove at the Archduke's flank on the Vistula, and Woyrsch's troops had to be flung across the stream to reinforce the Austrian army. At the same time the Russians attacked the Archduke's right wing above Turobin, and Mackensen had to hurry a large part of his forces across the difficult ground on the Wieprz river. Then the Russian troops attacked the Austrian centre, lying across the road to Lublin, and in a persistent, driving movement, lasting till Friday, July 9, they broke the Austrian centre, captured some 15,000 men and some dozens of machine-guns. The Austrians withdrew to the high ground around Krasnik, keeping in front of them a strong force on Hill 218, which dominated the country. The Russians made several attempts to carry the height, but the Austro-German machine-gun parties, helped by their artillery fire, countered all the attacks. In their turn, the Austrians swept down upon the hill, and tried to carry the village at the foot. But they were repulsed. By this time the two armies were fully entrenched against each other.

In so far as the Lublin army had aimed at breaking and routing the forces of the Archduke Joseph Ferdinand, and then getting on the flank of Mackensen's army, the great Russian counter-attack had failed; but in so far as it had been designed to check the enemy's advance, it had succeeded. The Austrian army of invasion was weakened in a very serious manner, and instead of being able to co-operate in a forward movement with Mackensen's force, it had to be saved from destruction by that army. This increased the weight of fighting thrown on Mackensen's men, and though they stubbornly moved forward to Cholm, they had to pay a terrible price for every mile they won. Mackensen's enormous battering-ram of heavy artillery had to have a railway built for it from Rava Ruska along the line where the Russian light railway had been destroyed.

There was only a single firm road running through the muddy Polish fields, and this causeway had been damaged as much as possible by the retreating Russians. The advance towards Cholm, after the extraordinary rainfall of the previous June, was a terribly exhausting struggle against Polish mud. Men and horses were severely strained, and the Russians inflicted severe punishment on the weary German advance forces in a series of flank conflicts along the eastern tributaries of the Wieprz. Mackensen could do nothing without thousands of guns behind him to command the battlefield, for his infantry had had much of its pugnacity knocked out of it.

On July 16 he tried to get into line with the Austrian forces at Krasnik by carrying by storm the Russian entrenchments east of the town of Tarnagora. But his men fell in heaps in front of the water-course, without effecting any advance. Again, on July 17, Mackensen tried to break across the river by massed infantry attacks, supported only by machine-guns and light field artillery. But the German troops were shattered at every point between the Bug and the Wieprz, and in the evening of that day the victorious Russian rearguard charged with the bayonet and cleared a forest of the enemy.

Mackensen succeeded after a fortnight's delay in getting his great howitzers dragged up to the battle-front, and in accumulating a great store of shells. By a hurricane fire he destroyed the Russian trenches on either side of the highway to Cholm at dawn on July 18, and captured the town of Krasnostav on the Wieprz river. This was a decisive success, for Krasnostav was only seven and a half miles from the railway running through Cholm and Lublin, and connecting Kieff with Ivangorod and Warsaw. In ordinary circumstances it was only an easy half-day's march for Mackensen's troops from Krasnostav to the railway. General Ivanoff's armies, of course, were able to make the short journey a matter of considerable difficulty to the invading force, but there were other circumstances which entirely changed the situation, and made the Lublin and Cholm battlefield for the time a scene of secondary importance.

Hindenburg had shown his hand. Either by design or from over-anxiety, the German commander-in-chief had tried to redeem the check to the Archduke Joseph's forces at Krasnik by a fierce attack from Prasnysch. The closing-in movement had begun on July 11, the day when the Russian army at

Lublin completed its great counter-offensive. Hindenburg should have waited until Mackensen retrieved the local situation between the Vistula and the Bug by bringing up his heavy artillery and clearing a path to Krasnostav. But his movement was not timed with precision, and the German plan was prematurely revealed by an exceedingly violent bombardment of all the Russian positions from Osoviec on the Bobr river to the trenches along the Wkra stream. The positions extended for nearly 140 miles north and north-east of Warsaw, with Prasnysch and Lomza as the central sector of the river line.

Hindenburg opened his bombardment at night on July 11, thus boldly revealing the position of his guns in the darkness by the flames they emitted, and challenging the Russian batteries to show themselves by their gun flashes. Naturally the Russian gunners attempted no reply, for each of their pieces would have been overwhelmed by the massed fire of the more numerous enemy batteries. Only the little fort of Osoviec, which commanded a road over the marshes where the Germans had only room to bring up a few guns, maintained an artillery duel. For three nights the artillery of Hindenburg's three armies swept the Russian positions with high-explosive shell. Then, on July 14, the German infantry advanced under the barrage, and captured Prasnysch, about 65 miles north of Warsaw.

The Russian forces holding the village, round which they had gained so many victories, did not resist the German advance, for an attempt to do so would have meant destruction. They fell back towards the Narew river, out of reach of the German artillery, which on part of the front seems to have included, from the start of the action, the great siege train under General von Beseler. The combined artillery power of Beseler's, Gallwitz's, and Scholtz's armies could only be met by bringing into action the fortress guns of Novo Georgievsk and the heavy position artillery behind the bridge-heads along the Narew river. In the meantime the movement of the German artillery forces was continually checked whenever they attacked without the help of the heavy howitzers, and great losses were inflicted upon the enemy in the river marshes north of Lomza and Ostrolenka, and also south of Prasnysch. But on July 19, which was the day when Mackensen drove forward towards the railway which connects Warsaw with southern Russia, Hindenburg also brought up his thousands of heavy pieces of artillery and his large army towards the Narew front, menacing the north-eastern railway communications of the Polish capital.

Warsaw was then clearly doomed, together with Novo Georgievsk and Ivangorod, and the fortress bridge-heads along the Narew River. There was no question of saving Warsaw. The problem was to save the central Russian army under General Alexeieff. The position of this army constituted a vast salient. The base of the salient stretched from Lomza on the Narew to a point near Lublin on the Vistula, the distance between the two points being about one hundred and thirty miles. From the base-line stretching from Lomza to Lublin the Russian salient extended forward nearly a hundred miles to the famous battle-line along the Bzura river. Could Alexeieff withdraw his forces from the Bzura river and from the upper Vistula, and entrench them strongly near Brest Litovsk before Hindenburg and Mackensen were able to smash through his right rear flank and his left rear flank, and surround, capture, or annihilate the principal Russian army?

The Russian forces holding the great salient were very large indeed, but against them were huge armies, with an artillery power of unparalleled magnitude. The guns of the great German fortresses in the east had been placed on special carriages, and moved first by train and then by motor tractors along the new roads which Hindenburg's armies made as they advanced. Two huge Austro-German siege trains battered in either side of the salient, and there was an immense number of lighter guns. The work of feeding the guns with shells and charges was enormous, and the estimated consumption of 250,000 shells a day was probably under the mark.

The main work fell on Hindenburg's armies, owing to the fact that Mackensen could not drive forward quickly enough. After weakening his forces to help the archduke, Mackensen was firmly held for some weeks by the Russian army at Cholm. But in the circumstances the delay in his advance to the railway line did not matter. It may have been subtly designed with a view to lulling the central Russian army into a feeling of false security, and inducing the Grand Duke Nicholas to risk holding on to the Warsaw front until Hindenburg's great hammer-stroke fell with terrific force on the right flank, when Mackensen was suddenly to strike with all his power on the other flank. The Grand Duke Nicholas, however, was not deceived. The success of his

Lublin and Cholm armies did not mislead him in his general strategy, for he gave the historic order for the abandonment of Warsaw on July 18. It was on this day that the remarkable strength of Hindenburg's armies was clearly revealed, in a drive down from Prasnysch to the Narew river. So close did the Germans come to the Russian river defences immediately above Warsaw that the guns of the Vistula fortress of Novo Georgievsk had to be brought into action to repulse the leading German columns. All the Russian forces in the centre swiftly concentrated round the doomed capital of Poland. The river lines along the Rawka were abandoned in the night, the guns being removed closer to Warsaw, to the Blonie lines, and the troops retiring under the protection of a strong rearguard, which in turn escaped to the new lines.

On this sector of the front the enemy forces were commanded by Leopold of Bavaria who did not display any initiative, and the Russian retirement was carried out without a hitch. General von Woyrsch, acting in the neighbouring sector between the Pilica and the upper Vistula, with Ivangorod as his objective, showed more driving power and grasp of the situation than Prince Leopold. Knowing that the Russian forces in front of him were certain to be preparing to retire, Woyrsch made a fierce attack on Radom along two roads which converged on this town. But the Russian commander sent out two strong forces west and north-west of Radom, so that the attack was met by counter-attacks and thrown back.

The army defending Ivangorod then fell back on its lines close to the Vistula and the bridge across the river. Ivangorod was no longer a fortress, its works of brick being too old to withstand the modern siege howitzers. The old-fashioned 6 in. guns had been removed and placed in pits behind the trenches in which the infantry worked. There were field-guns on some of the river islands and behind the wire entanglements in the riverside forests where the Russian infantrymen broke Hindenburg's first attack on the Vistula line in the autumn of 1914.

The Russian heavy artillery was sited across the river, thus making a retirement from Ivangorod a quick and easy operation. They had no difficulty at any time in holding back Woyrsch's forces. Only Mackensen's and Hindenburg's distant enveloping movements put them in danger. It was the Ivangorod army and the Warsaw army that the German field-marshals hoped to capture by their great flanking operations. General Alexeieff answered these flanking operations by withdrawing the menaced troops towards the Vistula and giving them shorter lines to hold, so that a considerable part of their forces could be at once sent through Warsaw and Ivangorod to reinforce the Narew front. In this way, the great Warsaw retreat was begun by a direct and strong movement of concentration against Hindenburg's group of armies.

Very great powers of judgment were needed in this intricate rearrangement of forces under the guns of the enemy. The German commander-in-chief had large reserves, kept on or about the railways in his rear. It was his object to mask the direction in which he intended to launch his reserve force and make his decisive stroke, while deceiving his opponent if possible by feints of new concentrations. This the strategical Prussian railway system enabled him to do. But Alexeieff divined the enemy's plan with such success that, after he had extracted his forces from the German noose and withdrawn them along the railway to Petrograd, the Tsar acclaimed him as the best Russian strategist and made him chief of staff to all the Russian forces.

All the while this rearrangement of the Russian forces was taking place in the salient, Hindenburg was drawing in on the bridge-heads of the Narew river. At the same time, his northern armies attacked all along the line from Riga to Kovno and thence down the Niemen and the Bobr streams. Far in the south-east an Austro-Hungarian army, under General Kirchbach, operating on the frontier of Galicia, made a violent effort near Sokal, on the Bug, and forced the passage of the river, threatening to divide the force under General Ivanoff. In the centre General von Woyrsch, with the Landwehr of Silesia and the infantry of Transylvania, closed down on Ivangorod, while Mackensen brought all his reserves into action and, with his guns again supplied with millions of shells, struck with great force at the Ivangorod-Lublin-Cholm-Kieff railway.

On Friday, July 23, 1915, the great blow fell in the direction foreseen by Alexeieff. For 1,000 miles the Russian troops were kept at tension by the attacking forces, each group of which advanced to the assault with the heightened energy of men who know that a great victory is within their reach. Between the Vistula and the Bug, Mackensen was breaking up the Russian trenches by a tornado of shell fire. In the bend of the Vistula, Woyrsch had broken the connexion between the army of Warsaw and the army of Ivangorod by capturing a river position between the two cities at Royienice. All the Russian forces between the mouth of the Pilica and Kozienice were forced across the Vistula. Prince Leopold of Bavaria was able to close in on Warsaw from the west and south and approach within 16 miles of the city. While all the Russian forces were thus apparently bent to breaking point, Hindenburg made what he thought was the decisive stroke.

Under his direction the army of General von Gallwitz, which for days had been bombarding all the bridge-heads of the Narew river, advanced in dense masses and stormed the redoubts at the crossing-places of Rozan and Pultusk. The losses of the attacking infantry were heavy, for the Russian commander had placed his heavy guns south of the river, in such sites as brought a cross-fire to bear upon any forces approaching the bridge-heads. These concealed guns had as long a range as anything made by Krupp and Skoda, and the only reason why they had avoided an artillery duel was the shortage of high-explosive shell. But there was a useful amount of shrapnel, and when the entire German army was deployed in the open field, the long-silent heavy Russian batteries got to work. Hindenburg had to use up the larger part of his reserve in order to force the river, and when this success had been achieved at enormous cost, it was found to be fruitless; for, far from being broken, the Russian forces on the Narew were in tremendous strength. So strong were they indeed that they defeated Hindenburg's design to make a rapid, sweeping movement across the Narew to the Lower Bug, in the rear of Warsaw.

The Russian commander had been holding the Narew line merely with a thin line of troops; his chief forces were concealed in the forests extending from the south side of the river. All the actions at the crossings were merely rearguard actions, fought to gain time for the new concentration of troops. Despite the fact that the evacuation of Warsaw was rapidly proceeding, and that all manufacturing plant and materials and workmen were being moved into central Russia, General Alexeieff seems to have been half inclined to stand and offer battle, for he was in a position of great advantage. His men were now little inferior in numbers to those of Hindenburg, and the over-powering hostile artillery was not able to work well; for as the region between the Narew and the Bug was marshy and thickly wooded, the movement of heavy guns was a slow and arduous business, and the field of fire was restricted.

Gallwitz's forces formed a salient between Novo Georgievsk and the Forest of Rozan, leaving him open to a combined attack on both flanks. This attack was delivered on July 26, and though Hindenburg threw into the field his last reserves from the direction of Sierok, the Germans were forced back to the Narew in disorder at several points. The Russians then closed on Sierok, which lies at the confluence of the Bug and Vistula, recrossed the Narew, and a long, fluctuating conflict went on day and night on both sides of the river until July 30.

So far as Hindenburg was concerned, Warsaw, with its protecting fortress of Novo Georgievsk, and its connecting northern entrenched camp at Grodno, might have stood firm throughout the campaign, with the Petrograd railway in the rear supplying the fighting-line. The German army under Below was held firmly in Courland. Eichhorn was vainly wasting men by tens of thousands in trying to approach Kovno. Gallwitz's troops were nearly exhausted. Scholtz's army had come into action on his right, without bettering the situation, and Novo Georgievsk was protected by a Russian army which prevented Beseler from getting his siege-guns within range of the steel-domed and concrete-walled forts.

But the failure of Hindenburg was redeemed by the success of Mackensen. On July 29 his famous striking force reached the railway track between Lublin and Cholm, thus turning by a flank attack all the Russian lines along the Vistula. Ivangorod, which had been munitioned and fed by the lost railway, had to be abandoned, and on its abandonment the armies of Prince Leopold, Woyrsch, the Archduke Joseph Ferdinand, and Mackensen's great force could link up and sweep forward in a vast enveloping movement on the east of Warsaw.

For more than two weeks the Russian armies, based on Lublin and Cholm, had stubbornly stood out against Mackensen. All that men could do, the old southern wing of the Russian forces had done. What had defeated them at last was the road-making plant of Mackensen's army. As the roads were made, the train of heavy howitzers came closer to the vital railway line. The lighter gunned and more mobile Russian army holding Lublin first tried to assail Mackensen's western flank by breaking through the Austrian army at Krasnik. When this desperate plan failed, the Cholm army essayed an equally hard task, and advanced directly against Mackensen's eastern flank, some thirty miles south of Cholm, at Grubieszov.

Mackensen's main artillery force was then slowly advancing towards the railway line, so that the quicker-moving Russian force was able to strike behind it. These were the usual Russian tactics in cases where the enemy was chained to a slow, cumbersome mass of extraordinarily heavy ordnance. They gave way on the sector in which the hurricane fire of large shells made their trenches untenable, but as they gave way they massed and struck out in a side attack on a sector where the enemy had to meet them on more equal terms in the matter of artillery power. The German commander was compelled, by the difficulty of finding hard roads for his great howitzers, and by the need for massing his artillery fire so as to obtain decisive effects, to keep his large pieces of ordnance close together.

Though Mackensen like other generals did not spare his men, he did not waste them without achieving definite results, and the greatest of all his achievements was the breaking of the Lublin-Cholm line towards the end of July, 1915. After he suddenly turned northward at Rava Ruska in the middle of June, his progress was slow. His average pace was only about a mile and a half a day. But though he was still faced by the armies he had broken on the Dunajec, the quality and temper of those armies had changed, and he had lost the advantage of surprise in his further conflicts with them. They had been thoroughly reorganized and placed under one of the ablest of Russian strategists, who was well informed of the artillery power and great infantry force which Mackensen wielded.

Yet the Russian considered he might fight the German to a standstill. He nearly succeeded in getting on his flank at Krasnik; and then at Grubieszov, Mackensen was again held up by a thrust towards his rear. He countered it by making a strong attempt to envelop the hostile forces, which were in a dangerously advanced position, at Grubieszov, on July 22. A German division was destroyed in trying to break through the Russian line of entrenched hills north of Grubieszov and reach the railway line at a point near the Bug. But this division did not die in vain. It was thrown away, with tens of thousands of other troops, in a fierce but misleading demonstration, and on July 29, when the Cholm army had massed eastward near the Bug after the victory, Mackensen's main force worked westward up the Wieprz river, from its old advanced base of Krasnostav, and in a conflict of extreme violence broke the Russian line between Cholm and Lublin, on the evening of July 29, and reached the railway at Biskupice.

The battle was waged on both sides of the Wieprz stream on a front of seventeen miles, and it was won by shell fire from thousands of pieces, many of the largest calibre. Deep as the Russian trenches were in places, they were wrecked by high explosives, and the sand-bag breastworks in the river marshes were more easily destroyed. In this way wide gaps were blown in the line of defence; and under this continuous stream of shells the Austrian army corps under General von Arz, which formed part of the German striking force, stormed into the Russian lines and held them. The hand-to-hand fighting that followed was desperate but the Russian counter-attacks, though at first successful, were at last shattered, and when night fell the railway was definitely lost.

The Ivangorod garrison then had to prepare to retire, and as the troops holding this section of the Vistula weakened, General von Woyrsch, who had secured a favourable position on the river between Ivangorod and Warsaw, threw two pontoon bridges over it and advanced to cut off Warsaw on Saturday, July 31. He was beaten back to his bridge-head at Maciejovice, but as the Russian line continued to weaken, owing to the pressure of Mackensen's forces eastward, General von Woyrsch poured his army over the river again, and on Sunday afternoon, August 1, he had four divisions across the water. The Russian troops in the neighbourhood were forced back a considerable distance towards Garwolin, and this new irruption into their lines definitely ended their stand on the Warsaw front.

The Polish capital, from which everything useful was removed, except food and private property belonging to the townsmen who chose to remain, was entered by Prince Leopold of Bavaria on the morning of August 5, 1915. A Russian rearguard held the last lines until the bridges were blown up. Then the defending troops marched through the lost city, having left the attacking forces a long task to restore the means of crossing the Vistula and getting guns and ammunition over to make a pursuit. It was Mackensen's new menace to the Brest Litovsk line, combined with the advance in the same direction by Woyrsch, largely brought about by Mackensen's manœuvre, that decided the fate of Warsaw and its neighbouring positions of Ivangorod and Novo Georgievsk.

The migration of the people from the country north and south of Warsaw, and from Warsaw itself, was a slow movement. Several million persons preceded the armies in the great retreat into Central Russia. Warsaw was emptied of material. Both factories and churches were stripped, one of the principal relics removed being the heart of the great Polish composer Chopin, which was taken to Moscow. Along the roads to Moscow, 1,000 miles away, moved all the carriages, carts, and horses, the vehicles being filled with household treasures. The direct route through Brest Litovsk was occupied with military business, troop trains and munition trains shuttling to and fro in answer to the pressure exerted by Mackensen and Hindenburg. The wealthy people in Warsaw, who stayed until the end, when all motor-cars had vanished, were glad of standing room in the cattle trucks. But the gigantic evacuation was managed with great organizing power, and when Prince Leopold's cavalry entered the city, there was nothing but an empty shell.

Though Warsaw had fallen, the Germans and Austrians had failed to envelop the Russian army and General Alexeiëff was solving the problem of withdrawal to a new line with considerable success. That problem was to withdraw a quarter of a million men from Warsaw towards Brest Litovsk, a distance of one hundred and thirty miles, while Hindenburg was pressing on his northern flank and Mackensen on his southern flank, and the armies of Prince Leopold of Bavaria and General von Woyrsch were assailing his retreating front. Mackensen, with his artillery, was the most dangerous assailant; so Alexeieff joined his left wing with Ivanoff's right wing, and between Ivangorod and Cholm the combined Russian forces made a surprise attack upon Mackensen's armies in a battle that lasted till August 9.

Mackensen's left wing was held up along the Wieprz river, while his centre and right wing were severely handled along the Bug some twenty-five miles south of the town of Vlodava. There was a Russian railway running from Brest Litovsk through Vlodava towards Cholm, and it fed the Russian defending forces more quickly than Mackensen could be supplied by the light railway he had built to connect his rear with the Lemberg system. It was not until August 10 that the army of General von Woyrsch, advancing through the Ivangorod region, got into touch with the Austrian force forming the left wing of Mackensen's army group, and on that day Mackensen's centre was only about eighteen miles north of the Lublin-Cholm railway, which he had reached on July 29. It had taken him twelve days to advance nineteen miles with his 2,000 heavy pieces of ordnance and the ordinary artillery corps of a group of armies numbering originally close upon a million men.

Hindenburg, however, who was working with another large army, from a point near Warsaw to a point near Riga, proved a very formidable opponent. His troops were fresher and less wasted than those of Mackensen, his siege artillery was less worn, and he had close behind him the double system of East Prussian railways, which had been extended by roughly-built lines across the frontier towards the Narew, Bobr, and Niemen battle-fronts. There were steam tramways for bringing up ammunition and food, with asphalted roads and motor-tractors; and deep beds of concrete were laid of ten to thirteen miles in length from the great Russian fortress towns of Novo Georgievsk, Osoviec and Kovno in preparation for the great siege-howitzers. In the open field fighting against Alexeieff's right wing, behind Warsaw, Hindenburg was not successful. He was held up between Lomza and Warsaw by struggles of a terrible kind in the forests and along the river-banks, and being impatient to carry out his part of the enveloping movement he used his infantry without waiting for his siege ordnance. On August 7, nine days after Mackensen had cut the Lublin-Cholm railway, Hindenburg began a series of superhuman efforts to storm the northern Russian front.

On the north, the Russian fortress guns broke the enemy; but on the west, in the difficult river country, where the Russian field artillery was protected by a couple of broad streams from the long-ranged German ordnance, the infantry battle was fiercely contested. The Russians held the Narew river line only with weak rearguards. These rearguards fell back immediately the pressure against them became severe. Every German commander thought it was a sign of weakness. The German infantry was thrown in great masses across the Narew. The result was that the Russian gunners along the second river line of the Bug were able to use their shrapnel with good effect.

Then, as they lifted on the German rear, the large main body of Russian infantry concealed in the riverside forests surged forward and recovered Sierok at the point of the bayonet. Hindenburg was also checked at Ostrov, where he attempted a lightning stroke against the Warsaw-Petrograd railway line.

His northernmost forces operating in the Riga region were likewise severely handled, and driven out of their trenches near the Dwina river. The beginning of the second week in August was thus marked by a series of defeats all along the immense line controlled by Hindenburg. Every other German or Austrian commander had some success to show. Prince Leopold of Bavaria was cutting off the Russian army corps at Novo Georgievsk by a movement on Praga, north of Warsaw. General von Woyrsch was at Garwolin, on the road to Brest Litovsk, and Mackensen was across the Wieprz river, and advancing in the same direction.

Hindenburg alone with his armies under Beseler, Gallwitz, Scholtz, Eichhorn, Below, and Lauenstein could not make any progress whatever, though they had the largest and the best armed forces. He appears to have attributed his delay to the long time required for making the concrete beds for the 16½ in. howitzers needed to batter down the chain of Russian frontier fortresses. As a matter of fact, there was ample room for him to have advanced between Lomza and Sierok in the south; and in the north, between Lomza and Grodno, only the small but important bridgehead fort of Osoviec barred his way. He had, in fact, concentrated his main forces between Lomza and Sierok; but on this section of the front Alexeieff clean outfought him by means of the use of forest cover and river marshlands.

The consequence was that Alexeieff moved southwards through the narrow corridor between the Warsaw-Petrograd railway line and the Garwolin-Lukov front—a distance of from 35 to 50 miles—in secrecy as complete as aeroplane reconnaissance would allow. When night fell and veiled his dispositions his main manœuvres for battle were conducted in the darkness. On August 9 he withdrew from around Novo Georgievsk, leaving much less than an army corps in the fortress and only half the fortress guns, with orders to hold out till the main forts were stormed. The troops, sacrificed to win time, formed his chief rearguard, and their most important duty was to sink every vessel that came up the Vistula. The enemy was using the river as his great line of communications and bringing up cartridges, shells, and charges by means of steam and motor tug-boats. For as the railway bridges at Warsaw and Ivangorod were destroyed, and the rails for some miles in front of both towns needed relaying, the Vistula remained the only quick means of supplying the armies of Prince Leopold of Bavaria and General von Woyrsch. In these circumstances the Russian commander thought it well worth while to sacrifice 25,000 men in Novo Georgievsk in order to delay supplies for the Austro-German forces.

The line of Alexeieff's retreat made it necessary for Hindenburg to strike as far north as possible, and as the fortress of Grodno was covered by a very strong line of Cossack sharp-shooters, fighting with the advantage of ground in the forests, swamps, and lakes west of the Niemen river, the city of Kovno, on the northern bend of the Niemen, was the only possible point at which vast massed German forces could be quickly concentrated for a belated attempt to obtain a decision.

Kovno lies only 50 miles from the Prussian frontier, at the confluence of the Niemen, the Vilia, and some small brooks. Originally it had a girdle of eleven forts, extending about two and a half miles from the old Lithuanian town. In times of peace a railway connected Kovno with the Prussian frontier town of Eydtkuhnen, and though the line had been destroyed the engineers of General von Eichhorn's army rebuilt the track and along it brought up a great siege train, including some 16½ in. howitzers and many 11 in. and 12 in. pieces.

The fortress could have been captured at a comparatively small expense of life by allowing the work to be slowly done by the siege train. But Eichhorn's assistant, General Litzmann, who directly controlled the operations at Kovno, began the attack across the western forest section, extending from the Jessia brook to the village of Piple. After a hurricane fire of two hours the German infantry threw out some skirmishing lines, and behind these came dense storming columns. But the wooded ground over which the assailers charged was pitted with land-mines, and behind these devices were the Russian wire entanglements and trenches, concealed in a tangle of trees and bushes. The mobile Russian field-guns, which had reserved their fire during the hostile bombardment, now came fiercely into action, and the German columns were so terribly shattered by shell fire, machine-gun fire, and rifle fire, that the Russian troops in the advanced trenches were able to make a daring bayonet charge into the enemy's front. By five o'clock in the morning the German infantry was thrown back into the ravines beyond the village.

The German gunners then tried to wipe out the Russian trenches with some hundreds of thousands of shells. The intense bombardment lasted all day on August 8, and when night fell the enemy columns again charged up from the forest ravines across the flame-lit rim of woodland between the Jessia and the Niemen. After a struggle of two hours they broke into the advanced Russian trenches, only to be driven out of them by high-explosive shell and hand-bombs. Then, just before dawn, Litzmann sent fresh masses forward, and the new columns managed to get a footing in a few trenches in front of the outer forts near Digry village.

All the force of the attack was concentrated against the western face of the fortress, but the outer defences were still resisting by August 12, after six days and six nights of fierce fighting. On Friday, August 13, Litzmann managed to capture a work in one of the Niemen woods, but his besieging army was broken by its enormous losses. Large forces had to be detached from the northernmost army, under Below, to enable the siege operations to continue. There was a lull of some days in the infantry attacks on Kovno, during which the heavy German artillery supplied with shell by the Prussian railway, maintained an unceasing storm of fire on the Russian trenches, redoubts, and forts. Then on Monday, August 16, the reinforced German infantry resumed its mass attacks. In the evening a small fort on the left bank of the Niemen was captured, and in the intervening spaces between other forts on the western sector the German columns stormed over the trenches. Fort after fort continued to fall under the overwhelming storm of heavy shell, while the mobile Russian field artillery operating in front of the forts was also overwhelmed. The Russian engineers had designed their cupolas to resist 8 in. shells, but the extraordinary explosive power of the $16\frac{1}{2}$ in. Krupp projectiles completely battered down the armoured domes.

The garrison withdrew over the Jessia brook, using its embankment as a last line of defence. For three days the struggle raged along the western bank of the Niemen and the

Jessia brook. General Litzmann had 2,000 pieces of ordnance; of these 600 guns were ranged in an unbroken semicircle, several rows deep, and they were all massed on a single fort until the work was completely smashed. Then the huge shells were directed upon another single fort. An air fleet of thirty aeroplanes and three large airships circled above the town, dropping bombs and controlling the gun fire. The front of Kovno cathedral was wrecked by a big shell, and much damage was done in both the new town and the old. Yet, though the garrison was hammered out of the forts, these works, with their supporting field artillery, wrought much slaughter before the guns were put out of action.

Since Hindenburg was ready to make this enormous sacrifice of life at a time when he possessed a terrific superiority in heavy artillery and shell supplies, the wonder is not that he captured Kovno, but that he failed to capture the garrison. The Russian troops, however, kept their line of retreat open at Janov, northeast of the town, and at Koshedari, eastward on the line to Vilna. Leaving only a rearguard in the last forts, they withdrew from Kovno on August 21, on which day part of their forces were still fighting on the west bank of the Niemen. Undoubtedly the fall of Kovno was an extremely disagreeable surprise to the Russian staff. Had the Russian armies been fully supplied with ammunition and big guns, Kovno could have been held, as Verdun was, by means of the new system of earthworks enveloping the forts at a distance of seven to ten miles from the town. But the supporting Russian field armies were still weak owing to the deficiency of munitions.

All the frontier fortresses upon which the Russian engineers had expended great treasure and labour became death-traps. The field armies could not hold them when the German siege trains came fully into action. The effect upon the mind of the Russian people, as stronghold after stronghold fell all along the line of invasion, was extremely disturbing. Kovno practically fell on August 17; Novo Georgievsk was occupied by the enemy on August 20. The next day Bielsk was captured. Osoviec was abandoned on August 22; the Austrian cavalry entered Kovel on August 24; and Brest Litovsk was occupied by the Germans and Austrians on August 25.

With the conditions then prevailing Hindenburg could not wait for the Vistula fortress to be reduced by gun fire. His need for the command of the river communications was urgent. He was racing against time, and the check to the munition supplies impeded the advance of his two southern armies, under Gallwitz and Scholtz, between Warsaw and Grodno, besides interfering even more seriously with the fighting power of the group of armies under Prince Leopold and Marshal von Mackensen. Hindenburg, therefore, used two armies against Novo Georgievsk, the besieging army under General von Beseler being reinforced by another 100,000 men.

Gallwitz cut off the fortress on August 9 by his thrust across the Narew river, while Beseler advanced along the Wkra river on the north, using artillery of double the calibre which the Russian forts were designed to resist. The comparatively small garrison had the odds of nearly eight to one against them in the matter of troops, and still more enormous odds against them in the matter of artillery power. But the German commanders lost much of their advantage through using their forces recklessly. As at Kovno, so at Novo Georgievsk, rushing tactics by close-packed columns, thinly screened by lines of skirmishers, were employed within the range of the Russian fortress-guns. Night after night there was a hurricane bombardment, followed by a tremendous infantry attack. The Russians lost trench after trench of their outer defences.

By August 14 the approach defences on the north-east sector were broken, and, pushing closer his siege ordnance, Beseler for sixty hours bombarded one of the chief forts and its two neighbouring smaller works. These were completely shattered and at last were carried by storm on August 18, so as to enable the railway running down from Mlava to be reconstructed closer to the doomed fortress. The Russian troops with their field-guns withdrew across the Wkra river, and fought in the angle between that stream and the larger breadth of water formed by the confluence of the Bug and the Narew, with the still wider expanse of the Vistula protecting them on the south. Beseler, however, brought his siege-guns round to the Vistula section on the night of August 18, and by another hurricane bombardment, lasting two days, all the outer works were destroyed. The remnant of the garrison withdrew on the night of August 19 to the forts round the citadel. The city fell on August 20.

After Kovno and Novo Georgievsk had fallen, the little marshland fortress of Osoviec was assailed. Osoviec consisted of a small system of earthworks, with some concealed concrete gun emplacements, lying on the causeway which connected the Prussian town of Lyck with the Russian town of Bielostok. It had been subjected to assault for nearly twelve months. Several 16½ in. Krupp howitzers were hauled up to blast away the defences of Osoviec, and altogether some two million shells were hurled upon the works. But the men of Osoviec held out when stronger Russian entrenched camps were battered down and stormed. This was due to the fact that no arc of hundreds of pieces of heavy artillery could be ranged against the little bridgehead. The fort was almost entirely surrounded by marshlands, and as the besieging army could only operate along the narrow causeway, the small garrison therein was quite able to hold the enemy back.

Eventually the progress of the German armies over the Narew front compelled the Russians to evacuate Osoviec. On August 21 the army of General von Gallwitz had advanced to the town of Bielsk, some thirty miles south of Bielostok and more than sixty miles south of Osoviec. So it was high time for the garrison to retire. Moreover, some ninety miles south of Bielostok the main forces of the Central empires were then closing round the great Russian entrenched camp of Brest Litovsk. There were seven German and Austrian armies engaged in a vast sweeping movement in the bend of the Bug river and along the forested country between the Bug and Bielostok. These armies were all converging towards the edge of the immense Pripet Marshes, where Brest Litovsk stood, at the junction of the roads and railways leading to Kieff and Moscow.

So long as the Russians held Brest Litovsk, they could keep all their armies for common action, with an intercommunicating system of railways behind them. But if the great junction fortress were lost, Ivanoff's army would lose touch with Alexeieff's army, and the two forces would be divided by the greatest stretch of difficult ground in Europe, the Pripet or Pinsk Marsh. The marsh formed a vast wedge with its point near Brest, and beyond Pinsk it broadened eastward to a width of more than two hundred miles of roadless bog, heath, and forest, quite impassable for an army. Since the age of Peter the Great, some 8,000,000 acres of swamp had been reclaimed between Brest and Pinsk, and a railway had been thrown across the morasses to connect the Moscow and

Kieff trunk lines. But, despite the immense labour spent upon it, the primeval marsh, 300 miles long and 200 miles broad, broke into two distinct portions any forces advancing on it or retiring by it. A scheme of attack had been planned soon after the fall of Warsaw, and though Hindenburg's southern wing, consisting of Gallwitz's and Scholtz's armies, did not move quickly enough, Mackensen's forces were able to sweep in a wide movement of envelopment round Brest Litovsk. In the north the army of Gallwitz's slowly moved towards the Bielovieska Forest, which extends to 396 square miles between the towns of Bielostok and Brest Litovsk.

The army group under Prince Leopold of Bavaria, which included General von Woyrsch's forces, advanced from Warsaw and Ivangorod towards Siedlce, on the road to Brest Litovsk. But about midway it turned leftward and crossed the Bug towards Wysoko Litovsk, and there thrust out along the south side of the Bielovieska Forest. The forest was thus hemmed in on the north-west and the north by Gallwitz's troops, and enveloped south-west and south by Prince Leopold's armies. It was barely fifteen miles from the southernmost skirts of the great northern forest to the northern sector of the outer defences of Brest Litovsk. Consequently, the mighty fortress was partly encircled near the only main line of retreat that was open to the garrison.

Mackensen in person operated with two armies, his own and that of the Archduke Joseph Ferdinand, on the western sector of the great entrenched camp. He also extended his forces northward towards the edge of the Bielovieska Forest in order to combine with Prince Leopold along the Russian line of retreat. Immediately south of Brest, General von Linsingen, who was supposed to have been retired after his disasters on the Dniester front in Galicia, unexpectedly appeared with another large army. He advanced on the south-western edge of the Pripet Marsh near the town of Vijva, through which ran the railway connecting Brest with Rovno. Then, about 15 miles south-east of Vijva, a large force of Teutonic and Hungarian cavalry, under General Puhallo, was fighting its way to Kovno, along one of the tributaries of the Pripet.

In order to batter down quickly the defences of Brest Litovsk the two thousand siege-guns of Mackensen's army were hauled up from Lublin on the rebuilt railway running through Lukov to Brest. For three weeks after the fall of Warsaw fighting went on in the hilly, water-threaded country stretching for ninety miles between Ivangorod and Brest Litovsk. At the beginning of the second week in August, Mackensen's artillery was hammering the Russian field army in front of Brest, while Prince Leopold's troops were making their surprising swerve far to the north of the fortress. But the Russian staff was fully aware of the fact that Mackensen's giant howitzers, though worn by fifteen weeks' work in which they had discharged an unparalleled number of shells, were still well enough rifled to outrange and overpower the smaller, older guns.

The Russian commander-in-chief therefore treated Brest Litovsk exactly as he had treated Kovno and Novo Georgievsk. The garrison removed about half the artillery, mainly pieces of 6 in. calibre that could be used in field warfare, and left about 20,000 infantrymen to hold out as long as they could in the spaces between the forts, while the gunners inflicted as much punishment as possible upon the attacking German and Austrian columns. Meanwhile the Russian field armies, under Alexeieff, withdrew northward in answer to the formidable pressure along the decisive line of attack.

In this way the siege of the greatest of Russian fortresses became a mere incident in the contest of the opposing field armies. Each side tried to deceive the other by attacking and counter-attacking with the utmost violence along the south-western and western sectors of Brest. The Germans had the mechanical advantage of superior artillery; but the Russians, by the slaughter they wrought in infantry fighting, could balance the losses they incurred in the bombardment. The problem was to continue the retreat along the railway to Minsk and the railway to Pinsk, while so misleading the enemy as to get full opportunity for two blows against Gallwitz, Prince Leopold, and Woyrsch in the north, and Mackensen and the Archduke Joseph Ferdinand on the west and southern fronts.

This object was achieved by the evening of August 25. Using the remaining guns of the fortress, the reduced garrison of Brest fought one of the most tremendous rearguard actions in the war, while the main Russian forces mowed down Prince Leopold's and Woyrsch's troops, and part of the northern wing of the Mackensen army group, in a battle in the open field by the Liesna river and the edge of the Bielovieska

Forest. The army of General von Gallwitz was also met and checked on the north-western side of the same forest, along the narrowing high-banked waters of the Upper Narew.

In the afternoon of August 25 the army corps of von Arz, stormed two forts on the south-west front of Brest, the Hungarian Landwehr leading the attack by the village of Kobylany. About the same time some of the new levies from Galicia and Silesia rushed a fort on the west front, and in a night attack Prussian regiments captured the citadel near the railway bridge. The Hungarians and Austrians advanced by daylight in the open in dense formations against the shattered forts.

As a matter of fact, the proper garrison of the great Russian entrenched camp was 100,000 men. But only a division was left to hold the forts along the Bug river. The small body of troops held out while the main army retired towards Pinsk. When this movement had been effected all the fortifications and bridges were blown up, the large railway-station was set on fire, the citadel was destroyed, and the market-place burnt. A very small rearguard checked the Brandenburg regiment during the night attack, and enabled the garrisons of all the forts to rejoin the field army.

Thus ended the progress of the great train of siege artillery which had begun four months before on the river-line of the Dunajec and Biala, in Western Galicia. When Brest fell Mackensen's enormous artillery train was found to be of no further use against the Russians. One thousand of the heaviest pieces of ordnance, all somewhat the worse for wear, were slowly hauled back to Warsaw, and thence sent through Berlin to the western front, where they arrived with the Prussian Guard Corps of the 1st and 2nd divisions about the middle of September. A large number of the 12 in. Skoda howitzers were returned to Austria and railed down to the Danube for use against the Serbians. Then a part of the Archduke Ferdinand Joseph's army, comprising the troops under the command of Kövess, were placed in reserve to refit and rest, preparatory to the new campaign against Serbia, with the general direction of which Mackensen was entrusted.

General Vass.tch commanded the Serbian forces in Macedonia. October, 1915.

Victor Emmanuel III King of Italy whose country joined the Allies, May, 1915.

The Duke of the Abruzzi, who commanded the Italian navy, 1915–17.

General view of Prizrend, Serbia, looking towards the old Turkish citadel. It was occupied by the Bulgarians on November 28, 1915.

An Austrian artillery observation post high in their mountainous frontier. This illustration gives an excellent idea of the arduous task confronting the Italians in their campaigns against the Austrians in 1915.

ALONG THE ITALIAN AND SERBIAN FRONTS

LANDING PLACE OF THE 2ND ROYAL FUSILIERS. This stretch of the Gallipoli coast shows the steep slope down to the beach which had to be carried with the bayonet by the invading troops against a rain of machine-gun fire in April, 1915.

Plate 38

Volume II

Enver Pasha, noted Turkish soldier in command against the Allies in Gallipoli, 1915.

General von Eichhorn, German leader in the East, who captured Kovno, August, 1915.

Ferdinand, tsar of Bulgaria, whose country joined the Central Powers in 1915.

Marshal von der Goltz was lent by the Germans to organize the Turkish forces.

Djemal Pasha, commanded the Turkish army attacking the Suez Canal

Prince Leopold of Bavaria entered Warsaw in triumph in August. 1915

During the Gallipoli operations in August, 1915, a British force landed unexpectedly at Suvla Bay, with the object of gaining control of the central heights of the peninsula. The advantage gained by the surprise element of the attack was lost by ensuing delay in advance and the Turks had time to consolidate before an assault in force was made on their positions. Substantially the project was a failure for the Allied arms.

SOME ENEMY COMMANDERS AND SUVLA BAY

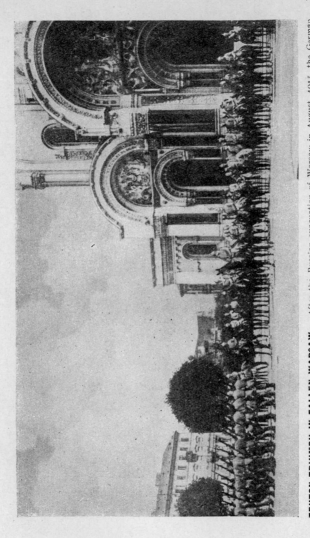

TEUTON TRIUMPH IN FALLEN WARSAW. After the Russian evacuation of Warsaw in August, 1915, the German troops, commanded by Prince Leopold of Bavaria, entered the Polish capital in triumph. This spectacular view represents the prince outside Warsaw's Russian church watching his regiments march past. The retreating Russians blew up the three bridges over the Vistula as they went away.

Plate 40

Volume 11

CHAPTER 21

The Battle of Loos

As early as June, 1915, the French general staff had begun to develop the plans which culminated in the battle of Loos in the following September. The object of this offensive was the recovery of the French mining district around Lens, and it was hoped that if it succeeded Lille would also be again in the possession of the Allies. It was to be timed to coincide with a French offensive in Champagne, so that the Germans could not move reinforcements northwards. After prolonged consultations between the British and the French high commands, it was recognized that an essential of success was an immense superiority in artillery and munitions. Sir John French maintained that this could not be achieved before the spring of 1916, and it was his wish to delay the operation until then. He was, however, overruled, and in the end it was agreed that the offensive which Joffre had originally planned for July should be undertaken in September, 1915.

While the British and French were accumulating men and munitions, the Germans were vigorously engaged in strengthening their position by the construction of a second line with deep barbed wire entanglements and many machine-gun emplacements. The existence of this second line was well known to Sir John French, and he once more attempted to induce Joffre to postpone the date of the attack, but again he was overruled. Yet when the time came to advance, the French were still not quite ready. The labour of bringing up three or four million shells, and transforming the larger part of the French railway system into a gun-feeding machine, required a long time. The British armies were readier to act by reason of the smallness of their front and the facility of their short sea-based lines of communications.

The British front had been extended from the village of Boesinghe, north of Ypres, to the hamlet of Noeux les Mines, near Carency. But even this extension only set free two French army corps, and the railway organization of supplying the French guns remained an enormous affair. No surprise attack on a grand scale was to be feared during the critical month of August when the principal forces of German artillery were completely occupied at Novo Georgievsk, Kovno, and Brest Litovsk. The German staff was well aware of the danger it was running; but it carefully watched the progress of French munitions and the transport of shell supplies and, meanwhile, urged Hindenburg and Mackensen to use up men in order to release quickly the heavy guns for service on the western front. This was the real reason why Hindenburg, for example, sacrificed a hundred thousand men for a rapid success at Kovno. The German staff was afraid that the new Creusot howitzers would come fully into action before a considerable portion of its own new siege trains, with the larger part of the output of the German shell factories, could be sent to the French front.

By the middle of September, 1915, the eastern German armies were able to send 1,000 heavy howitzers through Berlin and Cologne to strengthen their lines in Flanders, France, and Alsace, and the factories which fed with shells this multitude of great pieces despatched their trucks westward instead of eastward. Thus the fall of Kovno was a blow to the French and British as well as to the Russians; and in conjunction with the unexpectedly rapid destruction of Novo Georgievsk it added to the difficulties of Joffre and Sir John French, besides endangering the armies of Generals Russky and Evert. It is not extravagant to say that had the Russian line of fortresses held out a month, or even a fortnight, longer the German line in the west would have been broken by the new heavy ordnance of the French and British armies.

As it was, the result of the long-prepared campaign in France became largely dependent upon the race between the French and German railway organizations. Heavy German batteries passed through the Friedrichstrasse Station in Berlin on September 15, the day on which General Joffre issued the army order for a grand offensive, but though by this time the new Creusot guns were placed in position, the organization of the French railways was not completed.

Shells by the million were about to be employed. The local underground magazines near the batteries were utterly inadequate, as store places. Each main attacking army had to have some hundreds of trains in its service, bringing up a constant supply of ammunition, which had to be laboriously carted to the batteries and placed in the magazines beyond the reach of the most powerful enemy projectile. The work of preparation was of an unparalleled vastness and difficulty. Nearly all the ordinary goods traffic had to be stopped. It was a railway war absolutely. The troops were ready, the guns and the shells were ready, and the event depended on whether the German railway managers could get their guns and shells into France in time to cope with a hostile bombardment of incomparable length and intensity.

Orders for the offensive to be undertaken were issued on September 18. The chief advance on the German positions protecting the mining district was to be delivered by the 1st British army commanded by Sir Douglas Haig and by the 10th French army under General d'Urbal. While the main advance was made by these armies, the 2nd British army under General Plumer was to make a demonstration from Ypres to Armentières, while on that part of the front south of Armentières the 3rd corps, the Indian corps and the 2nd division were to demonstrate against the Aubers Ridge and the German positions north of the La Bassée Canal. The main force of the 1st army, consisting of the 1st corps in the north, and 4th corps in the centre, was to assault the German works between the canal and Loos, while in the south, on the right of the British, the French advanced against the defences of Lens and the Vimy Ridge.

The battle was of tactical interest for two reasons—for the first time troops of the British new armies, raised in 1914, were employed in offensive; and for the first time gas, emitted from cylinders, was used by the Allies against the Germans. The infantry assault was to be preceded by a four days' methodic bombardment of the German positions.

The enemy front had several points of strategical importance. The slag heap marked on the map as Fosse 8 lay about half a mile inside the German line, and commanded all the country to the south. About a mile and a quarter west of Cité St. Elie the Hohenzollernwerk, known to the British as the Hohenzollern Redoubt, had been pushed out some 500 yards in front of the line. This was considered the strongest work on the whole front of attack. Its face was prolonged to join up with Dump and Fosse trenches by two arms known to the British troops as Big Willie and Little Willie. Other important points were the Double Crassier and the Loos Road Redoubt.

Behind the German front were several mining villages—
Haisnes, Cité St. Elie, Hulluch, and Loos. Loos lies in a
hollow, and to the south-east rise further slopes, the highest
point being marked on the map as Hill 70. From Hill 70 the
ground falls away eastwards to the hamlet of Cité St. Auguste,
about a mile from Lens, and virtually a suburb of that place.
All these points were strongly fortified, and there were, in
addition, other slag-heaps, pits, and natural features which lent
themselves to defence. The most important were the Quarries,
the Chalk Pit, and the Pit No. 14 *bis*. The German reserve
position was roughly just west of Loos, and west of the Quarries.
The final position, so far as it was located, ran from west of
Cité St. Auguste northwards, behind the string of fortified
villages, Hulluch and Benifontaine, Cité St. Elie and Haisnes.

The position at this stage of the operations is described in the
Official History : Military Operations, as follows :

As regards observation the Germans held the advantage. In
the northern sector both the wheel-house and the dump of
Fosse 8, close to the German front line, gave complete command of the whole of the back area of the British lines . . .
A similar command over the southern part of the battle zone
was given by the combined wheel-house of a fosse and a puits
in Loos village, the standards of which were known as the Loos
Pylons, or " Tower Bridge." . . . . The British heavy
artillery strove in vain to destroy these watch-towers prior
to the battle. The principal British observation station
in the northern sector of the front was the dump of Fosse 9
de Béthune at Annequin on the La Bassée road, a great conical
mound rising to a height of 135 feet. . . . In the
southern sector the flat-topped slag heap of Fosse 5 de Béthune
. . . gave an extensive view of the German defences.
In consequence of preliminary conversations with the
French, it had been decided early in August to assemble as
secretly as possible the six divisions of the 1st corps (Lieut.-
General H. de la P. Gough) and the 4th corps (Lieut.-General Sir
H. Rawlinson) destined for the forthcoming operations, astride
and south of the La Bassée canal. . . . The 4th corps now
held the front from the Grenay-Lens railway, south-east of
Grenay, where its 47th division (Major-General C. St. L.
Barter) joined hands with the French 10th army to the Ver-
melles-Hulluch road. The 47th, a London territorial division,
had been in France since March, 1915, and had the experience
of the Battle of Festubert behind it. On its left, from the
Béthune-Lens road (inclusive) to the Vermelles-Loos track,

was the newly-arrived 15th (Scottish) division (Major-General F. W. N. McCracken), consisting entirely of Scottish battalions. Next on the left between the track and the 1st corps, was the 1st division (Major-General A. E. A. Holland).

The 1st corps, on the left of the 4th corps, held the line from the Hulluch-Vermelles road northwards across the canal to the right of the Indian corps at Givenchy. The right wing was the 7th division . . . under its original commander Major-General Sir T. Capper. In the centre and extending to enclose the salient of the German line called Hohenzollern Redoubt was the 9th (Scottish) division (Major-General G. H. Thesiger), also entirely composed of Scottish battalions. . . . The left wing of the corps . . . was the 2nd division (Major-General H. S. Horne), another of the original divisions of the B.E.F.

The decision to employ gas as an accessory for offensive operations dated back to May 3, 1915. Experimental work was carried on at home and at Helfaut, near St. Omer, and on August 22 a demonstration was given at Helfaut, which greatly impressed the army commanders who were present. On the 22nd Haig received Sir John French's fresh orders, based on Kitchener's instructions to co-operate in the operations planned by Joffre. It was decided to employ the gas on the whole front of attack south of the La Bassée canal, and to make a simultaneous assault with all six divisions, instead of attacking progressively, with at first two divisions only, as in Haig's original plan. At a conference Haig explained his changed intentions to his corps and divisional commanders. " The gas," he said, " is to be lavishly employed on the whole front of attack. It will be carried by the wind in front of the assaulting division, and create a panic in the German ranks, or, at least, incapacitate them for a prolonged resistance."

There was, however, one grave defect in the use of gases of any sort in a series of combined operations on a winding front. The army of Champagne faced north, while the armies of Artois faced east. Their attacks were fixed for the same hour—6.30 a.m. on Saturday, September 25, 1915. It was extremely unlikely that the wind would be blowing northward in Champagne and eastward in Artois at the same time. As a matter of fact, the new weather-gage seems to have fallen to the Champagne army, enabling it to stupefy a large proportion of the German forces in the opposite trenches. But the gas engineers of Sir John French and General Foch could not get a direct, steady stream of air flowing over the enemy's position at Loos and Souchez. The British troops did what they could by means of side-waftings of gas; and though some of their own men were incidentally caught by these gas waves, the grand infantry charges were punctually made with notable success.

It is proverbial that misfortunes never come singly, and General Foch suddenly found another difficulty in the way of his advance. Since the battles in the Carency region in May and June, 1915, there had been an important alteration in the geography of the country. With fine ingenuity the German engineers had turned the stream that used to flow through Carency, and had directed most of the water into a valley near Souchez, forming there a new and difficult bog. The existence of this bog was unknown to the officers of the French staff, as the Germans held a line of posts in front of it.

Even observing officers of the French flying corps could see nothing about the well-known patch of their own country calculated to arouse suspicion. The grass in the valley was very green, it is true, but there had been a good deal of rain all the summer, and hay crops everywhere were remarkably good, and the luxuriant quality of the herbage aroused little surprise. The stratagem therefore remained undiscovered until the French infantry forces attempted to advance and reach the new swamp. The German engineer who planned and carried out the diversion of the stream was then fully rewarded. It is scarcely too much to say that he saved the German armies on the western front, for not only did he check in a decisive manner the attack of the 10th French army, but he indirectly held up the more successful British advance on the north of Lens by robbing the British troops in the critical hour of the battle of the French support on which they were relying.

Fate was dead against the Allies on Saturday morning, September 25, 1915. In Champagne there was a heavy fall of rain which made the chalky ground sticky and slithery. In the Artois sector the rain at first was not a source of difficulty, but the artillery, the staff officers, and airmen were perplexed by a heavy mist. The aerial observers and the artillery could not trace the movements of their own troops or watch the enemy reserves mass against them, and then drop tens of thousands of shells in front of the advanced British positions. The staff officers, working between brigade and brigade and division and division, could not always quickly judge against what point the enemy was concentrating his main forces of resistance. Altogether the mist was disastrous to the conduct of the battle as arranged by Sir Douglas Haig, the commander of the 1st army, and controlled by Sir John French. And when in addition to the difficulty of the haze and the storm of rain that followed, the British reserves had to be held back to guard the gap left by the swerving movement of the French army, the struggle degenerated into an old-fashioned soldiers' battle.

The main attack was made by the 1st corps and the 4th corps between the La Bassée canal on the north and the German trenches opposite the village of Grenay, on the south. There were thus only 48,000 British bayonets engaged in the principal operation. The first brunt of the fighting fell on a London territorial division (the 47th), and on a Scottish division of the new army (the 15th). Acting with these two divisions were the 7th and 9th. Sir John French, however, did not expect Kitchener's men and the London territorials to perform miracles. He reckoned they would take the first or second German lines, but when this part of their work was done, he arranged to launch another large force forward to continue the breaking movement and complete the decisive attack.

With this object he held in reserve the 21st and 24th divisions, and the flower of all his infantry—the Guards division. It is easy to see what was in the mind of Sir Douglas Haig and his commander-in-chief. They were pleased with the appearance of the men of the new army and of the London territorials. But they could not feel the same trust in the newly-trained national troops as they felt in the well-tried regular corps. They therefore reverted to the method by which Hannibal, on the battlefield of Zama, endeavoured to use with safety a mass of new recruits of second-rate quality. They sent the new men forward to do their best in weakening the enemy and tiring him out, and reserved their veteran regiments to follow up whatever success the recruits obtained, and fall with fresh vigour upon the more fatigued Germans.

There is nothing striking in this disposition of forces. As has been remarked, it is as old as Hannibal, and the German commander-in-chief himself adopted it in the first Ypres battle, when he used up 250,000 new recruits in order to wear down the British troops preparatory to the grand charge of the Prussian Guard. Sir John French did not even feel secure when he had supported the London territorials and the new army division with the 7th division, the 9th division, the 21st division, the 24th division, and the Guards. But just before the battle opened he wired to the commander of the 2nd army to draw the 28th division to the town of Bailleul, from which it could move to reinforce the Loos front. In all, therefore, eight British divisions were to co-operate in the attack upon two weak German army corps entrenched between La Bassée and Lens.

The British artillery fire at first swept the whole German front with equal intensity. The Lille ridges were very heavily shelled from end to end in order to induce the enemy to believe that the British intended to renew their attack on the Rouges Bancs-Aubers line. The object, of course, was to induce the crown prince of Bavaria to put most of his men in a position in which they would not be wanted urgently. It was only with the closing burst of fire at dawn on Saturday morning that the direction of the coming British infantry thrusts could be discerned; for the Germans could then tell by their sufferings that most of the British batteries were collected on their wings at Ypres and in front of Loos and Hulluch. Sir John French seems to have had two plans. He intended first to attempt to break the German line in two places—in the north at Menin, and in the south at Lens, and to destroy the Bavarian army by thrusting around its right flank at Menin and its left flank at Lens. The result would be a gap of thirty miles in the German front.

But while preparing this grand scheme, with Sir Herbert Plumer at Ypres and Sir Douglas Haig at Lens working together, the British commander-in-chief contemplated the failure of the movement from Ypres, and devoted most of his energy to assuring the success of the smaller scheme of the Lens attack which, in co-operation with the advance of General Foch's armies, would still be of decisive importance. In any case it was necessary to hold the enemy all along the line while making the great thrust. So all the British army rose and charged, as the guns suddenly lifted soon after daybreak on Saturday morning.

At Ypres the 3rd and 14th divisions of the 5th corps attacked at 6 a.m., and by a magnificent effort stormed the great part of the enemy's front line. The German commander, Duke Albrecht of Württemberg, was alarmed both by the violence of the British artillery fire on the Ypres section and by the force of the British infantry advance. His infantry was terribly shaken by the preliminary bombardment, and it had been, moreover, severely handled in the previous actions at Hooge, the last of which occurred on August 9, 1915. The upshot was that the duke of Württemberg made an urgent request for reinforcements about the time when the principal British attack was developing thirty miles to the south. Most of the German reserves immediately available round Lille were sent towards Ypres.

The British advance on August 6 had given them the mine crater north of the Menin road, but the Germans still held part of the Hooge manor-house and the Bellewaarde lake. Then south of the Menin road they had a deadly redoubt in the corner of Sanctuary wood, from which they had directed an enfilading fire against the British right wing in the August action. The British opened the new battle by exploding a mine south of the Menin road, while their infantrymen were crawling forward with fixed bayonets towards the hillside under cover of the last intense bombardment. The British artillery had worked havoc in the German trenches; and when the British infantry sprang out in the pouring rain many of the defending troops fled helter-skelter to the second line, some three hundred yards to the rear. The remaining Germans were cleared out in a few minutes by hand-to-hand fighting.

The first German reinforcements came up at seven o'clock, and in some places the British troops retired, while the enemy bombarded his own trenches, and then charged and took them.

In turn the new garrison of German reserves was being battered by the British artillery and charged by the infantry, who again stormed the first enemy line. Both sides then settled down to a steady, fierce struggle, with all the guns curtaining off the scene of combat, and hammering at the supporting troops and the reinforcements. But the British not only regained the first German trench before the morning was out, but drove farther into the German position, and captured one of the ridges and some one hundred and forty prisoners. The great arc of heavy German artillery round Ypres was, however, exceptionally well provided with ammunition; and as the 5th army corps had fulfilled the main part of its work in drawing the enemy's reserves, Sir John French was disinclined to pursue further a secondary line of attack that could not be quickly pushed to a decision. So at nightfall the British troops in the Ypres sector returned to their own trenches, giving up all the ground they had won, with the exception of a few hundred yards of hostile trench by the Menin road which had a high tactical value.

A chain of similar events marked the movements of the 2nd army along its southern front. All the German trenches between Armentières and La Bassée were assailed. The right wing of the British 1st army took a notable part in this forceful demonstration. The British 3rd army corps resumed the attack on the Lille ridges at the hamlet of Le Bridoux, a little to the north of Rouges Bancs and Fromelles. The Indian army corps, co-operating in the Neuve Chapelle region, assailed Pietre Mill and the Aubers section of the great low horse-shoe plateau, while a part of the 1st army corps charged the German trenches at Givenchy, immediately in front of La Bassée. These attacks were at first successful all along the line, and it looked as if the heavy failure of the British against the Lille Plateau in May would at last be redeemed by a victory.

The Berkshires had a still more difficult task before them, as they had to carry a formidable work known as the Lozenge. After storming it, they found that it was lined with deep dug-outs in which the garrison could safely shelter from everything but the heaviest howitzer fire. The Lozenge protected the main German first line, and its machine-guns did terrible work among the Berkshires. But the Englishmen fought on with wonderful bravery. The Rifle Brigade also finely distinguished itself, by both its skill and its tenacity, in the holding battle of the ridges.

THE GAS AND THE WIND

The riflemen rushed to the assault, headed by a strong force of bombers. The bombers at once began to extend to the right and left, and in less than an hour and a half both the first and the second German lines were captured, and the British gunners lifted on the third line, north-west of Lille and close to the suburbs of the city.

The Germans, however, retained a wedge in the centre that checked connection with the battalion on the left of the Rifle Brigade. Both ends of the position captured by the riflemen were blocked with earth and sandbags. The enemy thus had time to recover from the first shock, and his reserves came up with a large supply of bombs; and by ten o'clock in the morning the men of the Rifle Brigade were compelled to abandon their conquest of the second line. But they held on to the first German line, and there repulsed with heavy losses another strong hostile attack. In the afternoon, however, all the captured positions had to be abandoned along the curve of the Lille plateau, owing to the fact that the German commander hurried up powerful reinforcements.

Judging from the number of prisoners taken in the British advance on Loos, the long-delayed British gas attack was not a very decisive success. Apparently it had taken British chemists nearly five months to provide the army with a weapon similar in operation to that employed by the enemy in April, 1915. No doubt, the new toxic fumes were reserved as an element of surprise for the great general offensive by the allied forces; but the wind, which had been blowing from a favourable quarter when the bombardment opened on September 23, appears to have veered at the critical moment on the morning of September 25.

The wind available at daybreak on Saturday seemed to have been too gentle and too aslant of the enemy's main positions. The British infantry had chiefly to rely upon the terrifying destructive work of their massed batteries and the swiftness of their own charge. Just before the guns lifted and the smoke clouds were formed the expectant British troops could safely catch through the haze glimpses of the bleak, ugly stretch of country which they were set to win. It was a poor, chalky ground, overgrown with long grass and rolling in two low, rounded swells of chalk towards Hill 70 near Lens. Hill 70 was more than two hundred and ten feet above sea level; but as all the land was a low chalk plateau, the summit of the hill was barely thirty feet above the neighbouring hollow in which Loos village spread in desolation. There was coal under the plateau, and what had been a hundred years ago as pleasant, lonely, and rural a countryside as the chalk edge of the weald of Kent, had been transformed into a hideous tract of Black Country. For tactical reasons, the possession of " Tower Bridge " was a matter of high importance to both contending armies. It formed one of the most perfect of observing stations, with a field of vision of forty miles in clear weather, and artillery officers working on it, in telephonic communication with their batteries, had the whip-hand of all enemy guns and howitzers in this sector of the front.

On Loos and its Tower Bridge, therefore, Sir Douglas Haig concentrated his forces of attack. The " Tower Bridge " was only about two and a half miles north-west of Lens, so that by the capture of it all British guns would be able to mass against the mining city and its important railway junction. The British artillery observers would also be able to reach the enemy batteries at Angers and Lievin, lying to the south-east and impeding the French advance on Souchez and the Vimy Ridge.

The British trenches, when the struggle opened, ran from a point near Cuinchy on the La Bassée canal, and curved round the formidable enemy position of Auchy-La Bassée to the village of Vermelles, continuing south, past mine-pits, with a railway line and blocks of miners' cottages, to the villages of Grenay and Bully les Mines, which were opposite to Lens. There was about one to five hundred yards of No Man's Land between the British parapets and the wall of dull grey sand-bags that formed the first German lines. On the first crest of the low downs rose a great German fortification some five hundred yards in diameter, built around the path from Vermelles to Loos, and dominating with its machine-guns and its sunken quick-firing turrets of steel armour the bare, grassy hollows through which the British had to advance. There were three lines of barbed-wire to get through, machine-gun positions sheltering behind slag-heaps to storm, and rows and large blocks of colliers' cottages—called, in French, corons—to master by desperate hand-to-hand fighting.

Great redoubts also extended along the second low swell of chalk, such as the Hohenzollern Redoubt and the Kaiser Wilhelm Redoubt, which defended the southern approaches to La Bassée and enfiladed any body of troops advancing on Hulluch. Then, like two deadly horns tipping this triple crescent of fortified swells of chalk, were the batteries of La Bassée and Auchy in the north, and the batteries of Angres, Lievin, and the Lens suburbs in the south. The main German batteries were ranged behind the centre of the triple crescent, with the heaviest and longest range ordnance in a stretch of woodland near Pont-a-Vendin. Pont-à-Vendin was a vital railway junction from which four tracks radiated, and through it the defending troops were supplied with munitions.

The attack was delivered by the Scotsmen of the 15th division in the centre, the Londoners of the 47th Territorial division on the right wing, and the veterans and new drafts of the famous 1st division on the left wing. The 1st division was held up on the enemy's second line, and the check enabled the Germans to collect local reserves along the rampart of chalk. The 1st brigade, however, found a gap, and its gallant brigadier showed extraordinary courage. Leaving his flank dangerously exposed, he pushed his troops ahead, and after capturing some gun positions and 500 prisoners, he won the outskirts of Hulluch.

The achievement of the London territorials was of even greater importance. Swinging out from Bully and Grenay, the Londoners were met by wild artillery fire which did but little damage, and they steadily advanced over the shrapnel-swept fields to the immense slag-heaps known as the Double Crassier. Here they stormed the German machine-gun positions which had been sheltered from the British artillery fire by the mounds of rubbish. Pushing on from the Double Crassier, the Londoners reached the western cemetery at Loos, where the fighting became terrific.

The Germans dug a trench at the upper end of the cemetery, and placed their machine-guns behind the burial mounds, using the tombstones as additional cover, and raising parapets among the graves. The Londoners who flung themselves on this disturbed resting-place of the dead rapidly added to the number of corpses in the cemetery. Leaping from one parapet to the other bombing and bayoneting as they went, they lost many men, but the Germans lost more. Yet so furious was the struggle that it was fifty minutes before the cemetery was cleared of living Germans. By that time the number of bodies outstretched among the fallen crosses and trampled wreaths greatly exceeded the number of coffined figures lying below the ground.

But the hand-to-hand fighting round the slag-heaps and colliers' cottages and cemetery was no worse than other features of the advance. It was the enemy's artillery that made the charging movements so costly of life. As soon as the British batteries, at 6.30 in the morning, lifted over the gas and smoke screens on to the enemy's reserve positions, every German gunner worked with furious intensity to maintain a curtain of fire between the British and German lines. A combination of high-explosive and shrapnel shells was principally used. It burst in thick black eddies of smoke over the advancing lines, and the British troops fell in thousands before they came into action. The enemy really possessed, in conjunction with his great number of machine-guns, sufficient artillery power to annihilate the British infantry while it moved for two to three miles on a wide front, stopping on the way in order to clear the slag-heaps and trenches from the gas. It is quite likely that the low-hanging mist was not wholly a misfortune. The British smoke-screen, with the mist and the curtains of rain, gave their troops most of the advantages of a night attack with the bayonet. A veil was thrown over the general operations, which no searchlights, flares, and star-shells could pierce.

In these circumstances, which made staff work difficult, not only did the London Territorial troops show great personal fighting power, but their officers displayed a skill in leading that provoked the admiration of Sir John French. In addition to getting hold of the cemetery, the division seized the chalk pits south of Loos, and, by strongly linking these gains with their conquest of the Double Crassier, they formed a firm defensive flank running from Loos to Bully and Grenay. In this manner they repaired the gap which had suddenly been produced between the French and British lines, when the marsh at Souchez caused General Foch's men to swerve southward. Sir John French in his despatch stated that the success of the London Territorial division removed his fear of a German thrust from Lens, and enabled him at last to release his reserve and throw it into the fighting-line.

Meanwhile, the Highlanders of the new army, the glorious 15th division, were making their wonderful charge through Loos and over Hill 70 to the Cité St. Auguste, a northern suburb of Lens. This fierce and rapid spring, across four miles of fortified ground, is probably the finest thing the Highlanders have done throughout their splendid history. The thing was accomplished, moreover, by men who knew little or nothing of warfare until the fateful month of August, 1914.

At ten minutes to six on the historic Saturday morning the heavy cloud of white-yellowish gas slowly rolled from the British trenches, and still more slowly floated onward. The launchers of a battleship could not be more anxious than were the British troops over the result of their first important gas attack. But unfortunately, the great cloud was carried too far northward, with the result that the enemy's second line was not overpowered by the stupefying fumes. At half-past six two brigades of the Highland division swept out towards the Tower Bridge. It was arranged that one brigade should make a direct attack on the Loos front, while the second brigade executed an enveloping movement to the north, bending round towards Loos and Hill 70. The third brigade was held in reserve, to be used as occasion required in either direction. There were thus only two bodies of newly trained troops, numbering each under four thousand bayonets, engaged in the main attack on Lens.

The first two brigades advanced in line against the first German position. Going forward by short rushes through a perfect tempest of shrapnel intensified by streams of bullets from machine-guns and rifles, the Highlanders took the whole of the first line in about half an hour. Then leaving some of their bombers to clear out the dug-outs, they smashed their way along the communicating trenches, or advanced in open order through the long grass, and quickly won a series of footholds in the German second line in front of Loos. Spreading out in furious fighting from each breach they had made, the Highlanders conquered the advanced defences of Loos as easily as they had stormed the first swell of chalk. The enemy was surprised by the speed and violence of the assault, and in less than an hour after the two brigades left their trenches they were fighting round the Tower Bridge and the outskirts of Loos. The fleeing Germans had crowded towards the village, where their officers got them well in hand and put up a rearguard fight.

But owing to the Scotsmen's plan of attack, which then came fully into operation, the enemy's stand at Loos did not greatly benefit him; for the brigade on the right began to work well north of Loos, where the enemy's resistance had weakened, and after getting without much difficulty well behind the village, the advanced brigade suddenly turned and stormed through some fir plantations to the summit of Hill 70. As the men charged they came under a terrible fire from a strong German position on their left flank at Pit 14-A, just between the chalk quarries and the hill. At the same time their right flank, as they climbed the down, was swept by German machine-gun fire from the eastern houses at Loos. But instead of stopping and seeking for cover, the furious Highlanders increased their pace until their brigadier-general lost control of them. He was a youngish man, with an agile habit of body, but when he arrived near Loos all that he could see was his men vanishing in the distance over the hill. The brigade crossed the road from La Bassée to Lens, captured the German third line on the opposite slope; and at twenty minutes past nine the survivors of the four battalions stormed Cité St. Auguste, a pitmen's village forming the north-western suburb of Lens.

Meanwhile, the division which had attacked Loos in front received the support of its 3rd brigade. The village was partly surrounded by two battalions, while the rest of the men undertook the difficult job of capturing the place by house-to-house fighting, with machine-guns playing on them from the first-storey windows, and splutters of musketry fire from the doors. By this time the Germans were squeezed badly on both sides of the village, with the London Territorials hammering them at the western cemetery, and the Highland brigade working round from the north and driving through the High Street. This street cut the village in half from east to west, being lined with poor shops and cafés, and leading to the cemetery. In the centre of Loos stood the ancient parish church, with the core of a once pleasant, old-fashioned village around it, from which spread rows of pitmen's cottages of a cheap and shabby quality. The cellars were packed with field-grey figures, and British bombing parties went down the side streets searching for these underground shelters, and marking their progress by explosions.

Loos had suffered severely from the British bombardment. The village church was almost levelled to the ground, not even the shell remaining. Of the 12,000 inhabitants only about three hundred men, women, and children remained. Six women and a child came out amid the British troops, but most of the unhappy people took refuge in their cellars. Snipers were brought down from the Tower Bridge, and some London territorials, who had worked round to a chalk-pit, south-west of Loos, climbed a slag-heap commanding a sunken road running to Hill 70.

The territorial battalions brought up machine-guns and linked forces with the Highlanders who had cleared the village, and when the Germans tried to return down the sunken road they were shattered by machine-gun fire and shells from a trench mortar which the " Terriers " had also brought forward. The London Irish, who had led the territorial division which closed the gap west of Lens, seem to have had a good share in the taking of Loos. After these extraordinary footballers had kicked their leather into the German trenches, crying " goal!" and had captured three German lines, another regiment came up to relieve them. The Irishmen of London had done their work, and the taking of Loos was not their job; but, swept on by the enthusiasm of battle, they worked away all the rest of the day, clearing house after house, or rather, what was left of the houses after the bombardment, and stabbing, shooting, and bombing until they felt ready to drop dead themselves. The 23rd Silesian regiment was wiped out by them.

All this was only the preliminary work of the London Irish and the splendid territorial division to which they belonged. The far-extended and exhausted Highland Division, which had pierced to Lens and then held on to Hill 70, was relieved on Saturday night. But the Londoners, whose losses were not so heavy, were set to hold the line they had won against the enemy's grand counter-attack. The Germans began by a bombardment lasting days and nights, and of extraordinary intensity. The Territorials of London were cut off from their army for three days by a wall of mingled shrapnel and high-explosive fire. Even water could not be brought up, and as most of their water-bottles were smashed the men learned what thirst was.

The weather was extremely bad, as it was raining on and off for the four days they held the line. Some of the troops hung out their muddy ground-sheets, and drank the water which collected in the waterproofs. Happily the new trenches, constituting the third German line, with the sand-bag parapets moved sack by sack to the other side, had been fairly well consolidated after the first victory, and by admirable foresight large quantities of supplies had been moved up. The men had food and ammunition, though they lacked water and sleep.

For the rest, the strength of the resisting line was a matter of racial character and individual power of endurance.

The troops holding the advanced trenches, which ran almost into the enemy's position, were continually attacked on both sides. When the German infantry held off, the German guns played on them in an almost incessant sweep of fire. All the ground held by the division was plastered with shells, and the men wondered whether they would be blown to atoms or buried in one of the human waves that kept surging against them. The strain on the nerves of these new soldiers was terrible. The soaked, miserable figures could at last hardly stand from fatigue, but still they fought on almost blindly. It was an incessant " Stand to!" for the entire division. The men could not afterwards tell how they kept themselves up.

The dawn broke on Sunday in a green haze pierced with flashes of light from rifles and guns. The men battled all day, and went out in shifts at night to the shell-holes to act as listening patrols. It was most necessary to guard against surprise in this way, as there was no barbed-wire available for putting up until the third night. In the darkness, some of the British troops obtained fresh bread from the packs of the Germans they had slain in front of the hard-fought line. In spite of the absence of wire entanglements, none of the German charges got nearer than a dozen yards to the trenches of the territorials.

Sunday passed in a tumult of bombardments and broken bayonet attacks, and no relief came. Monday went by like a nightmare. Yet on this day, when things were at their worst, the marvellous Territorials not only threw back the enemy, but bombed their way into the vital German position in the wood south of the chalk-pit. This extraordinary advance against the German reinforcements saved the situation. Then at daybreak on Tuesday the British guns were again so strongly massed and so well supplied with shells as to overpower the reinforced German batteries. Under cover of another great British bombardment, which broke down the German wall of fire, new troops were pushed forward, and the London division was relieved.

The men were afterwards addressed by the general.

Not only am I proud to have had the honour of being in command of such a regiment as yours, lads, he said to one, but the whole Empire will be proud whenever in after years the story of the Battle of Loos comes to be written. For I can tell you that it was the London Irish who helped to save a whole British army corps. You have done one of the greatest acts of the war.

And these remarks may be applied to every battalion of the London territorial division. First of all, it closed the gap between the French and British armies. Then, after helping to clear Loos, it protected the right flank of the British force, and enabled the Guards division to force back the German line and assure our hold on the new position.

We have seen that the veterans of the 1st division were held up, near Vermelles, in their advance between Loos and Hulluch. And, unfortunately, the check occurred to the brigade on the right which should have connected with the Highland brigade that took Hill 70. Had the British connecting staffs been more expert, the vehement movement of the Highland division might have been controlled and arrested at Hill 70, and touch maintained with the wing of the 1st division which had been thrown back at Hill 69. The Scotsmen should not have been allowed to drive into the suburbs of Lens; they could have done more important work by stopping at Hill 70, and using what surplus energy they possessed in an advance along the German trenches northward, thus weakening the resistance to the right brigade of the 1st division. The left brigade of this division had made a daring advance to the outskirts of Hulluch, and at ten o'clock on the morning of September 25 there was only a narrow wedge of German forces dividing the advancing British division between Loos and Hulluch.

Immediately north of the 1st division there was another scene of victory. The 7th division, reduced to little more than 2,000 strong in the first Ypres battle, then filled out with drafts from the New Army, and again wasted by ten months of trench warfare, and brought up to establishment by more of the new men, went forward to another great triumph. It was directed against the quarries, lying north of the road between Vermelles and Hulluch and defending the mining hamlet of Cité St. Elie, that straggled down the highway from La Bassée to Lens. St. Elie was practically the centre of the German position. The pitmen's houses had been transformed into a modern fortress by increasing the protection afforded by the cellars and placing the machine-guns and quick-firers behind slag-heaps where only a howitzer shell, falling almost vertically, could strike them. The quarries were furnished with deep, narrow trenches, profound dug-outs, easily excavated from the chalk, and barbed cable entanglements. Further westward, on the line of low downs between the quarries and the Vermelles road, another network of underground ways was dug in the chalk.

But the men of the 7th division took the ridge and all its machine-gun redoubts with terrible swiftness; and, after trying to help the 1st division, they swerved away from Hulluch, and, storming the western edge of the quarries reaching the La Bassée Road, broke into Cité St. Elie in fierce house-to-house fighting. Then from this pitmen's hamlet the leading brigade, headed by the 8th Gordon Highlanders, turned northward and smashed its way through a great German earthwork fortress to the village of Haisnes. At Haisnes, where a company of the Gordons broke through three lines of wire and held on from 8 a.m. to 5 p.m., fighting in the village, the enveloping movement of the 7th division should have been supported by the 9th division in a frontal attack. But this latter division, with its two leading brigades—the 26th and the 28th—was checked by one of the most formidable fortresses in the world. On the first swell of chalk, running alongside the Vermelles-La Bassée road, the German sappers had constructed northward, between the coal-mine Fosse 8 and the artillery position at Auchy, a masterpiece of fortification known as the Hohenzollern Redoubt.

This strong work was thrust out nearly 500 yards in front of the German lines, so that its fire-trench was close to the British parapets. The work was shaped like a bean, with its broadest end pointing north-west. The whole position was on a gentle rise, giving a wide field of fire, and was defended by an inordinate number of machine-guns. They were so placed as to be almost safe from shell fire, and so arranged that their streams of bullets could converge all along the front and sweep their own fire-trenches. The dug-outs in which the garrison sheltered were thirty feet underground—the depth of a three-storey house—and, being so massively roofed with chalk, they were beyond the power of penetration of the heaviest shell. No steel cupolas and slabs of concrete were employed; these mechanical aids to defensive strength would only have weakened the work.

Only a direct gas attack, carried out with a fair wind and maintained with full intensity for an hour, could have incapacitated the defenders of the Hohenzollern work. But, as in the case of the Loos advance, on the morning of September 25 the wind was too southerly for a successful attack of this kind. When the cloud of smoke and fumes rolled from the British position near Vermelles, it did not spread and thicken eastward, but floated rather towards the north, interfering in places with the movement of the British infantry. The troops garrisoning the Hohenzollern Redoubt were able to resist the attack upon them; for, though they lost some of their trenches in the fierce charge by the British troops, they won back part of the position by Saturday evening.

Meanwhile, the 26th brigade managed to capture Fosse 8, from which three communicating trenches ran into the Hohenzollern Redoubt. The British hold on the mine, however, remained weak, as the position was dominated by the guns and strong defences of the German troops at Auchy. The 26th brigade, struggling with desperate courage against an enemy possessing larger and more accessible supplies of grenades, and having a cross-fire of artillery from the north-west at Auchy, the north-east at La Bassée, and the east at Douvrin, stood against continual counter-attacks on Saturday night, Sunday, and Sunday night. But when day broke on Monday the 4,000 British infantrymen, weakened by heavy losses and worn out by attacks delivered from three sides, slowly gave ground and fell back to the eastern part of the Hohenzollern Redoubt. They seem to have needed more bomb-throwers and a larger supply of bombs, but as the enemy's batteries flung a terrible curtain of shell fire between the newly-won ground and the British bomb depots, it was practically impossible to bring forward abundant quantities of the special ammunition needed for the hand-to-hand struggle in the eight-foot-deep trenches. All the open field between the chalk rise and the original British position was swept clean by the Hohenzollern machine-guns, and rows of miners' cottages ran along the neighbouring roads, affording excellent observation posts for the German artillery and emplacements for the guns.

Using heavy, wooden-handled grenades that could rip the sides out of a chalk trench, and cause blindness by their mere concussion, the Germans bombed the British troops out of the trenches connecting with Fosse 8, and it was with marvellous heroism that the half-shattered brigade managed to stick to some part of the redoubt until fresh troops arrived. But as will afterwards be seen, the Hohenzollern work was to remain a place of contention between Briton and German for some considerable time, even as the Labyrinth for months was a scene of struggle between the French and the German. It was in the Hohenzollern trenches that the British tacticians clearly learned the lesson that all modern infantrymen needed to be as highly trained in bomb-throwing as in musketry; the hand-bomb was more important than the bayonet, in a parallel trench battle, at least.

The Hohenzollern position might have been turned by a combined attack north and south. This, indeed, had been planned, the northern British advance coming from Givenchy. But the troops at Givenchy—the 2nd South Staffs, 1st Liverpool Regiment, 1st King's Royal Rifles, and 1st Berkshires—were held up by unbroken wire and terribly smitten from the strongly fortified German work thrusting into their lines. The complete failures of the Givenchy attack and the Vermelles attack seriously limited the British advance.

When night fell on Saturday evening, September 25, and all the advantages of the long prepared British attack were exhausted, the new British line between Cuinchy and Hill 70 was an intricate affair. The enemy retained a wedge in it between Loos and Hulluch, and the position round Fosse 8 and Haisnes was a maze of battle. The London territorial division, the Highland division, and the 7th division had made three piercing thrusts that each reached to the third German line. The 1st division had also touched the enemy's final position at Hulluch.

All these great results, however, had practically been achieved by eleven o'clock in the morning. The German commander did not bring up his principal reserves until two hours later—at 1 p.m. on Saturday. In the Loos and Lens sector especially, where the enemy was thrown out of his third line by 9.30 a.m., and in the Fosse 8 and Haisnes sector, where the 8th Gordons reached the village by 8 a.m., there was ample time for British supports to advance; for the 24th division was waiting close at hand at Noeux-les-Mines, and the 21st division at Beuvry, east of Béthune. The Guards Division was preparing to march from Lillers to Noeux-les-Mines, and the 28th division was advancing.

The delay in bringing this powerful additional force into action against the retreating and badly shaken Germans was, of course, partly due to the check to the French 10th army. The French were not able to move until one o'clock on Saturday afternoon, and then they were checked and swerved away from the prearranged Franco-British direction of attack. Nevertheless, this grave accident to the allied plan of operation does not fully explain the fateful slowness in the movement of the British reserves. Sir John French states in his dispatch that the success of the London territorial division convinced him at 9.30 a.m. that there was no danger of a German rush between the British and French forces. He at once placed the 21st and 24th divisions at the disposal of Sir Douglas Haig. Some of the brigades marched past the British commander at Noeux-les-Mines and Béthune. At 11.30 the heads of the two columns of 24,000 bayonets were both within three miles of our original trench-line. They were barely more than five miles to the decisive new positions which the Highlanders were holding at Hill 70, the men of the 1st division at Hulluch, and the troops of the 7th division at the quarries and along the La Bassée-Lens road. Twenty-four thousand fresh British infantrymen, with their artillery and bomb supplies, thrown at once into the struggle against a half-beaten, outnumbered enemy, should have won a decision before the hostile reserves came into action.

At half-past eleven on Saturday the distance between the leading troops of the 24th division and the sorely-pressed brigade of Highlanders holding the western slope of Hill 70 was scarcely more than four and a half miles. Allowing for the mist and the rain and disorder of the newly-won ground, a couple of brigades could have come up with ammunition in two hours, arriving at 1.30 p.m. But no reserves arrived at the critical spot until nightfall, by which time the enemy had grown too strong to be broken. After the long delay, the men were at last launched on Sunday, September 26, along the line between Hulluch and Hill 70 won by the 4th corps. But the German commander, after more than 24 hours' grace, had been able to gather large forces, and by organizing a strong offensive east of the La Bassée-Lens road, he anticipated the British advance and threw back the foremost brigades of the 21st and 24th divisions.

Sunday, September 26, was a day of misfortune. One of the very finest of the younger British generals, Sir Thompson Capper, who had commanded the 7th division at the time of its great retreat from Ghent to Ypres, in October, 1914, was wounded during a terrific fight round the quarries, and died of his wounds. He was one of the greatest fighting men of Britain, adventurous and yet wary, magnificent in resistance, and also a grand thruster. The 9th division, which was fighting near the 7th, round Fosse 8, at the eastern end of the Hohenzollern Redoubt, also lost its commander, Major-General G. H. Thesiger, on the day Sir Thompson Capper died; and a third distinguished general of division, Major-General F. D. V. Wing, commanding the 12th division, fell soon afterwards by the Hohenzollern Redoubt. By Sunday evening the enemy's pressure against the new British line became very severe. The Germans continually counter-attacked, and the German gunners, using shells containing prussic-acid and other gas, tried to fill their lost trenches with poison fumes. But the British held on to the western slope of Hill 70, and the road from Loos to La Bassée as far as the western cottages of Hulluch. By dawn on Monday morning the British hold on Fosse 8 was lost, and the enemy prepared to make a grand attempt to win back all his lost positions.

The attack of the Guards division on September 27 was timed for 4.50 p.m. and at the same time it was arranged that troops of the 47th division should clear the enemy from the west end of the spinney. This operation was entirely successful. No one who saw it can ever forget the advance of the 3rd Guards Brigade to attack Hill 70, as they moved in artillery formation across the open ground down into the Loos valley. The Welsh Guards, in action for the first time, and the 4th Grenadiers led the attack, and met with heavy shrapnel-fire as they moved down the slope. But they moved on in perfect order. On Hill 70 they met with strong resistance, and suffered very heavily from machine-gun fire on the crest of the hill. They finally consolidated a line well up the slope. On the left the 2nd Guards Brigade had rushed, but were unable to hold Puits No. 14 *bis*, and held a line running through the chalk-pit on the Lens-La Bassée road. A second attack in the Puits on September 28 gained no further ground. During these days, while the Germans shelled the British lines heavily, the British worked hard at consolidating their positions and arranged to replace by reserves the more weary of the front line divisions. All round the Hohenzollern Redoubt there was constant fighting.

By October 2 the readjustment of the front was complete. The French took over the whole Loos sector. The 47th division was moved farther north and they, with the 12th division, completed the relief of the 4th corps. The 1st corps had received the 28th division as supports, and the Guards division was under orders to move to that part of the front which included the Hohenzollern Redoubt. The 46th (Territorial) division was moving south to take its place with the Guards and the 12th division in the 11th corps.

During the last days of September the Hohenzollern Redoubt was the scene of fierce and continuous fighting. The enemy, indeed, attacked all along the salient. But the loss of part of the redoubt galled him most, and his efforts to recover it were of extraordinary violence and persistence. Among the British troops that greatly distinguished themselves in the Hohenzollern work were the 7th Seaforths, the 8th Gordon Highlanders, and the 8th Royal Highlanders (Black Watch), who fought from September 25 to September 27. Towards the end of September and the beginning of October the 2nd East Surreys, the 1st Welch Regiment, and the Yorkshire Light Infantry gallantly maintained the defence of the main work and of the trench known as Little Willie.

On the afternoon of October 8 the Germans directed an intense attack all along the line from Fosse 8 on the north to the right of the French 9th corps on the south. At all parts of the line except two the Germans were repulsed with tremendous loss. On the right the attackers made a small lodgment on the Double Crassier held by the French, while on the left the trench held by the Guards division to the north-east of the Hohenzollern Redoubt was temporarily captured. The latter was speedily re-taken, and at midnight on October 9 the line held by the British 1st army was identically the same as that held before the German attack started. The preparations for the attacks against the Quarries and against the Hohenzollern Redoubt and Fosse 8 on October 10 were upset and delayed by the bombardment preceding the German attack on October 8, but they were at once resumed.

On October 13 the attack of the 1st army was begun at noon by a heavy bombardment, which lasted for two hours. After a discharge of gas and smoke the 1st brigade advanced in line to the assault. At first the British met with little resistance; then fire was opened on their front and on both flanks, and became more and more intense as they approached the German wire. They found it impossible to carry the position, and were withdrawn under cover of darkness. The day's fighting cost the 1st division 1,200 casualties.

On the front of the 11th corps, the attack on the Quarries was carried out by the 37th and 35th brigades, both of whom gained much ground after severe struggles, which resulted four nights later in their being able to occupy the greater part of the south-western side of the Quarries. On the right the 137th brigade gained a few yards of trench, and on the left the 138th brigade managed to take Fosse Trench. The position beyond the Hohenzollern became untenable, and after more casualties, the men retired to the Hohenzollern Redoubt.

Other attacks were made without any marked success, and after darkness had set in it was decided to evacuate the eastern face of the Hohenzollern Redoubt and dig a trench behind it, the trenches of the western face being also reorganized for defence. On October 14, with the exception of the small gains about Gun Trench, the footing on the edge of the Quarries and the recapture of the western portion of the Hohenzollern Redoubt, the battle front of the 11th corps remained unchanged. During October a succession of bombing attacks about the Hohenzollern and Big Willie by the Guards division did not prove very encouraging, and on November 4 General Haig informed the commander-in-chief that he was compelled to abandon any hope of continuing the offensive.

The British had altogether lost, between September 25 and October 16, 2,013 officers and 48,367 other ranks. Of this total some 800 officers and 15,000 men were killed, or missing and never heard of again. The German losses on the Loos front during the two ten-day periods September 21 to 30 and October 1 to 10 were 441 officers and 19,395 other ranks. As the official British account points out, however, this excludes the periods of heavy fighting on the 13th and following days and the German returns were computed on a different basis from the British. For example, many doing duty as officers were not included among the officer casualties, and the wounded who died in hospital were not included among the dead.

CHAPTER 22

Battles in Champagne

THERE is an ancient Roman road running from Reims to the Argonne forest. About twenty miles east of Reims this Roman way crosses the Suippes river near the small town of Auberive; thence it runs for about fifteen miles to the outskirts of the forest some distance south of the hamlet of Massiges. The country through which the old road runs is a barren tableland of chalk that continually swells into low, rounded hills, many of which have been planted with pine trees. The land is part of the Champagne district. The small stream of La Tourbe flows in front of Massiges. Then north of the hand-shaped down at Massiges is another stream, the Dormoise river. On the western side several streams flow into the Suippes river, the most important being the Py.

Immediately south of the Roman road is a vast circle of earthworks, known as the Camp de Chalons. Old tradition has it that the earthworks were made by Attila, king of the Huns, whose forces were for the first time broken on the plateau. A few miles due west of Attila's camp is the hamlet of Valmy, where the Army of the French Revolution won its first victory over the Royal forces of Prussia and Austria. For these reasons all this poor, mean country was holy ground to the French soldier, and despite the previous checks to the army of Champagne, the general opinion in France was that over the stretch of chalk between the Argonne and Reims the decisive advance against the German army would at last take place, for it was at this position that the breaking of the German front would be most disastrous to the enemy. All the invaders' lines, from Zeebrugge and the Yser to the northern heights of the Aisne, and the hills round Reims would be taken in flank and rear, and so menaced by a cutting of all the lines of communication, if a French army crossed the Dormoise and Py streams.

But the Germans boasted that their lines in Champagne were impregnable, and Von Kluck remarked to a German-American war correspondent that the position was that if he could not take Paris, neither could the French capture Vouziers.

Between Vouziers and the French front there were four fortified lines, each a mile or more apart. All the downs, on and between these lines were deeply excavated and transformed into underground fortresses, armed with quick-firing batteries, mortars for aerial torpedoes, cylinders for the emission of poison gas clouds, and thousands of machine-guns. Of all their military engineering works the Germans most prided themselves upon their Champagne defences. These defences had been greatly strengthened and extended since the French made their first great thrust in February, 1915. The French had then captured the first German line, running close to the Roman road by the hamlet of Perthes. But the loss of this line had put the German engineers on their mettle. They had fitted many of the sunken invisible forts with domes of hardened steel, and had driven a series of tunnels through the chalk to allow of supports being moved to the fire trenches safely in the heaviest storm of shrapnel and melinite shell.

The allied offensive movement was expected in the middle of August, 1915. It was then that the Germans began to re-inforce both the Champagne and the Lille-Lens sectors. At the beginning of September the Germans had 70 battalions in Champagne belonging mostly to their 3rd army (von Emem). These were gradually added to until, all told, they numbered 192.

Yet, despite the confused haste with which this large medley of forces was assembled, the German commander on the Champagne front, General von Emem, had so absolute an assurance of victory that on the eve of the struggle he invited German war correspondents to come and watch the spectacle of his triumph. One of these correspondents, Dr. Max Osborn, of the " Vossische Zeitung," has described the French bombardment. After telling how the French heavy artillery swept the German rear, seeking to explode hand-bomb depots and other magazines of ammunition, he added:

The violence of the bombardment then reached its zenith. At first it had been a raging, searching fire; now it became a mad drumming, beyond all power of imagination. It is impossible to give any idea of the savagery of this hurricane of shells. Never has this old planet heard such an uproar. An officer who had witnessed in the summer the horrors of the Souchez and the Lorette heights, told me they could not in any way be compared with this inconceivably appalling

A MESSAGE FROM JOFFRE

artillery onslaught. Night and day for fifty hours, and in some places for seventy hours, the French guns vomited death and destruction against the German troops and the German batteries. Our strongly-built trenches were filled in, and ground to powder; their parapets and fire platforms were razed and turned into dust-heaps; and the men in them were buried, crushed, and suffocated. One of our privates, a high-school young man who survived, amused himself by counting the shells that fell in his limited field of vision. He calculated that nearly a hundred thousand projectiles fell around him in fifty hours.

Another German war correspondent says that from the height on which he stood the southern sky-line looked like a vast volcanic eruption, and the unending roll of the French artillery sounded like " the kettle-drums of death." French artillery of every calibre was used, from the light mountain " 75's " to the latest howitzers from the Creusot and Bourges foundries, named by the workmen who made them, " The Conquerors."
The bombardment started on September 22, and was continued uninterruptedly for three days and nights against the whole German front. Besides being intended to demolish trench fortifications and the wire in front of them, long-range fire was directed against enemy headquarters, billeting areas, supply depots, and the Bazancourt-Challeranges railway.
On the eve of September 24 General Joffre issued the following order to his troops:

Soldiers of the Republic,—After months of waiting, which have enabled us to strengthen our forces and resources while our adversary has been wasting his, the hour has come to attack and conquer, and add fresh glories to those of the Marne, Flanders, the Vosges and Arras. Behind the tempest of iron fire, unloosened by the toil in all our workshops, where our brothers are labouring for us night and day, you will go to the assault all together, along the whole front, in close union with the armies of our allies. Your driving force will be irresistible. It will carry you, in one effort, as far as the adversary's batteries, beyond the fortified lines which face you. You will give him neither rest nor respite until victory is achieved. Go to it with all your heart, for the deliverance of our country, for the triumph of right and freedom.

Zero hour for the attack was at 9-15 a.m., at which time the infantry sprang to the advance along the whole French front of about 25,000 yards. For the first time the French had employed gas on a large scale as a preliminary to the assault—and conditions were favourable for its most effective use. Along the whole line the infantry invaded the German first trench system.

The first waves of the assault broke over the entire German front, from Auberive to the Argonne Forest, for a length of fifteen miles. But this was only meant to test the general strength of the enemy and pin his men down to every yard of the Champagne position. The main series of thrusts were then delivered at four points, the men advancing in narrow but very long and loose masses which spread out behind the first hostile line of downs. On the extreme left, at the village of Auberive, where the Germans held most of the fortified houses and the French were deeply entrenched along the southern outskirts, little progress could be made. Here the force of the attack was directed north-westward up the long slopes leading to the hamlet of L'Epine de Vedegrange. Another strong attacking force was directed from Souain through the Punch-bowl northward and against a line of fortified heights known as Hill 185, on which Navarin Farm lay, the Butte of Souain, and Tree Hill.

Eastward of Tree Hill was the height of Tahure Butte, with the village of Tahure south of it, and in the triangle of Tahure, Souain, and Perthes villages was the German fortress called the Trou Bricot, and nicknamed the Hollow of Death. East of this hollow was the fortressed escarpment of the Butte of Mesnil. Eastward of Mesnil was Bastion Crest, with the group of houses called Maisons de Champagne behind it, and still farther eastward, near the edge of the Argonne Forest, was a large, hand-shaped down, known as the Hand of Massiges, with south of it a quarried hill, called from its curious appearance the Earhole.

To sum up, the heights of (1) L'Epine, (2) Navarin Hill, Souain Butte, and Tree Hill, (3) Tahure Butte, (4) Mesnil Butte, and (5) Bastion Crest and the Hand of Massiges, formed five systems of defensive works against which the French army of Champagne worked forward. It was expected that some of the positions would prove too strong to be carried by storm, and it was arranged that in this case the most formidable fortresses should be left awhile unattacked, and then approached by a double flanking movement from behind. This is how Mesnil Butte, a down with a high, steep face thrusting into the French line, was dealt with.

A SYSTEM OF WARRENS

General de Castelnau's main scheme was to penetrate between each principal German hill position, and then turn and encircle it with two flanking columns. But before this could be done, the first German line had to be captured, the strength of each hostile fortress tested, and then the columns had to advance along the valleys and the slopes with enfilading fires sweeping them on both sides. It was afterwards calculated by careful observers of the conquered ground that along this front of 15 miles with a depth of two and a half miles, the German engineers had constructed nearly 400 miles of trenches. And, despite the extraordinary duration and intensity of the French bombardment, this enormous system of human warrens was only damaged badly on the front slopes and in the southernmost hollows between the downs. The high ramparts of chalk protected from destruction far the greater part of the vast earthworks. The new French howitzers threw to a height of 12,000 feet a very heavy shell that descended almost vertically. Yet this projectile could not destroy the sheltered trenches in the down on which the German sappers had been labouring for twelve months.

The German had first taught the Allies that no ordinary concrete and armour-plate fortress could resist his great howitzers. Then, when forced himself to remain on the defensive, the German had invented a new kind of underground fortress, with mobile defence guns, against which howitzers were of little direct use. There were lines of railways of narrow gauge spreading through the German works and connecting with the French railway running from Challeranges to St. Souplet. In the Trou Bricot there were even two railway tracks for bringing up supplies and moving heavy guns. The works resembled a system of sewers, half as large as those of London but more densely grouped, connected by tunnels of chalk as long as the London tubes, served by light railways, screened by a line of downs nearly six hundred feet above sea level, and lighted by electricity and comfortably furnished. Such was the German fortress of Champagne which Kluck proclaimed impregnable.

Nevertheless, the vehement attack of the French troops carried them in one hour through this fortress at two important points. At Massiges a colonial division, formed largely of Frenchmen born and bred in North Africa, reached in their first charge the Maisons de Champagne, a farm north of the Hand of Massiges Down. At Souain another French colonial division swept through the Punch-bowl and captured Navarin Hill. Between these two colonial divisions a column of Bretons and Vendeans, advancing from Perthes, reached the western slopes of the Butte of Tahure, while on the other side of this Butte an African division of Arab, Berber, Moorish, and Senegal troops took the eastern slopes, and there connected with the men of Savoy and Dauphiné in a flanking movement between the Butte of Tahure and Tree Hill. From 10 to 10.30 o'clock on Saturday morning, September 25, 1915, the situation on the battlefield of Champagne was similar to that obtaining at the same hour on the battlefield of Lens.

Both the French and British leading divisions had made advances. In particular, the position of the colonial troops at Maisons de Champagne resembled that of the Highland brigade at the Cité St. Auguste at Lens. The men had stormed through machine-gun fire, wire entanglements, rows of trenches, and gun positions, and had reached the last crest of chalk from which the valley of the Dormoise and the village of Ripont were dominated. Had supports quickly arrived, the road to Vouziers, Namur, and Liége might have been won. But, apparently, the battalion that reached the Maisons, having lost all its officers and being commanded by a sergeant, had moved too quickly.

The French staff could not get more men up there in time, and the half-shattered battalion, caught between two flanking fires from Massiges and Beauséjour, and attacked in front from Ripont, had to leave the heavy German and Austrian batteries it had captured on the crest, and fall back at two o'clock on Saturday afternoon. There was another battalion also in a still more advanced position at the entrenchments north-west of the Maisons. The men had held the hill for three and a half hours without help arriving, and it was only at the end of this time that the Germans at Ripont were able to re-form and return to the attack. As a matter of fact, the two wings at the height of the Hand of Massiges and at the Butte of Mesnil could not get forward as quickly as the centre had done. There had been a complete check at Mesnil, and this had thrown the operation out of gear. In the same way the British check at Vermelles interfered with the success of the Highland brigade beyond Hill 70. The commanders on either side had become very cautious, and wanted to feel that both their feet were firmly planted before making another step forward.

GERMAN MACHINE GUNS IN POLAND. In 1915 the Germans drove the Russians back all along the eastern front, overrunning Galicia and Poland. Warsaw fell to them in August and many other fortresses in Poland, but wherever they were pressed the Tsar's soldiers put up a stout resistance. The illustration shows a German machine gun section holding a barricade in the snow-swept wastes of Poland.

RUSSIANS IN THE CARPATHIANS. This photograph, which shows Russian troops moving to the attack in the Carpathians, was taken by Captain Adrian Simpson, A.D.C. to the Grand Duke Michael Alexandrovitch, commander of the Caucasian Native Division operating in Galicia. The struggle between the Russians and Austro-Germans in the Carpathian in 1915 was very severe.

Plate 42   *Volume 11*

Government buildings in Dar-es-Salaam, the former capital
of German East Africa, British fleet base in the war

General view of Windhoek, South-West Africa, capital of the former German
possession, entered by Union of S. Africa forces on May 12, 1915.

View of town and roadstead, Swakopmund, South-West Africa.
Developed by Germany to rival Walvis Bay, it was captured
by South African forces on January 14, 1915.

THREE AFRICAN TOWNS

Henri Manuel

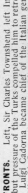

Vandyk

Swaine

THREE LEADERS ON THREE FRONTS. Left, Sir Charles Townshend left India in 1915 to lead a British Force in Mesopotamia. He advanced as far as Ctesiphon, but pressure of the Turks compelled him to retreat to Kut, which he was forced to surrender. He was knighted in 1916. Centre, Count Luigi Cadorna became chief of the Italian general staff in 1914, and was C.-in-C. from Italy's entry into the war in 1915 until the battle of Caporetto, 1917. After that disaster he was superseded by General Diaz. Right, General Sarrail commanded the French 3rd Army in 1914, taking part in the first battle of the Marne, September, 1914, and from August, 1915, until 1917 led the French forces at Salonica. In 1918 he joined the reserve.

Plate 44

Volume 11

The Germans at Massiges had a saying that Earhole down on Hill 191, rising south of the Hand, could be held by two washer-women with two machine-guns; for this trenched, caverned, wired, and tunnelled lump of chalk dominated the plain in which the French were camped. But in twenty-two minutes a colonial brigade, with the general charging at the head of his men, reached the quarry that formed the Earhole. The German regiments holding the hill had been too confident in the mechanical strength of their fortress. Many of their machine-guns, being worked from bomb-proof shelters, had escaped the French howitzer fire, but the speed of the infantry attack disconcerted and surprised the garrison. The French were supplied with light telephones, and the result was that, when the German machine-guns lifted above the damaged parapets and began to fire, the French batteries of mountain artillery came again swiftly into action.

The French mountain gun, first issued in small numbers to the Chasseurs in the mountains, had become a useful weapon for nearly all battlefields. It was a variation of the " 75," lighter, and shorter of range, but with a higher angle of fire. It was used close behind the troops, almost like a machine-gun, but while a machine-gun could not hit men behind a hill, the mountain-gun could shell or shrapnel enemy troops sheltering in a hollow or on the reverse slopes of a down. Under the cover of a bombardment of this kind the French bombers rushed to the German hill trenches, and flung in grenades, forcing the Germans to retreat. The hill was close to the Argonne, where the Crown Prince was fighting with a newly-reinforced army, directed by General von Mudra. In answer to telephone calls for help, Mudra sent some of his best troops to the Earhole.

Fighting went on day and night till September 30; for long after the original garrison was destroyed fresh troops poured into the northern works from the village of Rouvroy, coming from the Crown Prince's army a few miles to the east. Towards the north the French colonials reached Mont Tetu, overlooking the plateau, then, hour by hour, they pressed down eastward in the direction of the town of Ville-sur-Tourbe. The Germans were encircled in little groups in the trenches in the eastern valleys until a thousand prisoners were taken. The capture of a German bomb depot and 3,000 grenades greatly facilitated the operations on the Hand of Massiges and the Earhole.

Three French divisions were employed round Massiges. The first division captured Earhole Down; the second division stormed the middle finger and ringfinger of the Hand of Massiges; the third division took the height known as Bastion Crest, between the Hand of Massiges and the Butte of Mesnil. In all, five waves of French infantry swept up and over the heights and along the downland valley, which had been transformed into a maze of trenches and dug-outs. The enemy's gun-positions were reached and the French cavalry were thrown into the action. But the condition of the slippery, muddy ground prevented the horsemen from charging up the slopes where the guns and machine-guns were sited; so most of the men dismounted and fought on foot as supports to the infantry.

From September 25 to 30 the Germans round Massiges continually counter-attacked, with a view to winning back their lost line. It was then that they suffered losses quite as heavy as the French had done in their attacks. The last of the German counter-attacks came from Cernay, in the north-east. The troops deployed at the foot of the slopes of the little rounded down known as La Justice. But the French light guns shattered this counter-attack before it got under way, and the troops round La Justice broke and fled in a panic.

Westward, beyond the Butte of Mesnil, the French attack was directed on Perthes towards Tahure and the down north of the village known as the Butte of Tahure. The German guns and machine-guns on this butte crossed fires with the guns on Tree Hill, lying to the south-west. The road to the railway town of Somme Py ran in a long upward slope between the two fortified downs. The road was a death-trap, even when the village of Tahure had been captured; and it was necessary first to storm or mask one of the two heights before a decisive advance could be made. The French commander decided to attack Tree Hill, but instead of making a frontal assault on this formidable position, he launched at it two flanking movements. The Breton and Vendean troops advanced towards Tahure from the east, while the African troops set out westward from Souain, and reached the junction of the roads from Souain to Tahure and Perthes to Somme Py.

In practically every case the tactics of General de Castelnau consisted in bringing two French forces against a single German force. Nearly every German main position was assailed on two or three sides, by some 12,000 French soldiers on one flank and another 12,000 on the other. When, as in the case of the Butte of Mesnil, the enemy's flank defences proved too strong to be stormed by a swift movement, the troops veered as much as possible to the north-east and north-west, with a view to cutting the rear communications of the fortress.

At Perthes the Germans had a salient in a wood west of the village, the position being known to the French as the Pocket. It was attacked on two sides by the regiments of Savoy and Dauphiné, who captured it in seventeen minutes. The place was a labyrinth of trenches, caverns, and entanglements, but the Frenchmen went over it at the double and captured in the wood the guns that should have been playing on them as they charged. Two German officers were caught in bed. Then north of Perthes there was a large hollow between the downs, and across this the Germans had driven two lines of trenches. The Rhine Trench was in front, and about five furlongs behind it was the support line known as the Yorck Trench.

When the French attacked, their commander threw out battalions along his wings to mask the wooded slopes on right and left. The troops on the left wing had little to do but to dig themselves in, get good cover, and wait; for when the main Breton force of attack from Perthes linked up with the African troops coming from Souain, all the Germans in the western woods were completely encircled, driven in from the rear, and captured. East of the Punch-bowl, however, the process of encirclement was slower; for it was here that the great German fortress on the Butte of Mesnil dominated the field of conflict. There was an extraordinary series of redoubts on this long down.

From the Perthes side the Mesnil Butte seemed as impregnable as Gibraltar; for all the slope was very steep, and the Germans in the trenches above swept the incline with machine-gun fire, or broke up every attacking line with hand-bombs. So skilfully were the works constructed that the long, intense, preliminary bombardment had not injured them; and though the French brought up their light guns, and, placing them in the opposite wood across the Punch-bowl, maintained a storm of shell a few yards in front of their advancing infantry, the German garrisons above the steep survived the hurricane, and rose above their parapets in time to bomb back the wave of assault. It was not until October 6 that the Butte of Mesnil fell.

Meanwhile the main Breton force pushed along over the Punchbowl to the outskirts of the village of Tahure, and there a portion of them advanced with part of the African troops towards the two downs that crossed their fires over the road to Somme Py. All along this region, towards the Butte of Souain on the west and the Butte of Mesnil on the east, the third and last German line was approached; but progress was very slow in this decisive field of battle. The wire entanglements had not been reached by the French artillery, and behind the wire were numerous machine-gun positions which were but slightly injured by gun fire. The French gunners were pulling their pieces out of the pits which had been built in the spring, and their horses were being taken out of their underground stables and driven across the holed and slippery slopes of chalk to positions between the first and second German lines.

There, in a great downpour of rain, the Frenchmen worked their guns against the last chain of the Champagne downs. But in the thick weather their aerial observers could not mark the enemy batteries, especially those eastward, which enfiladed on the right flank the columns of attacking French infantry. The infantry were thus held up by three forces of the defence—wire entanglements, machine-guns, and artillery. Heavy, overwhelming, and exact howitzer fire was needed between the Butte of Tahure, Tree Hill, and the Butte of Souain. So the troops dug themselves in, and waited for clearer weather.

Work of great importance, however, went on south of this last line of downs. North-west of Perthes was Trou Bricot, connected with Souain by a rough country road. Here the enemy had built the most formidable of his underground fortresses. Two light railways ran through the position connecting with the main line near Somme Py. There were four cross tracks between the two parallel lines of light railway in the Trou Bricot salient. Thus munitions and supporting troops could rapidly be circulated through the fortress, one line of which connected with the Toothbrush Redoubt on the wooded Butte de Mesnil, and with the fortifications in the Bois Sabot towards the north-west. A fold of chalk ran from Trou Bricot to the Bois Sabot, passing by numerous systems of defence, some of whose picturesque names were the Satyr's Trench, Gretchen Trench, Kiao-Chau Wood, Elberfeldt Camp, and Von der Goltz Works. This fold of chalk formed a magnificent protection against the heavy French guns, and some of the lines on the reverse slopes were entirely intact.

Trou Bricot, seen first on the photographs taken by the reconnoitring French airmen, formed three round, pale blots, connected by a long white streak—the communication trench. Then there were six more whitish rounds, strung along the white line like balls on a string. It was on the white line that the French gunners began their work, and their heaviest shells fell in hundreds, at a range of five miles, on the main communication trench, cutting the telephone wires, destroying the shrapnel-proof passages, and choking the outlet. Then, at a signal from the watching airmen, a barrage of shells fell on Trou Bricot and on the great Elberfeldt Camp behind it. The German divisions that garrisoned the extraordinary fortress were so shattered by the bombardment that a single division of French African troops sweeping up the road from Souain to Tahure cut them off in the rear from Tree Hill and the position of Baraque, where the Breton division, advancing from the other side of the work, connected and formed a great net with the Savoy troops working forward from the Pocket in front.

The net of Arabs, negroes, Bretons, and Vendeans moved backward over Trou Bricot, and taking all the Germans in the rear, where only the low parados topped the trenches, they bombed and bayoneted the encircled enemy until the Germans surrendered in large numbers. The taking of Trou Bricot, with its many guns and machine-guns and its great garrison, holding one of the most important subterranean fortresses in the world, was a considerable achievement. And it is worthy of note that the conquest was made more by generalship than by the courage of the troops; for the immense stronghold, with its underground railways and caverns, could not have been taken by a frontal attack. It was by demonstrating against the Butte de Mesnil, attacking the frontal Pocket, and throwing out a line of troops to keep the defenders of the eastward down occupied, that the French general, by a sudden swerve westward, linked with the African division and gained the incomparable advantage of being able to attack the woodland fortress along its undefended rear.

While the African division was slanting off eastward from Souain towards the pine-woods round Trou Bricot, a famous colonial division, commanded by the hero of Fashoda, General Marchand, made a straight, swift leap northward up the road to Somme Py, midway along which was the down where rose Navarin Farm. General Marchand did not remain behind to watch the movement, and reinforce the leading brigades when they were checked. Instead, he advanced at the head of his 12,000 bayonets and led them to the attack. Marchand had already told his army commander, General de Langle de Cary: "Mon General, when the attack opens, we shall carry Navarin Farm in an hour." Though Marchand fell early in the attack, just as his men reached the first German trench, the fall of their gallant leader only made the troops more resolute to reach their objective.

There were two miles of German trenches and fortifications between the town of Souain and the hill-farm of Navarin. In fierce, desperate spurts the colonial division, with the Foreign Legion in support and a Zouave brigade and Moroccan division acting with it, worked through the Punch-bowl of Souain, where the enemy had built underground fortresses known as the Palatinate and Magdeburg Works. The last trench before Navarin Farm was taken, but then all progress eastward was stopped by the earthworks in Bois Sabot. The absence of Marchand must have been sorely felt.

The Bois Sabot was a horse-shoe shaped fortress, surrounding a pine-wood on the right of Navarin Farm. The work spread along the foot and sides of a gently-sloping hill, and it was laid out with such skill by the German engineers that they regarded it as one of the strongest points in their entire line of defence. The heavy bombardment had done little damage to its network of wire entanglements and deep subterranean lines; and in the evening of September 25 the French troops could only lie flat on their stomachs near this work, with the rain pouring on them and asphyxiating shells from the German batteries along the Py River blinding them. It was then that the Foreign Legion advanced through a curtain of shrapnel and flung themselves down by the colonials. The colonials were relieved in the night by the Zouaves and Moroccan troops, and the Legion crawled the following day into a stretch of woods to prepare for an attack. But the weather was so foggy that the French guns on September 26 and September 27 could not do any useful work, and, much to the disadvantage of the Allies, the fighting had to be temporarily suspended, so that the enemy won 48 hours in which to bring down reinforcements, guns, and ammunition.

At last, at half-past three in the afternoon of September 28, the air cleared sufficiently for the attack to be launched. The Legion had lost more than half its force in the great drive on the Vimy Heights in Artois in the spring, when it penetrated farther than any French troops. But two thousand recruits had since joined the Legion, and brought it up to full strength.

In the advance from Souain, in the pine-wood near Navarin Farm, the Legionaries had again lost nearly a quarter of their men from shell and shrapnel before firing a shot. They asked their colonel, in the evening of September 27, to beg the general at Souain to let the Legion, as a special favour, lead the grand charge against the enemy's last line.

The request was allowed, and the plan of attack was that the Legion should fling itself straight on the front of the fortress of Bois Sabot, and there engage the enemy with such fury that 12,000 other men—Zouaves, Moors, and colonials—could make a surprise attack on both flanks. The Legion gathered in the wood in two columns, and then, amid the cheers of the French troops occupying the trenches in front of them, they leapt across these trenches, over the heads of their comrades, and charged into the mouth of the Horse-shoe. First a rain of shrapnel met them: then the stream of bullets from machine-guns and rifles caught them in the front and raked them on both sides. With a dense curtain of shrapnel behind it and torrents of lead pouring on its front and flanks, the Legion was mowed down as by a gigantic scythe. Some men of the leading battalion lived through the enemy's fire and reached the wire entanglements; but only one man got through the wires. Then the second battalion followed, and a few men lived to get into the first trench and began to clear it out. Finally, the last battalions came forward and bombed and bayoneted their way into the fortress.

The Legion's heroism firmly established the army of Champagne in the region of Navarin Farm. West of the farm was a great stretch of downland, dotted with pinewoods, reaching to the town of Auberive. Midway between the farm and town a road cut across the down country, running from the village of St. Hilaire to the town of St. Souplet, on the Py river. Half-way along this road were the farm-buildings of Epine de Vedegrange, close to Hill 150. In this part of the field General de Castelnau's design seems to have been to carry Auberive by storm, and then attack Epine and the hill by two flanking columns, which should go on with their supports and light artillery, and break the last German position at St. Souplet. But Auberive proved to be impregnable. In the earlier Battle of Champagne the French had reached the outskirts of the town, and had afterwards sapped close up to the enemy's position. But later the ingenious German engineers had transformed Auberive into a subterranean city.

Hundreds of thousands of shells fell on the buildings during the bombardment, but the groundfloors were heaped with sand-bags, and the cellars were so strengthened with concrete that the troops in the caverns below were completely protected. A few observing officers sat among sand-bags in the attics, watching the French lines through periscopes and telephoning to their own batteries and to the various caverned headquarters. The only way in which Auberive could have been taken was by a grand attack in which a hundred thousand men would have been lost, or by a dense and immense gas-cloud, floating down gently on a steady, favourable wind. It needed, however, a direct south wind to carry the fumes over the town; and, as we have already seen at Loos, the wind on the morning of September 25 blew from the south-west. It enabled the French to clear the entrance of some of the valleys in the Champagne region, but it did not affect the hill defences, and it slanted away from Auberive. The consequence was that the frontal attack on this position at once became an affair of house-to-house fighting with hand-bombs against both bombs and machine-guns, in which the French troops made only very slow progress ; for north of the town the Germans had powerful groups of artillery which formed a fire curtain along the front and rear trenches of the French and checked the movement of their supporting troops.

In these circumstances, the principal French forces paused in the attack on Auberive, and swerved to the right towards the wooded slopes leading to Epine. At the same time the division operating from St. Hilaire, in a direct northward movement, also approached the crest. Only the first line of German defences in the Epine area had been destroyed by the French guns. The second line was erected on the northern slope of a ridge of chalk : it was practically intact and was defended by Württemberg and Hanoverian troops. There were eight lines of barbed-wire bound to the trunks of the pine-trees, with old-fashioned rows of sharp wooden stakes strengthening the great obstacle. Behind the wire and the stakes were machine-guns, so placed as to sweep all the slope fifty yards wide, running up to the crest.

When the French arrived their figures were silhouetted against the grey sky above the ridge and the German riflemen and machine-gunners had targets they could not miss. All the first line went down, but later waves succeeded in pushing on. Some made a path with the butt-ends of their rifles, others crawled under or cut the steel cables, while their bombers stood upright and pelted every German head within sight. After the battle it was seen that large stretches of wire still remained intact before the chief German machine-gun positions ; but there were gaps through which the German parapet was reached by the grenadiers, where the infantrymen pulled down the sand-bags, and, jumping to the trench, worked along it with dagger and revolver.

When at length a series of footings had been won in this line, the succeeding waves of French infantry, leaving their predecessors to finish cleaning out the work, dashed into the pine-wood behind it and descended into the long chalky bottom. There, some five hundred yards from the line below the crest, was a third system of German works with more unbroken wire entanglements, machine-guns, and many light field-guns. On the opposite slope of the long valley was another pine-wood, through which a road ran to Epine. Here there was a fourth German line with all the usual defences and a larger number of light field-guns, and the first heavy German howitzers which were placed in armoured casemates. The width of the valley was about a mile and a quarter, and when the French infantry appeared on the crest all the howitzers, guns, and machine-guns on both sides of the chalk hollow came into action at top speed. The German gunners had marked the range of every yard of the ground, and when the French were checked by the entanglements the storm of fire directed on them from the three German lines was of an appalling intensity.

The French won through chiefly by the skill and courage of their machine-gunners and their telephone signallers. The men of both these sections followed close upon the first lines of attacking infantry, though the burden they had to carry was heavier than that of their comrades. The French machine-guns were placed close to the German trenches to keep down the enemy's fire while the wire was being cut. The field telephones were even more quickly brought into action; and the French artillery officers worked out the ranges and telephoned to their batteries far away over the ridge. The third and fourth German lines were completely destroyed, and it was only the second line, just before the crest where the French soldiers were struggling within ten yards of the enemy, that gave very serious trouble. This barrier extended all below the crest of the long ridge, and the fighting was so close that the distant French howitzer batteries could not safely intervene. But, as we have seen, the Frenchmen worked through, some crawling under the wires, some blanketing them with their coats and then rolling over, others forcing a way with wire-cutter and butt. A wounded Zouave, returning on September 27 by the Wacques Farm, from the Epine position, stared at the two and a half miles of casemated batteries, sunken mazes, and entanglements through which he had stormed. " However did we get through all this? " he said in wonder.

The main second line of the enemy extended far along the crest eastwards, past Navarin Farm and Bois Sabot, to the fortresses of Tree Hill and Tahure Down; and after the troops on the Auberive—St. Hilaire section broke through the ridge entanglements, the general movement was still held up by the enemy's resistance at Bois Sabot, Spandau Wood, and Cameroon Trench, north of Souain. In the meantime, Tree Hill, which was the key position to the central German position, was masked.

The French position near Tahure rested on Hill 170, south-west of the village, along the road from Perthes. Immediately in front of the men from Normandy, Brittany, and Vendée was Tahure Down, which was some ninety-six feet higher than Hill 171. From the dominating height the German batteries and machine-guns poured so heavy a fire on the advanced French troops, in the afternoon of September 25, that the position seemed hopeless. Happily, several French batteries galloped down the Perthes road, through the curtain of fire by which the Germans were trying to keep off the opposing reserves. The French gunners unlimbered and worked their pieces in the open, and at close range beat down the covered German guns and howitzers on the high down northward, and so slackened the enemy's fire that the French infantry could lie out all night.

Throughout the night more guns and more supports were moved through the conquered German lines, and at dawn on

THE HORSESHOE POSITION

September 26 the attack upon the works stretching from the Butte of Souain to the Butte of Tahure was begun. The resistance offered by the Germans, however, was very formidable. They had the French in a great horse-shoe of heights, of which Souain Butte, Tree Hill, and Tahure Butte formed the centre.

The attacking forces were overlapped by two unconquered downs, nicknamed the Deux Mamelles, and by the long line of the Mesnil Down. Most of the German trenches in this protected stretch of downland had escaped the devastating effects of the French bombardment. The ground had been divided into compartments by the German engineers, and the systems of wire-fenced earthworks were so arranged that enfilading fire could be used by the defending forces at every important point. In some places the French troops in their first vehement movement had captured parts of the fire-trenches around this great horse-shoe. Some troops were struggling to maintain a hold on the steep western side of Mesnil Down, but they had to be withdrawn in the night of September 25, and some time passed before the two points of the Horse-shoe, Deux Mamelles and Mesnil Down, were definitely conquered.

The great Horse-shoe had originally formed the German third and last line. But when his first line was captured in the spring of 1915, he not only strengthened his second line, which was lost on September 25, but extended his third downland line, of which the Horse-shoe formed part, and then built a fourth line on the heights beyond the Py river. There seems also to have been a fifth reserve line south of Vouziers. The immediate objective of General de Castelnau was the old cross-country railway, running along the Py river, and connecting the army of the Crown Prince and the army of Metz with the army of Marshal von Heeringen, fighting in front of Reims and along the Aisne. This railway was already under the fire of the heavy French howitzers, but the gunners could only work from wireless signals received from aerial observers. When the country was covered with fog, as happened on September 26 and September 27, the heavy French batteries could merely fire at random at the railway. What they needed was an artillery observation post on a down overlooking the railway. The Butte of Tahure, with a summit only about a mile and a quarter from the railway line, overlooking some lower heights, was an admirable station for the French artillery officers.

Unfortunately for the French, all the German positions on the heights of the Horse-shoe were situated on the northern slopes. There was nothing in view that could be attacked by direct fire. The systems of parallel trenches with their wire entanglements were hidden behind the ridges. Only a few observing officers, sheltered in dug-outs and using periscopes, faced the attacking French forces. A little way behind them were a few machine-gun posts, widely spaced to escape destruction, and situated so as to command the slopes up which the French battalions must climb. Everything else was hidden below the crests. In these circumstances, General de Castelnau held back his troops for some days. He had some small successes on September 28 and September 29, when a Norman regiment took part of the Vistula Trench, west of the Butte of Tahure, and part of the position west of Navarin Farm near Chevron Wood was captured. In the last place the breach made in the enemy's lines was four hundred yards wide; but the French commander would not attempt to push his troops through it, for he knew that the heavy German batteries would come into play all round the Horse-shoe, and destroy his advanced battalions. So very little was done for eleven days.

In the meantime the French army was working energetically in the construction of a new front line on the ground they had conquered, driving communication saps down the valleys to connect with their old positions, while most of the French guns moved to new pits, new subterranean shelters and stables close to the fortressed hills behind which the enemy was massing. The idea of General de Castelnau was that he could afford to waste time in order to save the lives of his men. His great howitzers had rather a short range—five miles it is said—the length of their throw having been deliberately lessened in order to get a heavier projectile and a more vertical fall. They could destroy anything if they were brought close enough, but on widely-spaced lines such as the German they made the advance something of a crawl.

At last, on the night of October 6, the great new Creusot pieces were ready in their fresh positions, and all the smaller guns were thrown out well in front of them, close to the enemy's hill-line. A few days of clear weather had enabled the French airmen to photograph the wire entanglements and parallels behind the ridges; and all the French gunners used their pieces in howitzer fashion so as to get indirect fire effects. Even the ordinary light field-gun—the " 75 "—had a device which enabled it to be used somewhat in the fashion of a howitzer, so that it could throw shells high into the sky to an altitude at which they would fall behind an intervening hill-top. The arc of fire of a " 75 " was not as great as that of a howitzer; nevertheless, it was extremely useful in all this downland fighting.

The second French bombardment shattered the German defences around Tahure, and the great down of Tahure commanding the railway was captured by a Picardy division, which took some hundreds of prisoners. There was also a very fierce struggle among the downs north of Navarin Farm, where the Moroccan troops tried to thrust into Somme Py town. They took some of the heights along the road to Souain and Somme Py, but could not reach the river line. Yet they broke up a regiment of the German 10th army, which had been brought from the Russian front. The French guns curtained this force off from the Py river, so that the men had no water for four days, and lived on their " iron ration." Then the Moors burst among them, and the survivors of the 4,000—four hundred and eighty-two men and ten officers—surrendered.

This attack by the Moorish troops was more in the nature of a strong demonstration, designed to weaken the defences around Tahure, and in this respect it succeeded; for at Tahure the French drove strongly within a mile and a quarter of the enemy's supply railway. Meanwhile the great German counter-attack had been launched on the British front at Loos. The French army in Champagne profited by this weakening of the enemy, and the Breton and Vendean troops, having taken the Toothbrush Redoubt at Mesnil, closed round the Trapeze Redoubt on three sides, and blasted their way into it by aerial torpedoes and mines. In one of their mines they used more than twenty tons of high-explosive, which shattered two hundred and fifty feet of German trenches. Then day and night the French guns played on the position, until at last the surviving German garrison fled into their underground passages, and the Breton infantry met with scarcely any resistance. In all some 26,000 German prisoners were taken in Champagne, besides three hundred and fifty officers and one hundred and fifty cannon.

The action of the French 10th army in Artois, under the command of General d'Urbal, with General Foch as director of all the north-western front, was not a marked success. As has already been related, the creation by German engineers of a great new obstacle near Souchez checked at the outset the advance of the French 10th army, and prevented it from co-operating with the British 1st army in the drive on Lens. Then on the reverse slope of the Vimy Ridge, protected from French shell fire, the enemy had built a vast underground system of enormous strength. It was not until September 26 that the French forces in Artois were able to find a weak place in the German lines, and they were then held up on the north at Angres and Lieven, as the British had been at Auchy and La Bassée, and the main strength of their movement was directed against the Vimy Ridge.

On this occasion every yard of ground had to be won by desperate fighting; for on the south, above Arras, the Germans still held some communication trenches of the Labyrinth, and in the north they retained powerful gun positions from which the French troops were enfiladed. In all these adverse circumstances, with the chalk country slippery with rain, and the air thick with mist, General d'Urbal's troops pressed on in an effort of magnificent endurance, to capture Souchez, La Folie, and a footing on Hill 140, the highest hump of Vimy Ridge. For the most part the fighting consisted of ferocious hand-bombing work, in which ground was slowly won, trench by trench, until the enemy's reserves were brought up in sufficient force to immobilise the French army. What General d'Urbal aimed at was to facilitate the advance of the British 1st army, immediately on his left, by pressing the common foe strongly and forcing him to spread his army in full strength southward. When the charge of the British Guards' division and the advance of other reserve divisions did not produce any further marked deflection of the enemy's lines, the French 10th army relieved its British comrades in a more direct manner by taking over the Double Crassier, Loos, and Hill 70 trenches, and there beating back the left wing of the great German counter-attacking army on October 8.

CHAPTER 23

The Problem of Man Power

As the Great War progressed, a phrase, hitherto rarely if ever heard in Great Britain, came into use. It was man power. The struggle was certain to be a protracted one; the early hopes of a speedy entrance into Berlin had utterly faded away. The issue would not be decided by a single battle of the type of Zama or Hastings, Austerlitz or Sedan, one of those battles " without a morrow " of which German strategists had dreamed and written. Instead it had become a stern test of endurance, to which the nearest parallel was the American Civil War, resembling a tug-of-war rather than a boxing match. Under these conditions the fact that dominated all others, for even munitions were useless without men to use them, was the supply of men. Each combatant, it was fairly certain, was suffering casualties in much the same proportion, so victory would fall to the side that could longest keep up the supply of fighting men.

The great European countries, with their elaborate systems of compulsory military service, did not find it difficult to estimate their strength in this respect, but it was somewhat different in Great Britain. In Germany and France roughly one-tenth of the population, or one-fifth of the males, were sufficiently virile to bear arms, while perhaps a further 5 per cent. could be collected, in case of need, from the older and weaker men. Taking this as a basis, Great Britain, with her population of 45,000,000, had a maximum man power of some 7,000,000. Certainly not all these would be combatants. Indeed, Mr. Churchill is credited with the remark that it took six men to put and keep one soldier in the firing line, but this proportion was reduced later by the employment of women on munition and other work. However, it may be assumed that the fund of men upon which Great Britain could draw for the requirements of war was between 6,000,000 and 7,000,000.

By the autumn of 1915 the question how to maintain a regular and sufficient supply of recruits was causing great anxiety.

There had been a magnificent response to the appeals for volunteers. At the outbreak of the war hundreds of thousands of young men, the very pick of the nation, had flocked to the colours, many of them before any public call for recruits was made. Elaborate advertising schemes promoted by the War Office had forced the question upon every man in the country. Recruiting meetings, recruiting marches, military displays, public lectures, and private canvasses had all been used on a scale and with a persistence never dreamed of before. And the response to these had been larger than even the warmest advocates of voluntaryism would have deemed possible in the days preceding the war.

But if the response had been great, the requirements were still greater. The war was eating up men. In Gallipoli alone close on 200,000 were, up to the autumn, killed, wounded, missing, or invalided. In Flanders, infantry battalions were losing an average of 15 per cent. a month from one cause or another. At least 30,000 new men were required every week to make up wastage. By September, 1915, the voluntary system had apparently almost exhausted itself. Meetings were redoubled. Posters and placards calling for volunteers were more abundant, more artistic, and more persuasive than ever. But the recruits now joined in mere driblets. Skeleton battalions, their ranks swept by war and disease, called vainly for fresh men.

There were over 2,000,000 single men of military age in the country who had not offered themselves for enlistment. There were many more married men, with family claims, who felt it unfair and unjust that they, with wives and children to support, should be called upon to serve, while others, unmarried and having no one dependent on them, were going free. It was obvious that some among those who had not volunteered were engaged in necessary war work at home. But many had no good excuse; some said that they would not come until they were fetched. The Government tried, by a more liberal scale of allowances to soldiers' wives and families, and by other means, to make it possible for men to come who had others dependent upon them. But it soon became clear that something more must be done.

In endeavouring to form a fair estimate of the attitude of the British people at this time, it must be remembered that the greater part of the nation was by tradition and instinct strongly opposed to conscription in any shape or form. It had been their boast for generations that theirs was a voluntary army. " One volunteer is worth three pressed men " was a favourite but ridiculous English adage. The Englishman was accustomed to compare the British volunteer soldier with the Continental conscript, very much in favour of the British volunteer. In the mind of the average Briton, voluntaryism was associated with freedom, and conscription with the system of state regulation of the lives of its citizens, such as Germany maintained. Among the working classes, in particular, the feeling against conscription was deep rooted. There was a belief that conscription, if it came, would be the rich man's dodge to make the poor man's son serve, and that conscription for the army would be followed by conscription for labour purposes, forced work, low wages, and industrial servitude.

At the end of September the prime minister and Lord Kitchener met a representative group of Labour leaders in conference. Lord Kitchener put the facts before them. Men, many more men, must be secured for the army, navy, and also for munition work. There can be little doubt but that Lord Kitchener, backed by Mr. Asquith, solemnly warned the Labour leaders that if the recruits were not had by voluntary means, compulsion must follow. Mr. Will Thorne, M.P., told afterwards how Lord Kitchener said that if he could have 70 divisions —about 1,500,000 men—in the field, between then and the next spring, he would guarantee victory.

A discussion then followed, in which the premier was told that voluntary recruitment would be more successful if the Government would frankly state the actual requirements and the number of men who had come forward. Some speakers declared that many more men would volunteer but for the attitude of the employers. In the end, the conference pledged itself to do its utmost, and it set about organizing a big campaign. This campaign was to include meetings of the workers throughout the land, the preparation and distribution of special recruiting literature, and the sending of deputations to trades councils and other Labour organizations to explain the needs of the country and to secure their co-operation in meeting them. A recruiting rally was held throughout the country on the first Saturday in October, with marches of troops and special meetings everywhere. The rally was very successful, despite rain. But people were now coming to see that spasmodic efforts could scarcely ensure the regular inflow of men necessary.

A new and very important step forward was made on October 5, when the earl of Derby undertook, at the request of the secretary of state for war, the direction of recruiting for the army. Lord Derby had already done great public service. Head of the house of Stanley, and the leading territorial magnate in Lancashire, he was above all things a Lancashire man—blunt of speech, a hard worker, shrewd and genial, a good sportsman, and a born leader. As a young man he joined the Grenadier Guards. In the South African War he was at first chief press censor, and then private secretary to Lord Roberts. Returning to England, he became financial secretary to the war office, and later postmaster general in the Unionist ministry. Lancashire thought of Lord Derby not so much as a nobleman of ancient lineage and owner of some 70,000 acres, but as a man among men, who talked in its own speech, who knew its ways, and who was equally good at a directors' table, on the racecourse or hunting field, or in some great department of philanthropic work.

Lord Derby was himself a believer in national service, but since the beginning of the war he had sunk his personal preference and worked strenuously to make the voluntary system a success. He referred to his appointment at a meeting at Waterfoot, Rossendale, on October 5. He told how, ten days before, he had asked two questions of the Government—whether it had decided on the number of men it had to put in the field; and whether, having decided that, it was prepared, if it could not get enough men by voluntary means, to employ other means?

I had the question answered in a rather peculiar way. Lord Kitchener has asked me to become director of all recruiting throughout the United Kingdom. I have accepted out of personal loyalty and friendship to Lord Kitchener. It is not a position to be envied. I feel something in the position of a receiver who is put in to wind up a bankrupt concern; but I hope I shall be able to do it with such satisfaction as will enable the creditors to receive their 20s. in the pound. I myself am an advocate of national service, but I do not think that even those who have been my most bitter adversaries will deny that I have done my level best to make the voluntary system a success. I have done all I possibly could to get men under the voluntary system.

The appointment of Lord Derby was quickly followed by radical changes in the recruiting organization. Ten days after his appointment, he issued details of his new scheme, and these were elaborated in a notable speech at the Mansion House, London, on October 19. Every recruiting organization at work was to be employed, the parliamentary recruiting committees taking prominent place, for a grand canvass of unenlisted men of military age. Their work was to be systematized and thoroughly co-ordinated. The national register, which had been taken some weeks before, was to be used as a basis for this canvass. Civilians were to be asked to volunteer under a group system. There would be 46 groups—23 for single men and 23 for married men—arranged according to age. The single men who volunteered would be called up for service in the order of their groups; the men in the twenties being used in their order before the men in the thirties were called upon.

The married would not be asked to serve until the lists of single men were exhausted. Those who wanted to join the colours at once could do so. The others, after joining their groups, would go back to their ordinary vocations until wanted. Starred men—*i.e.*, men working at trades such as munition production, necessary for the war—and unstarred men found indispensable in their employments would be sent back at once to their employments after attestation, if necessary. But Lord Derby clearly intimated that even in starred trades there might be men who could be liberated from their employment. At the close of his speech at the Mansion House, London, he said:

There are people who seem despondent about the spirit of the country; I am not. I believe the heart of the country is right. Only the heart of the country has got to be touched. I believe we can do it. I believe that if men can only realise now that by their individual effort, they are going to secure for their children, and their children's children, a lasting and enduring peace, they will be prepared to make some sacrifice, or even any sacrifice. I believe implicitly that if we can get the country at the back of us, now, we are going, even at this eleventh hour, to make the voluntary system an unqualified success.

Lord Derby's proposals were received with a chorus of approval. The section of the press which defended voluntaryism was naturally pleased, because it realized that here was a possibility of saving its position. But those newspapers which upheld national service were also perfectly loyal, and declared they would do everything possible to forward Lord Derby's plans. They kept their promise. During the weeks of the canvass they gave the scheme the utmost publicity and the warmest advocacy. " The new recruiting campaign starts under the most favourable auspices, and without the slightest sign of opposition," The Times declared. " Everybody wishes it well, and Lord Derby has a host of eager helpers." The Daily Mail, which had good reason to be pleased that the plan of " single men first," for which it had fought for many months, was now officially adopted, pledged itself to co-operate. " We wish Lord Derby every success in his scheme," it wrote.

While the substitution of a direct canvass for the old haphazard system was widely praised, one weak point in the scheme was at once pointed out. If large numbers of married men volunteered and comparatively few single men, the married men might be called upon before they ought to be, despite the promise of single men first. Thus young slackers might still be seen walking about the streets, while married men with families were taking upon themselves the responsibilities of the firing line. This point was brought before Lord Derby by the town clerk of Chiswick. Lord Derby's reply was: " It is clear that if sufficient young single men do not enlist under the scheme, some other steps must be taken to fetch them. This would occur before the married men are taken."

People, however, asked something more than a general statement from the director of recruiting. It was felt that the prime minister himself should make a definite and unmistakable declaration of policy. Mr. Asquith did so in a notable speech in Parliament on November 2. He admitted that there had been differences of opinion in the Cabinet over the recruiting question. The question of compulsion was one of practical expediency. He admitted that the system of voluntary recruiting operated in time of war in a haphazard, capricious, and somewhat unjust way both as regard individuals and classes. His objection to the introduction of compulsion was that under existing conditions it would forfeit the maintenance of national unity. If it were applied without something in the nature of general assent, the nation would be disunited. He believed that the result of Lord Derby's recruiting scheme would be wholly satisfactory.

But if there should still be found a substantial number of men of military age not required for other purposes, who without excuse hold back from the service of their country, I believe that the very same conditions which make compulsion impossible now—namely, the absence of general consent—would force the country to the view that it must consent to supplement, by some form of legal obligation, the failure of the voluntary system.

Then he went on to refer to the doubt among married men whether they might not be called upon to serve, if they joined their group, while younger, unmarried men were holding back and not doing their duty. " Let them disabuse themselves of that idea," declared the premier, in a statement that affected the whole future history of Britain.

So far as I am concerned, I should certainly say the obligation of the married man to enlist ought not to be enforced, or binding upon him, unless and until—I hope by voluntary effort, and if not by some other means—the unmarried men are dealt with first.

Even this declaration did not suffice. Married men when canvassed said that the premier had merely given an expression of personal opinion. They wanted more than that. Nine days afterwards, on November 11, 1915, an official statement was circulated to the press which placed the matter beyond doubt:

Lord Derby is authorised by the prime minister to express his surprise that his statement in the House of Commons on November 2 should be considered in any way ambiguous. The prime minister on that occasion pledged not only himself but his Government when he stated that if young men did not, under the stress of national duty, come forward voluntarily, other and compulsory means would be taken before the married men were called upon to fulfil their engagement to serve. Lord Derby is further authorised to state definitely that if young men medically fit and not indispensable to any business of national importance, or to any business conducted for the general good of the community, do not come forward voluntarily before November 30, the Government will after that date take the necessary steps to redeem the pledge made on November 2.

The new scheme was further supported by a direct appeal from the King to the people of Great Britain:

At this grave moment in the struggle between my people and a highly-organised enemy, who has transgressed the laws of nations and changed the ordinance that binds civilised Europe together, I appeal to you.

I rejoice in my Empire's effort, and I feel pride in the voluntary response from my subjects all over the world who have sacrificed home, fortune, and life itself, in order that another may not inherit the free Empire which their ancestors and mine have built.

I ask you to make good these sacrifices.

The end is not in sight. More men and yet more are wanted to keep my armies in the field, and through them to secure victory and enduring peace.

In ancient days the darkest moment has ever produced in men of our race the sternest resolve.

I ask you, men of all classes, to come forward voluntarily, and take your share in the fight.

In freely responding to my appeal you will be giving your support to our brothers who, for long months, have nobly upheld Britain's past traditions and the glory of her arms.

GEORGE R.I.

Lord Derby and his assistants felt that their campaign would be greatly helped by introducing some badge that would openly and publicly mark off the volunteer from the slacker. This was provided by the adoption of an idea advanced some months before by Sir George Pragnell—the issue of armlets to all men who offered themselves for enlistment in the groups, and to other qualified persons. The khaki armlet was undoubtedly a dramatic stroke. The difficulty at first was that in some cities, particularly in London, young men did not care to wear their badges. They were driven to it more and more by public opinion, and by an appeal from the King.

An enormous mass of feeling in favour of military service had been gathering force in the country during the summer of 1915. Sometimes it found crude and foolish expression, as in white feather campaigns, when irresponsible young women presented young men in the streets and restaurants with white feathers, the symbol of cowardice. But essentially the feeling was sound. The young man out of khaki or without his armlet soon found himself in a painful position. Young women formed leagues, pledging themselves not to marry any man who had shirked his duty of enlisting. Mothers who had lost their sons, wives who had lost their husbands, would stop young civilians in the streets, or turn to them in omnibuses, and demand why they were not doing their duty. " I've lost my son and my husband in this war," said one lady in an omnibus, where three young civilians were sitting. " I am proud of them, and would not have kept them back; but I am ashamed when I see young fellows like you, as fit as they were, lolling in London and enjoying yourselves in place of doing your duty, and I hope you are ashamed of yourselves." This was the kind of talk which met the slacker at every turn.

The new canvass was launched on October 25, and was to last for six weeks. Leading men in different parts of the country accepted the posts of directors of recruiting for their districts. Thus, for instance, Lord Wimborne, the lord lieutenant, undertook the duties of director general of recruiting for Ireland. The machinery of political organizations was enlisted. Liberal and Unionist canvassers joined together, and many volunteered to do the necessary work of canvassing without pay.

The campaign began with a unanimity rarely witnessed in Britain. Every newspaper gave it day by day the leading place in its pages and urged its importance in its editorial columns. The Times published a special recruiting supplement. Municipal authorities gave up their public buildings to the workers. Every house in which a man of military age lived had to be visited and the man invited to join the army. If he refused he had to be asked his reasons for refusing. The local parliamentary recruiting committees responsible for the canvass in each district were at work often day and night, meeting difficulties, solving problems, and pushing on the campaign. The nation as a whole quickly came to learn that Lancashire's opinion of Lord Derby was right. He was an ideal man for the post, prompt in business, ready to face difficulties, frank and willing.

The campaign had its ups and downs. It was launched with what seemed to be a great boom, but that did not yield so many men as expected. All classes joined—civil servants, schoolmasters, many ministers of religion, and business men galore. In some cases the entire staff of a business house went and attested in a body. It seemed as though the great wave of enthusiasm would sweep in every eligible man. Then the

THE PROBLEM OF MAN POWER

boom suddenly exhausted itself. A statement made by Mr.
Asquith in the House on November 15—that no attempt would
be made to apply compulsion in any shape or form without the
consent of Parliament—was used in some quarters against the
campaign. An attempt was quickly made to remedy this, and
Mr. Asquith repeated and emphasized his earlier pledge to the
married men. " What the prime minister meant," said Mr.
Bonar Law, speaking for the Government, " and what we mean,
was not if they do not come in, but if there is a general shirking
of their duties, then they will be made to come in before the
men with wives and families."

The effect of the misunderstanding was, however, unfortunate,
and for a week or two things looked very bad. The time limit
for the canvass was extended to December 11, and Lord Derby,
in speeches at Edinburgh and Glasgow, reaffirmed the promise
to married men.

What more can I say to you on the subject, except that as
one who has been responsible for this scheme I should give
you my own personal pledge? To the fullest extent in my
power I will see that absolute faith is kept with those married
men who have joined under the assurance given. I am not
a member of the Government. I am only a recruiting
sergeant. I have no personal power, but I have behind me in
this matter an overwhelming power—the power of public
feeling of the country. The country is long-suffering, and
has stood a great many things, but it is not going to stand
anything that would be like bad faith with those ready and
willing to risk their lives for it.

On November 19, in order to leave no room for misunderstanding whatever, Lord Derby wrote a letter to the prime
minister, in which he clearly stated the position as he
understood it :

My dear Prime Minister,—As some uncertainty exists as to
the effect of the various statements recently made in Parliament and the Press on the subject of recruiting, may I
endeavour to put the position in a few words?

Married men are not to be called up until young unmarried
men have been. If these young men do not come forward
voluntarily, you will either release the married men from their
pledge or introduce a Bill into Parliament to compel the young
men to serve, which, if passed, would mean that the married
men would be held to their enlistment. If, on the other hand,
Parliament did not pass such a Bill, the married men would be
automatically released from their engagement to serve.

By the expression " young men coming forward to serve," I think it should be taken to mean that the vast majority of young men not engaged in munition work or work necessary for the country should offer themselves for service, and men indispensable for civil employment and men who have personal reasons which are considered satisfactory by the local tribunals for relegation to a later class, can have their claims examined for such relegation in the way that has already been laid down.

If, after all these claims have been investigated and all the exemptions made mentioned above, there remains a considerable number of young men not engaged in these pursuits who could perfectly be spared for military service, they should be compelled to serve. On the other hand, if the number should prove to be, as I hope it will, a really negligible minority, there would be no question of legislation.

Yours sincerely,
DERBY.

The prime minister replied as follows:

10, Downing Street, S.W.
November 19, 1915.

My dear Derby,—I have received your letter of to-day. It correctly represents the intentions of the Government.

Yours sincerely,
H. H. ASQUITH.

One of the urgent questions that arose during the canvass was how to decide which men were indispensable to the industries of the country, and which would serve the country better by enlisting in the army. Lord Derby here laid down the cardinal principle that it was for the state, not for the employer, and not for the man himself, to say whether he was indispensable or not. It was the duty of the man to attest, and then submit his case to the authorities. Local tribunals were appointed in which the various authorities interested were represented, and these authorities were empowered to decide. Besides local tribunals, a central appeal tribunal of five members was appointed. At the head was Lord Sydenham, a famous artillery officer and army organizer; Sir George Younger, the second member, was a Scottish Unionist whip, and chairman of a firm of brewers; other members were Sir Francis Gore, who was formerly solicitor to the board of inland revenue; Mr. Cyril Jackson, a prominent educationist; and Mr. G. J. Talbot, K.C., a distinguished ecclesiastical lawyer.

On December 3, despite all that had been done, it was felt by those behind the scenes that the net result of the scheme had been very disappointing. Lord Derby and the other leaders issued another appeal to all men of military age in the United Kingdom, pointing out to them once more that it was their duty to express their willingness to serve their country in the field. If they had difficulties which made it hard for them to do so, impartial tribunals would weigh their arguments, and, if necessary, exempt them from immediate service. " Let him " —the available man—" join the army under the group system, and show his country that he puts her interests before his own, and show the world, the Allies, neutrals, and enemies alike, that there are hundreds and thousands of our citizens who are ready to fight for her." At the same time the joint labour committee, which had been working hard among the working classes, issued its final appeal " to the free men of Britain to respond to the call of their country, and to enrol themselves at once in the great volunteer army which stands between us and the loss of our rights and liberties."

Four days before the end an amazing final boom began. The recruiting officers suddenly found themselves overwhelmed by thousands of men pouring in. From all parts of the country the news was the same. Long lines of men were waiting outside the doors of the recruiting offices to attest. In some cases the men had to wait for half a day before they could be attended to. In other cases the offices were kept open all night. It was not, however, really known how great this rush actually had been until Lord Derby published his report. Then it was shown that in these four days, from December 10 to December 13, a total of 1,070,478 men had attested.

In the last two days it became evident that it was impossible to make the medical examinations. The only way of coping with the rush was to swear the men in, take their names, pay them their attestation money, 2s. 9d., and let them go away, and be examined more carefully later. In Manchester on Thursday evening the long corridor of the town hall became so packed with men that the police decided to close the doors. In London bodies of young men marched to the recruiting depôts singing, and concerts were arranged for the crowds waiting their turn. Men in silk hats and men in fustian, employers and clerks side by side, lads not yet twenty and middled-aged men—

fathers of families—hustled one another to get in. Despite the fact that it had been repeatedly stated that no further extension of the time would be made, the time had to be extended in the end. It was found impossible to take the names of all offering themselves before midnight on Saturday, so attestations were continued during Sunday, December 12, and those whose names were taken on that day, who even then could not be attested, were allowed until the following Wednesday to offer themselves.

These dramatic and surprising closing scenes gave every encouragement to the advocates of the voluntary system. They proclaimed that conscription had been killed once and for all. Lord Derby's report was eagerly looked for. After a few days rumours began to be circulated that the total results were not quite so good as had been hoped. Very many men had joined —that much was certain—but a large number of these were married, and quite a considerable proportion of single men had not attested. Soon it became clear that there had been enormous numbers of single men slackers. Under the terms of Mr. Asquith's pledge, the Government must either compel these men to serve or not call upon the married men who had attested.

On Wednesday, December 15, Lord Derby made a significant statement in the House of Lords. He said that the first part of his report, dealing with the figures up to November 30, had been submitted to Lord Kitchener and Mr. Asquith, but as yet no judgment could be formed from it. Then Lord Derby added:

> I ask your lordships to support me in saying that it will be absolutely impossible for any action to be taken which will necessitate the calling up of married men until the country is absolutely convinced that the single man has come forward to such an extent as to leave only a negligible quantity unaccounted for. We must, above all things, keep faith with the pledge the prime minister gave to the married men.

The meaning of this was unmistakable. On the following day a group of some 30 resolute opponents of national service, led by Mr. J. H. Thomas, requested the prime minister to receive them as a deputation on the subject of the compulsion of the single men. The proceedings were private, but there can be little doubt about what the deputation asked. They were anxious to induce the prime minister to consent to a plan for yet another canvass of the remaining single men.

The majority of the nation had by now made up their minds that if the Derby scheme did not succeed, compulsion for the slackers must come. Men of all classes, Labour leaders, Liberal Members of Parliament, religious teachers, who had for years consistently fought conscription, now declared that circumstances alter cases. They did not like conscription, and they did not want it, but better conscription than that Britain should lose the war. If the Government decided, with all the facts before it, that conscription was necessary, they would submit. This was the loyal view of the overwhelming majority. A small group, however, still stood out, including some members of the Cabinet. They asked, in the hope of delaying conscription, that a measure should be passed directing all single men who had not attested to come before specially appointed tribunals and give the reasons why they did not join. If these reasons were satisfactory, the man should be marked off. If, however, in the opinion of the tribunal the reasons were not satisfactory, the man's name should be recorded. The total of the unsatisfactory men should be ascertained, and if this total was considerable then, and only then, should a measure of compulsion be passed for them.

During the end of December it was an open secret that a serious struggle was going on within the Cabinet. Lord Derby's final report was to hand, but the Premier had delayed giving it publicity. It was known that Mr. Lloyd George had taken a firm stand in favour of compulsion, declaring that to create further tribunals would merely be to postpone the struggle over the question. It was known, too, that Lord Derby had insisted rigorously on the maintenance of the pledge given by him. The compulsionists announced their faith in the prime minister's pledge, and said they were satisfied he would keep it to the full. Some newspapers, however, and a few politicians urged that the Government and Parliament were not bound by the prime minister's pledge, but that it was merely a personal promise which the Cabinet could break or not as it saw fit. Sir John Simon, the home secretary, led the opposition to compulsion in the Cabinet, and two other Ministers, Mr. Runciman and Mr. McKenna, were understood to be strongly against it. They feared the effect of a further considerable increase of our forces upon our economic position and our production of wealth, which must be maintained for success in the war.

THE DERBY FIGURES

On Tuesday, January 4, Lord Derby's report was made public. In it he gave a careful and luminous statement as to the whole recruiting problem, the difficulties raised by starred men, and the problems that often prevent single men as well as married men from offering themselves. But public interest fastened on the figures, which showed that over 1,000,000 single men of military age had not attested under the scheme, and that after allowing for those who were starred (or marked with a star as required for some indispensable post at home) there still remained unaccounted for 651,160. Here are the figures:

	SINGLE.	MARRIED.	TOTAL.
Total Men 18 to 40	2,179,231	2,832,210	5,011,441
Went to Attest	1,150,000	1,679,263	2,829,263
Did Not Attest	1,029,231	1,152,947	2,182,178
Of these are Starred	378,071	465,683	843,754
Unaccounted for	651,160	687,264	1,338,424
Total Attested	840,000	1,344,979	2,184,979
Of these are Starred	312,067	449,808	761,875
Unstarred	527,933	895,171	1,423,104
Deduct unfit, indispensable, and in reserved jobs	184,547	407,495	592,042
Actually Available	343,386	487,676	831,062

Lord Derby's comment on the 651,000, who were unaccounted for, took the following form:

This is far from being a negligible quantity, and in the circumstances I am very distinctly of opinion, that in order to redeem the pledge mentioned above (the pledge to married men), it will not be possible to hold married men to their attestation unless and until the services of single men have been obtained by other means, the present system having failed to bring them to the colours.

The groups were called up for active service on the principle of single men first, but it was evident before the end of the year that the scheme could not provide the necessary number of men, and everyone recognized that conscription was inevitable.

CHAPTER 24

Bulgaria Joins the Central Powers

IN the opening chapter of Vol. I is given an account of events in Bulgaria and the neighbouring Balkan states during the last half of the 19th century. An appreciation of this history is needed in order to understand the motives which caused Bulgaria to enter the war in 1915 on the side of the Central Powers.

The area to which the ranges of the Balkans have given their name was a veritable maze of mountains, broken only by small rivers, and devoid of valleys or plains suitable for large communities. Within the peninsula there was no natural centre around which, as a nucleus, a really great State could form and grow. This meant that among the inhabitants of the land intense rivalries were sure to develop. From north to south there was but one highway—or rather defile, for it was not unobstructed—the road from the Danube at the modern Belgrade to Salonica on the sea. It had been the avenue along which many armies had passed, and nothing was more significant of the terror it inspired than the fact that, with the exception of a few cities, the towns and villages hid themselves away from it in the hills. There were two other natural highways, both branching from the north-to-south road; one went south-east to the Bosporus—another blood-stained passage—and the other struck west to the Adriatic; both were difficult, being defiles rather than roads.

In modern times the story of the Balkans revolved round the slow, painful deliverance from the Turks of the races they had conquered centuries before, and the establishment of these races in the kingdoms of Greece, Serbia, Rumania, and Bulgaria. Montenegro, of close kin to Serbia, never had been entirely subdued, nor Albania. Serbia, Montenegro, Rumania, and Bulgaria were known collectively as the Balkan States; but, except between Serbia and Montenegro, and more loosely between Serbia and Greece, genuine cohesion did not exist.

Neither in race nor in religion did the Balkan states find a bond of union. The Serbians and the Bulgarians hated each other, though they came of Slav stock, and racially neither had anything in common with the Greeks, or with the Rumanians, who claim to be of Latin origin, and whose territory, properly speaking, lay outside the Balkans. Furthermore, of the monarchs who occupied the Balkan thrones only the kings of Serbia and Montenegro were natives. The faith professed by the bulk of the Balkan peoples was that of the Eastern or Greek Church, but the religious organization of each country was independent of that of the others, and all were at variance.

It was in union, and only in union, that the Balkan states could be really strong. Separately each was weak; but together their population approximated to 20,000,000, and, having universal and compulsory service, they would have been able to put into the field very nearly two million of men—a formidable army which not even a Great Power could despise. Mutual interests in commerce and industries did not suffice to unite them. Outside pressure might conceivably have welded them into one; outside pressure there was, but it was divided, and instead of leading to a confederation of the states, had the effect of making it impossible. They were overshadowed by Austria and Russia, both of whom showed the deepest concern with their affairs; but as these mighty empires were rivals, the one more or less offset the other.

It might be thought that at least in one direction the Balkan states would have presented a united front—that is, against Turkey; but the only union of the states against her did not include them all, and eventually led to further divisions, which seriously complicated the whole Balkan situation. This union produced the first Balkan War, and at its outset it appeared, as if the world were in sight of the achievement that had been held impossible—the formation of a veritable Balkan league, which was the title given to the allied states who declared war on Turkey at the close of September, 1912. Rumania stood aloof; because her interest in the struggle was less direct than that of the others. On the other hand, her very aloofness from it made her position decisive in the conflict which came afterwards. In spite of the fact that Bulgaria and Serbia had not been friends, and had tried conclusions on the battlefield of Slivnitza with disaster to the Serbians, they were the first members of the league. Greece joined them a little later, and with Serbia went Montenegro. This union of four of the states was in the main the work of three remarkable men—Pasich the Serbian, Gueshoff the Bulgarian, and Venizelos the Greek, each at the time prime minister of his state. But the union was soon shattered by the momentous happenings of 1914.

When the European war opened in July, and Serbia was involved with Austria, Bulgaria declared herself neutral, while her astute ruler, Ferdinand, kept a keen eye on the progress of events. The treaty which existed between Greece and Serbia against Bulgaria contained a provision for the lease to Serbia for 50 years of a small tract of land at Salonica, and for running powers over the Greek portion of the railway from that city to the north. It was in this way that Serbia was remunitioned by the French and the British in November and December, 1914, and was enabled to defeat the third Austrian invasion. King Nicholas of Montenegro identified himself and his tiny state with Serbia throughout. He it was who began the attack on the Turks in the first Balkan war, and when Austria declared war on Serbia in July, 1914, he took up arms to support her.

Although apparently favourable to the Entente Powers, the general situation in January, 1915, in the Balkan states, apart from Serbia and Montenegro, was thus in reality confused and doubtful. If in Rumania, in Greece, and even in Bulgaria there were pro-Entente elements, there also were elements which were distinctly pro-German; in Bulgaria opinion was biased by hatred of Serbia, and in a less degree of Greece and Rumania, and the Austrian predilections of the king materially affected the whole attitude of the country.

The best hope for the Balkan states themselves lay in their union, and as this union also was manifestly to the disadvantage of Germany, the Powers of the Entente worked assiduously to bring it about. The principal effort of the Entente was directed to the reconciliation of Bulgaria with the other states, who, she maintained, had robbed her of territory, though it was obvious that she had lost it in consequence of being defeated in a war which she herself had sprung on her former friends.

To placate Bulgaria meant concessions from the others, and the next eight months—until well into September—were chiefly concerned with the endeavours of the Entente to secure such concessions, and, having succeeded in their attempts, to get Bulgaria to accept them. But in this field, as in every other, the Entente Powers were faced with the persistent opposition

SIR JOHN FRENCH INSPECTING HIS TROOPS. By 1915 open warfare had given way to trench warfare, troops being drafted to the front and regularly relieved. The march past the British commander-in-chief was not a formal inspection but a frequent incident behind the lines. In this way Sir John French maintained the personal touch with his men which is so important a factor in the morale of an army, and satisfied himself as to their physical condition and equipment.

LOOS AFTER THE BATTLE. The ruins of the village of Loos, showing the famous " Tower Bridge," a pit-head structure, in the background. The battle, which was undertaken in September, 1915, with the object of recovering the French mining district around Lens, was preceded by a four days' methodic bombardment of the German positions. For the first time troops of Kitchener's New Army, raised in 1914, were employed.

Plate 46

Volume 11

of Germany. It is now known that in January a secret agreement had been negotiated between Bulgaria and Germany. This was signed a little later by Prince Bülow and M. Rizoff in Rome.

The respite given to Serbia at the end of 1914 by her great defeat of the third invasion by Austria proved to be a long one, as the attention of her enemy was almost entirely occupied for several months—first by the Austro-German campaign against Russia, and, secondly, by defensive operations against Italy, who joined the Entente Powers on May 23, 1915.

The striking triumph of Serbia had naturally a marked effect on the other Balkan states, who, as the new year opened, were still further impressed by the débâcle of the Turks which Russia brought about in the Caucasus and, later, by the Russian operations against Austria. Greece, allied by treaty with Serbia and inalienably hostile to Turkey, rejoiced, the great majority of her people showing openly their strong animosity to the Germanic league. Offers were made to Serbia early in the year by the Germanic Powers, which were eager to detach her from the Entente. She rejected their offers on receiving from the British Government pledges of solid support, provided she reorganized her army for a fresh campaign. She had not succeeded, unfortunately, in making good these pledges, and when her hour of desperate danger came the 500,000 allied troops needed to save her were not within easy reach.

Negotiations had been proceeding under the auspices of the Entente in furtherance of the union of the Balkan states, and some progress was made, but from the beginning Bulgaria pursued a tortuous course. Rumania had earlier received financial assistance from Austria, but in January a change in the direction of her policy was indicated by her obtaining a loan from Great Britain of several millions, most of which she applied to her army, then partially mobilised. On the other side of the account, Bulgaria had got money from Berlin. Attempts were made at the time to explain away the political bearing of the transaction by representing the advance as an instalment of a loan the terms of which had been concluded long before the war, but the essential fact was that the cash came from Germany at a time when she would not have permitted it to be paid out except for very substantial reasons.

In the same month Rumania tried to arrange with Bulgaria for common action by offering to restore to her part of the territory of which she had been deprived under the Treaty of Bukarest. Bulgaria coquetted with the proposal, but let it be understood that her price for joining in a union of the states which would support the Entente was the part of Macedonia allotted to her by the treaty of alliance between herself and Serbia before the first Balkan war, the valley of the Struma including the port of Kavala, the southern Dobruja, the whole of the territory Rumania had annexed under the treaty of Bukarest, and that area of Thrace which she herself had taken from the Turks in 1912.

Bulgaria asked a great deal. The Entente Powers took counsel with the other Balkan states, and in order to induce them to fall in, as far as possible, with the Bulgarian programme, suggested certain compensations for what they were asked to surrender. To Serbia, who at first was very averse from the idea of ceding the desiderated part of Macedonia to Bulgaria, they pointed out that she could find compensation in adding to her territory Bosnia, Herzegovina, and other Slav provinces and districts of Austria—that, in fact, she would be able to realise that confederation of the Southern Slavs which had been the ideal of Pasich, her ablest statesman. To Rumania, who already was willing to meet Bulgaria half-way, they said that Transylvania and Bukovina might be hers. To Greece, who had gained more at less cost from the two Balkan wars than the others, and so might be generous, they held out the prospect of obtaining a considerable area in Asia Minor, in which many thousands of people of her own race were domiciled. To Montenegro, who did not look for much, and who, in any case, might wish to attach herself to the projected confederation of the Southern Slavs under the headship of her friend Serbia, they stated that she could have Scutari and part of the Albanian coast. And as for Thrace, Turkey would have to yield not only the part of it Bulgaria wanted, but also a very large extent of her whole empire.

These suggestions of change and compensation were all dependent on the complete defeat of Germany, which the Entente Powers were confident was a certainty; but Bulgaria requested that at least some—and particularly one or two, such as Serbian Macedonia—of the proposed cessions should be actually made to her forthwith. Here was a great stumbling-block in the negotiations. The other Balkan states considered that, admitting even that the result of the war would be absolutely in favour of the Entente, these cessions might very well wait until the war had come to an end. In principle they were inclined to agree with the proposals submitted by the Entente.

Venizelos, in a memorandum to the king of the Hellenes, wrote that on the part of Greece concessions were possible to Bulgaria in return for compensation in Asia Minor, the concessions he had in his mind being the Struma Valley with Kavala. But the other states took exception to the evident intention of Bulgaria to aggrandise herself at their expense, before any of the suggested compensations were in sight. In February no real advance towards a settlement had been made, although a special French mission, with General Pau at its head, visited the Balkan capitals and tried to expedite matters.

But that month was signalised by an event—the bombardment of the Dardanelles by Allied warships—which had a considerable influence in the Balkans, Greece in particular being greatly stirred by it. Venizelos stated, in an interview some weeks later, that he was privy to this action, and had proposed despatching 50,000 Greek soldiers to aid in the attack, this number being afterwards reduced to 15,000 owing to the objections of the staff of the Greek army. In the end not one Greek was sent, because King Constantine could not see eye to eye with his great minister, and because the Greek staff was dissatisfied with the careless manner in which the Dardanelles operations were conducted. In the same interview Venizelos said that twice Greece had been requested by the Entente Powers to send men to help Serbia, but was compelled to decline through her fear of being set upon by Bulgaria.

In March the Balkans were convulsed by the sudden resignation of Venizelos because of insurmountable differences of view with his sovereign, the points in dispute being connected with definite action by Greece on the side of the Entente, which was urged by the statesman, but vetoed by the king.

On the last day of March the Parliament of Bulgaria was closed after a statement by M. Radoslavoff, the Premier, and a creature of King Ferdinand, that Bulgaria would preserve her neutrality, though Gueshoff, now in opposition, maintained that the real interests of the state were with the Entente. April opened with an occurrence that was pregnant with meaning. A feature of Macedonia under Turkish rule had been the activity of revolutionaries organized in komitajis, or armed bands of men, who kept up a guerrilla warfare upon the Turks. These societies, which were composed of Bulgar Macedonians, did not disappear with the transference of the country to Serbia, but, instigated by Bulgaria, remained in being and evinced hostility to the new owner of the land. On April 2 several of these bands made a raid in considerable force on the south-eastern frontier of Serbia, and after attacking with success outposts and block-houses in an attempt to cut the railway, were repelled only after severe fighting. Bulgaria loudly disavowed any participation in the affair, but Greece thought the occasion grave enough to demand a note of protest, which she sent to Sofia a few days later. Bulgaria again affirmed that she had nothing to do with the matter. Though now bound to Germany, she did not mean to strike as yet.

On the Balkans, as was inevitable, the triumphant offensive of the Germans against Russia had a tremendous effect; but as by the close of the month of May it was still in its first stages, that influence was not so manifest as it became later when further victories fell to the German arms in the eastern theatre. For one thing, Rumania saw any immediate prospect of seizing Transylvania vanish, and for another, Bulgaria became more and more pro-German. The Entente Powers, however, on May 29, made proposals to Bulgaria which, by offering her concessions, the fruit of their negotiations with the other Balkan states, were considered to be likely to lead her to fall in with their views. On June 15 Radoslavoff presented in return a note asking for further explanations.

During July Serbia was once more approached by Germany with an offer of a separate peace, but M. Pasich, the prime minister, passionately declared that she would agree to nothing of the sort, and proclaimed her unshaken loyalty to the Entente. On the 8th of that month Austria delivered a note to Rumania offering rewards in territory for her neutrality and substantially larger rewards for her early entrance into the war in favour of Germany and her allies. In the latter eventuality Austria dangled a tempting bait before her eyes by promising to conquer Bessarabia from Russia and transfer it to her as a permanent possession. In the meantime she was asked to permit at once the passage of munitions of war over her railways to Turkey, a permission which Rumania had steadfastly refused previously.

A CONVENTION SIGNED

Just a week afterwards Prince Hohenlohe-Langenburg, whose wife was a sister of the wife of the king of Rumania—both were daughters of the Duke of Edinburgh, who became duke of Saxe-Coburg-Gotha—arrived in Bukarest, and tried to induce his brother-in-law, King Ferdinand, to come to terms with Austria, or, at all events, to allow the transportation of munitions through the country, as requested. The prince's visit to the Rumanian capital had been preceded by a campaign in the German Press with the object of intimidating Rumania. But the king stood firm, and Prince Hohenlohe-Langenburg moved on to Sofia, where he met a more sympathetic soul in the other Balkan Ferdinand, who, at that moment, was endeavouring to get Turkey to conclude a treaty, for which secret negotiations had been going on for a long period, and by which Bulgaria was to obtain all the Turkish land on the west side of the Maritza river, and so free from Turkish interference the railway to Dedeagach. Ferdinand was successful, and on July 23 a convention gave Bulgaria sole possession of the line.

So far as Bulgaria was concerned, things did not look well for the Entente Powers, who could not but perceive the drift of affairs, and they made further efforts to procure her support. Early in August they made a collective representation to the Balkan states, and delivered to Bulgaria a reply to her note of June 15; in the one they spoke of the desirability of making further concessions, and in the other they stated that it was probable that the causes of friction would be removed and a union of the states brought about. Bulgaria, however, was not satisfied, and Radoslavoff, in an interview with an American correspondent, said that she would enter the war only on receiving absolute guarantees of achieving her national ideals. It afterwards transpired that a fortnight earlier she had completed her arrangements with Germany, Austria, and Turkey. This final treaty, which had been engineered by Prince Hohenlohe-Langenburg, explained the cession of Turkish territory on the Maritza, and promised Bulgaria a great deal more than the realization of her national ideals—Greek Macedonia being offered besides Serbian Macedonia. Unaware then of the existence of this or the earlier compact, the Entente brought additional pressure to bear on the other Balkan states.

The lion in the path now appeared to be Serbia, and, on behalf of the cause, she was again urged to surrender to Bulgaria all south-east Macedonia. The sacrifice was very great to her, but in a secret session of her parliament, held on August 24, she consented to make it. Rumania had been ready to agree to the stipulated concessions, and had advised Serbia and Greece to act in a similar way. On the 16th the Greek parliament assembled, Venizelos' adherents being in a large majority, and on the 17th the Gounaris government resigned. On the 22nd M. Venizelos was once again prime minister of Greece, and the Entente Powers, who still were ignorant of that fatal treaty, believed that the whole situation in the Balkans had become much more hopeful, from their point of view, than it had been for a long time. They were soon to be undeceived.

Perhaps the presence of Duke John of Mecklenburg, a relative of the Queen of Bulgaria, in Sofia, in the first and second weeks of September passed unobserved or was deemed unimportant, and nothing may have been thought of his going on to Constantinople, but as he was accompanied by Dr. von Rosenberg, a German diplomatist and a specialist in Balkan affairs, the Entente Powers might have been on their guard. Bulgaria, however, still kept the mask, yet her action on September 10 in calling for Macedonian Bulgars and Bulgars from Thrace to come forward and embody themselves in a Macedonian division, might have been deemed significant of her real attitude.

Like the rest of the world, the Balkan states were aware that during August and up to this time in September the Russians had suffered the most serious reverses and lost their best fortresses, while the British and the French had made no advance of importance in the west, and had failed of decisive victory in Gallipoli. It was of the utmost moment, therefore, for the Entente to bring to a favourable conclusion without further delay the negotiations between Bulgaria and her neighbours. On September 15 the Entente Powers presented a new note to Bulgaria, setting forth the concessions they had induced Serbia, Greece, and Rumania to offer to her in the interests of the projected union, provided that she should unreservedly declare against Germany.

Down to the very last days of September the British public enjoyed a cheerful conviction that the sympathies of every one of the Balkan states were entirely on the side of the Allies, in whose success their interests as a group were obviously bound up. The assumption in the mind of the ordinary man was that the interests and the honour of the Balkan states ensured their favour—their honour because every one of them owed their deliverance from the Turk to the nations of the Triple Entente, while they owed nothing whatever to the Central Powers, who were now in alliance with their old oppressor, the Ottoman; their interests, because Germans and Austrians had already given sufficiently convincing proofs of the treatment that might be expected by small states which should stand in the way of their aggrandisement.

It was supposed that Rumanians, Bulgarians, and Greeks were only restrained from flinging themselves actively into the fray on behalf of the Entente Powers by the prudence of rulers who wished to save their peoples from the burden of war, counting that the Allies would win without entailing sacrifice upon them, or that, at the worst, the door for their own intervention would remain open. What the British public did not reckon upon was that each individual state might hope for rewards at the expense of its neigh-bours if it should secure the good graces of the Central Powers, and the Central Powers should win. Also, it was by no means realized that the actual rulers of those countries were not popular assemblies, but monarchs whose personal sympathies were inevitably German, while they held in their hands the machinery for controlling the press and guiding public opinion.

Finally, it had hardly dawned upon British minds that the peoples of the Balkans could actually expect the Central Powers to win, or could believe that the way of safety lay in submission rather than in resistance. The Entente diplomatists were more alive to the danger of the situation, yet substantially they judged it very much as the public did—a remark certainly not less applicable to the French and the Russians than to the British. Only Bulgaria had certain recognised grievances; the rest of the Balkan states might, it was thought, have sufficient public spirit to consent to these being remedied for the sake of unanimity. So, as we have related, the diplomatists sought to persuade the other states to offer the inducements which were expected to bring Bulgaria into line, but they omitted to take the one step which, as a matter of fact, was necessary—a convincing display of military force; and, in the meantime, Ferdinand of Bulgaria at least had thoroughly duped all but a very few well-informed persons.

Even the mobilisation of the Bulgarian army was not at all conclusive. It could be construed as a wise precaution in the face of Austro-German armies concentrating upon the Danube. And when Greece also mobilised her army, her action was taken as a warning to Bulgaria that if the latter's intention was offensive, not defensive, if she meant to attack Serbia, she would find that Serbia did not stand alone.

In early October, at the invitation of the head of the Greek government, an Allied force was landed at Salonica. Unfortunately Venizelos had not a substantial backing, and he was dismissed by the king of Greece, who assembled a new ministry. Greece repudiated her treaty obligations to Serbia, and made it plain that she would not assist the Entente. It was not until the policy of seeking an autumn decision in the west was discounted by the limited success of the blow struck at the end of September that a fresh venture in the Balkans could be undertaken; nor, until Bulgaria dropped the mask, would such intervention have found military justification. The threat to the German lines in the west was the best security for Serbia. It was possible, on the other hand, to make ready for dealing with the Bulgarian intervention, but the Allies were deceived into assuming that they could count on the co-operation of Greece, and could regulate the scale of their own activities accordingly. It was only when they discovered that assumption to be a false one, after they had already occupied Salonica, that they found themselves forced to a new decision—whether they were to abandon the Balkans or were to organize their operations there with the knowledge that the Greek government, instead of giving active help, must be regarded as passively if not actively hostile.

The saving of Serbia from being completely overrun had become impossible from the moment when the defection of Greece paralysed immediate action. There was one excellent reason for retirement in the military maxim that it is a mistake to disperse your forces, especially at the dictation of your enemy. On the other side was the now patent fact that withdrawal would forthwith convert all the Balkan states into satellites of the Central Powers, with contingent effects in Western Asia certainly, in Egypt probably, and in India possibly, as well as on the Russian front. The decision, therefore, was definitely made to hold on to the Balkans.

CHAPTER 25

The Fighting in Africa

AFTER the British repulse at Tanga towards the end of 1914, neither the Germans nor the British in East Africa attempted any large scale offensive until 1916. A period of intensive preparation followed, both of the combatants endeavouring to build up their resources for the struggle which was ahead. For the moment Lettow-Vorbeck had reason to feel satisfied with what he had done, but he foresaw that the difficulties were only beginning, and he was not the man to wait quietly while his enemies collected their forces to crush him. His urgent problem would be the blockade of his coasts. Already it was far advanced, and by February 28, 1915, the British government declared that " ample steps had been taken to make the blockade thoroughly effective." Only on few occasions was the blockade broken.

The Germans were suddenly cut off from all those supplies for which previously they had been dependent upon Europe. But in dealing with the problem they displayed all the usual characteristics of German inventiveness and efficiency. Luckily for them, at the beginning of the war large supplies of European products had been accumulated in anticipation of the influx of visitors expected to attend the Dar-es-Salaam exhibition, and measures had been taken to supplement the food supply. This accident provided Lettow-Vorbeck with unexpected stores, and he took energetic measures not only to conserve them, but to augment his usual sources of replenishment. Dumps were formed all over the country, and to these the natives were required to bring large quantities of provisions.

Lettow-Vorbeck's chief personal achievement during 1915 was in the raising of recruits. As has been said in an earlier chapter, on the outbreak of hostilities he was possessed of an army of slightly under 5,000 men. When the struggle began in earnest in 1916, he had multiplied that number almost four times. Nor were his 20,000 men either raw or untrained. More than numbers he wanted efficiency, and owing largely to his personal abilities he succeeded in making his force a model of efficiency.

Of the total number about 4,000 were Europeans. The rest were askaris recruited from the most warlike of the native tribes.

The disastrous repulse at Tanga in November, 1914, was followed by another unfortunate affair for the British on the coast up which the Germans had advanced. The Germans were checked and thrown back across the frontier, losing Jasin, twenty miles south of it. On January 20, 1915, however, Lettow-Vorbeck, fearing that this move was a prelude to a second invasion in force, collected about 1,600 troops, attacked this post and compelled its surrender next day. It had been held by three companies of Indian infantry, who were without water and were compelled to surrender when their ammunition was expended. Help, which was attempted from the north, was unable to reach them owing to the skilful distribution of his forces which the German commander adopted. But they put up a splendid defence, and this was acknowledged by the Germans permitting the two British officers in command to retain their swords. About 240 men were made prisoners. Some 20 of the Kashmirs fought their way out of the place, and one of the King's African Rifles, a negro, succeeded in bringing his machine-gun into the British lines.

At the end of April, Brigadier-General Tighe, with the rank of major-general, was given command of the British in East Africa. While there was much desultory fighting, the summer campaign of 1915 contained no incident of great importance. German attacks on the Uganda railway were made repeatedly in the course of the year, but although carried out with great daring, produced little result. On Victoria Nyanza an expedition commanded by General J. M. Stewart, and consisting of detachments of the Royal North Lancashires, the 25th Royal Fusiliers (Driscolls Scouts), and King's African Rifles, captured the German's base at Bukoba, on June 25. In the south of the country, four weeks previously, a naval force under Lieutenant-Commander Dennistoun, with field artillery and some King's African Rifles, captured Sphinxhaven, a German town on Lake Nyasa. In June and July the Germans, in considerable strength, attacked Abercorn, a few miles south of Lake Tanganyika, but reinforcements arrived and the Germans retired.

All along the Rhodesian frontier, as all along the Belgian Congo frontier, raids and skirmishes were carried out by both sides. In the extreme south a rising of the natives in the Shiré

Highlands had taken place in January, and German complicity was suspected. It was organized by a fanatical negro preacher who had been educated in America, but with his death in a skirmish the revolt came to an end.

The allied forces in this area were composed of Belgians and British Rhodesians. Numbering about 3,000 in all they had the task of defending some 150 miles of frontier, against an active and well-led enemy. They were unable to check all the raids of the Germans, but splendidly led by Major J. J. Sullivan, they were able to repel all the advances which the enemy made in force. Thus, besides repulsing the Germans at Abercorn, they successfully defended Saisi against an even more vigorous attack in July.

General Tighe's task was difficult in the extreme. The Germans with their interior lines were able to throw the weight of their forces on any point with much greater speed than troops could be collected for its defence. Lettow-Vorbeck's worrying tactics were proving themselves admirably suited to the circumstances. During the whole of 1915, although it is doubtful whether he enjoyed any superiority of numbers, he managed to keep the Allies wholly on the defensive with the exception of the Lake Victoria expedition. By the middle of the year, plans had been arranged by the British and Belgian authorities for co-operative action. The urgent necessity was to pen the Germans in their own territory, and to make it impossible for Lettow-Vorbeck to continue his raids with his forces split "into guerrilla bands doubling back in all directions," as General Smuts subsequently described it. To this end it was arranged that while the Rhodesians in the south under General Northey and the Belgians under General Tombeur should advance slowly into German territory, occupy the frontier posts and thus prevent raiding, the British in the north should strike the main blow against the Germans round Kilima-Njaro. Preparations were at once begun, but little could be got ready before the end of the year, and the conquest of German East Africa was once more postponed.

Meanwhile, intense dissatisfaction had been expressed throughout Great Britain with regard to the failure of the British to achieve any vital success in East Africa. Questions were put in parliament, and the newspapers urged the Government to bestir itself and display much greater energy in the operations in this quarter. Eventually in December the announcement was made of the appointment of Sir Horace Smith-Dorrien to the chief command. A strong recruiting campaign was organized in South Africa, and many thousands of men enlisted.

Very different was the success attending the Allied arms on the other side of the continent. It will be remembered that in Cameroons by the end of 1914, the Germans had been driven from the coast and from most of the railway lines. They had taken up strong positions in the interior, the chief of which were centred in the mountainous districts of the north

EAST AFRICA. Map of the German colony conquered by Great Britain and Belgium during the Great War.

round Mora and the equally well-defined positions in the centre of the colony round Jaunde. In the south they were offering a strong resistance to the advance of General Aymerich's columns of French and Belgians, but they were gradually being hemmed in. Raids over the Nigerian border still occurred but with less frequency, and altogether the Allies had reason to be satisfied with the progress made.

Long after Sir Charles Dobell seized the port of Duala, on September 27, 1914, the Germans in the inland wilderness regarded themselves as unconquerable. But there was another side to their picture. The treatment of the natives by the Germans before the war, had done much to alienate any loyalty they might have won. Their conduct after the outbreak of hostilities was not calculated to allay the resentment they had stimulated earlier. The least sign of coolness on the part of the natives was visited with the most dire penalties and many natives were shot or hanged out of hand for conduct which the Germans maintained was treasonable.

Moreover, the methods of requisitioning supplies and labour were often brutal. It is not surprising that it was only in the north among the Fula Mahomedans that they received any support. The Bantus of the centre and south were invariably sullen and resentful servants. Only the askaris were treated with any consideration, but it must not be forgotten that the Germans' position was delicate and they were firmly convinced that any show of weakness on their part might possibly have precipitated a native rising in face of which they would have been helpless. The consequence was that the British and French commanders obtained from native enemy sources a good deal of valuable information about the movements of the German forces. The Germans, on the other hand, were often given by their own black spies misleading intelligence of their enemy's movements. In the immediate neighbourhood of any German garrison there was a condition of complete terrorism in native villages. But if any important movement of a German force occurred, some man or woman would slip at night into the thicket and get into touch with native watchers employed by the Allies. This is the explanation of the statement in Sir Charles Dobell's despatch concerning the great German attack on his main force: " I had obtained some knowledge of the German commander's intention."

In various regions the Germans held a number of enormously strong positions. Captain von Raben occupied the Mora mountain, that covered a rough circle about thirty miles in circumference and rose in cliffs to a height of 1,700 feet. In only a few places could the top be reached by men using both hands and feet in climbing, and in the rare breaks in the cliffs where this could be done, the slopes were covered with huge boulders that gave magnificent shelter for a defending force. Here he had pasture for his herd of cattle, a good supply of game, ample water, and such a system of defences as would require a Continental army to blockade and besiege. From his great mountain fastness Raben raided Nigeria and French Equatorial Africa.

About one hundred and fifty miles south of Mora was another great mountain fortress, Garua, on which two thousand native labourers had worked for nearly half a year. They had turned it into an entrenched camp that would have done credit to the engineers of a European battlefield. Here Captain von Crailsheim dominated the Nigeriⁿn line of the Benue river, with five guns, an unknown number of Maxims, and a large force of riflemen. A line of communication connected him with the Banyo mountain in the centre of Cameroons. Connected with this fortress was a mountain stronghold on the Ngaundere plateau.

Then in the heart of the broken highlands was the main German base, Jaunde, from which roads and paths radiated to entrenched heights and fortified fords in the country going down to the coast and to the Congo and its tributaries. The labour and the organization displayed by the Germans led some of the officers of the Allies to call Cameroons the fortress country. There was good reason for Commandant Zimmermann to look without anxiety at the capture of the port of Duala in September, 1914; for between Duala and Jaunde there was the mightiest system of natural defences in the world. It consisted first of a belt of estuary swamps and deadly mangrove forest. Above this great fever belt a primeval tropical forest rose in terraces of stifling gloom to the inland plateau.

Round these positions the Allied forces were gradually closing. A mixed French and British force under General Cunliffe was operating in the north, preparing to reduce Garua and then sweep south on Jaunde. The coast had been secured by General Dobell, and a French detachment under Colonel Meyer had occupied Edea, but was too weak to push farther into the swamps and jungle towards Jaunde. In the south-east, the French and Belgians under General Aymerich were approaching their objectives, the two German posts of Lomie and Dume.

General Aymerich sent a mission to Duala to arrange a scheme for a combined advance against Jaunde. The mission arrived at Duala on March 12, 1915, and asked the allied commander-in-chief, Sir Charles Dobell, to attempt a great thrust towards Jaunde. It was arranged that Brigadier-General Cunliffe should break into Garua, storm the Ngaundere plateau, and then move southward and unite near Jaunde with the forces under the command of Sir Charles Dobell and General Aymerich, who would by then have fought his way up from the south. General Aymerich, however, could not make the progress he had expected, and he remained for some months in the south-eastern corner of Cameroons with the enemy posts of Dume and Lomie strongly barring his way. Mayer's troops and Dobell's troops were in the fever belt along the coast, and suffering severely from disease. The British general did not want to move, as the great rains had begun in March and the forest tracks were difficult. On the other hand, while General Aymerich was attempting an advance against the other side of the fortress country, he could not allow the enemy to throw his full weight against the Franco-Belgian column. So to make at least a diversion, and compel Zimmermann to divide his army, Sir Charles Dobell undertook the operation to which he had demurred.

The only part of this plan which was successfully carried out was that assigned to General Cunliffe. General Cunliffe had two thousand native infantrymen, mainly from the Hausa tribes, one company of native mounted infantry, three guns, and nine machine-guns. With this Nigerian force there were seven hundred and fifty French native infantry, a squadron of cavalry, two guns, and two machine-guns. The French force was commanded by Lieut.-Colonel Brisset and the British column was under Lieut.-Colonel W. I. Webb-Bowen, both of these officers being under the orders of Brigadier-General Cunliffe.

The fall of Garua was brought about by a mutiny of the German black force. The Germans held out strongly until the last week in May, and not only defended themselves, but sallied out over the frontier and attacked the Allied force at Gurin. In the last week of May, Brigadier-General Cunliffe, relying on the profound indignation of the Bantu tribesmen, shifted the position of his troops. He moved from the south and south-west round to the fortified heights on the north. In spite of the time it took to carry all the French and British material and stores on the shoulders of native carriers and haul the guns through the wilderness, the German commander remained ignorant of the change in the direction of attack. In other words, the natives he sent out as spies refused to serve him. Then on May 28, 1915, three days after the attacking force had shifted to the north, Brisset received one heavy French gun, a 3.6 in., which outranged anything possessed by the Germans.

Lieut.-Colonel Webb-Bowen's column now pursued the German fugitives towards the Ngaundere highlands. In addition to the German force holding Garua, there had been outlying detachments linked with the mountain fortress and other points in the

German system of defence. These detachments were in the line of pursuit, and some were driven towards Banyo, after actions at Koncha and Maio Kelah on June 27. Then, on the other wing of the movement of pursuit, a British advance guard under Captain C. H. Fowle reached the steep paths leading up to the Ngaundere plateau on June 28. One of the terrific tornadoes of tropical Africa smote both the British and German forces, and amid this appalling tempest the two very different methods of discipline employed by the contending Europeans were put to a supreme test. The West African troops of the Allies, inspired by loyalty to their white officers, charged through the whirlwind and completely surprised and overwhelmed all the black German rearguards holding the cliff paths.

The British scaled the steep cliff, and with scarcely any loss captured the town of Ngaundere in the evening. During the night, when the tornado had blown over, the German officers succeeded in bringing up their main force and, collecting their other scattered troops, made a counter-attack upon the small advance guard. But the German native troops had no energy or courage left, and their assault was beaten off with ease. Lieut.-Colonel Brisset quickly arrived at Ngaundere from Garua and, with his comparatively strong body of French troops, firmly established the important new line won by Captain C. H. Fowle.

On April 7, 1915, a British native force under Lieut.-Colonel Haywood moved along the Midland Railway to Edea, to co-operate with the French native force under Colonel Mayer. The aim was to force the line of the Kele river, and from there to fight through the jungle, by Iseka and Wum Biagas, towards Jaunde. In a series of fierce actions the British and French columns took the line of the Kele river in April, and then found themselves opposed by the main German army. The leader, Zimmermann, had so completely checked the Franco-Belgian column four hundred miles away, that he was able to withdraw troops towards the coast to resist the Franco-British advance.

On May 1, Colonel Mayer's little army moved along the railway line to Iseka, and in spite of broken bridges and machine-gun ambushes, torrents of rain and great sickness, captured Iseka on May 11. Meanwhile, along the line of the road from Duala to Jaunde, Lieut.-Colonel Haywood, with two battalions of the Nigeria regiment, made a drive north of the Midland Railway, to outflank the enemy's main position on the permanent way. The road and railway were the only clear wide paths in the vast forest, and the Allied column had to cut through the bush, ford rivers and storm wayside posts in order to get an outflanking position on the Kele river, by Wum Biagas, which was on the Jaunde road. Then in a magnificent assault, in which both officers and men suffered very heavily, the entire position of Wum Biagas was stormed on May 4.

The Nigerians proved superb. They lost many of their white leaders, and yet fought up the steep ridges steadily and coolly, and though their victory left them with their two battalions badly shattered, they held their ground, and the French force at Iseka moved off and joined them. Colonel Mayer then took over the command of the allied column, and stores and supplies were sent forward by road, together with a naval 12-pounder gun. On May 25, Colonel Mayer, with all his force rapidly weakening by sickness, tried to push on before the heaviest rain fell and the bush became impenetrable. By this time it was known that General Aymerich's advance, 400 miles away, had failed.

But Colonel Mayer could not win through. In the first place Sir Charles Dobell, supporting him from Duala, could not get food supplies up. There were only three motor-cars available, and the ordinary carriers were suffering from sickness and also from hostile raids, for the German native troops were always working through the jungle and raiding the line of communication, forcing the Allies to send food and war material under armed convoys, and place guard posts along the track. At the same time the head of the Franco-British column was swept by machine-gun fire at every turn of the road, so that at every bend the troops had first to cut through the bush and outflank the enemy gunners. One mile a day was the average rate of progress of the allied column from May 25 to June 5.

Half-starved by raids on its line of supplies, shaken with fever and weakened by dysentery, the Franco-British force drew back to the Kele river. A great raid on its most important convoy of five hundred carriers was the immediate cause of Colonel Mayer's retirement. He had to race back to save his men from starvation. Sir Charles Dobell hurried up the last small force of troops in Duala, and after fierce and incessant rearguard fighting, the Kele river line was regained on June 28. In the rearguard actions the Allies were badly harassed but never broken, and as they in turn used machine-guns in continual ambushes, they inflicted heavy losses on the attacking force. But the casualties were serious.

The great rains had begun to fall during the retreat, and for some months the tropical torrents continued to wash through the forest. This, however, was an advantage to the Allies, as the downfalls checked the raiding operations of the victorious Germans. The rains which prevented all operations in Southern Cameroons did not hinder the movement of men in the north. Brigadier-General Cunliffe remained, therefore, free to attempt to extend his field of victories. The central German fortress of Banyo was the point of greatest strategic importance in his sphere of operations; but he knew that if he attacked it while General Dobell and General Aymerich were standing on the defensive, Zimmermann would swing his main force round to the central fortress and make it practically impregnable.

There remained the northernmost stronghold of Mora, which had been cut off from Zimmermann's army by the capture of Garua and Ngaundere. Under the arrangement which had been made after the failure of the main expedition, Brigadier-General Cunliffe's force was not wanted for any general enveloping movement until November, 1915. So he reckoned that he would be able to operate for three months against Mora. Towards the end of August he spent some days travelling round the mountain and reconnoitring for the easiest slopes up which his men could fight their way. He decided to attack from the north. Here he had already won a hill almost level with the northern end of the Mora mountain, and separated from it by a deep valley some six hundred yards wide. In the first week of September two or three mountain guns were hauled up the hill, and then, under cover of artillery fire, the 1st Nigeria Regiment made three gallant attacks across the valley and up the mountain.

In the final advance the Hausas reached the summit of this Gibraltar of the Cameroons, and were then stopped by machine-gun fire fifty yards from the German redoubt. For forty-eight hours the native troops clung to the Mora summit, near the dead body of Captain R. M. Pike, who had led the charge. No food or water reached the men, for the German machine guns swept all the slopes by which the supplies were bravely but vainly carried forward. On the second night Brigadier-General Cunliffe had to order them to retire as best they could. He resolved to sap across the valley, so as to provide his troops with cover from the German machine-guns, and he sent an urgent telegram to Lagos, asking for shells.

On September 15, Sir Charles Dobell and General Aymerich held a conference at Duala, at which the two commanders decided to resume the general enveloping movement against Jaunde early in October instead of in November. General Cunliffe was ordered to leave merely an investing force at Mora, and resume his main operations in the Middle Cameroons, where Captain C. H. Fowle had improved the line on July 23 by scattering a German force from Tibati.

In order to carry out the great sweep from the north, Brigadier-General Cunliffe had to capture a knot of fortified mountains some hundreds of miles in circumference. Towards the middle of October he flung half his force towards the Sanaga river and the highland country round Ngaundere, in order to hold back Zimmermann's central forces. Then, with two columns, he directed in person an advance from the north and north-west on the mountain knot round Banyo. All the German garrisons on the southern Nigerian frontier rallied round Banyo for the coming conflict. Some intercepted letters showed that they were quite confident of their ability to hold out, if necessary, to the end of the war.

Towards the end of October, however, they lost two of their main outworks by a surprise attack. A British column under Major Mann advanced from Gashaka, and, after a most arduous climb, overwhelmed and routed the German force holding the Gandua Pass. At a considerable distance to the north was another pass, where the enemy had prepared a system of trenches and redoubts to hold back Brigadier-General Cunliffe's main column. But when Major Mann took the more southern pass he got so close to the rear of the force opposing the British main column that he threatened to envelop it. The Germans, therefore, retired, and Brigadier-General Cunliffe's men had only a long, hard climb to the evacuated fortifications on the plateau. For a few days the advance continued across open rolling grass lands, and though the Germans tried to hold some isolated kopjes all their positions were turned without loss to the British troops. At the end of October the village of Banyo was occupied, and the German garrison retired some three miles away to their mountain fortress.

It seemed as if a large army were needed to capture the stronghold. Brigadier-General Cunliffe had only 1,250 infantry, and he was still short of shell. But hearing that two hundred more rounds of gun ammunition were on the way to him, he arranged his five companies of infantry on the northern, north-western, and southern sides, and spread out his mounted troops widely eastward to check there any attempt by the Germans to break out. On November 2 his infantry began to work over the foot-hills, but their great attack was postponed in order to allow time for the new shell supply to arrive. One company of Nigerians, under Captain Bowyer-Smijth, had amazing luck and amazing disaster. The company had been one of the most successful under General Cunliffe's command, and had conquered Gashaka the previous August by a great fighting climb that lasted twelve hours. Now the same company, while battling in the fog, found a weak point in the enemy's defences, and by noon it had forced its way right up to the summit of Banyo mountain. By this time, however, the fog had cleared off and the enemy's reserve caught the victorious company under a cross fire of Maxims and musketry. Captain Bowyer-Smijth was killed, and his shattered company fell back to the foot of the mountain.

The other four companies, however, found themselves, when the fog lifted, half way up the mountain slopes, and within thirty yards of one of the main systems of defences. Nothing more could be done in the clear tropical sunshine but to hang on to all the conquered positions and wait for the guns to get the shells they needed. When night fell, allowing food and water and cartridges to be brought up to the men, the Germans tried to light up every line of advance by fire-balls and rockets. Then rain fell, making the steep sides as slippery as glass; but the Nigerians reached the German entrenchments and hugged the southern wall of the great sangar.

When day broke the great sangar had been carried, and the advance slowly continued until the afternoon. Then it was that the British gunners got their fresh supply of 2.95 in. shells. With these projectiles the three mountain guns began to smash sangar after sangar, and make a shrapnel curtain before each main advance of the troops. When night fell on November 5 a violent thunder-storm broke over the mountain, and the German troops, divided into small parties, tried to escape. Most of the fugitives, however, were captured by posts of mounted infantry, and at dawn the fort surrendered. There remained only the business of sweeping up the retreating forces and to continue the advance cn Jaunde. In this great closing movement the northern force under Brigadier-General Cunliffe played only a subsidiary part. The main work of defeating the principal German force was done by the troops directed by Sir Charles Dobell and General Aymerich. As already stated, the two commanders met at Duala on August 25, 1915, and made a plan for a new campaign for the conquest of the Cameroons. By this time General Aymerich's troops, by very hard fighting, had captured the south-eastern German posts of Bertua and Dume. The French commander could, therefore, promise to make strong thrusts from Bertua and Dume towards the central German position at Jaunde, and he also arranged to send a third column under Lieut.-Colonel de Meillour to the Campo river, in the south-western corner of the Cameroons, to cut off the German retreat to Spanish Guinea.

Sir Charles Dobell was much strengthened by the arrival of the 5th light infantry of the Indian army. He also received more carriers from Nigeria and the Gold Coast, and trained some five hundred and thirty-six recruits enlisted in Nigeria. Also his full requirements in regard to motor transport were met, which enabled him to lighten the work of his carriers in the terrible forest region and thus accelerate his advance. The operations began in the first week of October, 1915, and followed the lines of the unsuccessful expedition of May. The French column under Colonel Mayer moved southward towards its former objective, Iseka, while the British column moved along the Jaunde road to the scene of its former pyrrhic victory, Wum Biagas. Naturally, the Germans had not been idle during the six months that had elapsed since the last expedition.

The position at Wum Biagas had been transformed into a great system of earthworks, from which fortifications extended for miles. The Nigerian force strongly demonstrated against this practically impregnable position, while three hundred men from the Gold Coast regiment attempted a turning movement on the left flank. For two weeks the little Gold Coast force cut its way through the bush, forded rivers, and made one of the most terrible marches imaginable through the forest. On the way the troops took a German mission-house which had been fortified, and then came to the Kele river, there hoping to get unexpectedly on the enemy's flank. The Germans were surprised at a place called Muin, where they had constructed rows of trenches, which they abandoned without a struggle. Recovering, they tried to attack from the rear, but were beaten off, without loss to the British.

At midday the Gold Coast force cleared the mountain precipice, and entered a bush path, with rising ground to the right and a steep hill to the left, both covered with a tangle of tropical growth. Everything looked quiet and peaceful as the officers went forward to reconnoitre. They found in front a deep river, on the opposite side of which was a high cliff. The land going down to the river on the side of their advance was as clean as an English meadow. All the trees had been felled and the brushwood cleared away. But the great bluff across the water was still clothed in trees and undergrowth, and they managed to make out the loopholes of a block-house and a longer series of loopholes running across the ridge. The commander of the flanking column brought up a small mountain gun, two machine-guns, and most of his men, hid the gun in the nearest clump of trees and then sent out the troops in skirmishing order. As soon as they were clear of cover, and visible in the open ground, there was a terrific burst of fire, not only from the block-houses and the loopholed ridge, but from trenches along the river bank and from both flanks.

The Gold Coast men dropped to the ground and found what cover they could. But the tiny mountain gun, with the two Maxims and the small reserve in support, had been able to get the range of the Germans when they made their great burst of fire. The German commander had acted too quickly. He should have waited until his enemy was swimming the river and trying to find the ford. As it was, he was subjected to a swift and accurate fire, with the result that the German black troops lost their nerve. Their firing went to pieces and their bullets flew well above the heads of the men in the advanced section, who were shooting at every rifle flash that they saw in front of them. After a fierce little battle, lasting four and a half hours, the Gold Coast force managed to threaten the left flank of their enemy and for some unexplained cause the German commander hurriedly retired.

With their flank thus turned by this small but quite extraordinary victory, the Germans hastily retired from their main position at Wum Biagas, where the Nigerian troops were attacking, and the force under Colonel Mayer was then able to make a successful thrust on Iseka. He had the good fortune to recapture a considerable amount of rolling-stock which had been left behind, and as his supply of engines and waggons was small, the recovered trucks greatly helped to improve the transport of supplies. The bridges between Duala and Iseka had partly been rebuilt, and the work of making good all this section of the Midland Railway was rapidly carried on during the first three weeks in November. The motor track along the Jaunde road was also much improved, and some 7,000 carriers served as means of communication off the two main lines of motor and rail traffic.

The British camp was pitched a little way beyond Wum Biagas at Angas. Thence a Nigerian force, under Colonel Gorges, moved against the enemy's position on the Jaunde road, while the French column under Colonel Mayer advanced along the railway towards the point at which another road from Kribi ran upward to Jaunde. In effect, however, the two forces, British and French, combined into a main body with two wings that swept towards the German base on a wide front. The German commander-in-chief, who was fighting at the same time the Franco-Belgian force under General Aymerich and the French column near Spanish Guinea, could no longer bring against all the main allied forces in the south a superior or even an equal number of troops. On a very small scale, he was in the same position as the armies of the German Empire afterwards were. He held the interior lines, but instead of being able to swing his main force from side to side and defeat each enemy in turn, he had to fight hard and incessantly on all fronts. Northward, Brigadier-General Cunliffe was closing in upon him; eastward, General Aymerich was stubbornly advancing; and southward, two French forces were moving along the Spanish frontier and towards the station of Ebolowa.

His chief danger lay in Colonel Mayer's force, and against this he decided to employ his main strength. If the French were able to smash in his position the only road of escape still open to him was cut off and his retreat to Spanish Guinea would be barred. Sir Charles Dobell tried to answer this concentration against Mayer by combining the Senegalese, Nigerian, and Gold Coast troops into a single army acting on a connected front;

but the lack of transverse roads through the bush prevented the British commander from transferring forces quickly from wing to wing. All that could be done was for the northern British wing, under Lieut.-Colonel Cockburn, and the British centre, under Colonel Gorges, to drive hard and incessantly at Zimmermann's flank and centre in order to compel him to weaken his attacks against Colonel Mayer's column.

In all that follows it must, therefore, be remembered that though Colonel Mayer made less progress than the British, he had the hardest task of all. His slow yet magnificent pushing movement was the pivot on which depended the victories of the British, French Equatorial, and Belgian Congo forces. Sir Charles Dobell, in his despatch, especially remarks upon the help he received from Colonel Mayer, not only in the skilled leading of the Senegalese, but in the perplexing strategical problems of the expedition.

While Colonel Mayer was fighting from the railway towards the Kribi road, the Nigerian troops made their main thrust on Jaunde along the upper road. The column set out on November 23, met the enemy's patrols the next day, worked past two German machine-gun parties, skirmished until November 26 in the rubber plantations, maize fields, and banana orchards along the road, and followed the enemy into the jungle beyond the clearings. Then, after topping a wooded ridge, the Nigerian column found the German battle position. At a point where the road sharply turned to the right the German force had lined up on a range of steep, heavily wooded hills, which they had previously deeply entrenched.

The Germans held advanced positions by two ravines, that opened on either side of the Jaunde road and left only a little neck of land running towards the entrenched heights. Three companies of the 1st Nigeria Regiment were ordered to take the ridge. The attack was opened by the second and third companies, commanded by Captain Balders and Captain Giles. On both flanks they were held up all the morning by the two gullies on each side of the road, and the sweeping machine-gun fire of the Germans.

Captain Balders fell when leading an attack against the main ravine, where the enemy had a machine-gun less than a hundred yards from the weakened British line. A Maxim had been pushed forward across the gully to help the two advanced sections of the

Nigerians, but they had suffered such losses that there were not more than a dozen rifles left in the line after seven hours' fighting. Of four British officers two were killed and one wounded. Lieutenant Ford, who was left in command, was inclined to retire with his twelve men to save his machine-gun from being rushed. But he hung on because Captain Balders, before falling dead with a bullet through his neck, had said: " This is a case where we've got to do or die." His audacity was justified. Suddenly the German fire slackened and then ceased. They were evacuating the ridge. By its tenacity a small British force, that had been reduced to twelve men and a Maxim, had forced a large body of Germans out of a strong position.

The Germans, however, only fell back to another entrenched ridge, and fighting went on furiously, over position after position, until the station of Ngung was captured on November 30. By this time the main British force was nearing the open and cultivated country. Only a narrow belt of bush remained, and the Germans, knowing that they would be outmanœuvred when the clear ground was reached, made desperate efforts to snatch a decision in the last patch of wooded jungle land. The British column stayed for some days at Ngung, in order to bring up supplies and clear its line of communication from hostile parties raiding through the jungle. Then, on December 7, 1915, the advance was resumed with a small part of the Gold Coast Regiment, under Captain Butler, acting as an outflanking force and cutting its way through the bush. Captain Butler, after an arduous march, succeeded in turning the flank of the last German fortified position in the bush, and its defenders were compelled to retire, leaving the way clear for the British advance into the open land to the east of the forests. The advance was speedily continued, and on December 17, Jang Mangas was captured.

This energetic movement completed the demoralisation of the German native troops, and Sir Charles Dobell decided not to wait until he was joined by Colonel Mayer, but to push on immediately to Jaunde. General Cunliffe's northern force was almost within striking distance of the German base, and a concerted advance was arranged. It was completely successful, the Germans falling back from position after position without a show of resistance, until on January 1, 1916, the head of the Allied column, under Colonel Gorges, entered Jaunde.

The wisdom of this advance in front of the French column had been justified by its success, but it had permitted the German forces to retire to Spanish Guinea. Had Sir Charles Dobell waited at Jang Mangas and assisted the advance of Colonel Mayer the German escape would have been cut off. The consequences, however, were not serious, for by this time the German force had become almost a rabble. Zimmermann, at the head of the few natives who still remained loyal, managed to effect his escape, and was interned in Spanish Guinea ; but by his retreat the whole of the southern region of the Cameroons passed into the hands of the Allies. Only Captain Raben's troops, shut up in Fort Mora, remained of all the German forces.

The immediate effect of the occupation of Jaunde was to relieve all pressure on Colonel Mayer's force, which reached the Jaunde-Kribi road early in January. The French and British forces swept south to Ebolowa and Kribi, picking up remnants of the scattered German garrison. Then Colonel Morrison, taking command of a strong French force, spread it out like a net towards the Spanish frontier, and, linking with the French force operating from the Campo river, cleared the Cameroons of Germans by the middle of February, 1916. At the beginning of this month Brigadier-General Cunliffe, having completed his sweep on Jaunde, turned back to the great mountain of Mora, brought up guns and shells to the hill level with the first ridge of the enemy's position, and prepared to besiege the place in earnest. But the affair ended without a battle, as Captain Raben surrendered with all his troops on February 18, 1916.

The conquest of the Cameroons was complete. With the exception of the help of one Indian battalion, the native forces of Nigeria, the Gold Coast, Sierra Leone, Senegal, French Equatorial Africa, and the Belgian Congo had carried out the difficult operations unaided. In this matter it must be remembered that the Cameroons was a fortress country specially adapted for a prolonged defence. If the Germans had treated their own natives fairly and had used more humane methods in both government and discipline, their strength of resistance in a country of such immense natural difficulties and intricate fortifications might have proved insuperable.

CHAPTER 26

The Overrunning of Serbia

IN the beginning of October, 1915, Serbia was called on to meet the fourth invasion of her territory since the opening of the Great War. The fighting which took place in the interval was comparatively unimportant; but during a considerable part of that time she had had to encounter foes of a different and exceedingly formidable kind. The Austrians, on being driven out of Valievo, had left behind them a dreadful legacy in the shape of typhus and other terrible maladies, and these diseases fastened themselves on the unfortunate Serbians, who succumbed in large numbers.

When the storm broke in full fury over the north of Serbia, and the dispositions of the hostile forces were disclosed, it was found that the Austro-Germans under Mackensen were divided into two armies in close contact with each other. One army was commanded by General von Gallwitz, who had distinguished himself by forcing the passage of the Narew two months before, and its composition was wholly German. The other army was led by General von Kövess von Kövesshaza, an Austrian soldier, and was partly Austrian and partly German, the former predominating. Gallwitz covered the line of the Danube from Orsova on the east to a point opposite Semendria on the same river, where he joined up with Kövess, whose troops thence extended along the Save and part of the Drina. Farther up the Drina an Austrian army was in position near Vishegrad.

The three armies consisted of at least 20 divisions, and their total strength was well above 300,000 effectives. Ten divisions were German, mostly war-hardened men withdrawn from the other fronts. Remembering their previous bitter experiences at the hands of the Serbians, the Austrians put some of their best infantry into the field. Mackensen's famous drive through Galicia had been triumphant owing to the overwhelming power of his artillery, and he now had upwards of 2,000 guns, many of them pieces of large calibre. His first task was to cross the rivers, and he relied on his artillery for its accomplishment.

THE OVERRUNNING OF SERBIA

Ever since their repulse of the Austrians in December, 1914, the Serbians had anticipated a renewal of the attack on them, and Marshal Putnik and his staff had taken all the measures that were possible in the circumstances to meet it. At the start of the fourth invasion their army mustered some 310,000 combatants, the vast majority of whom were well seasoned in war, and they had guns and munitions proportionate to the size of their forces, except that they were short of heavy artillery such as the enemy possessed. The force opposed to them was not too great in numbers, and if it had heavier guns this advantage was in a measure offset by the strong, natural defensive positions held by the Serbians. The entry of Bulgaria into the conflict made all the difference.

It was with the object of resisting assault on the north, the north-east, and the west that the army of Serbia had been disposed and the Serbian fortifications constructed and organized; the south-east—the Macedonian frontier and some distance north of it—was but little protected, and hence was easily vulnerable by any strong force. In other words, the position of Serbia, as a whole, was such that it could be turned, in military phrase, from the south-east.

At the outset of the fourth invasion the line south of the Save and the Danube was held by three Serbian armies, comprising seven and a half divisions, or about 150,000 men—nearly half of the whole military strength of Serbia. On the west the Serbian 1st army, of three divisions, which was commanded by Marshal Mishitch, occupied the angle between the Save and the Drina, with its headquarters at Shabatz. Next, eastward, came a force of a division and a half, under the leadership of General Zivkovitch, which was styled the army for the defence of Belgrade, a title that sufficiently indicated where it was placed. Farther east, and stretching towards the frontier of Rumania, lay the Third Serbian Army of three divisions, with General Jourishitch at its head; it was based on Pojarevatz, and the important valley of the Morava was its special charge. To oppose the Austrians concentrated in the vicinity of Vishegrad, Serbia had the army of Ushitze, of less than two divisions, under General Goikovitch, and the town of Ushitze was its centre.

It was upon these four armies, with some portion of the army of the Timok, a force which was based on Zaichar, on the eastern frontier, some 20 miles from Vidin, in Bulgaria, operating along the Danube towards Orsova, that the Austro-German invaders fell, the odds in favour of the latter being more than three to two. The rest of the Serbian army was deployed on the east facing Bulgaria, and had it not been for the menace from that country Serbia could have met her Germanic foes on fairly equal terms. As it was, Serbia felt compelled to keep more than 100,000 men to watch Bulgaria, with respect to whose aggressive intentions she had no illusions.

On September 23, Greece, then still under the guiding hand of M. Venizelos, mobilised her Army as a precautionary measure in face of Bulgaria and in support of Serbia. At the request of the great Hellenic Minister, France and Britain agreed to send to Salonica 150,000 troops to make up for an equal number which, by the terms of the Serbo-Greek treaty for mutual defence against Bulgaria, Serbia would have provided had she been able to do so. This force began landing on October 5, but on that very day Venizelos was compelled to resign because King Constantine disapproved of his pro-Entente policy. It was arranged, however, that under protest from Greece the troops of the Entente should continue to disembark with a view to assisting Serbia.

King Peter, on October 2, issued an order of the day which gave utterance to the feelings of himself and his subjects. He was well aware, he said, that every Serbian was ready to die for his country. It was in this spirit of absolute devotion that the Serbians defended their country against overwhelming odds, and the fight they made was one of the finest in all history. For three days and nights before October 6 the Austro-Germans, seeking to reduce the Serbian entrenchments to dust, heavily bombarded the whole Serbian line on the Danube, the Save, and the Drina, and under cover of their fire made further and more persistent attempts to get across these rivers, but the Serbians drove them back at all points. Fighting raged most fiercely at Ram, Dubrovitza, and Semendria, on the Danube; in and about Ciganlia, the island of the Gipsies, at Obrenovatz, Shabatz, and Jarak, on the Save; and at Badovintse, on the Drina. Von Gallwitz directed a tremendous bombardment upon Ram and Semendria, the two fortress towns which guarded the approaches to the Morava valley. On October 5 hundreds of shells were poured on this sector from the largest guns and howitzers of the enemy, yet the brave soldiers of Jourishitch held their ground.

But Belgrade itself, which the Austrians were very eager to recapture after their expulsion from it ten months before, was the centre of the most bitter struggle. Here the army of the defence of Belgrade, assisted by the naval missions of France, Britain, and Russia—in all, about 500 or 600 men, with naval guns, who had been in the city for some months protecting the river front—offered the most strenuous resistance to the attacking forces of Von Kövess. For one whole day the British naval mission, which was commanded by Rear-Admiral Troubridge, swept with their guns the great lake-like expanse, formed by the junction of the Save and the Danube, on the northern side of the Serbian capital, and sank every craft, including two gunboats, that came in sight. But on the afternoon of October 5 the Austro-Germans greatly augmented their fire.

Proud of their capital, the Serbians wished to preserve it from complete ruin, and, according to their own official statement, their troops for this reason evacuated it on October 8. But on October 6 and 7 the Austro-Germans, notwithstanding the valorous opposition of the Serbian armies, had effected the crossing of the rivers at several places, including Belgrade. After desperate fighting, the Serbians on the 6th threw back to the opposite bank of the Save the forces of Kövess which had got across at Jarak, Progorska island, and Zabrez, but the enemy came on again and succeeded in making good his footing on the south side. On the same day he captured Gipsy island in the Save, a short distance from Belgrade, and contrived to land under the lower fortress and on the Danube quay in the city itself. All his men at the lower fortress were either captured or killed, but the Serbians were unable to expel him from the quay.

On the following day the heavy guns of the Austro-Germans enabled them to overcome the opposition at other points on the rivers, and on October 8 the Austro-Hungarian troops of Kövess entered the northern part of Belgrade and took by storm the Citadel, an obsolete work in the same quarter of the town. Earlier in the day the German soldiers attached to Kövess's command captured the Konak, the royal palace in the centre of the capital, and hoisted over it the flags of Germany and Austria-Hungary. The Serbian troops had resisted magnificently, but the enemy's big guns had been too much for them. Their own gunners served their artillery until it was overwhelmed; the men of the French, British, and Russian naval missions fired until their guns were destroyed by the heavier metal of the enemy. On the afternoon of the 8th General Zikovitch ordered his troops to retire upon the positions lying immediately to the south.

On October 7 and 8 the enemy crossed the Danube between Gradishte and Semendria, near the village of Zatagna and the small fort of Kostolatz, but here he was held. On the 8th he took Ram, and tried with his heavy guns to batter a way southward, without making any advance. He attacked in force the village of Petka, but was driven back with considerable loss. He endeavoured to cross near Semendria from the island of the same name lying opposite the mouth of the Morava, but this attempt also failed.

On the same dates the Austro-Germans were checked between Obrenovatz and the village of Kratinska on the Save, failed in their night attacks on the Serbian positions near Zabrez, and were repulsed before Drenovatz, north-west of Shabatz. In this area the enemy was opposed by some of the finest soldiers of Serbia, the splendid Shumadia division being among them, and their commander, the old marshal, Mishitch, who had won great fame for his generalship during the third invasion, was the man to get the most and the best out of them. He also had charge of the defence of the Lower Drina, and opposite Badovintse several times repelled the Austrians.

Success attended Marshal Mishitch in a fierce battle at Zabrez on October 10, when the Serbians repulsed the Austrians and captured many prisoners. In spite of this and other Serbian victories in the region of the three rivers, the advantage, generally, lay with the invaders, for they had forced the crossing of the frontier. On October 11 headquarters in Berlin announced that on the front between Gradishte and Shabatz, more than 100 miles as the crow flies, the passage of the Danube and the Save had been completed. And at two or three points on the Drina the Austrians had reached its eastern side. In the meantime the enemy brought up large reinforcements, and continued a vigorous offensive east, south, and west of Belgrade, in a wide, sweeping movement along the whole front.

Mackensen concentrated his main effort on the east in securing possession of the Morava valley and its railway. Near Semendria, Gallwitz's right wing was in touch with Kövess's left, and the plan was that together they should fight their way up the Morava, one taking its east bank and the other its west; but before they could make any progress the fortresses of Semendria and Pojarevatz had to be taken. For more than a fortnight the former had constantly been subjected to a severe bombardment, to which it replied with energy; but here again the Serbian guns were overwhelmed. After being driven back near Ram, and repulsed on the sector between the Morava and the Mlava, a stream flowing a few miles east of the other, the Germans, under Gallwitz, had by October 10 made good their advance towards Semendria, which they occupied on the following day, the Serbians falling back on Pojarevatz. A desperate engagement took place at Lipe, near the fortress, which resulted in a victory for the invaders, but, thanks to Serbian bravery, at tremendous expense, the battlefield being thickly strewn with their dead. In no other encounter up to that time had the enemy suffered such terrible losses. After a siege of two days the Germans captured Pojarevatz, and the Serbians retired.

On the same day, October 12, Bulgaria declared war. She had assembled two large armies on Serbia's eastern boundary, and at the same time had sent a third army to watch the frontier of Rumania, of whose intentions she was not sure. Of the two armies which were to operate against the Serbians, the 1st army had a strength of 200,000 combatants, and it was concentrated on the north from Vidin to Zaribrod, so as to threaten the valley of the Timok and the part of the Belgrade-Sofia railway running through Pirot to Nish. The 2nd army, which was led by General Teodoroff, was only half as large as the first, but it was designed to operate in Macedonia, a country many of whose inhabitants were Bulgarian or in sympathy with Bulgarian ideals, a region, moreover, that was practically unfortified. Uskub was its chief objective, both on account of the strategic importance of that place as a railway centre, and as a point from which a wedge might be driven in between north and south Serbia. The main body of this force assembled at Kustendil, its left wing on Strumnitza.

Serbia's cry to her Allies for help did not fall on deaf ears. On October 12 Greece had definitely declined to assist Serbia as against the Austro-Germans; but the Entente Powers still strove hard to get her to change her mind, Great Britain going so far as to offer Cyprus to her as a gift if she would cast in her lot with the Serbians. The Greek king, who, since the second

IN A CAPTURED MINE CRATER AT LOOS The battle of Loos demonstrated that with adequate artillery preparation, a sing e line could be pierced and the multiple system (see Plate 36,) came into force. North of Loos on September 25, the attack was preceded by the explosion of a mine ; this photograph shows the crater after its capture but before the dead and wounded were removed.

The main street of Kralievo in Central Serbia. The flourishing centre of an agricultural district, it suffered severely in the war. It fell to the Austro-Germans on November 5, 1915, and from here the Serbians began their retreat on Mitrovitza.

A view of the harbour front and quays at Salonica, city of Greece, as it appeared in the war, when the port and surrounding country were turned into a vast fortified camp by the British and French forces.

THE CAMPAIGN IN THE BALKANS

Plate 48   Volume II

dismissal of Venizelos, was in full, though unconstitutional, control of the destinies of his country, rejected the offer of Cyprus, and would listen to no entreaties or arguments, but persisted in declaring his intention not to depart from the attitude of benevolent neutrality which he had taken up. On October 15 France and Great Britain declared war on Bulgaria, and announced a blockade of the Bulgarian coast on the Aegean. For some days the Allies had been rushing troops by railway up the Vardar valley beyond the Greek frontier, and on the day of the declaration of war French troops were attacked at Valandovo, by the Bulgarians, who were defeated and thrown back. The French, who were commanded by General Sarrail, gradually made their way northward along the railway as far as Krivolak and Gradsko, a few miles south of Veles, but their numbers were insufficient to make any change in the general situation of Serbia, daily becoming more critical, nor even to effect a junction with any of the Serbian forces.

Meanwhile the Bulgarians pursued their campaign with tremendous vigour and without mercy. On the north-east the Serbians repulsed three strong Bulgarian attacks near Zaichar, and much fierce fighting took place east of Kniashevatz and in the St. Nicholas Pass. Svinski Vis changed hands several times, but on the 19th the Bulgarians lay before Negotin. After Vraje had been taken the enemy were held up by the Serbians under Stepanovitch, who forced them to pay dearly for every step taken up the Nishava Valley.

On the south-east, in Macedonia, Teodoroff and the 2nd Bulgarian army had easier work and achieved success with correspondingly less effort. A large part of the vital railway from Belgrade to Salonica, via Nish and Uskub, passed through this section, and Teodoroff's first business, of course, was to get astride this railway. Detaching a strong force from his main body, he struck at the railway between Vrania and Zibeftcha, dominated the line with his guns, and cut it. The small number of Serbian troops, called the regiment of the southern Morava, fought him stoutly, but could not prevent him from capturing Vrania on October 17, 1915. On the same date Teodoroff took Egri Palanka, after having marched from the railhead of the Kustendil-Sofia railway, forced the pass on the frontier, and gained the highway en route for Kumanovo and Uskub. Farther south he penetrated the valley of the Bregalnitza, capturing the important strategic point, Sultan Tepeh, and the town of Kotshana, taking twelve guns. Pressing on through Ishtip, he occupied the portion of Veles, otherwise called Kuprulu, lying on the east side of the Vardar, on October 20th, thus cutting the railway again, and checking the advance of the French. Northward, he took Kumanovo on the same day, and after a violent battle, captured Uskub on the 22nd. Bojovic, the Serbian general, retired fighting to the Katshanik pass, north of Uskub, the prolonged defence of which, together with the defence of the Babuna pass, south-west of Veles, was one of the most memorable features of the struggle in Serbia.

While these grave events were taking place in the east and south-east of Serbia, the Austro-Germans continued their advance from the three rivers in the north in spite of the most heroic resistance of the Serbians. Immediately after the fall of Belgrade, Kövess attacked the heights south of the capital, and after three days of intense fighting took Mount Avala on October 18. Obrenovatz and Shabatz were also captured, both being important gains.

But the chief line of the enemy's advance southward lay along the Morava, his other movements being co-ordinated with it. Subsequently to the fall of Semendria and Pojarevatz, he assaulted the mountainous country of the Podunavlie, and after heavy loss drove the Serbians out of it. Gallwitz here had an exceedingly difficult task, owing to the peculiar formation of the ground, but by October 23 he had reached the southern bank of the Jasenitza, near Palanka, and had passed Rakinatz on the road to Petrovatz on the Mlava. About the same time his left wing, having shelled Tekia into ruins, crossed the Danube near Orsova, and took the heights overlooking the river. On the west, the Austrians got across the Drina at Vishegrad, and the whole three-river frontier of Serbia had been won.

Marshal Putnik was steadily carrying out his policy of a stubborn fighting retreat, holding his ground as long as possible, causing the enemy everywhere the heaviest losses, and avoiding anything in the nature of a general engagement. But his plans were greatly impeded by the exodus of practically the whole population of the northern area.

Gallwitz and Kövess kept on with their slow but persistent advance from the north, the Serbians retiring in good order and with undiminished morale During the fourth week of October

Gallwitz stormed the commanding heights east of Banitzina, south of the Jasenitza, captured Livaditza and Zabari on the Morava plain after severe fighting, and occupied the region south of Petrovatz. By the 28th he had gained Svilajnatz, beating down the Serbian resistance by sheer weight of men and guns, and on the 30th was within a day's march of Kragujevatz, the seat of Serbia's principal arsenal, and in former times the national capital. Situated on the Lepenitza, a tributary of the Morava, it lay about half-way between Belgrade and Nish, on a branch line of the main railway joining these two cities. The Serbian army, in accordance with the instructions of its commander-in-chief, on November 1 evacuated it, after destroying the arsenal and all its military stores.

The Serbians did not, however, withdraw from it without first giving their enemy a taste of their quality. The famous Shumadia Division, which was entrenched on the hills to the north of the town, weary of constantly retreating, begged their commander to obtain permission to attack, which to their delight, was granted. On a wet and misty day the gallant Shumadians fell on the Germans with remarkable effect who, by now accustomed to the purely defensive tactics of the Serbians, were taken by surprise and thrown into disorder. Fighting with irresistible fury they drove the Germans before them for a considerable distance, taking 3,000 prisoners and several guns.

On the right of Gallwitz, Kövess had simultaneously advanced his forces, marching along the railways from Belgrade and Obrenovatz towards the Western Morava, and constantly in contact with the Germans in the Morava region itself. South of Belgrade the Serbians resolutely defended the Kosmai positions, but had to yield before the enemy's heavy fire. On October 25 Kövess reached Ratcha, south of Palanka, on the right side of the Morava, and after severe fighting arrived at Gran Milanovatz on the 30th, and at Cacak (Tsatsak) on November 1, both places being a few miles west of Kragujevatz. He had now struck the western Morava and the railway passing along it eastward from Ushitze to the Belgrade-Nish railway. Farther west his cavalry, on October 26, had occupied Valievo on the Upper Kolubara, and one of his divisions crossed the Maljen ranges, which had been the scene of the Austrian rout in the previous year. Farther south, the Austrians, who had pushed on from Vishegrad, entered Ushitze on November 2.

During this time Bojadieff, at the head of the Bulgarian 1st army, was attacking the Serbians with success in two directions, one along the Timok against Kniashevatz, Zaichar, and Negotin, and the other along the Nishava against Pirot. Both efforts threatened Nish, but the more northerly had also the purpose of effecting a junction with the left wing of Gallwitz, which was advancing from Tekia, in the north-east corner of Serbia. This object was speedily realised, for on October 23 Bojadieff, here encountering very inferior numbers, took Negotin and Prahovo, the latter a port on the Danube, a few miles north of the former. This meant, when Kladovo was captured on the 25th, that the Serbian bank of the river, and the navigation of the Danube on that side, had passed to the enemy, who forthwith proceeded to utilise it, after clearing away mines, some of which were of Russian origin. Lower down, the Bulgarians occupied both Zaichar and Kniashevatz on October 28.

In spite of the desperate resistance of the Serbians, they were compelled on October 26-27, to abandon the commanding Drenova Glava height, 15 miles north-west of Pirot, and on the 28th Pirot had to be evacuated after a battle of remarkable intensity, in which the Serbians demonstrated their heroic quality to the full. With Pirot on the south and Kniashevatz on the north both in possession of the Bulgarians, the threat to Nish had become most direct and ominous, and the removal of the Serbian seat of Government from that city to Kralievo showed the gravity of the situation.

In the south-eastern area, or Macedonia, the Bulgarian 2nd Army, under Teodoroff, was not so fortunate as the 1st, under Bojadieff, but it was able to retain the ground which it had conquered earlier. After the occupation of Uskub, severe fighting took place for the possession of Katshanik Pass, and on October 22, the Serbians under Vassitch recaptured Veles, which they retained for a week against all Bulgarian assaults. On the 29th, however, the Serbians were forced to evacuate the town once more, and withdraw to the Babuna pass, the narrow defile over which the highway ran from Veles through Prilep to Monastir. At the opening of November, 1915, the Serbians were still holding the pass, and still were preventing the driving in of the wedge which was to sunder the southern from the northern Armies of Serbia, but it was already tragically clear that in spite of her heroism, Serbia was doomed.

With scarcely a halt at Kragujevatz, where they were disappointed to find no large amount of booty, the Austro-Germans crossed the Cacak-Kragujevatz road, and marched south on both sides of the Morava. Kövess moved over the Posetza, and the Germans entered Jagodina on November 3. The passage of both banks of the Western Morava was forced at Kralievo, and that town, from which the Serbian government had withdrawn in time, was taken on the 5th, being captured by Brandenburg troops after terrible fighting in the streets. Here the enemy laid claim to his first big capture of guns—130, but most of the pieces were of obsolete pattern, and the remainder had been rendered unserviceable.

Next day, or a day later, he was in Krushevatz, making prisoner, according to his own account, 3,000 unwounded soldiers, besides 1,500 wounded. The line of the western Morava was now in his possession. To the east of the Morava Gallwitz pressed on, took the series of heights south of Lugotznir, by storm, after the usual fierce struggle with Serbian rearguards, and on November 4 seized Parachin, on the Belgrade-Nish railway, from which a branch line extended through the hills to Zaichar. He was now very near the Bulgarians, who, as already narrated, had taken the last-named town, and on November 5 their armies joined up at Krivivir, a village lying midway between the two places. They were then about 30 miles north of Nish. On the same day German troops, by a surprise night assault, captured Varvarin.

Other forces of Bojadieff continued their advance in the direction of Nish. On November 2, at the village of Svrlig and on the Kalafat Hill, six miles from the city, a violent battle began, which Serbian heroism caused to last for three days, marked by the most determined and bitter fighting, the heaviest Bulgarian attacks being repeatedly repulsed with frightful slaughter, and many successful Serbian counter-attacks made. But owing to the dominatingly larger number of the Bulgarians, whose big guns wrecked the Serbian forts and trenches, and damaged Nish itself, the end was inevitable. The Serbians withdrew from the city on the 5th in good order, and Bojadieff occupied it, and here, it is said, he found still flying the flags to welcome the Allies who had never come, but discovered little plunder, the hundred guns he claimed to have captured being of no value. In some respects the loss of Nish was one of the worst of the blows which a hard fate had dealt Serbia, for if the city was only of subsidiary military importance, its fall had a decided political effect, coming second to that of Belgrade. The German newspapers described its capture as one of the greatest events of the war.

But the Bulgarians did not by any means have it all their own way in every quarter of the field at this time, for while Bojadieff was entering Nish in triumph, his colleague Teodoroff in the south-east was not only making no progress but was even suffering defeat. At the pass of Katshanik, by which entrance was effected from Uskub to the historic plain of Kossovo, the Serbians, under Bojovitch, with dauntless courage daily rolled back every attack. But it was in the Babuna pass that Serbian heroism most fully flowered. The sublime spirit in which this position was defended was nobly expressed by Vassitch when he declared that his soldiers would continue to fight desperately to the end, and that all Serbians would await without desertion at the foot of their cross the hour of their crucifixion, making their sacrifice live as an example to future generations. During that first week of November, 1915, Vassitch, in and around the Babuna pass, had only 5,000 men to pit against over 20,000 Bulgarians, who besides had much heavier artillery. From November 4 to November 6 an incessant and sanguinary hand-to-hand fight, in which the combatants made free use of their knives, raged in the deep and narrow gorges of the defile, ending in the complete rout of the Bulgarians, who were driven through Izvor pell-mell into Veles.

When Vassitch had recaptured Veles from the Bulgarians on October 22, it was hoped for a time that General Sarrail would be able to link up with him. The town lay along the railway some 35 miles north-west of Krivolak, but the French were not strong enough to push their way up to it. They gained possession of Kara Hodjali, a height three miles north of Krivolak, established their position and, having defeated furious enemy attacks, made an effective bridge-head on the east side of Vardar. But Vassitch had by then been compelled to evacuate Veles again and withdraw to the Babuna pass.

The French advance carried them to within ten miles of Vassitch in the Babuna pass, but they could not get across the hills, and Vassitch, fiercely assailed by the reinforced Bulgarians, could hold out no longer. On November 16, he retired. The French, still hoping to assist the Serbians in some way, retained their positions. It was November 20 before the Bulgarians renewed the attack, and they were again heavily checked, but Sarrail was unable to advance, the plain fact being that he neither had nor could get men in adequate numbers. And, meanwhile, in other parts of the country the progress of events, moving from disaster to disaster for the brave but unfortunate Serbians, had rendered it evident that the enemy's overrunning of the rest of Serbia was a question of but a very short time, on which the venture of the Allies in Salonica would exercise little influence.

On the north and north-east the crushing of Serbia went on unrelentingly, as the Serbian main armies were steadily pushed back towards the frontiers of Montenegro and Albania by Kövess, Gallwitz, and Bojadieff. The Serbians had no reserves from which to make good their losses, whereas the enemy kept bringing up reinforcements; his greater numerical strength and the efficiency of his long-range guns told heavily in his favour. Now becoming woefully short of supplies of both munitions and food, the Serbian armies, whose morale remained undiminished, fought bravely on in a struggle that grew daily more hopeless. The fortnight after the fall of Nish saw the development of a great converging movement of the three new enemy commanders on the historic Kossovo plain.

At the end of the first week in November Kövess with his Austro-Germans drove the Serbian rearguards out of the hills north of Ivanitza, and occupied that town on November 9. Four days later, having driven the Serbians from their positions in the district of the Stolovi range, he forced his way to Rashka, which he took on November 20, finding in its arsenal—the last the Serbians had left—fifty large mortars and eight guns that were, as the German official communiqué admitted, " of a somewhat ancient pattern." Farther east, Austrian troops were in possession of Sienitza and of Nova Varosh, close to the Montenegrin boundary, about the same date. Thrown back near Zhochanitza, the Serbians retired on Mitrovitza, from which Kövess on the 22nd was only five miles away.

East of Kövess, Gallwitz with his Germans had also been advancing southward, his objective being Pristina, on the east side of the plain of Kossovo and some twenty miles south-east of Mitrovitza. He had to negotiate the high mountain ridges of Central Serbia, and the Serbians, fighting desperately in the

Jastrebatz and other ranges, made him pay a heavy price for his progress, but on this front they furthermore had to endeavour to stem the Bulgarian tide of invasion under Bojadieff, and against the two they had no chance whatever.

Starting out from Krushevatz about November 8, Gallwitz struck southward towards Brus with one part of his troops, and with another due south across the high hills of the Jastrebatz in the direction of Kurshumlia. He soon reached Ribari and Rabaska Bania (Baths), and, storming the chief pass on the road over the mountains, gained entrance to the valley of the Toplitza. After a week's hard struggle Gallwitz entered Kurshumlia, which the Serbians had evacuated. Moving on, Gallwitz pushed across to Prepolatz, east of the Kopaonik mountains, occupying it on November 20, and then advanced southwards over the intervening ridges.

After withdrawing from Nish, the Serbians, under Marshal Stepanovitch, retreated to the west bank of the Morava, destroying the bridges as soon as they had got across, and, encouraged by the presence of King Peter in their midst, held up the Bulgarians there for some time. But farther north and farther south in the Morava valley they were at first less successful in checking the enemy. On the north the Bulgarians captured Alexinatz on November 7, the Serbian army of the Timok, in retreat from Zaitchar, barely succeeding in crossing the bridge over the river in time. On the south, and on the same day, the Serbians had to abandon Leskovatz. With the capture of these towns and other points on the line, the enemy secured complete possession of the great trunk railway from Belgrade through Nish to Sofia and Constantinople and of the Nish-Salonica railway as far south as the French entrenchments at Krivolak.

From Alexinatz the hard-pressed army of the Timok had only a single line of retreat, the road to Prokuplie and Kurshumlia, and, in danger of being cut off by the Germans on the west, it marched swiftly, though fighting rearguard actions all the while, and was able to unite with the army retiring from Krushevatz. Prokuplie did not fall to the Bulgarians till November 16. North-west of Leskovatz, where the pressure was not quite so extreme, Stepanovitch made a determined stand, on November 11 and 12, and heavily defeated Bojadieff's centre, throwing the latter's troops into confusion, and taking prisoners and guns. But this success could not, unhappily, be followed up; on the contrary, the Bulgarians, much reinforced, renewed the conflict two or three days later, and drove the Serbians down the road to Tulare and on to Pristina.

Meanwhile the Bulgarians were advancing on Pristina from a more southern direction—from Uskub. Here they were strongly opposed, and this sector of the campaign witnessed the battle of the Katshanik pass, in which the Serbians made their greatest effort subsequent to their magnificent resistance to the Austro-Germans on the Danube and the Save. By this time it had become apparent to the Serbian chief command that they could not receive from the Allies the expected assistance for their main armies. They now perceived that the only hope of saving their armies intact was by forcing a way to the south through Uskub. In order to achieve this the Katshanik pass and the road to the south had to be cleared of the enemy. Bojovitch's small army was reinforced, and on November 10, attacked the Bulgarians in the pass. The fighting, some of the most terrible in the campaign, continued until the 15th, but the enemy was too strong and the Serbians had to retire.

The plan for the retreat of the Serbian armies to the south had therefore collapsed, and its effect was immediately seen in the withdrawal from Mitrovitza of the Serbian staff, such members of the Serbian government as had remained there, and the personnel of the Legations of the Allies. On November 15 the Bulgarians captured Kalkandenen, and, driving before them the small Serbian force which had occupied it, took Gostivar on the following day, the Serbians retreating to Kichevo, on the road to Monastir. Bojadieff stormed the heights near Gilan and, occupying Gilan itself, advanced towards Pristina, being on November 22 no more than two or three miles from the last-named town.

The enemy had now succeeded in his great object of rolling back on to the Kossovo plain the Serbian main armies, which were united, but in considerable confusion and hampered by vast crowds of fugitives fleeing from all parts of the north, centre and east of the country. Near Mitrovitza, on the north of the plain, near Pristina on the east of it, and at Katshanik at its southern extremity, the Austro-Germans and the Bulgarians had, in the beginning of the fourth week of November, absolutely rounded up and hemmed in all the chief forces of the Serbians, for whom nothing really was left but surrender, destruction, or a terrible retreat into the mountains of Montenegro and Albania, now in the grip of winter. Kövess, having swept away the Serbian entrenchments north of Mitrovitza, entered that town on November 23, taking, by his own statement, 10,000 prisoners, 19 guns, and much railway material. On the same day Gallwitz, with his Germans, and the Bulgarians under Bojadieff captured Pristina, the former attacking it from the north and the latter from the south and east.

From Mitrovitza a part of the Serbian army, accompanied by multitudes of civilian fugitives, retreated to Ipek in Montenegro, and some proportion of them eventually arrived at Scutari, by way of Podgoritza, after suffering the cruellest hardships and privations—the rest perished miserably from cold and starvation. Retiring from the same town, another part of the force which had opposed Kövess stood and fought him again at Vutshitrin, but was beaten and pursued across the Sitnitza, on the western bank of which stream it was still fighting on November 25. But the main line of retreat of the Serbians was along the high road from Pristina to Prisrend, and the Bulgarians pressed on quickly behind in this direction, took the heights west of Ferizovitch, and also advanced northerly towards Ipek, against which town Kövess had sent a detachment. The retreat to Prisrend was covered by the Shumadia division. On November 27 upwards of 80,000 Serbians stood at bay in front of this town, but next day, after a most sanguinary conflict, and having fired their last shell, they spiked their guns, and fled across the frontier into Albania, while several thousand prisoners fell into the hands of the enemy.

As her forces still fighting in the south, in Macedonia, were inconsiderable, and were already being heavily pressed by the Bulgarians, the rout at Prisrend and the consequent flight signalised for the time being the end of Serbia. The Serbian government, with Pasich at its head, had left Prisrend a few days before the débâcle, and arrived without misadventure at Scutari on November 30. King Peter made good his escape, and after wandering among the snow-covered mountain paths, reached the Adriatic, whence he was conveyed to Brindisi, and later to Salonica. The Crown Prince Alexander, with the Princess Heléne, succeeded in getting to Cetinje. Marked by horrors unspeakable, the retreat of the Serbian army will remain one of the most terrible in history.

While the main Serbian armies were being driven out of their native land, the Bulgarians, after taking the Babuna pass and Kichevo, as well as Krushevo on November 20, did not at once advance to the capture of Monastir, and that city was subjected to many alarms for days, most of its population making haste to remove into Greece, whither the railway was still open. Vassitch had retired from the Babuna to Prilep, and there awaited the assault, which, however, did not materialise. When the Bulgarians at last moved, and took Brod with a view to cutting off his retreat, he quitted Prilep, and fell back on Monastir, which he evacuated on December 2, withdrawing his small band of heroes to Resna.

The last fight of importance by the Serbians took place near that town, from which Vassitch retired on December 5, and marching round the southern shore of Lake Ochrida, escaped with his men to Epirus. There were some encounters between small groups of Serbians and Bulgarians at Ochrida and Struga, but the retreat of Vassitch marked the conclusion of Serbia's glorious resistance against overwhelming odds. Just about ten weeks had passed since the Germans had begun shelling Semendria on September 21. While the struggle was still going on Serbia might have come to terms with the enemy, but she refused the offer made by Marshal Mackensen in November.

When Serbia was overrun, Mackensen redistributed his forces, various German and Austrian divisions being sent north to watch the Russians who, at that juncture, were rumoured to be about to make a diversion in the Balkans, either through Rumania or by a descent on the Bulgar shore of the Black Sea. German troops were transferred to Bulgaria and even to Turkey, but they were not withdrawn from the Montenegrin front.

With the disappearance from Serbia of her armies, the French and British forces which had come to endeavour to save them had no longer an object in remaining on Serbian soil. The rumours of military action by Russia on behalf of Serbia had proved unfounded. Italy had done nothing in the Balkans to help her Allies, except to shell Dedeagach on November 11. A month later she landed an army at Valona and elsewhere on the Adriatic coast. For several days after November 20, when the French on the west bank of the Tzerna repulsed the Bulgarians on that portion of front, nothing occurred. The first sign of what was about to happen appeared on November 27 in a

Paris official communiqué, stating that, in consequence of the situation of the Serbian armies at that time, the French troops which had occupied the west bank of the Tserna had been brought to the east side of that river—a movement which was made without any difficulty. A general withdrawal into Greece, with Saloncia as base, had been decided on by General Sarrail, in accordance with instructions from Paris and London.

It had been announced from Rome in November that Austria was assembling a force of three army corps in Herzegovina to attack Montenegro from that side. There were also available the Austrian troops already in Serbia on the Montenegrin eastern frontier, to say nothing of the Bulgarians who so far assisted Austria as to take Djakova on December 3. The whole expedition was placed under the direction of Kövess shortly after the fall of Mitrovitza. King Nicholas was not ignorant of what was coming. At the end of November, after Serbia had been crushed, he issued a proclamation to his people, in which he said that Montenegro, faithful to her traditions, would resist to the death, preferring death to slavery. He went on to state that the Allies had charged themselves with the supply of the army and population of Montenegro. Supply was always a great trouble in that poor little land, and when the Serbian refugees came flocking in, it became an insoluble problem.

Although the Austrians advanced during December some distance on the east or Sanjak front, capturing Plevlie, Ipek, and Bielopolie, their great offensive did not start until January, 1916. In the interval the Montenegrins had at least one considerable victory at Lepenatz, but in general they were driven steadily back. In the last days of 1915 Mount Lovtchen, the chief stronghold of the Montenegrins, and the position protecting Cetinje, was heavily shelled. On January 6, 1916, the Austrian commander Kövess attacked the Montenegrins on the Tara, Lim, and Ibar, and severely bombarded Mount Lovtchen from warships in the Gulf of Cattaro.

Berane, a town on the Lim, was captured on January 10, and Mount Lovtchen fell on the same day, the Austrians everywhere being in overwhelming force, and the Montenegrins short of guns, munitions, and food. With Lovtchen in the hands of the Austrians, the Montenegrins evacuated Cetinje, which was occupied by Kövess on January 13, 1916. Negotiations took place, the object of Montenegro being to gain time to ensure the retreat of her forces to Podgoritza and Scutari, and thence into Albania. The king and the royal family, with the government, escaped to Italy. Continuing their advance, the Austrians took Scutari on January 23, and San Giovanni di Medua on January 25, thereafter marching south to Durazzo. By the end of January, 1916, Austria was in full occupation of Montenegro.

Reverting to Salonica little happened for some weeks after the arrest of the enemy consuls and the clearing out of the spies. Everywhere the place was made stronger and stronger. East of it General Sarrail made its position still more secure by blowing up the railway bridge at Demir Hissar, on the line running towards Bulgarian territory. Additional reinforcements were constantly being landed at the Greek port. But up to the end of the first week of February, 1916, no attack had been attempted by the enemy except by occasional aeroplanes.

CHAPTER 27

The Evacuation of Gallipoli

THE final decision to evacuate Gallipoli was taken by the British Government in the middle of December, 1915. Among the reasons which influenced this decision was the lack of highly-experienced troops to meet the German, Bulgarian, and Austrian thrust at Salonica. The Salonica expedition had been planned by General Joffre and the French staff, and Sir W. Robertson and the British general staff were at first as much averse to this new adventure as General Joffre and General Castelnau had been to the Dardanelles scheme. But just as General Joffre had given way out of loyalty to the common alliance, and had sent a French army corps on what he considered was a hopeless business, so the British authorities and newly-reconstructed General Staff were moved by loyalty to co-operate with General Joffre in the Salonica expedition.

Another consideration was that the official casualty lists published in December showed that 25,000 officers and men had been killed, that the missing numbered over 12,000, and that nearly 100,000 cases of sickness, chiefly para-typhoid and dysentry had occurred among the troops. The task of evacuating the peninsula which fell to the lot of General Sir Charles Monro was one of supreme difficulty. The strength engaged amounted to three army corps and their numbers made it necessary that the evacuation should be gradual.

The British armies were now stationed at three points on the peninsula: the original landing places at the southern extremity of the peninsula and at Anzac Cove and the later one at Suvla Bay. Although the 10th division and one French division had already been withdrawn from Suvla and sent to Salonica, and the 2nd Mounted Division had left for Egypt, there remained somewhere about three divisions to be withdrawn from each of the original landing places. It seemed impossible that they could be re-embarked without serious losses—the estimates of what these would probably be varied from five per cent. to thirty-three per cent. The main difficulty lay in concealing the withdrawal from the Turks and in making such arrangements and dispositions of the forces as would keep the Turks under the illusion that all the British positions were manned in full strength and deter them from descending upon and annihilating the weakened forces which still remained.

The wintry conditions which set in during November and December materially helped in the task before the British commander-in-chief. Floods, frost and snow had brought both the British and Turkish armies to such a state of impotence that the attacks which might have disclosed the growing weakness of the British forces were impossible. The opposing forces held grimly on to their positions and did not attempt to move from them. Strangely enough the success of the Central Powers in another theatre of war had reactions in Gallipoli which greatly helped Sir Charles Monro's plans. The Serbian army had been signally defeated by the Austrians; Bulgaria had joined the Central Powers and thus a clear route was opened to Constantinople for the supply of munitions. The Turkish commander-in-chief therefore resolved to delay the final attack against the invaders of Gallipoli until he had at his command the new 12 in. howitzers and other heavy artillery now available. These pieces could only be slowly drawn into position by teams of bullocks. In many places the roads had to be widened and reconstructed in a solid manner to allow the great siege pieces to be hauled along. British warships shelled the route, destroying the bridge of Kavala, over which the new guns had to pass. A large part of the Turkish army laboured at road-making, and their work was much aggravated by the sodden condition of the ground at the end of autumn.

While the Turks were thus employed the evacuation went slowly on. Sir Charles Monro had decided that the armies at Anzac and Suvla Bay should be withdrawn first. Under cover of night the *matériel* was removed to ships and lighters which came close inshore and the fact that heavy fighting had stopped for the time being made it possible to get away most of the heavy guns without attracting the attention of the Turks to their absence. The embarkation of guns and stores fell largely to the navy, but the troops on land still had to do most of the work. They had to mine forward towards points of the Turkish line of tactical importance, so as to maintain the impression that they were preparing the way for the final, desperate assault. They had to intensify their bombing work and their use of aerial torpedoes, until even in the official Turkish communiqués remarks were made upon the renewed activity. Both the British and French armies threatened an advance. They blew up parts of the enemy's line, and when he rushed forward, filled his trenches, and brought up his reserves, the allied heavy artillery went into action and caused him heavy losses.

All this meant much hard work for the troops, but it was only a cover for the intense and sustained labour they were employing in secret directions. Excavation work went on in the trenches as though sappers were making tunnels against another and still heavier cloudburst. But the new diggings were filled with high explosives, and above the high explosives was placed a device of a deadly kind. Some of the things were trip-mines, which could be set so as to explode when anybody passed by. There were a good many miners in Anzac with much experience in explosives, and considerable powers of invention. According to rumour it was they who had suggested to the British War Office that donkeys would be very useful in transporting stores from the beach to the heights. The British official agreed that donkeys would save the lives of troops, but he wondered where they could be stabled, or something of that kind. The donkeys at Anzac were of course a simple mechanism used in the Australian gold mines, consisting of wires, up and down which suspended carriers could be hauled and lowered. The men who had first thought of these donkeys entered into consultation with the regular military engineers, and continuing their ideas they produced infernal machines, which were placed in large quantities at all spots where inquiring Turks were likely to venture.

None of the troops was informed of the intentions of the British commander. At Anzac and Suvla the armies were settling down to spend Christmas on the peninsula, when the news of the evacuation began to be known. The common opinion was that Sir Ian Hamilton had put down his probable casualties in a withdrawal at fifty per cent. of his men, and it was feared that the troops might be so disturbed at the possibility of such terrible losses as to fall into a panic towards the end. The first part of the evacuation was, therefore, conducted in such a way as to deceive the British forces. All the slightly wounded men, and the slightly sick, were first taken off at night, together with horses, stores, motors, and other machinery. But large quantities of empty boxes were piled up in conspicuous places to make the positions look as though they were going to be held for the winter.

The operation began on December 4, and by the 14th only the fit remained. On this day the regimental officers were told that, if the sea remained calm for one week, the withdrawal would be carried out. The whole thing was largely a gamble on the weather, with the odds against the British, for December was usually a month of heavy storms; and the moon was waxing, making the nights so much brighter that it seemed impossible for the Turks on the heights above to fail to see the ships which stole in empty after dark, and stole out full up at early dawn.

Gradually the troops became suspicious. They kept asking awkward questions about the destruction of serviceable material, and to their questions the officers had to return answers as non-committal as possible, and maintain an assumption of indifference in the matter which they were far from feeling. For the period of suspense was naturally extremely trying. The horrible thought of fifty per cent. losses weighed on every officer, and day by day their anxieties increased and the suspicion of the troops deepened. At last the withholding of general confidence could not be delayed, and the men were told exactly what was expected of each of them. The idea of anything like a panic, especially among the new troops at Suvla, was then seen to be absurd. The men behaved splendidly.

Setting immediately to work with a will, they destroyed beyond repair almost everything of use that had to be left behind.

The guns were removed, then the baggage was sent on three days in advance, till by the middle of December most of the heavy stuff had been got away. Then the Turks became much more active. They shelled the beaches and main positions continually, and some of their heavy howitzers began to cause considerable trouble. It was difficult to find their positions and knock them out. The gentle, moist south winds, which were making the weather perfect for embarkation, kept the clouds very low, and aerial observers could not see anything. But this lowness of the clouds saved the British from far more serious trouble than the heavy howitzer fire. For the Turco-German observers in turn were unable to find anything extraordinary about the British positions, and the enemy's bombardment was interrupted at night, when the beaches were crowded with furiously busy men, with hundreds of lighters by the water-edge, and transport steamers close at hand.

On the evening of Saturday, December 18, the British warships at Anzac trained every gun ready to shatter any attack on the weakened British lines. By seven o'clock in the evening the first big transport was in, and the embarkation began. It continued in absolute silence all night. The sky was clear, and the moon three-quarters full, yet the Turks never moved. Three-fifths of the total forces were embarked without mishap, and as the last transport slipped away at dawn, Sir Charles Monro, Sir William Birdwood, Sir John de Robeck, and their chief officers began to think that all might go well.

Sunday, December 19, was the critical day. Nobody could be sure that the Turks had guessed nothing, and were not concentrating for an attempt to break through Anzac and roll up the Suvla Bay forces. The warships remained broadside on to the Turkish positions, with all men waiting for the signal for action. But the day wore on, and still the Turks made no sign. They shelled the beach as usual, but the sight that cheered the departing army was the Turkish bombardment of a low hill from which every gun and every man had been removed. It seemed almost too much to hope that the Turks should be ignorant of what was going on beneath their eyes. But the only foragers in the half-deserted Anzac camp were a few men from Suvla Bay who had heard that among the medical comforts left behind for destruction were some cases of champagne. Suvla decided that medical comforts of this sort should not be wasted, and raided some of the abandoned stores.

On Sunday night the moon rose on a flat, oily sea, through a slight mist which hung low on the water and flowed on the wind into nullahs and valleys running up into the hills. Again the transports came in, miraculously unattacked in the clear moonlight, and the last men began to leave. The firing-line of trenches from Karakol Dagh, north of Suvla, to Lone Pine Plateau, south of Anzac Cove, was held by picked riflemen, one to seven or more yards. These " last ditchers," as they were called, were not so weak as they appeared to be. They had only six old guns behind them, but their guardian fleet had all the ranges nicely calculated to a yard, and could maintain an impenetrable curtain of shrapnel fire for a long period over all the first Turkish line and over the ground across which a charge must be made. There were also thousands of traps and mines with trip-wires, and a very ingenious bomb-thrower awaiting the enemy. But the Turks did not move. Even their patrols had been so severely handled that they had lost all their former spirit of adventure.

The Australians, however, could not bear to see so historic a scene end without some sort of struggle. Their brigades began to quarrel for the honour of being the last men at Anzac. Many soldiers paraded before their commanding officers, and protested vigorously against the orders to go on board the transport while men who had arrived on the peninsula later were staying with the rearguard. At Suvla two hundred men, who formed the ultimate rearguard, were selected from those who had made the first landing in the bay, and the final barrier they held was close to the spot where they had made their first rush and suffered heavy losses. The most touching thing about the withdrawal was the time the troops spent, during the last week, in the little mountain cemeteries and the burial-places.

On Sunday night some of the ambulance sections were called upon to show great courage. They agreed to be left behind if necessary with the rearguard, and attend the wounded during the evacuation, and remain with them and take their chance with the Turks. But the enemy made no attack. At about 3.30 on Monday morning, December 20, 1915, the embarkation was practically completed, and the rearguard at Anzac exploded a huge mine between themselves and the Turks on Russell's Top. This was a neck of land between the two ridges along which it was undesirable that the Turks should follow them. The terrific explosion had the desired effect; the Turks thought the Australians were attacking, and kept up a furious rifle fire for forty minutes. The retreating troops maintained a desultory but effective reply by a series of automatic devices. Along the now vacant trenches were candles and slow matches, so primed as to imitate rifle fire and make a show of activity sufficient to discourage Turkish snipers and patrols from reconnoitring the abandoned lines. About half an hour after the vast mine was fired, forty-five feet deep under the enemy trenches, a great fire blazed out at Suvla, and four large store-dumps burst into flame. There was soon one mighty bonfire two hundred yards long. The Anzacs also fired their abandoned heaps of bully beef, and a large motor-lighter, which had run ashore and could not be refloated, was blown up with a terrific report.

Still the Turks did not move, though the bonfires threw a red glow up to the sky, and dimming the moonlight, irradiated the whole scene with fiercer glow. The enemy pitched a few shells on a hill and a beach at Suvla, the total result of which was that one man was wounded. But the Turkish gunners did not make a curtain of fire as they so easily could have done. With watchful gait the rearguards came down in Indian file through the saps, followed by the happy forlorn hopes of the ambulance sections. After many stops and starts, and keeping well within the shadow of the saps, all the " last ditchers " reached the transports by four o'clock in the morning. The army of Anzac embarked at four o'clock, and the army at Suvla left a little earlier. By five o'clock both positions were evacuated, but some midshipmen in picket-boats waited by the piers to see if they could find any stragglers.

When the sun rose, the Turks began a grand bombardment, but instead of trying to reach the warships and transports, they shelled the vacated trenches, and the empty beaches, and in a state of utter mystification, even put large high-explosive shells into the flaming bonfires. The British warships also opened fire on everything that had been left behind—sunken lighters, the wrecked steamers forming breakwaters, and all structures likely to be of any use to the enemy. So there was the unique spectacle of Britons and Turks shelling the same targets simul-

THE EVACUATION OF GALLIPOLI

taneously. When the sun had climbed out of the morning mist, the Turks discovered at last that something was wrong, and trained some of their guns on the bombarding squadron. But their shooting was wild, and they never got within a hundred yards of the nearest ship. Late on Monday night one British battleship lay a dozen miles away from Suvla, and the glow of the bonfire was still visible.

The next morning a furious southerly gale sprang up and drove huge seas before it into the little bay, further wrecking the breakwaters of sunken sand-filled steamers, and breaking off all connexion between the coast and the sea. The departing armies had just escaped the storm by twenty-four hours. In the meantime, the Turks had become as over-rash as they had been over-cautious. They tried to crowd into the abandoned trenches, with the result that the automatic bomb-throwers, the trip-mines, land mines, and all the other hidden machines of death caught them by the thousand. A report from Athens said that five thousand men were killed or disabled in the vast death-trap between Karakol Dagh and Lone Pine Plateau.

This was probably an exaggeration; but there is no doubt that the Turks were badly punished during their first great rush for plunder into the abandoned lines. The total British casualties were one officer and two men wounded at Suvla, and four men wounded at Anzac; which was less than the ordinary daily casualties in the trenches under gun fire, sniping, and an occasional bomb. Two of the six guns left behind to support the rearguards in case of attack were venerable howitzers that had served in the South African War. All six guns were destroyed at the last minute, and though there seem to have been some stragglers who did not reach the Suvla beach till 8.30 a.m., not a man was lost.

The entire withdrawal was a wonderful piece of organization. It was practically staff work alone that achieved such a result. Sir Charles Monro oversaw all the arrangements, with Admiral de Robeck and Admiral Wemyss looking after the naval side, and General Birdwood looking after the military situation. In a special order of the day, Sir Charles Monro wrote an appreciation of the withdrawal from the Anzac and Suvla positions.

The arrangements made for withdrawal, and for keeping the enemy in ignorance of the operation which was taking place, could not have been improved. The general officer commanding the Dardanelles army, and the general officers commanding the Australian and New Zealand and 9th army corps, may pride themselves on an achievement without parallel in the annals of war. The army and corps, staffs, divisional and subordinate commanders and their staffs, and the naval and military beach staffs proved themselves more than equal to the most difficult task which could have been thrown upon them. Regimental officers, non-commissioned officers, and men carried out, without a hitch, the most trying operation which soldiers can be called upon to undertake—a withdrawal in the face of the enemy—in a manner reflecting the highest credit on the discipline and soldierly qualities of the troops.

It is no exaggeration to call this achievement one without parallel. To disengage and to withdraw from a bold and active enemy is the most difficult of all military operations; and in this case the withdrawal was effected by surprise, with the opposing forces at close grips—in many cases within a few yards of each other. Such an operation, when succeeded by a re-embarkation from an open beach, is one for which military history contains no precedent.

During the past months the troops of Great Britain and Ireland, Australia and New Zealand, Newfoundland and India, fighting side by side, have invariably proved their superiority over the enemy, have contained the best fighting troops in the Ottoman army in their front, and have prevented the Germans from employing their Turkish allies against us elsewhere.

No soldier relishes undertaking a withdrawal from before the enemy. It is hard to leave behind the graves of good comrades, and to relinquish positions so hardly won and so gallantly maintained as those we have left. But all ranks in the Dardanelles army will realise that in this matter they were but carrying out the orders of his Majesty's Government, so that they might in due course be more usefully employed in fighting elsewhere for their King, their country, and the Empire.

There is only one consideration—what is best for the furtherance of the common cause. In that spirit the withdrawal was carried out, and in that spirit the Australian and New Zealand and the 9th army corps have proved, and will continue to prove, themselves second to none as soldiers of the Empire.

While the armies of Anzac and Suvla were withdrawing, the allied forces south of Achi Baba, at the tip of the peninsula, undertook a diversion. The idea was to prevent the withdrawal of Turkish troops from the Cape Helles front for any closing attack upon the Anzac army and the Suvla Bay forces. The enemy had no offensive movement whatever in contemplation; but this could not be known to Sir Charles Monro, and, leaving nothing to chance, he ordered an attack upon the top of the Krithia Ravine. At two o'clock in the afternoon of December 19 all the artillery posts were manned beneath the rounded outline of Achi Baba—the familiar, unattainable object in the landscape, at which the men had been staring since April.

The country looked utterly peaceful in the warm sunlight. Nothing moved on land, though the smoke of cooking fires indicated something of the forces concealed in the trenches. But behind the eastern islands and in the northern mists the new British monitors were hidden with their 14 in. and 15 in. guns ready for action. And up by the Krithia Nullah, in seven mine galleries driven beneath the road the infantry was waiting in darkness with bomb, revolver, bayonet, and sand-bag. There was only about a foot of earth between them and the Turkish trench which stretched end on to the mine galleries. The mines had been driven so quietly that the enemy suspected nothing.

Instead of blowing them up and killing only a few Turks in their machine-gun posts, the British plan was to make seven infantry rushes through the mines, grab a few hundred yards of the trench before the Turkish brigadier knew that anything had happened, barricade the captured position, and work down the saps until the Turkish reserves arrived. The Navy began the operation by dropping a 14 in. shell into Krithia. Then, in a seemingly desultory manner, more heavy shells were pitched into the enemy second and third line, as in an ordinary daily bombardment. Meanwhile, more monitors emerged from the northern mists and the attack opened in force. Three mines were sprung under the Turkish first line, and all the land batteries let go with lyddite and tritol shrapnel, while the monitors and destroyers intensified their gun fire.

In about five minutes the Turkish gunners replied, but, being unable to perceive if a blow had fallen or if a blow had struck at all, they shot wildly about the peninsula. No movement of the British infantry could be perceived; yet, invisible in the dust and smoke, the soldiers had burst through their seven galleries. Some drove the Turks up the trench, while others built a barricade across the nullah, and with sand-bags made a parapet connecting their lines with the captured position. Eighty yards up, the Turks made a stand by their first barricade, and bomb-throwers replaced the men with revolvers and bayonets. In another direction a brave Turk pulled his machine-gun into the trench and caught one company, bringing down the captain and fifty men.

The rest went back to cover, but twenty yards behind them the new parapet was already four feet high. Five feet above the fighting infantry swept the shells from the British land artillery and ships, and crossing them, a little higher in the air, was another line of roaring missiles by which the Turkish gunners were trying to keep back supports of the attacking force.

What with the smoke and the noise, nobody could hear and nobody could see. Meanwhile, another trench had been taken with little difficulty, and the main group of Turkish soldiers remained ringed around by British infantry. The Turks fought on bravely behind their barricades where no help could reach them, and after fighting all night, the British only made another ten yards' progress. The affair ended with two pieces of Turkish trench being taken—two hundred yards in all—with the Turks sandwiched between the ground that had been gained.

Then the news came that Anzac and Suvla Bay had been evacuated without the enemy trying to move. There was then no reason for winning, at the cost of a man a yard, more of the ground which was so soon to be abandoned. So the demonstration at Krithia abruptly ended. No men could be spared for any general diversion, for with the evacuation of Anzac and Suvla the position of the forces at the southern point of the peninsula became one of great peril.

In the first place, the enemy was able to concentrate overwhelming forces of men and guns, with increased munitions of all kinds, on the short front at the edge of Achi Baba. In the second place, another surprise re-embarkation by the allied armies seemed impossible of achievement. Not only had the Turks been put on their mettle by the extraordinary stratagem used against them, but the German General Staff despatched a large body of picked officers to watch the position by the Dardanelles, and see that the army there did not again steal away without standing battle. In the third place, the period of very heavy storms had set in, making the approach of ships to the shore almost impossible, despite the rough-and-ready breakwaters erected round the landing-beaches. Moreover, the moon was nearing the full, so that the coast and a large stretch of sea were clearly visible. No transport could expect to approach the land without provoking gun fire, both from the Asiatic shore on the right flank and the Achi Baba lines in front.

Apparently the British Government could not make up its mind to run the terrible risks of evacuating the southern end of the peninsula. But it is very likely that this indecision was only another ruse to steady the nerves of the troops and mislead, if possible, the enemy. There were several good reasons for holding on. There was a considerable amount of elbow-room for the troops, enabling them to burrow away from the enemy's shell fire, while on the plateau which the British army occupied the flood-water from the hills inconvenienced the men less than it did the Turks on the higher slopes. The ground commanded the entrance to the Strait, giving the British some control of the historic waterway which led to Constantinople.

An American correspondent, Granville Fortescue, who had studied the position carefully from the Turkish side, and had talked to the German and Turkish officers there, published a pamphlet in London strongly advising the British people to hold on to the plateau at the end of the peninsula, and so remain the outer guardian of the channel between the Black Sea and the Mediterranean. The enemy was quite aware of the power the British could exert for generations on the traffic through the Dardanelles by maintaining their grip upon the southern plateau. He saw that the valid reasons for evacuating Suvla and Anzac, where the armies had been cramped, did not apply to the position on the tip of the peninsula. Therefore, he was not at all sure that an entire withdrawal was intended. The Turks were not pleased with this state of things; they would have much preferred to see an attempt at an evacuation, and then sweep down from the hills, with the possibility of inflicting heavy losses upon the retiring forces.

All the German commanders and advisers of the Ottoman Empire were determined to prevent another such withdrawal of the British and French troops as disastrous to their interests. They wanted to use the Turkish army to inflict a heavy blow, which would tell on both the material and moral elements of the allied strength. They reckoned that if they could only get their heavy howitzers in position and accumulate a great store of shells, they could employ the hurricane fire artillery tactics used on the Russian and French fronts. Only one of the landing-beaches was protected from the enemy's guns; the newly munitioned Turkish gunners with German, Austrian, and Hungarian artillerymen working the new heavy howitzers, would be able, it was calculated, to wear the invaders down.

By Christmas the Turks around Achi Baba had trebled their supply of ammunition; they had brought up guns from the Sari Bair area, and the heavy howitzers were being hauled along southward for the closing battle. New squadrons of German airmen were sent to Constantinople, and, reaching the Gallipoli front a few days before Christmas, they began to show unwonted energy and audacity in their scouting work. There had been sharp upbraidings and dismissals of commanding officers in connection with the Suvla and Anzac operations. The officers who were the Teutonic leaven in the Ottoman army were, at any rate, resolved not to be surprised again. German aeroplanes boldly hovered over British bivouacs, though gunners filled the sky with shrapnel all around them, and machine-guns spouted bullets at them when they swooped down to get a clearer view of the British activities.

At the beginning of the struggle to prevent the British from departing, the enemy used his new shell supplies in an alarming manner. As soon as the withdrawal from Suvla and Anzac had been effected, he tried to make life intolerable to the men at Helles. Every part of the ground was open to his fire. He shelled the communication trenches, along which the troops were to withdraw, and the beaches from which they had to embark. During the week after Christmas, the daily toll of casualties from shell fire became very heavy. So, by way of making the enemy anxious about his store of shells, Major-General Davies, commanding on the Helles front, launched another infantry attack against the Turkish lines. On December 29 a British division broke into the Turkish centre, and captured and held part of the fire trenches. This infantry movement was, of course prepared by a terrific bombardment, in which the great guns of the monitors joined with heavy howitzers in drenching all the enemy positions with shells that wrecked the deepest dug-out.

This show of activity by the British had the desired effect. General Liman von Sanders calculated what his available shell resources were and found that if he used them lavishly in desultory bombardments of the beaches and communication trenches, he might lack ammunition to repel a great and sustained attack in force. So he slackened his daily gun fire, especially at night, when his gunners were likely to waste shells by the hundred if the beaches were empty. He decided on a new and far more effective plan of action. He reserved his shells until his armies at Sari Bair and Anafarta were marched into position around Achi Baba. His idea was to test the strength or weakness of the British lines, by making a grand attack.

By this time Sir Charles Monro had come to Helles with General Birdwood, and these two experts in the art of perfect evacuation studied the more difficult problem of Helles with General Davies; then, with Admiral de Robeck, Admiral Wemyss, and the military and naval staffs, they worked out all the preparations. The French army corps started to embark towards the beginning of the new year. Their departure could not be hidden from the enemy, who soon found out that he had British uniforms and British voices in front of him on the Kereves Dere front. By this river gully the opposing trenches came within a few yards of each other, so any concealment was impossible. Happily, the enemy was not disturbed; for knowing that the French had set their heart on the Salonica Expedition, and disapproved of the Dardanelles campaign, the Turco-German commanders naturally supposed that the French had been freed so that they might work under their own commander-in-chief, General Sarrail. But a British division and the English yeomanry left about the same time as the French army corps, and the weakening of the lines went on in an apparently perilous manner until the first week in January, 1916.

At first the departing troops left their artillery behind them, so that the " last ditchers " could make a brave show of gun fire to the last possible moment. The method of embarkation was the same as that employed at Suvla and Anzac. The men came down to the beaches at night, and the transports came in under cover of darkness, loaded up, and stole out before dawn. Horses were used to drag down many of the big guns, which were then taken away by the French navy. Again it seemed extraordinary that the enemy could not discern, by means of star-shells, searchlights, and night-glasses, the difference between reinforcement and evacuation.

On January 7, 1916, however, it looked as though the anxious Germans, watching from the hill behind Krithia and from the large, round hump of Achi Baba, had discovered all that was going on. At eleven o'clock in the morning the British position on both sides of the great ravine was swept with gun fire which continued for hours, while British guns replied fairly vigorously. At three o'clock in the afternoon the enemy's fire suddenly assumed a speed and intensity exceeding anything known on the peninsula. It was a true drum fire, such as the French had invented in Champagne and Mackensen had perfected in Russia. It lasted only half an hour, so as to maintain the surprise effect, and prevent reserves from being brought up. At half-past three the enemy exploded two mines on Fusilier Bluff, which overlooked the sea at the extreme end of the British line. The moment for the great infantry attack had come. The left of the British line was shrouded in black smoke, trenches were blown in at many points, and several communication saps were blocked. But the Turks who came out were not many, and they were shot down. A real assault was only attempted opposite Fifth Avenue and Fusilier Bluff, where the Staffordshires broke up the movement by shooting most of the Turks. At the same time the Turkish trenches were enfiladed by fire from British destroyers which had got perfect bearings.

At this point there was undoubtedly an unwillingness on the part of the Turkish troops to advance. Great fighting race as they were the Turks had not the iron discipline which alone can induce troops to advance towards almost certain annihilation. The Turks, like the British, had gradually learned that the Gallipoli peninsula was to be evacuated by the Allies. In their many hand-to-hand encounters with Australasians, British, French and French Colonial troops they had learned to respect the forces opposing them. Those troubles which had affected the British troops had also affected the Turks. They, too, had suffered from frost-bite, enteric, dysentery, and poor food, and in addition the clothing provided for them was far less suitable to the severe climatic conditions of winter in Gallipoli than that which was issued to the allied troops. The Turkish troops having the intelligence to realize that the allies were about to abandon their positions did not see any reason why they should sacrifice themselves in order to bring about the retirement a few days earlier.

There were other factors which affected the moral of the Turkish troops. The naval bombardment with high-explosive shells had punished them severely. At this point in the operations it was clear that the British infantryman had definitely established his superiority over the Turkish infantryman. If it had been possible to reinforce the Gallipoli army with both men and artillery defeat might have been turned into victory. Two considerations made this solution of the problem of Gallipoli impossible. Sea communications which alone could supply men and munitions to the forces were interrupted by heavy storms, which would not lessen as winter came on, and the commitments of the British army in France, Flanders, Egypt, and elsewhere made it highly essential that the troops should be withdrawn from the Dardanelles in order to fight where immediate decisions seemed possible.

After the extraordinary check to the Turkish advance at Fusilier Bluff, the commander of the Ottoman forces decided that the British were resolutely fixed at the entrance to the Dardanelles. The weakness of his infantry forbade him attempting another attack, and in his drum-fire bombardment he had spent so much shell that he had to be very careful in using what remained in store. Thus all circumstances compelled him to await the arrival of the new German and Austrian heavy artillery, before trying to drive the invaders into the sea.

In the meantime, nearly all the British artillery was taken away. The Battle of the Bluffs ended in the evening of January 7, 1916, and by dawn on January 8 most of the field-guns and howitzers which had been used against the Turks had been taken to the beaches and shipped on gun lighters. January 8 was the culminating day at Cape Helles. It broke clear and calm, with a perfect sea for the great event, but about four in the afternoon a gale blew up, increasing in violence at night till the wind tore along at a speed of thirty-five miles an hour. This was an extreme peril. Had the Turks but known it, the remaining forces were at their mercy. The gale made one of the principal embarking places, Gully Beach, impracticable, and a lighter was wrecked there. At the chief place of embarkation, W Beach, just above Cape Helles, the connecting piers were washed away. There were collisions with rafts and hospital barges, troop lighters, and gun lighters, the engines of other lighters broke down, and another steam lighter was wrecked. Moreover, a hostile submarine had been seen off Cape Helles at nine o'clock in the evening.

In the thick weather the bombarding squadrons would not have been able to help the last weak line of infantry. However, though the great storm enormously increased the difficulties of the beach-masters, engineers, and lighter skippers, it saved them from extraordinary dangers. The German landsmen directing the Turkish army were certain that no large military force, with numerous heavy guns and immense stores of war material, could be embarked in a thirty-five-miles-an-hour gale. The result was that the Turkish gunners remained in their dug-outs. On the principal beach only six shells fell after darkness set in. It was pitch dark on land and sea, and the enemy was confident that the hurricane was working for him and preventing all traffic on the British beaches.

At midnight on January 8 the firing-line was quite empty of troops; but not a single Turk or German reconnoitred the trenches. The German commander and Turkish generals on the Gallipoli peninsula did not foresee that storm might be more favourable to the evacuation than calm. Owing to this fact, the evacuation of the southern part of the peninsula, in face of a much strengthened enemy, was conducted with as great success as the withdrawal from Anzac and Suvla. The total British casualties were—one man wounded. A few guns were destroyed and abandoned.

The programmes of embarkation at W Beach and Y Beach were completed at 2.30 a.m. on January 9, 1916. Meanwhile, the troops originally marked for evacuation at Gully Beach marched to W Beach, and got on the lighters by 4 a.m. As the naval beach party was just casting off, a military officer and three men, who had failed to clamber into a lighter at another pier, finished a two-mile walk, and barely arrived in time to catch the last boat. All the bonfires were already fused, and also the magazine piles and bomb stores. This small party just reached the last lighter and cleared the breakwater when the fires broke out. It was a close shave, for the lighter was barely 100 yards from the shore when the magazines exploded. Happily, the lighter was constructed with a splinter-proof roof and got away safely.

The beach was in flames, cliff high from end to end, and from this line of lowering fire the explosion burst. The magazine contained the gun-cotton store of the Royal Engineers, and near it were clumps of small-arm ammunition, bombs, and other explosives. But the end of the gun-cotton pile was accounted a magnificent spectacle by those who saw it. A huge crimson mushroom shaped mass rose in the reddened sky, with large lumps of black rock showing in the fearful flame. It shook the sea and the ship, and the men who had cleared the breakwater thought their end had come. But the larger rocks fell short of them, only the fringe of the volcanic shower striking the boat. Six men were cut, but none severely. It was then 4.30 a.m. The terrific explosion and the great line of flame aroused the Turk and the German, and their gunners began to shell the vacant lines and fiery beaches, and continued to waste ammunition until there was no enemy at whom to fire.

CHAPTER 28

The Campaign in Mesopotamia

BETWEEN the capture of Kurna, the last success of the British before the end of 1914, and the spring of 1915, the British force in Mesopotamia was actively employed in consolidating its gains and in reconnaissance. In April the position became serious, the Turks concentrating for an attack on Basra and threatening the oil pipe up the Karun river to the north-east. A second division was sent to reinforce the British expedition, and the whole force placed under the command of General Sir John Nixon, who arrived at Basra on April 9. Five days later the Turkish threat to Basra was successfully countered in a smart little engagement at Barjisyah and some successful fighting at Shaiba. These two victories allowed the force to consolidate its position; but although the fresh division was welcome it had arrived with less than half its proper scale of medical equipment and the river transport was utterly inadequate for its requirements.

Sir John Nixon's orders from the commander-in-chief in India were: 1. To retain complete control of the lower portion of Mesopotamia. 2. To secure the safety of the oilfields. 3. To submit a plan for the effective occupation of the Basra peninsula and for a subsequent advance on Bagdad. These orders, given on March 24, were not forwarded to the India office until May 3, and the secretary of state did not for some time realize that an advance on Nasiriyeh and Amara was involved. But after prolonged correspondence between India and England the secretary of state sanctioned successively the advance of the force to Amara and even to Kut-el-Amara.

With the small force that was left after providing numerous garrisons, General Townshend in command, had continually to attack an enemy who possessed overwhelming numbers. The enemy was, moreover, well equipped, armed with guns of superior power, directed by German officers, and entrenched in difficult positions with all the skill of which German engineers were capable. His only chance of success was to defeat the Turks before their reinforcements arrived. Before he could approach Bagdad he had to defeat a large Turkish force on the Euphrates at Nasiriyeh, which lay in a position to cut across the rear or to take in flank, the advance he designed to make high up the Tigris. Then at Kut-el-Amara, his small force had to meet the main Turkish army, strengthened by the force from Nasiriyeh.

The Turkish force which had been beaten at Shaiba had retreated along the Euphrates to Nasiriyeh, and had there been joined by strong reinforcements, who brought more artillery, including three heavy siege-guns, transported from Adrianople. The Euphrates route, by which the Turks had made their previous attack on Basra, was the only practicable line for an advance during the flood season. The town of Nasiriyeh was also important as being the capital of the warlike Mustafik tribe of Arabs; and its junction with the cross-desert canal of Shat-el-Hai, running towards the Bagdad region, greatly increased its military importance. The capture of the town would prevent the enemy from advancing on Basra by the Euphrates route, with the result that in the season when the Tigris was in flood the position would be absolutely secure. The enemy, however, had taken great pains with his defences. His army was entrenched on both sides of the wide river, with long lines of very strong entrenchments, extending for about a mile on either bank.

The Turks also had powerful detachments thrown out along the old channel of the Euphrates which runs through the vast sheet of water, Lake Hamar, to the junction with the Tigris at Kurna. There was a good deal of skirmishing round Lake Hamar between the British armed motor-boats and steamers and the Thornycroft-built warships which the Turks employed. This river fighting had been proceeding since December 9, 1914, when the capture of Kurna opened the old Euphrates channel to General Townshend's ships and gun-tugs. The Arab snipers were gradually cleared from the great lake, and then, at the beginning of July, a mixed force under General Gorringe set out to the Euphrates by way of Hamar Lake. The amphibious nature of the operations over flooded land, through creeks and lagoons pursued daily by flies and savaged nightly by mosquitoes, had no surprises for troops inured to this pestilential form of warfare; and fighting through the enemy's advanced position below Hamar Lake, the wonderfully-mixed flotilla arrived, at the end of the third week in July, 1915, at a distance of about seven miles from Nasiriyeh. The division was then split up. Two brigades were landed on the right or westerly bank, while to the other brigade was assigned the task of working through the groves of date-palms on the left bank. As a reserve, a fourth brigade was brought down from Amara, and held ready for action in river-boats. Each of these boats had four guns, and pushing slowly up the river they covered with their fire the British troops on either bank, and silenced some of the enemy's guns.

The battle began about half-past four on the morning of July 24, 1915. For half an hour the brigades had been moving forward; but before the infantry charged, all the howitzers, field, and mountain guns bombarded the enemy's foremost trenches with high-explosive shells. For a full hour the batteries continued to smash up the enemy's entrenchments and gun positions; and then the 2nd West Kents advanced through the date groves, while eight machine-guns, with the supporting battalions, covered the advance by rapid fire on the opposing trenches. Despite this covering fire, however, the West Kents were met by a terrible fusillade that swept their front lines. An officer in one of the regiments that was maintaining a covering musketry fire, said the most magnificent sight he had ever seen was the West Kents going on under the enemy's terrific fusillade. As soon as they got up to the Turkish trenches, they wheeled round to the right, and, while their comrades stopped firing for fear of hitting them, they leapt into the trenches and were at once engaged in fierce hand-to-hand fighting.

After the West Kents jumped into the Turkish trenches, the rest of the brigade advanced to support the attack, carrying all

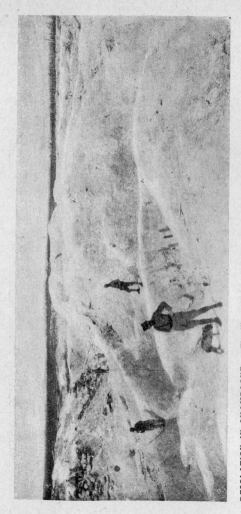

DESOLATION IN CHAMPAGNE. The illustration shows the effect of the heavy bombardment on the appearance of the country as a result of the fighting. Trees, cornfields, and vineyards are wiped out, and the result gives an impression of the Glacial Age. The battle of September–October, 1915, fought between the French and the Germans, resulted in heavy losses on both sides, and the French failed in the objects of their offensive

UHLANS IN THE OPEN. This remarkable picture shows a troop of German horsemen leaving cover in the Champagne district to charge the French. Only in open country such as this was it possible to employ cavalry on the Western front and then very infrequently. Heavy fighting took place in this region in the autumn of 1915.

Plate 50   *Volume II*

FRENCH TRENCHES IN CHAMPAGNE. View of the French lines before a German attack during the winter campaign in Champagne Some of the fiercest fighting of the whole war took place in this district

BRITISH PREMIER AND FRENCH WAR MINISTER CONFER. Mr. Asquith and M. Millerand are seen leaving Marshal Joffre's headquarters after a conference with Allied staff officers relating to the progress of the operations on the West front. The former is standing hatless at doorway, and M. Millerand is entering the car with Joffre next to him.

Plate 52

Volume 11

the ammunition they could collect. The brigade wheeled in the direction taken by its leading battalion, and picking their way through the terrible mounds of dead, emerged into an open space where the West Kents were taking cover by a low bank, and firing at the enemy in the date groves all around them. By this time the West Kents were using their last cartridges; but a battalion of Sikhs gave them some ammunition, and reinforced the firing-line by the low bank. Soon afterwards the order came to take two loopholed towers from which the enemy was maintaining a heavy fire. A double company of Sikhs and some twelve of the West Kents cleared the Turks out of the trenches on their right, and then fought their way along a communication sap, and took both towers in fifteen minutes.

After capturing the towers and a number of prisoners, the Sikhs and the handful of white men had ten minutes' rest, which they spent in binding up their wounded and putting them in the shade of the towers. Then the small force fought the Turks out of another long line of trench, running down to the edge of a creek which formed the extreme left of the Turkish position. Here there was a village with another couple of towers, and these were also stormed after long, terrible bayonet work above the last mat-covered trench. By this time the division had won the battle. The Turks could be seen running away on the left, and the Sikhs and the West Kents were signalled to hold the ground they had won, and not to advance any farther. So, posting guards, they slept by the last two captured towers that night.

Across the river the attack was equally successful. The Hants territorials shared the honours of the day with the West Kents; for, despite the fact that the enemy's position was protected by barbed-wire entanglements, the territorial battalion made a splendid storming charge. The Shushan, the Sumana, and other armed launches supporting the land attack had each in tow horse-barges containing a 4.7 in. gun, and these floating batteries did much to check the fire of the Turkish guns.

At the turning-point in the battle, the Shushan pushed up to the point where one of the main creeks entered the river, and shelled the Turks so heavily that they fled. At half-past five in the afternoon the Mejidieh steamer, from which the general and some of his staff officers worked, reached this point, and soon afterwards the enemy's camp was occupied, all the remaining Turks retiring towards the north. At the junction of the river and the creek the Mejidieh found four 15-pounder Turkish field-guns commanding the lower reaches of the river. After the battery had been discovered and silenced, Lieutenant Seymour pushed ahead in the Shushan launch and reached Nasiriyeh.

The riverside town of two-storied mud-brick houses was fluttering with white flags, and just beyond the town Lieutenant Seymour spotted two Turkish Thornycroft-built patrol-boats, one of which he sank with a 4.7 in. shell. As the Shushan returned past the town she was fired on from the white-flagged houses without, however, replying. The British and Indians camped in tents outside the town for the night, and on July 25 some of them went to the bazaar and peacefully bought what fresh fruit there was for sale. Nasiriyeh was a well-laid-out town, but its sanitary conditions were so bad that the troops were wisely kept in their tents outside till the engineers had cleaned up some of the worse filth.

The Turkish commander-in-chief, Nuredin Pasha, whose base was at Kut-el-Amara, had despatched a large body of reinforcements along the Shat-el-Hai canal. If this force had arrived during the battle, the overworked British division would have been compelled to retire. Happily, things fell out otherwise. The fresh Turkish troops met the routed army of the Euphrates, and were so impressed by the tales of the terrible valour of the British and the Indians, that they, too, turned tail and hastened back to Kut-el-Amara. Fourteen guns and 700 prisoners were captured, and some 1,800 of the Turks were killed at the cost of a casualty list of five hundred officers and men. The effect of the British gunfire was dreadful ; the hostile trenches were completely smashed, and nine hundred Turkish corpses were found in a small area. Towards the end of the month, when Nasiriyeh had been cleaned and garrisoned, the larger part of the force had another long voyage back to Amara on steamers and barges, with only grass mats shading them from the sun, leaving a small garrison behind. Meanwhile, General Townshend, based on Amara on the Tigris, was working his ships up the river and getting on friendly terms with the powerful tribes of the Beni Lam Arabs.

The victories on the lower rivers had made the sheikhs of the Beni Lam inclined to enter into a league with the British;

for, as some of the principal rivals had sided with the Turkish army, the Beni Lam had little to win if the expeditionary force were defeated, but they could look forward to acquiring new grazing grounds if they assisted against the other Arabs and against the Turks. As an ally, the Bedouin was a doubtful asset; he looked on battle as a sport, and quickly rode away from the conflict if he met with a slight reverse. But an agreement with the confederation of Beni Lam enabled General Townshend to use a long stretch of the Tigris with little danger of attack since the banks would be peopled with friendly Arabs.

Before Basra could be considered safe, apart from the greater objective of Bagdad, the town of Kut-el-Amara had to be secured. Accordingly early in August a move was made towards this town. Motor-boats explored the Tigris over the great distance between Amara and Kut-el-Amara. This work had been going on for nearly ten months, and had been undertaken with increasing vigour when the flood-water from the snows in the Caucasus had subsided. The captains of the Lynch steamers, who had studied the Tigris for years, could not give full information about its navigation; for the great winding stream was restless in its bed, and in every flood season it changed its shoals and sandbeds, tore away its mud-banks, and altered its course in small or large ways. Only actual reconnaissance could reveal if certain marshes dried in the summer sufficiently to enable troops to ford certain difficult creeks.

In the last week of September, 1915, the British forces were safely transported to the neighbourhood of Kut-el-Amara. There was still only a single weak division, with a brigade in reserve. The Turks were three divisions strong, with a large medley of mounted Bedouins acting as light cavalry. In their position, about ten miles from Kut-el-Amara, Nuredin Pasha's troops were deeply entrenched behind barbed-wire entanglements, and were supported by artillery heavier than could be brought up the river. On September 23 two British brigades advanced until they came within sight of the hostile tents and pitched camp on the south bank of the Tigris.

Though the summer was nearing its close, the sun was still very fierce, and the trying climatic conditions were to have an important bearing on the result of the battle. The two brigades demonstrated against the enemy on September 25, but it was then discovered that the Turks had placed mines all over the south bank of the river. Thereupon General Townshend altered his plan of attack. On the night of September 27 the two brigades crossed the river by a flying bridge, leaving their tents standing, as a dummy camp to delude the enemy. A Turkish division remained facing the empty tents, and it was the absence from the real battlefield of this enemy force, during the critical period of the struggle, that turned the tide of battle.

Between the town of Kut-el-Amara and the hamlet of Nakhailat, the Tigris makes a sudden southward bend. A little north of the bend was a swamp known by its shape as the Horse-shoe Marsh. Then north of this marsh was a patch of firm ground; and beyond this ground, still going northward, was a larger swamp, known as the Suwada Marsh. North of the Suwada Marsh was another narrow strip of firm ground, with a third swamp north of it, which we may call the circular marsh. The Turkish entrenchments extended between the river and the Horse-shoe Marsh, and continued between this and the Suwada Marsh; and were further prolonged from the Suwada Marsh to the circular marsh. The heaviest Turkish artillery was sited near the river behind the Horse-shoe Marsh, close to a place known as the Hundred and Twenty-one Tents. South of the Tigris the enemy's entrenchments stretched for some miles opposite the abandoned tents. The river was blocked by a line of sunken dhows and a line of thick wire just above the water.

The Turks, directed by German engineers, had spent months in fortifying their positions. Their trenches were ten feet deep, with bomb-proof communication trenches, overhead cover, and high wire entanglements, fronting which were wolf-pits, with pointed stakes at the bottom, and dynamite mines concealed beneath the sand. The Turkish guns were so dug in as to protect them from anything but a direct hit with a howitzer shell.

By the early morning of September 28, a column under General Fry, had gradually pushed its way up to within four hundred yards of the Turkish wire entanglements round the Horse-shoe Marsh. The troops went forward slowly and carefully, digging themselves in under continual shell and rifle fire. Guns in the open could not silence the Turkish artillery, which plastered the newly-made trenches and tried to curtain off the attacking troops during their swift, short forward rushes. Fortunately, the ground lent itself to attacking operations, as every hundred yards or so there were deep dry ditches, which gave good cover. Still more fortunately, the Turkish shells were of very poor quality. The attacking brigade only had 90 casualties all told, during its task of holding the enemy round the Horse-shoe Marsh and by the river.

While General Fry thus pretended to attack the Turks in their strongest position where they wanted to be attacked, the second column under General Delamain, consisting of the brigades which had crossed from the south side of the Tigris, marched all night east of the Suwada Marsh, and after resting for two hours, reached their new attacking position at a quarter to five in the morning of September 28. The position at which they arrived was a neck of dry land between the Suwada Marsh and the circular marsh, where the Turks had constructed their most northerly entrenchments. General Delamain's column, moving cautiously over ground which had been only partly examined, advanced for a mile between the marshes, and then came in full view of the enemy's trenches. But the airmen and scouts had reported that, right to the north of the last swamp, the circular marsh, there was no enemy position. So, before opening the decisive struggle, General Townshend detached part of the force under General Delamain, and, placing it under the command of General Houghton, directed it to march round the circular marsh northward, and make a flank attack on the Turkish entrenchments that barred the advance of General Delamain's troops.

The general's design was to outflank the enemy with General Houghton's column, and then to combine this column with General Delamain's column, and make another outflanking swoop on the enemy's main system of works around the horse-shoe marsh. The open road round the Circular Marsh seems to have been designed as a trap. There was a Turkish brigade hidden behind some ridges near the northernmost marsh; and so well was it concealed that the reconnoitring airmen do not seem to have suspected its existence. On the other hand, General Houghton's column set out in the darkness and moved so quickly round the marsh that the Turks were taken by surprise.

At 8.20 a.m. General Houghton was able to send a wireless message that he had reached the left rear of the Turkish lines. Thereupon, the skilfully-divided brigades of General Townshend's division attacked. Along the river the flotilla of armed steamers, launches, tugboats, and horse-barges had been bombarding the

Turkish main position since daybreak on September 27. The river fleet, headed by the Comet, first tried to dash in close to the bend in the stream, and work their guns at short range; but the Turks spotted the mastheads and wireless aerials, and they dropped their shells so close that the vessels retired and struck their topmasts. British batteries on shore co-operated at high pressure with the guns of the river fleet, and the armed launches crept closer and closer to the enemy's field batteries and succeeded by noon in killing or scattering the Turkish gun-crews. The ships were hit several times, but no vital damage was done to them. There was, however, one big Turkish gun that could not be silenced. A shore battery managed to get within range by galloping closer. The Turks put one shell into the battery, killing two gunners but that was the last shot the big gun fired, for a hail of shell put it out of action.

In the meantime, General Fry's brigade remained in front of the Horse-shoe position, under a violent fire all day long. A constant stream of shells burst, some hundred yards behind the troops, coming from a group of hostile quick-firers, which seemed to be worked by German gunners. But a more serious menace appeared when, early in the day, the Turkish division south of the river discovered that the camp there was a dummy affair, and about nine o'clock in the morning it crossed the Tigris by a flying bridge and entered fiercely into action.

The larger part of this fresh division was directed beyond the Horse-shoe marsh, in a counter-attack against General Dela-main's column. This column, operating between Suwada marsh and Circular marsh, began its assault at 8.20 a.m. All available British artillery between the marshes was concentrated against a small portion of the enemy's front, and, covered by the fire of the artillery and the machine-guns and rifles of their supports, a double company of the 117th Mahrattas made a desperate rush on the Turkish trenches. Nearly half the Indians were shot down before they reached the trenches; but the remnant, leaping into the enemy's line, forced their way along it with the bayonet. A double company of the 2nd Dorsets was then hurled at the enemy's trenches, and when by furious fighting they also had secured a hold, the rest of the battalion followed. The sappers were consolidating the captured position when the leading troops of General Houghton came into action round the rear of the Circular marsh. All the enemy's northern flank had been stormed in a frontal attack by a battalion and a half of Mahrattas and Dorsets. But the Turks still held courageously to their southern flank, from which they maintained a heavy fire.

Hurrying into action from his position of advantage, General Houghton threw the Oxfords forward with the other battalions of his wearied brigade, and in an action that lasted from half-past ten to two o'clock, the encircled Turkish force was either destroyed or captured.

General Houghton's long-enduring troops were already making steady progress southward to the west of the Suwada marsh. Early in the afternoon the Turkish division that had crossed the river at nine o'clock in the morning opened a furious counter-attack against the wearied brigade, while a force of Turkish cavalry tried to make an outflanking charge. After beating first the Turkish infantry and then the Turkish cavalry, General Houghton's troops still struggled on southward towards the river, a mile or more in the rear of the main Turkish entrenched forces round Horse-shoe marsh. But when the men had almost reached the water and completely encircled the enemy, the heavy Turkish batteries near Kut swept the ground with a storm of shrapnel. General Houghton's column had to draw back, away from the water for which it was thirsting, and rejoin General Delamain's force on the western edge of Suwada marsh. The men had been marching and fighting for thirteen and a half hours, and after General Delamain's force had gone to the assist-ance of General Houghton's column, most of the troops had to be given a rest. At five o'clock General Townshend ordered by wireless, a combined attack on the formidable Horse-shoe lines. General Fry's column, which had been making only very slow progress towards the Turkish centre, was ordered to wait until General Delamain's column got round to the enemy's rear.

Meanwhile, the two brigades under General Delamain and General Houghton wearily tramped along the south-west edge of Suwada marsh, and struck out once more towards the river, behind Nuredin Pasha's main position. Then occurred the most dramatic and extraordinary incident in this eventful day of tropical battle. A Turkish force of several battalions, with four guns, which had probably been detached to guard against General Houghton's outflanking movement, abruptly appeared through attack against the wearied brigade, while a force of Turkish column, when seen, was marching parallel with the British column, about a mile westward and slightly behind it. The effect of this surprising menace was electrical. With amazing rapidity, both brigades, which had seemed about to drop and die for want of water, wheeled to their right, and started to the attack as if it were morning, and they were fresh from sleep and breakfast. In one long, splendid charge, during which they hardly fired a shot, they broke in among the Turks with the bayonet, routed them in a single violent effort, captured all their guns, and shot them down as they fled in the gathering darkness towards the bridge of boats.

It was all over in an hour, and the exhausted troops, overtaken by the night, dropped down exhausted on the scene of their victory. As a result Nuredin Pasha was able in the night to evacuate his fortress, and move his troops across the bridge of boats to the southern bank of the Tigris. From there the Turkish force went by forced marches across the Shat-el-Hai, and on to Azizie, where another system of fortifications had been constructed for the defence of Bagdad. Nuredin was greatly perturbed at the thought of being overtaken by the British troops with their river transport. The first day he marched his men 35 miles towards Bagdad, and the following day they had to do 30 miles in 24 hours. This was no bad marching feat, even for Turkish regular troops, at the end of a Mesopotamian summer.

The Turks got away easily, and in good order. During the night the senior British naval officer, Lieutenant-Commander Cookson, decided to clear the obstruction in the river and give chase to the fleeing Turks. When his ship, the Comet, with two smaller vessels, rounded the headland, the enemy opened fire with rifles, and also reached the ships with hand-bombs. The sailors soon found the wire stretched across the river with dhows made fast to it, but as they were getting over their bows to cut the wire Lieutenant-Commander Cookson, who was leading them, was shot in seven places and killed. The ships retired, and when they steamed up again at daybreak, after burying their commander, they found the Turkish rearguard had vanished, and as a British wreck-party had dynamited the obstruction during the night, the flotilla proceeded to Kut-el-Amara, where the British cavalry were already in possession.

Kut-el-Amara, which General Townshend occupied on September 30, 1915, was 120 miles from Bagdad by road, and

220 miles by water. At about three-quarters of the distance was the riverside town of Azizie. Azizie was about 40 miles by road from Bagdad, and 116 miles by the winding river. The retreating Turkish army made a stand a little to the west of Azizie, to allow time for its engineers to prepare, near Bagdad, the last and most formidable system of defences in Mesopotamia.

Sir John Nixon had taken with him to Mesopotamia orders to submit a plan for an advance on Bagdad. This he had sent to the commander-in-chief in India at the end of August ; but for some reason neither the Viceroy nor the secretary of state was informed of it. However, on October 3 Sir John Nixon wired to the secretary of state: " I consider I am strong enough to open the road to Bagdad, and with this intention I propose to concentrate at Azizie." It would seem that he had in his mind that he could follow up the routed and demoralised Turkish army and reach Bagdad before they could rally.

There were available for General Townshend's force about 15,000 men, but no reserves, the rest of the troops in the area being required for guarding lines of communication. From Basra to Kut, these were 290 miles long: an advance to Bagdad lengthened them to 500 miles. The whole force was worn out by the summer campaign, and the British regiments were 30 per cent. under strength: the promised reinforcements had not even started from home, and even if they had arrived, it would have been a matter of two or three months to get them up to the front. In these circumstances it is not surprising that General Townshend reported early in October that if the advance was to be carried out successfully greater forces than those available would be necessary. Yet blind optimism was the order of the day, and urged as well by political considerations the doomed force went forward.

While the snow was only light on the Caucasian passes, most of the reinforcements for Nuredin Pasha's troops were apparently, hurried up from Syria by the half-built Bagdad railway line. At Azizie, which the British reached on October 13, 1915, it was rumoured that the enemy had already received thousands of fresh troops. General Townshend's division stayed at Azizie until the beginning of November, with part of the Turkish force entrenched four miles up-river. Skirmishing went on daily and hourly, the cavalry and the Royal Horse Artillery being busily and often heavily engaged. Meanwhile, the infantry were energetically digging trenches to strengthen their position against a possible grand attack. Naturally, the British commander would have preferred the enemy to return and attempt to recover his lost prestige among the tribes by flinging his troops on the trenches, while the shore batteries and armed vessels swept the ground with shrapnel. But the pasha, even with reinforcements, would not risk an assault.

The main factor in deciding the advance was probably the confident optimism of Sir John Nixon: the responsibility for the lack of reinforcements must be shared by the British and the Indian governments. Both these bodies seem all through, to have displayed a detachment amounting almost to indifference towards the campaign. For some reason, both Governments decided to let the conquest of Bagdad be a wild gamble, like the Dardanelles affair, instead of taking proper measures to ensure victory, or ordering Sir John Nixon and General Townshend to remain safely on the defensive in the Persian Gulf region, with Kut-el-Amara and Nasiriyeh garrisoned against attacks along the Tigris and Euphrates.

General Townshend continued to perform miracles with a force that never consisted of more than four brigades. Towards the end of October the Turks were so strongly established in their new fortifications near Bagdad that they left only a single brigade in their advanced position near Azizie. This rearguard had a large number of guns, by means of which it held the river against Townshend's gunboats, and pestered his camp with occasional shells. Townshend preserved a grim silence, with the object of lulling the Turk, and making him forget his danger. On one very dark night two British brigades made a long round-about march, with a view to getting on the enemy's rear and encircling him, while a third Indo-British brigade undertook a frontal attack at dawn. But the Turk showed himself capable of learning by experience. On this occasion his outposts were flung far into the desert, apparently with a portable wireless instrument well out on their flank. Long before the wide turning movement threatened their main position, the Turks were in full retreat, taking with them their guns and most of their stores.

The Indo-British division at once embarked in pursuit upon its picturesque flotilla of bellums, launches, paddle-steamers, horse-barges, and gunboats. An unending series of unchartered mud-banks continually interrupted the progress of this extraordinary river armada, boats sticking sometimes for a day on a shoal, and having to wait till steamers arrived to drag them off.

By November 9 General Townshend's officers knew that the great adventure was about to be undertaken. The small British force was set the task of breaking through to Bagdad with a view to linking on with the advanced columns of the Russian army in the Caucasus. One of these columns was rapidly working down the Persian border by Lake Urmia, and another was advancing much farther south towards the city of Hamadan. From Bagdad to Hamadan the distance was 250 miles, across difficult and mountainous country. But it seems to have been thought that, with the Turks beaten at Bagdad, and the German-Swedish-Persian force routed at Hamadan, the task of connecting the troops of Sir John Nixon and the army of the Grand Duke Nicholas would be fairly easy. On November 19 General Townshend's division, having captured the village of Zeur, marched against Nuredin Pasha's main system of defences. These works had been constructed 18 miles from Bagdad, near the ruins of Ctesiphon, half a mile from the Tigris. Nuredin Pasha's army was greatly increased and strongly entrenched at Ctesiphon, with a large reserve of good troops encamped a little farther up the river near Bagdad, and composed probably of forces detached from the Caucasian front during midwinter.

On the morning of November 22 the single Indo-British division stormed the Turks' fortress lines, wiped out an entire enemy division, taking thirteen hundred prisoners and a large quantity of arms, and bivouacked victoriously in the captured works of defence. The Turkish report of the battle, spread through the world from the German wireless stations, estimated the number of British troops at 170,000. As a matter of fact, General Townshend, at an extreme estimate, could not have had more than 25,000 men all told, and his striking force could not have exceeded 12,000 Indian and British infantrymen.

In spite of attacks by the reinforced Turkish army, the British troops held on to the Turkish position at Ctesiphon till the night of November 24, when want of water again robbed them of their full victory, and they had to retire four miles to the Tigris. The position by the river, however, was too weak to be held, and weakened by heavy losses, many battalions being reduced to less than half their strength, a withdrawal was necessary. The wounded were removed to the boats, 1,600 prisoners embarked, and then, after a rearguard action near Azizie, on the night of November 30, the British force retired in perfect order on Kut-el-Amara, fighting rearguard actions all the way. Two river-boats, which had been disabled by the enemy's shell fire, had to be abandoned after their guns and engines had been made useless. The British casualties at Ctesiphon were over 4,560. By December 3, the pursuing Turks were within two hours' march of Kut.

On the same day, the remains of the force which had set out with such high hopes six short weeks before staggered into Kut-el-Amara. Leg-weary, worn with continual desert fighting, they still maintained their high courage and methodically set to work to defend Kut. From west, north, and east the Turks closed in and Kut was a beleaguered town. The Turks, their line of communications fully open behind them, hurried heavy bodies of troops down the river and completely surrounded the place. Then began one of the most heroic, gallant, and long-drawn-out defences ever set down to the credit of British arms.

During the fateful seven days which had wrought such a momentous change in General Townshend's fortunes, he had taken every conceivable precaution to minimise its effects. Defences had been improved. All shipping, with sick and wounded, together with the prisoners captured at Ctesiphon, was despatched to Basra. The only vessel retained was the armed tug Sumana, which had rendered invaluable service during the retreat to Kut, and she was reserved in order to be used as a ferry-boat.

The adventures of the river flotilla in the interval deserve record. The heterogeneous fleet commanded by Captain Nunn, D.S.O., often under fire from both banks of the river, had afforded inestimable assistance in protecting the steamers and barges and refloating them when they took the ground, a matter of frequent occurrence. The shifting shoals and shallows of the treacherous Tigris served the enemy well. The Shaitan had stranded on the evening of November 28, and defied all efforts of the Firefly and Shushan to get her off, though they were fortunately successful in salving all her guns and stores. The hull, however, had eventually to be left.

On the morning of December 1, the Turks attacked the British at Umm-el-Jubail, but the Firefly, in company with the Comet, after making good practice on the attackers, received a shot in her boiler which completely disabled her. Her consort the Comet (Captain Nunn) immediately took her in tow; but luck was against them. As they were turning down stream in the narrow channel both vessels grounded. The strength of the current, combined with the dead weight of the Firefly, which was pressing against her, forced the Comet more and more deeply into the bank. Finding that his own position was hopeless until assistance arrived, Captain Nunn devoted all his energies to getting the Firefly clear, and finally succeeded in sending her careering down stream in the hope that she would escape.

The Sumana speedily came to the Comet's assistance, but all efforts to dislodge her proved unsuccessful. Meanwhile the enemy's fire had increased greatly in intensity. Several field-guns had been brought up within short range and were directed upon the two ships. They were, moreover, the target for the Turkish infantry, which poured volley after volley into them, and the Firefly (which had speedily taken ground again) at a distance of fifty yards. Very soon it became evident that the Firefly and the Comet would have to be abandoned, for each was badly damaged and in flames. Under an inferno of shot, shell, and rifle fire, the operation of rendering the guns useless and transferring the crews and stores to the Sumana, which seemed to bear a charmed life, was successfully accomplished.

On the same day, December 1, a fine feat of endurance was performed by the mixed brigade commanded by Major-General Sir Charles Mellis, V.C., consisting of the 30th Infantry and 1/5th Hants (Howitzer) Battery R.F.A., and the 16th Cavalry Brigade. It had been sent on, after taking part in the engagement at Umm-el-Jubail, to deal with hostile mounted troops which were interfering with the passage of steamers at Chubibat, some twenty-five miles below Kut. It became necessary to recall them, the increasing strength of the enemy rendering General Townshend anxious to concentrate his forces. So the mixed brigade retraced its steps, having marched eighty miles in three days, during one of which they had been engaged in fighting, and regained Kut without losing a single prisoner.

On the day previous to the completion of the investment (December 6), the cavalry brigade, with the exception of one squadron retained at Kut, and a convoy of transport animals was marched to Imam Ali Gherbi, some fifty miles down the river, there to be reinforced by infantry and guns from Basra.

They fought a rearguard action all the way, but fortunately with few casualties. Behind this detachment a force under Lieut.-General Aylmer, V.C., was collected with the object of relieving Kut as soon as concentration had been completed.

At Kut, the Tigris takes one of its innumerable bends in the shape of the letter U. Upon the peninsula thus formed, of about a mile in width and less than three-quarters of a mile in depth, General Townshend occupied an entrenched position, the village —it scarcely deserves the designation of a town—lying at the most southerly end. He also held the liquorice factory situated on the right bank, which he fortified and garrisoned with two battalions. To the east lay a bridge of boats covered by a bridge-head detachment on the right bank. The besieged were well supplied with stores and ammunition, but after the losses at Ctesiphon, there were only 10,000 men available for defence. Four Turkish divisions lay around the town.

General Townshend having complete confidence in himself and his troops, returned a determined refusal to Nuredin Pasha's summons to surrender. On December 9 the Turks made a fierce attack upon the bridge-head in sufficient force to oblige the defenders, who of necessity were compelled to husband their resources to retire. On the following night, December 9-10, the bridge itself was destroyed by a party of the Gurkha Rifles. During the next three days a continuous bombardment ensued, and a series of attacks was delivered, all of which were successfully repulsed, particularly on December 12, when the enemy's casualties in two days amounted to a thousand men. So far the casualties of the besieged force had only amounted to 470.

Of the difficulties in the path of the relieving force, the chief was the question of transport on the Tigris. The carrying capacity of the river, notwithstanding the ever-increasing number of craft of all descriptions and sizes which crowded it, was still inadequate. As far as Kurna, where the Euphrates joins it and they together flow seaward under the name of the Shat-el-Arab, the Tigris is navigable for ocean-going steamers of moderate draught ; but once above it, troubles not only begin but multiply. A draught of anything over five feet means certain and constant grounding, a source of interminable delay, and progress except in the flood season is a matter of impossibility at night.

The transports upon which the carriage of stores depended were mostly paddle-steamers drawing between four and five feet of water with a capacity of about five hundred tons. Each of them towed a couple of lighters, and together they moved no faster than the army which it was their business to keep supplied with the necessities of life. To every brigade was allotted a parent ship which met its wants, and was in turn supplied by attendant mahailas, craft peculiar to the river, and presenting with their high-sloping masts, lateen sails, pointed bows, and lofty stern an exceedingly picturesque appearance. They again were fed by the bellums described in a previous chapter.

When all other means of water transport were wanting, the navy enlisted the services of the gufar, which lays claim, not without justification, to be considered the oldest craft in the world. The gufar is built on the same principle as the Welsh coracle, but is completely circular in shape. An enormous basket covered with skins, or plastered with pitch, answering neither to the impulse of sail nor the control of rudder, it is cast upon the waters at any point between Tekrit and Amara—where, urged downward at varying degrees of speed by the current, it spins its way to its destination carrying a cargo according to its capacity and a complement of two men.

It became apparent at an early stage in the Mesopotamian campaign, that the relations between the Home and Indian governments were not tuned to the same note of mutual understanding and co-ordination which—none too soon—had been struck with such admirable precision in the concert of the Allies. The inevitable result—discord in lieu of harmony—ensued. As regards the medical service, the lack of co-operation between the two centres of authority was particularly and painfully noticeable. The whole organization of the medical department was deficient ; field hospitals were too few in number, while those which did exist were inadequately equipped.

Demand considerably exceeded supply. At Ctesiphon the available medical staff could give adequate attention and assistance to five hundred men. Nine times that number were in urgent need of both. Owing solely to lack of medical and nursing aid, the condition of even the slightly wounded was pitiful. Case after case was reported of officers and men, under the most trying climatic conditions, whether of heat or of cold, being left for days with no attention to injuries beyond that of the first dressing in the field, sometimes barely that; thrown into the same barges as stores, munitions, and horses; as many as six hundred under the charge of a single doctor and one orderly. The same conditions prevailed in the ocean-going steamers which transported the wounded from Basra to Bombay. That so many of the wounded died before they reached India, is one of the greater tragedies of this campaign, and one of the least excusable.

A lamentable spirit of parsimony, and of unconsidering optimism seemed to colour the counsels of the Indian government. Complaints of shortage were not restricted to medical officers, nurses, and supplies. They applied in ever-increasing volume to the deficiency of munitions, bombs and hand-grenades in particular, which played so prominent a part in the war, and whereof the troops in Mesopotamia stood badly in need. When they did arrive, at irregular intervals, the quality left much to be desired, and reflected seriously upon the source of their manufacture.

About other matters of grave import, the same conditions existed. River transport was unsuitable and scanty, and there was a lack of telephones and signalling apparatus. Whilst the Turks were busy with their railway line the British, with railway material at hand, did nothing.

To return to the beleaguered garrison at Kut. On December 14, 1915, the two battalions occupying the liquorice factory rushed the enemy's trenches, which were only two hundred and fifty yards away. Three days later a sally resulted in the bayoneting of thirty Turks. As Christmas approached, the fury of the enemy's attacks increased. He had received a formidable addition to his strength by the arrival of the 52nd division. Christmas Day saw the besieged hard pressed indeed. The garrison of the fort was unable to withstand a furious attack, and had to evacuate its position; but not for long, as a determined counter-attack, in which the enemy was repulsed, enabled the British to regain the lost ground.

Fighting of a desperate nature went on during the whole of Christmas Day, and was continued far into the small hours of the following day. Shortly before midnight a fierce onslaught was made on the northern bastion and a temporary footing secured. Forced to retire with heavy losses, the enemy came on again and again, striving to rush the breaches which had been made in the walls, and hurling innumerable bombs. But it was to no purpose, for their indomitable courage was opposed by a valour greater, and as the day broke they withdrew. On the 24th and 25th the British had lost over three hundred of their already depleted numbers. On the other hand, the enemy's losses were sufficiently heavy to warrant his asking on December 29 for an armistice to enable him to bury his dead and remove his wounded, who lay in heaps in front of the fort. During the first month of the siege the British casualties were 1,840; the Turkish were probably not less than 4,000. Finding it impossible to take the position by assault, except at a sacrifice of life which he was not prepared to make, Nuredin Pasha changed his tactics, and prepared to reduce it by starvation, keeping up a bombardment of an intermittent nature.

The grim spectre of hunger had not yet made an actual appearance, but its shadow was gradually creeping over the devoted defenders of Kut. Hopes of speedy relief still ran high within its walls, and of rations, if on a reduced scale, there were yet enough to go round. There were always the horses. Fortunately, on January 24, a large quantity of privately stored grain was discovered. The find proved of incalculable value. To reduce it to flour was now the difficulty. Grinding operations for so large a force were beyond the capacity of the solitary mill. In answer to Townshend's call, friendly aeroplanes dropped a large number of millstones into soft places.

Oil stored in the naval barges supplied the deficiency of fuel, which by this time was running short. General Townshend, with admirable forethought, had planted vegetable seeds, anticipating that he would shortly have to cope with the scourge of scurvy. So, indeed, it proved; and by the first week in February, by which time the stores of green food, rice, and sugar had run dry, and the milk at the hospital was reduced to a supply for ten days, the garrison was forced to add the bane of this disease to the sum of its sufferings.

Tobacco was at an end, and although some cigarettes were dropped by aeroplane the troops were reduced to smoking lime leaves, ginger and used tea leaves. All the horses and mules were slaughtered; one of the last to go being an Indian army mule which had served in three campaigns and was for a time reprieved at the earnest request of the men. The British troops were then receiving a daily ration of a twelve-ounce loaf of mixed wheat and barley flour, one pound of meat and a few dates and groceries.

CHAPTER 30

Battle of the Dvina

THE German attempts to bring about a complete encircling movement against the Russians had been unsuccessful mainly owing to the failure of their armies to move at a sufficient speed. In Galicia, Mackensen had progressed at the rate of three miles a day; but after the fall of Warsaw and Ivangorod his pace slackened to two miles a day, and ended at scarcely more than one mile a day. By the time he captured Brest-Litovsk, and arrived on the edge of the Pripet marsh, it was close on September, and wanted barely two weeks before the first fall of heavy autumn rain turned the earth-made roads into mud channels and the summer-dried surface of the marshes into yielding death-traps.

These climatic and physical factors had, of course, been taken into consideration by the Russians. Throughout the great retreat the Russian staff had chiefly been fighting for time, with a view to using the marshes in autumn as a defence against the enemy's heavy artillery. The first design of the Russian staff was to pit the lakes and morasses round the Niemen against Hindenburg's howitzers, and place the Pripet marsh in front of Mackensen's siege train, with the Bielovieska forest as the central link between the two boggy fronts. But the unexpected suddenness of the fall of Kovno, the chief fortress of the Niemen, made the execution of this design impossible. In the north, the Petrograd army of defence under General Russky had to withdraw its left wing from Kovno, and make a fighting retreat to the intricate lake district between Vilna, Smorgon, and Dvinsk.

Northward towards Riga, Russky's army still held to the river-line of the Dvina, with another immense stretch of lakeland behind it, which was being fortified by the peasantry of the Vitebsk and Pskov governments, as the ultimate line of defence for Petrograd. General Russky regarded his position as impregnable. Riga he was ready to lose in case of dire necessity, as his main scheme of defence was based upon the lake district, the rains of autumn, and the frosts of winter. Meanwhile, he held on to Riga in spite of the fact that on September 1, 1915, one of Eichhorn's group of armies, consisting of a very strong force under General von Lauenstein, had approached within fifteen miles of the famous seaport.

All the principal Russian generals, except one, were beginning to feel confident. Russky was gathering increased strength in the north, owing to the progress of munition making in the Petrograd region. On the southern wing General Ivanoff, with his brilliant army leaders, Brusiloff and Lechitsky and Cherbachoff, was growing stronger as the Russian factories increased their output, and products of the munition works of Japan reached his troops. The central Russian army, working north of the Pripet marsh and defending the Moscow line, was also growing stronger, after escaping at last from the siege trains of both Mackensen and Hindenburg.

After the fall of Kovno and Brest-Litovsk the lines held by General Evert's army formed another salient of great size on the Russian front. Hindenburg thereupon designed to concentrate in immense force against Evert with a view to retrieving his own mistakes and Mackensen's lack of decisive success. It was still the German aim to envelop and annihilate both Evert's and Alexeieff's armies. The main features of the scheme was a vast cavalry raid on the railway junction of Molodetchno, between Vilna and Minsk, and the larger part of the German and Austrian cavalry, numbering about 40,000 sabres, was collected for the purpose near Kovno, under General von Schmettau, with 600,000 German infantry behind them. It was foreseen that the thrust against the new Russian centre would be answered with a fierce counter-thrust by the northern Russian army under General Russky. The northern German wing, therefore, entrenched along a line of sandhills and stone-built farmhouses, turning the buildings into machine-gun redoubts, and bringing up more guns and shells to strengthen the fortified line.

While this work was proceeding, the German staff made two skilful moves to weaken the Russian centre. It was expected that the Russian staff would be well acquainted with the fact that Mackensen's chief forces had been redistributed after the fall of Brest-Litovsk, leaving the German centre weaker than the Russian. Naturally, the Russian staff would want to know to what new use Mackensen's troops would be put. Hindenburg, therefore, arranged that it should seem as though the direct, straightforward method of reinforcing the two Austro-German wings was being followed. In other words, it was made to appear that General von Lauenstein and General von Morgon would be strengthened round Riga with the object of an attack on Petrograd, while Böhm-Ermolli, Bothmer, and Pflanzer would be reinforced in Galicia, to attack Kieff.

The idea, of course, was to induce the Russian commander-in-chief to strengthen both his wings at the expense of his centre, so that the great German central thrust towards Minsk and Moscow would meet with less resistance. Undoubtedly, the project was well designed, and the Russian commanders all along the front were at a serious disadvantage in regard to the modern method of reconnaissance, owing to the superior numbers and equipment of the hostile aircraft. For nearly all practical purposes the Germans seem to have temporarily won the mastery of the air during the great retreat, with the result that they could conduct in comparative secrecy their new concentrations of great striking forces.

They opened their misleading attack on the Russian wings by a fierce attack on the fords of the Dvina, below Riga, and by a sudden assault, at the end of August, on the southernmost Russian positions along the Zlota Lipa and the Dniester. The attacks on the Dvina fords, near Kreuzburg, were repulsed, but the armies of Pflanzer and Bothmer carried by storm the Zlota Lipa lines, and forced the passage of the river, throwing Brusiloff's forces eastward towards the Strypa river. At the same time the army under Böhm-Ermolli advanced on Zloczow, and crossed the mountains where the Bug and Sereth rivers rise on the road to Dubno and Rovno. Then at Lutzk, a few marches north of Dubno, Linsingen's army progressed by fierce fighting along the southern edge of the Pripet marsh, in order to connect with the Austrian armies and menace Kieff.

This series of converging strokes against Ivanoff's southern army was calculated to perturb the Russian staff. It was not effected by any abrupt accession of courage in the troops or skill in their commanders; the result was merely obtained by greatly reinforcing the Austrian lines with Skoda guns from Mackensen's command and reserve troops that were no longer needed by the Archduke Joseph Ferdinand. A division of the Prussian Guard was also railed up through Lemberg for the movement of assault with another German division. Brusiloff's men, though strongly entrenched along a deep, winding river-course, were unexpectedly overwhelmed by a storm of shell fire from heavier artillery, heavier than that against which they had hitherto been contending. Their trenches were blown up by 8 in. and 12 in. shells, but though they were forced to retire, they made a desperate stand between the two rivers, and thus won time to strengthen their second line on the Strypa.

Again they were attacked all along the front from the Dneister to the southern fringe of the Pripet marsh, during the last two days in August and the first two days in September. Lutzk was lost, and Brody and Dubno, and the line of the Strypa river, and the enemy began to press strongly against the Galician railway junction of Tarnopol and the main Russian southern fortress of Rovno. Had Tarnopol fallen, the Russians would have completely lost their footing in eastern Galicia, and their chance of still connecting with Rumania along the Austro-Rumanian frontier. Had Rovno fallen, the road to Kieff and Odessa, the Black Sea, and Constantinople would have been open. The menace was thus a very serious one, and it seems to have been backed by a large part of the men and guns in Mackensen's group of armies. The railway from Brest-Litovsk to Lemberg had enabled the central Austro-German forces to be rapidly moved against Ivanoff's southern army group.

Mackensen delayed his Serbian adventure in order to direct in person, with the bulk of the new Danube army reinforcing Pflanzer's, Bothmer's, Böhm-Ermolli's, and Linsingen's forces, the sudden and very violent movement against Ivanoff's armies; for if Mackensen had succeeded in this drive towards Kieff and Odessa, he would have been able to exert a pressure on Rumania, on both sides of her frontier. Thus the violent attack on the southern Russian armies was a campaign of importance as high as the advance against the Serbians which followed it. The march towards Kieff and the Black Sea ports promised large results more speedily than the subsequent attempt to burst through the Serbian mountains. Indeed, Serbia was not seriously threatened until the greater movement was fought to a standstill. Meanwhile, General Ivanoff was not the kind of man to remain passive under hostile pressure. For some months his forces in Galicia and the Russian province of Volhynia had stood quietly on the defensive, guarding southern Russia, and drawing on the local factories and troop depots for small quantities of ammunition and small drafts. After the fall of Brest-Litovsk, the huge wedge of the Pripet marsh practically transformed Ivanoff's command into the independent army of southern Russia. Until the end of August Ivanoff's men lived on the resources of the Kieff and Odessa regions, with the Volhynian triangle of fortresses—Lutzk, Dubno, and Rovno— strengthening their flank near the Pripet marsh. But when Mackensen's guns and men returned to Galicia and were allotted to the forces of Linsingen, Böhm-Ermolli, Bothmer, and Pflanzer, General Ivanoff appealed to his commander-in-chief for heavy artillery and more rifles and ammunition. A large part of the supplies of munitions obtained from Japan reached him by the beginning of September, 1915.

When Ivanoff was in a position to strike back, he had to select the most telling point for his counter-stroke. He chose Tarnopol. It was his railhead in Galicia, by which he was directly connected with Odessa and Kieff. Tarnopol was more important to him than Rovno. It was a source of political prestige, as it lay in Austrian territory, and it was a great military base, by reason of its direct railway communications with the chief cities of southern Russia. There was also the advantage of quickness of movement from Tarnopol, as the fresh supply of munitions poured by railway directly into the town, and no delay in distribution was occasioned. So Ivanoff answered the unexpected blow by Mackensen, which had been delivered south-east of Lemberg at Brzezany, by an equally unexpected counter-blow delivered from the region of Tarnopol.

For the first time on the eastern front the German and Austrian troops were subjected to a heavy bombardment of high-explosive shells. To add to the difficulties of the enemy, the weather became very rainy at the beginning of September, with the result that the rough country roads in eastern Galicia were churned by the motor traffic into impassable swamps. All the mechanical transport, on which the Germans relied for quickness of manœuvre, was put out of action. It needed six horses to drag one motor vehicle, and the labour knocked up the ordinary army horse in a few days. Everywhere supply columns were bogged, and the task of providing the troops with food and munitions was terribly difficult. The condition of the ground grew worse on the north of General Ivanoff's front, which extended into the Pripet marsh along the lines of the

Styr and Goryn rivers, guarding the railway embankment running across the swamps and linking Pinsk with Rovno.

There were many morasses between the Styr and the Goryn, and the swamps were overtopped by hills, on which were the Russian forces entrenched with field-guns. General Ivanoff did not rely upon the Volhynian triangle of fortresses—Lutzk, Dubno, and Rovno—but based his northern wing on the more northerly village of Derajno, from which branched three small lines of light railways, connecting with the munitioning centre of Rovno. With the light railways he was able to waste Linsingen's forces by constantly moving to and fro between the Styr and the Goryn; for with his three light railways he could concentrate rapidly on a wide marshy front, and destroy the German troops mired between the rivers. In their attacks the Russians seldom went in pursuit farther than Kolki on the Styr, about 12 miles from the central light railway-head.

Tarnopol, in Galicia, however, remained the grand striking point for the southern Russian army, and it was against Tarnopol that Mackensen directed his main effort. In the first week of September the German commander brought up hundreds of his heaviest siege-guns by the railway running from Lemberg to Zloczov, and thence to Zborov towards Tarnopol. A division of the Prussian Guard—the 3rd division—with the 48th reserve division, and an Austrian brigade, advanced from Zborov on the night of September 7, for an assault on Tarnopol. Then, eighteen miles farther south, near the little riverside town of Trembovla, an Austrian army, with Skoda siege-guns, also advanced to break the Russian line on the Sereth, hoping thus to destroy Ivanoff's forces in Galicia.

Ivanoff, however, was not only a great general, but he had in his lieutenants, Brusiloff, Lechitsky, and Cherbachoff, three men who had experienced hurricane fire before, and were able to some extent to meet it. The two Russian armies moved out from their trenches in the darkness of the September night, followed by a strong force of Cossack cavalry, and squadrons of armoured motor-cars carrying machine-guns; and they were used along the road from Tarnopol to Zloczov in a daring manner. When the German and Austrian siege-guns began the usual hurricane fire on the Russian trenches, those trenches were empty. The troops which had held them were already breaking through the German and Austrian lines of advanced infantry, groping for the columns behind the skirmishing screens, and massing machine-guns on their flanks. As soon as the infantry struggle had so mixed the troops that the artillery on either side could not fire into the field of carnage, the new heavy Russian guns lifted on the enemy's arc of siege artillery, producing one of the great surprises of the war.

The German line was broken, but the arc of siege-guns was not reached by the Cossacks until daylight on September 8. Then, by massed shrapnel fire, the great guns and howitzers broke up the first charging squadrons of cavalry. The Cossacks, nevertheless, captured a large number of men and many guns. The enemy retired in haste to the Strypa river. The Russians followed them up, taking more prisoners and guns, and by September 12 the total Austro-Hungarian losses were sufficiently heavy to delay the contemplated new move against Serbia.

After the comparative failure of Mackensen, the German staff had one source of hope left. The new Russian army general, Evert, had hung too long on to the last great frontier fortress of Grodno. Grodno did not fall until the afternoon of September 3, 1915. General Evert stayed in Grodno till he had cleared it of everything and blown up all the works, bridges, railways, and buildings useful for military purposes. While he did so, the Vilna army with General Russky's southern wing held up a great German turning movement along the Vilia river, at a distance of nearly 100 miles north-west of Grodno. But this far-stretched Russian operation of retirement was in the circumstances daring to the point of national peril. Had General Evert been fully aware that Hindenburg was holding in reserve for a terrible lightning stroke a force of 40,000 cavalry with a hundred and forty pieces of horse artillery, and a large supporting army of infantry, he would not have waited to strip Grodno of every gun and shell. Evert's army was not harried in the first days of its retreat. A little pressure was exerted against it at Orany, where the great Trans-European railway line passed through the Grodno-Vilna section, on the route to Petrograd.

It was, however, not at Evert's army that Hindenburg was immediately striking. He designed to capture it only by the way, making a double turning movement against the northern army under Russky and against the central army under Alexeieff's successor. His point of attack was the railway junction at Molodetchno, nearly 150 miles in the rear of Grodno.

He intended to reach it by breaking through Russky's southern
wing in a hurricane of shell fire followed by the greatest cavalry
charge in modern history. All this part of the work was to be
done by Litzmann's army with Kovno as its base and
Schmettau's cavalry as its advanced guard. On the Niemen
front, facing the rearguard of Evert's army, was the army of
Scholtz, whose southern wing curled round Grodno and linked
with the army of Gallwitz, which was advancing north of the
Bielovska forest towards the town of Lida.

Still farther south, was the army of Prince Leopold of Bavaria,
connecting in turn southward with a large mixed force
of Landsturm and Landwehr troops, operating very slowly
along the Pripet marsh. The southernmost inferior force did
little more than hold the Russians by marsh entrenchments
bristling with machine-guns. The hammer blow against
Alexeieff's old army and the former Lublin and Cholm army
was designed to fall on their northern flank, when Prince Leopold
reached the railway junction of Baranovitschi. But all this
part of the front was, for the time, of little importance.

The critical sector was that between Sventsiany, on the
Petrograd railway, half-way from Vilna and Dvinsk, and
Baranovitschi, the railway junction between Minsk and Pinsk.
It was Russky who foresaw the extreme peril of the situation.
He came down from the Riga-Dvinsk sector on September 1,
and hurried Evert out of Grodno. Evert worked downwards
in a north-easterly direction towards Baranovitschi and Pinsk,
to counter the upward thrust of Gallwitz's and Prince Leopold's
armies. This part of the operation was just straightforward
hard fighting and incessant manœuvring all along the northern
curve of the huge salient, from Skidel, near Grodno, and thence
along the Upper Niemen, past the towns of Lida, Slonim, and
Novo Grodek to the critical railway junction at Baranovitschi.
The northern wing of Alexeieff's former army group co-operated
with Evert's retreating forces and greatly assisted in the defence
of the southern dent in the salient.

All the desperate difficulties of the great Russian retreat from
the last and most dangerous salient fell upon General Russky.
Coming down from the north, with part of the Petrograd army
of defence, he boldly threw a considerable portion of his forces
into the salient, bringing up the number of troops enclosed in
it to about 400,000. He reckoned that he would be half-encircled

by 600,000 German troops, and his estimate was correct. But
he does not seem to have been fully aware of the existence of
the 40,000 horsemen, with 140 guns, under Schmettau, who
moved his men by night northward towards Sventsiany, as
Russky pushed his men northwards towards Vilna.

Russky fixed on the angle between the Sventa and Vilia rivers,
between Kovno and Vilna, as the region of the German turning
movement. On September 1 he placed two divisions of the
Russian imperial guard on a hill, some seven hundred feet high,
by the village of Meiszagola. The position was 18 miles north-
west of Vilna, on the road to Vilkomir. It completely barred
the turning movement with infantry forces which General
Litzmann, the conqueror of Kovno, had been ordered to carry
out, for the famous imperial guard, a body of 24,000 bayonets,
with a considerable number of field batteries, fought with great
tenacity. For ten days and ten nights the battle lasted in a
narrow valley at the foot of the hill, below the trenches of the
guardsmen, whose well-designed earthworks became afterwards
the object of admiration of German soldiers. The Germans had
at last to haul up their siege-guns from Kovno, and after the
trenches were flattened out by a storm of big shells on
September 12, the guardsmen, reduced to the number of a
single division, made a slow rearguard fight across the low,
rolling hill country, trenching on every line of crests, and six
days' more fighting had to be done before the Germans got into
Vilna, on September 18, and found the city emptied.

As a matter of fact, Litzmann's army could not have entered
Vilna unaided, even with the aid of its siege ordnance. The
imperial guard at last retired before the shattered German army,
because of a startling event that happened some 50 miles farther
north. Here, near the town of Sventsiany, on the night of
September 14, the great enemy cavalry force under General
Schmettau found a gap in the overstretched line of Russky's
armies. Thence they were to drive down to Smorgon, along the
river line to the Vilia, entrench there, advance, with Smorgon
as their base of operations, and cut the railways to Minsk and
to Polozk and Petrograd at the junction of Molodetchno. This
they accomplished, in a movement of magnificent speed and
force, by September 17. They broke apart Russky's Dvinsk
and Vilna wings and penetrated his centre at Molodetschno,
which is 60 miles south-eastwards of Vilna. And Vilna at the

time had not been evacuated. The imperial guard was still defending the city, the earthwork defences of which were being bombarded uninterruptedly day and night. Meanwhile, south of the Vilia, a large German army was fighting on the Merechanka river, while still stronger enemy forces were making deeper turning movements south-eastward towards Lida and Slonim.

To all appearance, the Russians had not been in so perilous a position since Dimitrieff was broken between Tarnov and Gorlice, near the Carpathian line. Indeed, with 40,000 German horsemen 60 miles behind him, with 140 guns, and huge infantry supports coming to reinforce them, the situation of Russky seemed darkened by the shadow of impending doom. If Russky's side of the salient were suddenly driven in near the base, Evert's side of the salient would be quickly subjected to a similar cutting thrust. Then, with both Russky and Evert's forces partly enveloped and partly outflanked, the position of the central Russian armies round Pinsk and the Pripet marsh would also be disastrous.

The success of the German plan depended to a great extent on the weather. The German general staff had timed the blow with due regard to this factor, for meteorological records showed that September was the best month for operations in the Russian marsh district; the drying effect of the August sun made the morasses and swamps to some extent passable. But the summer of 1915 was a wet one, and the marsh roads had been soaked by August rain instead of being dried by August sun. The result was that Schmettau's force failed to achieve its full purpose for want of infantry support. Owing to this weakness, which continually increased through the delay in the advance of the German infantry and artillery, Schmettau's menace to Russky was nothing so great as Russky's menace to Schmettau.

After fighting for fourteen days in the salient, Russky preserved in his rear a passage 80 miles wide, from Molodetchno Junction to the Lebeda river between Grodno and Lida. It was wide enough for the largest army to pass through; it had two main roads and two lines of railway. It was indeed so broad and secure that, instead of rapidly retreating through it, General Russky entrenched on a line of hills and streams from Lida to Molodetchno, with a little cross-country railway running immediately behind his line, provisioning and munitioning the army. As soon as the tired German infantry arrived near the Russian lines they were flung forth in wide waves through curtains of shrapnel against the Russian hill trenches. Fighting went on day and night till the end of September on a gradually flattening curve stretching from a point near Slonim in the south to Sventsiany in the north. The Russians were well provided with artillery, machine guns, and munitions. By September 28 Russky was still holding out, well inside the salient on the Smorgon line, having fought Hindenburg to a standstill. The movement of envelopment had entirely failed. Everywhere the Russians were fighting for time. They had new levies, amounting to 4,000,000 men, which they were arming and training by the hundred thousand, as rifles and guns came from Japan.

Towards the beginning of December, Falkenhayn made one last effort to reach a more favourable line of fortified entrenchments. Linsingen and Ermolli, who had been trying for ten weeks to conquer Sarny and Rovno, gave up all attempts to make a serious advance, and dug themselves in near the Rumanian frontier. What fresh troops were immediately available were sent far north to Mitau, where Hindenburg made one more essay to capture Riga.

He selected for attack the large river island of Dalen, lying in the Dvina within gunshot of Riga. He advanced against this island from the south along the little stream Berse which flows into the Dvina at the farmstead of Bersemunde, fourteen miles south of the coveted seaport. The farm was captured by the Germans on November 24, and preparations were made to occupy the river peninsula to pass over to Dalen island, and thence force a passage across the Dvina at a spot where a series of islets half-bridged the main western stream. As a matter of fact, Hindenburg's forces had twice won a footing on Dalen island since the summer of 1915, and they had been driven out of it owing to their weak hold upon some dominating hills in the neighbourhood. These hills rose along the Berse stream near the farmstead, and on November 24, 1915, the Germans, besides occupying the farm and all the area between the rivers, stormed and occupied the heights.

The positions they had won, quite close to the city, and with excellent means of crossing the river, seemed to promise victory at a time when all hope of further conquest had been abandoned.

But most of the heavy guns had to be brought around the Tirul swamp, and across the marshy land and forests farther south, where both the Courland guerrilla bands and the Russian scouting parties were working actively; and long before the guns and reinforcements arrived, Dmitrieff, while repulsing an advance on Kemmern designed to distract his forces from the points of importance, launched a division against the lost farmstead and hills. For three days the struggle went on with increasing fury. The farmstead was recovered and lost and again recovered. Then after a hill had been carried and some machine-guns captured, the enemy was pressed back and thrown over the Berse. As in most of the struggles round Riga, the Russians had but few prisoners to show the extent of their victory.

The first new Russian army, which was armed too late to help Serbia, became ready to take the field in the last week of December, 1915. Had General Alexeieff, been able to choose his attacking point, he could have broken the German front as soon as the frost solidified the marshlands. The German centre especially was very weak, and as the Russian gunners had some millions of shells for immediate use, they could have equalled the hurricane fire effect of Mackensen's batteries. But the need of bringing pressure to bear on Bulgaria and helping Rumania to retain her freedom of action, and assisting the Serbians in Albania, compelled the Russian commander to attack the enemy on his right wing. In other words, General Ivanoff received the new army as a reinforcement, with orders to begin a strong offensive movement against the German and Austrian troops on the Styr and Strypa. The movement developed on December 30, 1915, and its immediate effect was to bring the famous German marshal August von Mackensen in haste from Serbia, check the Austro-German-Bulgarian attack upon the Franco-British camp at Salonica, and relieve the pressure upon the Serbian and Italian troops in Albania.

CHAPTER 30

The War in the Air

THOSE who, some few years before the Great War, crowded to the flying meetings and watched with fascination those gallant pioneers of aviation—the Wrights, Blériot, Hubert Lathan, Bertram Dickson, Colonel Cody, and the rest—disporting themselves in space, little guessed that they were assisting at the development of a science which was calculated to affect war more deeply than any invention since the magazine rifle. For the aeroplane has revolutionised warfare. Its effect has been more far-reaching than even the most sanguine supporter of the new arm ever dared to prophesy.

The two years before the War were years of progress and fruitful work. In April, 1912, the Royal Flying Corps was constituted by a Royal Warrant, and consisted of a naval wing and a military wing. In time the Royal Flying Corps Naval Wing dropped out of use as an official name, its place being taken by the Royal Naval Air Service; and the Royal Flying Corps became a sufficient description of what was a distinctively military body. After several fatalities to aviation in monoplanes, an order was issued by the War Office forbidding the use of monoplanes in the Royal Flying Corps, and training work at the Central Flying School at Upavon was at first delayed by this ban on monoplanes. In August, 1912, military aeroplane trials were held on Salisbury Plain.

An experimental branch was formed in March, 1913, under Major Herbert Musgrave, to whose work is due much of the success of British aviation. In the spring of 1914 a headquarters flight was placed at his disposal. When the War came, the headquarters flight was broken up, but the wireless section was attached for a time to No. 4 Squadron, and in September, 1914, a headquarters wireless unit was formed at Fère-en-Tardenois, in France, with Major Musgrave in command. From this unit the whole wireless telegraphy organization of the Royal Flying Corps was gradually developed. In December, 1914, the unit was enlarged, and became No. 9 Squadron stationed at headquarters. Having worked out all details for the supply of wireless machines to the squadrons in the field, Major Musgrave in March, 1915, left the Royal Flying Corps to take up duty with the staff of the Army. He was severely wounded in August, 1916, and in June, 1918, was killed inside the German lines.

With the original British Expeditionary Force the Royal Flying Corps took the field under the command of brigadier-general Sir David Henderson. Arrangements had been made some months earlier for its mobilization. The squadrons flew to France, and after a brief period at Amiens, headquarters and the majority of the Corps moved to Maubeuge and began to carry out reconnaissances over Belgium. The early reports of the observers gave valuable information as to the movements of the German troops.

When the retreat from Mons was ordered, the headquarters of the Royal Flying Corps was moved from Maubeuge to Le Cateau, and afterwards to various other places. While the aerodromes were being changed, reconnaissances were still being undertaken and produced useful information. Sir John French in his first dispatch spoke thus of the admirable work of the Royal Flying Corps:

> Their skill, energy, and perseverance have been beyond all praise. They have furnished me with the most complete and accurate information, which has been of incalculable value in the conduct of operations. Fired at constantly both by friend and foe, and not hesitating to fly in every kind of weather, they have remained undaunted throughout. Further, by actually fighting in the air, they have succeeded in destroying five of the enemy's machines.

The French commander-in-chief also paid tribute to their skill. Joffre's message ran:

> Please express most particularly to Marshal French my thanks for the services rendered to us every day by the English Flying Corps. The precision, exactitude, and regularity of the news brought in by them are evidence of their perfect organization and also of the perfect training of pilots and observers.

Important work was done in the photographing of enemy positions, and the early photography by the Royal Flying Corps was the forerunner of that immense photographic map of the western front in thousands of sections, constantly renewed, which played a great part in the later stages of the War.

During the fighting that took place in the spring and summer of 1915—the second Battle of Ypres, the British offensive on May 9 against the Fromelles ridge, the operations in the Festubert region and about the ruined Château of Hooge—aeroplanes continued to play their part quietly, modestly, usefully. But it was in the great Franco-British advance on September 25 that the airmen on the British front again had a great opportunity for showing what they had learnt in thirteen months' active service. They availed themselves of their opportunity to the full, and once more earned the admiration of the enemy and the warm eulogy of their commanders.

Probably all previous records for air mileage were eclipsed by the Royal Flying Corps in the three weeks or so preceding the British advance against Loos on September 25, 1915. The weather was by no means invariably favourable, but, notwithstanding this, the airmen were out daily on reconnaissances of the enemy trenches, watching for any indication of the Germans being aware of the great events taking place, or of taking measures to meet the " big push." On more than one occasion British aeroplanes remained for two hours at a stretch over the German lines, sometimes hovering at no greater altitude than 7,000 feet, the low-lying clouds preventing reconnaissance from anything like a safe distance above the enemy anti-aircraft batteries.

As the Allies improved both the material and the organization of their aircraft, the increasing power of their artillery enabled their airmen to show to more advantage. The work of the aerial scouts went on incessantly. They preceded both armies in the long race to the sea which began west of the Aisne in the third week in September and ended on the Yser in the second week in October, strategical reconnaissance being by far the most important part of their work, while tactical observation and photography also occupied them incessantly. There was also the unceasing work of directing the fire of the artillery. Now and then, when occasion offered, the airmen came out in large machines, carrying a store of bombs, with which they tried to injure the railway communications of the foe. They also worried any mass of hostile troops, the French airmen having small boxes of steel arrows for dropping on the enemy.

LAST ACT OF THE DARDANELLES TRAGEDY. The terrible, if magnificent, blunder of the Gallipoli campaign ended with a brilliant military operation when the peninsula was evacuated gradually throughout December, 1915, without the knowledge of the Turks. This photograph shows preparations for firing stores with straw and petrol, which were set off by time fuses after the last man had embarked on January 9, 1916. The total casualties in this operation at Helles amounted to one man wounded

SERBIAN RETREAT OVER THE MOUNTAINS. In October 1915 Serbia was attacked on the north and north-west by Mackensen, and on the east by a Bulgarian army. Her strength was reduced by earlier losses and by pestilence and her armies were forced to retreat into the mountains of Montenegro and Albania King Peter and escort are seen crossing the river Drin

Plate 54   Volume 11

Monastery of St. John overlooking the lake at Ochrida, Serbia The town was notable in the retreat of 1915.

Serbian troops retreating into Albania across the snow-covered plain ot Kossovo in the winter of 1915.

Statue to Lazar, the last Serbian tsar, at Krushevatz. The town fell to the Austrians, November, 1915.

SCENES IN SERBIA'S TRAGIC RETREAT

Royal Air Force, Crown copyright

THE CITY OF KUT AND THE RIVER TIGRIS. The geographical position of Kut, situated in a U-shaped bend of the Tigris, renders it liable to flooding and consequent isolation. This fate befell the British troops under Townshend in December, 1915, when the Turks invested the town. After a valiant defence, Townshend surrendered Kut in April, 1916.

A TERRIBLE WEAPON

This new aerial weapon, introduced by the French in October, was a terrible thing. It was a piece of steel rod a third of an inch in diameter, and about seven inches long. One end was pointed like a pencil for an inch or so, while the other end was machined out for five inches like the feathers of an arrow. They were packed in boxes of fifty, and released by the aviator opening the bottom of the box with a string. The speed at which the aeroplane was travelling distributed the arrows thoroughly, while the force of gravity endued the missiles, as they fell from a great height, with horrible power. The effect on infantry, when in close formation or when lying behind low trenches, was far more deadly than the same weight of bombs.

By lying flat on the ground a fighting man could escape the effect of a bomb unless it made a direct hit, which was extremely unlikely. But men lying flat, or even crouching, beneath a shower of aerial arrows, only exposed more surface to the missiles. The effect on cavalry was worse than on infantry, for there was a larger surface to hit. Altogether, it was a horrible weapon. But it was not more horrible than long-range gun fire, against which infantry was quite as defenceless.

Meanwhile, the allied aerial scouts continued their work of reconnaissance around the advancing armies. They were not always successful. An extraordinary case of an entire German army corps being lost by British airmen took place in the movement towards Arras. Two hostile army corps were seen marching through the forest at Vermand. A sharp look-out was kept on their movements. One corps was traced as it went to reinforce the German troops at St. Quentin. The other, however, vanished in a mysterious manner. A similar disappearance of a German army corps under the eyes of aeroplane scouts occurred some time before at Compiègne. In both instances it is supposed that the large mass of 40,000 to 50,000 men concealed themselves in the forest, where their movements could not be observed by the aerial scouts. Then they left the woods in small numbers at different times, and collected at a prearranged rendezvous. But the fact that the Germans had to undertake this lengthy and difficult operation of marching an army corps to a forest and scattering it, and then arranging for it to join together again by a time-table, after a long night march, is a telling example of the way in which the aerial reconnaissance of the Allies increased the difficulties of the enemy.

Towards the middle of October, 1914, there was a series of German aeroplane raids on St. Omer, Dunkirk, Calais, and Boulogne. But though the popular imagination was impressed by these bomb-dropping exploits, this was only an incidental purpose of the enemy airmen; their real business was the reconnaissance of the approaching movements of British troops. It is clear that the German General Staff expected the landing of a stronger British reinforcement than the 7th division and the 3rd cavalry division under Sir Henry Rawlinson. It was feared that a considerable number of British Territorials would at once be transported to help in strengthening the seaward front. Hence the far-ranging activities of the German airmen, who also went bomb-dropping to Paris while reconnoitring for General Joffre's reserve forces.

It was about this time that a German cavalry division was defeated by a few airmen. The large force of horsemen were pursued and harassed from the sky during the whole of October 15, and as evening drew on a well-aimed bomb attack completed their discomfiture. The allied airmen, however, did not have another amazing success of this sort. On the same day a chase occurred at St. Omer, in which three British aeroplanes tried to hunt down one German machine. It was expected that the enemy would be overtaken and put out of action. But two of the British machines proved to be slower than the German, and the other one met with an accident and had to give up the chase.

This was the first significant sign of a general improvement in German aeroplanes, that caused the allied commanders a considerable amount of trouble in the early part of the winter. Several things seemed to show that the superiority in the air, won by the Allies at the beginning of the War, was partly due to the fact that their opponents, drawn from the frontier air-stations, were at first using machines they had kept there for six, twelve, or eighteen months. They had mainly old-type Taube monoplanes, Aviatik biplanes, early-type Albatross, L.V.G. biplanes, and Jeannin monoplanes. These were heavy and slow, and many of them had only four-cylinder engines of 70 h.-p. instead of the 100 h.-p. six-cylinder engines of the new type.

In the middle of October a large supply of superior machines arrived in the western German lines. Some of them had been building before the War, others had been completed after the great struggle opened. The effect of this sudden and important improvement in the most useful kind of the enemy's aircraft was soon remarked. British pilots were surprised to discover that many of the German airmen began to climb better and fly more quickly than they used to. The British air service had, in fact, only a few machines that could keep up with them. Britain's main problem in aerial warfare then rested with her manufacturers. She had various new makes of aeroplanes capable of overtaking the best of the newest German types.

The Germans had largely recovered their lost ground by modelling their new machines on those of the British. Their latest type of tractor biplanes was almost indistinguishable from the British machine by an untrained observer. The Ago tractor resembled the Sopwiths or Avros, the new Aviatik, Albatross, and L.V.G. looked like the British B.E.'s. The popular chart, contrasting the silhouettes of German and British machines, and issued with the authority of the British Government, was therefore misleading in regard to modern types. The old-fashioned Taube especially, so continually mentioned in English newspapers, was rarely employed by the enemy. The new Aviatik seems to have been the common German machine.

While the Germans were imitating Great Britain's inventive manufacturers, progress in construction had continued in England. British airmen had the Sopwith Scout, the Bristol Scout, the remarkable Avros, so light and yet so strong, and the new Martinsyde Scout, possessing some fine qualities. Then the royal aircraft factory had developed out of the Sopwith and Bristol scouts a small machine with the enormous speed of 150 miles an hour. It was indeed so fast that it was hard to find pilots for it. Indeed, at that time there were very few men in the world who could manage it safely.

Thus, in combination with French makers, British aeroplane manufacturers were able to maintain a superiority against the better-organized efforts of the German aviation authorities. It was the old contest between the loose, free-branching activities of the muddling and yet finely-gifted British race and the careful, comprehensive, and efficient system of Government control on which the Germans have relied for the last hundred years. The British continued to retain the defects of their virtues; for no attempt was made to transform the royal aircraft factory into a general centre of aircraft research and construction, in which all the brilliant minds in enterprising private firms could co-operate. Though Sir John French pointedly asked for greater efforts in providing the growing armies with an overwhelming superiority in the machinery of the new arm, there was no complete and really efficient organization of the splendid resources which Britain possessed. The British still went along in the old free-and-easy way, managing on the whole to keep about level with the less inventive but better-organizing German.

The French aviators had the same zest for aerial warfare as the British, and on their improved machines they harried the enemy almost continuously at times. For instance, on September 18, 20, 21, and 22 they chased the German pilots on their front and compelled them to land. M. Pegoud, the famous inventor of the " looping the loop " operation, was one of the lords of the air. He took to night flying over the German lines, doing terrible damage in the darkness, and using a petrol flash on returning to land behind his own trenches. Sergeant Louis Noel, the Hendon flier, also became remarkable for his nocturnal flights. The whole of his squadron followed his example in habitually flying at night, much to the annoyance of the Germans, who would not imitate him. Noel, in the winter of 1914, was working on the Reims sector, where he achieved a great success. For it was by his efforts that the German fortress of heavy guns west of the city was put out of action.

Some weeks before this a combined squadron of British and French airmen made an attack upon the old forts of Lille. On November 4 they blew up Fort Englos; the next day they destroyed Fort Carnot. The forts were being used as magazines by the enemy and were important as points of support in the enemy's line of entrenchments. Their sudden destruction by aerial bombardment was an affair of some significance. Marksmanship in bomb-dropping was one of the special accomplishments of the allied aviators. It was born of the same qualities as made them the victors in most of the aerial duels. They had more imperturbable daring than their opponents; they swooped lower to get well on their target; in short, they risked their lives more frequently, and at the same time they lessened the risk by the brilliance with which they handled their machines.

The air raids of the flying men of the French and British armies were seldom so spectacular in interest as the expeditions of some of the Royal Naval Air Service aviators. They worked for the most part against the railway communications of the enemy, dropped bombs upon the motor transport columns of the German army, or attacked the German headquarters— striking at the brains of the enemy's forces. At the beginning of the War little or nothing was done by the Allies in these directions. What machines they had were urgently needed for other purposes, and the small experimental bombs first employed did not do enough damage. But when the battle of the trenches reduced modern warfare to strange new conditions, the quick-minded French had a machine ready for air raids on the enemy's communications. It was a large metal-built biplane, with a motor of 200 h.-p. It carried only a couple of very heavy bombs, charged with a new secret explosive. In the first experiment one of them made a hole in the ground ten yards wide and five feet deep. They were used for breaking down railway bridges and attacking trains. They were also employed in breaking up the permanent way in such a manner as to delay for days the supply of food and ammunition.

These great bombs weighed about 130 pounds. A smaller bomb of 20 pounds weight could be carried in larger numbers— in fact, most of the light and very swift machines could only take a few of the small missiles. The damage they did could quickly be repaired by the German engineers. But when a squadron of these light bomb throwers attacked a certain important point, in a circular movement to and from their base of supplies and their point of attack, the continual aerial bombardment became an important affair. When the Germans got their new machines, about the middle of October, 1914, they adopted the same tactics. In the middle of November especially they devoted much attention to the British Army Service Corps, killing some men and transport horses. It seemed as though the British had then lost for a while the supremacy of the air through not having enough fast and powerful aeroplanes to attack all the German pilots who approached their lines.

In the first week of December the German airmen were again active. They attacked the town of Hazebrouck, hoping to destroy one of the British headquarters, but only killed three children and three adult civilians. More effectual was their bombardment on December 7 of the junction of the Armentières-Dunkirk and Ypres-Calais railway line. Their bombs were small, and the damage they did was slight, but the operation was well planned. It showed, at least, that the Germans grasped the lesson of the Allies' repeated attacks upon their communications. British airmen had previously attacked the German headquarters at Thielt on November 1, when it was reported that the Kaiser narrowly escaped death from the thirty-two bombs thrown on the building in which he met his generals.

All the military air raids on either side, however, did no more than annoy and worry the respective enemy. Owing, perhaps, to the lack of machines and pilots, no men could be spared from reconnaissances and artillery direction duties in order to make a grand air attack on some point of importance. As cavalry reconnaissance was prevented on both sides by the barrier of the trenches, only the spy and the airman could obtain any information as to the movements of the enemy. The airman, therefore, became exceedingly valuable. It is not too much to say that he dominated the battlefield. In fact, he gave modern trench warfare its extraordinary character. It was to escape his observation that the life of the artillerymen became a laborious round of digging holes and hiding from sight. The entrenched infantry had continually to burrow deeper, and to conceal their burrows by all manner of devices in order to escape the notice of the airman. His bombs and air arrows were of small importance. What made him so terrible was the fact that he was the eye of distant batteries of hidden howitzers.

Without aerial fire control, the indirect fire of the howitzer would not have been the main influence upon the later western battlefields. The trench protected the soldier fairly well from the direct fire of ordinary guns. If he could have also avoided the almost vertical bombardment of high-explosive howitzer shells, the character of the fighting would have been changed. In particular, the French would probably have won the first turning movement they made under General de Castelnau towards the end of September. It was the heavy German guns and howitzers, directed by aerial observers, that saved the enemy's main line of railway communications at St. Quentin and east of Cambrai. And when the trenches along the Aisne were prolonged to Arras, Lille, and Nieuport, the long-range howitzer and its flying controller, with his range-finding instruments and camera was still the master-spirit of the campaign.

His vision reached 100 miles or more over the opposing front. The war became to him an intellectual pursuit of absorbing interest. If he had a genius for his work, he could read the mind of a hostile commander from the size and position of the bivouacs and the direction of the long string of motor-vehicles. No reconnoitring cavalry or scouts on motor-cycles could have accomplished what he accomplished. Beneath his eagle eye the fog of war was dissipated. The old grand, decisive element in strategy—the use of new large forces in unexpected times or places—became impracticable. The Germans effected one over-whelming thing of this sort at the opening of the war in the west by their vast, swift concentration of armies from the Sambre and Meuse, and the British army afterwards took General von Kluck by surprise by hiding in the forest near Paris, and chasing away his aeroplane scouts. But with these two exceptions, and the evasion of certain German army corps from aerial reconnaissance by scattering in thick woods, the mystery of war no longer obtained in the western field of struggle.

It was reckoned that from November, 1914, to February, 1915, British Army airmen flew altogether 100,000 miles. They always attacked any enemy craft which they sighted, except on the occasions when they were on some special duty from which they could not turn aside just for a sporting fight. If Britain had possessed more machines and men, the ascendancy over the enemy would have been far more completely maintained. As it was, the overworked British airmen did the best they could to interrupt continually the reconnaissance work of the enemy, and by a fortunate chance their efforts were, to some extent, helped by the enlightened policy of the Admiralty.

As an organizer in war, Mr. Winston Churchill was not without his critics, but he certainly had inspiriting qualities. He had little faith in the Zeppelin as an offensive weapon and believed that the fighting aeroplane rising above it and attacking it with incendiary missiles would be the proper reply to its menace; and his energies at the Admiralty were devoted to reducing wasteful expenditure on airships and to the encourage-ment of aeroplane construction. Early in the campaign, under his direction, the Royal Naval Air Service proved to be as efficient as the other branches of the British naval force. This may partly have been due to the fact that the Admiralty relied less upon the royal aircraft factory than did the War Office, and kept the enterprising private aeroplane makers going by Ad-miralty orders. Many of the best machines of the Sopwith

Company and the Avro Company were taken up by the Naval Air Service and put to excellent use. With this encouragement, it was only natural that the private manufacturer should offer his new products first to that branch of the Services which had been so good a friend to him in peace time. For the first year of the war, at all events, the Admiralty was the better served.

British naval aircraft patrolled the east coast, the North Sea and the Straits of Dover by daylight. The small airships often kept aloft for twelve hours, and, with the assistance of seaplanes working from a carrier steamer, the naval airmen kept continually under observation all the waters off the enemy's western coasts. This laborious, unending, unspectacular reconnaissance work, carried out, as the war proceeded, in bitter, dangerous weather, constituted the most important achievement of the men of the Royal Naval Air Service. Public attention was naturally fixed upon a few happy naval officers engaged in air raids. But these men were only able to be spared for picturesque and exciting work through the steady, silent, unnoted, but more important labours of their comrades.

From British weather stations on the edge of the Atlantic it is possible to foretell fairly the conditions of the air in the North Sea and the Channel. Thus British naval airships were able to operate with comparative safety. But as soon as the war broke out the English Meteorological Department kept its main weather information a secret, and in particular ceased to transmit to the Continent the facts gathered in observing stations in Ireland and elsewhere. The result was that Great Britain, through its happy position on the edge of the storm-brewing Atlantic Ocean, was as supreme over Germany in regard to aerial operations as in regard to naval operations. And this was the chief reason why no squadron of Zeppelins attempted throughout all the autumn, winter, and spring of 1914-15 to bombard London. Not only had they to face the attacks of aeroplanes and heavy anti-aircraft gun-fire but they had to take the immense risk of meeting adverse weather conditions. Nearly all anti-cyclones, representing mainly stable weather conditions, spread from the European continent to the British islands. Nearly all cyclones, representing weather disturbances, sweep across the Atlantic and affect the wind conditions in Great Britain a day before they spread to the Continent.

The British supremacy in weather lore was a great factor in the success of the British Naval Air Service. The German airships were superior in range of action. When the weather seemed to be quite settled they could venture far out into the North Sea, and there, at a height beyond the reach of British destroyers' guns, they could watch the movements of ships and telegraph their observations by wireless to the German naval base. The smaller patrolling British craft, with a less range of flight, could not operate from the British coast and keep all the waters between Denmark and Holland under constant observation. Britain had to use steamers fitted up as aircraft carriers in order to approach the German naval bases and to watch what went on round there. It was really the Britons' knowledge of coming weather conditions that enabled them to cope with the better-equipped German naval reconnaissance officers.

Throughout 1915 the naval wing at Dunkirk constantly performed good work, in spite of the fact that in June of that year the Germans brought out another new model, an Aviatik, which made rings round the fast British scouts. The Belgian coast was frequently raided by No. 1 Wing of the Royal Naval Air Service and other British naval airmen in the autumn of 1915 made extended flights over the North Sea and bombarded the German shore. Raids were made in the neighbourhood of Zeebrugge in the early part of the year, when much damage was done by the raiders. The submarine bases at Ostend and Hoboken were also attacked.

Late in 1915 a much-desired reform was made in regard to the connexion between the War Office and the royal aircraft factory. An army officer who was a good engineer was put in charge of all military aero-motors, with the result that engines were selected without any official bias against private makers, and with the sole aim of improving British aerial fighting power. But good engines could not be found, tested, made in large quantities, and built into admirable machines quickly under the conditions which prevailed at the time.

The Germans were leaving no stone unturned in their efforts towards supremacy in the air. They copied the fine features of the fast scouts and battle-planes which had been invented by private British manufacturers. They also copied the Morane-Saulnier and other French machines, and extended their own private aircraft works in an enormous manner. Dr. Hansen, who was in London just before the outbreak of war, took back with him drawings of the new Bristol scout biplane, which, with the latest Morane-Saulnier monoplane, was manufactured in a new aircraft factory founded in Cologne. Baron von Skoda, the maker of the famous 12 in. Austrian howitzer, established a large aircraft factory near Vienna, and a Dutch crack pilot, Fokker, after trying a machine of his own design that was of no use, undertook to manufacture Morane machines in Germany. The Bristol company's works at Halberstadt were commandeered, rechristened, and much extended; and many other German factories were greatly developed, and in many cases set to work on standardised designs in order to supply German needs. Britain in May, 1915, ought to have been in a position to help France and Russia in holding the dominion of the air on the combined lines of fifteen hundred miles, instead of having to cry for aid from French aeroplane makers to enable British airmen to hold their own on a thirty-mile front.

Generally speaking, the work of the principal British air force in Flanders and France during the spring and summer of 1915 was strongly influenced by the course of events on the Russian front. In April, 1915, the German staff thinned its western lines of fast, scouting aeroplanes, in order to exercise an overwhelming superiority in the war against the Russians. A purely defensive attitude was maintained against British and French airmen, and German battle-planes were seldom seen over the British trenches. Thereupon both the British and the French began to assume that they had recovered the command of the air, when, as a matter of fact, the enemy was as superior to all the Allies in aerial material as he was in artillery, the apparent decline in his power on the western front being merely the result of his most formidable concentration of forces on the eastern front.

It was in this deplorable condition of affairs that the air service of Britain and her Allies was strained to breaking point by the sudden appearance, towards the end of April, 1915, of swarms of the fast new German Albatrosses, followed by the improved Aviatiks and twin-engined battle-planes carrying guns. On the Dunajec front, especially, the Russian army was blinded, and Mackensen was able to prepare and deliver his terrific blow with such effect that it was a complete surprise. Great as was his heavy gun power, its destructiveness was enormously increased by his still more telling superiority in aerial power. Throughout the great retreat the Russians were almost in the position of blind men fighting against men with telescopic powers of vision. General Alexeiff at last had to manœuvre his forces under cover of night and conceal them in forests, in order to prevent all his dispositions from being closely studied by German observers seated in swift and far-ranging aeroplanes.

The French activity in the air was carried on on similar lines to that of the British, and their airmen made daily reconnaissances along the 500 miles of front. As the submarine and airship bases in Flanders were the main objective of the British, so the French directed their chief efforts to German supply bases and headquarters. A French aviator dropped bombs on an ammunition column near Middelkerke, and then bombarded the Kursaal at Ostend. Early in March another airman destroyed the powder works at Rottweil, which is situated nearly 100 miles from Belfort.

Damage was done to the airship sheds of Frescaty and the station of Metz, and other successful raids were carried out at Vigneulles, Ghent, and Friedrichshafen. In May a French squadron did much damage to an explosives factory at Ludwigshafen, and an early morning raid took place in June on the headquarters of the German Crown Prince. A raid on Brussels was followed by an attack on Karlsruhe as a reprisal for the bombardment of open British and French towns. French aviators also carried out successful raids on a gas factory in Alsace, the station of Freiburg, the petrol works between Hagenan and Weissenburg, the station at Dettweiler, and the aviation sheds of Pfalzburg. Considering the activity of the French aviators, their losses during the summer were small.

When Italy came into the war there was much aerial activity in the northern corner of the Adriatic. The Italian airmen bombarded the Austrian railways, attacked Pola, the Monfalcone dockyard, the torpedo works and submarine factory at Fiume, and made frequent assaults on the dockyards at Trieste. The Austrian aviators did not meet with much success. Venice was protected by a squadron of French seaplanes, and a German aeroplane was brought down in the lagoon. Austrian aeroplanes dropped bombs on Cettinje and the Serbian arsenal at Kragujevatz, but only a few civilians were killed.

The first Zeppelin raid on England took place on January 19, 1915, when the Norfolk coast was bombarded. On April 14, a more serious attack was made in Northumberland, the airship proceeding over Blyth, Wallsend, and South Shields, and dropping several bombs without, however, doing much damage. The following night a Zeppelin visited Essex and Suffolk and dropped bombs on Maldon and Lowestoft. On April 16 a biplane dropped bombs at Faversham and Sittingbourne, in Kent. Later in the month a Zeppelin attempted to visit Northumberland again, but failed, and early on April 30 another airship dropped bombs at Ipswich and Bury St. Edmunds, but no lives were lost.

On May 10 the Zeppelins began a serious succession of raids. About three o'clock in the morning bombs were dropped on Southend and the neighbourhood in great profusion. The Zeppelin apparently carried a load of 5,000 lb., and nearly one hundred bombs of 50 lb. each were used. One woman was burned to death in her bed; and damage to private property amounting to £7,000 was done. A six-months-old baby of a corporal of the Borderers had a narrow escape, and the soldier father sleeping with it was buried in the ruins of the house; but neither lost his life. Thus the 5,000 lb. of bombs achieved only the death of one woman.

Oblivious of danger, people were all anxious to see a Zeppelin in action, and crowded out into the streets to watch it, so that if the anti-aircraft batteries had poured shrapnel shell around the invader, the falling missiles would have killed more town-folk than did the bombs. This general spirit of curiosity remained in play throughout the year, despite the warnings given by the British Government of the great danger from the defence's own shells. On May 16 a Zeppelin attacked Ramsgate, dropping bombs in one of the most crowded parts of the seaside resort, killing two people and injuring more. On May 27 there was another raid on Southend, in which three persons were killed and others injured.

On May 3 the Zeppelin raiders at last approached their principal goal. The outlying district on one side of London was reached, and bombs were dropped at places in Essex and Kent. The German pilot claimed to have reached Finchley. Three large fires and many small fires broke out, but the British authorities reported that not all the fires could be definitely connected with the airship attacks. Only eight persons, however, were killed, among them being a child of eight, who was coming home from a picture-palace with a girl of sixteen. No public building was injured, but the damage to private property was considerable. Four children were killed, and two women were among the slain.

Another raid on the east and south-east coasts took place on June 4, but no casualties were reported. Yet the German Press and the German military authorities made extravagant claims in regard to the destruction done by their airships. From Leipzig it was learned that England had at last found her master in Count Zeppelin; along the coasts and in the inland cities of England flames and smoking ruins marked the path of the Zeppelins; unrest was being created over Britain which would have great influence on the course of the war.

During June more raids took place. On June 4 a visit was paid to Kent, Essex, and the East Riding, where several people were injured. Two days later an attack was made on Hull, Grimsby, and the East Riding, when twenty-four people were killed and forty injured. Nine days afterwards the north-east coast was visited by a Zeppelin, dropping bombs which killed fifteen persons and injured fifteen more. On August 9 a squadron of airships, under Dr. Sticker, attacked the east coast, claiming to have bombed Norwich. The night was very dark, and a thick fog over some of the coast towns rendered night flying by the British airmen very difficult. One Zeppelin was seriously damaged by gun fire from the British land defences, and in the morning of August 10 some enemy patrol ships found it and towed it towards Ostend. But a squadron of French seaplanes from their base at Dunkirk attacked the crippled monster. It was first hit by one of the British naval pilots, but the French airmen dropped upon it twelve 4.8 in. incendiary bombs and six 3.6 in. bombs. They quite destroyed the structure by an explosion of its gas, and then turned on the port of Ostend and dropped 49 explosive bombs among the vessels that were occupied in patrol work.

Thus this particular Zeppelin raid, in which 25 persons had been killed or wounded and only immaterial damage done to property, was not a success for the Germans, who had now lost more than twelve Zeppelins, without counting any hit by the Russians or any loss of Parsevals. This was the minimum verifiable loss of rigid airships on the western front, and the full losses of Zeppelins were probably greater.

Admiral von Tirpitz seems to have been the director of the air campaign against England as well as of the submarine campaign against all merchant shipping found in or near British waters. On August 12 there was another raid on the east coast by two Zeppelins that came over at 9.30 p.m. and 11.45 p.m. They killed and injured twenty-nine persons and destroyed fourteen houses. The British aircraft patrols went up, but could not overtake and outclimb the enemy airships, though one Zeppelin was thought to have been hit. Again, on August 17, the eastern counties were raided by three Zeppelins, one of which was struck by a British motor-gun. Again the British air patrols went up, but could not find and overtake the enemy. All the deaths and injuries occurred among civilians, one pathetic incident being that of a little girl killed in her sleep, and still clasping in her arms her cherished doll. A surgeon, performing the operation of tracheotomy at a nursing home on the east coast found the town electric current cut off, just when he was opening the windpipe of a child. Fortunately, the operator was prepared for Zeppelin effects. He had lamps ready, and with but trifling delay the operation was completed and the life of the child saved.

German newspapers were full of the tremendous exploits of their air fleet. By a stroke of the pen they had already destroyed most of the London docks, and they now went on and blew up Landguard Fort, at Harwich, by means of a Zeppelin bomb which penetrated into the magazine. The Dutch mail was destroyed at Harwich and postal communications interrupted for a week. But after reading all this, the Dutch were surprised still to receive the post from England in a regular manner, with no letters delayed except perhaps a few in which the British Censor was interested. The British Admiralty had settled on a policy of silence in regard to the places attacked by the raiders. Perhaps it was thought that strategical silence and the repression of long and detailed newspaper reports would tend to keep the nation calm. The Germans answered this move by getting their agents in England to start rumours of enormous loss of life after every important raid.

On September 7, according to the German statement, the western part of the London district was attacked, and large factories and harbour works and ironworks in the eastern counties. Between September 7 and September 8 the loss of life in the London district and the eastern counties was heavier than in any previous raid. Fires broke out, but happily were got under control, though the damage to small dwelling-houses was considerable. Yet the harm done by this aerial bombardment, maintained for two nights with all the power that Germany could spare, was insignificant in comparison with the dreams of destructiveness which the German populace had been cherishing for ten years. The German airship was first perceived moving at a fairly low level in the clear radiance of some of the London searchlights. The searchlight men caught her and held her, distinct and strangely picturesque, against the dim background of the starred autumnal sky. If a number of anti-aircraft guns, using incendiary shells, had been available on certain high places round London, the invaders would probably have been made to pay a heavy toll for the damage done.

At this period the system of attacking airships with aeroplanes had been practically abandoned. There was for some time a lack of nocturnal landing-places, with proper signal lights, and if any airman rose at night over London, he was only able to land in very hazardous circumstances. The defence of the capital appeared to consist of anti-aircraft guns of short range, firing almost useless shrapnel, because there were no high-explosive or incendiary shells available. Most of the men who manned the guns worked all day in bank and business offices, and were given no practice against kites or balloons.

The airship first seen over London, when the searchlights played upon her and the shrapnel came near, put up her nose and ascended into a cloud. Many Londoners took the matter in a sportsmanlike mood, standing in groups to watch the shooting, and confidently expecting the raider to be winged. Great was the general disappointment when she easily escaped eastward, without showing signs of any damage. The fault was not in the gunners, but in the responsible authorities, who had not provided effective anti-aircraft guns or trained the gunners by sending them in batches to the front for actual work against enemy machines. The new German aeroplanes were beginning to operate at a height of 10,000 feet, which was the altitude at which Zeppelins travelled at night over dangerous localities. Any gunner that could hit a small biplane at a good height could have brought down a Zeppelin, caught by searchlights, if he had a gun that carried far enough, and a shell to explode hydrogen gas. But no incendiary shells were then available.

On Sunday, September 12, the Zeppelins, according to the official German statement, tried again to reach the docks of London. The next night a Zeppelin crossed the east coast. In neither case was anyone injured, and very little damage was done. The anti-aircraft guns, fixed and mobile, were in action. They beat the raiders off. In the meantime, Sir Percy Scott was appointed to take charge of the gunnery defences of London against attacks by enemy aircraft. He it was who had raised the shooting in the navy to a very high level, and it was fairly certain that, if he were given the men, the guns, the fire-control instruments, and the special shell he needed, the Zeppelin flights over London would become very dangerous to the flyers. But the work did not go on in a rapid manner, and at intervals there were reports that Sir Percy thought of resigning from his position.

Both soldier and sailor gunners took part in the anti-aircraft artillery work along the coasts, and for some months the Admiralty and the War Office worked together without any close organization. Neither, seemingly, wanted the entire responsibility for failures to stop the nocturnal raiders. As the army relied mainly on the royal aircraft factory for machines, they could not mount their pilots with the efficiency needed for aerial bomb attacks upon the raiders. The War Office, moreover, could not spare flying officers for defensive raids on airship sheds between Emden and Hamburg, Antwerp and Düsseldorf. Yet in the end it was the War Office that took over the defensive work against hostile aircraft, though the sea patrols and Naval Wing exercised more or less control over the waters which the Zeppelins had to cross in reaching England.

The last Zeppelin raid of the year took place on October 13, when Zeppelins again visited the London area and the eastern counties; but, except for one chance shot, the damage was reported to have fallen wholly on property unconnected with the conduct of the war. The darkening of the metropolitan area helped to prevent the enemy from discovering the exact position of places of importance, but his bad marksmanship was still more attributable to the height at which he flew—some two miles—and to the speed with which he passed over the vast tract of dim streets. Sticker, in a private letter to a friend, claimed to have distinguished the bridges over the Thames and discerned the misses he made. But an airship going at 50 miles at a height of two miles could not have any hope of hitting a target the size of an acre. Unknown currents of air in the lower altitudes would deflect the bombs, even if it had been possible to loose them at the exact fraction of a second necessary to hit a mark in advance of the airship's route, which was being studied by an observer in the forward gondola. The officers of the Royal Flying Corps in Flanders, after hundreds of bombing expeditions in which they swooped down to 1,000 feet or less, confessed that they seldom got home on their targets. They thought a long-range heavy gun was far more effective than any bombing machine. On this reasoning, a Zeppelin, at a height of two miles and going at high speed to escape a shell fired at it, could not be expected to hit any building in London. It could only sow death and suffering indiscriminately amid the largest urban population on earth.

London, however, was not the most important object from a German point of view that could be attacked from the air. The bombing of the capital and the seaside resorts was a blunder as well as a crime. It was a blind expression of the Gott-strafe-England spirit, in which ferocious exasperation over Britain's entry into a well-planned war that she had upset misled the director of the Zeppelin squadrons. He aimed at London, in order to placate the German populace and carry out the tradition of the London bombardments of German toymakers and the pictures of the panic-stricken British capital given in German comic papers. Important military damage might have been done if all the 20 raids of 1915 had been directed towards the Midlands. On the other hand, the people of the midland counties had more energy of character than the vast, unorganized population of London. It was almost worth while, from the German point of view, to let the sleeping dogs of the midlands lie, and from the middle of October, 1915, to the middle of January, 1916, no Zeppelin raid occurred.

CHAPTER 31

V.C. Heroes of the War (II)

FOLLOWING out the plan adopted in our first volume, this chapter on the heroes who won the V.C. in the Great War covers a full year of the struggle, carrying the story from August 4, 1915, to August 3, 1916. In that period 78 officers and men were gazetted as having been awarded the Victoria Cross. A first analysis shows that eight V.C.'s went to the Navy in the second year of the war, as compared with four in 1914-15. The Air Service also doubled its total of V.C.'s, earning four in the second year of the war as against two in the first twelve months. Of the sixty-six crosses which went to soldiers, twenty were won in Gallipoli, and of these nine fell to Anzac soldiers and one to a Gurkha. Crosses were won in Mesopotamia and in East and West Africa, and the remaining 42 fell to soldiers fighting on the western front.

The magnificent services rendered by the navy in the landing operations upon Gallipoli on April 25, 1915, were rewarded by six crosses on August 16. Five of these were won at the landing on V Beach, when a collier, the River Clyde, was crammed with troops and run aground in order to provide cover for the soldiers until the actual stepping ashore. Its commander, Edward Unwin, had specially prepared the vessel for this work and his gallantry in handling it was fittingly rewarded with a V.C.

Two midshipmen associated with him in this work were similarly honoured. The first was Midshipman George L. Drewry, R.N.R. He stood under the hail of bullets in the numbing water, and worked oblivious of the danger in which he stood. Twice he tried to swim with a line from one lighter to the other, though he was wounded in the head and suffering from loss of blood. After his double attempt to pass a line from one lighter to the other had failed, another gallant lad, Midshipman Wilfred St. A. Malleson, R.N., attempted the task, and succeeded in reaching the second lighter with the line. Unfortunately it broke, and he had to make the attempt again. Twice more he tried, being taken out of the water each time in a state of extreme exhaustion.

SOME NAVAL HEROES

Two able seamen of H.M.S. Hussar also won the V.C. during these difficult and dangerous operations. One of them, Able-Seaman W. C. Williams, exposed himself breast-deep in water for an hour under the heavy fire, holding a line. In the end the gallant fellow was killed. Seaman George McK. Samson, R.N.R., also of the Hussar, worked all day under fire in one of the lighters, tending the wounded and hauling on the lines. Eventually he was dangerously wounded.

Nearly a year after his death, the V.C. honour came to the name of one more naval hero of V Beach, whose glorious bravery was described at the time, but whose identity was not traced until long after his death. Sub-Lieutenant Arthur Waldene St. Clair Tisdall, R.N.V.R., heard wounded men calling for help from the beach, while the attempts were being made to effect the landing from the River Clyde. He jumped into the water, and pushing a boat before him as cover, went to the rescue of the men on the beach. Four or five times he made the journey, assisted by Chief-Petty-Officer Perring and Leading-Seamen Malia, Curtiss, and Parkinson. Before he was identified as the hero of this daring, Sub-Lieutenant Tisdall was killed, leading his men on May 6.

The seventh naval V.C. of the year was earned by Commander Eric G. Robinson, R.N., who was in command of a party put ashore from the fleet at Cape Helles on February 6, 1915, their mission being to destroy the guns of Fort Seddul Bahr. The men were dressed in white, and so made a good mark for the snipers concealed in the rough ground behind the fort. For this reason Commander Robinson would not let them advance, but undertook the work of destruction single-handed. Under heavy fire he advanced alone to the guns, not knowing whether a force had not been left there to protect them. He blew up one 4 in. gun, and returned for another charge of explosive. With this he succeeded in blowing up the second gun.

The scene of the exploit which won the eighth naval V.C. for the year was laid at Kut-el-Amara, and its hero was Lieut.-Commander Edgar Christopher Cookson, D.S.O., R.N. The Turks had placed an obstruction in the river, to the great disadvantage of the relieving force, and on September 28, 1915, Lieut.-Commander Cookson took the river-gunboat Comet, with other river-gunboats and similar craft, to examine the obstruction, and to destroy it if possible. The enemy was in ambush, waiting for them, and as they approached the obstruction the little flotilla came under heavy fire. It was found that a number of dhows had been fastened by wire ropes in the centre of the stream, completely closing the fairway. An attempt to sink the central dhow, which was the pivot of the barrier of boats, was made with gun fire; but it proved unsuccessful. Then Lieut.-Commander Cookson ordered the Comet to be taken alongside this dhow, and with an axe in his hand he jumped aboard her and tried to sever the wire ropes which bound her to the other vessels. While at this work he was struck by several bullets and killed.

Airmen are only awarded the V.C. under most exceptional circumstances, as the exploits of the airmen V.C.'s of the second year of the war will prove. The first was Captain John Aidan Liddell, of the 3rd battalion (Princess Louise's) Argyll and Sutherland Highlanders and R.F.C. On July 31 he was engaged upon a long-flight reconnaissance over Ostend-Bruges-Ghent. While flying at a great height he was wounded by anti-aircraft artillery, a piece of shell breaking his right thigh. The pain and shock of the wound rendered him unconscious, and his observer found the machine dropping with an ever-increasing velocity, while he was quite powerless to avert the imminent catastrophe. Captain Liddell recovered partial control after a drop of 3,000 feet, and by a great effort righted the 'plane. He was continually fired at, but stuck grimly on. His magnificent grit was rewarded by his bringing the aeroplane back to the British lines, after half an hour of indescribable effort and agony.

A few days before, on July 25, Temp.-Major Lance George Hawker, D.S.O., of the Royal Engineers and R.F.C., put up a remarkable fight against three German aeroplanes which engaged him at the same time. Each enemy 'plane had machine-guns, pilot, and observer; but Major Hawker met them single-handed in the air and routed them utterly. One machine he tackled at a height of 10,000 feet and drove it to the ground in the British lines, both pilot and observer being captured. The second was badly damaged and compelled to descend, and the third then took to flight.

The third airman V.C. of the year was Second-Lieutenant Gilbert S. M. Insall, No. 11 squadron R.F.C. With an observer, First-Class Air-Mechanic T. H. Donald, he was patrolling the

German lines on November 7, 1915, in a Vickers' battle-plane, when a German machine was sighted. Lieutenant Insall gave pursuit, and the German led him over a rocket battery, the only effect of the manœuvre being that the Vickers' machine made a great dive, which brought it so close to the German that the gunner was able to fire a drum of cartridges into the enemy machine at close range. This had the effect of stopping the German's engine, driving him to the desperate remedy of diving through a cloud, with the British machine hot in pursuit.

Again the English mechanic got a chance, and this time brought the German down. The two occupants of the fallen machine scrambled out, and Lieutenant Insall made another great swoop of five hundred feet, permitting his gunner once more to get into effective range. The two men were driven away, one obviously wounded, and then the lieutenant completed his work by dropping a bomb upon the fallen machine, which was last seen wrapped in smoke. The two airmen had then to run the gauntlet of the German trenches at an elevation of only 2,000 feet, and they passed this barrier, the lieutenant driving his machine and the gunner working cheerfully away at the machine-gun.

A naval airman won the fourth and last airman's V.C. for the year. This was Squadron-Commander Richard Bell Davis, D.S.O., R.N. He took part in an aerial attack upon Ferrijik Junction, in company with Flight-Sub-Lieutenant Wyllie. The latter officer had his machine brought down, and in order to prevent it falling into the hands of the enemy he set fire to it. While he was at his work, Commander Davis swooped down and, in spite of the near approach of the enemy, picked him up, and reached the aerodrome in safety with him.

The soldiers who won the Victoria Cross number sixty-six, of whom thirty-one were officers, and thirty-five non-commissioned officers and men. Forty-one of these sixty-six were won by officers or men of line regiments, and three more by Guardsmen, making a total of forty-four for the regular infantry. The remaining twenty-two included nine Anzac soldiers, one among them being a light horseman, five members of the Indian army, one Canadian, two engineers, one yeoman, one chaplain, one officer from the R.A.M.C., one from the Indian Medical Service, and an artilleryman. The honours were widely distributed, but the outstanding feature of the awards, next to the

Anzac record of nine V.C.'s in a month, was the number won by Lancashire regiments. The Lancashire Fusiliers took three crosses, the East Lancashire Regiment two, the York and Lancaster Regiment two, the Manchester Regiment two, the Royal Lancasters one, and the Loyal North Lancashires one. Other regiments with two V.C.'s were the Coldstream Guards, the Cameron Highlanders, the Royal Inniskilling Fusiliers, and the King's Royal Rifles.

The V.C. awards to the navy for the miraculous landings on Gallipoli on April 25, 1915, have already been detailed. A number of army awards were also made, and notable among these were the V.C.'s awarded by the process of election. Three companies of the Lancashire Fusiliers were concerned in the exploit for which the three crosses in question were given. On landing, these companies were met by a deadly fire from hidden machine-guns, causing extremely heavy casualties. The uninjured men charged boldly up the face of a steep cliff, being checked in their advance by thick wire entanglements, which they cut. In the face of a murderous fire they gained the summit of the cliff and seized a position which made it possible for their comrades to land more safely. Where all had shown such dash and bravery, the selection of the three men for special honour was left to the soldiers themselves. Their choice fell upon Captain Richard Raymond Willis, Sergeant Alfred Richards, and Lance-Corporal William Keneally.

On the day following the landing, April 26, Corporal William Cosgrove, 1st battalion Royal Munster Fusiliers, took part in an attack on the Turkish positions east of Cape Helles. He led his section into action from the beach with great dash, and on the way encountered a high entanglement of barbed-wire. He approached it single-handed and under heavy fire, and actually pulled down the posts which supported the wire. This fine example of resource and courage was effective in making a way through this formidable obstacle.

The whole Gallipoli campaign was resplendent with single-handed feats performed in extreme emergency and against overwhelming odds. Of this character was the conduct by which Lieutenant Herbert James, of the 4th battalion Worcestershire Regiment, won the V.C. Two gallant feats stood to the credit of this young officer. On June 28, when an attack was being made in the southern zone of Gallipoli, a portion of a regiment near him had been checked in its advance, owing to all its officers having been put out of action. Lieutenant James, acting on his own initiative, gathered some men together and advanced under heavy fire. Leaving these new-comers to collect the checked soldiers, he went back for another party, whom he also brought up, with the result that fresh life was instilled into the attack on this section of the line. Later, in the night of July 3, he led a party of bomb-throwers up a Turkish communication-trench, and in the fight that followed lost all his men. Single-handed, he kept the head of the trench under a heavy fire and showers of bombs until a barrier had been built behind him and the position made secure.

A similar feat was performed by Captain Gerald Robert O'Sullivan, 1st battalion Inniskilling Fusiliers, on the night of July 1-2, at Krithia. An important section of trench had been lost, and although Captain O'Sullivan did not belong to the troops detailed for its recapture, he volunteered to lead a bombing party for the purpose. They had to advance across the open, under heavy fire, and having reached their objective, to bomb the Turks out of the captured position. In order to see where his bombs were falling, this officer climbed upon the parapet, and from this exposed position directed the assault.

Another Inniskilling Fusilier, Sergeant James Somers, also of the 1st battalion, remained alone in a sap which the Turks were attacking, waiting for bombs to be brought up for the defence. When they came, he climbed over to the Turkish trench and made a spirited attack upon its occupants. Later, he crossed the open under heavy fire, in order to bomb the Turkish flank, and several times ran back under fire for fresh supplies of bombs.

The first important military operation by the British forces in the second year of the war was the ill-fated landing at Suvla Bay. This operation was covered by a number of gallant demonstrations executed by the Anzacs, who already held the beaches nearer Fort Gaba Tepe; and among these assaults the capture of Lone Pine Plateau stands out by itself. The overwhelming charge of the 1st brigade of Australian infantry which carried the Turkish positions, and the stubborn defence during the ensuing four days, in which the 2nd brigade of Australian infantry also participated, will rank among the most glorious of all the brave deeds of the Anzacs. In those four days no fewer than seven V.C.'s were won, three by officers, and the others by men who had not then attained commissioned rank.

Captain Alfred John Shout, of the 1st battalion, had won the Military Cross when the Anzacs landed on Gallipoli and was the hero of a dozen dazzling exploits in subsequent affrays. On August 8, 1915, he was attached to the headquarters of the 1st brigade on Lone Pine Plateau, when a large body of Turks came down a long communication-trench which led from their position across the plateau. They came into sight around the last traverse, within fifty yards of headquarters, under the astonished eyes of Brig.-General Smythe himself. They were checked, and then Captain Shout and his friend, Captain Sass, resolved to drive them back by the way they had come. Captain Shout went first, with a liberal supply of bombs, and his fellow-officer supplemented his efforts with a rifle. They drove the Turks back, bit by bit, inflicting loss upon them at each traverse. When a satisfactory spot was reached, they decided that a barricade should be erected, and in order to drive the Turks effectively away during the execution of this work, Captain Shout endeavoured to throw three bombs, which he lit at the same time. The third exploded in his hand, inflicting mortal injuries. A memorial to him has been erected in Darlington, New South Wales, the town from which he came.

Captain Frederick Tubb, of the 7th battalion, was in charge of a small band of men belonging to that battalion in the morning of August 9th. They were holding a newly-captured section of trench at Lone Pine, the preservation of which was of vital importance to the whole position. The Turks persisted for some hours in their attempts to capture it, renewing their bomb attacks from time to time with fanatical bravery. Three times they succeeded in blowing down the barricade behind which the Anzacs sheltered, and as often Captain Tubb led his men forward, drove them back, and rebuilt the shelter. He was wounded twice, and almost every man of his small company shared the same fate. But they retained the position through the crucial hours. For this work Captain Tubb was awarded the V.C., as were two of his non-commissioned officers, Sergeant William Dunstan and Corporal A. S. Burton. Burton paid for the honour with his life, and Dunstan was seriously wounded.

During the night of August 8-9, Lieutenant William John Symons, also of the 7th battalion, was in charge of another section of trench not far from that so bravely held by Captain Tubb. The fury of the Turkish attack was divided between the two places. All night the enemy kept up their bomb attacks, but always they were driven off. Early in the morning the lieutenant was called to a sap-head, where six officers had been killed or wounded in succession, and where a portion of the sap had been captured by the enemy. Revolver in hand, he led a charge which drove the Turks out of the sap. He then superintended the construction of a barricade across the sap, holding up a wooden screen to shelter his men from the Turkish rifle fire. The Turks came close to this screen, and managed to set it on fire, but the lieutenant extinguished the flames without allowing the work to be interrupted. He held the position until relief came.

Lance-Corporal Leonard Keysor, of the 1st battalion, was awarded a V.C. for continuous bravery in the south-eastern corner of Lone Pine Plateau, extending without intermission from August 7 to August 9. Keysor was one of the best bomb-throwers in the Anzac ranks, and in this engagement he threw and fielded live bombs for fifty hours without rest. The bombs used by the Turks were furnished with a ten-second fuze, and Keysor caught many of these as they landed, and returned them among the enemy, where they exploded. Keysor was wounded and marked for hospital, but he declined to go. Later he was again wounded, and ordered back to the dressing-station; but on his way there he encountered a company which had lost all its bomb-throwers and volunteered for service with them. He continued fighting until a very difficult situation was eased.

Dare-devil bravery of a different kind was shown by Private John Hamilton, of the 1st battalion, who won the V.C. at Lone Pine on August 9. He was stationed in a section of trench from which a view of the main Turkish communication-trench could be obtained by taking extreme risks. Hamilton climbed up on to the parapet, exposing himself fully, and from this post gave warning of the approach of each party of Turks which passed along the communication-trench. His comrades attempted to build a sand-bag shelter around him, but could only succeed in covering the lower part of his body. Hamilton stuck to his self-imposed task, shooting at the Turks whenever any came in sight, and risking his life every minute he stayed there. He escaped wounds for five hours.

V.C. HEROES OF THE WAR (II)

While the Australian infantry were holding Lone Pine, the New Zealanders made an irresistible assault on the hill mass of Chunuk Bair, from a point nearer to Suvla Bay. In this attack, which began on August 7, Corporal Cyril Royston Guyton Bassett, of the New Zealand Divisional Signal Company, won the V.C. for the most conspicuous bravery. Bassett's name had been a synonym for devotion to duty ever since the New Zealanders first landed on Gallipoli, and the deed of August 7 is but one among many with which he is credited. The New Zealand infantry had taken the ridge, and the work of establishing telephonic communication was undertaken by Bassett, among others. In broad daylight, and under a heavy and continuous fire, he succeeded in laying a line to the advanced position, and was awarded the only V.C. which fell to New Zealand during the first two years of the war.

The last Anzac to win the V.C. on Gallipoli was Second-Lieutenant Hugo Vivian Hope Throssell, of the 10th Australian Light Horse. His chance came in what was practically the last British offensive operation on the Peninsula—the capture of Hill 60 on August 29-30. A section of trench at the foot of the hill was taken by a charge of the Light Horse, in which Captain Fry, the leader, was killed. Lieutenant Throssel then assumed command of this important section of trench, and defended it against repeated attacks delivered by the Turks in overwhelmingly greater numbers than the defenders. The attacks were maintained all through the night of August 29, and well into the morning of August 30. The young officer lost most of his best men, and was himself wounded twice. His good spirits never flagged, and by his unfailing courage and resource he encouraged the handful of men under his orders to maintain the defence until the last. He succeeded in holding out until relief came, when he went away to have his wounds dressed.

Of the Suvla Bay contingent, Captain Percy Howard Hansen, adjutant, 6th (Service) battalion Lincolnshire Regiment, won the V.C. for remarkable bravery at Yilghin Burnu on August 9, 1915. The advance of the regiment was checked by scrub fire, and eventually it had to retire, leaving some seriously wounded men behind it. Captain Hansen, gathering a few volunteers, dashed back through the scrub, and under a terrible fire crossed the open to the assistance of the men. He did this several times, and saved from death by burning no fewer than six men.

A MANCHESTER MAN

Private Frederick William Owen Potts, of the 1st Berkshire Yeomanry (T.F.), won renown and the V.C. by dragging a wounded comrade to safety a distance of six hundred yards on a shovel. The incident took place at Hill 70, Gallipoli, on August 21. Potts was himself severely wounded in the thigh, but he stayed with his comrade, who was unable to move, for two days under the very parapet of the Turkish trenches. He was fired at by the Turks when he started in the dark for the British lines with his comrade on his novel sledge, but escaped further hurt, and arrived in the camp about 9.30 p.m. on August 23.

Another Gallipoli V.C. was Lieutenant William Forshaw, 1/9th battalion Manchester Regiment (T.F.), who maintained an unequal fight against overwhelming numbers of Turks through the days August 7-9 in the north-west corner of the position known as the Vineyard. Three separate trenches converged at this point, and the Turks attacked by all three trenches at once. Lieutenant Forshaw was the soul of the defence, directing his men to great advantage, and all the time throwing bombs with fine effect. For forty-one hours he was throwing bombs incessantly, so that he could not move his stiffened arm when he was finally relieved. After the first twenty-four hours of this work, the detachment to which he belonged was relieved, but he volunteered to stay on. A crucial point of the defence was a sand-bag barricade, and over this the Turks managed to climb on August 8th. Lieutenant Forshaw led a charge against them, shot three with his revolver, and recaptured the position.

West African fighting yielded one V.C. during the year; but though gazetted on September 2, 1915, the feat by which Captain John Fitzhardinge Paul Butler, King's R.R.C., West African Frontier Force, earned it was actually performed on November 17, 1914. With a party of thirteen men he went into the thick bush of the Cameroons, and attacked an enemy force of one hundred, including several Europeans. His little band gained a victory and succeeded in capturing a machine-gun and a large quantity of ammunition. Later, on December 27, 1914, he made a reconnaissance under fire, by swimming the Ekam river with a few men. Having completed his observation, he swam back again, with a loss of only two men wounded.

East Africa provided an actor-hero in the person of Lieutenant Wilbur Dartnell, who left the stage to join the Royal Fusiliers

(City of London Regiment). In an engagement at Maktau, East Africa, on September 3, 1915, it was necessary to retire, leaving several wounded men in a dangerous place. Lieutenant Dartnell knew that the black soldiers against whom we were fighting invariably murdered our wounded, and though himself wounded, remained behind to die in their defence.

Among gallant deeds performed in Mesopotamia that of Major George Godfrey Massey Wheeler, of the 7th Hariana Lancers, Indian army, was rewarded with a V.C. He took out his squadron at Shaiba, Mesopotamia, on April 12, 1915, in an attempt to capture a flag which was the rallying-point of the enemy. The sortie was a gallant one, in which the enemy suffered heavily, and on Major Wheeler's retirement they came out of cover to retaliate, forming an excellent mark for the Royal Horse Artillery's guns. On the following day, April 13, Major Wheeler was killed in leading an attack upon a position known as North Mound. When last seen he was spurring his horse against the enemy, far in advance of his squadron.

Another hero of Mesopotamia was Private (Shoeing-smith) Charles Hull, of the 21st (Empress of India's) Lancers. Captain Learoyd, the adjutant of the regiment, had his horse killed in a very hot engagement, and though the enemy was but a few yards away, Hull checked his own mount under heavy fire and took up the dismounted officer.

Rifleman Kulbir Thapa, 2nd battalion 3rd Queen Alexandra's Own Gurkha Rifles, won his V.C. on September 25 by bravery and self-sacrifice that will ever be remembered when the splendid fighting qualities of the gallant little Indian hillmen come under discussion. He was himself wounded, and behind the first German line. Making his way back, he found a soldier of the 2nd Leicester Regiment badly wounded and helpless. The British soldier urged him to save himself, but the brave Gurkha preferred to remain with him, which he did throughout that day and night. Taking advantage of a patch of mist in the early morning, he carried him on his back to a place of comparative safety. Leaving the Englishman there, he went back twice into the German lines for two of his wounded comrades. It was now broad daylight, but he finished his work by carrying the wounded Briton in on his back, under the enemy's fire.

Two other brave Indian soldiers were awarded the V.C. for similar devotion to wounded Britons. Sepoy Chatta Singh,

9th Bhopal Infantry, Indian army, seeing his commanding officer lying wounded and exposed, left his safe cover to render assistance to him. First binding up the officer's wound, he afterwards stood up under heavy fire to dig cover with his entrenching tool for the wounded man. From early afternoon till dusk fell, a vigil of five hours, he lay beside his officer, and between him and the enemy. When the friendly dark came at last, he went back for help, and returned to assist in bringing his officer back to safety.

Lance-Naik Lala, 41st Dogras, Indian army, rivalled this courageous and devoted conduct. Finding a British officer lying near the enemy lines, he dragged him into a comparatively safe place, where were already lying four wounded men whom he had rescued and bandaged. From this shelter he heard the calls of the adjutant of his own regiment, lying wounded and helpless within a hundred yards of the Germans. Facing almost certain death, Lance-Naik Lala crawled out to the officer, and wished to crawl back with the wounded man on his back. As this could not be done, he remained by him, and actually divested himself of the major part of his clothing to keep his charge warm. When dark fell he made his way back to his shelter, carried the wounded officer he had first tended to safety, and then returned with a stretcher to rescue his adjutant.

Two V.C.'s won at Ypres were gazetted during the year, the first going to Sec.-Lieutenant B. H. Geary, 4th battalion East Surreys. He held the left crater at Hill 60 on April 21, 1915, with his own platoon and some men of the Bedfordshire Regiment, and had to submit to a night-long bombardment which broke down the defences. Furious bomb attacks followed, till the crater was choked with dead and wounded men. The officer was the life and soul of a spirited defence. At times he used a rifle; again he could be seen hurling bombs at the enemy or mounting to the edge to scan the approaches. In these operations he continually risked his life, and eventually was wounded. He found time to arrange for fresh ammunition supplies, and to send reinforcements. Five days later, on April 26, Acting-Corporal Issy Smith, 1st battalion Manchester Regiment, also won the V.C. at Ypres. Leaving safe cover on his own initiative, he went out a long way towards the enemy lines to assist a severely wounded man. Later, he displayed great courage in tending and bringing in other wounded under fire.

V.C. HEROES OF THE WAR (II)

Among the last of the Neuve Chapelle V.C.'s to be gazetted was Captain Charles Calveley Foss, D.S.O., 2nd battalion Bedfordshire Regiment. Captain Foss led a handful of eight men in a gallant counter-attack upon a section of trench which the Germans had captured from us. His attack was delivered with so much dash that the position was taken again, and the fifty-two Germans who held it were made prisoners. The position was a most important one.

The V.C. which fell to Canada was won at Givenchy on June 15 by Lieutenant Frederick William Campbell, 1st Canadian Battalion. Lieutenant Campbell took a machine-gun over the parapet to the German first line, and under heavy fire and bombing maintained the position he had taken up until every man with him had fallen. Finding himself single-handed, he advanced with his machine-gun, and occupied a higher and still more exposed position, from which he fired 1,000 rounds with excellent effect. To him is largely due the credit of holding back a counter-attack delivered by the Germans. In a subsequent engagement Lieutenant Campbell was so seriously wounded that he died of his injuries.

The second year of the war also saw the first V.C. allotted to a British chaplain. The Rev. Edward Noel Mellish, temporary chaplain, was formerly curate of St. Paul's church, Deptford. At St. Eloi he displayed a marvellous devotion throughout three days of terrible fighting, and brought in single-handed no fewer than twenty-two wounded men, besides taking part as a volunteer in many concerted movements for rendering succour to the wounded. On the first day he passed continually from our original trenches to those we had captured, always under heavy fire. On this day he brought in ten men; and some idea of the risk he ran may be gathered from the fact that three of them were killed before him, when he was in the very act of dressing their wounds. On the second day he brought in twelve more men under similar circumstances, while on the night of the third day he headed a party of volunteers who performed similar dangerous work.

The magnificent bravery displayed in the September and October fighting at Loos, Hill 70, and the Hohenzollern Redoubt was productive of a large number of V.C.'s, the first to be gazetted being Lance-Sergeant Oliver Brooks, 3rd battalion Coldstream Guards. Brooks had to meet and stem a desperate rush of German bombers on the night of October 8 near Loos. They had captured two hundred yards of trench, when the Coldstreamer, acting on his own initiative, led a counter-attack of bombers, and drove the enemy out of the trenches.

The award to Brooks was followed by a batch of eighteen other V.C.'s, won at Loos and in the neighbourhood. Temp.-Lieutenant Colonel Angus F. Douglas-Hamilton, commanding 6th Cameron Highlanders, was killed at the head of his men on September 26 at Hill 70. The troops on either side of him having fallen back, he led his own battalion to the charge four times. At the fourth charge he had only fifty men left, and in this gallant charge he fell. It was no useless sacrifice he made, for owing to his efforts the advance of the enemy at this point was checked. Another V.C. hero of Hill 70 was Second-Lieutenant Frederick H. Johnson, 73rd Field Coy., R.E. Though severely wounded, he led several charges against the German position, and that under very heavy fire. His example was contagious, and was instrumental in saving the position which had been taken. He remained at his post until relieved. At Hill 70 Private Robert Dunsire, 13th battalion Royal Scots, went out under heavy fire on the night of September 26 and rescued a wounded man from No Man's Land. Later on the same night he heard a wounded man close to the German lines calling for help. He crawled amid a hail of bullets across the open and brought in that man also.

Hulluch also supplied its quota of V.C.'s, foremost among whom was Captain Anketell M. Read, 1st battalion Northamtonshire Regiment, who paid with his life the price of the valuable services he rendered. When the first attack was made on September 25, 1915, he was partially gassed. None the less he struggled out to rally disorganized and retiring units. Several times he led such parties back to the firing line, and under a heavy fire, moved about among them, inspiring them with fresh confidence. In this brave work he met his death. Private George Peachment, 2nd battalion King's Royal Rifle Corps, lost his life and won the V.C. at the same place on the same night. Peachment died in trying to save his company commander, Captain Dubs. The captain was lying wounded in the open, and Peachment crawled out to him under heavy fire. He knelt there in the open, indifferent to his great danger, attempting to render aid to his wounded officer. There was a shell-hole close at hand, in which a number of men had taken cover, but this brave fellow had no thought for himself. He was wounded by a bomb on this errand of mercy, and later met his death from a rifle bullet. Private Arthur Vickers, 2nd battalion Royal Warwickshire Regiment, displayed most serviceable heroism at Hulluch in this attack. Finding that the advance of his battalion was held up by the German wire, he went out upon his own initiative, under very heavy shell, machine-gun, and rifle fire, and cut the wires. It was broad daylight at the time, and his escape from what appeared certain death is miraculous.

At Hohenzollern Redoubt many brave deeds were performed, and for one notable act Second-Lieutenant Arthur J. T. Fleming-Sandes, 2nd battalion East Surrey Regiment, was awarded the Cross. He had to take over a company which had run short of bombs, and had been much tried by continuous bombing and heavy machine-gun fire. Their own store of bombs was nearly exhausted, while they could see the men on their right retiring. The lieutenant at once grasped the critical nature of the situation, and collecting as many bombs as he could gather, sprang on the parapet and hurled them at the Germans. The enemy was only twenty yards distant and the officer was fully exposed. He was soon wounded, but he disregarded the wound and continued his bomb-throwing until he was wounded a second time.

At Hohenzollern Redoubt Second-Lieutenant Charles G. Vickers, 1/7th battalion Sherwood Foresters (T.F.), also won his V.C. by a fine single-handed performance on October 14. He had lost nearly all his men, and had to meet an attack from front and flank. There was only a barrier between him and the enemy and he had but two men to carry bombs for him. Yet he held the barrier single-handed for some hours. In order to strengthen the precarious position, he further ordered that a second barrier should be built behind him, thus cutting off his only means of retreat if the first barrier should be captured. He held his barrier long enough to allow the second one to be finished; and then he fell, dangerously wounded.

The bravery and initiative of Corporal J. L. Dawson, 187th Coy. R.E., saved a great many men from being gassed at Hohenzollern Redoubt on October 13, 1915. The trenches were full of men at the time, and a heavy gas attack was in progress. Dawson, in order to get the infantry out of the trenches that were full of gas, walked up and down upon the parados in full

The bridge of boats across the Tigris at Amara, and (left) Arab boatmen on the river.

Part of the palace of Ctesiphon, once the winter residence of the Parthian kings. From here Townshend retreated to Kut.

The wharf at Amara, showing some of the flat-bottomed river vessels. This town of Mesopotamia was the scene of a battle between the British and the Turks, May 31,–June 4, 1915. The Turks were routed, the British taking 1,800 prisoners and 17 guns.

CAMPAIGN IN THE CRADLE OF CIVILIZATION

Façade of the cathedral at Nish, Serbia. The town was captured by the Bulgarians, November 5, 1915.

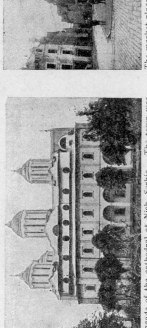

The market place and ruined church of Bethune, France which figured prominently in the war.

General view of Notre Dame de Lorette, France, with ruins of the church of Ablain-St.-Nazaire in right foreground. Fierce fighting took place here in 1915.

PLACES PROMINENT IN THE FIGHTING EAST AND WEST

FRENCH MACHINE GUNS AT NEUVILLE ST. VAAST The trench shown had been captured from the Germans, and the photograph was taken by one of the official French photographers. The village of Neuville St. Vaast was stormed by the French on June 8. 1915. Its site was almost obliterated

Metropolitan church of Petrovna, at Novi Pazar, in S.W Serbia. The town was taken by the Austrians in 1915

The arch of Galerius at Salonica. During the war a Franco-British force occupied the town as a base.

The ruined main street of Pervyse, Belgium. The village was severely damaged by German bombardment.

BELGIAN RUINS AND TWO BALKAN SCENES

Plate 60   *Volume II*

view of the enemy, giving directions. He discovered three cylinders of gas that were leaking and rolled them away from the trench, where he fired bullets into them to let the gas escape.

" Pluck, endurance, and devotion to duty beyond praise " won for Private T. Kenny, 13th (Service) battalion Durham Light Infantry, the V.C. With his officer, Lieutenant Brown, Kenny was on patrol duty in a thick fog near La Houssoie on November 4. They drew the fire of some Germans who were lying in front of their lines in a ditch, and the officer was shot through both thighs. Kenny hoisted him on his back and began to crawl about with him in the thick fog. Eventually he sank down utterly exhausted, to find himself lying in a ditch with which he was familiar. Leaving Lieutenant Brown there under cover, he went back for assistance, and the officer was brought in under heavy fire.

The coolness and bravery of Corporal James D. Pollock, 5th battalion Cameron Highlanders, checked a German attack made on the Hohenzollern Redoubt by way of " Little Willie " trench. The enemy were working dangerously along the trench, when Pollock climbed out, and from the top of it threw bombs down upon them. He was exposed to heavy machine-gun fire, but he held them for an hour single-handed. In the end he was wounded, but he had checked the rush.

In the same neighbourhood there was a heavy bombing attack made on September 29 by the Germans at " Big Willie " trench. Bombs were desperately needed to meet the attack, and Private Samuel Harvey, 1st battalion York and Lancaster Regiment, volunteered to fetch them. The communication-trench was choked by wounded men and by the supports who were coming up to the fight; so Harvey had to run across the open under heavy fire. He made many such trips, and had carried thirty boxes of bombs to the front before he fell wounded in the head.

The devotion to duty shown by Lieutenant George Allan Maling, R.A.M.C., in the heavy fighting with which the Loos attack opened, was rewarded with the V.C. He worked in the open near Fauquissart, and during the twenty-four hours which began at 6 a.m., September 25, 1915, treated more than three hundred cases under heavy shell fire. Early in this trying experience he was knocked over and stunned by the bursting of a big high-explosive shell, which killed several of the men who were waiting for treatment. Another shell soon afterwards buried him and his instruments in debris; but he could not be deterred from his duty. His only assistant was wounded, yet he persevered with his work of mercy until he dropped from sheer exhaustion.

Hooge was the scene of the devoted action by which Second-Lieutenant Sidney Clayton Woodroffe, 8th battalion Rifle Brigade (Prince Consort's Own), lost his life while winning the V.C. on July 30, 1915. On that day the Germans used liquid fire, and drove back the British centre so far that Lieutenant Woodroffe found his position attacked from the flank and finally from the rear. In this emergency he showed the greatest skill in withdrawing his men. Then he organized a counter-attack under extremely heavy fire and was shot down while attempting to cut the German wire. At Hooge, again, between September 25 and October 1, Second-Lieutenant Rupert P. Hallowes, 4th battalion Middlesex Regiment, behaved with unexampled bravery and energy throughout four heavy and protracted bombardments, heartening his men by his wonderful courage. On several occasions he climbed upon the parapet, heedless of danger, in order to put fresh courage into the men. He is credited with a number of most daring reconnaissances of the German positions, and when bombs were needed he went back and brought them up under heavy shell fire.

Piper Daniel Laidlaw, 7th battalion King's Own Scottish Borderers, won the V.C. by one of those acts which will live for ever in history. His regiment was to open the attack between Loos and Hill 70, but while waiting for the signal, it was severely gassed. Noticing that the men were shaken by this experience, Laidlaw mounted the parapet and played his company into action, marching up and down on the edge of the trench. The sound of the pipes acted like a charm, for the men dashed out of cover and went to the assault like inspired beings. Laidlaw continued to pipe until he was wounded.

" The bravest of the brave " was the epithet applied by his colonel to Second-Lieutenant Alexander B. Turner, 3rd battalion Royal Berkshire Regiment, who was awarded the V.C. for services at Fosse 8, near Vermelles, which cost him his life, on September 28, 1915. A great bomb fight was going on in Slag Alley, and it was only too apparent that the regimental bombers were held in check. Lieutenant Turner therefore volunteered to lead a fresh bombing-party. He rushed down a communication·

trench, almost unsupported, hurling bombs with such effect that the Germans were driven back one hundred and fifty yards.

Posthumous honours were also paid to Sergeant Harry Wells, 2nd Sussex, who took command when his platoon officer had been killed in the advance of September 25, near Le Rutoire. He led them to within fifteen yards of the German wire, losing men at every yard. When half the platoon had fallen the men were checked, but Sergeant Wells rallied them splendidly and led them on again. He fell while once more urging the scanty remnant of the platoon forward to the attack.

A double deed of splendid courage and self-sacrifice is credited to Acting-Sergeant John C. Raynes, of A Battery, 71st Brigade R.F.A. On October 11, at Fosse 7 de Bethune, he rushed forward forty yards under heavy fire to the assistance of Sergeant Ayres, who was badly wounded. He bandaged him, and went back to his gun, only to return when the " Cease fire " order was given. With two gunners he carried Ayres in, when a gas-shell burst before the dug-out into which the wounded man had been carried. Raynes gave his smoke-helmet to the wounded man, and then, though badly gassed himself, he crept back to serve his gun. Next day, October 12, Raynes, when rescued from the debris of a wrecked house in Quality Street, assisted his wounded comrades to safety under heavy fire.

Another dogged Briton was Lance-Corporal George H. Wyatt, 3rd battalion Coldstream Guards, who was awarded the V.C. for two separate acts of bravery. The first occurred at Landrecies on the night of August 25-26. The enemy had kindled some straw stacks in a farmyard by means of incendiary bombs, and Wyatt knew that if they continued to burn, the British position would become untenable. The enemy was only twenty-five yards away, but twice he rushed from the trench, daring the bullets that were poured at him, and extinguished the flames. Later, he was wounded in the head at Villers-Cotterets, but continued to fight till the blood pouring into his eyes prevented his seeing. His wound was dressed, and he was ordered to the rear; but he preferred to return to the firing-line.

Corporal Alfred A. Burt, 1st battalion Hertfordshire Regiment (T.F.), well earned the V.C. for his promptness in tackling a huge trench-mortar bomb at Cuinchy on September 27. The bomb fell in the front trench just when Burt's company was preparing to scale the parapet for a charge. He knew the great destruction its explosion would cause, and though he might have saved himself by taking cover behind a traverse, he disdained that course. He went forward to the fizzing bomb, placed his foot upon the fuse, and wrenched it out of the bomb, rendering it innocuous. The fuse he threw over the parapet.

Two V.C.'s were won in the fighting at La Brique in November, the first falling to Private John Caffrey, 2nd battalion York and Lancaster Regiment. Caffrey first went out with Corporal Stirk to the assistance of a wounded man of the West Yorkshire Regiment, who was lying about three hundred yards from the enemy lines. The two men were turned back by heavy shrapnel, but were not content with the rebuff. They ventured again, and this time they reached their man, though they had to run the gauntlet of accurate sniping and machine-gun fire. While Stirk was lifting the wounded man upon Caffrey's back he was himself wounded in the head. Caffrey put down his burden, bandaged Stirk, and helped him back to safety. He then went out alone to the wounded man, this making his third journey across the danger zone.

Similar devotion was shown at La Brique, on November 23, by Corporal Alfred Drake, 8th battalion Rifle Brigade. With an officer and two men he was patrolling near the German lines when the party was discovered and fired upon. The officer and one man fell wounded. Drake devoted himself to the officer, while the remaining man carried in his wounded comrade. The last glimpse he had of Drake revealed him kneeling by the officer under heavy machine-gun fire, calmly bandaging his wounds and tending him. A rescue-party went out later and, crawling carefully close to the enemy lines, found the two men. The officer was unconscious but living, with his wounds bandaged.

Another November V.C. was that won by Corporal Samuel Meekosha, 1/6th battalion West Yorkshire Regiment, in an isolated trench near the Yser on the 19th of the month. The trench was held by a platoon of twenty men, of whom six were killed and seven wounded by a heavy bombardment. Then came a shell and buried all the sound men remaining, with the sole exception of Meekosha. The corporal managed to obtain a runner, by whom he sent a message for assistance. He himself set about the work of digging out the buried men. Big shells were falling all about him, something like a dozen landing within twenty yards of the spot where, in full view of the enemy and at close range, he was stolidly digging for his comrades. At least four men owed their lives to his courage, justly described in the official record as magnificent.

One of the noblest sacrifices of the war was that of Second-Lieutenant Alfred Victor Smith, 1/5th East Lancashire Regiment (T.F.). When in the act of throwing a grenade he slipped, with the result that the live bomb fell near a group of officers and men. He shouted a quick warning and was able to get into cover. But as soon as he was safe he realized that the others could not find cover in time. Without a moment's hesitation he threw himself upon the grenade in the moment of its explosion, paying with his own life for those of others whom he saved.

The feat of the private who tore the fuse from a large minnenwerfer bomb was rivalled by the conduct of Second-Lieutenant George Arthur Boyd-Rochfort, Special Reserve, 1st battalion Scots Guards. While in the trenches between Cambrin and La Bassée, at 2 a.m. on August 3, 1915, a huge bomb from a German trench-mortar landed on the parapet near a working-party. The lieutenant could easily have taken cover, but he rushed forward with a warning shout and seized the big thing in his hands. One great cast sent it spinning clear of the parapet, where it forthwith exploded.

Another act of supreme devotion, performed amid the explosions of the large bombs cast by the minnenwerfer, won the V.C. for Private Harry Christian, 2nd battalion Royal Lancaster Regiment. With half a dozen comrades he was holding a crater in front of the trenches when the men were driven back by a heavy bombardment from the German trenches. Christian found, after retiring, that three men had not come away from the crater; he therefore returned alone to the place and found them buried. Under showers of bombs he dug them out one by one and carried them back to safety.

Repeated acts of bravery and devotion to duty resulted in the award of the V.C. to Captain John Alexander Sinton, M.B., Indian Medical Service. Though shot through both arms, he worked under very heavy fire, dressing the wounded, and refusing to go into hospital while there was light to work.

Even the records of the Great War hold few parallels to the endurance of Lance-Corporal William Richard Cotter, 6th East Kent Regiment. His right leg had been shattered at the knee and he was wounded in both arms, yet he made his way unaided to a crater fifty yards distant, where his men were in a critical position. A fresh counter-attack of the enemy was imminent, and Cotter made a new disposition of the men in order to meet it. For two hours he directed the defence by word of mouth, and only when the attack had quieted down did he allow rough dressing to be applied to his wounds. It was fourteen hours later before he was moved back to a dressing-station.

Another splendid soldier, who continued to fight when his foot had been blown off, was Captain Arthur Forbes Gordon Kilby, 2nd South Staffordshire Regiment. By his own request he was selected to lead a forlorn hope against a strong enemy redoubt, his well-known courage marking him out for this dangerous service. He ran at the head of his company along a narrow tow-path, under heavy machine-gun fire and a shower of bombs, and brought his men to the enemy's wire. Here he was shot down, and his foot was blown off by a bomb; but he continued to fire a rifle and cheer his men on by word of mouth. He never returned from the attack.

Severe and painful wounds did not deter Private William Young, 8th East Lancashire Regiment, from going to the rescue of his sergeant, who was lying wounded under heavy fire in No Man's Land. As soon as he left the trench, Young had both jaws shattered by a bullet, but persisted until, with the help of another man, he had brought the sergeant in. When he got to the dressing-station it was found that he had also been wounded severely in the chest by a bullet.

Another Lancashire hero was Private Henry Kenny, 1st battalion Loyal North Lancashire Regiment. Six times in one day he went out into the open under heavy fire, and every time he returned with a wounded man. As he was handing the sixth man over the parapet he fell wounded in the neck. Sergeant Arthur Frederick Saunders, 9th Suffolk Regiment, earned the V.C. by magnificent work with machine guns. When his officer was wounded, the sergeant took charge, and supported four charges of another battalion. After being hoisted in the air with his men, by the explosion of a mine, Lieutenant Eric Arthur Archibald McNair, 9th Royal Sussex Regiment, was still capable of leading them with such great gallantry and skill as to be awarded the V.C.

PERSONALIA OF THE WAR

I N each volume we provide concise and authoritative biographical information concerning the outstanding personalities of the war. For clearness and ready reference they are grouped according to nationality. The most suitable volume in which to include these biographies is that wherein the subjects figure most prominently.

BRITISH

Sir Sackville Carden

SIR SACKVILLE HAMILTON CARDEN was born May 3, 1857. He entered the navy in 1870. He saw active service in the Egyptian War in 1882, at Suakin in 1884, and with the Benin expedition of 1897. In 1908 he was made a rear-admiral and from 1912 to September, 1914, was superintendent of the dockyard at Malta. In the autumn of 1914 he commanded the fleet that operated against the forts of the Dardanelles, but in March, 1915, he resigned through illness. Knighted in 1916, he was promoted admiral in September, 1917, and placed on the retired list in November of that year. He died May 5, 1930.

Sir John de Robeck

SIR JOHN MICHAEL DE ROBECK, son of the 4th baron de Robeck of Naas, county Kildare, was born June 10, 1862. His father's title was a Swedish one, dating from 1750. The 2nd baron, who fought in the armies of Sweden and France, became naturalised in England about 1800. John Michael entered the navy in 1875, and by 1911 was a rear-admiral. From 1912-14 he was admiral of patrols, and in March, 1915, was appointed commander of the force sent to assist the landing in Gallipoli and directed operations off the coast until the conclusion of the evacuation in January, 1916. In June, 1919, he was made commander-in-chief in the Mediterranean, and he acted as high commissioner at Constantinople. In 1916 he was knighted, in 1919 he was made a baronet, and in 1920 a full admiral. He died January 21, 1928.

Lord Wester-Wemyss

ROSSLYN ERSKINE WEMYSS, 1ST BARON WESTER-WEMYSS, better known as Sir Rosslyn Wemyss, was born April 12, 1864. He entered the navy in 1877. He was commander of the Ophir, in which King George and Queen Mary visited the Dominions, 1901; commodore R.N. barracks, 1911-12; and commander of the second battle squadron, 1912-13. In the Great War he commanded the squadron at the landing in Gallipoli, April, 1915, and at the evacuation, and in 1916-17 was commander-in-chief East Indies and Egypt. He was first sea lord, 1918-19, and in that position directed naval affairs at the time of the armistice, and was Britain's chief naval adviser at the peace conference in Paris. Captain in 1901, he was promoted rear-admiral, 1912, vice-admiral, 1916, admiral, 1919, and admiral of the fleet, 1920. He was knighted in 1916, and in 1919 was raised to the peerage. He died on May 24, 1933. In 1924 he published The Navy in the Dardanelles.

Sir Reginald Tyrwhitt

SIR REGINALD YORKE TYRWHITT was born May 10, 1870, and entered the navy in 1886. He was promoted lieutenant in 1892, and, two years later, he served with the squadron that was prominent in protecting British interests in Nicaragua.

Promoted captain in 1908, he was in command of the second destroyer flotilla from August, 1912, to December, 1913. At the beginning of the war he had been serving for about six months as a commodore of the 2nd class in charge of the destroyer flotillas of the first fleet, flying his broad pennant in the Amethyst. One of the vessels of this command, the Lance, figured in the first notable incident of the operations in the North Sea, sinking the German mine-layer Königin Luise on August 5, 1914. Tyrwhitt commanded the destroyer flotilla in the battle of Heligoland Bight, August 28, 1914, flying his flag in the light cruiser Arethusa, then just out of dockyard hands.

Tyrwhitt next came under the favourable notice of the Admiralty as commander of the destroyers which helped to convoy the British seaplane pilots who bombarded German warships lying in the roads off Cuxhaven on December 25. He led the destroyer flotillas at the battle of the Dogger Bank, January 24, 1915, when the Arethusa torpedoed the Blücher, and was in command of the Arethusa when she was wrecked in February, 1916. Tyrwhitt had a part in the exploit of blocking the harbours of Zeebrugge and Ostend in April and May, 1918, when he led out a portion of his Harwich force to guard the British raiders against interference from the German bases in the Heligoland Bight. In January, 1921, he was given command of the third light cruiser squadron in the Mediterranean, and from 1923 to 1925 he was commanding officer, coast of Scotland. Tyrwhitt was commander-in-chief, China squadron, 1927-29, and in 1930 became commander-in-chief at the Nore. Promoted rear-admiral, December, 1919, he was made a knight, 1917, and a baronet in 1919.

Sir Reginald Bacon

SIR REGINALD HUGH SPENCER BACON was the son of a clergyman. He entered the training ship Britannia in 1874, and became a lieutenant in 1883. In the Benin expedition of 1897 he was chief of the intelligence department, winning the D.S.O., and later conducted the first submarine trials. From

1907 he was director of naval ordnance and torpedoes, becoming director of the Coventry ordnance works in 1909. Having re-joined soon after the outbreak of war in 1914, Bacon went to France as colonel of the Royal Marines and commanded one of its heavy howitzer brigades. In 1915 he was appointed vice-admiral in command of the Dover Patrol, a post he held until January, 1918, when he was made controller of the munitions inventions department at the Admiralty. He was knighted in 1916. In 1919 he published an account of the operations of the Dover patrol in the Great War.

Sir Ian Hamilton

SIR IAN STANDISH MONTEITH HAMILTON, the son of a soldier, was born at Corfu, January 16, 1853. Educated at Cheam School and Wellington College, he entered the Gordon Highlanders in 1873, and first saw active service in the Afghan War of 1878-79. He served in the Boer War of 1881, being taken prisoner at Majuba Hill, where he was wounded, was with the expedition up the Nile in 1884-85, and in Burma, 1886-87. In 1891 he became colonel, and, after service in the Chitral campaign, 1895, led a brigade in the Tirah, 1897-98. He then commanded the school of musketry at Hythe.

In 1899, when the South African War began, Hamilton was in Ladysmith as chief of the staff to Sir George White, and he was in command of the infantry at Elandslaagte and other engagements. After the relief of Ladysmith he commanded some mounted infantry, was chief of the staff to Lord Kitchener, and was in command of mobile columns in the Transvaal until the end of the war in 1902, when he was made quartermaster-general to the forces. During the Russo-Japanese War he was military representative of India, being in Manchuria with the Japanese, an experience which led to his book, A Staff Officer's Scrap Book. From 1905-9 he was general officer commanding the southern district, from 1909-10 adjutant-general and a member of the army council, and from 1910-15 commander-in-chief in the Mediterranean and inspector-general of oversea forces. In 1915, having been just made a full general, Hamilton was chosen to command the force that landed on the Gallipoli peninsular. He led it in its terrible fighting until he was superseded in October. In 1920 he retired from the army.

The failure of the expedition was bound to react on the general in charge of the operations, and the commission that inquired into the matter censured him, although only on minor points. A charming personality, Hamilton is a writer with distinct gifts of style, shown not least in his dispatches, and something of a poet. His works include Icarus and Fighting of the Future, and Gallipoli Diary, 1920.

Sir William Birdwood

SIR WILLIAM RIDDELL BIRDWOOD was born in India, September 13, 1865. A nephew of Sir George Birdwood, he belonged to a family long connected with the government of India. Educated at Clifton and Sandhurst, he joined the Scots Fusiliers in 1883, transferring to the 11th Bengal Lancers in 1886. It was on the North-Western Frontier of India, the physical features of which approximate in no small degree to those of Gallipoli, that Lieut. Birdwood had his first experiences under fire. He took part, in 1891, in the Black Mountain (Hazara) Expedition under General Elles, an expedition which passed through many a hazardous enterprise in a roadless and storm-beaten country, sometimes at an elevation of ten thousand feet. In the South African War he served on the staff, and was severely wounded. Kitchener, with whom he returned to India in 1902, made him his military secretary, and he acted as chief staff officer on the Mohmand expedition, and on its conclusion was given command of a brigade. This was followed by his appointment in 1912 as quartermaster-general in India, and almost immediately by that of secretary to the Indian Government for military affairs and member of the viceroy's council. In 1914, being then a K.C.M.G., he was selected to command the Australian corps, which he led in Egypt and in Gallipoli.

On Sir Ian Hamilton's retirement Birdwood assumed command of the army in Gallipoli, prepared the plan for the evacuation, and superintended its execution. He remained at the head of the corps when it was moved to the western front, only leaving his post in May, 1918, to take over the command of the Fifth Army, as reconstituted after the disaster in March. After the armistice in November, 1918, he commanded the Australians in England. Birdwood was made a full general and a K.C.B. in 1917, and was created a baronet and G.C.M.G. in 1919, receiving a grant of £10,000 for his services in the Great War. In 1931 he was made master of Peterhouse, Cambridge.

Sir Aylmer Hunter-Weston

SIR AYLMER GOULD HUNTER-WESTON was born September 23, 1864, the son of an Ayrshire landowner. He was educated at Wellington. Having passed through the R.M.A. at Woolwich, he entered the Royal Engineers in 1884. In 1891 he saw active service on the Indian frontier, as he did in 1894-95, when he was wounded; in 1896 he was in Egypt. He went through the South African War, being first with the engineers, then on the staff and finally in command of a column. While there he made his name known to the public by a daring act in cutting the railway north of Bloemfontein in March, 1900. Hunter was employed on the staff 1904-11, when he became assistant director of military training. In 1914 he was in command of the 11th infantry brigade, and this he took to France in August. In 1915 he went to Gallipoli as general of the 29th division, assuming in May command of the 8th corps. In this year he was knighted. He left Gallipoli on account of his health, but was in France early in 1916, and led the 8th corps in the battle of the Somme and elsewhere. In 1916 he was returned as M.P. for North Ayrshire, and he retained the seat at the subsequent general elections.

Sir Charles Monro

SIR CHARLES CARMICHAEL MONRO was born June 15, 1860, and entered the West Surrey Regiment in 1879. He was in charge of the London division of Territorials, 1912-14, and when the Great War began he took the 2nd Division to the front. In 1915 he was given command of the 1st Corps, and when the Third Army was formed was placed at its head. Soon afterwards, sent to report on the position in Gallipoli, he succeeded Sir Ian Hamilton as commander-in-chief and superintended the evacuation. Returning to the western front early in 1916, he took command of the First Army, but later in the year was sent to India as commander-in-chief, which post he resigned in 1920. In 1915 Monro was knighted, in 1917 was made a general, and in 1921 a baronet. He died December 7, 1929.

Sir Walter Braithwaite

SIR WALTER PIPON BRAITHWAITE was born November 11, 1865. He entered the Somerset Light Infantry in 1886, and saw active service the same year in Burma. From 1906-9 he was employed at the Staff College, Camberley, and he commanded the Staff College at Quetta, 1911-14. In September, 1914, he became director of staff duties at the War Office, and in March, 1915, chief of the staff to the Mediterranean Expeditionary Force, serving in Gallipoli until October, 1915. Transferred later to the Western Front, he led the 62nd Division in March, 1918, and the 9th Corps later in the year. In 1918 he was knighted. He was adjutant-general to the forces 1927-31.

Sir Frederick Stopford

SIR FREDERICK WILLIAM STOPFORD was born February 22, 1854, son of the 4th earl of Courtown. He entered the army as a second-lieutenant in the Grenadier Guards, 1871, saw service in Egypt, the Sudan, and Ashanti, and in the South African War was military secretary to Sir R. Buller, 1899-1900. Director of military training, 1904-6, G.O.C. London district, 1906-9, he was lieutenant of the Tower of London, 1912-14.

In 1915 he was in command of an army corps in Gallipoli, and until superseded on August 14 had charge of the operations at Suvla Bay. He was promoted lieutenant-general, 1909, and created K.C.M.G., 1900. He died May 4, 1929.

Sir John Maxwell

SIR JOHN GRENFELL MAXWELL was born July 12, 1859. He was educated at Cheltenham College, and in 1878 joined the Black Watch, with which he served in Egypt in 1882, being present at Tel-el-Kebir. In 1884 he served in the Nile expedition as a staff officer, and took part in all the campaigns there during the next twelve years, winning the D.S.O. at Giniss and commanding a brigade of Egyptians at Omdurman. In the South African War he commanded a brigade and afterwards was military governor of Pretoria, being knighted in 1900. After some years on the staff in England, Maxwell held the command of the force in Egypt, 1908-12, and again 1914-15. Early in the latter year he defeated the attack of Djemal Pasha, the Turkish commander, against the Suez canal. Maxwell's forces in this campaign consisted of British territorials, Australian and New Zealand contingents, Indian cavalry and infantry and units of the Anglo-Egyptian army. When the Irish rebellion broke out in April, 1916, he was sent to Ireland as commander-in-chief; but in a few months he was appointed to the northern command, which he retained until April, 1919. In 1919 he was made a full general.

Sir Alexander Godley

SIR ALEXANDER JOHN GODLEY was born February 4, 1867. He was educated at Haileybury and Sandhurst. In 1886 he joined the Dublin Fusiliers, and in 1896 saw active service with mounted infantry in South Africa. Having passed through the staff college, he was in South Africa when the war broke out in 1899, and after assisting in the defence of Mafeking, took command of a mounted brigade. From 1903-5 he was commandant of the school of mounted infantry at Aldershot, and in 1910 was sent out to New Zealand. On the outbreak of the Great War he went to Egypt and Gallipoli at the head of a division of Australians and New Zealanders. After an arduous year on the peninsula he went to France, where he led a division for some time and was put in command of the 22nd corps, which he led in the closing stages of the war. He was in command of the New Zealand Expeditionary Force throughout the war, and a corps of the army of the Rhine. He became military secretary to the secretary for war, September, 1920, resigning in 1924 to become commander-in-chief of the Southern Command. Godley was knighted in 1914.

BRITISH

Sir Edward Alderson

SIR EDWARD ALFRED HERVEY ALDERSON was born April 8, 1859, the son of E. M. Alderson, of Ipswich. He entered the West Kent Regiment in 1878. His earliest active service was with the mounted infantry in South Africa in 1881-2, and he served in the Egyptian campaigns in 1882 and 1884-5. He was in Mashonaland in 1896, and during the South African War in 1900-1 was in command of the Mounted Infantry. From 1903 he commanded an infantry brigade at Aldershot, and from 1908-12 the Poona Division in India. During the Great War he was commander in France of the Canadian Division, which he directed at the second battle of Ypres, and when a Canadian Corps was formed he was placed at its head. In 1916 he was made a K.C.B. and returned home, being then a lieutenant-general. He died December 14, 1927.

Sir James Willcocks

SIR JAMES WILLCOCKS was born April 1, 1857. He entered the Leinster Regiment in 1878 and saw service in the Afghan War, 1879-80; in the Sudan, 1885; in Burma, 1886-87; and on the Indian frontier. Joining the West African Frontier Force, he became its commandant in 1898, and led the expedition to the relief of Kumasi. For this exploit he was knighted. In 1914 Willcocks was chosen to command the Indian Corps sent to the Western Front, and he led this in the difficult winter of 1914-15. Later in 1915 he returned home, and he was governor of Bermuda, 1917-22. He was advanced to the rank of general in 1915. He died December 18, 1926.

Sir Michael Tighe

SIR MICHAEL JOSEPH TIGHE was born May 21, 1864. He joined the Leinster Regiment in 1883, transferring to the Indian staff corps two years later. He served in the Burmese war, 1886-88, and in various frontier expeditions, and in 1895 took part in the East African expedition, and later in the operations in Makran and South-east Persia. In the Great War he was in command of the British troops during the earlier stages of the campaign in East Africa. He was created K.C.M.G. in 1916. He died September 5, 1925.

Sir Percy Girouard

SIR EDOUARD PERCY CRANWELL GIROUARD was born in Montreal, January 26, 1867. He was educated at the Royal Military College, Kingston, and entered the army in 1888. He served with the Dongola expeditionary force, 1896, when he gained the D.S.O., and in the Nile expedition, 1897.

He was railway traffic manager, Woolwich, 1890-95, director of Sudan railways, 1896-98, director of railways, South Africa, 1899-1902, and, during the next two years, was commissioner of railways, Transvaal and Orange River Colony. In 1906 he was A.Q.M.G. of the western command, Chester; high commissioner of North Nigeria, 1907-8, and governor and commander-in-chief of East Africa, 1909-12. In 1912 he joined the board of Armstrong, Whitworth & Co. When Lloyd George became minister of munitions in May, 1915, he appointed Girouard his chief organizer, with the title of director-general of munitions supply. He was created K.C.M.G. in 1900. He died September, 26, 1932.

Commander Samson

CHARLES RUMNEY SAMSON was born in 1883. He entered the navy in 1898, and served in Somaliland, 1903-4, and in the Persian Gulf operations, 1908-10. When first-lieutenant of the scout Foresight, he was chosen by the admiralty for training in aviation at Eastchurch, and took his pilot's certificate in 1911. He had a distinguished career in the Great War. He was in command of the aeroplane and armoured-car support of the R.N.A.S. in the autumn of 1914. Based on Dunkirk, his squadron carried out daring and successful raids. In January, 1915, he dropped bombs on the German positions in Brussels, and in February commanded the aeroplane attack on Zeebrugge and Ostend. In that same year he served in Gallipoli, and later in Egypt. He was also in command of the seaplane carrier Ben My Chree on the Syrian coast. In 1930 he published Fights and Flights, a record of his adventures. He died on February 5, 1931.

Earl of Derby

EDWARD GEORGE VILLIERS STANLEY, 17th earl of Derby, was born April 4, 1865. He was educated at Wellington College and served for some years in the Grenadier Guards. He entered the House of Commons in 1892, and during the earlier part of the South African War was chief Press censor and private secretary to Lord Roberts. In 1895, then Lord Stanley, he joined the Conservative government as a lord of the treasury, and in 1900 became financial secretary to the War Office, being promoted postmaster general in 1903. He succeeded to the earldom in 1908. In 1915 as director-general of recruiting, he organized the Derby scheme, a method of obtaining recruits for the army on a voluntary basis. In 1916 he became under-secretary for war, and soon after war secretary in succession to Mr. Lloyd George. He remained at the War Office till 1918, when he was appointed ambassador to Paris, a position which he resigned in September, 1920. He was secretary for war in the Unionist ministry October, 1922, to January, 1924.

Edith Cavell

EDITH LOUISA CAVELL was born December 4, 1865, at Swardeston, Norfolk, the daughter of the Rev. Frederick Cavell, who was 40 years vicar of that parish. She completed her education in Brussels, travelled on the Continent, and having studied German methods of medicine and hygiene, returned to England and underwent the course of training as nurse at the London Hospital. In 1900 she was appointed superintendent of the Highgate infirmary. In 1906 she returned to Brussels, where she became matron of the Ecole Belge d'Infirmières Diplômées, later known as the Ecole Edith Cavell. When the Great War broke out and the German army invaded Belgium she decided to remain at her post, where she continued to succour the sick and wounded. On August 5, 1915, she was arrested by the Germans, charged with harbouring refugees and assisting them to escape. On October 7 her trial took place; on October 11 she was sentenced to death, and, despite the mediation of neutral diplomatists, she was shot in the Tir National, Brussels, at 2 o'clock the following morning, among her last words being, " I am glad to die for my country." In May, 1919, her body was brought to England, and, after a memorial service at Westminster Abbey, was buried in the precincts of Norwich Cathedral.

In Britain many memorials, homes for nurses, etc., were established. In Canada one of the lofty peaks of the Rocky Mountains was named Edith Cavell. A monument to her was erected in St. Martin's Place, London, a short distance to the north of Trafalgar Square. It is of grey granite, standing 40 feet high, and contains the statue of Miss Cavell shown standing erect in her nurse's uniform. It was designed by Sir G. Frampton, R.A., and unveiled by Queen Alexandra, March 17, 1920.

Mrs. St. Clair Stobart

MABEL ANNIE ST. CLAIR STOBART was born in 1862, daughter of Sir Samuel Boulton, Bart. She married, first, St. Clair Stobart, and secondly, John Herbert Greenhalgh. After spending some years in South Africa, she founded the Women's Sick and Wounded Convoy Corps, commanding a detachment of it in the Balkan Wars, 1912-13. In the Great War she organized hospitals (women's units) in Belgium and France for the St. John Ambulance Association. She was taken prisoner by the Germans, and condemned to be shot as a spy, but released. In 1915 she took a unit to Serbia, where she established a military hospital, roadside tent dispensaries for the civilian population, and did a wonderful work during the terrible retreat of the troops to Albania. She wrote The Flaming Sword—in Serbia and Elsewhere, 1916.

FRENCH

Admiral Guépratte

EMILE PAUL AIMABLE GUEPRATTE, the noted French sailor, distinguished himself in 1914-15. He took part in the naval operations in the Dardanelles, succeeding Admiral du Fournet as commander of the French squadron in that theatre of war. He served under Vice-admiral de Robeck in the attack of March 18, 1915. He was promoted vice-admiral in October, 1915.

General d'Amade

ALBERT GERARD LEO D'AMADE was a son of Adolphe d'Amade, military intendant. He was born at Toulouse, on December 24, 1856, and was educated at La Flèche and at the lycée of Lorient, Morbihan. He entered the French army as a lieutenant of Algerian infantry at Constantine on October 1, 1876. He was military attaché at Peking, 1887-91, and military attaché with British Headquarters in the South African War. He was promoted colonel in 1903 and was military attaché in London, 1903-6. Advanced to the rank of general in 1907, he commanded the French forces in the operations in Morocco, 1907-9. In 1914 he became a member of the Conseil Supérieur de la Guerre, and on the outbreak of the Great War was in charge of the mobilisation of the army of the Alps. Later in the same year he commanded a group of territorial divisions, and in April-May, 1915, he led the French troops which landed in Gallipoli.

General Gouraud

HENRI JOSEPH EUGÈNE GOURAUD was born at Paris, November 17, 1867. He joined the French army as a lieutenant of the Chasseurs à pied in 1890. He saw service in the Sudan in 1898; in the Congo, Senegal, and Morocco. He was at the head of the 1st Colonial Army Corps in February, 1915. In July, 1915, he was severely wounded while in command of the French forces in Gallipoli. Returning to France, in December he was given command of the Fourth Army. In 1916 he was appointed resident commissary-general in Morocco, but in June, 1917, was again in command of the 4th army. In

1919 he became high commissioner of France in Syria and Cilicia, and commander-in-chief of her army of the Levant. It was to Gouraud that Marshal Foch confided the tremendous task of meeting the first shock of that offensive which the enemy were confident would clear the road to Paris. The German attack began on July 15, 1918, on a fifty-mile front east and west of Rheims. Between Prunay and Massiges, to the east, where the 4th army was, they were held, as Gouraud, in his address to his men on the 7th, said they would be.

Alexandre Millerand

A LEXANDRE MILLERAND was born in Paris, February 10, 1859. He studied law, was admitted to the bar in 1881, and attained immediate prominence by his defence of the miners of Montceau-les-Mines in 1882. Elected deputy for Paris in December, 1885, he quickly acquired a leading position in the Radical-Socialist party, and in 1887 was made a member of the Budget Committee. He defended the syndicates that were prosecuted as illegal organizations, and became parliamentary leader of the Socialist party and editor of La Petite République, the party organ, vacating that position in 1896 to become managing director of La Lanterne. Waldeck-Rousseau chose him as minister of commerce in 1899.

After the fall of the Waldeck-Rousseau cabinet in 1902, Millerand continued to work on the completion of the legislative programme he had initiated for the betterment of the workers. In July, 1909, he was appointed minister of public works, an office he held until November, 1910, organizing the State railway system. Poincaré appointed him minister of war in January, 1912, and when he left that office in 1913, he devoted himself chiefly to military questions, urging energetic preparation against the German invasion, which he foresaw. Directly war broke out Millerand was made president of the committee on supplies at the ministry of war, and on August 25, 1914, returned to the ministry of war, remaining in office until the Viviani cabinet resigned in 1915. Millerand was elected a member of the Academy of Moral and Political Sciences in 1917, and on the conclusion of the armistice in 1918 he was appointed commissioner-general for Alsace-Lorraine.

Millerand succeeded Clemenceau as premier after Deschanel's election to the presidency of the republic, also undertaking the office of foreign secretary, and formed his cabinet on January 19, 1920. He was a prominent figure of the Allied conferences at Lympne in May and August of that year. Deschanel, who had been elected president over the head of Clemenceau, was compelled to resign in September. The election for a new president, held on September 24, resulted in an overwhelming majority for Millerand, who received 695 votes as against 69 received by M. Delory, the Socialist candidate. He resigned the presidency in June, 1924, following an adverse vote in the chamber. He was a member of the senate 1925-27, and later. His publications include Socialism réformiste en France, 1903, and La Guerre Liberatrice, 1918.

ITALIAN

King Victor Emmanuel III

VICTOR EMMANUEL III, King of Italy, son of Humbert I, was born at Naples, November 11, 1869. He entered the army in 1887, and showed great ability in military matters, frequently visiting Germany to obtain information and ideas. In 1896 he married Princess Helena of Montenegro. He ascended the throne on the assassination of his father, July 29, 1900, and proved a wise and tactful monarch. When Italy joined in the war he assumed the supreme command of all his land and naval forces. A man of wide culture and interests, he became known for his knowledge of numismatics.

General Cadorna

COUNT LUIGI CADORNA was born at Pallanza, September 4, 1850, son of Count Rafaele Cadorna, the leader of the Italian army that invaded the Papal States in 1870. Educated at the military school Turin, he entered the Italian army in 1868, and saw active service on his father's staff in 1870. By 1905 he had risen to the rank of lieutenant-general. In 1914 he succeeded General Pollio as chief of the general staff. When Italy, in May, 1915, entered the Great War, Cadorna was appointed commander-in-chief, and continued to hold that position until immediately after the battle of Caporetto, 1917, when he was superseded by General Diaz. He then represented Italy on the military council at Versailles, and was placed on the retired list in September, 1919. He died December 21, 1928.

Duke of the Abruzzi

LUIGI AMADEO, DUKE OF THE ABRUZZI, third son of Amadeo, duke of Aosta and king of Spain, 1870-3, and cousin to Victor Emmanuel III, king of Italy, was born in Madrid, January 29, 1873. He ascended Mt. St. Elias, Alaska, July 31, 1897, being the first to do so. He organized an Arctic expedition, 1899-1900, and from his ship, the Stella Polare, sent out sledging parties, one of which attained lat. 86° 33′ N., the then highest recorded. His expedition determined the N. coast of Franz-Josef Land. In Africa he ascended Mt. Ruwenzori in 1906, and in 1909 he established a new record in mountain-climbing by ascending Mt. Godwin-Austen, Kashmir, to an altitude of 24,600 ft. Meanwhile he had served in the Italian navy, commanding a squadron during the war with Turkey, and on Italy's entry in the Great War in 1915 became commander-in-chief, holding that position till 1917. He died March 18, 1933. His writings include Farther North than Nansen, 1901; and On the Polar Star in the Arctic Sea, 1903.

Signor Salandra

ANTONIO SALANDRA was born near Foggia on August 31, 1853. He studied at Naples and became a lawyer. Elected to parliament as a conservative, 1886, he served in the treasury, 1891-96; was minister of agriculture, 1899-1900; and of finance, 1906, 1908-10. In 1914 he became premier, and was at the head of the government which placed Italy on the side of the Allies and entered the Great War, 1915. Criticised for lack of initiative and want of energy, he resigned in 1917. He was one of Italy's representatives at the Paris Peace Conference, 1919. He wrote on legal and political subjects. After the Fascist coup of 1922, Salandra was asked to form a ministry, but on the refusal of three Fascist deputies to accept office under him, he recommended the king to send for Mussolini. He was nominated a senator in 1928 and died December 9, 1931.

Baron Sonnino

BARON SIDNEY SONNINO was born at Pisa, March 11, 1847, his mother being an Englishwoman. He joined the diplomatic service, and was attached to the Italian legation in Madrid, Paris, and Vienna. He entered parliament in 1877 as a liberal-conservative, and was under-secretary for finance in the Crispi cabinets, 1887-90 and 1893-96. Afterwards he became minister of the treasury, and saved Italian credit by his drastic financial and fiscal reforms. He was premier in 1906 and again in 1909-10. From 1914-19 he was foreign minister, and enhanced his reputation by his skilful and tactful conduct of the negotiations leading up to Italy's participation in the Great War, and of those with the Allies which led to the pact of London. He was one of Italy's representatives at the Peace conference in Paris in 1919, in October, of which year he retired from political life. A noted authority on economics and finance, he published Contadini in Sicilia, 1876, and edited Rassegna Settimanale, 1878-82. He died November 24, 1922.

General Zupelli

VITTORIO ZUPELLI was born in 1862. After a distinguished career in the army he was a general of division at the outbreak of the Great War. On the entry of Italy on the side of the Allies, May, 1915, he was war minister, and took an active command in April, 1916. He succeeded Dall' Olio as minister of munitions in May, 1918, and in 1919 was for a time minister of pensions.

RUSSIAN

General Kuropatkin

ALEXEI NIKOLAIEVITCH KUROPATKIN, the noted Russian soldier, entered the army in 1864, first saw active service in Turkistan and served as a volunteer with the French army in Algeria in 1874. During the Russo-Turkish War (1877-78) he was chief of staff to General Skobelev. During 1880-81 he was again in Turkistan and distinguished himself by a brilliant march of some 500 miles to Geok-Tepe, and at the storming of the fortress. In 1898-1904 he was minister of war, and in 1904 he was given the command in the war with Japan.

After the defeat at Mukden he was superseded by General Linievitch, and for the remainder of the war served as commander of the first Manchurian army. During the Great War he was commander-in-chief of the armies on the Northern front, but in August, 1916, was appointed governor of Turkistan. A year later he was placed under arrest on a charge of distributing arms among the Russian colonists. His death was announced from Moscow, February 10, 1921.

SERBIAN

King Alexander of Yugo-Slavia

ALEXANDER, KING OF YUGO-SLAVIA, who was Crown Prince of Serbia during the Great War, was born at Cettinje, December 17, 1888, the second son of King Peter of Serbia. He took the oath as heir apparent March 27, 1909, when his elder brother George renounced his right of succession. He distinguished himself in the wars of 1912-13 against Turkey and Bulgaria, and was commander-in-chief of the Serbian army in the Great War. He was proclaimed King of Yugo-Slavia August 19, 1921. In 1924 he dismissed his parliament and set up a dictatorship.

General Stepanovitch

STEPHEN STEPANOVITCH was born at Kumodra, near Belgrade. He joined the Serbian army as lieutenant in 1876. He saw service in the Serbo-Turkish wars, 1876-78, and in the war against Bulgaria, 1885-86. A colonel in 1891, he was general in 1906, and acted for a considerable time as minister of war. He took part in the Balkan Wars, 1912-13. Raised to the rank of field-marshal (voivode) shortly after the outbreak of the Great War, he took part in the defeat of the Austrian invasions, 1914-15. In the autumn of 1915 he commanded the army which bore the brunt of the Bulgarian onslaught in Northeast Serbia, and in September, 1918, he was one of the chief Serbian commanders in the offensive which resulted in the overthrow of Bulgaria. He died April 27, 1929.

General Vassitch

GENERAL VASSITCH had a distinguished career in the Great War. At the outbreak of war he was a colonel. In October, 1915, he commanded a Serbian force in Macedonia which made an heroic attempt to stem the Austro-German advance, and won a victory over the Bulgarians at the Babuna Pass. In 1916, in command of an army corps, he helped to recover Monastir, and in September-October, 1918, as commander of the first Serbian army, took a leading part in the defeat of the enemy and the liberation of Serbia.

GERMAN

Admiral von Hipper

FRANZ VON HIPPER, the German sailor, was born September 13, 1863. He held the rank of rear-admiral at the outbreak of the Great War, and was in charge of the German naval raid on Scarborough and the Hartlepools, December 16, 1914, and commanded the cruiser squadron at the battles of the Dogger Bank, January 24, 1915, and Jutland, May 31, 1916. He was one of several German admirals whose surrender was demanded by Great Britain. He died May 25, 1932.

Admiral von Tirpitz

ALFRED FRIEDRICH VON TIRPITZ was born at Küstrin, March 19, 1849, and educated at the gymnasium, Frankfort, entering the Prussian navy, April 24, 1865. He was Prussian minister of state in 1898, and thereafter devoted his energy to the creation of a navy capable of challenging that of Great Britain. In 1903 he became grand admiral of the German navy and head of the naval staff. Shortly after the outbreak of the Great War, he announced the submarine campaign against the Allies, but in the end disputes in Germany as to the real value of this campaign brought about his fall in March, 1916. In his retirement he was the active head of the Fatherland Party, which was particularly hostile to Great Britain. He published My Memories, 1919 and died March 6, 1930.

Prince Leopold of Bavaria

LEOPOLD, PRINCE OF BAVARIA, the son of Prince Luitpold, regent of Bavaria, and the Archduchess Gisela, daughter of Francis Joseph of Austria, was born at Munich, February, 9, 1846. He entered the Bavarian army in 1861, and was made a field-marshal of Germany in 1904. During the Great War he commanded, in 1915, the German 5th army, which lay along the line from the Vistula south by the Bzura to the Pilitza, and he occupied Warsaw on August 5, after its evacuation by the Russians. In 1916 he was nominally commander of the German 9th army, operating in Russia. He died September 28, 1930.

General von Bernhardi

FRIEDRICH VON BERNHARDI, German soldier and writer, was born at St. Petersburg while his father, Theodar von Bernhardi, was attached to the Germany embassy, November 22, 1849. He was educated at the gymnasiums of Berlin and of Hirschberg in Silesia. He entered the German army in 1869, and took part in the Franco-German War of 1870-71. From 1891 to 1894 he was military attaché at Berne, and for the next three years he lectured to young soldiers on military history. In 1907 he was given command of an army corps, but he retired from the army in 1909. He returned to it on the outbreak of the Great War and served first in the eastern and then in the western theatre.

At the close of the 19th century Bernhardi was known only in military circles as a general of a studious character, and a writer on the technical aspects of warfare. In 1912 he startled Germany with the deadly earnestness and frankness of his Germany and the Next War which at once ran through a number of editions, and was translated into English by A. H. Powles the same year. A disciple of Treitschke, Bernhardi popularised the ideas of his master. The time of his outburst was significant. The embroilment with the French over Morocco had given the military folk every reason to hope that "the day" had come. It was, however, settled in humane and civilized fashion, and the indignant soldier poured out his scorn on the civilians of Germany who had thus preferred the peace and prosperity of their homes to the expansion of their country by war. Borrowing a little from the newer prophet, Nietzsche, he was able to improve on the older master, and show how struggle and the triumph of the stronger was a law of life itself, millions of years older than the demoralising dreams of the pipe-of-peace smokers. Like Nietzsche, he misunderstood Darwinism, and thought that civilization could make progress only by warfare.

Then followed significant and fatal miscalculations of Britain, Russia, and worst of all, of the situation at sea. The British fleet would, of course, be so superior that it would drive the German ships under the shelter of the forts and blockade Germany, but Germany would be able to raid British commerce disastrously, and would get adequate supplies through Denmark and Scandinavia. Belgium would be part of the theatre of war, and he sneered at its "paper bulwark" of neutrality, and thus gave a useful phrase which the German chancellor employed in August, 1914. In fine, he scorned the kind of diplomacy which would conceal this aggressive enterprise under pretexts that Germany was merely defending herself against jealous rivals. The Great War, he said expressly, must be brought about by Germany. She must foment trouble in the oversea possessions of the rival Powers and march out with her drilled forces to world-power or downfall. He died July 10, 1930.

Field-Marshal von der Goltz

KOLMAR VON DER GOLTZ was born August 12, 1843, at Bielkenfeld, near Labiau, East Prussia. He entered the Prussian army as a lieutenant in 1861. In the Franco-Prussian War he was on the staff of Prince Frederick Charles and afterwards served on the historical section of the general staff in Berlin. In 1883 he undertook the reorganization of the Turkish army, with the rank of pasha, and remained in Turkey for twelve years. In 1908 he became field-marshal, and he headed a German mission to Constantinople where he remained for some years and had much to do with the Young Turk movement.

When the Great War broke out Goltz accompanied the German army into Belgium, and was made governor-general, first of Brussels and then of Belgium. Early in 1915 he went to Turkey, and he commanded a Turkish army near Constantinople during the allied attack on Gallipoli. For some time he directed Turkish operations in the Middle East, but died of spotted fever at his headquarters on April 19, 1916. His most notable book, The Nation in Arms, 1883, had much influence in strengthening the fighting spirit in Germany. Among his other works were The War History in Germany in the Nineteenth Century; and the Campaigns of Frederick the Great.

The field marshal's nephew, General von der Goltz, commanded the German forces in Latvia in 1919, and captured Riga in October of that year. He carried on a campaign in the Baltic provinces after Germany had been ordered to evacuate them.

General Seeckt

HANS VON SEECKT was born in Schleswig on April 22, 1866. At the age of 19 he entered the Kaiser Alexander grenadier regiment, in 1897 he was appointed to the general staff, and in 1913 he became chief of staff of the 3rd army corps (Berlin). He had reached the rank of colonel in 1914, and on the outbreak of war was appointed chief of staff to General von Lochow. He took part in most of the battles on the west front in that year, and in 1915 he planned the German offensive at Soissons. He then became chief of staff of the group of armies that, under Mackensen, broke into Galicia and overran Serbia. In 1917 he took command of the Turkish army. In 1919 Seeckt was Germany's military representative at Spa, and from 1920 to 1926 he was commander-in-chief of the army of the republic and was responsible for its military organization under the peace treaty. In 1928 he published Thoughts of a Soldier, and in 1929 The Future of the Reich.

General Liman von Sanders

OTTO VICTOR KARL LIMAN VON SANDERS, the son of Karl Leonhard Liman, was born at Stolp, Prussia, June 16, 1855. He entered the German army as a lieutenant of cavalry in 1874. In 1913 he attained the rank of general, commanded the 22nd division, and, being ennobled, added von Sanders to the family name. In 1914 he was sent to Constantinople, and, having been appointed a Turkish field-marshal, was commander-in-chief of the Turkish forces opposing the Allies in Gallipoli in 1915. After the death of von der Goltz, he directed the operations of the Turkish armies in the Middle East, and in 1918 was in chief command in Palestine and Syria, when Allenby conquered those countries. After the armistice he surrendered to the Allies, was interned in Malta, and released in August, 1919, when he returned to Germany. He published Five Years of Turkey, in 1920, an English edition of which appeared in 1928. He died August 24, 1929.

Prince von Bülow

BERNHARD HEINRICH MARTIN KARL, PRINCE VON BÜLOW, was born at Klein-Flottbeck, Holstein, May 3, 1849. He was educated at the universities of Lausanne, Leipzig, and Berlin, and entered the army in 1870. He took part in the Franco-Prussian War, 1870-71. He joined the diplomatic service in 1873, served as junior secretary in the embassies at St. Petersburg and Vienna, and was one of the officials of the Congress of Berlin in 1878.

Bülow was first secretary at Paris, 1878-84, at St. Petersburg, 1884-88, minister at Bukarest, 1893, and ambassador at Rome, 1893-97. From 1897-1900 he was foreign secretary, and in October, 1900, was appointed chancellor and president of the Prussian ministry, in succession to Prince Hohenlohe. He was made a prince of the German Empire in 1905, and retired from the chancellorship in 1909. In December, 1914, he was sent to Rome as ambassador, but failed in his efforts to prevent the entry of Italy into the Great War. His Imperial Germany, translated into English by M. A. Lewenz, 1914 (revised edition, 1916), is a defence of the policy of Germany, and contains his theories of autocratic rule and popular submission to authority. He died October 28, 1929.

BULGARIAN

Ferdinand, Tsar of Bulgaria

FERDINAND, tsar of Bulgaria, was born at Vienna, February 26, 1861. He was the youngest son of Augustus, prince of Saxe-Coburg-Gotha, and Clementine, daughter of King Louis Philippe. He was well educated, and with his brother Augustus published a book on his botanical observations in Brazil. He entered the Austrian army, but soon his ambition led him in another direction. In 1887 Alexander, prince of Bulgaria, abdicated, and after much intrigue Ferdinand was chosen as his successor. Russia was opposed to him, but he won through and by 1896 most of the objections to him had ceased. In 1908 he proclaimed the independence of Bulgaria, and called himself king or tsar, winning recognition from the powers shortly afterwards. He was an advocate of the Balkan League, and was one of the instigators of the war of 1912-13. On the outbreak of the Great War, Ferdinand was cautious enough to wait developments before committing himself to any definite policy. His strong German tendencies became more apparent, however, and finally, having exhausted the prevarications of diplomacy, he declared war on Serbia, October 13, 1915.

He played no conspicuous part in the war itself, and, on the final breakdown of the Bulgarian effort, he abdicated, October 4, 1918, in favour of his son Boris, and retired to Germany. Ferdinand married first, in 1893, a daughter of the duke of Parma; and secondly, in 1908, Eleanor, a princess of Ruess.

TURKISH

Enver Pasha

ENVER PASHA was born at Constantinople in 1882 of humble parentage. He entered the Turkish army in 1896. He first came into notice in connexion with the Young Turk movement in 1905 at Salonica, and three years later joined the revolutionaries, who in July, 1908, captured Monastir, where a constitution, accepted by the sultan Abdul Hamid, was proclaimed. Enver soon afterwards was appointed military attaché at Berlin, but on the outbreak of the Turkish counter-revolution in March, 1909, he returned to Salonica, and assisted in the deposition of Abdul Hamid.

Enver then went back to Berlin, and in 1910 paid a visit to London. In 1911 he organized the Arabs of Tripoli against the Italians in the Tripoli War. In the second Balkan War he recaptured Adrianople from the Bulgarians in July, 1913. Shortly before he had become minister of war with the rank of pasha, and married one of the imperial princesses. One of the leading spirits of the Committee of Union and Progress, the central organization of the Young Turks, he was personally pro-German, his influence being one of the factors that brought Turkey into the Great War against the Entente. After the submission of Turkey in 1918 Enver fled to the Caucasus. He was condemned to death in 1919, but fled to Russia. He was next concerned with the furtherance of Soviet propaganda in Asia Minor, but afterwards turned against Russia and led an unsuccessful insurrection against that country in the mountains of Russian Turkistan. He encouraged the Turks in their active resistance to the terms of the Peace Treaty in 1920, and engaged in plots. He was killed in Bokhara, August 4, 1922.

DIARY OF EVENTS
1915

DIARY OF EVENTS

From January 1, 1915 to December 31, 1915.

1915
JAN. 1.—H.M.S. Formidable torpedoed in Channel, loss of nearly 600 lives; 2 officers and 68 men rescued by the Brixham fishing smack Providence.

An Army Order defines the new organisation of armies, each consisting of three army corps.

JAN. 2.—King George's New Year message of confidence and friendship to President Poincaré published. Cheery reply sent by President.

Cardinal Mercier, Archbishop of Malines, made a prisoner in his palace by the Germans for issuing a pastoral on " Patriotism and Endurance."

Successful operations at Dar-es-Salaam by H.M.S. Fox and Goliath.

JAN. 3.—Turkish transport sunk by mine in the Bosporus.
JAN. 4.—New German move in Poland reported. Endeavour to cross to north of the Vistula, to join hands with forces from East Prussia, and descend upon Warsaw for the north.

French take Steinbach in Upper Alsace.

JAN. 5.—First auction of five prize steamers in the Baltic Exchange yields £130,725, which is placed to credit of a poundage fund for the Fleet.

Turkish transport sunk in Black Sea.

JAN. 6.—Russian victory in Caucasus, near Kars.

Albania in revolt against Essad Pasha.

Earl Kitchener states in House of Lords that over 218,000 names have been registered under the household canvass of those willing to serve.

German supply ship sunk by H.M.A.S. Australia in Pacific.

Arrangements made for exchange of British and German prisoners of war who are incapacitated for further service.

JAN. 7.—President Poincaré signs decree making permanent the prohibition of the sale of absinthe.

JAN. 8.—Cancellation of interdict against export of tea; prohibition of export of coffee.

French attack around Soissons.

JAN. 9.—King George and Queen Mary visit Indian troops in hospital in Brighton.

JAN. 10.—Sixteen German aeroplanes attempt to cross English Channel, but return without reaching England. Later they drop bombs on Dunkirk.

JAN 11.—French successes won near Soissons and Perthes maintained. Burnhaupt-le-Haut reoccupied by enemy.

In Caucasus Turks assuming vigorous offensive in neighbourhood of Karaugan.

JAN. 12.—Sir E. Grey's reply to United States Note on subject of contraband favourably received in America.

JAN. 13.—Indian Viceroy, at Delhi, states India has despatched, or is despatching, nearly 200,000 men to fight overseas.

Redoubt north of Beauséjour Farm the scene of a desperate struggle.

JAN. 14.—Tabriz, capital of Persian province of Azerbaijan, occupied by a Turkish force.

Resignation of Count Berchtold, Austro-Hungarian Minister of Foreign Affairs: he is succeeded by Baron Stephan Burian.

French report loss of eastern side of spur of Hill 132, north-east of Soissons; succeed in establishing themselves between Crouy and Missy.

South African force occupies Swakopmund.

JAN. 15.—North of Arras, Zouaves brilliantly carry German position.

German bridges across the Meuse destroyed by French, and in the Vosges enemy thrown back.

Transfer of German ship Dacia to American ownership discussed by London and Washington.

JAN. 16.—Price of wheat in Great Britain increases considerably.

JAN. 17.—French retake foundry at Blangy, near Arras, which had been seized by Germans.

Paris follows London in darkening streets.

JAN. 18.—German losses to date estimated at $2\frac{1}{2}$ millions.

JAN. 19.—Important British financial step announced. No company can invite fresh capital, and no fresh company can be formed unless the State approves. No capital can go abroad except under Government control.

German Zeppelin attack on English coast towns.

JAN. 19-20.—Twenty-six Turkish supply ships sunk by Russian torpedo-boats between Batum and Trebizond.

JAN. 20.—Loss announced of French submarine Saphir, engaged in patrol work in Dardanelles.

JAN. 22.—British airmen drop 27 bombs on German submarine base at Zeebrugge.

German airmen drop 66 bombs on Dunkirk.

JAN. 22-23.—M. Millerand, French Minister of War, visits London and Aldershot, and is received by King George.

JAN. 24.—Battle of Dogger Bank. German warship Blücher sunk by squadron under Vice-Admiral Beatty.

JAN. 25.—German Chancellor, in interview published in New York, essays explanation of his " scrap of paper " allusion. (Sir E. Grey promptly replies.)

Mr. Bryan issues statement proving that United States had not broken the spirit of neutrality in favour of Germany's enemies.

H.M.S. Natal, the British armoured cruiser, which was sunk by explosion in Cromarty Firth, December 30, 1915.

Sir Sackville Carden, who was in command of British naval forces at the Dardanelles.

Sir John de Robeck, who commanded the force assisting the landing in Gallipoli.

Sir Rosslyn Wemyss, who commanded the squadron at the evacuation of Gallipoli.

The German light cruiser, Dresden, showing the white flag off Juan Fernandez, March 14, 1915, after being put out of action by the British cruisers Kent and Glasgow and the auxiliary ship, Orania.

THREE BRITISH ADMIRALS AND TWO ILL-FATED SHIPS

A BELGIAN OBSERVATION BALLOON. Balloons were used by the intelligence department for reconnoitring over the lines. The type here shown possessed remarkable stability, and could remain aloft during a gale. The observers, whose main work was to search the terrain for German artillery positions, were provided with parachutes, so that in case of attack by aeroplane they could reach the ground in safety.

Plate 62   *Volume 11*

JAN. 25-27.—Fighting at La Bassée, Craonne, the Argonne, the Woevre, and the Vosges.

JAN. 26.—King George decorates the first Indian soldier to receive the Victoria Cross.

Turks advance on Egypt.

JAN. 27.—British loan of £5,000,000 to Rumania.

JAN. 29.—Loss of H.M.S. Viknor reported.

JAN. 30.—Takomaru (with New Zealand supplies for suffering Belgians) and Ikaria torpedoed in English Channel, and towed into port by French torpedo-boats.

Japanese sword of honour presented to King Albert.

JAN. 31.—National Relief Fund, £4,500,000.

FEB. 1.—German force, battalion strong, attacks trenches to north of La Bassée-Bethune, but repulsed. Attack south-east of Ypres repulsed.

Announced that Germany to be put on siege rations of bread.

Attempt by German submarine to torpedo British hospital ship Asturias off Havre.

FEB. 2.—German Admiralty warns neutral shipping to avoid the Channel, as it intends shortly to act against British transports by submarines.

German attack near Bagatelle in the Argonne repulsed.

Fighting of fiercest character reported along the Warsaw front.

British forces defeat Turkish advance body near Ismalia.

Authorities of the State of Maine arrest a German officer for bomb outrage on Canadian Pacific Railway bridge over St. Croix River.

FEB. 3.—Germans send fire-boats down River Ancre above Aveluy (north of Albert), but these contrivances stopped by French before they explode.

Kemp, one of rebel leaders in South Africa, surrenders with his commando.

FEB. 4.—Kaiser inspects fleet at Wilhelmshaven, and hands Iron Crosses to crew of submarine U 21, which torpedoed British merchant ships in Irish Sea.

German Admiralty declare blockade of whole of Great Britain and Ireland from Feb. 18.

British Foreign Office issues warning of importance that Great Britain may have to consider the adoption of re-taliatory measures against German trade should Germany persist in her apparent intention to sink merchantmen by submarines, regardless of loss of civilian lives.

Battle for Warsaw still raging.

FEB. 5.—Russians take offensive to cross the Bzura, capturing part of enemy's position near Dakoro.

Capture of German trenches in the neighbourhood of Lille.

British Army Estimates issued, in which noted that number of men which Parliament will be asked to vote for the Army, Home, and Colonial establishments, exclusive of those serving in India, is 3,000,000.

FEB. 6.—British capture brickfield east of Cuinchy. Announced that struggle for Warsaw reaching its climax.

FEB. 7.—Foreign Office issues statement that " secret British orders " have been given to merchantmen to fly a neutral flag, that " the use of the neutral flag is, with certain limitations, well-established in practice as a ' ruse de guerre.' "

Russians holding important point north of Vitkovitza, on the extreme German left, and capture whole series of trenches near Borjimov.

Allied compact regarding finance : British Chancellor of the Exchequer returns from Paris, from a conference with the Finance Ministers of France and Russia. Important agreement concluded, by which they pool their financial resources, and will float a loan jointly, at the same time providing for advances by the three Powers in equal shares to such countries as have taken, or may take up, arms for the common cause.

FEB. 8.—Violent infantry battle at Bagatelle, in the Argonne.

Mr. Asquith announces in Parliament British casualities up to February 4 are 104,000.

Navy Estimates presented to Parliament give power to raise strength of the Navy in men from 218,000 to 250,000.

German cruiser Breslau bombards Yalta and Russian cruisers in reply bombard Trebizond.

FEB. 9.—Enemy bombard Ypres and Furnes and pour incendiary shells on Soissons.

Austrian official report issued in Vienna admits breakdown of their offensive in Carpathians.

FEB. 11.—Russian retreat in East Prussia in consequence of great German advance.

FEB. 12.—In the Vosges French Chasseurs carry Hill 937, in region north of Hartmannsweilerkopf, in violent snowstorm.

Great air raid against German submarine bases in Zeebrugge, Blankenberghe, and Ostend districts. Thirtyfour aircraft took part.

FEB. 13.—United States Note to Germany regarding blockade published. It warns Germany that if German vessels destroy an American ship and lives of American citizens on high seas, the German Government will be held to " strict accountability for such acts." The Note to Great Britain states American Government will view with anxious solicitude any general use of the United States flag by British vessels in the zone of operations.

FEB. 14.—Reims again bombarded by Germans.

Russian retreat in East Prussia. Farther to north, Russian troops fall back to fortified line of River Niemen, under pressure of German forces.

FEB. 15.—Important speech by Mr. Churchill in House of Commons, in which stated that British reply to German " system of piracy and murder " at sea would be an increase in restrictions now placed on German trade, pointing to a blockade of German coast.

Count Bernstorff, German Ambassador to United Sates, presents Note to its Government, to effect that Germany is ready to consider abandonment of policy of attacking British merchantment if Great Britain will cease her efforts to prevent foodstuffs from being conveyed to civilians in Germany.

FEB. 16.—Second great air raid by Allies on German positions on Belgian coast.

British steamer Dulwich (3,289 tons) blown up twenty miles off Cape Antifer (Havre). French steamer Ville de Lille sunk off Barfleur by German submarine.

Russian official message announces Germans advancing from East Prussia, attempting to envelop Russian forces in neighbourhood of Augustow on either wing.

British Naval losses since commencement of war published: Killed, 348 officers, 5,812 men; wounded, 45 officers, 352 men; missing, 8 officers, 5 men. In Royal Naval Division: Killed, 5 officers, 36 men; wounded, 4 officers, 184 men; missing, 7 officers, 968 men; interned, 39 officers, 1,524 men.

FEB. 17.—Sir Edward Grey, in his Note to United States, replying to complaint regarding British interference with neutral shipping, points out that complaint founded on a misconception.

Zeppelin L 4 destroyed on Danish island of Fanoe, and another German airship lost on Danish coast.

FEB. 18.—German " Official " Blockade of Great Britain begins.

FEB. 19.—The 200th Day of the War. British Notes to United States published. In one Sir Edward Grey replies to representations of United States Government as to use of latter's flag by the Lusitania. Other Note deals with Wilhelmina case. Both explain British attitude in view of Germany's " paper " blockade and repeated violation of international law.

American ship Evelyn mined off Borkum.

Bombardment of Dardanelles Forts.

FEB. 20.—Serious fighting in the neighbourhood of Ypres.

s.s. Downshire sunk by a German submarine off the Calf of Man and s.s. Cambank torpedoed off Anglesey.

FEB. 21.—Russian success in Galicia.

German aeroplane raid over Essex.

Russian counter to the German advance from East Prussia and Posen begins.

Announced from Holland that United States ship Evelyn, carrying cotton from New York to Bremen, was sunk by a mine off Borkum.

Reims again bombarded and cathedral severely damaged.

FEB. 22.—Mr. Asquith announces in Parliament that the Allies are considering what action to take by way of reprisals for the German blockade.

Zeppelin attack on Calais, five civilians killed.

Sir Edward Grey, in message to Washington, denies German assertion that British intended to destroy an American ship in the war zone to precipitate a crisis between the United Sates and Germany.

South African Union forces occupied Garub, 70 miles east of Lüderitz Bay, without opposition.

FEB. 23.—Admiralty restricts navigation in the Irish Channel by proclamation of a prohibited area.

German submarine attacks Folkestone-Boulogne cross-Channel passenger boat, the torpedo passing 30 yards ahead of the ship.

First neutral vessel sunk in blockade. The Norwegian collier Regin torpedoed in the English Channel; crew saved.

Fifteen hundred shells rained upon Reims Cathedral.

Rioting among Indian troops at Singapore.

FEB. 24.—Loss of H.M.S. Clan McNaughton, armed merchant cruiser, missing since February 3, announced by Admiralty.

FEB. 25.—Allies bombard forts at the entrance to Dardanelles.

FEB. 26.—Government and Clyde Strikers. In a letter to the Engineering Employers' Federation and various engineering trade unions, Sir George Askwith, chief industrial commissioner, states that the Government must call for a resumption of work on Monday morning, March 1.

Fierce battle on the Polish front in progress, severest struggle around Prasnysch.

French Ministry of Marine states that dredging for mines in the Dardanelles passage has begun.

FEB. 27.—Seizure of the Dacia. The German ship transferred to a German-American owner with cotton for Germany stopped by a French warship in the Channel and brought to Brest.

FEB. 28.—British blockade of German East African coast takes effect at midnight.

French make marked progress in Champagne on the whole front from Combres to the north of Perthes.

Important speech by Mr. Lloyd George, at Bangor, on the question of labour troubles.

MAR. 1.—Blockade of Germany by Great Britain. Mr. Asquith, in Parliament, announces that a real blockade of Germany is to be undertaken; no goods of any kind to enter or leave Germany.

Russians advance eleven miles in Poland.

MAR. 2.—Text of the American note to Germany making suggestions which would free commercial ships from some of the risks they run in the waters of the belligerents, together with the German reply, published in a message from Amsterdam.

MAR. 3.—The Clyde engineers who went on strike resume work, but stipulate for no overtime, and if the advance of 2d. an hour be not granted by March 9, to work at low pressure.

MAR. 4.—Further Admiralty report on Dardanelles operations, in which it is stated that to date forty enemy's field-guns destroyed.

Russian success in Carpathians and Eastern Galicia.

MAR. 5.—British squadron shells Smyrna.

Turkish oil depot destroyed at Said (near Gaba Tepe) by French battleship in Dardanelles operations.

MAR. 6.—War Crisis in Greece. The Cabinet of M. Venizelos resigns.

Operations in Dardanelles continue. The Queen Elizabeth, supported by Agamemnon and Ocean, attack forts by indirect fire across the Gallipoli peninsula, firing at 21,000 yards.

German casualty list published by French Press Bureau gives total of 3,000,000, including killed, wounded, and prisoners.

MAR. 7.—British air raid on Ostend by six aeroplanes.

British Losses in Persia. Indian Office announces a force of 12,000 Turks and Arabs has inflicted a check on a British reconnoitring detachment in the valley of the Tigris.

In Dardanelles four French battleships cover the direct bombardment of the defences of the Narrows by H.M.S. Agamemnon and Lord Nelson.

MAR. 8.—Greece and the War. Crisis still continuing. M. Zaimis declines the task of forming a Cabinet, while Greek people and Parliament support M. Venizelos, who resigned owing to King Constantine's unwillingness to declare war on side of Triple Entente.

In Champagne Germans attempt to retake captured woods west of Perthes, but repulsed.

MAR. 9.—National War Workshops. Mr. Lloyd George announces that Government is taking powers to commandeer factories and divert them, if need be, to make munitions.

German submarines sink three British merchant ships.

Crisis in Greece relieved by new Ministry of M. Gounaris.

MAR. 10.—Battle of Neuve Chapelle. Striking British advance in La Bassée region, village of Neuve Chapelle carried and 1,720 prisoners captured. German casualties very heavy.

French gain a valuable success in Champagne.

German submarine U 12 rammed and sunk by British destroyer Ariel.

MAR. 11.—French official communiqué regarding recent operations in Champagne states 10,000 Germans killed and 2,000 taken prisoners.

MAR. 12.—Despatch from Sir John French giving details of brilliant success achieved by British troops in capturing Neuve Chapelle on March 10. All enemy's counter-attacks repulsed.

MAR. 13.—Announced that H.M. auxiliary cruiser Bayano torpedoed by German submarine; only 27 saved out of crew of 216.

MAR. 14.—A train at Don station blown up by British aircraft.

Sudden assault makes Russians masters of the enemy's positions near the village of Malkovice, in the Przemysl region; an Austrian battalion captured.

German cruiser Dresden sunk near Juan Fernandez island by H.M.S. Glasgow, Kent, and the auxiliary cruiser Orama.

MAR. 15.—Important Speech by Lord Kitchener in which he reviews recent British progress, commends the Bill to commandeer factories for war work, and speaks most gravely of the arrears of output.

The " Real Blockade." Text of the Order-in-Council as a reply to Germany's piratical submarine campaign issued. No merchant vessel may proceed to or sail from a German port. Goods for German ports must be discharged in an allied port; if not contraband or requisitioned, they will be restored to the person who has forwarded them. Goods from German ports will be seized and sold, and the proceeds of sale retained till peace. Goods of German origin in neutral ships may be seized and sold.

MAR. 16.—Sir John French reports that in recent fighting about Neuve Chapelle, German loss was between 17,000 and 18,000. A casualty list issued gives total of losses among British officers at 191 for the period of the Neuve Chapelle fighting.

Russians report advance on both flanks of their immense front.

MAR. 17.—Russia's offensive in North Poland successfully continued.

British blockade defined. A White Paper issued shows that American Ambassador asked Sir Edward Grey whether our reprisals are a blockade of Germany or not. Sir E.

Grey replied that it is a blockade, " effectively controlling by cruiser cordon all passage to and from Germany by sea," but we shall not exact from neutrals full penalties for breach of blockade.

MAR. 18.—Zeppelin attack on Calais, seven people killed.

First neutral vessel arrested by British cordon of cruisers under the Order-in-Council—the Swedish steamer Geheland, laden with cargo of provisions, alleged to be consigned to a German port.

Fresh Russian invasion of Prussia.

Battle of the Narrows. An action between the combined squadrons of Great Britain and France and the great fortresses of the Narrows in the Dardanelles fought.

MAR. 19.—Reported that Russians have occupied Memel.

MAR. 20.—Admiralty announce that there is every reason to believe that German light cruiser Karlsruhe was sunk in neighbourhood of the West Indies at the beginning of November.

New Chief of the General Staff. Announced that Lieut.-General Sir W. R. Robertson appointed Chief of General Staff.

MAR. 21.—Zeppelin raid on Paris. Four German airships visit Paris early in morning, a few bombs dropped upon the north-west district, but only cause trifling damage.

Russians take 3,954 men of the Przemysl garrison, which made an unsuccessful sortie from that fortress.

Occupation of port of Memel notified officially by Russians.

Lord Kitchener's grave warning in a letter to secretary of the Dock Labourers' Union, warning the workers against persistence in their refusal to work overtime.

MAR. 22.—Fall of Przemysl. The great Austrian fortress surrenders after a six months' siege. The prisoners number 126,000.

Important speech by Sir Edward Grey on the origin and objects of the war. One essential condition of peace, he says, must be the restoration of Belgian freedom and reparation to her.

MAR. 23.—Russians withdraw from Memel.

Turk raid on Suez Canal. Turkish force 1,000 strong attacked and routed by a British detachment under Sir G. Younghusband.

MAR. 24.—Naval air raid on Antwerp. Five machines of the Naval Wing operating from Dunkirk fly to Hoboken, near Antwerp, and bombard the submarine building.

In the Carpathians, Russian troops seize several fortified heights on the front between the roads leading to Bortfeld and Uzsok; 4,000 prisoners captured.

MAR. 25.—German submarine U 29 sunk, with all hands. She was commanded by the officer who sank the three Cressys, and had distinguished himself as " the polite pirate."

German submarine U 28 sinks Dutch steamer Medea off Beachy Head.

MAR. 26.—French air raid on Metz.

MAR. 27.—British liner Falaba torpedoed to the south of the St. George's Channel by German submarine, and sinks in ten minutes. About 140 survivors picked up; 136 persons missing.

MAR. 28.—Black Sea Fleet bombards the outside forts and batteries of the Bosporus, on both sides of the Straits.

MAR. 29.—Campaign against alcohol. Mr. Lloyd George receives a deputation, representative of the leading shipbuilding firms, who urge total prohibition during the war of the sale of liquor.

MAR. 30.—Home Secretary appoints a Committee to consider the conditions of retail trade in regard to the further enlistment of men.

General Hughes, the Canadian Minister for Defence, announces that the Government is prepared to keep 50,000 Canadian troops in the firing-line throughout the war, if necessary.

MAR. 31.—German submarine U 28 sinks British steamers Flaminian and Crown of Castile.

Campaign against alcohol. King George's letter to Mr. Lloyd George expressing his " deepest concern " at " the grave situation " now existing in our armament factories published.

French airmen successfully bombard the maritime station of Bruges and the aviation camp of Gits.

APRIL 1.—Moonlight raids by British airmen. Flight-Sub-Lieutenant F. G. Andreae carries out successful air attack on the German submarines which were being constructed at Hoboken, dropping four bombs. Flight-Lieutenant J. P. Wilson attacks two submarines at Zeebrugge. Both these officers start in the moonlight.

APRIL 2.—Bulgarian raid into Serbia.

APRIL 3.—Turkish cruiser Mejidieh strikes a mine near the Russian coast and sinks.

Union forces seize Warmbad, the southern capital of German South-West Africa.

APRIL 4.—French progress in the Woevre continued.

APRIL 5.—Russian Black Sea Fleet fights indecisive action with the Goeben and Breslau.

Russian progress in the Carpathians. Heavy defeat of Austrians at Bartfeld, south of the Dukla Pass.

Reply of the United States Government to the British

Note regarding the Allies' reprisals against German trade published by Foreign Office.

APRIL 6.—British mine a trench. Sir John French reports the successful explosion of a mine under the German trenches near La Bassée.

APRIL 7.—Austrians driven back across the main range of the Carpathians, and on a wide front forced to retreat twelve to fifteen miles.

APRIL 8.—By a night attack at Les Eparges, on the heights of the Meuse, French troops make great progress, despite desperate resistance by the Germans, who leave over 1,000 dead on the field.

APRIL 9.—French capture Les Eparges, an important position dominating the Woevre plain.

APRIL 10.—The Russians report that the enemy's attacks, made in great strength, were repulsed, and that several heights towards the Uzsok Pass have been carried.

APRIL 11.—The German cruiser Kronprinz Wilhelm arrives at Hampton Roads, Virginia.

APRIL 12.—In the direction of Stry Russians repulse attacks on the front, Rosochacy-Orawezyk-Kosziowa-Roriunka, inflicting enormous losses on the enemy.

APRIL 13.—Rear-Admiral Hood's despatch published, describing the work of the Franco-British flotilla in checking the German advance on Calais.

Committee for Munitions of War. Appointment of a strong committee, under the chairmanship of Mr. Lloyd George, with full powers to deal with the problem of national output of munitions of war.

APRIL 14.—Zeppelin Raid on Tyneside.

APRIL 15.—Field-Marshal Sir John French's despatch on Battle of Neuve Chapelle published. The British losses were 12,811 (killed 2,527, wounded 8,533, missing 1,751).

French success near Arras.

Allied squadron of 15 aeroplanes drops bombs with great success on German military buildings at Ostend.

APRIL 16.—German air raid on the English East Coast. Bombs dropped on Lowestoft and other places.

APRIL 17.—Victory in Persian Gulf. Officially announced that a severe defeat has been inflicted upon a Turkish force of 15,000 men by the British and Indian troops near Zobier.

British Submarine E 15 stranded off Kephez Point, in the Dardanelles.

British transport Manitou attacked in the Aegean by a Turkish torpedo-boat, which is chased, driven ashore, destroyed, and her crew captured.

APRIL 18.—Heroic feat in Dardanelles. British submarine E 15, stranded on April 17, destroyed by picket boats from

Triumph and Majestic, in face of heavy Turkish fire, to prevent her falling into hands of enemy.

Notable British Success near Ypres. A successful action, commencing on April 17, culminates in the capture and complete occupation of an important point known as Hill 60, about two miles south of Zillebeke, east of Ypres.

APRIL 19.—French progress in Alsace. Attacks carried out on both banks of the Fecht increase French advance by forcing the enemy to evacuate Eselsbrucke, above Metzeral.

APRIL 20.—Mr. Lloyd George announces in House of Commons that Lord Kitchener is very gratified by the response which has been made to the appeal to the country, and intimates that the Government considers conscription unnecessary.

APRIL 21.—Mr. Lloyd George states in the House of Commons that the British armies now in France are more than six times the six divisions of which the Expeditionary Force was originally composed.

A bold and successful aeroplane attack made on the German airship harbour shed at Ghent.

APRIL 22.—Second battle of Ypres opens.

Germans launch sudden attack to north of Ypres and make considerable advance, due to use of asphyxiating gas.

APRIL 23.—Canadians save the situation. War Office announces that the fight for the ground between Steenstraate and Langemarck laid bare left of Canadian Division, and four Canadian 4.7 in. guns passed into hands of enemy. Some hours later the Canadians made most brilliant and successful advance, recapturing these guns, and in the official words, "saved the situation."

APRIL 24.—New German attack on extreme left of Allied line repulsed.

APRIL 25.—Landing at the Dardanelles. A large allied force successfully lands on the Gallipoli peninsula.

APRIL 26.—Sir John French reports severe fighting north-east of Ypres.

APRIL 27.—French recapture summit of Hartmannsweilerkopf, and advance 20 yards down the eastern slope.

Dardanelles land fighting. Troops in the Gallipoli peninsula under Sir Ian Hamilton made good their footing with the effective help of the Navy.

Mr. Asquith on reparation. In House of Commons the Premier states that " when we come to the end of this war we shall not forget this horrible record of calculated cruelty and crime, and we shall hold it to be our duty to exact such reparation against those who are proved to be the guilty agents as it may be possible for us to do."

French armoured cruiser Léon Gambetta sunk by Austrian

submarine at entrance to the Otranto Straits. Rear-Admiral Sénès and nearly 600 of crew perish.

APRIL 28.—German offensive definitely stopped. Sir John French announces that allied operations definitely stopped the German attack. In resisting allied counter-attacks, Germans again made use of asphyxiating gases.

APRIL 29.—French, in co-operation with Belgian troops, make progress in Belgium towards the north. On the right bank of the Yser Canal 150 prisoners and two machine-guns taken.

Mr. Lloyd George introduces into House of Commons the Government drink proposals. They include increased taxation of spirits, heavy beers, and wines, and powers to control the sale of intoxicants in certain districts.

APRIL 30.—Zeppelin raid on the East Coast. Several incendiary bombs dropped in Ipswich and Bury St. Edmunds, doing heavy damage.

MAY 1.—Announced that allied troops at the Dardanelles have established themselves firmly at three separate points, two on the European and one on the Asiatic coast.

Two German torpedo-boats and one British destroyer sunk off the Dutch coast.

Continued success of General Botha's campaign in German South-West Africa reported.

MAY 3.—More German attacks at Ypres. Sir John French reports enemy attacked Hill 60, using asphyxiating gas.

Reported Russian check. The German headquarters claim to have inflicted a great defeat on the Russians in Western Galicia.

MAY 4.—Second War Budget introduced in the House of Commons. Mr. Lloyd George foreshadows a possible expenditure of £1,132,654,000, but announces no further new taxation.

Heavy Turkish defeat in Persia reported. Russians completely rout enemy after three days' fighting.

MAY 5.—Renewed Battle for Hill 60. The Germans obtain a footing under cover of poisonous gases and favoured by weather conditions.

Owing to the great strength of the enemy in Western Galicia some Russian units fall back to the second line.

British recapture some of lost trenches on Hill 60, south-east of Ypres.

MAY 6.—Announced that German Commander in South-West Africa admitted in a letter to General Botha that orders had been given to poison wells.

Officially announced that General Botha has occupied the important railway junction of Karibib (German South-West Africa).

MAY 7.—Lusitania torpedoed and sunk. The giant Cunarder

torpedoed by German submarine about ten miles south of Kinsale. 1,195 lives lost.

MAY 9.—Zeppelin Raid on Southend. Early in morning a Zeppelin attack made on Southend; ninety bombs dropped in the town, and fifty more in the vicinity. One woman killed, and two persons injured.

British unsuccessfully attack Aubers Ridge.

Sir John French reports that enemy, under cover of poisonous gases, made attack east of Ypres in neighbourhood of the Menin road.

MAY 11.—Growing resentment against Germans in Great Britain as a result of the Lusitania outrage. German shops wrecked in London and provinces. Troops called out.

MAY 12.—Sir John French reports the repulse of a German attack east of Ypres.

Anti-German riots in London and elsewhere.

MAY 13.—Announced that United States has decided to send a Note in severe terms to Germany, demanding that sinking of merchant and passenger vessels shall cease.

Campaign in German South-West Africa. General Botha enters Windhoek at the head of Union forces.

H.M.S. Goliath torpedoed in Dardanelles Straits. Five hundred lives lost. About 20 officers and 160 men saved.

E 14 reports sinking of two Turkish gunboats and a transport.

MAY 14.—Italian Cabinet resigns. Many demonstrations in favour of war take place in Italy.

Petrograd, admitting the retirement of the Russian armies in West Galicia, reports that a defensive concentration on the banks of the River San is being carried out.

MAY 15.—Reported resignation of Lord Fisher, First Sea Lord.

MAY 16.—Sir John French reports 1st Army made successful attack between Richebourg l'Avoué and Festubert (northwest of La Bassée), breaking the enemy's line over the greater part of a two-mile front.

MAY 17.—Zeppelin raid on Ramsgate, forty or fifty bombs dropped. The aircraft appears later over Dover Harbour.

MAY 18.—Germans bombard Przemysl.

Lord Kitchener announces that British troops must be adequately protected from asphyxiating gases by the use of similar methods; and that 300,000 more recruits are required.

MAY 19.—Political crisis. Premier announces that the Government is to be reconstructed.

Government requests stewards of the Jockey Club to suspend all race meetings, except Newmarket.

MAY 20.—The Italian Chamber gives its approval to the declarations of the Government, which is interpreted as security for the Government and a free hand for the prosecution of war against Austria-Hungary and Germany.

MAY 21.—French attack on the southern slopes of Notre Dame de Lorette has brilliant results.

Italy and war. By the enormous majority of 262 votes to 2 Italian Senate passes the Government Bill providing for the measures necessary in the event of war.

MAY 22.—Disaster to British troop train conveying the 7th Royal Scots southwards, which collides with a local train near Gretna, and Scottish express from Euston dashes into mass of debris. Over 200 killed and many injured.

MAY 23.—Italy Declares War. Italian Ambassador in Vienna presents a declaration of war against Austria.

MAY 24.—Italo-Austrian War. Austrian aeroplanes attempt an attack on the arsenal at Venice, but are driven off.

General Count Cadorna, in command of the Italian Armies, leaves for the Front.

MAY 25.—Italian Army crosses Austrian frontier in north-east corner of Venetia, and occupies a number of villages in and near the valley of the Isonzo.

Germans renew their attacks north of Przemysl.

Brilliant Exploits by Submarine E 11. In Sea of Marmora she sinks an ammunition vessel, chases and torpedoes a supply ship, enters the waters of Constantinople, and fires a torpedo at a transport.

MAY 26.—New British Cabinet announced, composed of twenty-two members, a National Government to win the war; Prime Minister, Mr. Asquith.

MAY 26.—H.M.S. Triumph sunk by submarine off Gallipoli peninsula.

Zeppelin raid on Southend, over forty bombs dropped, killing two women and wounding a child.

MAY 27.—H.M.S. Majestic torpedoed off Gallipoli.

Minelayer Princess Irene accidentally blown up in Sheerness Harbour.

Eighteen French aeroplanes carry out air raid against Ludwigshafen, dropping many bombs on the works of the Baden Aniline Dye Company, where high explosives and asphyxiating gases are manufactured.

MAY 28.—Admiral Sir Henry B. Jackson, K.C.B., appointed First Sea Lord of Admiralty in the place of Lord Fisher.

French take a big work in the direction of Souchez.

A Petrograd communiqué announces Russian success on the San.

MAY 29.—French in possession of Ablain. They annihilate or put to flight three German companies.

MAY 30.—French capture all German trenches on Hill 17 about three miles north-east of Ypres.

Italians occupy Ala, the Customs station on the Brenner route, seven and a half miles from the frontier.

MAY 31.—Messages between King George and the King of Italy, expressing mutual confidence and gratification at the alliance in arms of Great Britain and Italy, published.

Russians attack along the line. German offensive brought to a standstill. In Eastern Galicia over 7,000 of enemy captured, and reported to be retiring in disorder.

German reply to U.S. Note on the sinking of the Lusitania generally described in the American Press as insulting.

Zeppelin Raid on Outer London. Admiralty issues a statement that Zeppelins reported near Ramsgate and Brentwood, and in certain outlying districts of London. Many fires reported, but these not absolutely connected with the visit of airships. Ninety bombs dropped, four persons killed.

JUNE 1.—Italians develop vigorous offensive on their north-eastern front.

Przemysl forts attacked by Austro-German forces. After obstinate battle, enemy repulsed with enormous losses.

JUNE 2.—Italians cross the Isonzo, north of Trieste.

A French communiqué reviews events between May 9 and June 1 in the sector north of Arras. The division which captured Carency, Ablain, St. Nazaire, the Malon Mill, and the Souchez Sugar Refinery, took 3,100 prisoners, including 64 officers, and buried 2,600 Germans.

German transport torpedoed by British submarine in Sea of Marmora.

JUNE 3.—Przemysl retaken by Austro-Germans, after heroic resistance of Russian garrison.

Announced that on May 31 the British force in the Persian Gulf attacked a hostile force north of Kurna, seized the heights, captured three guns, ammunition, and two hundred and fifty prisoners. Amara occupied.

The new Ministry meets Parliament. Sir John Simon introduces the Bill creating a Ministry of Munitions.

Great French air raid on German Crown Prince's headquarters; one hundred and seventy-eight bombs dropped.

JUNE 4.—General attack delivered upon the Turkish positions in southern area of the Gallipoli peninsula.

Zeppelin raid on east and south-east coasts of England; few casualties.

JUNE 5.—Five German counter-attacks east of the Chapel of Lorette repulsed with heavy loss to the enemy.

JUNE 6.—French success on the Aisne.

Zeppelin raid on East Coast. Five deaths and forty injured.

JUNE 7.—Flight-Sub-Lieutenant R. A. J. Warneford, R.N., attacks a Zeppelin in the air between Ghent and Brussels at 6,000 feet. He drops six bombs, and the airship explodes and falls to the ground; twenty-eight of crew killed.

Flight-Lieutenants J. P. Wilson and J. S. Mills attack Zeppelin shed near Brussels, setting it on fire.

Naval encounter in Baltic. Russian mine-laying transport Yenissei sunk by German submarine.

JUNE 8.—Resignation of Mr. Bryan, U.S. Secretary of State, owing to his disapproval of the second U.S. Note to Germany regarding Lusitania.

JUNE 9.—Mr. Asquith announces total number of British casualties up to May 31 as 258,069. Killed, 50,342 (officers, 3,327); wounded, 153,980 (officers, 64,980); missing, 53,747 (officers, 1,130).

Canada announces she will raise a further 35,000 men.

JUNE 10.—Italians take Monfalcone, nineteen miles from Trieste.

Two British torpedo-boats, Nos 10 and 12, torpedoed by a German submarine off the East Coast.

JUNE 11.—Text of the Second U.S. Note to Germany published.

JUNE 12.—Petrograd officially announces that in the three days' battle on the Dniester, in the region of Zurawna, which lasted from June 8 to June 10, Russians captured 348 officers, 15,431 soldiers, 78 machine-guns, and 17 cannon.

JUNE 13.—General Election in Greece. M. Venizelos gains one hundred and ninety-three seats out of a total of three hundred and sixteen.

JUNE 14.—Italians bombard the fortress of Malborghetto.

JUNE 15.—Karlsruhe bombarded by twenty-three Allies' aeroplanes; one hundred and thirty projectiles dropped.

Zeppelin raid on North-East Coast, sixteen killed, forty injured.

In Commons, Mr. Asquith moves a Vote of Credit for £250,000,000; and announces average daily expenditure on war services since April 1 as £2,660,000.

JUNE 16.—German first line trenches captured by British north of Hooge.

Mr. Lloyd George takes the oath as Minister of Munitions.

JUNE 17.—French gain important success in the Souchez neighbourhood.

Italians occupy whole of Monte Nero.

JUNE 18.—Petrograd reports enemy losses of 120,000 to 150,000 east of the Dniester in preceding month, along a front of forty miles.

JUNE 19.—French carry the Buval Bottom, which had been obstinately defended by enemy since May 9, and in Alsace completely invest Metzeral, to which Germans set fire before evacuating it.

JUNE 20.—Italian official report describes many enemy positions on the line of the Isonzo taken by storm.

JUNE 21.—In Lorraine the French press their former gains, taking all the enemy first-line trenches on a front of 1,500 yards. In Alsace they take Metzeral.

Second War Loan at 4½ per cent. announced in Parliament, unlimited in amount, and available to public in denominations as small as five shillings.

JUNE 22.—French progress in Lorraine continues. In Alsace they have pushed past Metzeral, and advanced beyond the Andasswasser.

De Wet sentenced to imprisonment for six years and to a fine of £2,000.

Lemberg recaptured by Second Austrian Army under General Böhm-Ermolli.

JUNE 23.—In the Vosges French continue their advance up the valley of the Fecht towards Münster, and occupy the village of Sonderbach.

Mr. Lloyd George introduces Munitions of War Bill in House of Commons.

JUNE 24.—Germans bombard Arras, where a hospital is struck.

JUNE 25.—Heavy enemy defeats in Galicia.

Union Forces operating in German South-West Africa occupy post on Swakopmund-Grootfontein line.

JUNE 26.—Lieutenant-Commander M. E. Nasmith awarded V.C. for submarine exploits in Sea of Marmora.

Resignation of General Sukhomlinoff, Russian Minister of War. General Polivanoff succeeds him.

JUNE 27.—Battle of Bobrka. A fierce fight developed here, eighteen miles south-east of Lemberg. The Russians capture during counter-attacks 1,600 prisoners.

JUNE 28.—Further retreat of Russians to Bug River.

British attack on Achi Baba in Gallipoli.

JUNE 29.—National Registration Bill introduced in Parliament.

JUNE 30.—French capture trenches in Gallipoli.

JULY 1.—German repulse in Galicia. In the sectors of the Front from Kamionka to Halicz great loss inflicted on enemy. 1,000 prisoners taken.

Announced that Leyland liner Armenian sunk by German submarine U 28 off Scilly Isles.

JULY 2.—German naval defeat. Submarine torpedoes and sinks German battleship Pommern in the Baltic. In same action German mine-laying cruiser Albatross driven on shore and destroyed.

JULY 3.—South Africa offers to organise and equip an oversea volunteer contingent. Offer accepted July 6.

JULY 4.—British force from Aden is attacked and retires before superior Turkish force from the Yemen.

Allies inflict heavy losses on Turks in violent attack on our positions in Gallipoli.

German cruiser Königsberg, which had sheltered up Rufiji River, German East Africa, destroyed by monitors Severn and Mersey.

JULY 5.—Announced that Lord Fisher appointed Chairman of the Inventions Board.

A despatch from Sir Ian Hamilton describes attacks by Turks upon his positions. These failed, and Turks' losses amounted to over 20,000 men.

JULY 6.—Sir John French reports gain of ground south-west of Pilkem, near Ypres.

JULY 7.—Sir Ian Hamilton's despatch on Dardanelles operations published.

Germans, in taking offensive near St. Mihiel, penetrated French first line on a front of seven hundred and sixty yards.

JULY 8.—Austrians admit defeat of their army under Archduke Joseph, which had advanced north-east of Krasnik. In the direction of Lublin, Russians developed the offensive, and captured 11,000 prisoners, and many machine-guns.

French advance on Souchez.

Italian cruiser the Amalfi torpedoed by Austrian submarine in Upper Adriatic.

National Registration Bill passed in Commons.

JULY 9.—Botha's final triumph. Officially announced General Botha has accepted surrender of entire German forces in South-West Africa.

JULY 10.—German reply to U.S.A. Note published. The arguments in justification of the sinking of the Lusitania are repeated, and Americans are told that if they sail in British ships they do so at their own risk.

Austrian retreat in Poland. Russian army defending Lublin takes over 15,000 prisoners.

JULY 12.—Despatch on Second Battle of Ypres and the operations in the Festubert region, by Sir John French, published.

Souchez Cemetery taken by Germans, also some parts of the adjacent trenches.

JULY 13.—French air raid in the Woevre. Squadron of thirty-five aeroplanes rain one hundred and seventy-one bombs on Vigneulles, the junction for the field railways running from region of Metz.

Success of War Loan. Mr. McKenna announces that £570,000,000, not including subscriptions through the Post Office, had been subscribed.

JULY 14.—New German move north of Warsaw. Officially announced from Russia that the Germans are trying to reach Warsaw from the north.

Registration Bill passed by the Lords.

JULY 15.—Dardanelles Success. Sir Ian Hamilton reports that as result of attack by British and French troops in Gallipoli, four hundred yards were gained on both flanks.

Strike of 200,000 Welsh miners begun.

JULY 16.—In Central Cameroons the Allied forces occupy the town of Ngaundere.

JULY 17.—Fighting renewed in Argonne, all enemy attacks checked.

JULY 18.—Hindenburg's new move. German troops in east under Von Hindenburg forcing Russians back towards the line of fortresses of the River Narew.

Heavy fighting in the West. In the Argonne, on the Heights of the Meuse, on the Lorraine border, and in the Vosges.

Italian cruiser Giuseppe Garibaldi sunk by Austrian submarines in the Adriatic.

JULY 19.—Splendid stand made by Russians against German attacks north and south of Warsaw.

German attack west and south-west of Souchez repulsed by French, also one to the south-east of Les Eparges.

Officially announced that Italians have obtained a substantial success on the Isonzo front, capturing formidable lines of trenches, 2,000 prisoners, and guns.

Dardanelles losses. Announced that up to end of June total naval and military casualties were 1,933 officers and 40,501 men.

Mr. Lloyd George, Mr. Runciman, and Mr. Henderson confer with miners' leaders at Cardiff.

JULY 20.—Russian troops fall back to places on River Narew and line of fortresses protecting main railway line from Warsaw to Petrograd.

Sir John French reports that the British east of Ypres sprung a mine and occupied 150 yards of trenches.

French aerial raid on railway station of Colmar, also on Conflans, junction between Verdun and Metz.

Coal strike ended; terms of settlement drawn up by Mr. Lloyd George.

JULY 21.—Advance on Warsaw. Russians reported still holding the Blonie defences, fifteen miles from Warsaw, and offering strong opposition to General Mackensen south of the Lublin railway (south-east of Warsaw).

JULY 22.—Enemy reported closing in on Warsaw from the west and south-west.

Gallipoli gains. Despatch from Sir Ian Hamilton reports that since July 18 our forces have made steady progress in consolidating captured trenches.

Convention signed ceding to Bulgaria Turkish portion of the Dedeagatch railway, with the territory between the River Maritza and the frontier.

JULY 23.—Officially reported that on the Carso Italians inflict defeat on enemy; 1,500 prisoners taken.

JULY 24.—Text of third American Note to Germany published.

JULY 25.—French success in Vosges. German defensive positions from La Fontenelle to Launois stormed, and over eight hundred prisoners taken.

JULY 26.—Russian official report admits that Germany crossed the Narew between the fortress of Rozen and Obryte Pultusk. Mackensen's forces south of Lublin—Cholm railway have been fought to a standstill.

Officially announced that Italian naval forces have occupied island of Pelagosa, in the Adriatic.

Announced in Parliament that Turkish and Arab troops have been heavily defeated up the Euphrates.

German destroyer sunk by British submarine in North Sea.

JULY 27.—Italians gain a height on the Carso plateau.

Russia reports that German troops who crossed the Narew between the fortresses of Rozen and Poltusk have been checked.

Mr. Asquith in Parliament states total British military casualties to July 18 numbered 330,995; and total naval casualties to July 20 as 9,106.

JULY 28.—Struggle for Warsaw. Enemy held at nearly all points.

JULY 29.—On the Bug River above Sokal Russians repulsed two Austrian attacks. Von Mackensen breaks through Russian line on the Lublin-Cholm railway.

German aeroplanes drop bombs on Nancy, and French aeroplanes bomb Passchendæle.

JULY 30.—Sir John French reports that by using liquid fire enemy penetrated our trenches north and south of Hooge.

Leyland liner Iberian sunk by German submarine.

JULY 31.—Russians evacuate Lublin, and Austro-German forces seize Lublin-Cholm railway.

AUG. 1.—Germans occupy Mitau.

Italians occupy Mount Medetta, in Carnia.

AUG. 2.—Feats of submarines. Admiralty announces that British submarine in Sea of Marmora torpedoed large steamer. Torpedoes were fired at lighters alongside the arsenal at Constantinople. Railway cutting one mile west of Kara Burnu bombarded and line blocked.

AUG. 3.—Press Bureau announces that in Gallipoli a successful

attack was carried out against a network of Turkish
trenches, with gain of crest of important ridge.

Aug. 4.—Fall of Warsaw.

Rumanian Cabinet votes a military credit of £4,000,000.

Aug. 5.—Fall of Ivangorod. New Vosges battle.

Italy reports capture of big entrenchments on the Carso.

Russians evacuating Riga.

Aug. 6.—Fighting in the Argonne with great intensity around
Hill 213.

Petrograd officially announces that Warsaw was evacuated
in order to save the city from effects of a bombardment.

New landing at Suvla Bay, Gallipoli.

Aug. 7.—Germans held near Riga. Enemy dislodged from the
region between Dwina, the Eckau, and the lower course of
the Aa.

Aug. 8.—H.M.S. Ramsey, small armed patrol-vessel, sunk by
German auxiliary Meteor.

H.M.S. auxiliary cruiser India torpedoed in Norwegian
waters.

Germans cross the Vistula east of Novo Georgievsk.

German naval repulse in Gulf of Riga; nine battleships
and twelve cruisers driven off.

Germans heavily shelled whole Belgian front on the
Yser.

Aug. 9.—British Advance near Hooge.

Austrian attack on Serbia in attempt to cross Danube
defeated.

Turkish battleship Hairredin Barbarossa sunk by British
submarine.

French air raid on Saarbrück; one hundred and sixty-four
bombs dropped on the station and factory.

Zeppelin Raid on East Coast. Twenty-eight casualties,
including fourteen deaths.

H.M.S. Lynx, a destroyer, sunk in North Sea after
striking a mine. Four officers and twenty-two men saved.

Gallipoli advance. Sir Ian Hamilton reports gain east
of Krithia road.

Aug. 10.—Severe fighting in Gallipoli. Australian and New
Zealand troops treble the area they had held.

Admiralty announces sinking of a Turkish gunboat,
Berk-i-Salvat, by British submarine in Dardanelles.

Aug. 11.—Poison shell attack in Argonne. French line penetrated temporarily.

Austrian submarine U 12 torpedoed by Italian submarine
in Upper Adriatic.

Russians holding in check the German flanks south of
Riga and in South-East Poland. Furious enemy attacks on
the fortress of Kovno.

AUG. 12.—Turkish transport sunk by British seaplane (Flight-Commander Edmonds) in Dardanelles.

Belgrade again bombarded.

Zeppelin raid on East Coast. Six killed, twenty-three injured.

AUG. 13.—Austrian submarine U 3 sunk by French torpedo boat Bisson in Adriatic.

AUG. 14.—British transport Royal Edward sunk by submarine in Aegean Sea, 1,000 men missing.

AUG. 15.—Raid by nineteen French aeroplanes on a German park and depot in the valley of the Spada.

National Register Day.

At Suvla, in Gallipoli, British advance five hundred yards.

AUG. 16.—English coast towns shelled.

Von Mackensen and Prince Leopold of Bavaria closing in on Brest Litovsk and Kovno. Russians partly evacuate Bielostok.

Greek Ministry resigns, and a Venizelist President (pro-Ally) elected.

AUG. 17.—Kovno falls after desperate resistance, and Von Mackensen's army cuts Cholm-Brest-Litovsk railway.

Zeppelin raid on Eastern Counties. Ten persons killed, thirty-six injured.

AUG. 18.—Allies' naval victory in Gulf of Riga; two German cruisers, eight torpedo boats, and four barges full of troops which had attempted to land at Pernau reported sunk. German Dreadnought Moltke reported torpedoed and sunk by British submarine. Russian gunboat Sivoutch sunk.

AUG. 19.—White Star liner Arabic torpedoed; 391 saved out of a total of 423.

Severe Fighting in Gallipoli. Sir Ian Hamilton reports that the recent operation included a fresh landing at Suvla Bay. After very severe fighting the position at which the British aimed was won.

Turkish defeats in Caucasus announced by Russia. Fall of Novo Georgievsk.

AUG. 20.—Italy declares war on Turkey.

AUG. 21.—M. Venizelos again Greek Premier.

Cotton declared absolute contraband by the British Government.

AUG. 22.—German destroyer sunk off Ostend.

AUG. 23.—Bombardment of Zeebrugge by forty British ships.

AUG. 24.—Report of German plans to invade Serbia through Bulgaria. German troops concentrated at Brasso, opposite Rumanian frontier.

Count Bernstorff's apology to U.S.A. regarding the sinking of the Arabic.

AUG. 25.—Important statement issued by Press Bureau, in

which announced that although attacks at Anzac and Suvla have gained ground, at no point has the real objective yet been attained.

Fall of Brest-Litovsk.

Allied air raids. Great concerted attack by British, French, and Belgian Army and Navy aeroplanes on Forest of Houthulst.

AUG. 26.—Sir Edward Grey's reply to German Chancellor's recent speech at opening of Reichstag published.

British aeroplane destroys submarine. Squadron-Commander A. W. Bigsworth, R.N., destroys single-handed a German submarine by bombs dropped from an aeroplane off Ostend.

Count Bernstorff states that German submarines have been ordered not to attack mechantmen without warning.

French airmen bomb poison-gas factory at Dornach and station at Mulheim.

AUG. 27.—To the north of Arras some German trenches wrecked and munition depôt destroyed.

Fresh trouble in South Wales mining district.

AUG. 28.—Mr. Balfour says total casualties from Zeppelin raids up to date are eighty-nine civilians and two hundred and twenty wounded; no soldiers or sailors killed, but seven wounded.

Further advance at Suvla Bay.

AUG. 29.—Germans storm Lipsk, on the Bobr, twenty miles from Grodno; and make progress towards Vilna.

AUG. 30.—Russian success on the Strypa in East Galicia; three thousand prisoners, thirty guns, and twenty-four machine-guns captured.

AUG. 31.—Russian success in the direction of Lutzk (Luck); one hundred officers and seven thousand men captured.

SEPT. 1.—General Alexeieff appointed Chief of Russian staff. Germany accepts United States demands regarding submarine warfare communicated by Count Bernstorff.

SEPT. 2.—Fall of Grodno.

Rumanian Government stops further export of cereals and transit of gold.

Announced from Paris that four Turkish transports have been sunk by British submarines in Dardanelles.

German intrigue precipitates rising in Persia. British Consul-General at Ispahan attacked and wounded.

SEPT. 3.—Germans storm bridgehead at Friedrichstadt on the River Dwina.

General Joffre visits Italian front.

SEPT. 4.—Allan liner Hesperian torpedoed without warning off coast of Ireland; twenty-six persons missing.

SEPT. 5.—Tsar assumes supreme command of Russian armies.

Grand Duke Nicholas appointed to the command in the Caucasus.

Indian frontier raid on Mohmand country driven off.

Mr. Balfour describes losses of German submarines as " formidable."

SEPT. 6.—Air raid on Saarbrück by forty French aeroplanes. The station, factories, and military establishments successfully bombarded.

SEPT. 7.—Zeppelin raid on Eastern Counties. Fifty-six casualties; seventeen killed.

Russian victory near Tarnopol; 8,000 men and thirty guns captured.

Germans announce loss of submarine U 27.

SEPT. 8.—Zeppelin raid on London; one hundred and six casualities; twenty killed.

SEPT. 9.—Russian triumph in Galicia. Officially reported that in fighting in Galicia between September 3 and 9 over 17,000 prisoners were taken, and nearly one hundred guns.

SEPT. 10.—Russian victory near Trembova, in Galicia. Seven thousand prisoners and thirty-six guns captured.

SEPT. 11.—Zeppelin raid on East Coast, no casualties.

SEPT. 12.—Continued Russian success in Galicia. North of Tarnopol, ninety-one officers and 4,200 rank and file of enemy captured.

Zeppelin raid on East Coast, no casualties or damage.

SEPT. 13.—Dvinsk-Vilna railway cut by Germans at Sventsiany. German aeroplanes dropped bombs on Kentish coast; seven persons injured. Chased off by two naval aeroplanes.

Another Zeppelin raid on East Coast.

SEPT. 14.—Announced Admiral Sir Percy Scott appointed to take charge of the gunnery defences of London against attack by enemy aircraft.

More Russian successes in Galicia.

British success at Maktau in East Africa.

SEPT. 15.—Lord Kitchener announces that Sir John French has received eleven divisions of reinforcements, and has taken over from the French about seventeen miles of additional front. The provision of men to keep up the strength in 1916 " has caused us anxious thought. We shall require large additions."

Mr. Asquith announces the enlistments in both Services were not far short of 3,000,000; the daily war bill should not now exceed £5,000,000.

Sir John French reports that during past week there had been twenty-one air fights over the German lines, and in eleven cases the hostile aeroplanes were driven to ground.

Battle for Dvinsk and Vilna continued, the Russians counter-attacking vigorously. In Galicia Russians dislodged enemy, crossed to other bank of the Strypa, and took over 1,500 prisoners.

SEPT. 16.—Considerable German progress on the road to Dvinsk.

Admiralty announces British submarine E 7 lost in Dardanelles.

Announced that casualties in Dardanelles up to August 21 amount to 87,630.

SEPT. 17.—Official account of Zeppelin raids on London district gives the week's casualties as thirty-eight killed and one hundred and twenty-four injured.

SEPT. 18.—Fall of Vilna.

Anglo-French bombardment of German positions on Belgian coast.

SEPT. 19.—Bulgaria mobilises and announces armed neutrality.

SEPT. 20.—French gain footing on Aisne-Marne Canal and progress at Hartmannsweilerkopf in the Vosges.

SEPT. 21.—Great War Budget introduced in House of Commons by Mr. McKenna. New taxes estimated to bring in additional revenue of over £100,000,000 in a full financial year.

SEPT. 22.—Russians make vigorous attack between Friedrichstadt and Riga, recapturing a bridge-head on the Dwina at Lennewaden.

SEPT. 23.—French aeroplanes bombed railway line from Verdun to Metz.

Fierce artillery duel in region of Arras.

SEPT. 24.—Mobilisation of Greek Army.

SEPT. 25.—Belgian coast bombarded. French batteries co-operate with British Fleet in bombarding German positions of Westende and Middelkerke.

Battle of Loos. British capture the western outskirts of Hulluch, the village of Loos, with the mining works around it and Hill 70, and also make at attack near Hooge, on either side of the Menin road. The attack in the south gains five hundred yards of enemy's trenches, 1,700 prisoners, and eight guns, besides machine-guns captured.

In Champagne the French penetrate the German lines on a front of six miles; 12,000 prisoners taken. In Artois, cemetery at Souchez, and last trenches of enemy east of the "Labyrinth" taken.

SEPT. 26.—Fierce German counter-attack on ground won by British, with result that all ground gained is held, including whole of Loos, except some ground just north. Number of prisoners totals 2,600, and nine guns.

The attack to north of Arras results in fresh progress. Whole of village of Souchez occupied. Farther south La Folie reached. 1,000 prisoners taken in this fighting. In Champagne more ground gained. Number of prisoners to date exceeds 16,000 unwounded men.

SEPT. 27.—North-west of Hulluch British repulse counter-attacks. East of Loos the offensive progresses. Captures to date amount to fifty-three officers, 2,800 men, eighteen guns, and thirty-two machine-guns.

SEPT. 28.—Russians ocupy Kovel.

Severe fighting round Loos, where progress made to the south. Total prisoners to date 3,000, and twenty-one guns and forty machine-guns.

French take nine hundred more prisoners in Champagne, and threaten the Crown Prince's supply-line in the Argonne.

Defeat of Turks at Kut-el-Amara, on the Tigris. They retreat towards Bagdad.

SEPT. 29.—French progress east of Souchez continued, and Hill 140 on crests of Vimy commanding Lens reached after obstinate fighting.

Announced that British force in Mesopotamia captured Turkish positions on the Tigris, in front of Kut-el-Amara. Enemy in full flight towards Bagdad.

SEPT. 30.—More Champagne gains at Hill 185, the Butte de Tahure, and before Ripont.

Details of victory on the Tigris show that British captured 1,650 prisoners and four guns, and that the pursuit to Bagdad is in full swing.

Petrograd reports Russians abandoned Lutzk, the Volhynia fortress.

OCT. 1.—Sir E. Grey announces that German officers are taking control of the Bulgarian Army.

Allied aviators attack German railway communications radiating from Valenciennes and Vouziers.

OCT. 2.—Sir John French reports British counter-attack recovered two trenches south-west of Fosse 8 and to the north-west of Loos.

OCT. 3.—Petrograd reports that the enemy has been " crumpled up " near Vileika.

OCT. 4.—Russian Ultimatum to Bulgaria.

Turks defeated in the Caucasus near Van.

OCT. 5.—Allied Forces land at Salonika.

Diplomatic relations between Russia and Bulgaria broken off.

Lord Derby appointed Official Director of Recruiting.

OCT. 6.—M. Venizelos, Greek Premier, resigns.

OCT. 7.—Invasion of Serbia by German and Austro-Hungarian troops.

OCT. 8.—Great German attack on Loos completely repulsed.

British submarine sinks German transport in the Baltic.

OCT. 9.—Sir John French reports British trenches pushed steadily forward north-east of Loos between Hill 70 and Hulluch.

Belgrade occupied by Austro-German troops.

Oct. 10.—In Champagne, French progress to the north-east of Tahure.

Oct. 11.—Sir John French's despatch proves that German attack on the allied positions at Loos was executed on a great scale. He reports that a very severe reverse was inflicted on the enemy.

Bulgarians invade Serbia.

Oct. 12.—Miss Edith Cavell, English nurse, shot by Germans in Brussels.

Russian victory in Galicia.

Oct. 13.—Zeppelin raid on London. Fifty-six persons killed, and 114 injured.

British gas attack in the West. After a bombardment, attacked German trenches under cover of a cloud of smoke and gas south-west of Hulluch to the Hohenzollern Redoubt.

Oct. 14.—Great Britain declares war on Bulgaria.

Oct. 15.—Germans retake the summit of the Hartmannsweilerkopf in the Vosges.

Oct. 16.—Officially reported that British submarines sank five German transports in the Baltic Sea.

Russians pierce German lines at Ustie, on western shore of Lake Boginskoe.

Oct. 17.—French regain Hartmannsweilerkopf.

Italian occupation of Pregasina.

Oct. 18.—General Sir Charles C. Monro succeeds Sir Ian Hamilton as commander-in-chief of Gallipoli operations.

Allies occupy Strumnitza (Strumitza).

Oct. 19.—New German thrust at Riga.

Salonica railway line cut by Bulgarians.

German attack at Hulluch. Enemy's losses very severe.

Oct. 20.—General Ivanoff carries by assault town of Chartoryisk on the Styr; 750 prisoners and 9 guns taken.

Oct. 21.—Russians carry German positions east of Baranovitschi; 3,500 prisoners taken.

Russian fleet bombards Varna.

Oct. 22.—Allied Fleets bombard Dedeagach.

Oct. 23.—French troops cross Greek frontier and join forces with Serbian troops.

Oct. 24.—British submarine near Libau attacks and sinks German cruiser Prince Adalbert.

Russian warships shell Bulgarian ports of Varna and Burgas.

Strong German salient on the northern slopes of Hill 196, one and a quarter miles to north of Mesnil les Hurlus, known as the Courtine, carried.

British occupy Banjo (Cameroons).

Oct. 25.—Germans counter-attack on the whole front of the

Courtine work, and reoccupy in the centre some portions of trenches.

Franco-Serbians recapture Veles.

OCT. 26.—British transport Marquette torpedoed in the Aegean, ninety-nine men missing.

OCT. 27.—Austrians across the Drina, east of Vishegrad.

Uskub retaken by Serbians.

Varna bombarded by Russian fleet.

Total Italian captures for the week along the Isonzo front over 5,000.

German attack to the east of Reims launched on a great scale, backed with use of poisonous gas, is repulsed.

OCT. 28.—French Ministry resigns. M. Briand forms new Cabinet.

H.M. cruiser Argyll grounds off East Coast of Scotland. All her crew saved.

Announced that Lieutenant-General Sir Bryan Mahon is in command of British forces in the Balkans.

OCT. 29.—H.M.S. Hythe, auxiliary mine-sweeper, sunk after being in collision with another ship off Gallipoli peninsula; 155 men missing.

General Joffre arrives in London to take part in important war consultations.

Total British casualities to Oct. 9 published—493,264.

OCT. 30.—Germans retake summit of the Butte de Tahure.

OCT. 31.—Fierce struggle for possession of portions of trenches recaptured by Germans east of Neuville St. Vaast; French regain possession of some of them.

NOV. 1.—Battle for Nish.

H.M. torpedo-boat No. 96 sunk in Strait of Gibraltar, after being in collision with a mercantile fleet auxiliary.

NOV. 2.—Serbian Campaign. On the north-west front the enemy attacks in force the south-east bank of the Lepenitza. He is repulsed in the centre with heavy losses.

NOV. 3.—Russian success in Galicia.

British cavalry operating in Serbia with the left wing of the Southern Serbian Army are thrown across the path of the Bulgarians advancing towards Prilep and Monastir.

The Austro-German army of invasion occupies Ushitze.

NOV. 4.—Greek Ministry defeated in Chamber by party of M. Venizelos. The Prime Minister, M. Zaimis, resigns.

French positions in Champagne round the Chausson Farm taken by Germans, retaken by the French, and again violently attacked by the enemy.

On the Russian front fighting took place west of Dvinsk and on the Strypa. Both sides claimed successes.

NOV. 5.—Press Bureau announces Lord Kitchener's temporary absence from the War Office on public duty.

Sinking of British transport Ramazan by shell fire from an enemy submarine on Sept. 19 in the Aegean Sea. Of 380 Indian troops on board, 75 were saved.

H.M. armed boarding-steamer Tara sunk by enemy submarine in Eastern Mediterranean.

Bulgarians enter Nish.

Nov. 6.—On the Riga front Russians successfully attack the Germans near Olai.

In Champagne a fresh German attack against French trenches in the Courtine earthworks completely fails.

Announced that Lord Kitchener has left England at request of his colleagues for a short visit to the Near East.

Nov. 7.—Italian liner Ancona torpedoed off Sardinia by Austrian submarine, 222 persons missing.

German cruiser Undine sunk by submarine in Baltic.

Nov. 8.—Austro-German invaders of Serbia enter Krushevatz.

To the north of St. Mihiel French batteries demolish a German anti-aircraft gun.

Nov. 9.—Main line through Nish to Sofia and Constantinople reported almost wholly in enemy hands.

Nov. 10.—British transport Mercian attacked by gun fire from enemy submarine in the Mediterranean; 103 casualties.

Near Kolki, on the River Styr, Russians break enemy's line, and in the pursuit take 50 officers, 2,000 men, and 20 machine-guns.

Nov. 11.—New War Committee of the Cabinet announced. During the temporary absence of Lord Kitchener it consists of five members—Mr. Asquith, Mr. Balfour, Mr. Lloyd George, Mr. Bonar Law, and Mr. McKenna.

Germans reported to have abandoned part of the country west of Riga.

Nov. 12.—The Greek Government, having failed to come to any working arrangement with Venizelist majority, dissolves the Chamber.

Nov. 13.—Russian troops in the Schlock region pursue the enemy, inflict great losses on him, and advance west of Kemmern.

Nov. 14.—French army slowly pushing up the Valley of the Vardar towards Veles.

Germans penetrate the French trenches in the Labyrinth, but are dislodged by a counter-attack.

Air raid on Verona by three Austrian aeroplanes, seventy-eight persons killed and injured.

Nov. 15.—Successful attack on Turkish trenches in Gallipoli; 160 yards on east of the Krithia Nullah and 120 yards in the west gained.

Continuance of fighting in the Labyrinth in Artois.

Officially reported from Petrograd that during the past

month Russians took 674 officers, and 49,200 men prisoners, capturing 21 guns and 118 machine-guns.

Nov. 16.—Despatch from Sir John French reports that, since November 10, artillery on both sides have been active, specially south of the La Bassée Canal, east of Kemmel, and east of Ypres. He also reports considerable mining activity.

Nov. 17.—Allies' War Council. Announced that Mr. Asquith, Sir Edward Grey, Mr. Lloyd George, and Mr. Balfour have gone to Paris, accompanied by naval, military, and diplomatic advisers, for the purpose of consultation with the French Government.

Slight improvement in Serbian operations reported. Bulgarians driven back on the Babuna front.

Hospital ship Anglia strikes a mine in the Channel and founders; 4 officers, 1 nurse, and 129 men missing.

Nov. 18.—Sir John French reports that south-west of Messines his troops forced an entrance into the enemy's front trench.

Nov. 19.—Attempted enemy air raid on Luneville. Fresh German attempts to cross the Dwina north-west of Friedrichstadt failed.

Nov. 20.—Lord Kitchener has audience of King Constantine in Athens.

Nov. 21.—Artillery engagements in Artois (around Loos and Hulluch).

Nov. 22.—Sir John French reports organised bombardment on many portions of the hostile lines during the past four days, and the capture of a German aeroplane.

Nov. 23.—Serbian capital removed from Mitrovitza to Prizrend. British Victory in Mesopotamia. Big battle fought at the ruins of Ctesiphon, eighteen miles south-east of Bagdad. Turkish position captured, together with 800 prisoners and war material. British losses 2,000 killed and wounded.

Russians capture a first-line enemy trench in the Dwina district.

Nov. 24.—In Serbia the plain of Kossovo carried by enemy.

Note presented to Greece by the Entente Powers as to the security of the Allied troops in Macedonia.

Nov. 25.—In Galicia, near Siemikowice, on the Strypa, Russian troops attack the enemy, and drive him to the river, where many are drowned.

Nov. 26.—Battle of Ctesiphon. General Nixon reports that Turks retreated from scene of battle on November 23-25 to Ctesiphon, a point ten miles south of Bagdad; 1,300 prisoners taken.

Nov. 27.—German poison-gas attack between Forges and Bethincourt, to the west of the Meuse, failed.

Nov. 28.—German submarine destroyed on Middelkerke by British aeroplane.

Nov. 29.—British forces withdrawn from Ctesiphon, owing to Turkish reinforcements.

Nov. 30.—Prisrend taken by Bulgarians.

Lord Kitchener returns to London.

Dec. 1.—In Belgium, east of Boesinghe, Allied batteries inflict important damage to enemy defensive works.

Russians rout Turks near Lake Van.

Dec. 2.—Baron Sonnino announces that Italy has signed the Pact of the Allies to make no separate peace.

Fall of Monastir.

Dec. 3.—General Joffre appointed Commander-in-Chief of the French Armies, with General de Castelnau as his Chief of Staff.

Dec. 4.—Announced that General Townshend, on the night of Nov. 30-Dec. 1, fought a rearguard action at Azizie against greatly superior Turkish forces. Two river-boats disabled by shell-fire and abandoned. Total British casualties in the various actions amounted to 4,567.

Dec. 5.—In Artois British batteries vigorously reply to violent bombardment of trenches at the double slag-heap south-west of Loos.

Dec. 6.—Rumanian military authorities commandeer all vessels of foreign ownership anchored in Rumanian ports.

British submarine exploits. Admiralty announces that British submarine operating in the Sea of Marmora fired at and damaged a train on Ismid Railway, torpedoed and sank Turkish destroyer Yar Hissar, and sank a supply steamer off Panderma by gun fire.

It is announced that General Townshend's force has reached Kut-el-Amara without further fighting.

General Joffre presides at first general meeting of Allies' Military Council of War in Paris.

Dec. 7.—In Champagne fighting continues for possession of the advanced trench south of St. Souplet.

Dec. 8.—British losses in action at Ctesiphon amounted to 643 killed, 3,330 wounded, and 594 missing.

German attacks in Champagne. East of the Souain Hill French counter-attacks succeed in overcoming the German attack, launched on Dec. 7.

Dec. 9.—Hard fighting on the Champagne front. A counter-attack by the French east of the Butte de Souain pushes enemy back.

Dec. 10.—Russian stroke in Persia. Petrograd announces Russian success between Teheran and Hamadan, in which several thousand Persian rebels were defeated.

Dec. 11.—On the Heights of the Meuse, in the sector of the Bouchet Wood, the French artillery causes serious damage to the German first line and supporting trenches.

DEC. 12.—An official bulletin shows that one British division in the Balkans had to fight its way back against heavy odds. The gallantry of the troops, especially of three Irish regiments, enabled the withdrawal to be successfully accomplished. Eight British guns were lost; casualties 1,500.

Text of American Note to Austria on sinking of Ancona issued.

Close of first Derby Recruiting Campaign.

DEC. 13.—Despatch about Kut-el-Amara published. Turks attacked British positions on December 10 and 11. On latter day enemy repulsed with heavy loss.

Announced that Greece has agreed to allow the necessary freedom of action for Allied troops at Salonica.

Arab force in Western Egypt defeated by British under Colonel Gordon.

DEC. 14.—Messages from Greece show that the Allied troops have completely retired from Serbia into Greek territory. Salonika fortified by the Allies.

General Sir Horace Smith-Dorrien appointed to supreme command of the British forces in East Africa.

DEC. 15.—Sir John French's successor. Announced that General Sir Douglas Haig has been appointed to succeed Field-Marshal Sir John French in command of the army in France and Flanders.

DEC. 16.—General Townshend reports that in the attack against British positions at Kut-el-Amara by the Turks, on December 12, the latter lost 1,000 men.

DEC. 17.—Heavy artillery actions in Champagne north and east of Massiges and east of the Mesnil Ridge.

Russian troops under Grand Duke Nicholas occupy Hamadan.

German cruiser Bremen and a torpedo boat accompanying it sunk by Allied submarine in the Baltic.

DEC. 18.—French aeroplanes attack Metz.

DEC. 19.—German gas attack against British lines north-east of Ypres frustrated.

DEC. 20.—Men enlisted under Group System who are classified in Groups 2, 3, 4, and 5, notified by Public Proclamation that they are to be called up for service forthwith.

Gallipoli Evacuation. Announced that all the troops at Suvla and Anzac, together with guns and stores, have been successfully transferred with " insignificant " casualties (three men wounded) to another sphere of operations.

Another report from General Townshend at Kut-el-Amara published. On night of December 17-18, British and Indian troops surprised Turks in their advanced trenches. In actions on December 1 and during night of December 12-13 the Turks lost 2,500 men.

Dec. 21.—Announced that Sir William Robertson, Chief of the General Staff of the Expeditionary Force, has been appointed Chief of Imperial General Staff.

General De Wet and 118 other prisoners released.

Russians reported to have occupied Kum, 100 miles south-east of Teheran.

Japanese steamer, Yasaka Maru, sunk by submarine in Mediterranean.

Dec. 22.—In Alsace, the French force their way from the summit down the eastern slopes of the Hartmannsweilerkopf.

Sir Charles Monro appointed to command the First Army Corps in the West, in place of Sir Douglas Haig.

Dec. 23.—Renewed fighting in Alsace.

Total Dardanelles casualties to December 11 announced as 112,921. Total British casualties on all fronts up to December 9 announced as 528,227.

Dec. 24.—Montenegrin troops attacked near Mutchido.

Dec. 25.—Another German attack on the Hartmannsweilerkopf repulsed.

Dec. 26.—Russian forces in Persia occupy Kashan.

Dec. 27.—Germans, after a bombardment, attack near Hill 193 in Champagne, but are easily repulsed.

India Office reports that Turks have been repulsed in attacks upon a fort at Kut-el-Amara, on the right flank of the British position. Their loss 900; British, 190.

Dec. 28.—Indians leave France. Official communication gives text of stirring message of thanks from King-Emperor to the Indian Army Corps, and states that this corps has departed from France, as its services are required " in another field of action."

Cabinet decides by a majority that they are bound by the Prime Minister's pledge, and approves the principle of compulsion.

Dec. 29.—More gains by the French in the Vosges. Since beginning of the operations 1,668 prisoners taken.

Dec. 30.—Austrian destroyer sunk and another blown up by a mine in sea fight off Cattaro, between Austrian and Allied vessels of war.

German, Austrian, Bulgarian, and Turkish Consuls arrested at Salonica, and placed on board French warship.

French occupy island of Castellorizo, between Rhodes and the mainland.

P. & O. liner Persia torpedoed; 192 missing.

British cruiser, H.M.S. Natal, sunk in harbour, the victim of internal explosion; 14 officers and 373 men saved.

Dec. 31.—German infantry attack in the Vosges completely repulsed by the French.

END OF VOLUME TWO.